EDUARDO GALEANO

EDUARDO GALEANO

Through the Looking Glass

Daniel Fischlin • Martha Nandorfy

Montréal/New York/London

Black Rose Books No. EE304

Hardcover ISBN: 1-55164-179-8 (bound) Paperback ISBN: 1-55164-178-X (pbk.)

Canadian Cataloguing in Publication Data
Fischlin, Daniel, 1957-
Eduardo Galeano : through the looking glass

Includes bibliographical references.
Hardcover ISBN: 1-55164-179-8 (bound) Paperback ISBN: 1-55164-178-X (pbk.)

1. Galeano, Eduardo H., 1940- --Criticism and interpretation. 2. Galeano, Eduardo H., 1940- --Political and social views. 3. Latin America--Politics and government--1948- 4. Authors, Uruguayan--20th century--Biography. I. Nandorfy, Martha, 1957- II. Title.

PQ8520.17A4Z65 2000   868   C00-900453-X

We wish to thank Eduardo Galeano for permission to use all visual materials related to *Crisis* and to his own books. Although every effort has been made to secure permission for materials reproduced herein, in some cases, we have been unable to locate a copyright holder.

Cover design: Kathe Gray / electric pear

BLACK ROSE BOOKS

C.P. 1258	2250 Military Road	99 Wallis Road
Succ. Place du Parc	Tonawanda, NY	London, E9 5LN
Montréal, H2W 2R3	14150	England
Canada	USA	UK

To order books:

In Canada: (phone) 1-800-565-9523 (fax) 1-800-221-9985
email: utpbooks@utpress.utoronto.ca

In United States: (phone) 1-800-283-3572 (fax) 1-651-917-6406

In the UK & Europe: (phone) London 44 (0)20 8986-4854 (fax) 44 (0)20 8533-5821
email: order@centralbooks.com

Our Web Site address: http://www.web.net/blackrosebooks

A publication of the Institute of Policy Alternatives of Montréal (IPAM)

Printed in Canada

The Canada Council Le Conseil des Arts
for the Arts du Canada

Table of Contents

Illustrations

Chapter 4

Chapter 5

End of Chapter Images
Acknowledgements

Chapter 1

Chapter 2

Chapter 3

Chapter 4

Chapter 5

And each day that passes it seems more logical and necessary to approach literature—whether we are writers or readers—as one approaches the most basic encounters of one's existence such as love or death, knowing that they form an inseparable part of the whole, and that a book begins and ends much before and much after its first and last word.

—JULIO CORTÁZAR, "REALITY AND LITERATURE IN LATIN AMERICA"

In order to survive, we must keep hope alive.

—WILLIAM PARKER, "THE PEACH ORCHARD"

How untell the lies
How pray for forgiveness
When the departed made wise
Demand restitution?

—KEN SARO-WIWA, "THOUGHTS IN TIME OF WAR"

Acknowledgements

This book, conceived several years ago in relation to an unproduced documentary filmscript, owes its genesis to many people. Malcolm Guy and Marie Boiti and their staff at Productions Multi-Monde in Montréal offered an initial home to many of the ideas we develop in this book. Numerous librarians, independent booksellers (all over the world), and students participated in the task of gathering materials from a wide range of sources. The interlibrary loan staff at Princeton University was particularly generous in releasing holdings of relevant periodicals, notably the earliest and very rare versions of *Crisis* that were so crucial to the writing of this book. Librarians at the University of Guelph were exceedingly helpful in sorting through some particularly vexatious referencing problems. The undergraduate students in a seminar at the University of Guelph on "Eduardo Galeano: Literature, History, Human Rights" provided a lively forum for debating the issues that inform this book, as were participants at two Brock University international conferences entitled "Love's Aspirations at the Millennial Turn" (2000) and "Storytelling in the Americas" (2001), where small portions of the chapters on utopian thinking and storytelling were presented.

Research assistance from Benjamin Lefebvre was singularly supportive, informed, and efficient—without his diligence, expertise, intelligence, and good humour the book would never have been completed. The significant range of materials that we consulted as we prepared this book, listed in the Works Consulted, would never have been assembled without his help. Mark Fried, Eduardo Galeano's current English translator, was kind enough to open his files to us over the years it has taken to assemble the information for this book. Diana Palaversich (University of New South Wales), author of the only full-length monograph on Galeano (in Spanish) before ours was providentially generous as we entered the final phases of writing. Liz Monasterios (SUNY Stony Brook) also provided much-needed context for evaluating materials from Latin America.

Eduardo Galeano, though not directly involved in the production of this book, was gracious in accommodating the initial attempts to develop a documentary filmscript—he gave generously of his time in an extended series of unreleased video interviews made in Montevideo by Productions Multi-Monde with the help of a Telefilm Canada grant. These interviews formed an important backdrop to the writing of the book, as were other film materials listed in the works consulted. We are also deeply grateful to Galeano for giving us copyright permission to use the rare materials from *Crisis*, the remarkable journal he edited from 1973-76. Mario Jacob at Imágenes, a film and video production house in Montevideo, was kind enough to make his production facilities available to us for the transfer of rare film footage, particularly the sobering and inspiring documentary on *Chile Crea* in which Galeano was a key participant. Our publisher at Black Rose Books, Dimitri Roussopoulos, who commissioned this work, showed (much appreciated) understanding and patience as we missed one deadline after another and as we struggled with the acquisition of rare materials and a range of information that proliferated well beyond our initial expectations. Linda Barton, also of Black Rose Books, was a delight to work with. Her talents facilitated many of our design ideas as the book went into production. Susan Bergholz, of Susan Bergholz Literary Services in New York, provided much needed support at crucial stages of the book's development.

We deeply appreciate the support of many colleagues and friends, including Olga Araujo-Mendieta, Irene Blayer, Christine Bold, David Chato, Carina DesRochers and family, Karen and Todd Edmunds, Eduardo Falero, María Figueredo, Katou Fischlin, Helen Hoy, Janice Kulyk Keefer, Thomas King, Harry Lane, Neena and Harish Naidu, Donna Palmateer Pennee, Mercedes Rowinsky, Elena Siemens, Ann Wilson, Tracy Wynne, Richard Young, and many others. Financial support from the offices of Jack Miller, Jacqueline Murray, Wayne Marsh, and Carole Stewart, at Brock University and the University of Guelph, respectively, as well as a grant from the office of the Provost of the University of Guelph, Alastair Summerlee, enabled the final phases of research and writing. Sharon Ballantyne, at the School of Literatures and Performance Studies in English (University of Guelph), constantly proved her ability to resolve even the thorniest of details and eased the final stages of the book's completion. Kathy Hanneson of the Media Centre (College of Arts, University of Guelph) did a superb job organizing the visual materials for the book. Michael Keefer repeatedly demonstrated his collegiality and generosity in myriad ways. Both David Clark and Ajay Heble took time from punishing schedules to read the manuscript in its entirety—and the book has benefited from their acute insights, suggestions, and the spirit of their own critical work. Belinda Leach, Ross Butler, and Rachel and Charlotte Butler provided everything from books to informed and critical conversation to babysitting. Their help with this book was instrumental and deeply appreciated. Dorothy Hadfield, with whom we have worked on a number of other projects, once again proved herself utterly indispensable in producing the index that provides a detailed map of many of the topics we cover. We would especially like to thank *pachamama* Marta Nandorfy for her unstinting generosity when most we needed it. We are grateful for permission to reprint short sections of work by Daniel Fischlin published in *Ariel*, *Border Crossings*, and *Revista canadiense de estudios hispánicos*. Finally, we thank the editor of *Border Crossings*, Meeka Walsh, for her encouragement in the earliest phases of work on this book. None of these people holds any responsibility for the views expressed in this book, though to our minds this book does express a community of concern without which it could not have been written.

As we completed the book we were frequently asked about the nature of the co-writing process this book represents. For the record, a chapter trajectory was devised after extensive discussion and each of us undertook to compose initial drafts based on our own interests and areas of expertise. Once that process was begun, the drafts were opened to ongoing criticism, intervention, and change. Each of us had complete freedom to alter, interrogate, or delete materials written by the other as the book took shape; in fact, the majority of the book has extended passages whose authorship is the complementary writing identity that emerged from our shared efforts.

We dedicate this book to Damian, Hannah, Zoë, and Esmé, for whom we wish, as we do for children everywhere, the promise, reality, and responsibility of a better world. It was Esmé, our four-year-old daughter, who provided the succinct question that allowed us to complete this book: "Is it tomorrow?"

August 2001, Kipawa, Québec

Chapter 1

The Cemetery of Words: Alien Memories, Resistance, and Restitution

In the Guaraní language, *ñe'ẽ* means both "word" and "soul."

The Guaraní Indians believe that those who lie or squander words betray the soul. (Galeano, *Walking Words* 40)

Beginnings: Critiquing the "Falsified, Unseen, Betrayed Reality of the History of America"

 Incisive and ironic, with a compelling sense of social justice and little tolerance for meretricious literary display. Allegorical and keenly attuned to telling details, hidden contradictions, inverse relations, striking paradoxes. Dissonant and resistant, giving shelter to hope ("*abrigar esperanzas*" [Barsamian, "Eduardo Galeano" 9]), indebted to memory and its disappearances, an expositor of betrayed realities, gatherer of lapidary words, a doubter who "distrust[s] those *compañeros* who only offer certainty" (NACLA staff 14), and a writer with a profound aversion to "schematic formulations" (Sherman 4). Eduardo Hughes Galeano, born in Montevideo in 1940, has emerged as one of the major literary voices in Latin America whose concern with human rights issues animates both his revisionary historical writings and his alternative, recuperative forms of storytelling. Author of the monumental trilogy *Memoria del fuego* (*Memory of Fire*; 1982, 1984, 1986), an unprecedented emendatory history of the Americas, Galeano takes on the task set by Walter Benjamin "to brush history against the grain" ("Theses" 257). But he does so by brushing literary discourse against the grain too, through contrarian narrative strategies, inventive generic disruptions, and a sobering critique of the way in which literary culture must rethink its relation to the public sphere.

The great-great-grandson of Welsh and Genoese families, Galeano has Uruguayan roots that lie in a "traditional Catholic landowning-cum-business family fallen on hard times" (Martin, "Hope Springs Eternal" 148). After only two years in secondary school, Galeano dropped out to work at a number of different jobs: "I never learned in school. I didn't like it. I felt like George Bernard Shaw who said 'when I was seven years old I was obliged to stop my education by going to school'" (Bach 17). As an exceptionally precocious fourteen-year-old, in September 1954, he published his first article (Martin, "Hope Springs Eternal" 18) after already having published political cartoons for the socialist weekly *El Sol* (Galeano signed these cartoons Gius, the Spanish equivalent for his Welsh patronymic, Hughes, which he later abandoned in favour of his mother's family name). "From the beginning of his working life," as Gerald Martin states, "he was involved in trade-union activities" and, in 1960 only twenty years old with little formal schooling, he became the managing editor of *Marcha*, "which its founder Carlos Quijano had made one of Latin America's most influential political magazines" ("Hope Springs Eternal" 148-49), a position *Marcha* retained until it was shut down by the military in 1973.

As editor of other major Latin American publications like *Epoca* (executive editor, 1964-66) and *Crisis* (co-founder and editor, 1973-76) and as director of the University of Montevideo University Press, Galeano was exposed to an enormous variety of writing practices and people at very early stages in his writing career. These relationships would set the stage for his emergence as novelist, essayist, journalist, chronicler, revisionist historian, and rights activist, while perhaps also accounting for his extraordinarily prolific output, widely disseminated in numerous languages besides his own native Spanish. Prior to seeking asylum in Argentina in 1973 after the June 27 coup in Uruguay, Galeano had published a novel (*Los fantasmas del día del león* [*The Phantoms of the Day of the Lion*], 1967), works of political criticism that examined China and Guatemala, and most importantly, the book that made his reputation throughout Latin America, *Las venas abiertas de América Latina* (*Open Veins of Latin America*, 1971), an economic and political analysis of the exploitative relations of European and North American cultures to Latin America. Written in just three months, this book gained an enormous readership for Galeano, making him "one of Latin America's most widely read writers" (Martin, "Hope Springs Eternal" 148). As Martin observes, "the editors of Monthly Review Press, which published the book, claimed with some justice that the work is 'a history which is at the same time a political economy, a social and cultural narrative of the highest quality, and perhaps the finest description of the primary accumulation of capital since Marx'" ("Hope Springs Eternal" 150). *Open Veins* has since "appeared in more than fifty editions in Spanish and has been translated into more than a dozen languages" ("Hope Springs Eternal" 151). Diana Palaversich states that *Open Veins* "represents the first truly alternative and popularised version of [the] history of Latin America" and was "written under the influence of Andre Gunder Frank's Dependency theory" ("Eduardo Galeano's *Memoria del fuego*" 135). *Open Veins* was followed by *La canción de nosotros* ([Song About Us], 1975), a novel that won Galeano the prestigious *Casa de las Américas* prize for fiction in 1975 and that was highly praised by Julio Cortázar for its depiction of state terror. Galeano later repudiated the novel's hopeful ending ("Hope Springs Eternal" 151).

In 1976, Galeano fled Argentina to Catalonia where he made a living as a writer and journalist before returning to Montevideo in 1985. This period of exile proved enormously important: it marked the period during which he began to write *Memory of Fire*, the history of the Americas that brought him even wider international recognition. During the same period Galeano produced *Days and Nights of Love and War* (1978; also winner of the *Casa de las Américas* prize in 1978), a largely autobiographical series of vignettes from his life that anticipates the kind of literary structures he would later formalize in *Memory of Fire*. Subsequent books include *El libro de los abrazos* (*The Book of Embraces*, 1989), further vignettes that chronicle autobiographical events, dreams, conversations with friends, insights about hope and despair, and reportage; *Nosotros decimos no: crónicas (1963-1988)* (*We Say No: Chronicles, 1963-1988*, 1989), a collection of writings, speeches, and journalistic pieces; *Patas arriba: la escuela del mundo al revés* (*Upside Down: A Primer for the Looking-Glass World*, 1998), a scathing denouncement of the new world order that builds on observations made in earlier work; two children's books, *La piedra arde* ([The Rock Burns], 1980) and *Las aventuras de los jóvenes dioses* ([Adventures of the Young Gods] 1984); and a host of other books, articles, speeches, and interviews in different languages.

Throughout all this, Galeano has survived a suicide attempt (*Days and Nights* 45), malaria, a heart attack ("my heart had broken from so much use" [*The Book of Embraces* 195]), imprisonment (in 1973 in Uruguay, following the right-wing coup), the disappearance of close friends and colleagues and the threat of disappearance to himself (his name "turned up on a list of those condemned by the death squads" in Argentina [Walljasper 34]), exile and dictatorships, penury and political persecution.[1] Moreover, he has been a forceful presence at major social actions taken in resistance to oppression and injustice, especially in the Americas. His attendance as the keynote speaker at *Chile Crea* (July 1988), a gathering of activists that met in Santiago prior to the plebiscite on General Augusto Pinochet's reign, not to mention his presence at the first *Zapatista Encuentro* in Chiapas (1996), both of which we address in this book, mark an engaged and active presence on the world stage. Galeano is someone who takes the public sphere seriously and who acts on it through more than just his writings. Throughout the life trajectory we have briefly outlined, he has sustained and developed his unique vision with a rare integrity and forcefulness, developing a style that combines "formidable powers of literary evocation…with the journalist's skill in collecting and synthesizing different sorts of information" (Martin, "Hope Springs Eternal" 150). In 1999, Galeano received the first Cultural Freedom Award from the Lannan Foundation (Santa Fe) in recognition of his outspoken critique of systemic injustice and the enormous and growing body of work he has produced dedicated to improving the conditions of human freedom generally.[2]

From this brief summary of a rich, varied, and productive life, it is apparent that Galeano's cultural presence is significant, even though his work has been largely ignored as unworthy of critical attention by academic scholarship in various disciplines. If anything, the relative absence of scholarly attention is telling. Not only does it signal the ways in which critical canonization works on exclusionary principles with writers whose work is inimical to the politics underlying much that passes as legitimate criticism, it also highlights the degree to which Galeano's work is disruptive of, if not a direct challenge to, the way in which the critic (as writer) functions in the public sphere. Deeply politicized, intensely concerned with issues of historical context, a populist who does not sacrifice content at the altar of vacuous entertainment, relentlessly informed, a *rhétoriqueur* with lyrical flare, a genre-breaker with a visceral regard for form, an anti-academic with formidable scholarly abilities, a sensualist with keenly honed analytic abilities, a historical pointillist with a deep sense of context, Galeano defies literary norms and expectations. His work not only challenges the relevance of criticism *as* criticism but also interrogates its underlying formal and structural principles, the very materials that ground its cultural presence and are crucial to its legitimation. Galeano's writing practices critique reductive forms of academicism that confine criticism to a domain of the aesthetic separated from lived reality. From Galeano's perspective, the responsible and independent analysis of that reality in all its material and existential complexity—and, importantly, the ethical discriminations and the political choices and commitments that follow from such an analysis—must find new forms that trouble the generic orthodoxies governing different forms of critical and aesthetic expression.

This book is an attempt to understand Galeano in relation to what we identify as four key configurations that consistently recur in Galeano's writing practice: the relationship between literary expression and issues of social justice (grouped under the rubric of human rights issues); the practices of *testimonio* and storytelling as challenges to the arbitrary but effective divide between literary high culture and lived experiences, especially in relation to the most pertinent issues of human agency (those having to do with oppression and equality, understanding and acceptance of difference, resistance to injustice, story and memory); the problem of writing revisionary history that challenges historiographic conventions, especially those that eliminate the specificities of traditionally marginalized experiences in favour of universalist, unifying theories that serve hegemonic interests; and finally, the notion of alternative communities to current political, economic, and social organizations largely modeled on neoliberal, pseudo-democratic, capitalist principles (grouped under the rubric of utopian theory or what Immanuel Wallerstein calls "utopistics").[3]

Neoliberalism we understand in the sense provided by Lesley Gill, an American anthropologist who has worked extensively in Bolivia, as "an economic, political, and moral doctrine that posits the individual as the fundamental basis of society" and as an ideology that "places unlimited faith in the 'magic of the market' to resolve all social problems. The most compelling aspect of this ideology lies in the conceptualization of the market as a neutral, even beneficent, arbiter rather than a metaphor for capitalist processes" (3). Neoliberalism legitimizes the tyranny of the market and enshrines the individual as the normative measure of economic and social achievement, a position radically at odds with the communitarian vision Galeano proposes as its antithesis. Moreover, neoliberalism disregards the deep historical contingencies that have produced the market as a space in which players are positioned in far from equal positions of advantage and power. The injustices associated with the neoliberal view are profound and contribute to Galeano's historical project insofar as it relates to human rights. Galeano's hybridized literary voice produces critical alternatives to the stories "we" are told (allegories of the beneficence of the free market as a source of equal opportunity), making possible an understanding of memory as possessing the emancipatory potential to transform the world from as it *is* into what it *could be.*

This book, then, examines the central motifs in Galeano's writings that function in direct relation to issues surrounding neoliberal doctrine and the response to it—historical amnesia, alternative communities, globalization and (under)development, human rights and freedom of the press, ecocriticism, indigenous cultures, the power of the word, dissonant history, testimonial and narrative, story and memory, and so forth. Our book also examines more indirectly the relation between such issues and some of the events that have shaped Galeano's life, from the dictatorships in Uruguay and Argentina that forced him into exile (after the disappearance and execution of many of his friends and colleagues) through to the ongoing epistolary relationship between Galeano and Subcomandante Insurgente Marcos, nominal leader of the Chiapas rebellion. In locating our readings of Galeano in relation to these particular configurations, we have no intention of limiting the field of critical play, much less of foreclosing on other possible interventions that adumbrate additional aspects of his work. Nor do we intend to suggest that Galeano's writing practices can be confined within purely ideological structures void of aesthetics and craft. Galeano, despite the efforts of many critics to paint him as a *canoso* or grey-haired dogmatist, is an artist whose resistance to reductive categories emerges from an allusive, allegorical style predicated on the transformation of found materials into narratives that interrogate simplistic genre-divides between fictive and lived experiences.

The title of this introductory chapter outlines a precise allegorical trajectory that, for better or worse, we have chosen to overlap with the chapter structure that moves through issues of rights, memory and story, history, and alternative communities. The cemetery of words (*Days and Nights* 173) is Galeano's trope for writing practices that deny meaning and relevance to pressing issues of social justice. Moribund language that has no active presence in addressing the here and now of human reality resides in the cemetery of words. Dead words numb humanity, narrow the ability to see things critically, and thereby reduce the capacity not only to envision alternatives to deadening structures but also to act upon those insights. As Caleb Bach notes, "Good writing, for Galeano, 'must reflect the struggle between what one *wants* to say and what one can *actually* say. Without that tension between *desafío* (panic/horror) and *euforia*, it emerges lifeless, dead'" (18). Alien memories, resistance, and redemptive storytelling counterbalance the death force of the cemetery of words. Reshaping memory through that which has been evacuated, suppressed, or seemingly annihilated from it is in Galeano's general literary philosophy an active, liberating force, one small part of a larger dynamic related to how humanity seeks to challenge and transform itself. Resistance to anything that demeans the basic dignity and integrity of a humanity that is at once shared but constituted by enormous differences can be born of how memory is restituted via literary means. Ultimately, restitution involves a renewed capacity to interrogate the world in a way that balances social justice and appreciation of difference, the ideal and the real, the shape of what *is* against the shape of what *could be*.

In the mode of such restitutions, this book offers the first full-length critical study of Galeano in English. It neither aims for comprehensivity in its coverage of Galeano's writings (though we have examined his entire body of published work) nor aspires to be biographical: in fact, except for the summary outline of his life's trajectory provided at the beginning of this chapter, we have largely resisted the biographical mode, if only because of its tendency to seduce interpreters, according to their biases and commitments, into opposing extremes of demonization or hagiography. Instead, we have striven to write a book that stylistically respects the anti-generic and disruptive strategies evident in Galeano's own writing practice. To do so has meant producing a text that speaks from a variety of different critical positionings: these include a deployment of literary and cultural theory, which are foregrounded throughout what follows, especially in relation to central issues involving the telling of history and the relations between literature and human rights. As the book took shape and we addressed the diverse materials (visual, filmic, photographic, journalistic, literary) that characterize Galeano's output, it became evident to us that adhering to single chapter headings would not work because the scope of Galeano's work eludes pressures of straightforward categorization. As an alternative, we chose to use single chapter headings with multiple sub-headings as a way of gathering diverse but related materials into a recognizable and flexible structure in which the profuse forms and voices of Galeano's work might be given their best space to breathe. What emerged was a blend of critical readings that were highly dependent on comparative juxtapositions, structures of fable and parable, fictive interventions, phantom memories, and historicized appositions in which encounter narratives and their legacies figure prominently. Moreover, we have deliberately sought to place Galeano in a transcultural and transliterary context that evokes unexpected conjunctions, strange disparities, unlikely contiguities and synergies, and discrepant engagements (a term coined by the African American writer Nathaniel Mackey that we return to at greater length in the next chapter). We recognize that we have in many ways produced two books—one that addresses Galeano's writings in a wide variety of contexts, another that addresses the larger issues toward which Galeano inevitably points his readers.

Because some of the materials related to the book can only be found in Spanish, Portuguese, and French, we have chosen for accuracy's sake to cite extracts in the original language along with our English translation whenever no translation has been published. Unless otherwise indicated, all translations are our own. Where translations of Galeano's work already existed in English we have used them. Also, because many of the materials from the 1970s activities of Galeano and the journal *Crisis* are crucial to understanding the contexts that shaped Galeano's later writing practices, we have chosen to include extracts from that journal and associated publications, some appearing for the first time in English. These extracts are important for their context, especially in light of the very real pressures of torture and disappearance faced by the people associated with these journals. (Haroldo Conti, for instance, a well-known contributor to *Crisis*, was disappeared while Fico Vogelius, who financed the publication, was jailed and tortured.) They are significant, too, for how they represent an alternative and admirable methodology (let alone aesthetic) of publication in the "infotainment" world of supposedly diminished alternatives. We discuss the publication practices of *Crisis* at some length in our chapter on story and memory and we have sought in some degree to echo them in our own writing practices.

In response to the lacunae evident in most previous critical responses to Galeano, we have given extended emphasis to the relations between human rights and literary inquiry. This issue, largely neglected in the realm of literary and cultural studies, is where we decided to focus the conceptual thrust of the book in the hope that the critical repressions motivating that neglect may be converted into more constructive energies. The interconnectedness of literary culture and human rights culture has only recently begun to draw any attention, not surprisingly through organizations like PEN and Amnesty International, in which the plight of writers in repressive regimes receives only moderate publicity as a function of how the efforts of such organizations are largely ignored by the mainstream media. Much slower off the mark have been literary theorists, who—despite the work some have produced to challenge preconceptions about race, gender, sexual orientation, power, nationalism, colonialism, and so forth—have largely avoided theorizing on general issues of human rights, especially the language used in crucial human rights documents and instruments. Because of this lack, our long chapter on rights discourse and literature dominates the shape of this book. More importantly, though, we see Galeano's writing practice as actively engaged with achieving social change and justice within a transnational context as a direct result of the experience of the post-conquest Americas. One aspect of this engagement is Galeano's production of a consistent critique of structures of thought that shape orthodox understandings of how such change is to be (limitedly) achieved (as a function of the rhetoric of "being realistic"), denied, or restricted altogether. In our reading, it would be fatuous to place a writer of Galeano's range in any one pigeonhole. Hence, critical receptions of

Galeano, as Virginia Bell astutely observes, need to work against reductively portraying him as a "substitute figure for the multiplicity of voices participating in the contest over the design of the Americas" (115). Nonetheless, it is clear to us that understanding his literary work in relation to the emergence of a discourse of human rights in the last half of the twentieth century is a productive avenue to follow.

Only a small number of formal essays in English and Spanish, whether scholarly or not, have been written about Galeano. No book in English has dealt with him as a major literary figure; only two books in Spanish, Palaversich's academic monograph (based on her doctoral dissertation) *Silencio, voz y escritura en Eduardo Galeano* (1995) and Hugo Riva's belletristic *Memoria viviente de América latina: La obra de Eduardo Galeano* (1996), have done so, though neither of these latter sources is widely available or cited, either in Spanish or in English. With few exceptions major critical studies devoted to such topics as decolonization, postcolonial theory, and Latin American history bypass Galeano, despite the fact that in many ways his writing practice has anticipated and exceeded their own critical positionings: Palaversich states, "despite being quoted in hundreds of works dealing with a wide range of subjects such as economics, history, health, sociology, and culture, Galeano's writings…have encountered surprisingly few responses from literary critics" ("Eduardo Galeano's *Memoria del fuego*" 135). Martin echoes this view, observing that:

> It is striking that although his works are so widely diffused, and he has received the unusual distinction of winning literary prizes both in Cuba and in the United States, he has received almost no attention among academic critics. In this regard, and in others, he is reminiscent of George Orwell, a writer of immense influence who cannot easily be pigeonholed and whose devotees are among the wider reading public rather than among scholars, who have hardly written about him at all. ("Hope Springs Eternal" 148)

And Bell comments that "recent U.S. critical acclaim [of Galeano's work] may have to do with the perception that the Cold War has ended. Galeano's 'socialism' is no longer perceived as a threat. The post Cold War context allows an aestheticized and de-politicized appreciation of his work" (265–66).

From our perspective, understanding Galeano's work involves avoiding any simplistic privileging of either his aesthetics or his politics. He is no simple aesthete, no simple ideologue, and his work consistently refuses to centre itself in either of these reductive categories. Palaversich identifies the current biases behind the critical silence (or repudiation) as a function of the fact that many of Galeano's texts are not ambiguous and do not invite plural interpretations: in many cases, Galeano speaks so plainly as to seem to not require interpretation at all. Moreover, his crossing of genres—writing lyrical and popular retellings of concrete historical events and people—throws both literary critics and historians for a loop. Our reading of Galeano would argue that such plain talk as Galeano produces is not to be dismissed as either reductive or simplistic, the anti-literary machinations of a writer with a journalistic background. Galeano does not, as the preceding statements might suggest, renounce allegory or ambiguity so much as put their traditional uses to the question. In conjunction with a writing technique that strips things to the bone (in the mode of Juan Rulfo, the Mexican writer who produced a very small body of work, one that has clearly been an important literary influence on Galeano), ambiguity and allegory as used by Galeano produce a perspective that challenges literary traditions (and readers) grown comfortable in familiar styles of production and reception.[4] Historians bent on "objective" accounts of events devoid of any ideological point of view or ethical interpretation are just as put off by Galeano's work as are literary critics dedicated to examining the intricate, self-referential discourses of experimental, postmodern literature. But what to do with a writer who challenges both these conventions, such as they are, and, moreover, places his challenge firmly in the domain of public discourses about global issues of social justice?

The critics who do pay attention to Galeano are not always distinguished by their insights, a fact exemplified in the commentary of Danubio Torres-Fierro's essay "Los mercaderes de la virtud" ["The Merchants of Virtue"]. This thinly-veiled apology for neoliberalism parading as postmodern wisdom accuses Galeano of the very characteristics that he himself clearly despises in theory and practice: "el gusto por las frases sonoras e inofensivas sobre las que todo el mundo se pone fácilmente de acuerdo" (57) [a taste for grandiloquent and inoffensive pronouncements easily agreed upon by everyone]. The quotation from Jules Romains, the French author, used as the epigraph to Torres-Fierro's piece, sets the vitriolic tone for the essay's sole and unfounded charge that Galeano speaks in a "*langue de bois* (una jerga de carácter ideológico hecha de lugares comunes y dominada por el vacío de sustancia)" (57) [wooden language (ideological jargon made up of clichés lacking any substance)]. At two decisive moments in the essay, Cuba—a highly problematic signifier that requires deep contextualization for any semblance of reasonable dialogue to occur—is vaguely alluded to as a sign of Galeano's fossilized idealism and a source of political resentment. And the reader is expected to collude unquestioningly with Torres-Fierro in his facile linking of socialist, humanitarian principles with a revolution that supposedly no longer holds any interest for sophisticated intellectuals. As is the case with most critics who equate ideological principles with dogmatism, Torres-Fierro accuses Galeano of ordering binary characteristics representing capitalism and socialism in a way that is both Manichean and imprecise, revealing a loathing for context (58).

Admittedly, counterpointing binaries is one of Galeano's many techniques for producing stark imagery and clear language that nevertheless resists being reduced to any simplistic representation of causes. The play of opposites is schematic but symbolic and, in some cases, invites the reader to contemplate human folly, as in the poem "Fin de siglo" [End of the Century]:

Está envenenada la tierra que nos entierra o destierra.

Ya no hay aire, sino desaire.

Ya no hay lluvia, sino lluvia ácida.

Ya no hay parques, sino parkings.

Empresas en lugar de naciones.

Consumidores en lugar de ciudadanos.

Aglomeraciones en lugar de ciudades.

Competencias mercantiles en lugar de relaciones humanas.

No hay pueblos, sino mercados.

No hay personas, sino públicos.

No hay realidades, sino publicidades.

No hay visiones, sino televisiones.

Para elogiar una flor, se dice: "Parece de plástico." (Apuntes para el fin de siglo 95)

[*Poisoned is the earth that buries or banishes us.*

There's no air, but despair.

There's no rain, only acid rain.

There are no more parks, but parking lots.

Companies instead of nations.

Consumers instead of citizens.

Agglomerations instead of cities.

Commercial competition instead of human relationships.

There are no pueblos, just markets.

There are no persons, just spectators.

There are no realities, just advertising.

There are no visions, just televisions.

To praise a flower, we say: "It looks like plastic."]

Bleak and to the point, this kind of negation in Galeano's writing is held in balance with the optimism expressed in another example of contrastive terms relating to the new millennium, "The Right to Rave," a text in which the negative terms of the upside-down world are prophetically turned right-side up:

People shall not be driven by cars, or programmed by computers, or bought by supermarkets, or watched by televisions;

People shall work for a living instead of living for work. (*Upside Down* 334)

This strategy of inversion and reversal, a strategy of seeing through things disguised to mask the way the world wants to be, can be located in important hybrid voices that emerged in the post-conquest Americas of the sixteenth century. Felipe Guaman Poma de Ayala, for instance, an Andean, Indio-ladino "contemporary of Shakespeare's, called the post-conquest world in which he lived and wrote *mundo al revés,* 'a world in reverse.' For him and his people, the invasion of America turned the world upside down" (Wright, *Stolen Continents* 8). Galeano consistently explores the topos of the "world upside-down" as a function of his inverted narrative strategies from very early work through to *Patas arriba* (*Upside Down*), a book based wholly on this conceit. An entry from *Memory of Fire* on the American writer Charlotte Perkins Gilman, for example, posits this upside-down world in gendered terms:

> What would happen if a woman woke up one morning changed into a man? What if the family were not a training camp where boys learn to command and girls to obey? What if there were daycare for babies, and husbands shared the cleaning and cooking? What if innocence turned into dignity and reason and emotion went arm in arm? What if preachers and newspapers told the truth? And if no one were anyone's property?
>
> So Charlotte Perkins Gilman raves…This stubborn wayfarer travels tirelessly around the United States, announcing a world upside down. (*Century of the Wind* 18-19)

Galeano does not privilege any one form of social or cultural analysis in relation to this upside-down strategy. The rhetorical form of the inversion presupposes an ironic capacity to see the world as it really is, as opposed to how its image has been constructed by the interests that control dominant forms of representation. Galeano persistently punctures these latter forms in the name of resistant narratives that enable alternative forms of seeing. We do not wish to discount the power and playfulness of such inversions as a mode for framing narratives and specific tropes. Bell, for instance, identifies "*llueve hacia arriba*" (the rain falls up) as a key phrase that undergirds the second volume of *Memory of Fire* (75).

Yet another effect of the play of opposites in Galeano's writing is to unveil the real motives behind the political hypocrisy of the U.S. government and of the mass media, as in "In Defense of Nicaragua":

> The pitiless, ever-growing siege and blockade are not taking place because democracy does not exist in Nicaragua, but so it never will. They are not taking place because a dictatorship exists in Nicaragua, but so one may again. They are not taking place because Nicaragua is a satellite, a sad pawn on the chessboard of the great powers, but so it may be one again. (*We Say No* 200)[5]

Galeano clarifies the contrast between his preoccupations and the rhetoric of literary theorists who label and denounce him as a propagator of communism or male aesthetics. He ends "In Defense of Nicaragua" by framing his essay as a modest but crucial show of solidarity, voicing a motive for writing that does not usually occur to either historians or literary critics who are trapped in objectivist modes of pseudo-scientific expression:

> Nicaragua is not looking for walls to hide behind, but it needs shields with which to defend itself. These words I put down here, which have nothing neutral about them,

are an attempt to give some of that help, even though it be of small import. Ambiguity and fog have become fashionable now, and taking sides is considered a sign of stupidity or poor taste. But this writer feels a joy in choosing and he confesses to being one of those antique creatures who still believe that joy gives meaning to the mysterious adventures of the human animal on this earth. (*We Say No* 204)

Torres-Fierro's insistence on atomizing elements of culture is presented in his essay as reflective of his own critical integrity and appreciation of complexity, a term that keeps reappearing in predictable ways in a mode of criticism that refuses to see the oppressively homogenizing effects of economic globalization.[6]

Throughout this book, we will examine in multiple contexts how Galeano's practice of fragmenting narratives differs from this desire to obfuscate the not-so-complex economic principles aimed at yielding maximum profits through minimal investment, both ethical and financial. For instance, Graciela Tomassini interprets Galeano's mosaic fragmentation in *Memory of Fire* as a technique to include the reader in history-making since, as she suggests, the transformation of the fragments into history depends on the reader's encyclopedia, on his or her ideological perspective, and on the task of reading (119). In direct contrast to this interpretation of Galeano's participatory aesthetics, Hispanist scholar Jean Franco reduces the complex synthesis of the revisionary history *Memory of Fire* to an attempt at foundational documentary, rather than a sophisticated act of resistance using the very tools of what is (mis)perceived to be foundational in a free-form reconstruction that blends fictive writing techniques with chronicle, *testimonio*, journalism, social analysis, storytelling, and so forth. Furthermore, while the term "foundational" has negative connotations of stability and institutional legitimation, these are not the only meanings and do not adequately describe Galeano's search for what is fundamental in the cultural sense of recuperating the sources of communities. Much North American cultural theory is blind to the issue of solidarity in communitarian ethics and adopts a self-righteous tone in policing practices and language that exceed its own unreflective individualism and amnesia. Franco suggests that "whereas those authors [Carlos Fuentes, Mario Vargas Llosa, Augusto Roa Bastos, Edgardo Rodríguez Juliá, Homero Aridjis] establish a dialogue between history and literature, Galeano is unwilling to grant historical discourse its due" ("The Raw and the Cooked" 184).

Such a view gives precedence to traditional literary means of addressing history via the novel. But the precise point of Galeano's project is that new, bastardized literary forms are needed to reshape conventional and over-determined relations between history and literature. Reshaping involves overwriting the monolithic ordering of space and time that is characteristic of traditional novelistic discourse through the (re)invention of a genre that recognizes fragmentariness, incoherence, multiple points of view, myth, and dream. These are crucial constituents, aesthetic and substantive, of the experience of history and memory as literary constructs. While many of these characteristics are lacking in the Anglo-American canon, they are the most celebrated features of recent Latin American literature. However, self-referentiality, virtuosity, and an imprecise locale and time evocative of universal or at least trans-continental realities (as in the case of Latin America) are other features that distinguish Latin American fiction from the more urgent writings of Galeano, Marcos, and even novelists like García Márquez—all of whom, in particular instances, choose to return to journalism to tell a story that demands more precise limits and immediate responses than a novel.

Moreover, writers concerned with history and social justice can no more rely on traditional forms (like the novel) than they can on traditional sources (as designated by official history). How many writers of history or literature have spent as much time as has Galeano with the state policy documents and annual reports of NGOs (non-governmental organizations) like Human Rights Watch, Amnesty International, and Survival International to construct their narratives? Though we address these issues more fully in our chapters on rights and history, suffice it to say that one of Galeano's key projects as an innovative writer has been to experiment with the aesthetics of historical writing practices. Such experimentation will always merit—if not beg—criticism as part of an ongoing dialogue about why memory and story are such crucial features of any civil community. To diminish Galeano's work as "more problematic, perhaps because, unlike the 1950s when Neruda wrote his *Canto General*, it is now beyond the scope of one person to rewrite the entire story of Latin American resistance" (Franco, "The Raw and the Cooked" 184) is to not entirely get the point of what Galeano is up to.

Galeano's method consistently resists monolithic ordering of historical narratives (though necessarily as writer he is responsible for the ordering of his materials) in a series of writings based on his own multiple sources, reliable and unreliable, authentic and inauthentic, up-to-date and out-of-date. Moreover, it was never even within the scope of Neruda[7] (another of Galeano's crucial influences, along with José Martí) to "rewrite the entire story of Latin American resistance." The last poem in Neruda's epic *Canto General* states, contrary to Franco's point, that "At last, I'm free within beings" (399), an explicit gesture toward narrative multiplicity. The line denotes the way in which narrative is contradictorily located in a single person but then emerges from a complex backdrop of multiple voicings that both produce the narrative and respond to it (what Marcos, spokesperson for the Zapatista insurgency in Chiapas, frames as "An echo that reproduces its own sound, yet opens itself to the sound of the other" [*Our Word Is Our Weapon* 122]). Neruda's closural lines to the *Canto General* effectively capture this communitarian vision of voice and action and provide a crucial *mise-en-scène* for Galeano's own work:

Amid beings, like live air,
and from corralled solitude
I set forth to the multitude of combats,

free because my hand holds your hand,
conquering indomitable happiness.

Common book of mankind, broken bread
is this geography of my song,
and a community of peasants
will one day harvest its fire
and will again sow its flames
and leaves in the ship of the earth. (399)

Such an aesthetic context is far from Franco's imaginings of a unified historical narrative, though solidarity, narrative (dis)continuity, ongoing struggle and combat, and authorial solitude all figure as part of the complex representations that produce narrative. Historical writing that emerges from such a context implicitly resists being reduced to a univocal position, as Franco would have it with Galeano.

Franco, in reading Galeano as someone who "views Latin America's history as personified geography rather than as discourses initiated from different and often antagonistic positions of power and authority," interprets Galeano's conception in *Memory of Fire* as a gendering of America as a woman: Franco bases this assessment on Galeano's claimed attempt "'to…rescue the kidnapped memory of all America, but above all of Latin America, that despised and beloved land: I would like to talk to her, share her secrets, ask her of what difficult clays she was born, from what acts of love and violation she comes'" ("The Raw and the Cooked" 184). The astonishing diversity of source materials used by Galeano argues against Franco's reading here.[8] How many historians take seriously, as does Galeano, indigenous creation myths as part of a historical narrative of origins? To imply sexism in the highly conventional language of gendering nation is an all-too-easy mark to shoot at. This is especially so for someone whose politics are questioning the very conditions of that gendering, using conventional and recognizable literary tropes as a means to overturn such unthought stereotypes based on *both* love and rape. Is this another case of the self-censoring, political correctness that insists "I can only speak for myself" while also censoring anyone else who thinks they can empathize, and speak *with* others in solidarity?

The basis of this solidarity resides in the indigenous conception of Mother Earth, *La Pachamama*, which Galeano describes in his anthology of writings about women, *Mujeres*:

En el altiplano andino, *mama* es la Virgen y *mama* son la tierra y el tiempo. Se enoja la tierra, la madre tierra, la Pachamama, si alguien bebe sin convidarla. Cuando ella tiene mucha sed, rompe la vasija y derrama. A ella se ofrece la placenta del recién nacido, entrerrándola entre las flores, para que viva el niño; y para que viva el amor, los amantes entierran cabellos anudados. La diosa tierra recoge en sus brazos a los cansados y a los rotos, que de ella han brotado, y se abre para darles refugio al fin del viaje. Desde abajo de la tierra, los muertos la florecen. (37)

[In the Andean highlands, *mama* is the Virgin and *mama* is the earth and time. The earth, Mother Earth, *Pachamama*, gets angry if someone drinks without offering her any. When she is very thirsty, she breaks the jug and it spills. To her we offer the newborn's placenta, burying it among the flowers, so that the child will live; and so that love will live, lovers bury strands of their hair knotted together. The earth goddess gathers in her arms the tired and the broken who have flowered from her, and she opens herself up to give them refuge at the end of the journey. From beneath the earth, the dead make her flower.]

Dangerous and Fertile Embraces 1. Frida Kahlo, "The Love Embrace of the Universe, the Earth (Mexico), Diego, Me, and Señor Xólotl" (1949).

Many women authors and visual artists also represent their nations and the Earth as feminine, since—like Galeano and other men who do the same—they are not gendering an inanimate object but recuperating the holistic cosmogony of indigenous Latin American culture, according to which the universe is animate and the Earth is figured as the mother of all. Frida Kahlo's painting "The Love-Embrace of the Universe, The Earth (Mexico), Diego, Me, and Mr. Xólotl" (1949) depicts Kahlo holding Diego Rivera shrunk to the size of a baby, while she herself is cradled by Mother Earth/Mexico whose breast oozes milk and who in turn lies in the arms of a pre-Columbian deity.[9] Is it critically suspect for a male writer to express a similar mythic conception of a feminine source and space? We will argue throughout the book that Galeano's plurivocal aesthetic cannot be reduced to academic historiography, and that the lyrical and mythic elements of consciousness are meshed with empirical data, producing texts that appeal to the reader's emotions and intellect simultaneously.

Our critique of Franco's reading of Galeano is not meant to suggest that Galeano is above criticism or beyond reproach. No writer who enters into the dialogic process of narrative can be so considered. We do not mean to foreclose either on debate about sexism in the narrating of the Americas or on other concerns critics have expressed over, for example, Galeano's sometimes overly truncated narrative style, as in Paul West's analysis in *Latin American Literature and Arts Review* of the last volume of *Memory of Fire, Century of the Wind*.[10] The standard critical gesture against Galeano has been to label him an apologist for leftist views, even when these labels are held to be virtually meaningless and over-determined in the individualistic social morality of the "First World," where terms such as "socialism" and "imperialism" are emptied of significance or, as Palaversich suggests, "rendidas obsoletas y 'metafísicas' en el Primer Mundo" [rendered obsolete and 'metaphysical' in the First World] in a process of "deideologization" that Galeano fervently opposes (*Silencio* 126-27). According to the logic of some of his critics, Galeano is an ideologue who flies the intellectual banner of an outmoded, non-pragmatic, unattainable utopic idealism. Within such a view Galeano's attempt to imagine the possibility of alternative social, cultural, political, and economic formations is deemed a perversion of the "complex" forces that currently determine those realities.

But attentive reading of Galeano's many pronouncements on precisely these issues reveals quite the opposite. A tempered optimist ("My certitudes have doubts for breakfast. I distrust full-time optimism" [Manrique 59]), Galeano also works to produce a writerly frame of reference that recognizes diversity and its potential:

But the world contains other sources of energy. This is real richness: so many worlds within the world, so many worlds the world contains! Sources of energy and hope. We are not doomed to a way of life that obliges you to choose between dying of hunger and dying of boredom. But it's not easy nowadays to rediscover those alternative fountains. They are suffering, let us say, a crisis of low esteem. (Manrique 58)

At once a mordant metaphorician and skilled allegorist (from the Greek *allos* for other and *-agoria* for speaking), Galeano sets these qualities to work in the name of the liberatory potential of social and historical transformations that emerge from a practice of reading the world critically:

> The black legend asks us to enter the Museum of the Good Savage, where we can shed tears over the obliterated happiness of a few wax figures that have nothing in common with the flesh-and-blood beings who people our lands. The pink legend, on the other hand, invites us into the Great Temple of the West where we can add our voices to the Universal choir, intoning hymns in celebration of Europe's great civilising mission, to conquer the world in order to save it.
>
> No to the black legend. No to the pink legend. To reclaim reality: that is the challenge. *To change the reality that is, to reclaim the reality that was, the falsified, unseen, betrayed reality of the history of America.* (Galeano, "A Tale of Ambiguities" 34; our emphasis)

In this passage, Galeano explains why he refuses to be duped by any reductive legend that produces simplistic arrangements of complex relations, especially in regard to the encounter narratives that ground notions of American cultural identity. Reclaiming betrayed and unseen realities requires the rejection of deterministic myths of the good savage or of the civilizing mission of European culture. There is a truth hidden away between the two poles of these stereotypical understandings of the foundation of the Americas: another story to be fashioned.

What interests us in the polemical criticism Galeano's work has engendered are the underlying operative principles that shut discussion down by overlooking alternative paradigms that seem alien to individualistic, self-interested, highly canonical critical perspectives. One of the most frequently recurring charges against Galeano is that he appropriates the other's voice to speak for the disenfranchised, to speak from "a plural place, which nevertheless is [neither] ambiguous nor indeterminate," according to Tomassini's positive take on how voice can be collective, even when written by an individual author (111). The concept of "otherness," so much a part of postcolonial theory, is invaluable in critiquing discourses that absorb and annihilate the other or convert it into an exotic object. But the other can also become fetishized by the individualistic discourse that posits it as completely inaccessible, thus disallowing the allegorical "other-speaking" that Galeano deploys as a crucial writing strategy. In contrast to the concept of inalienable otherness, Galeano's commitment to critical solidarity—that is, solidarity that emerges from the critique of deeply embedded structures like the black and pink legends—does not mean self-interest specific to a particular group of people. Solidarity understood in this way (as a function of the critique of imposed models that betray reality) is challenging and hope-inspiring when it seeks to bridge cultural, ethnic, racial, gender, and economic differences in striving to transform humanity.

Much postmodern criticism passes from offering a healthy dose of skepticism about how desires are voiced and how one can represent an "other" to completely cynical negation of any trans-individual empathy or expression. The limitations of academic discourse would not be of interest if it were not for the fact that this anti-ethics based on the principle that "I can only speak for myself" permeates a broader cultural reality and has disturbing sociopolitical implications. Angel Rama sees Galeano's project as a search for the "new man" in which people from different backgrounds can share, given their common goals to change inequitable dispositions of power in accordance with communitarian principles that evolve out of an ongoing dialogue and sense of reciprocal respect.[11] The concept of community is often dismissed in the North American context as a fatuous myth that inhibits people from understanding the benefits of globalization unless it is co-opted into the advertising myth of the global village.[12] Against such a view, Noam Chomsky addresses the commonality of purpose in the pedagogical context and says that students "should not be seen merely as an audience but as a part of a community of common concern in which one hopes to participate constructively" (*Chomsky on MisEducation* 21). Many of those who critique Galeano's socialist views confuse this speaking to "a community of common concern" with "preaching to the converted." Since these critics misunderstand the historical and theoretical context for Galeano's sense of what constitutes community, they attribute expressions of desire for transforming society to the individual author, seen as reaffirming the beliefs of his or her own comrades while boring everyone else. Galeano's work encourages a reexamination and recontextualization of what is meant by didactic intentions. Such intentions, as Palaversich observes, are automatically dismissed as "paternalistic" in a Western criticism that theorizes postcolonialism while largely ignoring both neocolonialism and the social responsibility of a writer like Galeano, who considers Latin America as a (still) colonized space and whose writing is consequently a liberatory project (*Silencio* 14, 20).

In *Pedagogy of the Oppressed*, Paulo Freire addresses the problems of miseducation and the culture of silence in which oppressed individuals suffer an alienating division between self and reality and do not discern the causes inhibiting both individuals and communities from achieving fulfillment. Freire's vision of a pedagogy of the oppressed goes far beyond literacy programs and indoctrinating the newly educated individual as "end-product" into the existing market economy under the slogan that the sky is the limit when it comes to personal entrepreneurship. Education for Freire is not just the teaching of literacy and some technical skill enabling the individual to find a job, but a radical process of *concientizaçao* [the making conscious of] the dialogic cultural action "by means of which the people, through a true praxis, leave behind the status of *objects* to assume the status of historical Subjects" (141). Freire envisions pedagogy as a revolutionary means of transforming individuals into community members who work together to achieve justice and the end of the dehumanizing paradigm of oppressors and oppressed:

The object of dialogical-libertarian action is not to 'dislodge' the oppressed from a mythological reality in order to 'bind' them to another reality. On the contrary, the object of dialogical action is to make it possible for the oppressed, by perceiving their adhesion, to opt to transform an unjust reality. Since the unity of the oppressed involves solidarity among them, regardless of their exact status, this unity unquestionably requires class consciousness. (155)

The concepts of a libertarian politics based on solidarity and the desire to end the oppression resulting from social inequality and dehumanizing work permeate much of the writing that emerges from Latin America. These concepts are so alien as to be incomprehensible to those who subscribe to the purely individualistic aims of the "American Dream": the paradigm of community effort is completely at odds with one that centres on the individual, as in the neoliberal model. Galeano's intentions, then, can only be understood from a communitarian perspective whose aims are to end the suffering and the numb silence of the majority and to work towards the creation of non-oppressive, liberatory social structures where words circulate freely and decisions are made collectively through participation and not representation. The suffering and silence cannot be alleviated through simply increasing income and material goods, because one's humanity does not depend on purchasing power but on being integrated emotionally, spiritually, intellectually, and socially into a common project that strives to fulfill these capacities in *all* community members without regard to class, gender, sexual orientation, or ethnic status.

According to Riva, Galeano's didactic project helps create an anti-schematic, reflective context that resists any attempt to reduce human community through discourses that posit the "masses" as a tenable concept in relation to the inexhaustible richness of humanity. This perspective opposes negative pedagogies predicated on the individualistic assumptions that conceive of didacticism as a paternalistic feeding of knowledge from above to the ignorant below. By contrast, in the Latin American context of libertarian ideals, teaching is seen as a shared dialogue in which all participants learn from each other, and the "intellectual" or member of the dominant social class, however revolutionary an individual, has a great deal to learn from the oppressed and not vice versa:

En esa línea de trabajo podemos insertar la obra de Galeano, pues se considera que el ser es inagotablemente rico aunque las realidades sociales imponen duras frustraciones; hay confianza en que es posible desarrollar lo mejor de cada uno con un sentido solidario, que identifica más allá de las discrepancias. Se induce a la reflexión, se procura evitar todo esquematismo, se acentúa la actitud indagatoria sin caer en el escepticismo, reconoce que la masa es anónima y sólo número, en tanto el pueblo es un organismo viviente que tiene tradición y futuro. (*Memoria viviente* 70-71)

[It is in this line of work that we can include Galeano's writing given that he sees human beings as inexhaustibly rich, although the social realities impose hard frustrations on them; there is confidence in the possibility of developing the best in each and every person with a sense of solidarity, which he never loses sight of despite all the differences. His work leads to reflection, avoiding a schematic attitude and encouraging instead an attitude of inquiry without falling into skepticism; he recognizes that the masses are anonymous and only made up of numbers, while the people (*pueblo*) are a living organism that has a tradition and a future.]

A major linguistic problem confronting any work on culture in both Spanish and English is the difficulty of translating the word *pueblo*. By translating this term as "the people," many of the connotations of the Spanish term, evocative of a class distinction including rural and urban working people and the severely disenfranchised majority, are lost. Consequently, the Spanish *pueblo* is also "the poor." In English "the people" is virtually indistinguishable from "the masses," thereby making Riva's distinction hard to comprehend. Palaversich observes that *pueblo* comes closest to how postcolonial theorists use the term "subaltern" in opposition to "hegemony," which in the Latin American context refers most frequently to imperial oligarchies (*Silencio* 168).

However, we would add the important distinction of "subaltern" as a negative term, literally meaning "of inferior rank," while *pueblo* has the more positive connotations of being the "magma" or foundation of any nation, as well as resonating with a tone of solidarity lacking in the English "the people" except in very specific contexts of political discourse. It becomes increasingly clear when comparing North American and Latin American discourses on development, revolution, and human rights that *pueblo* with its positive resonances drops into a silent, barely thought, or forgotten void in English. Argentine liberation theologian, historian, and cultural theorist Enrique Dussel argues for an understanding of *pueblo* in relation to its indigenous cognates in "colonial and Amerindian contexts," a move that further troubles *pueblo*'s signification: "When we talk of the people [*pueblo*], this had to do with the *antepetl*, the *nahuatl* concept [coincident with the idea of *comunidad* as a non-Western, indigenous formation]. We could include the parallel meanings in Maya, Inca, et cetera. This notion of people is not people [*pueblo*] as we articulate it in Spanish. Today, after the naming of the conquistadors, we call them peoples [*pueblos*], yet if we still wish to use the notion, we must give it the kind of resonance that it still has in Latin America lest we forget the colonial and Amerindian contexts" ("Ethics Is the Original Philosophy" 69). Such linguistic distinctions are significant for what they say about lived cultural realities: as Anthony Pagden reports,

When the Franciscan Alonso de Molina came to compile his Spanish-Nahuatl dictionary the only words he could find to stand for *hombre* were terms designating social groups…[There was] no word to translate the expression *homo sapiens*. For the

Mexica, man, once he has left the group, ceased, in all important respects, to be 'man'…De-humanisation is, perhaps, the simplest method of dealing with all that is culturally unfamiliar. (*The Fall of Natural Man* 17)[13]

What initially appears to be simply a linguistic difficulty suggests a much greater cultural divide when it comes to thinking about the past in relation to social alternatives. According to the smug logic of capital-centric thought prevalent in the First World, "the poor" constitute an aberration of the "American Dream." Myth would have it that they are the losers who had the means to catapult themselves into wealth but failed to do so through lack of intelligence, imagination, or initiative. Dussel distinguishes between the two ethical systems that come into play in this kind of comparative cultural study: community ethics and the social morality growing out of isolated individualism. In his exposition of liberation theology, Dussel argues for embracing community ethics and for recognizing the severe limitations of individualism:

> The "poor"—still in the negative sense—are those who, in the face-to-face of the person-to-person relationship must confront the person possessed of money. And yet they have not sold themselves. They are poor because they have their own corporeality to sell, their bodiliness, their skin, their "hide," in their absolute nakedness, their radical poverty—without food, clothing, housing, health, protection. They are but miserable beggars. The word "economy" comes from the Greek *oikos* and *nomos*, and means, etymologically, "law of the house." The homeless, then, are nothing, non-being, worthless, to the economists of domination. The "poor"—this time in the positive sense of the word—are the miserable unemployed, precisely in their carnality, their fleshliness. They ask the person with money, the capitalist (or abstractly, capital) for work. And yet they are subject, the creative subject, of all possible value. These starving poor, who beg for work, for a wage, are the very Christ of the *ecce homo*. And yet it is they who constitute the foundation and groundwork of the whole current system of domination. They abide only on the outside, "thrown into the ditch and robbed." But there is no Samaritan to help them. (*Ethics and Community* 125-26)

Dussel's empathic definition of the poor comes much closer to what is meant by *pueblo* than to "the people," with its socio-moralistic connotations of individual voting citizens. According to Galeano's communitarian ethics, as voiced consistently throughout his work, writing contributes to the process of decolonizing Latin America. And it does so through the recuperation of a language that dissents in the terms proposed by Dussel. To read Galeano with any understanding, then, is to learn this language anew, to be open to its symbolic and intertextual relations with histories and cultures that lie beyond the purview of normative Western culture. Ironically, these relations that are excluded from the norm are part of the hybrid, mestizo culture that the Americas represent.

While many critics accept the notion of decolonization as an ongoing process in Latin America,[14] they often deny writers the right to speak in solidarity with others who continue to suffer the consequences of colonization unless they can be classified by critics as purely testimonial participants or witnesses. Román de la Campa turns the tables on those who "[preempt] contestation" and "[wallow] in manic triumphalism," attributing these characteristics to the political culture of neoliberalism that also "reads Third World claims of redress as nothing but chronic conflicts of underdevelopment, inexplicable civil wars, or irrational residues from outdated master narratives" (33). But like other critics who see communitarian concerns as belonging to a naïve and outdated ideology, de la Campa ignores the motivating force of solidarity and criticizes the narrative strategies in Galeano's *Guatemala: Occupied Country* on the basis that "ethnic, national, and even linguistic elements of difference are ignored, even though they are crucial factors separating the Uruguayan writer from a Guatemalan guerrilla force"; de la Campa further attributes this glossing over of crucial differences to a 1960s male aesthetic (44-45). Here, Galeano is seen as suspect because he presents the historical and socioeconomic context of Guatemala's brutal régime and the massacre of the Maya from a third-person omniscience, even though "these [contexts] are interspersed with various dialogues, interviews, and other first-person speakers" (44). He is suspect not only for his narrative strategies that situate his voice "in the background as a passive interlocutor" (44), but even for not abandoning his profession and privileged position, as did Fidel Castro and Che Guevara (45). This position, which dismisses Galeano's personal history (and especially the conditions that led to his exile), is dependent on an outmoded notion that separates writing from action. It would be akin to accusing a soldier in the Zapatista army of shirking duties because he or she did not publish the motivations and contingencies that led to specific political actions. What recourse does such criticism leave the author (let alone the political actant) who believes intensely in the circular movement of storytelling emanating from the people and traversing the writer and the reader, not as isolated individuals but as members of a community of common concerns? What recourse does it leave the author who sees a continuity between action and the various means of discourse he or she deploys?

Galeano is painfully aware of the economic forces responsible for the high illiteracy rate in Latin America and the prohibitive cost of even paperback books, as well as of the ways in which these economic forces function as an effective form of censorship by excluding the vast majority from readership or from access to reading materials. In one text in particular, he asks himself whether he should stop writing, but then concludes that to write is a moral and social obligation rather than an intellectual privilege:

> In Latin America a literature is taking shape and acquiring strength, a literature that does not lull its readers to sleep, but rather awakens them; that refuses to stir the ashes but rather attempts to light the fire. This literature perpetuates and enriches a powerful tradition of combative words. (*We Say No* 142)

Moreover, Galeano refuses to be labeled an intellectual, seeing such empty categories as symptomatic of the deformation that results from economic paradigms that reduce people to their employment functions: "In reality, both the *intellectuals*, an expression that reduces people to heads, and the *manuals*, people reduced to hands, are the result of the same fracturing of the human condition. Capitalist development generates mutilated people" (*We Say No* 159). Where would the revolutionary guerrilla fit in this scheme of employment functions? Did Fidel Castro and Che Guevara give up their heads to fight with their hands? And why is it that academics who are only read by other academics can disqualify writers from the sphere of action, while people of both action and writing, such as Subcomandante Marcos (an accomplished author himself), thank other writers for inspiring them to take action and to continue writing?

In an open letter to Galeano (11 May 1995) published in a recent collection of Marcos's selected writings, Marcos explains how a passage in Galeano's *Walking Words* keeps dancing around in his head (*Our Word Is Our Weapon* 254), how he is embarrassed to tell Galeano that he abandoned the book in February's "lucky escape" from capture by the Mexican Army, and how it was serendipitously returned to him by Ana María, an indigenous Tzotzil who is an infantry major in his army (255). Marcos tells Galeano other disturbing stories to which we will return, but the point here is that Marcos, guerrilla fighter, speaks back to the "writer" and expresses how the book circulates not among "intellectuals" but in his own army, and how it makes him question his own efficacy. Keeping in mind Torres-Fierro's contemptuous dismissal of both Galeano and fellow Uruguayan writer Mario Benedetti as "merchants of virtue," it is worth noting that Marcos ends his letter to Galeano with the following postscript: "p.p.s....which is unlikely. If you should see Benedetti, please give him my regards. Please tell him I whispered words of his into a woman's ear and they took her breath away. Words like that move all humanity..." (258). The implied exchange between Galeano and Marcos suggests that it is impossible to separate history *making* from history *writing* when the writer is seen as an active (even necessary) participant in social change. Aside from Galeano's work, Neruda's *Canto General*, and a handful of other texts and artistic forms widely divergent in genre and focus (including those by, among others, muralist Diego Rivera, filmmaker Fernando Solanas, and authors Ronald Wright and Gabriel García Márquez), how many historians and cultural critics have undertaken the thrust and scope of this revisionary project?[15] As John Ramsay puts it, "If someone other than Galeano has devoted a career to insisting that we understand that 'the other Americans' live both north and south of the Rio Grande, I don't know who that is" (24).

Attempts to paint Galeano as a naïve utopian clouded by sentimental ideals—about the material conditions required for effective historical change that leads to social justice, about the importance of indigenous culture as a source of alternative forms of community-making, about resistance to neoliberalism as a necessary critique of, if not a synecdoche for, the power relations that (de)structure global relations of state power, globalization not as "internationalism, but [as] rather the universal imposition of a culture of consumerism and violence" (Manrique 58), and so forth—are almost entirely wrong-headed but nonetheless predictable responses from the very forces Galeano resists. Typically, Galeano evinces a much more sophisticated positioning than his critics allow him. Ramón Eduardo Ruiz, in his reading of *Open Veins of Latin America*, claims that "Galeano's views, which will please few North American scholars, add little to what is already known. They may, in fact, even distort some of the truth. Clearly he writes with scant objectivity. Yet few will deny that he speaks for a majority of Latin America's intellectuals and scholars. In that rests the value of his book" (582). Ruiz's comments exemplify a kind of criticism that sycophantically sets up the North as the arbiter of scholarly value, makes claims about distortions of the truth (without once showing where, how, or why such a distortion occurs), establishes objectivity as a norm while evading the issue of how objectivity is a social construction that serves particular interests, and then makes claims on behalf of "a majority" of Latin American intellectuals and scholars by associating them with Galeano's non-objective distortions of the truth.

This form of vacuous critical attack does little justice to the breadth and integrity of Galeano's writing practices. Those practices, contrary to the rebarbative polemicists who dismiss Galeano's work as tired idealism or predictable dogmatism, are realistic and reasonable in their assessment of complex issues. With regard to indigenous traditions as a model for "another possible world," for instance, Galeano states:

> I am not one of those who believe in tradition for tradition's sake: I believe in the spiritual inheritance that increases human freedom, and not in one that puts it behind bars. When I refer to the remote voices of the past that help us find an answer to the challenges of today, I am not suggesting reclaiming the sacrificial rites during which human hearts were offered up to the gods, nor am I praising the despotism of Inca and Aztec kings.
>
> Rather I am celebrating the fact that America might draw, from her oldest sources, her youngest energies. The past tells us much about the future. If the values represented by real, living Indians were of nothing but archaeological interest, the Indians would not continue to be the object of bloody repression, nor would those in power be so intent on keeping them away from the class struggle and popular liberation movements. In our day and age the conquest continues. The Indians continue to atone for their sins of collectivity, liberty, along with other effronteries. ("A Tale of Ambiguities" 36)

And on the links between deforestation and profit:

> In the last twenty years, while humanity tripled in number, erosion killed off the equivalent of all the arable land in the United States. The world, transformed into

market and merchandise, is losing fifteen million hectares of forest each year. Of these, six million become desert. Nature has been humiliated and subordinated to the accumulation of capital. Land, water, and air are being poisoned so that money will generate more money without a drop in the rate of profit. Efficient is he who earns more in less time. ("To Be Like Them" 121)

Both positions demonstrate an agile vision, balanced between critique of idealized notions of indigenous society and frank analyses of market economics and power relations. No blind adherence to myths of the good native or of the superiority of Western civil culture. No simple defeatism or triumphalism. But an appeal to the compelling possibilities that arise from a critique that identifies the way in which reality is betrayed by those who advance such notions.

Dangerous and Fertile Embraces:
Speaking in the Name of the Other

Understood in light of our previous comments, Galeano's work is comparable to Chomsky's in its ideological thrust, though Galeano himself might resist such reductive comparisons if only for the fact that his work subversively crosses into many genres that Chomsky's does not. Nonetheless, Chomsky's and Galeano's writings share a fierce commitment to social justice and to establishing the conditions for effective critiques of the institutions and geopolitical realities in which the Americas figure. Where Chomsky's relentlessly informed empiricism ends, Galeano's rigorous blend of fictive, autobiographical, and historical chronicling begins. Where Chomsky's work is ascetic, leaving aside "aesthetic dimensions" ("Writers and Intellectual Responsibility" 55), Galeano's is fully aware of the affect associated with the aesthetics of writing—what he calls in his foreword to the work of the Argentine poet Juan Gelman "the crime of marrying justice to beauty. From such a dangerous and fertile embrace, a general uneasiness must issue" (xi). Dangerous and fertile embraces that come of the marriage of justice and beauty typify Galeano's writings, which explore the relationship between aesthetics and social justice, between embracing lost and uneasy memories and the incipient awareness of being human as a function of the embrace of community. Thus, the writer embraces story and memory as an act of restitution to all those stories and memories expelled from official history, a dangerous and fertile embrace that releases repressed or forgotten human energies.

A striking example of this "embrace" occurs in Galeano's retelling in *Memory of Fire* of a myth from the Cashinahua, a Panoan-speaking people of the western Amazon who occupy small portions of what is now Brazil and Peru.[16] The Cashinahua's language is spoken by little over 1,000 people (according to Kenneth Kensinger's 1993 estimates) and, as such, their use in a key opening passage to *Memory of Fire* exemplifies the kind of memorial restitution of lost and disappeared cultures so crucial to Galeano's project generally. Entitled "Love," the vignette focuses on the symbolic embrace that inaugurates human community:

In the Amazonian jungle, the first woman and the first man looked at each other with curiosity. It was odd what they had between their legs.

"Did they cut yours off?" asked the man.

"No," she said, "I've always been like that."

He examined her close up. He scratched his head. There was an open wound there. He said: "Better not eat any cassava or bananas or any fruit that splits when it ripens. I'll cure you. Get in the hammock and rest."

She obeyed. Patiently she swallowed herb teas and let him rub on pomades and unguents. She had to grit her teeth to keep from laughing when he said to her, "Don't worry."

She enjoyed the game, although she was beginning to tire of fasting in a hammock. The memory of fruit made her mouth water.

One evening the man came running through the glade. He jumped with excitement and cried, "I found it!"

He had just seen the male monkey curing the female monkey in the arm of the tree.

"That's how it's done," said the man, approaching the woman.

When the long embrace ended, a dense aroma of flowers and fruit filled the air. From the bodies lying together came unheard of vapors and glowings, and it was all so beautiful that the suns and the gods died of embarrassment. (*Genesis* 14)

Dangerous and Fertile Embraces 2. José Francisco Borges, from *Walking Words* 285.

As a myth of origins that transgresses against antiseptic, Edenic myths at the heart of Christian culture, the story reinforces the linkages between the natural world and the human experience (the natural here is a model for human encounter), while linking human beginnings with the compassionate and reciprocal discovery of sexuality. Readers tempted to read this passage as a reinstatement of male paternal privilege over an abjected woman would do well to note the derisory, ludic humour aimed at the male's stupidity and error in trying to cure the woman of her putative lack. The detail subverts the dominant male position, suggesting male ignorance as the impediment to the culminating embrace that will produce human community.

The moment, for all the humour of its description, points to the danger of the embrace. The embrace is doubly dangerous. In its primary sense the embrace signifies an attained knowledge of the foundational intimacy that will produce human community. But the trope of the embrace also highlights how Galeano appropriates the Cashinahuan myth, a speaking in the name of the other that cannot be disregarded as part of the context in which the story gets told. The embrace sensualizes the world: intimate human relations become a metonym for the pleasure of the natural, thus killing gods, themselves figures of alienated forms of power.[17] And it points to the ethical issues that arise from the embrace of the other, an allegory implicit in the story as told by Galeano. The unease provoked by forms of human love, solidarity, and community suggests deinstitutionalized and intimate encounters as a defining human characteristic, the beginning of *being* and *becoming* human. Human intimacy summons beauty and death, complicated and problematic tropes that are at the heart of Galeano's project as a writer of allegories of encounter.

Consider another narrative of encounter in which a radically different form of "love" or embrace occurs relating to Las Casas's presence at the Caonao massacre. The cultural critic Tzvetan Todorov cites a passage from the third volume of Las Casas's *Historia de las Indias*, in which a young indigene is murdered by a conquistador:

> "And just as the young man came down, a Spaniard who was there drew a cutlass...and gives him a cut through the loins, so that his intestines fall out...The Indian, moaning, takes his intestines in his hands and comes fleeing out of the house. He encounters the cleric [Las Casas]...and the cleric tells him some things about the faith, as much as the time and anguish permitted, explaining to him that if he wished to be baptized he would go to heaven to live with God. The poor creature, weeping and showing pain as if he were burning in flames, said yes, and with this the cleric baptized him. He then fell dead on the ground." (qtd. in Todorov 169)

Todorov's analysis of this passage concludes that "by performing this action Las Casas is certainly moved by love of his neighbor"; he also acknowledges that "there is something ludicrous about this baptism *in extremis*" (169), all the while silently effacing the possibility that the "love" in question is a rhetorical conceit in which the suffering position of the other is turned into a figure of acquiescence at the mercy of Christian salvation. The rhetoric of the Lascasian account—with its hellish "flames," its elision of the problem of reception (does the dying Indian understand Las Casas? What precisely does the cleric tell the dying man? And what god was the dying man thinking of when and if he so acquiesces?), and its unwitting closural moment that links the effect of baptism with death—is frank in its depiction of the instrumentality of the Christianizing mission, even on the threshold of a painful death. Institutional imperatives guide Las Casas as much as any metaphysics of love.

The love that will not speak its name here is based on the missionary position, literally and figuratively, in which the disemboweled indigene is doubly abjected in death and baptism. The cut to the Indian's loins figures colonial dominance, a symbolic registering of the native's impotence in the face of the technology of power (the cutlass thrust). The creation myth Galeano tells, in which the man assumes that the woman is missing the thing that will make them self-same, echoes the cut to the Indian's loins, the very thing that marks the difference of the indigene in the Las Casas story. While the creation myth involves the man's attempt to "cure" the woman, to make a restitution that is revealed to the man through his observation of the "natural" world (monkeys copulating), the Las Casas incident imposes the institution of baptism on the symbolically emasculated native, thus regulating the Indian's status as non-Christian interloper. Galeano restitutes (in his version of the creation myth that we cite above) that imposed impotence, suggesting the fertility of an encounter in which traditional, institutionalized forms of power, whether church or state, have no place.

The singular lack of compassion evident in Las Casas's story, except of the institutionalized, self-interested sort, is carried forward by Todorov in the iron grip of the passage's dissimulative and self-serving rhetoric. The ludicrousness is not in the baptism itself so much as it is in understanding the baptism as an expression of "love." Todorov's and Las Casas's narration of the baptism denotes the language of colonial affect, in which the logic of colonial relations is reinforced as a function of a deeply perverse use of language. Todorov's unease at his own curious embrace of Lascasian rhetoric, despite his sympathy with anticolonial analyses, suggests an encounter that endangers the "justice" of his own narrative. In the apposition of this telling of a telling—Todorov's account of Las Casas's experience as narrated by Las Casas in a manner that may, it must be emphasized, be entirely constructed so as to reveal a particular form of the history of this encounter—with Galeano's reconstruction of a creation myth, we note the revisionary force of Galeano's parable. The story exemplifies how to undo a deeply entrenched rhetoric of colonial abjection through a language that embraces justice as a function of human intimacy.

These two versions of the twentieth-century reinscription of the notion of "love" from colonial and pre-colonial cultures are themselves narrative representations multiple steps away from the putative source events themselves. Todorov constructs the source in realist mode, whereas Galeano mythifies source, ambiguating its meaning. Both speak in the name of the other, a strategy of literary impersonation known as prosopopoeia, the "presentation of absent, dead, or supernatural beings, or even inanimate objects, with the ability to act, speak, and respond" (Dupriez 357). Prosopopoeia, a rhetorical construct deeply embedded in colonial narrative structures, allows the narrator the illusion of appropriation, of speaking for an absent voice in a manner that closely follows the logic of colonial encounter narratives. Prosopopoeia is what permits Columbus's narrative (itself a prosopopoeia written by Las Casas) to speak in the name of the indigenous other whose language he does not know.

> WEDNESDAY, 24 OCTOBER. Last night at midnight I raised anchor from Cabo del Isleo on the north side of the island of Isabela, where I had lain, and set sail for the island of Colba, *which these people tell me* is very large and has much trade. *They say* that it contains gold and spices and large ships and merchandize and *have told me by signs* that I should steer west-south-west to find it, and I think this is right, for *if I am to believe the indications of all these Indians and those I have on board—I do not know their language*—this is the island of Chipangu [Japan] of which such marvelous tales are told, and which in the globes that I have seen and on the painted map of the world appears to lie in this region. (73; our emphasis)

The passage resonates with the paradox of a speaker speaking in the name of a people whose language he does not know and thus seeing the world as a function of an image of the "painted world" *always already* in place. Thus, a doubly false knowledge is instituted at the inception of the colonial project of discovery through prosopopoeia, in which the lack of knowledge of the other's language does *not* prevent a speaking in the name of the other. This is the false consciousness of the Mandevillean traveller who does not travel, in which the narrative repeats precedent perspectives based on assumptions of the globe as it was known to Europeans at the end of the fifteenth century.

Like hypotyposis, a close rhetorical cousin, in which things are painted "so vividly and with such energy that they in some way become visible" (Dupriez 219), prosopopoeia is thus an instrumental factor in the narrator's control of textual affect, its presumption and transmission of knowledge. As Rolena Adorno notes in discussing Todorov's work on colonial representations, "Todorov seems to invest in those who control the text…Todorov does not interrogate the texts he uses as his sources but treats each statement as though it were straightforward and not part of its own larger rhetorical scheme" ("Arms, Letters, and the Native Historian" 207). Though we would agree with this assessment generally, it becomes inapplicable to Las Casas's narrative, specifically because Todorov does not treat Las Casas's "straightforward" account of baptismal blackmail as such but converts it into a narrative that emblematizes Las Casas's "love" for the abjected indigene. Todorov reads "love" in its literal meaning into the narrative, dragging in his own prosopopoeitic intervention in Las Casas's voice-over of the dying indigene.

In contrast, Galeano's account names love as a frame for the story but effaces its textual presence in the actual narrative, leaving instead an unspoken and unknowable embrace that resonates in the natural world even as it kills its divine observers. The lovers have no name yet for what it is they do. Allegory is an issue for both narrators: for Todorov, though, the allegory involves authorial impositions, whereas for Galeano, the allegory involves unsettling structures of ambiguity and resonance. The Todorov account imposes a form of coherence that Eurocentrizes and Christianizes (those reciprocal terms of engagement) the event, a form of writing that Peter Hulme notes is the "touchstone of bourgeois aesthetics" (178). In this latter regard, Galeano is candid in *We Say No* about literature not being a "frozen institution of bourgeois culture" (141), suggesting instead that the "primordial function of Latin American literature today is the rescue of the word, frequently used and abused with impunity for the purpose of hampering and betraying communication" (142).

Betrayed communications are instrumental in allowing dominant régimes of truth to deform reality in their own interests. Cannily, Galeano recognizes that the same tools used to deform can be deployed to inform: as he states in *We Say No*, "'Freedom' in my country is the name of a jail for political prisoners, and 'democracy' forms part of the title of various regimes of terror; the word 'love' defines the relationship of a man with his automobile, and 'revolution' is understood to describe what a new detergent can do in your kitchen" (142). Thus, Galeano's writing practice is as much informed by the turns of phrase and thought that consistently foreground the way in which words deform reality, rendering false accounts of human relations and giving false names to things that matter. Moreover, the "true name of things" (142) is sometimes best left unnamed in order to preserve its resonance and meaningful potential.

Galeano's account of the Amazonian creation myth, with its ironic humour and its devolution into the impenetrable heart of human communion that rattles the divine birdcage, does not present a coherent narrative so much as it represents its own unspeakability: love dare not be named in this incident for fear that the illusion of naming in language will destroy it. Speaking directly in the name of love risks its radical deformation. Moreover, the collective nature of myth-making, that is, a myth's representation of a narrative that resonates symbolically for an interpretive community, is clearly invoked by Galeano's tale, making for a very different form of prosopopoeia than the one observed in the Todorov or the Columbus examples we have cited. Myth represents the collective nature of writing. And literary creation in this mode signals solidarity with(in) community. The word emerges from the other (of the writer) as a gift that is returned to the other by the writer, in the form of "inspiration and prophecy [aliento y profecía]" (*We Say No* 140). Storytelling at this mythic level evokes the human bonds of reciprocal responsibility, enacting human solidarity via the multiple embraces engendered by the narrative as it brings together interpretive communities: at the heart of every such community lie the fertile and dangerous possibilities of human potential to reshape the world through acts of narration and through actions engendered by narration.

Narrative structures of this sort are part of a larger frame of human intercourse to which the writer contributes. At the same time as Galeano observes in *We Say No* that "To claim that literature on its own is going to change reality would be an act of madness or arrogance" (140),[18] he also notes that writing plays a crucial role in the "denunciation of those who stop us from being what we can become" (139) and in articulating an "authentic collective identity" that "is born of the past and...nourished by it" (138). The denunciatory function of the writer is "linked to the need for profound social transformations" (137) even as "the possessors of power continue to carry out with impunity their policy of collective imbecilization, through the instruments of the mass media" (137). Literary structures enact intimate structures of engagement with reality—"to narrate is to give oneself" (137). In short, the silent scene of reading is a crucial battleground where transgressive and irruptive forces can be incarnated, even as that scene also locates the struggle to contain its radical potential, the fertile and dangerous embrace of the writer who denounces collective imbecilization and amnesia.

Border Thinking and the Occidental Barbarian: Impersonating Civility

There is no document of civilization which is not at the same time a document of barbarism. And just as such a document is not free of barbarism, barbarism taints also the manner in which it was transmitted from one owner to another. (Benjamin, "Theses" 256)

Barbarism: 1. The effectual base consists of Gr *barbaros*, non-Greek, also n, esp. in pl *barbaroi*: *hoi barbaroi*, the non-Greeks, are lit. 'the Unintelligibles, The Stammerers': cf the Skt adj *barbaras*, stammering... (Partridge 39)

R1: Barbarisms are alterations, obtained by composition, derivation, or linguistic 'patching'; they always result from ignorance or confusion. This does not prevent them from finding a place in literary works. (Dupriez 77)

The epigraphs to this section centre on one of Walter Benjamin's memorable pronouncements from the "Theses on the Philosophy of History," some of which were written on newspaper wrappers and passed on by Benjamin just before he committed suicide in 1940 with a morphine overdose: the Jewish emigré fleeing fascist persecution was refused entry by Spanish border authorities for lack of a French exit stamp, and the refusal clearly contributed to his suicide. Both the suicide and the fragmentary text it bequeathed to posterity haunt modern historiography. But it is as a symbolic act in which attempted border crossings produce a haunted and haunting text whose explicit contexts bring together historical crisis (1940 and the onset of World War II) and human rights (the right of freedom of movement subsumed under Article 12 of the Universal Declaration of Human Rights, belatedly enacted in 1948) that Benjamin's text signals major concerns to be found in

Galeano's work in which historical crisis and human rights are consistently foregrounded. We remain largely critical of dehistoricized textual strategies that impose Eurocentric modes of analysis on Latin American literary writers like Galeano, a problem we have attempted to resolve through our ongoing hybrid readings of his texts. Nonetheless, Benjamin's comments on the nature of barbarism in relation to civil and civic discourse provide an influential model for our work as a function of our own cultural formations in the Americas as Canadians of European ancestry who were trained in Eurocentric, highly Occidentalized forms of knowledge, many of which we critique. We are aware that aggregate designations like Western, Eastern, Occidental, Oriental, First World, Third World, Northern, Southern, European, and American can be read as "mythical abstractions" that are "lies": "cultures are too intermingled, their contents and histories too interdependent and hybrid, for surgical separation into large and mostly ideological oppositions like Orient and Occident" (Said, *Representations of the Intellectual* xii). While we agree with this, we also recognize that such historical designations (usually based on falsely oppositional binaries) have been used to support specific ideological ends (as represented by conglomerate entities like the state or state coalitions) that are less than enlightened, especially in relation to obstructing different forms of human solidarity. Moreover, we would argue that one of the ways in which such terms can be shown to be misrepresentations of complex realities is through the kind of inversion we pursue in this section of the book, based as it is on a critique of the standard equation between the Occident (as a trope that stands in for a dominant power relation) and civil society.

Galeano's project, literarily contrarian as it is, documents the barbarism of oppressor to oppressed out of which the Americas have emerged. Galeano identifies the indigene as bearer of civil discourse and settler culture as exemplifying a shocking incapacity to address difference in any but the most predictable ways, involving violence, suppression, and effacement. The importance of this radical inversion of the position of the barbarian cannot be emphasized forcefully enough. The continuity of quotidian brutality is one of Galeano's thematic constants, as is the resistance to this structure, a resistance that posits transgressive acts of hope and dissidence. Benjamin's parable remembers that civilization emerges as a function of barbarous acts, and that the transmission of civil history is itself complicated by the barbarism that assures it continuity from "one owner to another" (Benjamin, "Theses" 256), generation to generation. This is one reading, largely derived from an interpretive tradition that makes of "barbarism" a general trope for violence and oppression, forged in the fire of civil European society on the eve of its most destructive and self-indicting calamity, the shame of World War II.

To Americanize the trope of the "barbarian," to bring it into the reading context that Galeano consistently tries to establish via his rehistoricizing of the Americas, is to see it in the fullness of its etymological and philological origins. Barbarism is the unintelligible, the otherness of the "non-Greek," the stammering of a hybrid language spoken by civilization's barbarous other. Todorov notes language as the decisive factor in attributing the difference constitutive of the "barbarian": "if he does not speak our language, it is because he speaks none at all, *cannot* speak…It is in this fashion that the European Slavs call their German neighbors *nemec*, 'mutes'; and the Cakchiquel Mayas refer to the Mam Mayas as 'stammer-ers' or 'mutes'" (76). As a literary trope, then, barbarism signals alterity. Remember: "Bar-barisms are alterations, obtained by composition, derivation, or linguistic 'patching'; they always result from ignorance or confusion" (Dupriez 77). Barbarism, in this usage, repre-sents the patchwork language of derivative composition, that is, composition dependent on an otherness that is barely known or wholly unknown. "Ignorance" and "confusion" mark its entry into the literary work. But the other side of this story is the imagined barbarian's side, the side that has its own culture and language of which so-called civil culture is igno-rant or unaware. Galeano is greatly concerned throughout all his writing projects with how this other culture writes back, asserting its knowledge, its language, and that right to resist what has been stereotyped as "barbaric."

The contrast between European civilization (deemed superior) and imagined autochthonous barbarism (deemed inferior) resonates throughout Latin American history and literature. In some ways, it is definitive of both. The city, for example, populated by ed-ucated Europeans, is represented in the nineteenth century as the locus for enlightened and democratic society. But Domingo Faustino Sarmiento, author of the famous work on the relationship of politics and culture entitled *Life in the Argentine Republic in the Days of the Tyrants or, Civilization and Barbarism* [*Facundo: civilizacion y barbarie, vida de Juan Facundo Quiroga* (1845)], continues to be heralded in the twentieth century by many Latin Americans as "the very ideal type of the schoolmaster" (Mann 8). While Sarmiento's de-nunciation of the system of *caudillos* and warlords that would spawn such tyrants as Juan Manuel de Rosas was prophetic, the one-sided appreciation of Sarmiento's democratic in-tentions belies a blindness to the ulterior motives of tyrants, represented as sources of salva-tion by Mary Mann in her preface to the English translation of Sarmiento's text:

> The study of education also led [Sarmiento] to the study of legislation at home and abroad, and in those two paths he has been of incalculable benefit to his country, not only convincing its most advanced men that public education is the only basis of a republic, but aiding them essentially in modeling their government upon that of the United States, which is their prototype, and to which they now look, rather than to Europe, for light and knowledge. (8-9)

The passage details the transition from Eurocentric to American influence as undergone by Latin American statesmen. This shift in influence is represented in highly idealized terms that seem to have no connection to the economic impetus of imperial capital, as though the imperial powers were disseminating some transcendental knowledge for spiritual develop-ment. But Galeano reveals another side to Sarmiento's discourse, one rarely cited because it does not fit the image of the statesman who preached enlightened tolerance. Beneath the civil mask of Sarmiento's discourse lies a face distorted by intolerance and racism. Sarmiento represents the national hero of Uruguay, José Artigas, as a "highwayman" and an aberration of white civility:

> Thirty years of practice in murdering or robbing are indisputable qualifications for the exercise of command over a horde of mutinous Indian peasant scum for a political revolution, and among them the fearsome name of Artigas is encrusted as bandit chief…Uncouth, since he never frequented cities, foreign to all human tradition of free government; and although white, commanding natives even less educated than himself…Considering the antecedents and actions of Artigas, we feel a sort of revolt of reason, of the instincts of the man of white race. (*Faces and Masks* 162)

Issue 14 of *Cuadernos de Crisis*, written and compiled by Carlos Machado, is dedicated to Artigas, who is identified as "el general de los independientes" [the general of the independents]. Machado presents a very different portrait from Sarmiento of Artigas's role as the leader who inspired epic democratic achievements. According to Machado, the rebellion that spread across the eastern grasslands led by Artigas in the 1820s embodied a true rural agrarian protest of the poor against the urban oligarchy (5).

Artigas's vision of indigenous sovereignty and self-government expresses a democratic ethics that was inconceivable to representatives of bourgeois white culture like Sarmiento, regardless of their commitment to fight European political colonialism (though they were not nearly as committed to opposing commercial colonialism):

> Yo deseo que los indios, en sus pueblos, se gobiernen por sí, para que cuiden de sus intereses como nosotros de los nuestros…Recordemos que ellos tienen el principal derecho, y que sería una desgracia vergonzosa para nosotros, mantenerlos en aquella exclusión que hasta ahora han padecido, por ser indianos…lo que dictan la razón y la justicia es que los indios nombren los administradores de ellos mismos. (Artigas qtd. in Machado, *Cuadernos de Crisis* 14: (1975) 41)

> [I want the Indians, in their *pueblos*, to govern themselves, in order to safeguard their interests just as we do ours…Let us remember that they have the principal right, and that it would be a shameful disgrace for us to keep them in the exclusion which they are condemned to until now, for being Indians…reason and justice dictate that the Indians elect their own administrators.]

Artigas's ideas continue to be opposed by those who collude with national governments to deny indigenes the right to recuperate and practice their own traditional forms of communitarian governance. In a recent publication that won the Donner Prize (an award given by the Donner Foundation to a book on Canadian policy issues that encourages "individual responsibility and private initiative to help Canadians solve social and economic problems" from a free market perspective [Kappler A18]), the political scientist Tom Flanagan suggests that certain terms be kept under tight institutional control, proposing (not surprisingly) that universities are good places to keep the lid on potentially dangerous ideas: "Sovereignty [for Canadian indigenes] has become such a tangled concept that it might be better to leave it to the academics and banish it from popular discussion of politics" (50).[19] We wonder where someone like Chomsky would fit into this neat dichotomy, which assumes coherent, separable spheres in which academic and the public (popular) have little or no relation.

Amazingly, Flanagan's thinking about aboriginal sovereignty is explicitly in accordance with the racist paradigm that Sarmiento inherited from the conquistadors, showing that ideas die hard, however irrational and obviously biased they are, especially when they validate colonial dominance over peoples and resources: "[But] if, as I have argued, the distinction between civilized and uncivilized is meaningful, then the doctrine of *terra nullius* [no one's land] comes into play, because sovereignty in the strict sense exists only in the organized states characteristic of civilized societies" (58-59). The "masters of the universe" mentality evident here cannot even conceive of the other's inherently human sense of justice and law outside of the machinations of "civil" institutions. The naïve assertion of freedom shows itself to be a contradiction due to Flanagan's restricted and totalitarian concept of justice: "In a free country like Canada, aboriginal leaders can talk all they want about their own inherent sovereignty, but the expression is only a rhetorical turn of phrase. It may produce domestic political results by playing on guilt or compassion, but it has no effect in international law or...in domestic law" (61). The possibility of hearing the other is contemptuously dismissed as misguided sentimentalism, and the other's voice as inconsequential rhetoric aimed at gaining small victories that hit a brick wall when it comes to meaningful legal recognition. What clearer statement on how the law—international or domestic—is undemocratic?

In the same kind of rhetorical move found in the earliest colonial writings justifying the imperialist motivations of nationhood, Flanagan's vision of justice overrides community and usurps the name "Canada": "In short, the claim to possess an inherent right to self-government, as that phrase is understood in Canada today, is an assertion of sovereignty contrary to the history, jurisprudence, and national interest of Canada" (66). Sadly, such assertions exclude all those Canadians who disagree on what constitutes national interest, who find revisionary histories more truthful and compelling than the history that Flanagan appeals to, and who question the narrow and undemocratic theories and practices of jurisprudence that produce social inequality. Reiterating exactly the same "free" market ideology that we will examine in numerous cultural contexts, Flanagan attacks communitarian ethics and insists that aboriginal survival is dependent on embracing the imperative of private property. Flanagan's forked tongue speaks not-so-subtle contradictions that in plain English translate to the assertion that people are more free (more "civil") when they trade their own leaders for the logic of the "free" market:

Civil society cannot thrive without containment of political power and wide dis-
persal of private ownership. The challenge for self-government is to 'civilize' aboriginal communities in the sense of creating the conditions for civil society to emerge.
Above all, that means getting government out of the way—especially the kind of
'self-government' that exercises total control over community affairs. (198)

The simplistic alliance of civil society with private ownership is a massively un-
der-historicized account of different practices of community and of management of property that indigenous examples, all but eradicated from official history (let alone political
theory), afford so-called democratic culture. Corrupt band council governance is no doubt
a major problem for aboriginal communities in Canada and elsewhere. But to suggest that
the only tenable alternative is the imposition of a free market logic, one with no connection
to traditional modes of governance that have largely been obliterated by the so-called free
market imposed by colonial culture, is to be entirely misguided. Moreover, to structure the
terms of the encounter as Flanagan does is to reinforce colonial thinking that equates settler
culture with civility and indigenous culture with barbarism, a highly fraudulent representation of reality.[20] At the beginning of the nineteenth century, Artigas called precisely this
kind of reasoning shameful, thereby provoking Sarmiento's openly racist attack on him.
Sarmiento is uncomprehending of how a member of a settler (white) culture could identify
with the underdogs instead of seeking out the privilege that his race putatively secures him.
Artigas bears the brunt of Sarmiento's slurs for organizing non-white peasants, in a blanket
condemnation of those who are non-urban, non-European, non-criollo, and most importantly non-bourgeois, and therefore barbarian.

In *We Say No*, Galeano rejects the historian's "objective" language in framing
Sarmiento's racist and self-interested description of the "enemy": "Sarmiento praised the
long struggle of the Araucanian Indians for freedom: 'they are wilder, that is, more stubborn
animals, less apt for Civilization and European assimilation'" (308). Writing against the official history lesson on Sarmiento's civilizing influence, Galeano chooses to look beyond the
Argentine hero's crusade against rural *caudillo* despots to expose a more pressing historical
problem that has left a legacy of deep cultural division along racist and classist lines.
Galeano remembers that Sarmiento, whom he calls an "effective" writer, "blessed with the
slogan 'civilization and barbarism' the exterminating wars that the port of Buenos Aires
waged against the rebellious provinces. The dilemma still lives and still wrecks havoc: Civilization, culture of the few, against barbarism, the ignorance of all the rest" (159).

Seen in this light, Galeano's various references to Sarmiento are a response to the enshrining of this man's writings in official history. Galeano sees in Sarmiento not an individual luminary as official history portrays him but a typical representative of the class that
dominated nation-building: "The most ferocious racism in Latin American history is to be
found in the words of the most famed and celebrated intellectuals of the end of the nine-

teenth century and in the documents of liberal politicians who founded the modern state" (308). The same attitude continues to characterize the rich enclaves of white, imported civilization in Latin America. Galeano accuses these of alienation from everything but their own self-interest, inverting Sarmiento's paradigm to show that the urban élites do not belong to any culture other than consumer society: "Los puertos y las grandes ciudades, que arrasaron al interior, eligieron los delirios del consumo en lugar de los desafíos de la creación. En Venezuela he visto bolsitas de agua de Escocia, para acompañar el whisky. En Nicaragua, donde hasta las piedras transpiran a chorros, he visto estolas de piel importadas de Francia" (*Apuntes para el fin de siglo* 51) [The ports and large cities, which razed the interior, chose the delirium of consumption instead of the challenges of creation. In Venezuela, I have seen little bags of water imported from Scotland to drink with whiskey. In Nicaragua, where it is so hot even the rocks sweat buckets, I have seen fur stoles imported from France]. It is typical of Galeano's consequential vision of the past that he not only revises the official representation of heroes and villains, in some cases like that of Sarmiento and Artigas inverting them completely, but that he also traces how that official history has contaminated the present. History, for Galeano, exposes the roots of the problems of injustice and oppression even when it is official history that must be read against the grain to reveal its inadvertent messages.

Galeano's second vignette about Sarmiento, "The Road to Underdevelopment: The Thought of Domingo Faustino Sarmiento" (appearing in *Faces and Masks*), summarizes the utter lack of vision and common sense that typify Latin American hegemons who are seemingly incapable of establishing the conditions for their countries' self-sufficiency: "*We are not industrialists or navigators and Europe will provide us for long centuries with its artifacts in exchange for our raw materials*" (169). The attack on Artigas in the self-incriminating quotation from Sarmiento's seminal text typifies the kinds of racist and self-negating stereotypes that Galeano is at pains to show as deeply influential in shaping Latin American culture and history in *Memory of Fire*. Carlos Fuentes's *The Buried Mirror*, a more conventionally organized overview of Latin American history, also shares Galeano's anti-imperialist critique and calls for a re-evaluation of native forms of social organization that characterize Galeano's more future-oriented exploration of memory:

> The true barbarism of this ideology was that it excluded from the notion of civilization all indigenous models of existence. Black, Indian, communitarian, and all property relationships other than those consecrated by liberal economics were left out—most notably, the centuries-old style of life based on shared agricultural produce and properties, such as the *ejido* in Mexico and the *ayllu* in Peru. These alternative cultures subcribed to a different set of values from those of the cities. Tradition, mutual knowledge, a knack for self-government among communities that knew their own people well, an attachment to nature, and a suspicion of abstract laws im-

posed from above were all denied by the progressive mentality of the nineteenth century. This blatant disregard would come back to haunt Spanish America in the twentieth century, when the example of the alternative society as a Mexican agrarian Arcadia was proposed by the peasant leader Emiliano Zapata. (285)

Fuentes, like Galeano, inverts Sarmiento's (in)famous dichotomy to level the accusation of barbarism against white colonists whose lack of communitarian ethics blinds them to the possibilities presented by the cultures that they subjugated instead of embracing. In short, then, barbarism points toward a liminal relationship with the otherness that always threatens so-called civil culture with confusion, unintelligibility, and inversion. But barbarism hints, too, at the need to restore the reciprocity of relations between self and other, the need to think beyond and across borders. The unintelligibility imposed on the other by civilizing culture in order to sustain its own fantasies of superiority and domination is, in this regard, a profoundly corrupt structure for imagining encounters with difference.

For Walter Mignolo, the "subaltern perspective defines border thinking as a response to colonial difference" (*Local Histories/Global Designs* x); Benjamin's trope, thus read, mutates into the inescapable legacies bred of colonial difference. The opposed images of civilization and barbarism, each a reductive trope based on strategic impositions of meaning that establish relations of difference, are haunted by the spectre of colonial difference. The supposedly barbarian other occupies the space between giving civilization meaning and the civilization that gives itself meaning through the effacement, neutralization, and possession of the other. Mignolo, discussing the Nahuatl word *nepantla*, "coined in the second half of the sixteenth century" and meaning "To be or feel in between," argues that the word "was possible in the mouth of an Amerindian, not of a Spaniard," suggesting a conceptual space that can only be understood from the other side: from the side of the supposed subaltern's relation to hegemony (*Local Histories/Global Designs* x).

The subalternizing of the subaltern, a frequent gesture in the critical discourses of colonialism, is itself a legacy of the same logic as that under which the barbarian was created. The subaltern, as an essentialized form of inferiority, is as much a fantasy as is the barbarian, except in terms of the political and linguistic contexts that energize such deformative concepts in strict alignment with colonial imperatives. Thinking the "other side" is a form of "*Border thinking*...[which] works toward the restitution of the colonial difference that colonial translation (unidirectional, as today's globalization) attempted to erase" (Mignolo, *Local Histories/Global Designs* 3). Moreover, for Mignolo,

> Border thinking is...the denial of the denial of 'barbarism'; not a Hegelian synthesis, but the absorption of the 'civilizing' principles into the 'civilization of barbarism': a 'phagocytosis' of civilization by the barbarian...rather than the barbarian bending and entering civilization...What we are facing here are no longer the spaces in between or hybridity, in the convivial images of contact zones, but the forces of

'barbarian' theorizing and rationality…integrating and superseding the restrictive logic behind the idea of 'civilization' by giving rise to what the civilizing mission suppressed: the self appropriation of all the good qualities that were denied to the barbarians. (*Local Histories/Global Designs* 303-04)[21]

Galeano's writing consistently invokes this other side, this "border thinking" with all the attendant difficulties of appropriation and distortion. But border thinking also has the salutary effects of imagining civilization from the position of an alterity that is entrenched in the collided space between the colonist and the perverse construction of the colonial subaltern. Born of that collision is a dissident relation to Benjamin's allegory that refigures its meaning as a function of colonial difference in the Americas. Consider the following short parable that tells via other means the story we have just framed in the language of literary criticism:

The preacher Miguel Brun told me that a few years ago he had visited the Indians of the Paraguayan Chaco. He was part of an evangelizing mission. The missionaries visited a chief who was considered very wise. The chief, a quiet, fat man, listened without blinking to the religious propaganda that they read to him in his own language. When they finished, the missionaries awaited a reaction.

The chief took his time, then said: *"That scratches. It scratches hard and it scratches very well."*

And then he added: *"But it scratches where there isn't any itch."* (*The Book of Embraces* 30)

The passage, entitled "The Function of Art," is doubly purposeful. First, it narrates its own utility (its "function" as art) in destabilizing clichéd notions of civilization as a function of propagandistic evangelization (an ancient colonial trope literally buried in the significance of Columbus's name, Cristobal Colón, meaning "bearer of the Christ" and "repopulator" [Todorov 26]). Second, it stages the act of reading against the position of the indigene as barbarian, using wit, comic timing, and rhetorical concision to score the point that the other's civil position can remain impervious to the blandishments of Occidental civic rhetoric and posturing. Who is more barbarous in the exchange Galeano narrates? Has not the position of barbarian been evacuated from the narrative frame? Or, if not evacuated, have not the conditions for thinking the relations between civil self and barbarian other been forcefully recast in the exemplary mode of Mignolo's border thinking?

Brun's story, retold by Galeano, becomes a tainted document of civilization in Benjaminian terms, but only insofar as it reflects on the barbarism of European culture as it struggles to address its encounter with difference. Interestingly, as such a document is passed from owner to owner (from Brun to Galeano), a process of transmission that subverts the concept of enduring property so critical to Occidental notions of legality and community, the document acquires force as a critique of civil discourse, as a critique of the perversity of "right" as a trope that always beckons toward the difference it excludes ("my right, not yours"), the object on which it imposes. Moreover, the story gains meaning not only in its puncturing of the alignment of right with civility but also in terms of its reinstatement via the figure of the chief of a form of civility and cultural integrity that rattles the Eurocentric cage. Missionary zealots impersonate civility even as the discursive elegance of the indigenous chief reflects badly on the Occidental barbarian who would convert at any cost, even that of the perversion of his own spiritual belief system. And yet the chief's deflection is tactful and polite, a way of suggesting that the discrepant engagement of encounter need not necessarily be governed by fanaticism or violence as it so often was in the post-conquest Americas.

Read via Galeano's parable, then, Benjamin's allegory, *mutatis mutandis*, suggests the contingent relationship of civilization (a hopelessly reductive trope that is itself synonymous with violence and brutality) to that which it figures as resistantly other, beyond its borders, incapable of its language. Further, it figures the ongoing contagion of that relation as it is "transmitted from one owner to another." After all, does the force of Brun and his fellow missionaries' rejection by the chief not indicate that a form of dialogue has been entered into, in which clever counter-indications produce the "itch" of so-called civil society's own bad faith to its colonial mission? In effect, Benjamin's allegory and Galeano's parable suggest that civilization and barbarism have intertrammeled and reciprocal relations. These relations continually challenge the imaginary border that separates them, even as relations of dominance and subordination are powerfully and deterministically at work in the reciprocity of the image.

The force of this thinking is, as we aim to show, consistently interrogated by Galeano's writing practice in relation to the Americas, in which the borderland or frontier becomes a site where opposition occurs, not as a rigid form of rejectionism so much as a way of inviting new possibilities of community that border thinking allows. Galeano's writings resist any and all simplistic taxonomies. Border crossing, contradictory hybridities, the violation of frontiers, the abhorrence of reductive labels that pin writing like an insect to a collector's blank board are all recurrent figures in Galeano's work. As he explicitly states in an interview with David Barsamian:

> I hate to be classified. This world has an obsession with classification. We are all treated like insects. We should have a label on the front. So many journalists say, "You are a political writer, right?" Just give me the name of any writer in human history who was not political. All of us are political, even if we don't know that we're political.
>
> I feel that I am violating frontiers, and I am very happy each time I can do that. I suppose I should be working as a smuggler instead of a writer, because this joy of violating a frontier is, indeed, revealing a smuggler inside me, a delinquent. ("Eduardo Galeano" 6)

Lines from a poem by the Chicana poet Gina Valdés—"Hay tantísimas fronteras / que dividen a la gente, / pero por cada frontera / existe también un puente" (4-5) [There are so many borders / that divide people, / But for every border / there is also a bridge]—aptly summarize Galeano's hybrid writing practices. Such a context is radically contrary to the often narrowly reductive depictions of him as an old-school socialist with rabidly fixed views on imperial culture and its operations.[22] Rather, Galeano's work invites thinking toward the border crossings, thinkings, and smugglings that define "Nuestra América" [Our America]. The latter is a term used by Cuban revolutionary, journalist, and poet José Martí for a form of hemispheric—as opposed to national—thinking, which "relies on the premise that there is a fundamental geocultural distinction between those American societies produced respectively by Iberian and British imperialisms" (Belnap and Fernández 5). Galeano's debt to Martí is significant, especially in its envisioning of the Americas as a space where border crossings have led to pillage and rapacious exploitation at the same time as they are enabling, here and now, the emergence of profound hemispheric alternatives to hegemonic relays of power, influence, and capital. From Galeano's perspective, writing plays its role in memorializing exploitation. But writing also enables alternative formations that lie in the here and now of the creative moment as well as in the horizon of a future yet to be made:

Does writing have any meaning? The question lies heavily in my hand.

Custom houses for words, incinerations of words, cemeteries for words are organized. So we will resign ourselves to live a life that is not ours, they force us to recognize an alien memory as our own. Masked reality, history as told by the winners: perhaps writing is no more than an attempt to save, in times of infamy, the voices that will testify to the fact that we were here and this is how we were. A way of saving for those who we do not yet know, as Espriu had wanted, "the name of each thing." How can those who don't know where they come from find out where they're going. (*Days and Nights* 173)

The word can kill: memory, self, history. Cemeteries of words are complicit with false histories and alien memories that serve institutional state culture in the Americas.

But words that escape this formulation can resist infamy, restore hope, and restitute loss. Redemptive and alive, these words give a shape to memory, thus enabling future possibilities. Galeano's thoughts on the relevance of writing as action return to the most ancient of memories in Mayan culture, which gives as the primary attributes of the first created humans the capacity to make words:

These are the names of the first people who were made and modeled.

This is the first person: Jaguar Quitze.

And now the second: Jaguar Night.

And now the third: Not Right Now.

And the fourth: Dark Jaguar.

And these are the names of our first mother-fathers. They were simply made and modeled, it is said; they had no mother and no father. We have named the men by themselves. No woman gave birth to them, nor were they begotten by the builder, sculptor, Bearer, Begetter. By sacrifice alone, by genius alone they were made, they were modeled by the Maker, Modeler, Bearer, Begetter, Sovereign Plumed Serpent.

And when they came to fruition, they came out human:

They talked and they made words. (Tedlock 146)

Galeano's work emerges from a similar foundational moment: the genesis of words as the fundamental attribute of being human, not begotten but made through talk and word. The memory of the power of this making and the restitutional energies that such a memory releases is the meaning of writing, one that links the present with a deep past that is the genesis of human words. Words that speak echo this deep past into the resistant horizon of human potential: mortuary words necrotize memory, masking the real and obliterating human identity. The writer walks the knife's edge between the cemetery and the sky.

Writing Mirrors and Windows, Mapping Distortions

As with a two-way mirror, literature can show what is visible, and what is not but still is there. And since nothing exists that does not contain its own negation, it often works as revenge and prophecy. (Galeano, *We Say No* 171)

Latin America still constitutes an enigma in its own eyes. What is the image the mirror gives us of the dominant cultures? A broken image. Pieces. Just disconnected pieces: a mutilated body, a face to be put together. (Galeano, "The Revolution as Revelation" 9)

One of the recurrent motifs in Galeano's work is the mirror and the reflected image of a distorted truth that it creates in the alienating context of colonialism both "post-" and "neo-." The mirror held up to Latin Americans and the "Third World" (a term whose problematic construction we will discuss later in this book) by the multinational image-makers throws an inverted reflection: it frames, thus limiting context. It is narcissistic, creating a self-enveloping structure of the gaze. And as observes the Vietnamese filmmaker and cultural theorist Trinh Minh-ha, "the mirror [in Western culture] is the symbol of an unaltered vision of things" (22), thereby fixing the state of affairs by capturing the alienated reflection of the colonized subject. It promotes the tyranny of synchrony. When placed facing each other, two mirrors condemn the viewer trapped between them to a limited perspective within infinite horizons of recurrence. The mirror proliferates false images and lies voraciously. It transposes the image of the conqueror on the conquered in a gesture of false community that is really an advertising ploy to flatter and seduce through a perverse identification with impossible images. The dazzled spectators are either submerged in a fantasy world where their desires and preoccupations are grafted onto them like masks, or they suffer the difference between image and reality by regarding their own faces with contempt. Within this paradigm, assuming the gaze of the conqueror leads to self-loathing.

The former possibility is satirized in a series of cartoons by Pancho, published in an issue of *Crisis* as part of an article on the control of ideology by large corporations. One cartoon depicts an appliance salesman showing off his product to a woman outside of a shack constructed from odd and ends scavenged from the dump (as is often the case in urban slums). The woman, hands clasped to her chest and eyes wide with awe exclaims: "¡La enceradora es hermosa!...pero no tenemos parquet ni electricidad!" [The polishing machine is beautiful!...but we don't have floors or electricity!] To which the salesman replies: "¡Magnífico!...En ese caso puedo hacerle un descuento especial!" (24 [1975]: 6) [Great! In that case, I can give you a special discount!]

The Floor Polisher. Pancho, from *Crisis* 24 (1975): 6.

In front of another shack constructed of old billboards and boxes sporting famous brand names like Reader's Digest and Marlboro with a Coca-Cola sign as a roof, a slum dweller tells a man in a suit doing a survey: "Sí, en mi casa también pensamos que todo va mejor con Coca-Cola..." (7) [Yes, in my house, we also think that things go better with Coca-Cola]. Two ragged dump scavengers dragging their findings along in homemade carts argue about the comparative virtues of the Fairline and the Mercedes 350 S.E. (9). Seen in the false reflection of commercial reality, the enormous disparities between the dump and the dream of wealth are mitigated. The mirror mercilessly reflects this distorted dream in the name of obscuring the conditions that produce such disparities:

> They sell newspapers they cannot read, sew clothes they cannot wear, polish cars they will never own and construct buildings where they will never live. With their cheap arms they present cheap products to the world market. (Galeano, "The Other Wall" 7)

EDUARDO GALEANO

The Coke Shack. Pancho, from *Crisis* 24 (1975): 6.

Luxury Vehicles. Pancho, from *Crisis* 24 (1975): 6.

The mirror enlarges small spaces, creates doubles where there are none. Good for the prison of everyday life and the solitude it engenders, mirrors falsely cure the diminished social space of its restrictions and emptiness. The mirror fills emptiness with emptiness. Vanity, lack of interest, self-loathing, and boredom glaze its surfaces: "Some time ago, I saw a chicken pecking at a mirror. The chicken was kissing its own reflection. In a little while, it fell asleep" (*We Say No* 178). The appearance of verisimilitude is just that: an appearance, a reflected dissimulation. In a document from the 1996 *Encounter for Humanity and Against Neoliberalism*, the Zapatista Army of National Liberation (EZLN) uses the trope of the mirror that falsifies identity and blinds people to the conditions governing their existence. In this document, it is clear that *who* holds the mirror and *who* fashions the context that gives meaning to its images is crucial:

A new lie is sold to us as history. The lie about the defeat of hope, the lie about the defeat of dignity, the lie about the defeat of humanity. The mirror of power offers us an equilibrium in the balance scale: the lie about the victory of cynicism, the lie about the victory of servitude, the lie about the victory of neoliberalism.

Instead of humanity, it offers us stock market value indexes, instead of dignity it offers us globalization of misery, instead of hope it offers us an emptiness, instead of life it offers us the international of terror. (12-13)

But the mirror is also instructive, a tool for teaching, and it has specific positive associations in its symbolic usage by the *tlamatinime*, a Nahuatl (Aztec/Mexica) word for "wise ones."[23] As Miguel León-Portilla notes,

> The *tlamatini* is a light and a thick firebrand that never smokes. He is a pierced mirror, a mirror perforated on both sides...He is writing and wisdom...He transmits wisdom and follows the truth. Master of truth, he never ceases admonishing. He makes wise the faces of others, he makes them take on a face and develop it...He holds up a mirror before others...so that their own face appears...He applies his light to the world...Thanks to him, the people humanize their desiring and receive disciplined instruction. (qtd. in Dussel, *The Invention of the Americas* 96-97)

León-Portilla, in his seminal work on Aztec culture, suggests further that the "perforated mirror" alludes to the "*tlachialoni*, a type of scepter with a pierced mirror at one end. The object was part of the equipment of certain gods, who used it to scrutinize the earth and human affairs...Applied to the wise man, it conveys the idea that he is himself a medium of contemplation, 'a concentrated or focused view of the world and things human'" (*Aztec Thought and Culture* 11).[24] In this indigenous context, then, the perforated mirror symbolizes the one capable of wisdom (itself a function of seeing differently), of admonishing to seek after wisdom, of giving others face through the act of holding the mirror before them thus humanizing desire through disciplined instruction. Dussel glosses the "mirror" in the crucial phrase here—"to place a mirror before others"—as symbolizing the "critical, speculative reflection by which one looks at oneself and overcomes meaninglessness. The *tlamatini* places a mirror before the other's visage and enables self-discovery, self-reconstruction, and self-development" (*The Invention of the Americas* 185).

In such a context, Galeano's use of the mirror trope is double-edged, signifying at once the dangers of deception and the ability to discover via "critical, speculative reflection." It is no coincidence that the second book of *Memory of Fire* is entitled *Caras y máscaras* (*Faces and Masks*), which gestures toward the *tlamatini*'s task of giving face to the faceless while at the same time acknowledging that the world is masked, in need of revelation, both crucial strategies underlying Galeano's historiographic project. Bell states that "Because in Spanish *máscaras* (masks) is also a play on words meaning *más caras* (more faces), the title [*Caras y máscaras*]...suggests that there are/were other truths" (99). Read in this way, the pun operates as a reminder to the *tlamatini* of the extent of the work (giving face to the faceless) that needs doing. Galeano clarifies the way in which he understands the mask/face to work in a passage from *The Book of Embraces*:

It's the age of the chameleon: no one has taught humanity so much as that humble little creature.

Experts in concealment are highly respected, homage is paid to the culture of the mask. We speak the double language of master mimics. Double language, double accounting, double morality: one morality for speech, another morality for action. The morality for action is called realism.

The law of reality is the law of power. So that reality should not seem unreal, those in charge tell us that morality must be immoral. (178)

Exposing the doubleness of language, the doubleness of morality via inverted narrative strategies is at the heart of Galeano's writing project: this exposition is linked to showing how the "morality of the real," what is reflected in the narcissistic, self-interested mirror of civilization, is a construction in the service of relations of power.

The mirror, in its derivation from the Latin word *mirari,* means to "wonder (at)," to "look [at] with attention" (Partridge 407). But critical contemplation of the mirror and being trapped in its inverted gaze are two very different things, for the mirror is an instrument and metaphor of the system Galeano denounces. Galeano calls upon readers, in the manner of the *tlamatini*, to wonder and look at (see through) the spectacle of their own distorted images as mirrored by the system:

The System

We walk along the Barcelona boulevards, fresh tunnels of summer, and we draw up to a stall where birds are sold.

There are cages for one and for several birds. Adoum explains that in one-bird cages a little mirror is placed inside so the birds won't know they are alone.

Later, at lunch, Guaysamín talks about New York. He says he has seen men there drink by themselves at counters. That behind the row of bottles there is a mirror and sometimes, late at night, the men throw their glasses and the mirror shatters to bits. (*Days and Nights* 30)

Shattering the mirror is the work of disgusted drunks or dissident writers. The shattered mirror is a recurrent trope in Galeano's work and is perhaps emblematic of the function he sees for his own work, which repeatedly stages the will to destroy reality's mirror. In *La canción de nosotros*, an early novel, Galeano describes the workings of the state machine as it breaks dissident prisoners using the mirror:

Vio una cara. Pobre viejito, desfigurado por el miedo. Pobre diablo. Daba lástima. Era la cara de alguien que se había perdido en la selva, con barba y mugre de años y los rasgos hinchados y borrosos. Y sin embargo, era un espejo. Descubrió que era un espejo. Era un espejo lo que tenía delante...él quiso reventar el espejo, hacerse saltar en pedazos, convertirse en una telaraña de vidrio o en un montón de vidrios rotos de una trompada: quiso romperse, y se dijo: arriba brazo, arriba mano. Pero los brazos y las manos tampoco le pertenecían y descubrió: soy mis jirones, soy los restos de mí mismo. (119-20)

[He saw a face. Poor old man, disfigured by fear. Poor devil. It was pathetic. It was the face of someone who had been lost in the jungle, with a beard and grime from several years, swollen features, out of focus. And yet it was a mirror. It was a mirror he had facing him...he wanted to break the mirror, smash himself to pieces, transform himself into a glass spider's web or into a pile of glass shards broken by his fists: he wanted to break himself and thought, lift the arm, lift the hand. But his arms and hands were no longer his and he realized, I am my shreds, I am the remains of myself.]

The technology of terror deploys the mirror to reflect the prisoner's abjection and disempowerment. The mirror reproduces an effaced, distorted identity without even the power to destroy itself. To break the mirror is to break the abjected identity it reflects. The passage is particularly effective for how it describes a double process of destruction: torture both destroys identity and the capacity to imagine identity beyond the context of torture. All that remain are fragments, shards, shreds.

As the emblematic stuff of "civilization," the goods given to credulous indigenes, mirrors bear a special relation to the colonial and the so-called developing world: "Sin embargo, nuestro fino olfato para los negocios nos hace pagar por todo lo que vendemos y nos permite comprar todos los espejos que nos traicionan la cara" (*Úselo y tírelo* 119) [However, our (Latin Americans') fine sense of business makes us pay for all that we sell and permits us to buy all the mirrors that betray our faces]. Betrayal and commodification go hand in hand: these are made to seem normal, quotidian. The mirror has become the window through which we see inverted images of what it means to be human: "One hundred and thirty years ago, after visiting Wonderland, Alice stepped into a mirror and discovered the world of the looking glass. If Alice were born today, she'd only have to peek out the window" (*Upside Down* 2). Galeano parodically reinforces the inverted pedagogy of the mirror and what it teaches:

The looking-glass school is the most democratic of institutions. There are no admissions exams, no registration fees, and courses are offered free to everyone everywhere on earth as well as in heaven. It's not for nothing that this school is the child of the first system in history to rule the world.

In the looking-glass school, lead learns to float and cork to sink. Snakes learn to fly and clouds drag themselves along the ground. (*Upside Down* 5)

The mirror teaches inversion and has been doing so throughout the history of the conquest.[25] Perversely, the mirror teaches the other to disfigure itself in a regulatory sameness:

1538: Santo Domingo
The Mirror

The noonday sun makes the stones smoke and metals flash. Uproar in the port. Galleons have brought heavy artillery from Seville for the Santo Domingo fortress...Amid the bustle and pandemonium, an Indian girl is searching for her master. Her skin is covered with blisters, each step a triumph as her scanty clothing tortures her skin. Throughout the night and half the day, from one scream to the next, this girl has endured the burns of acid. She herself roasted the *guao* tree roots and rubbed them between her hands to make a paste, then anointed her whole body, from the roots of her hair to the soles of her feet, because *guao* burns the skin and removes its color, thus turning Indian and black women into white ladies of Castile.

"Don't you recognize me, sir?"

Oviedo [mayor of Santo Domingo] shoves her away; but the girl insists in her thin voice, sticking to her master like a shadow, as Oviedo runs shouting orders to the foremen. (*Genesis* 98)

The illusory sameness produced by self-mutilation is physically inscribed on the body, internalized self-hate converted into an externalized sign. Checked in the mirror. Motivated by the mirror. The technology of such a distortion and perversion of human difference is also the technology of colonial power, and it is systemic.

A pertinent example of how this structure of distortion finds other venues is exemplified in Galeano's treatment of yet another emblem of colonial power, the map. Galeano consistently refers to maps as indicative of the extent to which human relations are deformed by technologies of representation at the service of hegemonic control. Jerry Brotton's discussion of the Treaty of Saragossa (23 April 1529) provides a useful example of this effect. The treaty was signed between Charles V and the Portuguese crown over possession of the Moluccas, an island group in Indonesia also known as the Spice Islands because they were the source of a lucrative trade in that commodity. The maps associated with the making of the treaty, which apportioned strategic territories, "were by no means impartial," according to Brotton. Instead, Brotton argues that

...the ritual construction of the map, and the fantasy of its ability to implement a form of maritime policing (that was in reality unenforceable), stood as the object through which the diplomatic transactions which carved up the Moluccas came to be ratified. Having been established as a 'capital good' which entered the marketplace alongside the spices and cloves it projected, the map now appeared in the more restricted arena of the political economy of diplomatic negotiation. It was this politically sensitive arena which appreciated the map as a type of visual contract. (137)

Early modern cartographic practice clearly used maps as political and economic instruments, a visual signifier for imagined power relations. José Rabasa, in an extended reading of Gerhard Mercator's never-completed compendium of maps *Atlas sive cosmographicae meditationes de fabrica mundi et fabricati figura* (1595), suggests that "What is particular to Mercator's *Atlas*...is that it reintegrates America into a global perspective that not only privileges Europe but also institutes European subjectivity as universal" (207-08). Similar strategies typify modern usage, the notorious borderlands between Mexico and the U.S. being a classic example of how maps express territorial imperatives even as they conceal the history of their production, the histories upon which they are overlaid and which they obscure.[26] For instance, Galeano notes that "In the United States, the environmental map is also a racial map. The most polluting factories and the most dangerous dumps are located in pockets of poverty where blacks, Indians, and Latinos live...The residents of Convent, the Louisiana town where four of the dirtiest factories in the country operate, are nearly all black. Most of those who went to the emergency room in 1993, after General Chemical rained acid on the northern part of Richmond on San Francisco Bay, were black" (*Upside Down* 221). Charles Bowden documents this effect in Juárez, a maquiladora twin city to El Paso, Texas, where "Mexican children from Colonia Felipe Angeles play in one of the most contaminated areas in Cd. Juárez—on the border, near the premises of the U.S. company Asarco, which concentrates on the smelting of copper in El Paso" (14-15).[27]

On the world map, as a representation of the distorted "real," Galeano is equally critical, challenging readers to see through the deforming mirror of false representation:

> The equator did not cross the middle of the world map that we studied in school. More than half a century ago, German researcher Arno Peters understood what everyone had looked at but no one had seen: the emperor of geography had no clothes.
>
> The map they taught us gives two-thirds of the world to the North and one-third to the South. Europe is shown as larger than Latin America, even though Latin America is actually twice the size of Europe. India appears smaller than Scandinavia, even though it's three times as big. The United States and Canada fill more space on the map than Africa, when in reality they cover barely two-thirds as much territory.
>
> The map lies. Traditional geography steals space just as the imperial economy steals wealth, official history steals memory, and formal culture steals the word. (*Upside Down* 315)[28]

The implicit questions Galeano poses here are many: how does such deformed knowledge get produced? Transmitted? To what end? The map as false mirror of reality must be seen through, overturned, torn apart in order to understand the specific historical realities that have shaped its purposes, if only because imagined reality (however illusory) contributes to the shape of lived reality.[29] Those who imagine the world in the deformed arrangement of size relations deconstructed by Galeano are challenged to reconsider what it would mean to see the world differently, a persistent interrogative mode that characterizes Galeano's literary method. In the case of maps, Galeano suggests the following:

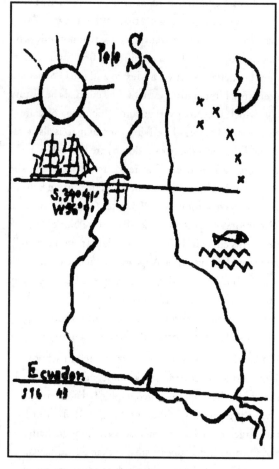

In the twelfth century, the official geographer of the kingdom of Sicily, al-Idrisi, drew a map of the world that Europe knew about, with south on top and north on the bottom.

That was common in mapmaking back then, and that's how the map of South America was drawn eight centuries later, with south on top, by Uruguayan painter Joaquín Torres-García.

"Our north is south," he said. "To go north, our ships go down, not up."

If the world is upside down the way it is now, wouldn't we have to turn it over to get it to stand up straight? (*Upside Down* 337)

Our North is South. Joaquín Torres-García, from *Upside Down* 337.

The visual inversion used here is a characteristic Galeano strategy in which normalized relations of power and representation are reversed to produce the possibility of alternative vision so crucial to revisioning a corrupt, distorted world order.[30] Canadian artist Greg Curnoe captures the spirit of this sort of method in his 1989 painting "America," which effectively elides the geographical space of the United States, joining Mexico with Canada, a visual pun that disrupts orthodox visual conventions that figure the Americas as centred on the United States.

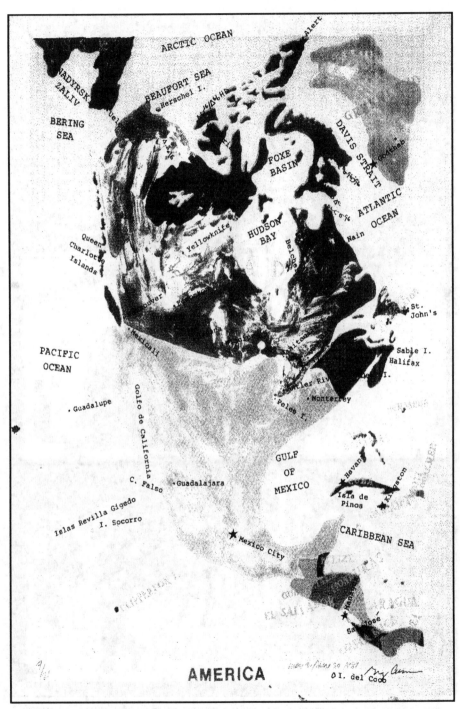

Greg Curnoe, "America" (1989).

Gregorio Selser, from *Los marines: Intervenciones norteamericanas en América Latina, Cuadernos de Crisis* 9 (1974): front cover.

La expansión territorial de los Estados Unidos

Km²

1776 – En el año de la Independencia **160.000**

1790 – Al consolidarse los Estados constituyentes **2.300.805**

1803 – Se añaden, por compra de la Louisiana a Francia, con la protesta de España, 2.141.600 Km² **4.442.405**

1819 – Se agregan, por compra compulsiva a España de las Floridas occidental y oriental, 186.416 Km² **4.628.821**

1845 – Por la incorporación del territorio de Tejas, arrebatado a México, 1.010.080 Km² **5.638.901**

1846 – Por incorporación del territorio de Oregón, cedido por Gran Bretaña, 739.367 Km² **6.378.268**

1848 – Por botín de guerra arrancado a México por el tratado de Guadalupe Hidalgo, 1.369.625 Km² **7.747.893**

1853 – Por la "Compra Gadsden", impuesta a México como "añadido" a lo precedente, 76.737 Km² **7.824.630**

1867 – Por compra amigable de Alaska al Zar de Rusia, 1.518.220 Km² **9.342.850**

1898 – Por anexión compulsiva de las islas Hawaii, 16.699 Km² **9.359.549**

1899 – Por incorporación compulsiva de las islas de Puerto Rico y Guam, 9.442 Km² **9.368.991**

1900 – Por adquisición compulsiva de islas del archipiélago de Samoa, 196 Km² **9.369.187**

1904 – Por adquisición con trampa (vía espúreo tratado Hay-Bunau-Varilla), 1.431 Km² de la llamada Zona del Canal **9.370.618**

1937 – Por adquisición amistosa de las Antillas Danesas o Islas Vírgenes, 344 Km² **9.370.962**

1947 – Por fideicomiso de las islas del Pacífico (islas Caroline, Marshall y Mariana, exceptuando Guam), 21.980 Km² **9.392.942**

— Veinticinco islas y atalones del Pacífico (Line Islands, Phoenix Islands, Ellice Islands, reclamadas también por Gran Bretaña; y Union —Tokelau— Islands y Northern Cook Islands, reclamadas también por Nueva Zelandia), con un total de 110 Km² **9.393.052**

Gregorio Selser, "La expansión territorial de los Estados Unidos," from *Los marines: Intervenciones norteamericanas en America Latina, Cuadernos de Crisis* 9 (1974): 22.

A history of such resistant, interrogative strategies is to be found in the social and intellectual contexts that have formed Galeano. A good instance of these contexts occurs in *Cuadernos de Crisis,* directed and edited by Federico Vogelius and Aníbal Ford, an adjunct publication to the banned journal *Crisis* that Galeano edited. The ninth issue of *Cuadernos de Crisis* entitled *Los marines: Intervenciones norteamericanas en América Latina,* written by Gregorio Selser (1974), contains an account of territorial expansion that has produced the United States' territory as it is now known. From 1776 to 1947, U.S. territory changed from 160,000 square kilometres to 9,393,052 square kilometres, an extraordinary territorial makeover. Most of the expansion occurred in the nineteenth century. After the Louisiana Purchase of 1803 and the purchase of Alaska from Russia in 1867, the single largest acquisition of territory occurred with the Treaty of Guadalupe Hidalgo (1848), which ended the Mexican-American War, and in which 1,396,625 square kilometers (two-thirds of Mexico's territory) were sold to the U.S. for $15 million U.S. dollars. Gore Vidal's summary account of the events leading up to the treaty of Guadalupe Hidalgo suggests that "in 1846, [the U.S.] produced [its] first conquistador, President James K. Polk. After acquiring Texas, Polk deliberately started a war with Mexico because, as he later told the historian George Bancroft, we had to acquire California. Thanks to Polk, we did. And that is why to this day the Mexicans refer to our southwestern states as 'the occupied lands,' which Hispanics are now, quite sensibly, filling up" (12). Polk, as Selser notes, wanted to extend the territory of the States to the size of Europe (7).

Seen in this light, the rapid expansion of American interests and territories in the nineteenth century sets the stage for what followed in the twentieth, during which the military consolidation of international space became an objective: "But in the decades where the United States has largely resisted the ratification of the UN treaties [on various aspects of human rights], it has established three hundred major military installations abroad, covering 2 million acres with 474,170 United States military personnel overseas, not including 250,000 United States military personnel afloat" (Drinan, *Cry of the Oppressed* 196). Galeano's writing strategies set the stage for the production and transmission of this sort of knowledge in a hybridized literary space. An admixture part social-scientific, part ethico-moral, part lyrico-testimonial, his writings attempt to shatter illusory representations, literally and figuratively, to see through them in the name of transformative critique.

Galeano's resolute anti-academicism is closely tied to a wariness of generic boundaries that map the orthodoxies of literary expression. Insofar as genre is a compulsive recapitulation of what is always already known, an antecedent reading and writing structure that subordinates difference in the expectation of a projected self-sameness, escaping genre becomes for Galeano a crucial element in formulating the "emergency" that is meaningful discourse. Genre is a crucial construct of literary academic culture, producing a form of knowability that presumes an epistemological field that can be mapped then converted into the dull energy of conventional reading practices. The sentimental romance, the historical fiction, the tale of origins, all fulfill presumptive expectations and formulae. Writing that defamiliarizes genre or plays with its conventions may evade the trap of expectation but falls into yet another—one in which patterns of defamiliarization themselves become generic and predictable adaptive practices in the name of a difference that is not. In a chapter of the anthology *The Writer and Human Rights*, titled "The Imagination and the Will to Change," Galeano recognizes this dilemma and the relationship it has to the revolutionary ideals and dissident values embedded in some forms of textuality: "Like a two-way mirror, literature can show both what can be seen, and what cannot be seen but is there. And since nothing exists which does not contain its own negation, literature often acts as a sort of vengeance and as a prophecy" (122). Vengeance is visible; prophecy is not. Both can exist simultaneously in the same transparent and endangering space. And the vengeance of the literary text is precisely its capacity to contain via the visibility of its own textuality the invisible threads that make the jaguar's mouth roar with bloodlust over a fresh kill, the spider's thread resonate with the lives of uncaught flies and grasshoppers.

The simultaneity of the dissonance between what is and is not in the text, its vengeance and its prophesy, locates what Galeano names the "prescience of change": dangerous writing presumes that "In a system of silence and fear, the power to create and to invent and to imagine attacks the rootedness of obedience" (122). Galeano argues that "To deny literature which is not part of an emergency is as serious a mistake as to despise the literary forms of expression which escape the boundaries of genre or which have no place on the altars of academic culture" (123). Emergency, crisis, escape from generic boundaries and academicism—all typify the resistance to "a system of silence and fear," one enabled by embracing memory "as it flashes up at a moment of danger" (Benjamin, "Theses" 255). A writing that challenges generic orthodoxies disavows the formalist obedience that makes genre recognizable as such, that gives genre an historiographic form coincident with false boundaries. This, then, is the danger of genre to Galeano: "However revolutionary it pretends to be, work undertaken without risk ends by being conformist in fact. Even though it arouses fervor, it provokes drowsiness. It is said to be directed at the multitudes, but it really converses in solitude with the mirror" (123).

Self-regarding and self-reflexive literary structures, so the lesson goes, stand before the mirror of their own making in the name of conformity. Meta-narratives of their own lifelessness, such texts mirror a preformed, predictable ideology shared by creator and audience in which the perverse distortions of self-same reflections provoke neither change nor risk. Literary critical texts are particularly susceptible to the isomorphic logic of the mirror, reaffirming critical orthodoxies in the name of the mirror's ideology of narcissism, distortion, and contented self-regard—infatuated by the visible absence of difference. Galeano pointedly makes this observation in discussing the identity politics of Latin American emigrants to "America":

I'm always saying that our worst sin in Latin America is the sin of stupidity because we enjoy looking at our own caricature. For instance, when I meet Latin Americans here in the States, they say "Now I'm in America." Ah, you're in America now, because you are in the States. Before you were where? Greenland? Asia? Japan? We have accepted this distorted vision of ourselves looking at the mirror which despises and scorns us. (Barsamian, "Eduardo Galeano" 4)

The ideology of the mirror is the ideology of deceptively hard surfaces, the emptying out of the boundary spaces between here and there, subject and object, self-interest and reciprocity. Simultaneity and self-sameness reinforce the impunity of the subject *as* subject. The space of knowing is the same space as that of seeing, an always dangerous arrangement of perspective that presumes singular epistemologies, singular event-horizons. For Galeano, mirrored relationships of this sort contribute to a relationship of dominance and submission: "The oppressor wants the mirror to give back to the oppressed just a blank reflection, and certainly no process of social change can urge forward a people who don't know who they are or where they come from" ("For Haroldo Conti" 15). Blank reflections efface identity, even when the seer sees his or her own image reflected. The insight recalls a moment in the fourth part of the Mayan sacred text, the *Popol Vuh,* in which the "first people [Jaguar Quitze, Jaguar Night, Not Right Now, and Dark Jaguar] who were made and modeled...By the Maker, Modeler, Bearer, Begetter, Sovereign Plumed Serpent" achieve an intensity of seeing and knowledge that allows them to "under[stand] everything great and small...And so the Bearer, Begetter took back their knowledge" (Tedlock 146-48). The danger that these first people will gain too much knowledge and thus become godlike forces the gods to reform their creation:

And when they changed the nature of their works, their designs, it was enough that the eyes be marred by the Heart of Sky. They were blinded as the face of a mirror is breathed upon. Their vision flickered. Now it was only from close up that they could see what was there with any clarity.

And such was the loss of the means of understanding along with the means of knowing everything, by the four humans. The root was implanted. (Tedlock 148)

The Mayan allegory of lost sight, of a fogged mirror, is an allegory of human subjection to the gods' will, born of a fear that human vision allowed to achieve its full intensity will compromise the relationship of creator to created. Galeano responds to this passage with the following parable:

Jealousy From On High

The Maya believe that at the beginning of history, when the gods gave us birth, we humans could see beyond the horizon. We were newly established then, and the gods flung dust in our eyes so we would not be so powerful.

I thought of this jealousy of the gods when I learned of the death of my friend, René Zavaleta. René, who possessed a dazzling intelligence, was struck down by cancer of the brain.

Half a century earlier, Enrico Caruso had died of cancer of the throat. (*The Book of Embraces* 210)

The gods, emblems of hegemonic power, seek to blind, whether through dust in the eyes or through the breath that fogs the mirror. These tropes allegorize how the powerful seek to restrict seeing, to contain the knowledge that comes with the "means of knowing everything."

But even the clear mirror perpetuates blindness figured in the inverted certainty of what one sees reflected. Dispelling that blindness, rethinking the epistemology of self-cognition from outside the frame of the mirror, however utopian or idealist such a project may seem, is critical to any understanding of Galeano's project, which is neither wholly political nor wholly aesthetic but both at once. The emptying out of memory, implicit in the short narrative just recounted from the *Popol Vuh*, is as much a project of the gods as it is of the people who use the gods in the name of oppressive fantasies: "Those who approach the people as if they were hard of hearing and incapable of imagination confirm the image of them cultivated by their oppressors. Those who use a language of boring, stereotyped sentences, who create one-dimensional, papier-mâché characters, without fears, doubts, or contradictions, who mechanically carry out the orders of the author, are blessing the system they say they are fighting" ("The Imagination and the Will to Change" 121). Oppression, loss of sight, deafness: the recurrent and aligned tropes insist on their opposites as mediated by a writing that challenges oppression while seeking the clarity of contradiction and the resonance of imagination.

Writing plays its role in this struggle because it "makes a choice by the simple fact of its existence. In directing itself to others, it inevitably occupies a position and takes sides in the relationship between society and power. Its content, whether liberating or alienating, is in no way determined by its theme, by its subject" ("The Imagination and the Will to Change" 121). Which is to say that the discourse of thematics, so much a part of genre criticism generally, is misleading as a criterion against which to judge the effect of a given text. The writer who evades or betrays the mirror-effect that equates theme with intent and effect chooses the guise of an anti-genre (in all the forms that may take, whether through fragmentation, hybridization, collage, bricolage, radical contrarianism, and so forth) that begins the disruptive process of destructuring orthodoxy and cant.

The invitation implicit in such a technique is to see anew, to recuperate a lost seeing associated with a revisionary aesthetics, but also with alternative forms of governance. As Martí states, "To govern well, one must see things as they are" (113). Through the looking glass, perhaps, lies one such way of seeing "things as they are," which is to argue that so much seeing is compromised by historical amnesia, deeply ingrained narrative structures that produce particular subject-positions in readers (who are thus subjugated), and the blindness perpetuated by seeing oneself wherever difference is located. This is the blindness of self-alienation masquerading as self-recognition. In the Americas that emerge from Galeano's literary imaginings, the struggle is to undo the self-alienation resulting from the mirrored relations with America as a reductive trope for the geopolitical entity of the United States. Literary art, then, plays a crucial role in undermining the selective vision imposed by reflected surfaces. Thus, Galeano associates the role of the artist, whether literary or otherwise, with a seeing beneath and through surfaces:

> One fine day the mayor's office commissioned [a famous sculptor] to make a huge horse for the city plaza. A truck brought a gigantic block of granite to the shop. The sculptor began to work on it, standing on a ladder, hammering and chiseling away.
> The children [in the neighbourhood] watched him work.
> Then the children went away to the mountains or the seaside on vacation.
> When they returned, the sculptor showed them the finished horse.
> And one of the children asked him, wide-eyed,
> "But…how did you know that inside the stone there was a horse?" (*Days and Nights* 173)

Who else but the sculptor, here a metonym for all artists, is capable of freeing form from stone, of penetrating through to the hidden promise in granite? Identity is hidden from Latin Americans in a similar way, given that the majority has a life-long contact with television, that most deforming of mirrors, as compared to only a few years (three or four) spent in schools. An article in *Crisis* called "El control de la ideología" [The Control of Ideology] examines how alienated the majority of Latin Americans are thanks to having their dreams manufactured for them by multinational advertising firms: "los campesinos pobres, los villeros, las empleadas domésticas y los peones reciben casi todo lo que aprenden del mundo exterior a través de las imágenes y slogans de la publicidad" (24 [1975]: 4) [Poor peasants, slum dwellers, domestic employees and unskilled workers all receive almost everything they learn about the external world through advertising images and slogans].

In *El descubrimiento de América que todavía no fue y nuevos ensayos* [The Discovery of America Yet to Come and New Essays; 1991], Galeano asks what possibility there is of change when people never see images of themselves, let alone any critique of the reasons behind why the television and advertising images bear no relation to their own reality: "Qué proceso de cambio puede impulsar un pueblo que no sabe quién es, ni de dónde viene? Si no sabe quién es, ¿cómo puede saber lo que merece ser? ¿No puede la literatura ayudar, directa o indirectamente, a esa revelación? (18) [What process of change could stimulate a people who do not know who they are, or where they come from? If they don't know who they are, how can they know what they deserve to be? Can literature help, directly or indirectly, in this revelation?]. The enemy ("el opresor") whose interest is assured by those alienating images is repeatedly identified in Galeano's writings and not just accepted as an integral part of modern civilized life: "El elitismo, el racismo, el machismo y el militarismo impiden que América reconozca en el espejo su rostro múltiple y luminoso" (160). [Élitism, racism, machismo, and militarism impede America from recognizing its multiple and luminous face in the mirror]. Herein lies the main stimulus for Galeano's writing: to rediscover, record, and converse with that multiple and luminous face. Notwithstanding his own limitations—"Yo, blanco y macho pero no militar ni rico" [I, white and male but not military nor rich]—

> ...escribí *Memoria del fuego* contra la amnesia de las cosas que vale la pena recordar. No soy historiador. Soy un escritor, que se siente desafiado por el enigma y la mentira, que quisiera que el presente deje de ser una dolorosa expiación del pasado y que quisiera imaginar el futuro en vez de aceptarlo: un cazador de voces, perdidas y verdaderas voces que andan desparramadas por ahí. (150)

> ...[wrote *Memory of Fire* against the amnesia of things that are worth remembering. I'm not a historian. I'm a writer who feels challenged by the enigma and the lies, who would like the present to stop being a painful atonement of the past and who would like to imagine the future instead of just accepting it: a hunter of voices, lost and real voices that wander about scattered.]

The allegory of the tarnished, shattered, or buried mirror, also alluded to by Carlos Fuentes, is not a call to recover a lost object (as if identity could be singular) but an accusation against those who deny Latin America its own struggles, visions, and victories. The *Zapatista Encuentro* documents often break into poetry. In one of these instances the mirror is miniaturized and becomes an audio instrument uniting all individuals in "a network of voices that not only speak, but also struggle and resist for humanity and against neoliberalism" (48):

> *A pocket mirror of voices,*
> *the world in which sounds may be listened*
> *to separately, recognizing their specificity,*
> *the world in which sounds may include*
> *themselves in one great sound, continues...* (49)

Galeano searches for such mirrors and holds them up in the manner of the tlamatini, revealing fragments entitled "windows" through which the reader is invited to see. The true mirror thus becomes indistinguishable from a window, an aperture on the reciprocity of personal and collective realities.

It is said that the writer's choice is always a two-way choice. Whether one assumes it clear-sightedly or not, by writing one situates oneself vis-à-vis both society and the nature of literature, that is to say, the tools of creation. The way I encounter or incorporate the former, in other words, is the way I confront merge into the latter, for these are the two inseparable faces of a single entity. Neither entirely personal nor purely historical, a mode of writing is in itself a function. An act of historical solidarity, it denotes, in addition to the writer's personal standpoint and intention, a relationship between creation and society. (Trinh 20)

Galeano makes this "writer's choice" clear-sightedly. Not a writer in search of himself as a solitary individual in search of his fate so much as a voice comprised of multiple other voices that engage him in storytelling. "I belong to a land that is still unknown to herself. I write to help her reveal herself—to reveal, to rebel—and seeking her out I seek out myself, and with her, in her, I lose myself" (*We Say No* 175). In the image of the writer as seeker of voices converge key impulses in Galeano's work: the solidary spirit linking self to other in a process of dialogue that demands an ethics of reciprocal engagement, the revelatory relations of past, present, and future, and the persistent hope of transforming the alien present into "another possible world" (*Upside Down* 336). We would argue that these impulses connect Galeano's work in important ways to an emergent understanding of human rights in relation to literary discourse, a subject to which we now direct our attention.

NOTES

1. In a 1979 essay, Galeano discusses his exile in relation to the fate of a number of writers who were disappeared or tortured by military régimes, suggesting that "*Some literature is incompatible with the military's pedagogy of amnesia and lies*...To de-dramatize the plight of writers in exile, you needn't search far. A few examples from Argentina and Uruguay that recently scarred my soul: poet Paco Urondo, shot dead; authors Haroldo Conti and Rodolfo Walsh and journalist Julio Castro, lost in the sinister fog of kidnapping; playwright Mauricio Rosencof, broken by torture and now rotting behind bars" (*We Say No* 143-45).

2. For further summaries of available biographical information on Galeano, see among others: Martin, "Hope Springs Eternal"; Palaversich, *Silencio*; and Bach. To the best of our knowledge, no biography of Galeano has been written and, at the time this book went to press, none is in progress.

3. Wallerstein asserts that "Utopistics is the serious assessment of historical alternatives, the exercise of our judgment as to the substantive rationality of alternative possible historical systems. It is the sober, rational, and realistic evaluation of human social systems, the constraints on what they can be, and the zones open to human creativity. Not the face of the perfect (and inevitable) future, but the face of an alternative, credibly better, and historically possible (but far from certain) future" (*Utopistics* 1-2).

4. Galeano commemorates Rulfo's 1968 death in *Century of the Wind*, noting that "Fifteen years ago he said what he had to say, in a small novel [*Pedro Páramo*] and a few short stories, and since then he says nothing. Or rather, he made the deepest kind of love, and then went to sleep" (202).

5. The Spanish version of this essay published in *El tigre azul* is more complete: this paragraph ends "No ocurren porque Nicaragua difunda armas en los países vecinos, contagioso ejemplo de independencia nacional y participación popular" (81) [They are not taking place because Nicaragua provides arms to neighbouring countries, but to stop it from providing an example: its dangerous, contagious example of national independence and popular participation].

6. American labour historian and cultural critic Mike Davis states of Galeano that "No one has focused greater moral clarity on the inhuman conditions and radical inequalities that sustain the mirage of the New Economy" (qtd. in Sherman 2).

7. Gwen Kirkpatrick argues that the *Memory of Fire* trilogy "takes its format, in large part, from Neruda's *Canto General*" and cites Galeano's self-assessment of the multiple forms his work exemplifies: "'It is not an anthology but a literary creation, based on solid documentation but moving with complete freedom. The author does not know to what literary form the book belongs: narrative, essay, epic poem, chronicle, testimony'" (170-71).

8. Virginia Bell offers a different critique of Franco's assessment of Galeano, stating that "[Franco] concludes that 'Canada is left out altogether' in the trilogy and that *Memoria del fuego* ends up 'caught in the old gendered discourse which considers America to be a woman of clay or territory'...There are entries which warrant these comments, to be sure, but it should be quite clear from the numerous examples I have given that Canada is very much included and that the trilogy's discourse on gender is not at all monologic" (111). Since Franco's critique, Galeano has collected his vignettes about women and republished them in *Mujeres* (1995). To further counter Franco's point, Bell discusses Galeano's use of women as historical actants in relation to the stream of indigenous narratives in *Memory of Fire*. She argues that "Galeano goes to great length to include women as major actors in the events he recounts" and that he "relentlessly involves women in the histories of social upheaval, privilege, and resistance movements" (108). At the same time, "regardless of Galeano's intentions, narratives about women's history in the Americas sometimes stand in conflict with narratives about, for example, indigenous resistance. There is no single alliance between a variety of subordinate positions" (109).

9. Hayden Herrera identifies the same theme and pre-Columbian vision in her commentary on two other paintings by Kahlo: "*Roots* can also be seen as a reversal of *My Nurse and I*. In the latter Frida is a baby nourished by the plantlike breasts of a Mexican earth mother; in *Roots* the adult Frida nourishes the Mexican earth" (91).

10. Even West's highly critical position on how Galeano presents some historical information is potentially debatable via aesthetic arguments that place economy of form over prolixity, narrative gaps over diachronic comprehensivity.

11. Rama's use of the term "new man," however much an echo of its use as a widely used referent in Latin America for Che Guevara as an embodiment of revolutionary principles, works against his communitarian argument insofar as it suggests, however unconsciously, an androcentric view of the world.

12. As with many of the terms used in this book, we do not associate globalization with any singular expression of reality. Alexander Stille argues that "globalization has the homogenizing effect of allowing multinational corporations to extend their reach into virtually every corner of the world. But at the same time, by making it easier for members of small minorities (beekeepers or Gaelic speakers) to communicate at a distance, it creates openings for niche cultures to thrive" (12). The unspoken question in Stille's analysis is what happens when large majorities begin to use global opportunities to address so-called "niche" ideas regarding the practice of democracy, the influence of multinationals, the abuses of nation-states, the ma-

nipulations of unaccountable transnational organizations, and so forth. June Nash, the distinguished American anthropologist, gives one instance of the extent to which state sovereignty has been undermined by banks whose "international business…has jumped from $55 billion annually in 1965 to over $2,200 billion in 1981, [which] means that an enormous pool of wealth lies outside of the control of nations and of international agencies" (11). See also John Keane's argument that "global public spheres—when they function properly—can help to ensure that nobody monopolizes power at the local, regional and world levels" (15).

13. Further discussion of notions of the "human" in relation to how rights are enacted occurs in the following chapter.

14. Wright is blunt in his assessment of the realities of decolonization: "no country in America has really been decolonized. Indians may form half the population of Peru, three-quarters of Bolivia, and sixty percent of Guatemala; but the rulers are Ladinos—whites and mestizos—whose blood, or at least whose culture, came with the conquistadors. Only dead Indians are heroes" (*Time Among the Maya* 37).

15. In his review of the third volume of *Memory of Fire*, Gerald Martin places Galeano's revisionary historical work in a genealogy that includes "Rivera's multitudinous murals, Neruda's monumental *Canto* [and] Fernando Solanas's blockbusting *Hour of the Furnaces* (1968)" ("Preaching to the Converted" 183).

16. For further information on the Cashinahua's culture, see Kensinger. When Kensinger "arrived on the Curanja River in 1955, four years after an epidemic had killed four-fifths of the adult population," there remained "fewer than one hundred Peruvian Cashinahua" (270). Generally, Galeano's position is in line with anthropological work that documents "the ingenuity and adaptability of subsistence-based economies, defined as those in which the producers consume a majority of production and sell only to meet basic needs of food, housing, and health" (Nash 12). June Nash summarizes a number of examples of these sorts of cultures, including ones in Somalia, Amazonia, southeast Asia, and Tanzania (12).

17. We recognize the constructedness of the notion of "natural" here as well as the deep cultural gap that opens up between an Amazonian indigene's notion of the natural (as conceived in relation to a myth of genesis) and a twentieth-century reconstruction of that space and concept. Further, the story may be read as reinforcing a form of gender relations that perpetuates notions of female passivity in relation to male initiative. The alternative reading would be that the man's initiative is pointless, derived from his own ignorance, thereby devaluing the notion of initiative (the woman can lie back passively because she possesses knowledge and recognizes that there is no problem to be solved). The male stereotype is further subverted and imbued with the positive attitude expressed in his nurturing concern for the woman: her laughter is hardly passive in the face of the man's concern over how to make love, suggesting a further inversion of gender stereotypes.

18. Galeano also states that the "function of political and intellectual work will depend on how…objective reality responds to it; and that it will often have a very modest function, which is nonetheless worthwhile" (qtd. in Davis 24).

19. Flanagan's win of the Donner Prize came *after* his book received support from the Donner Canadian Foundation, which "financially support[ed] my research as well as the publication of the book" (Acknowledgments). The sequence says a great deal about how public legitimation of ideology coincident with dominant interests operates in the production of knowledge. How many books that take an informed position counter to Flanagan's receive anywhere near the level of support (in their production) or public recognition?

20. Flanagan is not the first, nor will he be the last to make this sort of assertion. Ronald Wright notes how the Guatemalan historian Severo Martínez Peláez, in his *La patria del criollo*, "sees postconquest Indian culture as somehow inauthentic—not a survival or development of Maya society but 'the historical consequence of colonial oppression'" (*Time Among the Maya* 183). Wright also cites Martínez Peláez's uninformed opinion that "The Indians [Maya] do not know their history" (253). Both comments efface indigenous realities in favour of the historical authenticity of colonizing culture, a deeply perverse model of encounter and its aftermath.

21. Mignolo borrows the Argentine philosopher Rudolfo Kusch's troubling notion of "phagocytosis," one step removed from the barbarized figure of the cannibal.

22. Consider, for example, the continuity of the tone and content evident in the following reviews—both anonymous—of two of Galeano's books, spread over a period of eight years:

On *We Say No*; from *Kirkus Reviews*, 1 May 1992:

Uruguayan journalist Galeano, author of the portentously pastiched *Memory of Fire* trilogy, collects here almost 30 years of occasional pieces that exhibit a mind set so tightly over its blind convictions that apparently nothing by way of observation or analysis has pierced its essence for three decades. From a pious interview with Che Guevara to a screed decrying the Gulf War ("Who will live to say that their crime was our suicide?"), Galeano most often almost chokes with Marxist rage and gall: The pieces are short and barked, the style strictly loudspeaker: "For us capitalism is not a dream to be pursued, but a nightmare come true. Our challenge lies not in privatizing the state but in deprivatizing it. Our states have been bought up at bargain prices by the owners of the land, the banks, and everything else." Or—especially choice—"The elections in Nicaragua were a very cruel blow. A blow like hatred from God, as the poet said. When I heard the results, I was a child lost in the storm. A lost child I remain, but I'm not alone. We are many. Throughout the world we are many." For connoisseurs of propaganda only. (585)

And on *Upside Down*; from *Kirkus Reviews*, 15 July 2000:

Galeano (The *Memory of Fire Trilogy*, etc.) has set to paper an astonishingly straight-faced indictment of *yanqui* capitalism that—for all its freshness and wit—could well have been freeze-dried at about the time of Che Guevara's assassination. The author views the world as essentially a matter of conflict between North and South, rich and poor, First World and Third World, big business and the small guy, and man against nature. Big business pollutes the Third World, uses their cheap labor, and sells them Big Macs, unleashing its power (and power is everything to Galeano) on the poor and voiceless. Galeano sees the US as heavy-handed and heavily armed—using its might to quell any uprising it doesn't like and to impose any government it prefers. The North he holds responsible for most social injustices—"free trade" being his euphemism for the slave trade. He also believes that whites are responsible for the annihilation of Jews, Gypsies, blacks, and gays during the Holocaust. Hitler, he points out, sterilized Gypsies—not very different, he believes, from the sterilizations performed in America during the 1930s on criminals, blacks, and alcoholics. Yet Americans, he believes, feel inexplicably superior. Blacks have been treated poorly in both the northern and southern hemispheres; dark-skinned black or Indian Brazilians form an underclass, rarely seen in the media or at universities. The author writes of the Argentine death squads, and he sees drug trafficking as a plot of the banks and gun manufacturers: "An illegal industry of death thus serves the legal industry of death." Galeano brings an almost Manichean dualism to his disquisitions on stock markets, capitalism, unemployment, nuclear arms—and much, much more. Old-time agitprop from south of the border. (1009)

The mode of both reviews is dismissive even as the respective reviewers cannot turn away from the force of Galeano's content: the so-called "agitprop," in other words, has obviously had its effect. If anything, both reviews indicate the critics' own capacity for agitprop, especially when reducing as complex a positioning as Galeano exhibits to the terms of a simplistic Manichean dialectic that Galeano's vision of the Americas artfully rejects. The critical blindness of this sort of argument lies precisely in its own appropriation of a mode of reductive discourse that it seemingly critiques. The fact that both polemics are unsigned, as is typical with all reviews published by *Kirkus*, points to a form of critical cowardice that is deeply unethical, however instrumental.

23. Dussel describes the word's meaning as follows: "From *mati*: 'he knows, is familiar with'; *tla*: 'thing or something'; *ni*, 'giving the substantive character': *the one who knows. Tlamatini*: 'he who knows something'" (*The Invention of the Americas* 184).

24. In a short essay entitled "Word and Mirror: Presages of the Encounter," León-Portilla examines how Moctezuma, the Aztec leader defeated by Hernán Cortés, contemplated portents of encounter in a mirror found on the "head of a rare, ash-colored bird that looked like a crane" (96). There, Moctezuma saw "people of war, and they rode what looked like large deer" (97). The mirror used in this sense signifies "what is about to happen. There are also prophetic words pronounced by soothsayers and, at times, even

by circumspect men renowned as philosophers. Such words and mirrors are magic bearers of presages; they are early images of portents" (96). A form of deep-seeing, if one can see far enough into them, or even through them, the mirror has a long symbolic history of reflecting both deceptive and potential elliptical realities. The real is deceptive in some cases precisely because of its potential, a critical reading strategy that shapes Galeano's writing practices.

25. Octavio Paz's essay on Mexican-American relations, "The Telltale Mirror," opens with the following description of mirrored reality: "Before becoming a reality, the United States was an image to me. That is not surprising: we Mexicans begin as children to see that country as the *other*, an *other* that is inseparable from us and that at the same time is radically and essentially alien" (164).

26. For useful attempts to think through the possibilities of recuperating indigenous relations to material space, see Verdesio, de Vorsey.

27. David Sibley argues that "There is a history of imaginary geographies which cast minorities, 'imperfect' people, and a list of others who are seen to pose a threat to the dominant group in society as polluting bodies of folk devils who are then located 'elsewhere.' This 'elsewhere' might be nowhere, as when genocide or the moral transformation of a minority like prostitutes are advocated, or it might be some spatial periphery, like the edge of the world or the edge of the city" (49). From Galeano's perspective, such an imaginary is enacted as a function of geographies of disadvantage and exclusion.

28. See also Galeano's slightly more polemical comments on maps in *We Say No*:
    We learn world geography on a map that doesn't show the world as it is, but rather as its owners would have it. In the conventional projection, the one used in schools and virtually everywhere, the equator is not located in the middle: the Northern Hemisphere takes up two-thirds and the Southern Hemisphere one-third...*The map that makes us small is symbolic of everything else.* Stolen geography, plundered economy, falsified history, daily usurpation of reality: the so-called Third World, inhabited by third-class peoples, encompasses less, eats less, remembers less, lives less, says less. (209)

29. Important epistemic and moral considerations arise from such a statement. Sibley, for instance, argues that "the control of knowledge [such as that provided by the image of the map] has an important moral dimension. Excluded knowledge is a narrative concerning groups and individuals who have been relegated to the margins of society because the values they represent undermine the moral consensus. This knowledge becomes dangerous and threatening when it is brought to the centre and presented as a legitimate perspective on social relations" (132). Bell's account of "Los fundadores" [The Founders], a vignette from the second volume of *Memory of Fire*, is telling in this last regard:
    'Los fundadores' describes French explorer Pierre de La Vérendrye's room in which he imagined and constructed a preliminary map of Canada...'The map of Canada occupies a whole wall. Between the East coast and the Great Lakes, a few cities, a few small forts. In the background, an immense mysterious space. On the other walls, scalps of enemy Indians darkened by tobacco smoke hang beneath the crossed muskets'...The *retablo* narrative that follows paraphrases travel writing that criticizes the Chippewa because of their egalitarian gender roles and 'libertine' sexuality...Chippewa cultural practices have been replaced with hierarchical gender roles; and human experience of the land in terms of topography has been replaced with U.N. borders that now divide the Great Lakes region between Canada and the United States. Galeano's narratives imply that the scientific claims of cartography and nation building mask the ideological desires of control, violence, and mutilation of the body's and the earth's topography. (103-04)

The excluded knowledge of alternative ways of imagining sexual relations, let alone geographical space are as threatening as the "immense mysterious space" that de La Vérendrye imagines. Bell comments that Galeano consistently attacks European spatial organizations, showing them to serve specific ideological purposes, whether in "expos[ing] the hallucination of 'El Dorado' and the instability of the 'real' in cartographic space" or in "charg[ing] cartography and other physical sciences with serving the interests of the British empire" (see 267n31).

30. Ignacio Ellacuría articulates a similar strategy of inversion in relation to the traditional narratives circulating round the "discovery" of the Americas where the oppressed discover the oppressors rather than vice versa. See our comments in the following chapter.

Chapter 2

Literary Culture and Human Rights Theory

The legitimacy of human rights is not…its authoritative universalism, so much as its capacity to become a moral vernacular for the demand for freedom within local cultures. (Ignatieff, "Human Rights" 320)

The Claims of the Universal

 It is a sad irony that the fifty-odd years since the Universal Declaration of Human Rights (1948) have continued to produce an astonishing legacy of bloodshed, violence, and situations in which human rights abuses have proliferated. The notion of a "universal" declaration of rights is itself deeply flawed since, in fact, the 1948 declaration was not ratified by most African or Asian nations (100 nations had yet to be decolonized) and was instituted in the year in which apartheid was made legal, both factors suggesting that the universality of human rights as stated in this particular document was (and is) highly problematic. Further, the document was passed in the same year that George Kennan, American State Department Policy Planning chief, was advocating "that if we are to maintain the 'disparity' between our [American] wealth and the poverty of others we must put aside 'idealistic slogans' and keep to 'straight power concepts'" (qtd. in Chomsky, *Year 501* 99). Paul Gordon Lauren notes that out of a total of 56 member states, 48 voted in favour, none opposed, and eight abstained (among the abstentions included the Ukraine, the Soviet Union, South Africa, and Yugoslavia) (237, 345). Even more damning perhaps is Lauren's claim that "at the time of the adoption of the Universal Declaration of Human Rights no state—not one—regardless of location, level of development, or culture, could meet its standards of achievement" (240). Indeed, it remains debatable whether today much has changed in this latter regard.

Johannes Morsink, author of a major study on the genesis of the Universal Declaration, states that "the process used to draft the Declaration was a very inclusive one" but adds that "this process was dominated by nations from around the North Atlantic (with their friends and former colonies) and from Latin America, and that large regions of our world, such as Asia and Africa, were grossly underrepresented at the drafting table" (36). This tale of inclusivity in the name of domination and under-representation characterizes the kind of doubletalk associated with rights discourse in general, a discourse that we analyze through Galeano's Latin American perspective.[1] Robert F. Drinan, a prominent American rights advocate, suggests that "The UN charter assumes that there is enough conviction and consensus in the entire world about the value of human rights that all nations, whether their governments have a sacred or secular orientation, can adhere to the charter and carry out its mandates. That assumption has not been openly challenged by any of the one hundred nations who did not participate in the founding of the United Nations because they were not then independent countries" (*Cry of the Oppressed* 9). This is the regrettable and highly troubling language of assumed consensus that underlies universalist accounts of rights doctrine.

The problem deepens as definitional specificity intensifies: Article 7 of the Universal Declaration proclaims that "All are equal before the law and are entitled without any discrimination to equal protection of the law" but does little to address the diverse nature of the law (it is not a universal, transcendent principle so much as a culturally-constructed discourse specific to time, place, economy, culture, politics, dominant ideology, and so forth). Nor does the article address how malleable a concept is the notion of "equality before the law." Even in the most liberal-democratic of countries, with highly developed legal systems, equality is mitigated by race and ethnicity, education, class, and access to fiscal resources. Egalitarianism, or as Fredric Jameson puts it, "the radical demand for equality" (*The Jameson Reader* 391), is the defining feature of democracy, whether in material or in theoretical terms. But identifying democracy's presence as a function of equality requires careful evaluation of the evidence. Edward Said, for instance, qualifies the relevance of the Universal Declaration and other international agreements in the following way: "Most, if not all, countries in the world are signatories to a Universal Declaration of Human Rights, adopted and proclaimed in 1948, reaffirmed by every new member state of the UN. There are equally solemn conventions on the rules of war, on [the] treatment of prisoners, on the rights of workers, women, children, immigrants and refugees. None of these documents says anything about *disqualified* or less equal races or peoples" (*Representations of the Intellectual* 97; see also Said's "Nationalism, Human Rights, and Interpretation"). The lamentable situation in regard to Canadian aboriginals and African-Americans, groups whose members are imprisoned in disproportionate relation to their representation in the general population, is proof enough of what is implicit in Said's observation, namely that universality is highly fraught because of sustained and unrecognized inequalities. As Drinan observes, "50 percent of prisoners in the United States [the country with the largest prison population in the world, with as of 1999 "up to 1.8 million inmates," a tripling of the number from 1980] are African Americans, although only 12 percent of the general population is black" (*A Worldview of Human Rights* 141, 146). The other side of the problem of equality before the law is that the legal system is dependent on highly evolved and expensive modes of litigation with lawyers operating as independent businesses whose motive is profit, not justice. Until both sides of the equation are addressed, no legal system will be capable of guaranteeing the tenets of Article 7 regarding universal equality before the law.

Universal declarations or not, then, the twentieth century has been marked by a simultaneous increase in the rhetoric of rights and the perpetuation of genocidal violence. But the recognition of genocide, its increased presence as a focal rights issue in the media and its place as the focus of much late-twentieth century "peace-keeping" efforts, has effectively obscured other forms of violence. Economic and class inequities, for instance, produce the conditions for other forms of less visible abuse that are deeply pervasive. Galeano notes, following a United Nations Development Program report, that "Ten people, the ten richest men on the planet, own wealth equivalent to the value of the total production of fifty countries, and 447 multimillionaires own a greater fortune than the annual income of half of humanity" (*Upside Down* 28). The *Human Development Report 2001* establishes in no uncertain terms the staggering disproportion between excessively wealthy and excessively poor: "World inequality is very high. In 1993 the poorest 10% of the world's people had only 1.6% of the income of the richest 10%. The richest 1% of the world's people received as much income as the poorest 57%. The richest 10% of the US population (around 25 million people) had a combined income greater than that of the poorest 43% of the world's people (around 2 billion people)" (19). Gilberto Dimenstein, in *Brazil: War on Children*, reveals that there are millions of street children in Brazil and that they are the casualties of a hidden war waged against them by the state and the economic system. In relation to these staggering figures of abandonment, suggestive of an enormous and collective abrogation of responsibility toward children generally, Galeano asks: "How many does the development of Brazil develop?" (*We Say No* 253). Noam Chomsky, to cite but one further example from an exhaustive list culled from multiple state and local contexts, adds that "India alone is reported to have some 14 million child laborers, aged six and up, many working under conditions of virtual slavery for up to 16 hours a day" (*Year 501* 175). When placed in apposition to the multiple instances of genocide perpetuated in the twentieth century, these structural inequities that affect the material circumstances of both the "haves" and the "have-nots" on a day-to-day basis suggest that universality, however idealistic in principle, is a rhetorical sleight of hand, virtually meaningless in relation to the material circumstances of how the majority of people on this planet conduct their daily lives.[2]

As a rhetoric of deception, though, universality has its uses. The arguments made by Henry Kissinger, for example, against the concept of universal jurisdiction and by extension against the International Criminal Court (ICC), which would "submit international politics to judicial procedures" (86), bear commenting on in this regard. First, the notion that international politics are somehow above and beyond judicial procedure is a characteristically retrograde notion of social justice. Is justice thinkable in the aftermath of the catastrophic derogations of responsibility and abuses of power (let alone the philosophical underpinning of key rights instruments like the Universal Declaration that were a response to these abuses) that have marked the twentieth century generally? Jacques Derrida, the French philosopher, affirms that "No justice...seems possible or thinkable without the principle of some *responsibility*, beyond all living present, within that which disjoins the living present, before the ghosts of those who are not yet born or who are already dead, be they victims of wars, political or other kinds of violence, nationalist, racist, colonialist, sexist, or other kinds of exterminations, victims of the oppressions of capitalist imperialism or any of the forms of totalitarianism": in short, how to think justice without a form of responsibility that is concerned with "those who *are not there*, of those who are no longer or who are not yet *present and living*"? (xix). We would modify this question somewhat: how to think justice in terms of *those who are responsible* for those who are not there, in the sense of not yet present and living or long since dead, *as victims of responsibility's seeming absence*? In the historical context of the Nuremberg trials, for example, which sought to place direct responsibility on specific human beings for specific actions taken, decisions made, and which Kissinger himself cites as one of the judicial standards enacted to address such catastrophes (87), "sovereign immunity" and "the sacrosanct nature of national frontiers" (86) were all but done away with in the name of a higher moral purpose—namely, the effort to place responsibility on those answerable for appalling abrogations of duty to the other.

Moreover, in the face of efforts to achieve multilateral trade agreements that permit the free movement of global capital (as a function of the pre-established dominance of U.S. capital in the world market) with limited responsibility for its effects and deployment, any argument against universal jurisdiction is particularly cynical and illogical. Kissinger's position against universal jurisdiction is perfectly consistent though with the Monroe Doctrine of 1823, which restricted European intervention in the Americas, and which has been used to create the "American sphere of influence," a precursor to the concept of the "new world order." Ironically, the concept of non-intervention in the Americas establishes a form of universal restriction in the name of self-interest, a position at the heart of U.S. foreign policy and a position deeply at odds with alternative notions of international community making ostensibly provided by the rights movement. As Chomsky states:

> It is hard to improve upon the formulation by Woodrow Wilson's Secretary of State, Robert Lansing, which the President found "unanswerable" though "impolitic" to state openly: "In its advocacy of the Monroe Doctrine the United States considers its own interests. The integrity of other American nations is an incident, not an end." (*Year 501* 157-58)

The doctrine of universal self-interest as a justifiable sovereign disposition (even as it is used by Kissinger and others to justify attacks against universal jurisdiction) is grounded in some of the worst aspects of Western political philosophy (see our comments below on Grotius, Hobbes, and Hegel). Galeano is emphatic on this sort of logic as the basis for systemic self-interest, which takes its most catastrophic form in militarization, while offering the following sort of counter-analysis:

> I have spent five minutes searching for words as I gaze at a blank sheet of paper. In those five minutes, the world spent $10 million on armaments and 160 children starved to death or died of curable illness. That is to say, during my five minutes of reflection, the world spent $10 million on armaments *in order that* 160 children could be murdered with utter impunity in the war of wars, the most silent, the most undeclared war, the war that goes by the name of peace. (*We Say No* 250-51)

This perspective coincides with Chomsky's argument that points to "evidence that 'democracy' and 'human rights' are regarded [by imperial interests] purely as power instruments, of no intrinsic value, even dangerous and objectionable; precisely as any rational person with some knowledge of history and institutions would expect" (*Year 501* 211). Chomsky references the situation in Haiti following the election of liberation theologian Jean-Bertrand Aristide in 1990, in which significant amounts of U.S. aid were directed at the conservative opposition to Aristide in the name of "Democracy Enhancement"—an outrageous subornation (done in the name of democracy) of a nation's sovereign enactment of democratic principles. Stanley Hoffman is equally categorical in his assessment of U.S. foreign policy initiatives in relation to international concepts of rights: "American power has been used to strengthen or to preserve regimes whose attitudes toward human rights were anything but compatible with democratic values. The promotion of human rights abroad is not synonymous with 'the expansion of American power.' Neither the pluralism of our institutions nor our own liberal-democratic values have guaranteed us against the misuse or corruption of power abroad" (48).

In arguing against international jurisdiction, which effectively limits the accountability (and therefore responsibility) of sovereign states to a larger, more complex context, Kissinger further avers that "The danger lies in pushing the effort [to prevent genocide, human rights violations, and so forth through the application of the principle of universal jurisdiction] to dangerous extremes that risk substituting the tyranny of judges for that of governments; historically, the dictatorship of the virtuous has often led to inquisitions and even witch-hunts" (86). It is precisely the failure of sovereign nations' governments to address issues extending beyond their own self-interest in just ways that has led to the pressure to create thoughtful and effective alternatives that are supra-sovereign (and this for only the most egregious of crimes against humanity). The key problem with the nation-state is precisely that its sovereignty can supersede collective interests. Friedrich Nietzsche understood this well enough in affirming that "the state has a very special mission in the world system of egoism that is to be founded: it is supposed to become the patron of all prudent egoisms in order to protect them with the might of its military and police forces from the horrible eruptions of imprudent egoism" (155-56). But when the state itself is the source of "imprudent egoism," the problem arises as to how that condition is to be managed and resisted if it wreaks havoc with more prudent states. Kissinger's argument is Nietzschean insofar as it advocates the tyranny of the state as the ultimate arbiter of justice. That said, countless examples of state excess exist to counter this position.

The Italian political philosopher Norberto Bobbio has consistently emphasized that "the critical problem facing our times [is] not one of finding fundamental principles for human rights, but that of protecting them" (12). Bobbio makes the following related assertion about the concept of international jurisdiction: "Thus one will only be able to talk of international safeguards for human rights when an international jurisdiction will be able to superimpose itself on the national jurisdictions, and the safeguards *within* the state, which are the main feature of the current phase [of development of human rights], are transformed into safeguards *against* the state" (26). Rather than an "indiscriminate court" (Kissinger 92) like the ICC, Kissinger argues to make the ICC more compatible with U.S. constitutional practice (a gesture that manifests its own self-serving indiscriminacy) while noting that the "extraordinary attempt of the ICC to assert jurisdiction over Americans even in the absence of U.S. accession to the treaty has already triggered legislation in the Congress to resist it" (94). In the Americas, the failure of the U.S. to address adequately its own role in major rights abuses, not to mention the fear that there are legitimate claims against its citizens for crimes against humanity, has prompted these resistances in the name of anti-universalism.

The very fact that Kissinger's argument substitutes the generality of the U.S. as a nation for the specific people responsible for specific decisions and actions suggests an important slippage between the universal and the specific. The American political philosopher John Rawls argues—in a critique of the fire-bombing of Tokyo and other Japanese cities in 1945 and of the use of the atom bomb on Hiroshima and Nagasaki—that "it is the leaders and not the common civilians of nations who finally initiate war" (95). Moreover, in relation to outlaw states, Rawls is even more explicit: the bringing on of war "was done by the leaders and officials, assisted by other élites who control and staff the state apparatus. They are responsible; they willed the war; and, for doing that, they are criminals" (95). Rawls's formulations evade the issue of how supposedly non-outlaw states (i.e. "well-ordered peoples") are to be dealt with when they are complicit with or responsible for what he calls "very grave wrongs" (95) and what others might call crimes against humanity. When such a nation abrogates its responsibility to judge its own actions justly (that is, seeks its own sovereign self-interest over that of the community of nations), clearly some form of supra-sovereign jurisdiction is called for. Kissinger's move in calling this a form of "universal jurisdiction" takes advantage of the speciousness of the metaphysical construct of the universal in the legal and political contexts of specific lived experiences. Daniel Singer's comments on universal jurisdiction are mindful of the way in which such jurisdictions inevitably end up being aligned with the interests of the most powerful: "Can you imagine…encroachments against human rights being measured by a yardstick unconnected with American commercial interests? Yet, if you institutionalize such a body, under the sponsorship of the United Nations or otherwise, and put armed forces at its disposal, you will merely strengthen the status quo" (212). Singer also advocates for a "genuine international authority" based on the "ecological predicament," which is an issue of planetary survival, a problem completely evacuated from Kissinger's narrow political argument (212).

The fundamental recognition that states are simply not to be trusted in the international safeguarding of rights can only begin when an adequate analysis of their actions is presented. This recognition is certainly one important key to Galeano's literary work insofar as it presents a vision, largely determined by the historical experience of the Americas, which resists generic classification and can hardly be grasped from a Western perspective that distinguishes art from critical inquiry.[3] Galeano's expressive mode entails the artistic synthesis of mind, body, and spirit, a synthesis that some indigenous storytellers centre in the belly:

> The words passed down from mouth to ear (one sexual part to another sexual part), womb to womb, body to body are the remembered ones. S/he whose belly cannot contain (also read "retain") words, says a Malinke song, will succeed at nothing. The further they move away from the belly, the more liable they are to be corrupted. (Words that come from the MIND and are passed on directly "from mind to mind" are, consequently, highly suspect.) (Trinh 136)

Similarly, Galeano situates memory (words passed from mouth to ear) in the belly that is both sanctuary and destination:

Window on Memory (II)

> A refuge?
> A belly?
> A shelter to hide you when you're drowning in the rain, or shivering in the cold, or spinning in the wind?
> Do we have a splendid past ahead of us?
> For navigators who love the wind, memory is a port of departure. (*Walking Words* 113)

The breadth of Galeano's poetics radically repositions the storyteller and chronicler in relation to political discourse and activism, while infusing his writing with a degree of versatility and intellectual agility impossible to achieve in any discourse that is trapped in its own univocal and self-serving paradigm. In contrast to those who fear that universal perspectives may reveal the true source of so many nations' subjugations, Galeano's probing questions and speculations travel the globe and constitute an accusation for anyone who can discern the obvious pattern that emerges:

War of the Fallacies. 1. First Day: Some Questions

War. For what?

To prove that the right of invasion is a privilege reserved for the great powers? And that Hussein cannot do to Kuwait what Bush did to Panama?

So that the Red Army can with impunity beat up on the Lithuanians and the Latvians?

So that Arabs finance the butchery of the Arabs?

So that everyone understands the oil is not to be touched?

Or so that it remain absolutely essential for the world to continue wasting $2 million a minute on arms, now that the Cold War is over?

And what if one of these days, from so much playing at war, this world, turned into an arsenal, blows up?

Who sold the destiny of humanity to a handful of crazy, greedy killers?

Who will live to say that their crime was our suicide? (*We Say No* 298)

It is precisely the interconnectedness of world events that reveals the cynical desire of the guilty to cover up the double standards separating the U.S. and its allies from the rest of the globe. Kissinger's talk of humane behaviour and his lament over the violent times (as if violence were simply a symptom of modernity and not the result of dirty politics) parody the twisted logic of "newspeak," implied as the opposite of Galeano's innocently dangerous questions and answers.

"In the end," Kissinger claims, "an excessive reliance on universal jurisdiction may undermine the political will to sustain the humane norms of international behavior so necessary to temper the violent times in which we live" (96). The veiled threat of this conclusion is noteworthy, especially in the contexts of how Galeano analyzes the hypocrisy surrounding Kissinger's intervention in Chile after the democratic election of Salvador Allende in 1970: "At the beginning of the seventies, when Chile tried to take democracy seriously, Henry Kissinger dotted the *i*'s and crossed the *t*'s of the White House decree against that unpardonable foray. 'I don't see why,' he said, 'we need to stand by and watch a country go communist because of the irresponsibility of its own people'" (*Upside Down* 313). The imposition of values whose moral enforceability is thought to have universal application led in Chile to the Augusto Pinochet coup d'état (supported by the U.S. government), in which democratic choice was supplanted by a dictatorship *in the name of* democracy.[4] In this case, one of many, the imposition of so-called universalist democratic norms led to years of brutality and suffering and severe abuses of the "humane norms" cited by Kissinger as an end of responsible political action. The impersonation of civility masks abuses of power, a pervasive structure we locate throughout this book in post-Columbian, European modes of encounter with the indigenous other. Until accountability of action is a meaningful concept with international legal consequences that have been carefully adduced and agreed upon from the full range of particular juridical practices and national contexts, there will be little to mitigate against the most cynical abuses of political will by the powerful. Anti-universalism in this context is a highly suspect and self-serving concept; we distinguish our own critique of universalism from it in the following way.

The political will to sustain universal "humane norms" has all too often been (and is) lacking in "international behavior" and has done little to temper the violence of the times in which we all live and out of which we have all emerged. Rights discourse that fails to account for this from the start is severely compromised. Galeano's example is particularly intriguing in the sense that he combines narrative ability (one explored throughout this book) with the kinds of critical analyses that explode unthought truisms, pervasive clichés, and deceptive structures of thought circulating in the master narratives that ground universalist notions of rights. The closural anecdote from Galeano's *We Say No* about the relations between oppressor and oppressed, a crucial issue in all rights discourse, one of whose primary aims is the establishment of equality and "brotherhood,"[5] is telling:

> Some time ago the Spanish priest Ignacio Ellacuría told me that to him the notion of the Discovery of America seemed absurd. The oppressor is incapable of discovery, he told me:
>
>> "It is the oppressed who discovers the oppressor."
>
> He believed that the oppressor couldn't even discover himself. The true reality of the oppressor can only be seen from the point of view of the oppressed. (316)

Here, Galeano undoes the orthodox narrative of discovery in which the conquerors benignly come upon their victims in order to save them from their supposed barbarity. Galeano's vignette, to which we will return later in this chapter, inverts the ethical relations between oppressor and oppressed, discoverer and discovered in a way typical of his approach to narrative, inversion being a crucial dimension of his critical aesthetic. Another example of this sort of inversion occurs in a scene where Galeano has God confess to him about the creation and the Edenic scene of Adam and Eve's passion:

> *Errata*: where the Old Testament says what it says, perhaps it should say what its main protagonist has confessed to me:
>
> *In keeping with the principle of authority, I resisted the desire to congratulate them [Adam and Eve] for having suddenly grown wise in human passion.*
>
> *Then came the misunderstandings. They understood "fall" where I spoke of "flight." They thought that a sin deserved punishment if it was original. I said that those who fail to love are sinners; they understood that those who love are sinners. Where I spoke of a meadow of joy they understood a vale of tears. I said that pain was the salt that gave flavor to the human adventure; they understood that I was condemning them by granting*

them the glory of being mortal and a little nuts. They got everything backwards. And they believed it. (The Book of Embraces 90-91)

The inversions here presume an interpretive rigidity that is in need of the kind of narrative undoing (defamiliarizing) where the divine confesses to the human. The human misinterpretation of divine precept is thus authorized, not only by Galeano's imaginary but also by his divine interlocutor. As we show throughout this book, this strategy is crucial for thinking issues of rights discourse, especially different modes of narrative (fictive, testimonial, historical, and so forth) that enable the production of meaningful alternatives to orthodoxies that limit human expression and fulfillment.

From this inversion of power relations emerges an insight that has direct bearing on the way in which rights are construed. If reality as seen by the dominant culture is a distortion that can only be remedied by the reality of the disempowered, what value does the discourse built upon the distorted reality actually have? The question has deep roots in encounter narratives related to the Americas and is implicit in what Nahua wise men, the previously discussed *tlamatinime*, had to say in response to attacks on indigenous customs made by missionary friars in 1524.

Our lords, our very esteemed Lords:
great hardships have you endured to reach this land.
Here before you,
we ignorant people contemplate you...

And now, what are we to say?

What should we cause your ears to hear?
Perchance, is there any meaning to us?
Only very common people are we...

And now, are we
to destroy
the ancient order of life?...

Hear, oh Lords,
do nothing
to our people
that will bring misfortune upon them,
that will cause them to perish. (qtd. in León-Portilla, *Aztec Thought and Culture* 63, 65, 66)

The oration begins with an acknowledgement of the other's presence (remember that the "other" here is the European) and of that other's suffering, an oration that is not merely rhetorical: literally, it signals the recognition of difference that permits the dissenting discourse the *tlamatinime* will present. Here, the "annihilated" other (66) recognizes the pain of the oppressor and acknowledges the reality of the new power relations in place. Ignorance and contemplation go hand in hand in this opening gesture, a speech act of profound importance for how it establishes an alternative structure of encounter, one that requires both a recognition of one's ignorance of difference as well as the need to contemplate that difference in a meaningful way. The interrogatives that follow set the stage for establishing a dialogue based on the conjoined position of contemplative ignorance: "And now, what are we to say?" Following on this invitation to imagine a new space of discourse, the *tlamatinime* question *their* own meaning, a gesture of solidarity with the unimagined dialogue that could potentially emerge from the encounter and an acknowledgment that new meanings remain to be created through encounter.

The invocation not to cause harm to "our people" iterates a fundamental ethical principle within the theological space in which this discourse occurs, suggesting yet another ground on which the basis of encounter can be established. In many ways, the brief fragment discussed here addresses an ethics of encounter to which Europeans were antithetical and (with few exceptions) unsympathetic. This ethics of encounter anticipates Ignacio Ellacuría's position, mentioned earlier, which proposes an ethics predicated on the position of the oppressed that, as the *tlamatinime* example shows, can provide sophisticated ethical modes for establishing the terms of encounter. The imposition of a universal structure of how "we" know the other, based on the normative relationship of oppressor to oppressed, would in such a perspective be entirely specious. The intolerance of the system for such a reversal of the gaze, which in essence reflects on the system's inability to know itself (and thus to know the other as well) cannot but produce a perverse universalist structure that suppresses the false relations so cannily observed by Ellacuría and his *tlamatinime* predecessors.

Universality, in this latter sense, is a cultural construction that serves particular post-conquest imperial ends having to do with the production of common qualities in the face of individuation: as philosopher Charles Landesman explains, "the problem of universals is to explain how different things can have common qualities, [whereas] the problem of individuation is to explain how things with all their qualities in common can be different" (17). Harnessed to particular ideological purposes, the universal effaces difference in the name of a homogeneity that promotes a self-governing, self-regulating, self-same citizenry whose very imagined uniformity is best expressed in concepts like nation, community, empire, science, equality, and, importantly, "right" and "tradition."

Richard Falk assesses the last half-century of "achievement" with regard to human rights traditions in a way that aligns with our arguments to this point. Falk notes how different spaces of national self-identification produce very different notions of rights discourse:

> It became clear that the normative framework of the Universal Declaration, even if one includes the two subsequently negotiated human rights covenants, had serious deficiencies if it was meant, as claimed, to address the full range of human rights

concerns. As representatives of indigenous peoples began to make abundantly clear, the mainstream human rights tradition did not speak to their general circumstances. It was especially insensitive to their view that human rights had to include the protection of traditional ways of community life in the face of state- and market-driven modernization. Somewhat more controversial were the various contentions that non-Western civilizations did not participate fully in the standard-setting process, making the human rights tradition both insufficiently responsive to non-Western values and lacking in any truly global legitimacy. Islamic and Confucian scholars have both complained about the excessive individualism and permissiveness of the human rights tradition as written into international law. They have also complained about its failure to balance the rights of the individual against responsibilities to the community, and about the selectivity of emphasis in which civil and political rights are privileged. (191-92)

Falk's assessment of the ethical loopholes in the Universal Declaration echoes those we have cited earlier in this chapter. We would argue that to speak of a human rights "tradition" in such a context is to distort the degree to which the tradition is in fact under extreme critical pressure as a function of the anomalies that underpin it. Falk's citation of Bobbio's three stages in the evolution of human rights (from *The Age of Rights*), beginning with the Roman stoics through to the American and French revolutions through to the production of international rights instruments like the Universal Declaration (Falk 60), excludes anything but Western-centric sources for the ideas that form the basis of rights discourse today.

Pertinent examples abound of the indebtedness of Western rights discourse to foundational ideas that are under severe pressure, from G. W. F. Hegel to Thomas Hobbes, who introduced the term "right" into political philosophy. In the case of Hegel, Chomsky scathingly notes how "Hegel pondered 'the contempt of humanity displayed by the Negroes' of Africa, 'who allow themselves to be shot down by the thousands in war with Europeans. Life has a value when it has something valuable as its object,' a thought beyond the grasp of these 'mere things.' Unable to comprehend our lofty values, the savages confound us in our quest for justice and virtue" (*Year 501* 119-20). Enrique Dussel also states how Hegel formulated notions of the right in his *Encyclopedia*: "against the absolute right of that people who actually are the carriers of the World Spirit [Germany and especially England], the spirit of other peoples *has no other right (rechtlos)*" (*The Invention of the Americas* 24); Dussel then associates this sort of absolutist thinking with the cruelty and cynicism underlying the "*Aufklärung*" (25). The despicable self-interest of Hegel's account of European and African encounters finds its echoes in Hugo Grotius, "a leading 17th-century humanist and the founder of international law" who "determined that the 'most just war is against savage beasts, the next against men who are like beasts'" (Chomsky, *Year 501* 22).

It gets worse. Hobbes, who developed Hugo Grotius's concept of *jus*, says: "The right of nature, which writers commonly call *jus naturale*, is the liberty each man hath, to use his own power as he will himself, for the preservation of his own nature; that is to say, of his own life; and consequently of doing any thing, which in his own judgment, and reason, he shall conceive to be the aptest means thereunto" (84). Hobbes goes on to argue that "the condition of man...is a condition of war of every one against every one" and that "it followeth, that in such a condition, every man has a right to every thing; even to one another's body" (85). Hobbes's formulation is the dominant sense of state-defined right in the West. Self-preservation (with its underlying paranoid logic), self-interested will, and the doing of "anything" one's discretionary reason permits are the means to effecting the "right of nature." As an influential idea in the conception of Western notions of right, Hobbes's right of nature would allow the most egregious of actions in the name of self-preservation— which, as with any other key term, is open to interpretation. Further, the right of nature so defined excludes alternative notions of right based on international contexts of community and solidarity among individuals, among peoples, among nations.

The culmination of such a viewpoint is embodied in Rawls's comments on Quakers' rights to high office in a liberal democratic régime. Rawls denies Quakers this right on the basis that they oppose war and therefore would compromise the interests of self-defense held by a liberal democracy: "they could not in good faith, in the absence of special circumstances, seek the highest offices in a liberal democratic regime" (105). Absolutizing the ethics of leadership, as Rawls does, excludes the possibility that even a Quaker might come to "admit of a case where it might be immoral or amoral not to use force, if not to defend oneself then to defend others" (Hitchens, "Covenant With Death" 9), just as it empties out the moral force of Quakerism's resolute pacifism. Rawls's position merely translates Immanuel Kant's perverse notion that "In the present state of human culture...war is an indispensable means to the still further development of human culture. Only in a state of perfect culture would perpetual peace be of benefit to us, and only then would it be possible" (67). This highly compromised genealogy is a serious problem that traduces the rights "tradition" in the name of a linear and highly selective form of history.

Coming out of such a questionable intellectual genealogy, universality permits the free flow of concepts like nation, tradition, and rights into spaces of difference in the name of producing self-sameness, a contradictory effect that human rights theory struggles to recognize and resolve. *The Human Development Report 2000*, an annual document put out by the United Nations that examines key indicators of human well-being throughout the planet in relation to particular issues like rights and technology, states:

> There is tension between the universality of human rights and cultural specificity. Between national sovereignty and the international community's monitoring of human rights within countries. Between the indivisibility of human rights and the

need to establish priorities because of resource allocation. Between the supremacy of international laws and that of national laws. Between international norms and the norms set by regional human rights systems. Between ratifying international treaties and enforcing them nationally. (30)

The key to addressing the tensions described in the report is to establish an agreed-upon balance (as well as a forum for the establishment of discourse about such a balance) between principles and concepts like "crimes against humanity" (which implies a universalist position) and the local and specific agencies involved in establishing the particular ways in which such a concept is meaningfully enacted on the international scene. In other words, transnational justice can never be universally applied, let alone achieved, without an ongoing negotiation between the specificity of agency and context "in the everyday life of living and breathing social actors" (Preis 315) and the rights principles against which they are apposed.[6]

Galeano is particularly trenchant on the way in which the local has been destroyed in the name of a universalist logic of democracy, economic modernization, and global imperatives. In contrast with the kind of logic that allows Kissinger to make U.S. constitutional and democratic norms the basis for international practice (in spite of the fact that "Western social reality is alienated from its own criminal past to an alarming degree, and is therefore encompassed by it" [Falk 90]), Galeano suggests that

> History is unambiguous: the U.S. veto has blocked or closed off to the point of strangulation most of the political experiments that have sought to get at the roots of violence [such as those in Chile, Nicaragua, and Cuba]. Justice and solidarity have been condemned as foreign aggression against the foundation of Western civilization, leaving it plain as can be that democracy has limits and you'd better not test them. (*Upside Down* 313)

According to Falk, "In the case of Nicaragua…the U.S. State Department grounded its objection to the Sandinista government on the failure of the Sandinistas to grant adequate democratic space to the political opposition. This position was argued even though the Sandinista government was probably the best human rights government that Nicaragua ever had and the most impressive government in the region" (61). Falk's assessment reinforces the structure of intolerance of difference that Galeano sees as the limits of democracy. How, in such a context, can a universal concept of rights that emerges from the limitations of democratic discourse be just or meaningful in how it addresses human difference? How can such a universalist notion of rights become, in Michael Ignatieff's terms, a "moral vernacular" that forms the basis for "freedom," when the very terms "moral vernacular" and "freedom" are themselves so thoroughly dependent on universalist assumptions? ("Human Rights" 320)

"And I Shall Do All the Evil and Damage to you that I Am Able": Rhetorical Violence, Discursive Rape, and the *Requerimiento*

The imposition of universal standards is fraught with hypocrisy and under the rubric of democratic rights follows a particular and deep-rooted pattern found in the earliest structures of encounter in the Americas. The Spanish *Requerimiento* [Requirement], the self-interested "legal" document read to indigenous peoples by the conquistadors as part of the extension of a putatively Castilian juridical space, is exemplary for its (ab)use of universalist principles:

> [I] hereby notify and inform you...that God Our lord, One and Eternal, created Heaven and Earth and a man and a woman from whom you and I and all the people of the world are descended...God placed one called Saint Peter in charge over all these peoples...And so I request and require you...to recognize the [Catholic] Church as your Mistress and as Governess of the World and Universe, and the High Priest, called the Pope, in Her name, and His Majesty [king of Spain] in Her place, as Ruler and Lord King. (qtd. in Wright, *Stolen Continents* 65)

Read in a language (Spanish) that could not be understood by its presumed auditors, the document assumes a universal linguistic context congruent with its universalist legal presumptions. The logical extensions of this form of universalism are pervasive in structures of colonial domination—whether repeated in popular culture's massively successful television and film series *Star Trek*, whose colonialist mode (to seek out and explore new worlds) structurally repeats the linguistic universalism evident in the *Requerimiento* via alien encounters in which the *lingua franca* is always English or in the institutional structures that make of any form of difference a threat (thus justifying, for instance, the disproportionate numbers of minorities—Black, Hispanic, or aboriginal—to be found in American or Canadian prisons). Moreover, the *Requerimiento*'s concern to express a singular genealogy for all humanity is based on a universalist discourse that thus allows and requires the governance of St. Peter, who in turn stands in as a metonym for the Catholic church as a universal site of governance: *this* church is the mistress and governess of the "World and Universe."

Palacios Rubios, author of the *Requerimiento,* was a civilian lawyer who along with Matías de Paz wrote "the first full length legal and ethical considerations of the justice of the conquest to have survived" (Pagden, *The Fall of Natural Man* 50). Rubios found Amerindian promiscuity, which promoted matrilineal/matrilocal genealogies, particularly threatening to Eurocentric notions of "the origins of civil society" founded on the family whose "natural ruler was the father. Any community where, because there was no marriage, there was no proper family structure, and where women ruled over such loose unions as did exist (in the crucial sense that they were responsible for the education of the children), was not only guilty of sanctioning unnatural practices, it was no community at all but a mere horde" (53). The naturalization of universal assumptions about the family (still deeply pervasive in

Occidental thought and a topic to which we will return at the end of this chapter) produced the vicious ethnographic response to Amerindian culture that made it exempt from so-called natural law, and permitted the barbarities that were inflicted on that culture in the name of civil (universal) society.

The link between such universalist assumptions and the military imposition of homogeneity is made egregiously clear in the *Requerimiento*:

> And if you do not do this…with the help of God I shall come mightily against you, and I shall make war on you everywhere and in every way that I can, and I shall subject you to the yoke and obedience of the Church and His Majesty, and I shall seize your women and children, and I shall make them slaves, to sell and dispose of as His Majesty commands, *and I shall do all the evil and damage to you that I am able*. And I insist that the deaths and destruction that result from this will be your fault. (qtd. in Wright, *Stolen Continents* 66; our emphasis)

Refusal to accept this universalist logic will result in universal destruction ("I shall make war on you everywhere and in every way I can") and evil being unleashed ("I shall do all the evil and damage to you that I am able") with the attribution, paradoxically, of specific blame on those who do not conform to the universal doctrine espoused by the Requirement ("the deaths and destruction that result from this will be *your* fault" [our emphasis]). This universalist structure is arrogantly self-righteous, pathological, presumptuous, and violent—a form of discursive rape. As a textual structure that signaled material consequences in the reterritorialization of the "new" world, it advocates a rhetorical mastery predicated on the uncivil notion that specific cultural difference can be eradicated through violent rhetoric.

To what extent does such an exemplary structure of conquest, which depends on the imposition of universal values, get reiterated in a document like the Universal Declaration, in spite of its presumed intention to establish a "universal" structure of shared values that ensure a basic standard of rights recognized in international law from one nation to the next, from one local context to the next? At this point, where universality as a rights discourse collides with recent literary theories that attempt to account for the specific agencies registered in human difference, a productive dialogue emerges between the dominantly legal and juridical language of rights and the deep skepticism of literary criticism. At its most trenchant, literary criticism promotes the slow and careful reading of textual structures that remain largely unexamined, self-perpetuating, and seriously compromised by a general disregard in ethical terms of human values seeking to promote carefully articulated notions of justice that weigh the balance between local and global contexts.

When "universal" becomes a trope for the eradication of human difference and for a form of equality that compromises identity even in the name of putatively shared values, something is awry. Galeano, for instance, explicitly links equalization with inequality by stating that

...the machinery of compulsory equalization works against the finest trait of the human species, the fact that we recognize ourselves in differences and build links based on them. The best of the world lies in the many worlds the world contains, the different melodies of life, their pains and strains: the thousand and one ways of living and speaking, thinking and creating, eating, working, dancing, playing, loving, suffering, and celebrating that we have discovered over so many thousands of years. (*Upside Down* 25-26)

To Galeano, equalization makes "us all the same," a devastating process tied into the way in which the emergent global system encourages a dissipate uniformity through transnational corporations, media conglomerates, and international political, economic, legal, and juridical structures:

No computer can count the crimes that the pop culture business commits each day against the human rainbow and the human right to identity. But its devastating progress is mind-boggling. Time is emptied of history, and space no longer acknowledges the astonishing diversity of its parts. Through the mass media the owners of the world inform us all of our obligation to look at ourselves in a single mirror. (*Upside Down* 26)

The mirror's singularity distorts vision. In such a context, any structure that proclaims universal values merits suspicion and careful critical evaluation if the right to identity is to be sustained in any meaningful way. Given that rights talk is textual, discursive, framed in language, and thus subject to the deforming vagaries that mark how language goes out into the world, it is imperative when thinking through the notion of universal rights in the name of *all* peoples on this planet that extraordinary care and precision mark the critical dialogue over how rights are elucidated and given form. Textual forms reflect cultural practices that have material consequences for those who live within their mirroring frame: it is within such a context that we place Galeano in relation to emerging discourses that link human rights theory to literary and cultural theory.

In this last regard, the gap between theory and practice of human rights has never been greater, perhaps reflecting on the quality and nature of the theory itself. Moreover, the persistence of that gap or cultural deformation, in which rights theory proliferates even as its ostensible object becomes increasingly remote, has prompted little resistant countercriticism. Galeano's interventions into issues of human rights are closely tied to his notions of writerly responsibility towards the power of the word. He is scathing in his criticism of structures of thought, particularly the lie of universalism, that promote the cultural deformation that allows for such a gap between theory and practice to exist. Instead, Galeano offers modes of critical and aesthetic engagement with the memory, history, and forms of expression that have direct pertinence to thinking human, thinking rights. This portion of the book addresses several overlapped issues, including the degree to which writing and human rights can be co-located as extensions of each other, the influence of Galeano's ideas on human rights discourse, and the need to rethink the theoretical bases of human rights talk generally as Galeano consistently does in his varied writing practices.

We would argue that the key to understanding rights discourse and Galeano's position therein lies in notions of universality and its critique. A telling example of how this critique might be applied occurs in a late-nineteenth, early-twentieth-century anarchist formulation on rights, in which Peter Kropotkin reiterates ideas from his book *Mutual Aid*:

> In fact, all that was an element of progress in the past or an instrument of moral and intellectual improvement of the human race is due *to the practice of mutual aid*, to the customs that recognized the equality of men and brought them to ally, to unite, to associate for the purpose of producing and consuming, to unite for purposes of defense, to federate and to recognize no other judges in fighting out their differences than the arbitrators they took from their own midst. (139)

The passage ostensibly proclaims a universal moral doctrine of equality based on the practice of mutual aid. Progress, association for the purposes of production and consumption, equality of "men," defense—all these operative terms are highly suspect. Progress for whom? As defined by whose interests? Moral and intellectual development as measured by whose standards? Whose definition of equality? Economic? Social? Political? And why the isolationist fear of arbitrators not "from their own midst"? And especially, why the rhetoric of violence in a passage devoted to mutual aid? Kropotkin's ostensibly progressive ideas depend on an implicit assumption that Occidental geocultural and geopolitical interests are the foundation for thinking what it means to produce the conditions of mutual aid, let alone its "progressive" goals and moral relevance.[7]

Consider, though, the degree to which any of these ideals, coming as they do from an emergent discourse of human rights, begin to collapse when placed in relation to the Latin American concerns articulated by Galeano: "We all have the right to know and to express ourselves, which is nowadays very difficult as long as we are obeying the orders of an invisible dictatorship. It is the dictatorship of the single word, the single image, the single tune, and perhaps it is more dangerous than other dictatorships because it acts on a world scale. *It's an international structure of power which is imposing universal values that center on consumption and violence*" (Barsamian, "Eduardo Galeano" 3; our emphasis). Crucial here is Galeano's rejection of the universality of consumption as a relevant language for discussing rights. The rejection is important for how it addresses the degree to which literary discourses of rights as a marker of "civilization" are dependent upon tropes of consumption. Kropotkin's bleak and paranoid view of mutual aid in the name of a progress that foregrounds production, consumption, and an equality and unity based on defense and the belligerent "fighting out" of differences inscribes an Occidental nationalist discourse. In that discourse, state sovereignty ("no other judges") and principles of economic production reign in the name of anarchist critique. That the vision Kropotkin advances of mutual aid is riven with metaphors of antagonism and isolationism is no small accident, given the enormous pressures upon even the most radical of thought to conform to a worldview that cannot think otherwise or imagine elsewhere (a topic to which we will return in our final chapter).

Kropotkin recapitulates a foundational form of Occidental liberal discourse that emerges from what Walter Mignolo has described as the reciprocal relations of colonialism and its perverse notions of mutual aid and production (as extraction) with the inception of modernity.[8] Dussel argues that modernity is inaugurated when Europe affirms itself as the "*center* of the 'world-system', of the first world-system, through the incorporation of Amerindia"; the colonial periphery thus becomes a necessary element in the centre's self-definition, since "Modernity is not a phenomenon of Europe as an *independent* system, but of Europe as center" ("Beyond Eurocentrism" 4). The Occident's position entails an ethics of alterity that is always already seriously compromised by the myth of independence in the face of the reality of dependence. By extension, such an ethics (centre/periphery) presumes a notion of human rights that is also highly compromised. Todorov argues, for instance, that Columbus's motivation to "discover" was based on the ostensible project of extracting enough wealth from the new world to finance the retaking of Jerusalem, thus leading to the following formulation: "Paradoxically, it will be a feature of Columbus's medieval [Crusade] mentality that leads him to discover America and inaugurate the modern era" (12). A telling example of these seemingly reciprocal relations, here based on the ability to enter into commercial relations, occurs in the digest from Columbus's logbook (as transcribed by Bartolomé de Las Casas from the original logbook that has since disappeared) of his first voyage (dated Tuesday, 16 October): "The people here...seem to me rather more civilized, more tractable and more intelligent [than those on other islands], for they are better able to bargain for the cotton and other trifles which they have brought to the ship than were the other peoples...The people are more friendly *and the women wear a small piece of cotton in front which just hides their private parts*" ["*y las mugeres traen por delante su cuerpo una cosita de algodón que escassamente les cobija su natura*"] (Columbus, *The Four Voyages* 64 and Columbus, *Journal of the First Voyage* 40; our emphasis). The passage clearly equates civil virtue and intelligence with a recognizable form of commerce, even as the passage culminates in the erotic charge of a barely seen pudendum.

This latter moment is worth further thought. In our reading, it indicates the degree to which colonial imperatives regarding the recognizability of indigenous culture in economic and therefore European civil terms (also in a gesture of simultaneous diminishment) reduces the native other to an exoticized object of thinly-veiled eroticism. The Spanish word *natura* as a substitute for genitalia is highly charged in what it reveals about the allegory at work in this incident. The recognizability of the native other as a civil being paradoxically requires that her *natura* be covered. This requirement succeeds in overwriting the indigenous difference that sustains the lustful thrust of the passage (commerce and sexuality share the same colonial discourse) even as it firmly places the native other in a position of abjection in comparison to the standard of civilization of the Spanish colonizer. "Nature" must be covered as an expression of the discoverer's perverse relations to body: civilizing gestures that cover women's genitalia parallel the covering over of "nature" more generally by the colonial, civilizing imperative. Covering the body is symptomatic of a pervasive will to power that is the very opposite of dis-covery, as Dussel points out: "Europe never discovered (*des-cubierto*) this Other as Other but covered over (*encubierto*) the Other as part of the Same: i.e., Europe. Modernity dawned in 1492 and with it the myth of a special kind of sacrificial violence which eventually eclipsed whatever was non-European" (*The Invention of the Americas* 12). Galeano's position in *We Say No* is virtually identical in this regard to Dussel's:

> It's already been said that in 1492 America was invaded, not discovered, since thousands of years previous it had been discovered by the Indians who lived there. But it could also be said that America was not discovered in 1492 because those who invaded it did not know *how to see it*, or simply could not do so…No imperial undertaking, neither the old kind nor today's, has the capacity to discover. An adventure of usurpation and plunder does not discover: it covers up. It doesn't reveal: it hides. To be successful it needs ideological alibis that turn arbitrariness into law. (179-80)

Galeano further skewers this perverse ordering of things in an episode on Columbus's geographical conception of the world he has "discovered":

1498: Santo Domingo
Earthly Paradise

In the evening, beside the Ozama River, Christopher Columbus writes a letter. His body creaks with rheumatism, but his heart jumps for joy. The discoverer explains to Their Catholic Majesties *that which is plainly evident*: Earthly Paradise is on the nipple of a woman's breast.

He realized it two months ago, when his caravels entered the Gulf of Paria. *There ships start rising gently toward the sky*…Navigating upstream to where the air has no weight, Columbus has reached the farthest limit of the Orient. *In these the world's most beautiful lands*, the men show cleverness, ingenuity, and valor, and the extremely beautiful women wear only their long hair and necklaces of many pearls wound around their bodies. The water, sweet and clear, awakens thirst. Winter does not punish nor summer burn, and the breeze caresses what it touches. The trees offer fresh shade and, within arm's reach, fruits of great delectability that arouse hunger.

But beyond *this greenness and this loveliness* no ship can go. This is the frontier of the Orient. Here waters, lands, and islands end. Very high and far away, the Tree of

Life spreads its enormous crown and the source of the four sacred rivers bubbles up. One of them is the Orinoco, *which I doubt if such a great and deep river is known in the world.*

The world is not round. The world is a woman's tit. The nipple begins in the Gulf of Paria and rises to a point very close to the heavens. The tip, where the juices of Paradise flow, will never be reached by any man. (*Genesis* 51-52)

The trope of the earthly paradise as breast, in a supposedly civilizing discourse of encounter and discovery, is coincident with the gendering of the discovered as a passive female body to be exploited.[9] Erotic fantasy and the imposition of a Christian worldview of paradise are inseparable, a curious relation that will produce unspeakable acts of barbarity as recounted by Las Casas and others.

Paradise in such an erotic context is a highly ambiguous signifier for both an unattainable utopian space of the spirit as well as a space of physical temptation. Out of this ambiguity arises an inexorable logic of destruction. Kill that which tempts your body so that your spirit may be worthy, a logic that eventually reduces to kill in the name of self-interest:

On another occasion a troop of soldiers on a pillaging expedition had happened upon a mountain region where a large number of natives had sought refuge from the reign of terror the Christians were conducting in their towns and villages. Taking the fugitives by surprise, they carried off seventy or eighty women and young girls, killing at the same time as many men as they could. The following day, the survivors regrouped and, sick with worry about their wives and daughters, set off in pursuit of the soldiers. Finding themselves hard-pressed and loath to allow their pace to slacken, the soldiers stuck their swords into the guts of the women and young girls, massacring every single one of them. (Las Casas, *A Short Account* 35)

Here, in a passage that typifies the brutality of the Spanish conquistadors, the initial perverse imaginings by Columbus of a paradisaical space likened to a woman's body have been transformed into the brutal reality of colonial domination. The expulsion from paradise necessarily calls for its destruction, a pernicious logical deformation of Christian symbology that disconnects Christian principles from enacted realities. This structure must be carefully analyzed and understood in relation to human rights discourses that silently incorporate a similar logic masked by a rhetoric of ethics dependent on such a disconnection. A key figure in the production of originary documents relating to human rights in the "New World" some fifty years after Columbus's "discovery," Las Casas recognizes:

From the very beginning, Spanish policy towards the New World has been characterized by blindness of the most pernicious kind: even while the various ordinances and decrees governing the treatment of the native peoples have continued to maintain that conversion and the saving of souls has first priority, this is belied by what has actually been happening on the ground. The gulf that yawns between theory and practice has meant that, in fact, the local people have been presented with an ultimatum: either they adopt the Christian religion and swear allegiance to the Crown of Castile, or they will find themselves faced with military action in which no quarter will be given and they will be cut down or taken prisoner. (*A Short Account* 32)

The surpassing contradiction of the policy—convert in the name of Christ or we will kill you in direct violation of Christian principle—is foundational to the colonization of the Americas that simultaneously signals the inception of modernity.

The passages relating Columbus's feminization of the space of discovery along with the Las Casas account of the murder of women are one step removed from an incident described by one of Columbus's Italian lieutenants, Michele de Cuneo, which shows the extent to which notions of human rights were materially absent from the discourses of early colonial encounter. This absence, when read via the relation of modernity to the colonial project, suggests the need for assiduous attention to the way in which literary structures and human rights theory produce a form of knowledge coincident with actions that are far from enlightened.[10] As we have argued, the rhetoric of violence and the literal and figural rape that discourse enacts toward the other suggests a pervasive mode of encounter that deforms the apparent civility of the so-called civilizer. Cuneo describes an infamous early modern encounter that also reads as a possession and rape scene:

> *While I was in the boat, I captured a very beautiful Carib woman, whom the said lord Admiral gave to me. When I had taken her to my cabin she was naked—as was their custom. I was filled with a desire to take my pleasure with her and attempted to satisfy my desire. She was unwilling, and so treated me with her nails that I wished I had never begun. But—to cut a long story short—I then took a piece of rope and whipped her soundly, and she let forth such incredible screams that you would not have believed your ears. Eventually we came to such terms, I assure you, that you would have thought she had been brought up in a school for whores.* (Columbus, *The Four Voyages* 139)

The scene (one that links rape with its narration in writing) reflects on the European standard of civilization that Columbus consistently advances in terms of writing and rhetorical skill. In this rhetoric, possession is always figured as a function of writing, one that bears witness to the act of possession itself initiated in and through discourse ("the required declarations"): "The Admiral…demanded that they should bear faithful witness that he had taken possession of the island…He further made the required declarations, which are recorded at great length in the evidence there set down in writing" (Columbus, *The Four Voyages* 53). The sheer, unappeasable gluttony of desire for possession is also figured through a familiar rhetorical dodge that involves synecdoche, a rhetorical figure that promotes endless associative claims in the name of the part for the whole: "Generally it was my wish to pass no island without taking possession of it. Though having annexed one it might be said that we had annexed all" (Columbus, *The Four Voyages* 60).

These narratives all figure possession as a function of the narrative voice imposing the tyranny of signification on indigenous culture even as that voice purports to advance a notion of the civil procedures that enable its capacity to possess via writing and storytelling. The key lesson to be learned here, we suggest, is that foundational narratives governing the "discovery" of the "new" world, tropes of high subterfuge in their own right, are heavily inflected with the absence of what might now be considered to be a language of civil rights, even as the notion of civil rights is authoritatively linked to European language and writing practices. This foundational structure, against which we see Galeano mounting a devastating critique, is aptly captured in the contradictions that gather in Cuneo's rape story, which betrays the truth value of the narrative and of the language used to tell it: the beautiful Carib woman is both captured and given to him, unwilling then willing (as a function of his violence). "Schooling" in Occidental values is predicated on violence, rape, and the commercial exchange value of the prostitute, another imposition on the *tabula rasa*, in this case, of indigenous sexuality. Difference is troped as acquisition, resistance as acquiescence, and abduction as gift.

The Cuneo rape scene is a touchstone moment in colonial encounter narratives, one that a number of commentators, including Todorov and Galeano, have returned to for analysis. Is this critical voyeurism or is there something in the narrative that is insistently telling about the symbolics of encounter? Todorov's reading suggests that a "double rape" occurs, because it involves both a woman and an Indian (49), thus a rape of a particular woman (who remains nameless) as well as a cultural rape. Galeano, taking writer's liberties with the story, adds detail, even as he performs the journalistic illusion of the self-absenting narrator who merely "reports" on the incident. Both Todorov and Galeano note the paternalistic structure of the human gift given from one male to another, Columbus giving "women to his compatriots as readily as he distributed little bells to the native chiefs" (Todorov 49). Galeano's version of the incident concludes with the following sequence:

> Miquele hurls himself upon the bleeding body and thrusts, gasps, wrestles. The air smells of tar, saltpeter, of sweat. Then the girl, who seems to have fainted or died, suddenly fastens her nails in Miquele's back, knots herself around his legs, and rolls him over in a fierce embrace.
>
> After some time, when Miquele comes to, he doesn't know where he is or what has happened. Livid, he detaches himself from her and knocks her away with his fist.
>
> He staggers up on deck. Mouth open, he takes a deep breath of sea breeze. In a loud voice, as if announcing an eternal truth, he says, "These Indian women are all whores." (*Genesis* 49-50)

Adding descriptive, forensic detail to a scene that Cuneo describes in a more detached manner, Galeano's self-absenting narrator paradoxically intervenes in the ethical crisis this incident makes present.

By pushing the grim details of the rape into a more descriptive mode, Galeano invites the question of how narratives imprint on the reader in relation to questions of ethics. The distance of Cuneo, which involves a first-person narrative position, suggests the matter-of-factness of Cuneo's *right* to do as he pleases in relation to the doubly subalternized figure of the Carib woman. Galeano imagines the encounter in sensorial detail, thus enhancing the affect of the story—its deeply troubled sense of a "right" that involves the violence of the rape, the surprise of the surrender (which itself remains suspended ambiguously over the narrative as if to suggest a supplement to the story that can never be revealed), self-disgust (isn't that what Cuneo wanted all along?), and the final, damning trope of universalizing knowledge (necessarily false) that emerges from the encounter, namely that all Indian women are whores. This last point is perhaps the most important. Where Cuneo reflects on the particular woman, Galeano reshapes the story to reflect on Spanish attitudes toward indigenous culture in a way that universalizes the experience of encounter. What is implicit in Cuneo is thus made explicit in Galeano.

Universal structures of knowing the other depend on violence and abuse of power, even when performed by supposedly civil beings who have the power to introduce their stories into the realm of supposedly civil discourse: "In countries around the world, government agents [like Cuneo] use rape and sexual abuse to coerce, humiliate, punish, and intimidate women. When a policeman or a soldier rapes a woman in his custody, that rape is no longer an act of private violence, but an act of torture or ill-treatment for which the state bears responsibility" (Alston and Steiner 168). Read in this light, the Cuneo story shows the structure of the relationship between the oppressor and oppressed in brutal detail: the key element of that structure involves the absenting of the perspective of the oppressed from the telling of the story. Civil discourse is founded on such narratives in which the odd irruptive moment, exemplified by Cuneo's story in its different manifestations, represents the civilizing mission (unknowingly in the case of Columbus, knowingly in the case of Galeano) as the failure—or absence—of rights. This structure must be interrogated in relation to any supposed universal discourse of rights.

If the Occidental notion of the civil is an impersonation, and moreover a deep structure that goes back to the inception of modernity in the colonial moment of encounter, to what extent does such a structure inhabit emergent discourses of universal human rights particular to the twentieth century? This question lies at the heart of Galeano's retelling of the indigenous rape by Cuneo. And it lies at the heart of our critique of the claims of the universal made by a rights discourse fashioned in the name of hegemonic power that has extraordinary trouble seeing itself through the eyes of the oppressed other. The colonial moment, seen as the inceptive moment of modernity in which the dissonance of the European is registered in the "natural" world of the Carib, is thus the moment in which writing tells the story of the violence of inscriptive and material practices that elide the imagination of any other form of encounter, any other form of civil discourse between cultures, any other standard of rights except that of the discoverer. Read in this way, the distance from Kropotkin's radical anarchist imaginings of mutual aid and Columbus's rhetoric of possession is not so vast: universalist structures of power and its imposition are figured by consumption, commodification, and violence (whether material or scriptive, literal or figural).

Earlier we called this structure the impersonation of civility in which the imagined universal values of Christian fantasies of possession are aligned with a false notion of equality associated with so-called civil discourse. Todorov notes—especially in relation to Paul's famous dictum in the Christian bible that "There is neither Jew nor Greek, there is neither slave nor free, there is neither male nor female: for ye are all one in Christ Jesus" (Gal. 3:28)—how this sort of thinking "does not combat inequalities (the master will remain master, the slave a slave, as if this were a difference quite as natural as that between man and woman); but it declares them irrelevant with regard to the unity of all in Christ" (106-07). Impersonating civility requires this rhetorical sleight of hand, one that establishes the seeming egalitarianism of a world devoid of difference, free of specific subject positions (some inimical to this view), while at the same time allowing inequality to remain in place. The "unity of all in Christ" transcendentalizes the vast array of human agencies and specificities in relation to a form of colonial discourse predicated on the unity trope and reinforced by the divinely unknowable authority of Christ.

The erasure of difference guarantees that identity be subsumed in unity and that egalitarianism remain a passive form of an equality occuring in the metaphysical realm of Christian symbology rather than in the realm of local, material circumstance. This universalist structure of the right to be united in conditions of unaltered subjection subsumes even the most seemingly radical of Occidental versions of what constitutes civil discourse and human rights based on equality, "the consideration of every human individual as being worthy of universal moral respect" (Benhabib 10) and "the conviction that every human being is sacred" (Perry 11). In Columbus's terms, culture is a function of imposition and genealogies of possession (as the anxious rhetoric of self-interest that is captured in Las Casas's transcription betrays):

> Therefore having expelled all the Jews from your dominions in that same month of January [1492], your Highnesses commanded me to go with an adequate fleet to those parts of India. In return you granted me great favours bestowing on me the titles of Don and High Admiral of the Ocean Sea and Viceroy and perpetual governor of such islands and mainland as I should discover and win or should in future be discovered and won in the Ocean Sea, and that these rights should be inherited by my eldest son and so on from generation to generation. (Columbus, *The Four Voyages* 38)

It is no accident that the expulsion of the Jews from Spain in 1492 in the name of Christian reterritorialization coincides with Columbus's fantasies of patrilineal empowerment.

In Kropotkin's terms, progressive human culture is capable of a mutual aid that is self-benefiting and a function of cultural isolationism. Such a universalism informs the culture of encounter and its narrated histories and is embedded in the notion of the "progressive." Moreover, this form of universalism serves the interests that benefit from notions of the "civil" constructed in relation to violence and commodification. Novelist Chinua Achebe, in the spirit of denouncing such structures in relation to African writing, critiques the concept of universalism in a manner similar to that of Galeano:

> In the nature of things the work of the Western writer is automatically informed by universality. It is only others who must strain to achieve it. So and so's work is universal; he has truly arrived! As though universality were some distant bend in the road which you may take if you travel out far enough in the direction of Europe or America, if you put adequate distance between you and your home. I should like to see the word *universal* banned altogether from discussions of African literature until such a time as people cease to use it as a synonym for the narrow, self-serving parochialism of Europe, until their horizon extends to include all the world. (9)

Substitute "Latin American literature" for "African literature" and the point becomes all too clear: why have literary cultures and the values they inscribe been put into play as a function of the European centre in relation to the African or South American margins or peripheries (itself a false structure of geopolitical and geoliterary realities)? In what way do the values inscribed in that dialectic presume and reinforce an oppressor/oppressed hierarchy? To what extent does literary discourse play a role in forming the basis from which notions of human (and the rights inherent in that multiply complex subject position) are to be constructed, disseminated, and categorized? Here, Galeano's notion of an "invisible dictatorship," discussed earlier on in this chapter, is pertinent: patterns of thought exist that are foundational in the history of narrating the relations between colonialism and modernity. Those patterns have relevance to the discourse of universal rights that began to emerge after World War II. Moreover, the linkage between those patterns and a notion of human progress is highly compromised. As Ignatieff suggests:

> Most histories of international law regard the dense fabric of international human rights law and the number of states who ratify these covenants as self-evident signs of progress. But there are historical traditions that vigorously dissent: postmodernists who insist that progress and especially moral progress are incoherent; those Marxists who represent human rights as bourgeois ideology; those within the Islamic world who dispute the universality of human rights standards; those who interpret the proliferation of international human rights as a continuation of European imperialism by cultural means. ("Human Rights" 314)

Note how the dissenting voices Ignatieff cites are attached to monolithic ideological structures, whether postmodernist, Marxist, Islamic, or anti-imperialist. But within these reductive categories, troubling their stability as meaningful designations for critical activity, are specific voices mounting sophisticated critiques from within no single category. Galeano is one of these voices, despite the reductive way in which his severest critics have addressed him. Further, he is doubly subversive for his choice of literary discourse as the context for his critique and for his articulation of multiple narratives drawn from history's shadows and phantom presences.

"This Hangman's Shadow, Does it Come From My Body?": Early Modern Recognitions of Rights

Unspeakable genocidal violence has taken place in the twentieth century, but Todorov argues that it is the sixteenth-century genocide in the specific geopolitical and hemispheric location of the Americas that exceeds all others: "the sixteenth century perpetrated the greatest genocide in history" (Todorov 5). Implicit in this declaration is the assumption that one genocide is comparable to another, a structure of thought that ranks the specificity of human suffering caused by genocidal cruelty as greater or less than in relation to other such acts. The move evacuates the specificity of historical agency associated with particular acts of surpassing cruelty, an extraordinarily dangerous position to take since it reduces the understanding of human suffering to a crude hierarchy of relations of greater or less than, an implicit diminishment of *specific* sufferings via a context that only understands (and imagines) *relative* suffering. Nonetheless, an uncanny parallel should be noted in Todorov's suggestion. As we note at the beginning of this chapter, the coincident relations in the twentieth century between genocidal violence and human rights discourse is a fact. But in the sixteenth century, a century that announces the dawn of modernity in the name of "discovery," a parallel emerges in relation to the School of Salamanca, a group of sixteenth-century theologians (Dominican and Jesuit) who produced an emergent rights discourse of their own, one prompted by questions relating to Amerindian enslavement. The English historian Anthony Pagden observes that "the Indian 'problem' became, at base, the problem of the nature of the relations between the different groups of men within as [Francisco de] Vitoria termed it, 'the republic of all the world (*respublica totius orbis*)'" (*The Fall of Natural Man* 65).

Discourses of conscience with regard to encounters with the other *do* occur in the early modern period, and not only in relation to the School of Salamanca. In the latter half of the sixteenth century, for instance, Michel de Montaigne's essay "Of the Caniballes" undertook a critique of European barbarity to indigenous American populations. Montaigne's ethnographic description of the origins of cannibalism among indigenes presents a striking indictment of European encounter strategies. For Montaigne, cannibalism is not "natural" to indigenous culture but rather a response to the barbarity of Europeans (especially the Portuguese). After describing the elaborate and respectful ceremonies that indigenes take prior to killing their victims, in which ritual care is taken not to "offend" the prisoner, Montaigne states the following:

> ...in the presence of all the assembly [they] kill him with swords: which done, they roast, and then eat him in common, and send some slices of him to such of their friends as are absent. *It is not as some imagine, to nourish themselves with it* [the roast flesh] *(as anciently the Scithians wont to doe), but to represent an extreme and inexpiable revenge.* Which we prove thus; some of them [the indigenes] perceiving the Portugales, who had confederated themselves with their adversaries, to use another kinde of death, when they tooke them [the indigenes] prisoners; which was, to burie them up to the middle, and against the upper part of the body to shoot arrowes, and then being almost dead, to hang them up; they [the indigenes] supposed, that these people of the other world (as they [Europeans] who had sowed the knowledge of many vices amongst their neighbours, and were much more cunning in all kindes of evils and mischiefe than they) undertooke not this manner of revenge without cause, and that consequently it was more smartfull, and cruell than theirs, and thereupon began to leave their old fashion to follow this [cannibalism]. *I am not sorie we note the barbarous horror of such an action, but grieved, that prying so narrowly into their faults we are so blinded in ours. I thinke there is more barbarisme in eating men alive,* than to feed upon them, being dead; to mangle by tortures and torments a body full of lively sense, to roast him in peeces, to make dogges and swine to gnaw and teare him in mammockes [portions of flesh] (as wee have not only read, but seene very lately, yea and our own memorie, not amongst ancient enemies, but our neighbours and fellow-citizens; and which is worse, under pretence of pietie and religion) *than to roast and eat him after he is dead.* (166-67; our emphasis)

Montaigne's ethnography attempts to speak from the position of the other, recognizing that there is inhumanity on both sides of the equation at the same time as he locates cannibalism's origins in the egregious evils perpetrated on indigenes by Europeans. The inversion is unfamiliar for Western readers and one that Galeano ironizes in his vignette "On Cannibalism in America": there, the battle over power among Europeans (Francisco Pizarro and Diego de Almagro) struggling for ascendancy in the Americas is shown to produce a cycle of executions and escalating violence in which Europeans kill each other (*Genesis* 114-15). Montaigne's critique is clearly associated with earlier debates about the status of the "Indian's" humanity and is thus part of a genealogy of emergent discourses of conscience linked to rights discourse generally. Amazingly, the twentieth-century manifestation of a universal discourse of rights (the 1948 Universal Declaration) is predicated on atrocities committed in World War II, which simultaneously staged the forgetting of post-conquest atrocities that characterized European encounters with indigenous populations, a point we will return to later in this chapter. Thus, the recuperation of early modern critiques of encounter narratives that struggle with ethical questions of indigenous rights is crucial to re-historicizing this errant genealogy.

Galeano, in episodes devoted to the key figures in the early modern European debate over indigenous rights (Bartolomé de Las Casas and Juan Ginés de Sepúlveda), is explicit about the arbitrary conditions that produce the lived realities of enslavement in the name of freedom (the latter a key signifier of, if not the precondition for, rights). Two episodes from *Memory of Fire* bear recitation for how they inform the kind of critique of rights discourse that we argue is one of the implicit animating principles of Galeano's work. Both episodes comment on emergent rights discourses in the early modern period.

In an episode dated *1545: Royal City of Chiapas* and entitled "The Bad News Comes From Valladolid," Galeano marks the following circumstances:

> The Crown has suspended the most important new laws, which set the Indians free. While they lasted, barely three years, who observed them? In reality, even Indians marked *free* on the arm in vivid red continued to be slaves.
>
> "For this they have told me I was right?"
>
> Fray Bartolomé feels abandoned by God, a leaf without a branch, alone and a nobody.
>
> "They said yes to me so that nothing would change. Now not even paper will protect those who have no more shield than their bowels. Did the monarchs receive the New World from the pope for this? Is God a mere pretext? *This hangman's shadow, does it come from my body?*"
>
> Wrapped in a blanket, he writes a letter to Prince Philip. He announces that he will visit Valladolid without waiting for a reply or permission. (*Genesis* 110; our emphasis)

Galeano's vignette depends on multiple anomalies: a law giving freedom to the indigenes with no bearing on their lived reality as slaves; then the suspension of the same law giving them freedom, thus suggesting the arbitrariness of the law as a source of authority; the paradox of corporeal markings to denote freedom; the illusion of change in the name of stasis; the contradictory faith in "paper" as a metonym for Western legal and juridical discourse even as that faith is shown to be groundless; the odd image of the prophylactic bowels, signaling the visceral reality of domination and torture; the shameful discourse of possession with the pope giving the new world to the Castilian monarchs; and finally, the self as a destroyer of the other. This latter question, framed in the trope of the "hangman's shadow," addresses the dawning suspicion of responsibility for the destruction visited on the Indian slaves, in itself an incipient recognition that rights have been violated.

The brief episode sets the stage for the famous debates between Las Casas and Sepúlveda that took place in 1550-51 in Valladolid. Galeano neatly captures the outcome of these debates in an entry dated *1554: Mexico City*, which begins with Mexico's city council deciding to award Sepúlveda "two hundred pesos in gold in recognition of his services" (*Genesis* 123), pesos that will be added to his already considerable fortune. Galeano continues the story:

> In rebuttal to Bartolomé de Las Casas's assertions, Sepúlveda maintains that Indians are serfs by nature, according to God's will, and that the Holy Scriptures contain examples to spare of the punishment of the unjust. When Las Casas proposes that Spaniards learn the Indians' languages and Indians the language of Castile, Sepúlveda replies that the difference between Spaniards and Indians is the same as that between male and female and almost the same as that between man and monkeys.[11] For Sepúlveda, what Las Casas calls abuse and crime is a legitimate system of dominion, and he commends the arts of hunting against those who, born to obey, refuse slavery.
>
> The king, who publishes Las Casas's attacks, places a ban on Sepúlveda's treatise on the just causes of the colonial war. Sepúlveda accepts the censure smiling and without protest. In the last analysis, reality is more potent than bad conscience, and he well knows what those in command all know in their hearts: *The desire to make money, not to win souls, is what builds empires.* (123-24; our emphasis)

Sepúlveda may, in this account, be the subject of a ban that is ultimately meaningless because it will not prevent the economic, cultural, and military exploitation his ideas support.[12] Sepúlveda's vitriolic attack (in the form of a Socratic dialogue) on the Amerindians in support of Spain's right to conquest, titled *Democrates secundus sive de justis causis belli apud Indos*, is frequently cited as the nadir in the attacks on Amerindian culture by so-called civilized Europeans. Pagden argues that what was controversially thought to be a theological work was a "work of literature," the "work of a man who…was best known for his literary achievements" (*The Fall of Natural Man* 111-12).

We make this observation in relation to Galeano only insofar as it places one of the key voices in the emergent discourse of rights in early modern Europe (Sepúlveda) not in relation to legal or political discourse so much as to a literary genre (the dialogue) in which rhetorical figures like *antitheta* (the contrast of opposites) are used in conjunction with characteristic modes of address like the exhortation and the eulogy (*The Fall of Natural Man* 114-17). For Pagden, *Democrates secundus* "was certainly intended to be read as a work of literature. It is a skilful exercise in political rhetoric on behalf of the Castilian crown's Indian 'wars'" (*The Fall of Natural Man* 114). It is no small irony, then, that the rapacious conquest ideology supported by the literary and political rhetoric of this treatise, which addresses basic issues of rights that were to follow a trajectory largely congruent with Sepúlveda's racism,[13] has found in Galeano one of its fiercest and most skilled opponents in a similarly literary forum.

The literary dimensions of the "origins" of rights discourse are a neglected and misunderstood element in the genealogy of rights discourse generally. Galeano, in responding in kind to the provocations offered by Sepúlveda (that is by using literature as an arena for engaging in critique and resistance), is no aberrant dissident writer in this regard. Rather, he is an interlocutor in an especially significant and long-standing debate about the form and content that rights discourse may take, a debate that has been misread in relation to the historical precedents that form part of its genealogy. The two episodes we cite here, then, summarize a lengthy and complicated debate about indigenous rights that form a crucial literary site for locating emergent modernist rights discourse in the ideology of the post-conquest period. One discourse is marked by the "hangman's shadow," the other by the absence of conscience and a self-legitimating structure of appropriation and abuse. The latter discourse (Sepúlveda's) will prevail and produce the empire that places itself at the centre of human rights discourse in the twentieth century. What does it mean, then, to have such a perverse discourse, with its emphatically literary roots, as one of the key sources from which the torrent of rights talk flows?

Mignolo offers a useful summary of the significance of these early debates related to emergent rights discourse, discovery narratives, and the onset of genocidal modernity:

> …in the sixteenth century the Atlantic was organized according to a different and opposed principle: the "rights of the people," which emerged from the Valladolid early debates between Ginés de Sepúlveda and Bartolomé de las Casas on the humanity of the Amerindians and was followed up by the long debates in the School of Salamanca on cosmopolitanism and international relations…"rights of the people" was the first legal attempt (theological in nature) to write down a canon of international law, that was reformulated in a secular discourse in the eighteenth century as the "rights of men and of the citizen"…the first ["rights of the people"] is at the heart of the colonial, hidden side of modernity and looks for the articulation of a new frontier, which was similar neither to the Moors nor to the Jews. The second ["rights of men and of the citizen"], instead, is the imaginary working within the system itself, looking at the "universality" of man as seen in an already consolidated Europe, made possible because of the riches from the colonial world flowing west to east, through the Atlantic. (*Local Histories/Global Designs* 29)

The dilemma of rights theory pits a universal structure whose universality is used to perpetuate an illusion of justice and egalitarianism against a relativist approach that deflates universalist principles in the name of local self-interest and context. Universality—in the sense that Perry defines it as an absolute—involves a troubled distinction between the practical and the theoretical: "Even if *no* human rights are, as moral rights, absolute, some human rights, as international legal rights, should be—and, happily, are—absolute"; the theoretical contingency of *all* human rights ("Many human rights are, both as moral rights and as legal rights, conditional, not unconditional" [106]) suggests a responsibility to local context and conditions of reciprocal engagement that cannot be enacted (unless the very principle of universality becomes an imposed condition for thinking rights, itself highly problematic for what it implies about *who* articulates the interpretation of the universal principles and *who* gets chosen to impose them in a just and equitable manner).

Local principles of self-affirmation in which dissonant and resistant dialogues are enabled as a function of a community that follows principles articulated by Seyla Benhabib are critical for evaluating the applicability of the universal across multiple human contexts: these multiple contexts require the "*principle of universal moral respect*" and the "*principle of egalitarian reciprocity*" in which "each has the same symmetrical rights to various speech acts, to initiate new topics, to ask for reflection about the presuppositions of the conversation, etc." (29). Further, these principles necessitate in Benhabib's terms a "historically self-conscious universalism" (30). Such a concept bears interrogation in relation to those who use self-consciously universalist histories to promote their own interests or to silence those who resist the imposition of a history whose supposed universality betrays their reality. As Galeano pointedly observes, "In 1948 and again in 1976, the United Nations proclaimed long lists of human rights, but the immense majority of humanity enjoys only the rights to see, hear, and remain silent" (*Upside Down* 334). How does this resonant silence jibe with the universality of rights so proclaimed in 1948? How are the foundational structures of this silence perpetuated in relation to the universality of rights?

In the next section, we will address how influential literary structures (at both the narrative and etymological levels) are deeply complicit with this silence. At the same time, emergent writing practices, of which Galeano's is a distinctive example, are struggling to displace silence in the name of a dialogical community that has relinquished the cemetery of words for a life-affirming space of critical resistance and empowerment based on egalitarian reciprocity.

The Literariness of Obedience:
On the Threshold of Rights and Literary Theory

One of our purposes in writing this book has been to examine how foundational discourses, critical and otherwise, serve to reinforce systems of thought that obscure significant, lived realities. A writer like Galeano plays a crucial role in destabilizing these restricted forms of thought, providing a forceful example of alternatives to the norm. In his listing of the "never-proclaimed right to dream" at the end of *Upside Down*, in a chapter itself entitled "The Right to Rave" ("El derecho al delirio"),[14] Galeano provides a counterpoint to the Universal Declaration's listing of rights, itself based on the rhetorical structures of biblical declamation. In the case of human rights discourse, one of the key foundational documents for thinking rights has been the Judeo-Christian bible. Micheline Ishay's anthology *The Human Rights Reader*, for instance, locates the early origins of human rights in Exodus

20:1-21, the biblical passage in which the ten commandments (the Decalogue) are given to Moses by God. The irony of the passage is that it replaces one form of bondage with another: "And God spake all these words, saying, I am the Lord thy God, which have brought thee out of the land of Egypt, out of the house of bondage" (Ishay 1). In return for freedom the Israelites surrender their autonomy, the first commandment being "Thou shalt have no other gods before me," a fiat that ensures God's transcendental authority will form the basis of all further commandments. These commands may be construed as the basis for an emergent doctrine of human rights in which blasphemy, adultery, murder, thievery, false witness, and desire for property not your own are all proscribed.

We take this to be an exemplary structure for how human rights get theorized and for the literariness of structures of obedience that articulate a nascent form of human rights thinking. What does it mean in such a narrative of displaced obedience—flee the Egyptians, enslave yourself to a transcendental principle—to surrender one's rights to this demanding god? We note how the first four commandments given by God to Moses have virtually nothing to do with shared, material human realities but have everything to do with instituting a radical subservience to the principles of monotheistic practice. What we would suggest lies at the heart of the meaning of this passage is that subordination, bondage, and enslavement (as transcendent principles grounding human relations to an ethics) are foundationally linked to ethical discourses in Judeo-Christian and Occidental thought, and hardly the basis for universal declarations that imagine emancipatory and enabling conditions for *all* humanity. It is not our purpose to digress into a history of how this grounding transcendental principle is consistently used to oppress and limit expressions of humanity; instead, suffice it to say that from this inaugural moment through to the structures of absolutist government in place in Europe at the time of the conquest, through the extended period of colonial encounter, and through to the closural, rhetorical device used by American presidents in addresses to the nation ("God bless America"),[15] a certain continuity is to be discerned. Thus, a literary narrative about obedience that assumes a theological and metaphysical dimension is also the locus for conceptualizing emergent rights discourses. Obedience to a transcendental principle grounds shared, "wannabe" universal values.

Galeano neatly undoes the pious assumptions built into such a structure by exposing its less-than-universal nature: "the Church, holy mother, shall correct the typos on the tablets of Moses and the Sixth Commandment shall dictate the celebration of the body; the Church shall also proclaim another commandment, the one God forgot: You shall love nature, to which you belong" (*Upside Down* 336). Scriptural typos, the evasion of the body, an amnesiac God, the fundamental absence of a basic relation to nature, something inscribed at the core of virtually every indigenous culture's religious and ethical beliefs, all point to the deeply flawed structure of divine law amended in Galeano's "rave/*delirio*."

The emergence of a legally defined discourse of human rights in the postwar period, marked by the 1948 Universal Declaration, has yet to be studied in relation to the concurrent emergence in literary culture of modes of criticism marked by overlapping concerns with issues of gender, race, ethnicity, nation, class, and sexual orientation. In fact, much of the study of human rights has been relegated to the realm of legal, political, philosophical, or historical modes of inquiry. The role of literary culture in imagining what constitutes freedom, equality, and inalienable rights has been forgotten or dismissed. Human rights theory, as promulgated primarily in legal, political, and juridical discourses, unrelentingly points to the gap between desired effect and actual practice. Human rights have been influenced and shaped by theories of reading, which is to say, by theories that envisage alternatives to well-established models for thinking about literature and its history. Galeano's writings are also readings of literary and critical history mediated by an emergent discourse of "universal" rights theory.

Galeano, for instance, consistently addresses the role of the writer in relation to human rights discourse: "We writers are neither gods nor insects. The consciousness of our limitations is not a consciousness of impotence, but a consciousness of reality. Literature is a form of action...the writer can lay claim to his part in the process of change—even in the narrow field in which he may work—without pride or false humility, but knowing himself to part of something vaster than himself" ("For Haroldo Conti" 15). Galeano has further theorized that "Writing makes a choice by the simple fact of its existence. In directing itself to others, it inevitably occupies a position and takes sides in the relationship between society and power...The literature that is most political, most deeply committed to the political process of change, can be the one that least needs to name its politics" ("The Imagination and the Will to Change" 121). Both comments, anchored in the belief that writing acts upon the world in tangible ways, provide a starting point for theorizing the relations between literary expression and human rights theory, between the rhetoric of imagination and the legal and state rhetoric that sets the formal limits upon that imagination.

Not surprisingly, given the historical relevance of rights discourse to lived experience in Latin America, some of the most pertinent work relating rights discourse to literary theory is coming from Latin American critics, whose work remains largely unknown (and untranslated) in North America. Hernán Vidal's work, *Crítica literaria como defensa de los derechos humanos: Cuestión teórica* [Literary Criticism as Defense of Human Rights: Theoretical Issues], focuses on the notion that a crucial component in the creation of the "universal" ethical conscience imagined by such legal documents as the Universal Declaration is, in fact, literary culture. Moreover, Vidal argues that literary works are an important repository of the history of the defense of human rights, one that can be traced back through various genres of literature and criticism. Interestingly, Vidal is concerned with laying out the theoretical foundations of this relationship without necessarily exploring in any detail the archive of specifically literary texts he imagines. In what follows, we link Vidal's work on rights and literary studies to Galeano's to show how the two have significant relations to each other while expressing contradictory attitudes to heterogeneity and social dynamics.

The operative terms in Vidal's critical discourse—"hegemony," "nation," and "institutionalization"—are phenomena he accepts unquestioningly as the necessary framework for articulating social structure and change. The debate is then limited to which group will occupy the dominant position and how this is most rationally and democratically determined in order to reorganize institutions and create a national culture based on consensus. The change of consciousness envisioned by Vidal is from top to bottom, the proposal being to reorganize institutions such as universities to reeducate a traumatized people who have been violently severed from their past and their destiny by the fascist régime that sold them to transglobal capital. Vidal's views on literary studies are refreshingly interdisciplinary and committed to the idea that education and writing forge cultural, social, and political consciousness. But his envisioning of how recanonizing national literature will create the knowledge and ideology required to resuscitate the nation as such seems both megalomanically ambitious and too restrictive in its institutional basis and complete control by intellectuals.

Vidal's call to engage the critical consciousness associated with textual analysis in order to re-envision national history and culture through the defense of human rights is promising, and not just as a form of revitalizing academic literary studies. He sees this sociological approach to rethinking the literary canon as a "poderoso foco de cohesión y de movilización ciudadana consensual" (*Cultura nacional* 426) [a powerful source of cohesion and consensual mobilization of the citizenry]. It must be remembered that Vidal speaks to a specific context: the rebuilding of Chile after the Pinochet dictatorship and the monumental task of reconciling people who hold radically opposed political views, as well as educating those who have been completely emptied of social consciousness by the alienating authoritarian propaganda machine. The collective trauma caused by the brutal repression resulting in the torture, disappearance, and exile of thousands of Chileans is suffered as festering wounds by some, repressed guilt and denial of reality by others. While this context understandably informs the basis for Vidal's nationalist vision, ironically, his language betrays his libertarian intentions. The positing of this project in nationalist terms results in a totalizing discourse in which consensus necessarily suppresses difference in the name of order, consolidation, hegemony, and hierarchy.

Virginia Bell qualifies Galeano's *Memory of Fire* as a "narrative of treason," his project as "postnational historiography,"[16] while reading his work against precisely the kind of national historiography Vidal seems to fall into almost inadvertently. Whereas both Galeano and Vidal envision literature as an important forum for defending human rights, reevaluating the past, and democratizing the future, it would seem that Galeano's polyphonic interweaving of narrative threads that include and even foreground dissonant voices would disqualify him from Vidal's consensual canon. Vidal proposes, in no uncertain terms, that the current hegemonic void be filled by the Communist Party whose self-evaluation he considers sufficient rationale to authorize assuming the power that was forcefully taken from Allende's Popular Unity Party:

En el contexto chileno este debate se ha centrado sobre el diagnóstico del impacto militar sobre la cultura de izquierda. El Partido Comunista Chileno asigna al golpe militar la categoría de derrota momentánea, por lo que queda implícita la noción de que los núcleos institucionales más básicos del movimiento popular—la organización, teoría y línea partidista, sus nexos con las bases que tradicionalmente han dado sustancia a su organización, generando sus cuadros y mandos medios y superiores y, por tanto, su capacidad de movilización de masas—han quedado esencialmente incólumes. Esta visión permite al Partido Comunista la elaboración de propuestas organizativas para la oposición y la resistencia antimilitar con actitudes discursivas de gran certidumbre y convicción, además de continuar haciendo proposiciones globales para la futura conducción de la cultura nacional hacia el socialismo, asumiendo los intereses del proletariado chileno. (*Cultura nacional* 432)

[In the Chilean context, this debate has centred on the evaluation of the military impact on leftist culture. The Communist Party of Chile classifies the military coup as a temporary defeat, implying that the most basic institutional nuclei of the popular movement—the organization, the party theory and line, its connections to the bases that have traditionally substantiated its organization, generating its ranks and intermediate and superior leadership and, consequently, its capacity to mobilize the masses—have remained essentially intact. This vision allows the Communist Party to elaborate proposals for organizing antimilitary opposition and resistance with discursive attitudes of great certainty and conviction, besides continuing to make global propositions for the future orientation of the national culture towards socialism, adopting the interests of the Chilean proletariat.]

What initially comes to mind when reading Vidal's argument is Galeano's reflection on how "a certain militant literature aimed at a public of the converted" mirrors the same closed system as the hermetic discourse of élitist academics: "For all its revolutionary rhetoric, a language that mechanically repeats the same clichés, adjectives, and declamatory formulas for the same ears seems conformist to me. It could be that this parochial literature is as remote from revolution as pornography is remote from eroticism" (*Open Veins* 288). But this is more than a question of style: such terms as "leftist culture," "the masses," and "Chilean proletariat" suppose a homogeneity of interests that allow those blind to difference to voice a discourse of great certainty.

Vidal's proposal is profoundly ahistorical, even anti-historical in implying that the Communist Party could assume power with any legitimacy because it deems its own institutions ready to appropriate hegemony—as if they could simply pick up the threads after almost thirty years of fascist rule exactly where they had left off before the 1973 coup. Such a notion could only come from a vision of society governed exclusively by economics and highly conventional partisan divisions. Vidal brushes aside José Joaquín Brunner's concern for a democratic nation with an extraordinarily heterogeneous identity:[17] "Brunner da mayor importancia a esos grupos de identidad difusa, frágil e inestable que a aquellos otros que, como el Partido Comunista Chileno, todavía conservan la memoria de una identidad forjada con anterioridad al advenimiento del fascismo y han logrado reconstituirse de acuerdo con ella en la clandestinidad" (452) [Brunner gives greater importance to those groups whose identity is diffuse, fragile and unstable than to those, like the Communist Party of Chile, that still conserve the memory of an identity forged prior to the advent of fascism and that have managed to reconstitute themselves through an underground identity]. Since the heterogeneous groups are deemed to be diffuse, Vidal divests them of identity, or at least fails even to ask who they are and what they have to say. Only an organized, institutionalized body's identity is recognized and thereby forms the basis for the "consensus" that will integrate the diffuse groups into that same identity. Who will shoulder the responsibility of defending human rights? Whose rights is Vidal referring to? How is democratic consensus formed? Vidal states categorically that this imagined consensus should include those social groups *capable* of creating a consensus and democratic institutional order (453).

Consensus here is assumed to mean adherence (obedience) to the Communist Party's agenda; hence, communication simply becomes a means of mobilizing the masses, the militaristic terminology suggestive of repositioning machines that await orders instead of expecting interlocution. Curiously, Vidal cites Brunner's critique of the *mito de izquierda* [leftist myth], presumably as a mistake not to be repeated. Vidal outlines the causes of the crisis that resulted in the Chilean coup as follows:

1) en su estrategia de transición al socialismo la Unidad Popular continuó con la concepción mesocrática de que era el Estado el instrumento fundamental para la reorganización de la cultura nacional; 2) en la conducción de su política la Unidad Popular desconoció la heterogeneidad cultural incubada durante las décadas anteriores y, de acuerdo con un consenso de los sectores más importantes de la izquierda—ellos mismos disímiles—se propició la restricción institucional e ideológica de la propuesta transición al socialismo en torno a lo que Brunner llama "un preciso mito de izquierda." (448)

[1) in its strategy of transition to socialism, the Popular Unity held on to the mesocratic concept that the State is the essential instrument in the reorganization of national culture; 2) in carrying out its program, the Popular Unity ignored the cultural heterogeneity incubated during the previous decades and, in agreement with a consensus of the most important sectors of the left—themselves dissimilar—it caused the institutional and ideological restriction of the proposed transition to socialism to what Brunner calls "a precise leftist myth."]

These same causes are fatalistically replicated in Vidal's discourse of certainty and conviction. Heterogeneity sounds almost like a disease (*incubated* during the decades prior to Allende's victory) and the dissimilarity between leftists becomes synonymous with divisiveness from a perspective that sees hegemony as harmony. Galeano's critique of the mass media as an instrument by which "the owners of the world inform us of our obligation to look at ourselves in a single mirror" (*Upside Down* 26) can also be leveled at Vidal's vision of hegemony and consensus, where the latter term is an index of submission to an inflexible vision of reality. Paradoxically, Vidal claims that Brunner's most significant contribution to the discussion of Chile's crisis is his analysis of how the militarized neoliberalism of the "bourgeois nation" attempted to homogenize the heterogeneous national culture by reducing all cultural activity to market function. The conclusion? Bourgeois homogeneity is bad because it alienates, but socialist homogeneity is good because it is consensual. Furthermore, Vidal's partisan politics allows him to summarize Brunner's analysis as trite in order to criticize the Popular Unity Party without mentioning in his closing chapter the U.S. intervention that destabilized the Chilean economy and was directly involved in what Cockroft calls "destroying democracy in the name of saving it" (Salvador Allende 19).[18]

Anticipating criticism of how his analysis may represent the key players in Chilean politics as static, Vidal appeals to the Cuban experience: "En ella fue la dialéctica de cambio revolucionario—con sus debates, conflictos y confrontaciones para responder a coyunturas internas y externas—la que fue creando una conciencia y una voluntad consensual entre sectores democráticos de clase e ideologías diferentes, que más tarde sentó las bases para la fundación del nuevo Partido Comunista Cubano" (*Cultura nacional* 449) [In it the dialectics of revolutionary change—with its debates, conflicts, and confrontations in response to internal and external situations—initiated a process of creating conscience and consensual will amongst democratic sectors from different classes and ideologies, which later established the bases for founding the new Communist Party of Cuba]. The fact that the Cuban Revolution is a touchstone for many Latin Americans does not mean that Cuba's relevance is always interpreted in the same way. Galeano, for instance, expresses admiration for Cuban ingenuity, integrity, and survival in face of the constant threat of invasion and severe economic hardship imposed by the United States embargo, a topic we will return to in greater detail in our last chapter.

But again, Vidal focuses on achievement in terms of hegemony: a stable Communist Party, with consensus assumed to be eternal once it is achieved, rather than an ongoing process involving debate, conflicts, confrontations, and resolutions. A good example of disagreement and dissent involves the presumed consensus in Cuba that excluded gay rights, not just by ignoring gay and lesbian people but through active persecution and deportment.

Yet many Cubans did not accept this official policy and have traditionally shown much greater acceptance of difference than the Communist Party did in this instance. Filmmakers like Juan Carlos Tabío and Tomás Gutiérrez Alea, who collaborated on *Fresa y chocolate* (1993) [Strawberries and Chocolate] and *Guantanamera* (1995), are joined by a multitude of voices that challenge the reactionary immobility of institutions. The many Cubans who do this cannot be labeled dissidents, since they struggle constantly to renew the dialogue needed to ensure true consensus in diversity and a collective envisioning of their communitarian future that can only be democratic if it is capable of accommodating this diversity. "The Party" is inevitably condemned to sclerosis if it dissociates itself from the dynamism and multiplicity of the "people" who tend to resist being homogenized and "dealt with" as "the proletariat masses."

Vidal's internationalist rhetoric, however, does just this. Besides splitting the people into two arbitrary categories labeled the "proletariat" and the "diffuse, fragile, and unstable" group, he does not deal with their specificity, their regional, ethnic, and sexual differences, or the possible contributions they could make to re-envisioning a communitarian ethics from, for example, indigenous or feminist perspectives. Vidal pretends to address this possibility in a chapter entitled "Discurso cultural chileno: ciencia social militarizada y redemocratización feminista" ["Chilean cultural discourse: militarized social science and feminist redemocratization"], already problematic in structural terms since he juxtaposes his examination of the work of a conservative pro-military sociologist with the work of a group of female anthropologists who gather *testimonios* from poor rural women. First, Vidal contrasts the women's project with Hernán Godoy's obvious élitism and identifies the different social groups each intends to write into Chile's cultural history:

> Ese integralismo democratizante amplía los parámetros espaciales, étnicos, geográficos y comunicativos de la actual cultura chilena en su versión oficialista. Demuestra la voluntad de incluir la expresión oral de una clase social subordinada, de grupos étnicos marginados de la conciencia nacional, como los aymarás, o sólo simbólicamente incorporados a ella, como los mapuches, y la totalidad geográfica del territorio nacional, a diferencia de la restricción que hace Godoy de la cultura chilena al reducirla a un verdadero enclave geopolítico dentro de la zona central del país. (213)

> [This democratizing integrationism widens the spatial, ethnic, geographic and communicative parameters of contemporary Chilean culture in its official version. It demonstrates the will to include the oral expression of a subordinate social class, ethnic groups that are marginalized in relation to national consciousness, like the Aymaras, or only symbolically incorporated into it like the Mapuches, and the entire geography of the nation's territory, in contrast to how Godoy restricts Chilean culture by reducing it to a mere geopolitical enclave in the central zone of the country.]

Ultimately, both projects are rejected as the products of misguided partisan, bourgeois "specialists." Vidal accuses the women's collective of appropriating the voices of the subjects interviewed and of homogenizing them into a totalizing discourse. How this is any different from how Vidal or the Communist Party speaks for the proletariat is unclear. While the problem of bourgeois women speaking for "subaltern" women is a constant preoccupation in feminist politics and is continually addressed in feminist critical theories, Vidal does not allow that these debates can have a potentially constructive impact on how these scholars conduct their projects. He chooses instead to write them off as inauthentic because of their official status, together with the marginalized ethnic groups and the women who gave testimony.

Vidal expresses contradictory intentions when he calls for Chileans to unite in re-evaluating literary texts as a means of understanding, in broad cultural terms, the full impact of colonization on all social sectors, not just in economic terms that would highlight class difference. But he also proposes that the Communist Party simply assume the leadership to promote the proletariat's interests. It is not clear why the consideration of human rights should be limited to the national literary canon, and why the notion of a canon, even if recanonized, should remain operative. There is no sense in Vidal's writing that thinking is provisional and dynamic, indefinitely open to revision. His ultimate goal of forging "una identidad nacional cohesiva" (454) [a cohesive national identity] as the collective basis for the defense of human rights falls prey to the totalizing and exclusionary discourse of all nationalisms, and within this discourse, consensus cedes its communitarian and libertarian values to a partisan politics based solely on economic factors. If this is the outcome of the "interdisciplinary" scope of a critical approach combining sociology and literary studies, then "we say no": Galeano's defense of human rights could never be contained in a canon whose function is to be a repository of a single national identity, however revolutionary and inclusive it imagines itself.

In their discussion on envisioning revolutionary societies based on diversity instead of national unity, Paulo Freire and Antonio Faundez (another Chilean critic) identify the reactionary and colonialist underpinnings of nationalist agendas:

I would say that, since the Revolution, and even before it, the modern state, as a nation-state, has complied with the authoritarian demands of one social group which imposes unity on the nation by reducing or eliminating the cultural differences which could exist in the nation-state, or state-nation. As I see it, since the creation of the modern state, there has been a persistent tendency to achieve unity by eliminating diversity, rather than by discovering the Other as an enriching element...This conception of the modern state inspires not only the modern state as at present constituted and structured by the politics of the right, but sadly also determines the structure of "progressive" states. (*Learning to Question* 72)

In contrast to this tendency, Freire elaborates on his participation in the Nicaraguan revolution and how it was decided that the Spanish literacy campaign should not be forced on the Miskito Indians who speak an English-based Creole.[19] Instead, members of community projects were to learn from the Miskitos "what they had to say about [the Revolution] and what were their hopes and dreams...I insist that such a position is part of democratic revolutionary commitment to organizing and reorganizing society. By contrast, in an authoritarian situation, it is decreed in the name of the Revolution what has to be done" (*Learning to Question* 75).

This democratic attitude on the part of the Sandinistas is flatly denied in a document from the Indian Law Resource Center in Washington, D.C., according to which the Miskitos were already in an on-going war against the Sandinistas when the Contras became involved. Sandinista sympathizers claim that the English-Creole speaking Miskitos were easily infiltrated and manipulated by the Contras. The fact that the Indians "were subjected to economic and political pressures by United States and Honduran officials for trying to negotiate 'unilaterally' with the Sandinistas" and that "these officials had demanded that there be no Sandinista-Indian talks without prior approval of the contras" demonstrates the undemocratic, interventionist, and conspiratorial attitude on the U.S.-Honduran side ("Report on the Nicaraguan Indian Peace Initiative" n.pag.). The document is full of innuendos and contradictions that make it difficult to interpret the allegations against the Sandinistas. Tomás Borge (principal official who we will return to in the last chapter) is discredited for flip-flopping on such details as who is to be included in the talks and where they are to be held. He is made out to be either paranoid or to be stalling the process when he cannot decide on which North American advisors and observers should stay, since "Sandinista officials had called three of them CIA agents" (n.pag.). Several paragraphs later, the report confirms CIA involvement: "Opponents of an independent Indian resistance and independent Indian peace initiative, particularly CIA and Honduran military officials, intensified their pressures on the Nicaraguan Indians in Honduras" (n.pag.). This conflict among minority groups, factions within a nation-state, and foreign intervention makes it abundantly clear that democratization is a complex process that cannot be simplified through authoritarian nationalism. Regardless of whether Freire's testimony to the Sandinistas' commitment to democracy is accurate, given in good faith, or as a retrospective corrective to Sandinista abuses (difficult to ascertain because of the contradictory testimonies), it is indisputable that the spirit of listening and responding to minority needs and vision is the only path to democracy. The practical and theoretical implications of democratization discussed by Freire and Faundez contrast with the authoritarianism implicit in Vidal's attitude to reorganizing the State in accordance with a monolithic view of nationalist unity.

We have dedicated this much space to discussing Vidal's views on reading literature in light of the defense of human rights because his work is a rare proposal in the current academic climate of sectarian interests and also because his approach poses serious ideological obstacles to pursuing this line of study. Examining Vidal's views on the (re)canonization of literary texts sheds light on the libertarian power of Galeano's words willed by him to take independent flight once uttered, in order to circulate in a richly heterogeneous world unfettered by national borders and nationalist mentalities. Galeano's weaving together of threads from vastly diverse cultural sources produces a literary space that invites unceasing interpolation. His writing practice continually renews itself by engaging wholeheartedly with the inexhaustible resources of popular culture. Far from being an aesthetic concern with formal experimentation, Galeano's dialogue with the otherness embraced in his own discourse is a form of communication that does not lend itself to the positivistic divisions of self and other, form and content, art and politics. It is in such a hospitable yet oppositional space that the discourse of human rights can speak. At once highly polemical and scrupulous, ironic and earnest, the fabric of these voices expresses the most radical forms of alterity and solidarity.

Galeano's insights are deemed poetic not because they adhere to the tenets of some literary genre but because, like the following lyrics of a popular song about the desire for freedom, they create metaphorical confluences for the envisioning of rights without boundaries even beyond human boundaries:

Por el pájaro enjaulado
por el pez en la pecera
por mi amigo puesto preso
porque ha dicho lo que piensa
por las flores arrancadas
por la hierba pisoteada
por los árboles podados
por los cuerpos torturados
yo te nombro libertad.

Por los dientes apretados
por la rabia contenida
por el nudo en la garganta
por las bocas que no cantan
por el beso clandestino
por el verso censurado
por el joven exilado
por los nombres prohibidos
yo te nombro libertad.

[*For the caged bird*
for the fish in the fishbowl
for my friend taken prisoner
because he said what he thought
for the ripped-up flowers
for the trampled grass
for the pruned trees
for the tortured bodies
I name you liberty.

For the clenched teeth
for the repressed rage
for the knot in the throat
for the mouths that don't sing
for the clandestine kiss
for the censored verse
for the young exile
for the forbidden names
I name you liberty.]

These lyrics—based on the poem "Liberté" by Paul Eluard, rewritten by Gian Franco Pagliaro, and sung by many popular performers including Nacha Guevara—express a commitment to freedom in both cosmic and specifically political terms, reminiscent of Galeano's previously mentioned "The Right to Rave." The highly concrete references weave an all-encompassing web of solidarity with the oppressed in terms that are so panmaterialist that they embrace all forms of otherness and make no distinction between nature and human beings. The poetics of this song, like the poetics of Galeano's writing, think of beauty in terms of justice, peace, and solidarity. This kind of poetics speaks with urgency to the listener/reader's capacity to feel empathy not just through reductive identification with a given group but through a form of being that is most opposite to self-interest and easy self-identification. The breadth of this poetics extends human rights beyond a narrow legalistic or political discourse towards an ethical horizon that challenges us to imagine the full potential of our humanity as an integral part of nature.

The Earth-Born Nobody:
Being Human, *Having* Rights / *Thinking* Human, *Thinking* Rights

We are all equal under the law. Under what law? Divine law? Under earthly law, equality grows less equal every day and everywhere, because power usually sinks its weight onto only one tray on the scales of justice... (*Upside Down* 201)

For the period immediately preceding the establishment of the Universal Declaration, two facts are worthy of notice. The first is that when the United Nations Charter (1945) "recognized the fundamental rights of the individual," this recognition for the "first time in history transformed individuals from mere objects of international compassion into actual subjects of international law" (Lauren 206). The astonishing legal vacuum in which the individual was construed by international legal and juridical practices is one of the great conceptual failures of modernity. And the absence of the legal concept of the individual from the legal contexts shaping international law says a great deal about what it meant to *be* human and *have* rights through pre- and post-conquest history, not to mention what it meant to *think* through the notion of humanity and its concomitant rights. The second feature of the pre-Universal Declaration period entails the International Military Tribunal at Nuremberg (1945-46), in which for the first time in history "a legal proceeding attempted to make government leaders internationally responsible as individuals for crimes against humanity": crimes against humanity was a conceptually "new" category of crime within legal discourse (Lauren 209) and one that Nazi atrocities had been ironically instrumental in constructing via Hermann Goering's abysmal plaint that the atrocities were "*our right!* We were a sovereign State" (qtd. in Lauren 210; our emphasis). This specious argument has astonishing parallels with the justifications used by sovereign nations like the United States to *not* ratify major human rights instruments. Further, it points to the problems with any state-based theory of rights, since such state-based theories are profoundly (in)formed by self-interest, the definitive feature of sovereignty.[20] How then to construe a theory of rights across multiple state boundaries when the very fact of those boundaries suggests the limit of the universal and the periphery of the particular? Imagining alternative rights structures from within such a "national" context is highly compromised. This position leads back to Rosa Luxemburg's notion that "Speaking of the right of nations to self-determination we dispense with the idea of a nation as a whole." To the recognition that the nation as a universalist structure of consent is as theoretically compromised as any universalist notion of rights Luxemburg adds: "under slogans like 'national self-determination' or 'freedom of the citizen,' 'equality before the law'"—all of which are to be found in international human rights discourse—"there lurks all the time a twisted and limited meaning" (qtd. in Bookchin 70).

Remarkably, as recently as the mid-twentieth century, the absence of a credible concept of the individual in the face of international law and the perpetuation of the myth of absolute state sovereignty as disembodied from the specific individuals who embody its actions were simultaneously being promulgated. Both facts indicate the shocking and embattled fragility of human rights construed as legal entities over a long historical period. Darryl Robinson's overview of the historical development of the concept of "crimes against humanity" suggests that these are based on "general principles of law recognized by the community of nations" (44). This history begins only as recently as 1899 and 1907 with the

Hague Conventions, which "referr[ed] to the 'laws of humanity'; the Joint Declaration of May 28, 1915, condemning 'crimes against humanity and civilization'; and the 1919 report of the Commission on the Responsibility of the Authors of War, advocating individual criminal responsibility for violations of the 'laws of humanity'" (44). Drinan suggests that the "human instinct to abhor cruelty found its first mention in Anglo-American law in the English Bill of Rights in 1689. It declared that 'cruel and inhuman treatment or punishment' would not be allowed" (*A Worldview of Human Rights* 130). The lag in legal theory, let alone juridical and legislative activity, between the lived reality of post-conquest European and American cultures' barbarity and its moral-ethical pronouncements on what it means to be human is one of the significant failures of Western culture generally.

The advent of the Universal Declaration ostensibly presented a challenge to both these shameful structures of intellectual and moral failure. In this section, we examine through Galeano's literary practices what it means to *be* human, *have* rights, *think* human, *think* rights. Our starting point is to suggest that if the latter forms of thinking had absented themselves from international legal and political practice, except in the most perverse of ways, they were well-located in the discourses of literature and the humanities generally, in which a struggle to embody the notion of the human in relation to an emergent discourse of rights was (and is) evident. Nowhere is this more pronounced than in the actual history of the term "human" in English discourse, which, as we will show, has a rather instructive moral to it in relation to theorizing rights discourse. Chomsky notes the gap between concepts of personhood in the Universal Declaration and grim reality:

> ...a major innovation of the UD [Universal Declaration] was the extension of rights to all persons, meaning persons of flesh and blood. The real world is crucially different. In the US, the term "person" is officially defined "to include any individual, branch, partnership, associated group, association, estate, trust, corporation or other organization (whether or not organized under the laws of any State), or any government entity." That concept of "person" would have shocked James Madison, Adam Smith, or others with intellectual roots in the Enlightenment and classical liberalism. But it prevails, giving a cast to the UD that is far from the intent of those who formulated and defend it. (*Rogue States* 117)

A "corporation," to cite one interesting example in the line of terms linked to "person" that Chomsky cites, is defined in the Oxford English Dictionary (hereafter the OED) as a "united body of persons, esp. one authorized to act as an individual; fictitious person created by charter, prescription, or act of the legislature, comprising many persons"; or as an "artificial person." Hence, even as the historical concept of the individual has been evacuated from international law, its use-value in terms of defining corporate identity as an impersonation of personhood is unquestioned. The person or individual has been invaluable as an enabling concept for associative legal constructs, giving those the presumptive rights of the individual (minus the accountability) at the same time as the actual rights of the individual were circumscribed or ignored as a transnational legal concept. Thus, as Chomsky observes, "Through radical judicial activism, the rights of persons have been granted to 'collectivist legal entities,' as some legal historians call them; and more narrowly, to their boards of directors, 'a new "absolutism" bestowed by the courts'" (*Rogue States* 117).[21]

The OED definitions of "human" are similarly instructive in what they do *not* say about *being* human. Consider the following OED definitions of "human" for their empty, culturally laden assumptions predicated on notions of superiority:

A. *adj.*1. Of, belonging to, or characteristic of mankind, distinguished from animals by superior mental development, power of articulate speech, and upright posture...

2.a. Of the nature of humans; that is human or consists of human beings...

3.a. Belonging or relative to human beings as distinguished from God or super-human beings; pertaining to the sphere of faculties of mankind (with implication of limitation or inferiority); mundane; secular. (Often opposed to *divine*.)...

b. Belonging or relative to humans, relating to or characteristic of activities, relationships, etc., which are observable in mankind, as distinguished from (*a*) the lower animals; (*b*) machinery or the mechanical element; (*c*) mere objects or events...Also *human engineering* orig. *U.S.*, the scientific study of the interaction of human beings and their working environment and the exploitation of this interaction in the interests of efficiency...

B. *sb.* 1. A human being, a member of the human race...

2. ...that which is human, that which relates to mankind or humanity.

The curious feature of such canonical definitions of human is how they empty the term of any meaning, replacing it with a circularity of meaning in which being human is defined as a function of having the features or attributes of humanity. A similar circularity drives Alan Gewirth's virtually empty notion of rights: "We may assume, as true by definition, that human rights are rights that all persons have simply insofar as they are human" (119). Gewirth's formulation is congruent with Bobbio's critique: "Most of the definitions [of human rights] are pure tautology: 'The rights of man are those which are due to a man in as much as he is a man'" (5). In such a decontextualized, dehistoricized, assumptive (of shared or implicit values, means, and objectives) formulation, human rights obviously become more a matter of "who" has the power to interpret the emptiness of their definition, rather than of any intrinsic substantive content they may be said to have. The power of interpretation we are associating with the counter-narratives proposed by Galeano are crucial to presenting alternative definitions that are meaningful beyond the legal, national, and juridical interpretations whose effect and instrumentality have been limited, to say the least.

Where human faculties are hinted at in the OED definitions we cite above, they are in an undefined position of limitation or inferiority, a perverse definitional strategy if only for how it eradicates qualitative attributes in which limitation or superiority are *not* normative. The definition hints at an ideological superstructure guiding its purpose, one that relies on hierarchy as a key structuring feature. When faced with the logic of such a definition further compromised by the tautological structure that argues "a human is a human is a human," it is clear that even our most sophisticated resources of attributing linguistic meaning and origin are severely flawed when it comes to *thinking* human, theorizing what it means to be human. What does such a curiously compromised definition tell us about how post-Enlightenment structures of knowledge like the dictionary have contributed to or have become symbolic of the ideological forces pressuring as crucial a concept as the "human"?

The reference in section 3.b. of the definitions just cited to human engineering (which as the OED states is of U.S. origin) in relation to "exploitation in the interests of efficiency" is an extraordinarily perverse rendering of "human" in relation to the range of behaviours, knowledges, and cultural differences subsumed under its rubric. To what extent does this notion of "human" figure, however discretely, in the notion of "human" conjoined with the concept of rights? To what extent does the human need to be rethought in order to produce a more forceful and theoretically viable notion of rights? And how are such alternative forms of knowledge-making to be found? It is our contention that one of the important sources of this kind of theoretical and critical consciousness is apparent in literary activities that conjoin such a focus on theorizing the human with a nascent discourse of rights (as influenced by poetic structures of thought). Furthermore, we would argue that Galeano is one of the key contemporary figures exemplary of such a conjunction.

When the OED defines human as hierarchical difference (a binary structure that allows for élitist and racist discourses), that is, as a function of speech, walking erect, and being either superior to animals or distinguished from machinery, the definition presupposes too many variables to be of much use. Is a deaf mute less human for not having oral language? Are humans necessarily superior to animals, and how does that superiority function as an obstruction to a universal declaration of human rights, in which the bestialization of non-white indigenous culture is a crucial feature? Why frame human subjectivity through inter-species comparisons based on wildly unethical and antiquated presuppositions about humanity's place in the "great chain" of being? On this last point Galeano is explicit:

> But the oldest tradition in the Americas, the great cultural heritage, teaches that we are brothers and sisters of everything that has legs, paws, wings, or roots. The so-called civilization has been fighting against this certitude since the so-called Discovery of America. First in the name of God, later in the name of Progress. Who knows how many Indians were tortured or killed for the sin of idolatry? Nowadays, everybody speaks about protecting nature. But nature continues to be something strange to us, something seen as a landscape. We don't belong to nature, and we are

unable to realize that any crime against her becomes a suicide. We are still suffering this cultural divorce. (Manrique 59)

As we have been arguing, this divorce is apparent in the crucial definitions that lie at the heart of epistemologies of the human, however blind these are to the kind of alternatives proposed by Galeano.

Note, for instance, the enormous divide between the definition cited in A.1. of the OED (above) and the first recorded use of the term "human" in an English context in 1398: "This creatour thenne made man, and nature humayne comune" (OED). Where the definition seeks to "distinguish" the human from the animal, a metonymic literary structure for the disarticulation of nature and the human, the actual supposed first usage suggests the opposite, implying the colloquy of nature and human community. One issues from reciprocal relation to the other. Clearly, the presumptive ideology of the close reading practices associated with the production of the definition is divorced from the actual meaning implicit in the first recorded usage. The divorce also exists in the lamentable state of theorizing, whether in legal, literary, or social scientific circles, on the gap between the reality of *being* human and *thinking* human.

Sophisticated (and sophistical) attempts to direct the nature of this theorizing have been in place for centuries. These theories advocate a number of tenets: technological intervention as a supreme expression of human difference from the natural; progress and growth as infinitely positive and necessary directives of human endeavour; exploitation in the name of efficiency, expediency, and exigency; miseducation as a consistent strategy to ensure a compliant, self-replicating citizenry (as in for instance the androcentrism of economic theory where the cost of environmental side effects and collateral damage caused by a particular profit motive or business plan are generally not accounted as part of the real cost of doing business);[22] and the fervent (irrational) belief in the rational as supervening all other forms of being and thinking, thus foreclosing on the imaginative resources that are also acutely if not definingly expressive of what it means to be human. Further, there are cultural uses that gather round the sense of "human." Raymond Williams, for instance, examines the meaning constructs of sin and fallibility as they pertain to the "human":

"He had a human side to him after all" need not mean only that some respected man was fallible; it can also mean that he was confused or, in some uses, that he committed various acts of meanness, deceit or even crime…The sense relates, obviously, to a traditional sense that it is *human* not only to err but to sin. But what is interesting about the contemporary use, especially in fashionable late bourgeois culture, is that 'sin' has been transvalued so that acts which would formerly have been described in this way as proof of the faults of *humanity* are now adduced, with a sense of approval that is not always wry or covert, as proof of being *human* (and *likeable* is usually not far away). (151)

What meaning does a "human" right have in such a context of implicit approval for, or association with, the ethically questionable—the sense that it is likeable to be morally suspect? A reasonable outcome of this line of argument is that all key terms in the debate over human rights, whether justice, reciprocity, equality, freedom, and so forth, require rigorous examination: both for what they actually mean *and* for how those meanings produce material effects. These examinations must observe at least two criteria. The first relates to the plural forces and contexts acting on a word that give it meaning (as a function of that plurality). The second involves the practical implications of these words' meanings in social practices related to rights in different social spheres, different cultural and historical spaces. The enormous pressure to conform to the mode of thinking and being in the world, implicit in Williams's definition of human, finds resistances in those forces (whether artistic, scientific, historical, or otherwise) that produce imaginative alternatives to such narratives.

The OED definition also does little to address the actual etymology of the word "human," which derives from Old Latin "*hemo* (whence *nemo*, nobody)," meaning the "'*earthy* one, the *earth*-born' from L *humus*, earth (soil, ground)" (Partridge 292). In this etymology, at least a more forthright definition of human is explicit: *the earth-born nobody*. Galeano ends *The Book of Embraces* with a brief meditation on the relationship between the earth-born nobody who is human by definition of a relation to the telluric that makes the two virtually indistinguishable: "I am naked...I am my face in the wind, against the wind, and I am the wind that strikes my face" (272). Mayan creation myths tell the story of an incomplete "man" fashioned from earth, wood, and leaves, who is only made flesh once corn is discovered in the quartered remains of a coyote and mixed with the blood of the tapir and the serpent ("brought from out of the sea") to form the dough of creation (*The Annals of the Cakchiquels* 46-47). The myth is uncannily in sync with the English etymology we describe for "human," with the important distinction that earth alone is not enough to "make" someone human. An act of co-creation is required in order for the earth and that which issues from it (maize) to become meaningfully human. The Latin derivation of "human" is also related to the Greek *khthōn* ("on the ground") with its connection to the *autokhthōn*, "of or from the earth, of the land," itself the derivation for an aboriginal or indigene, as in autochthonous.

How did the early conception of the word "human" mutate, via its association with the telluric, into a signifier for solely the aboriginal, as opposed to the full-range of human difference? One of the ways in which this concept of the earth-born as an expression of the human has been corrupted is through Aristotelian philosophy, which suggests that imperfect biological creatures, like insects and reptiles,

> ...were generated spontaneously from the earth or were the product of some fusion of rotting matter...By suggesting that the Indians had originally been created in this manner [Andrea] Cesalpino, Paracelsus, Girolamo Cardano and even Giordano

Bruno were, in effect, classifying them along with insects. The belief in spontaneous generation…was generally held to be blasphemous and heretical as a dire threat to the unity and integrity of the human race…For if men can be made out of the sod, then 'is not our own health in doubt and our own redemption?' (Pagden, *The Fall of Natural Man* 22-23).

The conceptual dissociation of "human" from the "earth" in the early modern debates about the intrinsic humanity of the Amerindians diminished the Amerindians' humanity. The move allowed for the conquest to be sanctioned by religious and legal authorities and was a major failure in how European culture constructed relations of difference as a result of encounter. To what extent would a full understanding of this definition of human (the earth-born nobody), widely disseminated and applied through different pedagogical, artistic, and scientific contexts, transform the ethical thoughtfulness with which humans actually are human? To what extent would such a definition influence what Jim Merod calls the "conditions of knowing in which we are placed, the *here* and *now* of our potential understanding" all "equally a part of every text's way of being in the world"? (100).

Thinking the rights of being human necessitates a critical responsibility to such base definitions. Rights, it cannot be emphasized enough, are profoundly influenced by the critical pressures brought to bear on these concepts. A legal document, a rights report from an NGO, a poem, a *testimonio*—all are opportunities for re-envisaging the responsibilities of the here and now as mediated by critical reflection. Merod states this succinctly enough when he argues that "intepretation seizes texts as available (and more or less suitable) occasions for asserting meaning, for ideologizing or de-ideologizing as the case may be. The question is: Whose meaning, whose ideology, whose politics are in play?" (100). Significant pressure has been placed on this "human" to move it from its richly suggestive etymological roots to the bland and reductive definition that appears, for instance, in John Walker's nineteenth-century dictionary. There, "human" simply (and tautologically) means "having the qualities of a man," a familiar betrayal (*pace* OED) of the imaginative and epistemological range of qualities expressive of the human condition.

Similar etymological and critical pressures can be brought to bear on the notion of "right," which has an extensive linguistic pedigree and is granted an enormous amount of space in the OED by comparison with the definition of "human" (10 pages as opposed to two). Again, the kind of critical consciousness that typifies Galeano's method across the many genres in which he writes is instructive when it comes to thinking the concept of the right. The OED definitions are pertinent and exemplary of why such a critical consciousness is necessary. "Right" is defined in the following ways, from a myriad and substantial listing:

1.1. The standard of permitted and forbidden action within a certain sphere; law; a rule or canon…

2. That which is proper for or incumbent on one to do; one's duty...

3.a. That which is consonant with equity or the light of nature; that which is morally just or due. (Often contrasted with *might* and *wrong*, and in M.E. freq. coupled with *reason* or *skill*.)

Further definitions include "Justifiable claim, on legal or moral grounds, to have or obtain something, or to act in a certain way"; "A legal, equitable, or moral title or claim to the possession of property or authority, the enjoyment of privileges or immunities"; and "Agreeing with some standard or principle; correct, proper. Also, agreeing with facts; true" (OED). Typically, the divorce we have already noted (between usage and meaning) in *thinking* "human" is also apparent in the term "right." As a "standard," a right assumes a norm against which actions are measured, a meaning that leads to the legal and canonical sense of the term. What this primary definition leaves out, however, is *who* sets the normative standard "within a certain sphere." What relative contexts inform the way in which action is permitted or forbidden? Whose master narrative is operative? What cultural constructions produce the norms of the authorized and the criminal? What essentialist notions of the permitted and forbidden, the legal, are operative in that "certain sphere"?

Galeano observes that fear "among other things is a source of law" (*Upside Down* 206). If so, how valid is a legal discourse of rights predicated on fear that simultaneously addresses issues of equality and solidarity? To what extent is such a discourse an attempt to contain fear and as such a function of ethically suspect motives, rather than an expression of human solidarity, community, and social justice? Moreover, *whose* fear is being acted upon—that of the legislators' or that of the subjects of the legislation? What historical contexts have led to the production of that "certain sphere"? Such questions are far from pragmatically irrelevant to thinking the concept of right. Apartheid, for instance, emerged as a concept in seventeenth-century South African settler culture before being used as part of political discourse in 1943, prior to its formalization in legal statues in 1948. In the South African concept of apartheid, a right so defined would include the "certain sphere" permissive of a legal environment in which racial discrimination of a minority of 4 million people who happened to be white overruled that of the majority of 26 million people who happened to be black. The monstrosity of such a situation is permitted by the OED definition, by which apartheid would constitute a *right* (as a "standard" operative within a "certain sphere") without necessarily *being* right within the global contexts of establishing human rights that overrule specific national and supposedly sovereign contexts.

Similar problems arise when these critical pressures are brought to bear on the other definitions of "right" we have cited. For instance: how to define duty as a non-relative concept, dependent on specific historical location and agency, the kind that permitted Nazi soldiers the defense of having committed crimes in the line of duty (a defensive plaint heard in the American My Lai massacre trials, and countless other situations in which soldiers have committed horrors in duty's name)? How to define "That which is consonant with equity or the light of nature" when these are hazy legal and moral terms fused to a semi-literary trope ("light of nature")? Who determines what is "consonant with...the light of nature"? What cultural constructs are at work in determining the meaning of the "light of nature" as it applies to equity?[23]

The latter definitions of right from the OED consternate in similar ways. These link right with possession of property or title, whether moral or otherwise (already a highly dubious criterion in which a particular cultural construction is at work vis-à-vis property), and the right to privilege (another usage heavily burdened with classist and élitist freight). And the last definition we cite—"Agreeing with some standard or principle; correct, proper. Also, agreeing with facts; true"—is distinguished by its definitional slackness ("some standard or principle") in which agreement with the facts and the truth are contingent. The way in which fact is constructed as a particular narrative that can distort as well as illuminate is not addressed by the definition. When read in light of the relationship between the word "right" and the Indo-European root *reg.* (meaning "to stretch, straighten, straight, right; to lead, direct, rule" [Klein]) from which it derives, "right" can simply mean to rule, with the implication that to do so is to right a state of affairs that requires it. Thus, contextual issues around how such a "right" is construed to serve particular ideological ends are effectively sidestepped, a process Galeano consistently debunks as pervasive and deforming: "In our countries, numbers live better than people. How many people prosper in times of prosperity? How many people find their lives developed by development?...In Central America, the more wretched and desperate the people, the more the statistics smiled and laughed. During the fifties, sixties and seventies, stormy decades, turbulent times, Central America boasted the highest economic growth rates in the world and the most extensive regional development in the history of human civilization" (*The Book of Embraces* 81). Evasive notions of rights lacking a thoroughly developed, consistently theorized sense of the constructedness of the facts and hence of the truth that in turn produces the property and privilege of a right are theoretically empty and fatuous.

"The Child of No One":
Gender, Imagined Families, Rights (In)Equality

Feminist legal scholar Catharine MacKinnon analyses the way in which rights discourse is heavily inflected by male-gendered constructs, one example of the degree to which the underpinnings of rights discourse require strenuous theoretical pressure along the lines that Galeano and others propose:

> Male reality has become human rights principle, or at least the principle governing human rights practice. Men have and take liberties as a function of their social power as men. Men have often needed state force to get away with subjecting other

men; slavery, segregation in the United States, and Hitler's persecutions were explicitly legalized. So the model of human rights violation is based on state action. The result is, when men use their liberties socially to deprive women of theirs, it does not look like a human rights violation. But when men are deprived of theirs by governments, it does. The violations of the human rights of men better fit the paradigm of human rights violations because that paradigm has been based on the experiences of men. (93)

MacKinnon further argues that "'a man' defines what 'an individual' means, and human rights are mostly 'individual' rights" (91). Hence, normative constructions govern key definitions of what it means to be human and what it means to have rights; these definitions must be thoroughly interrogated if *being* human and *having* rights are to have any meaning in terms of how the majority of people on this planet actually live their lives. Galeano observes, for instance, that "The United Nations preaches equality but doesn't practice it: at the highest levels of this, the highest international organization, men occupy eight out of every ten positions" (*Upside Down* 71). The issue, as MacKinnon rightly points out, revolves around "whose experience grounds what law" (84), a formulation we would revise to read "whose experience grounds the meanings of the multiple discourses that reflect the actual lived circumstances and conditions of all peoples." The perversion of rights realities as a function of the patriarchal sovereign state understood as the normative legal, cultural, and political entity in the determination of rights cannot be underestimated, a construct that John Rawls tries to circumvent in his troubling description of the "law of peoples" insofar as it produces just social relations.

One problem with Rawls's analysis arises from his notion of the "veil of ignorance," which, as Elaine Scarry describes,

> ...requires that one become temporarily ignorant about one's own physical, genetic, psychological, and even moral attributes. We enter into decisions about the best social arrangements without knowing what position within that social arrangement we occupy...the act of making oneself featureless accomplishes the same outcome as making oneself a composite of all possible features...By becoming featureless, by having a weightlessness, a two-dimensionality, a dryness every bit as 'impoverished' as the imagined other, the condition of equality is achieved...we create what Rawls describes as 'the symmetry of everyone's relations to each other.'" (293)

Assuming that such a hypothetical state is thinkable, let alone its opposite assumption—namely, that we are fully knowledgeable about all aspects of our being at all times (and assuming that these aspects are constant)—Rawls projects the universal structure of imagined featurelessness as a condition for imagining equality. In so doing, the very contingency that provides the potential basis for reciprocity and acceptance based on difference is evacuated from the act of coming to know the other. The latter act implies the real of ongoing, processual dialogue, as opposed to the abstraction of devolving oneself of the context that shapes specific enactments of equality (itself a term whose local lived meaning must be thought over and above the universal meanings that attach to it). Rawls assumes that self-interest *necessarily* dominates judgement; the veil of ignorance simply serves as a safeguard by dissembling the self without allowing for the empathy that produces moral reasoning. One might just as easily argue that the veil of ignorance is a condition necessary to enact the most egregious of crimes, a sociopathic rejection of the particular affect and knowledge that enable responsible conduct toward the other. The veil of ignorance produces the illusion of the featureless nobody who is everyone, a deformation of human agency that is precisely aligned with the nation-state's dream of a homogeneous, passive, ignorable citizenry.

Galeano, in extensive and persistent critiques of the "system," figures the problem of the nation-state as norm in the following way:

> Whoever is against it [the system], the machine teaches, is an enemy of the nation. Whoever denounces injustice commits treason against the country.
>
> I am the country, says the machine. This concentration camp is the country: this garbage heap, this immense wasteland empty of men.
>
> Whoever thinks that the country is a house which belongs to everyone shall be the child of no one. (*Days and Nights* 41)

The parable, part allegory, part ideological critique, with its reliance on modernist rhetoric (machine, concentration camp, garbage heap, wasteland) suggests that the imagined "family" of the nation is illusory, citizens as bastard children of an instrumental, mechanical, and rationalized state in ruins, a wasteland. If such a state is the progenitor of rights discourse, how meaningful can such a discourse be, especially if the denunciation of injustice is treasonous? What does it mean to *be* human or to *have* rights within such a framework? Why use such a state as the model upon which to build an alternative rights discourse?

Deracinated citizenship becomes meaningless and a betrayal of solidarity, troped here in the language of familial and domestic vulnerability. Necessarily, alternative constructions of that solidarity and familial structure that the nation betrays are called for, ones based on non-hegemonic structures of dialogue, acceptance of difference, reciprocity, and duty:

> You cannot reconstruct the world or society, nor rebuild national states now in ruins, on the basis of a quarrel over who will impose their hegemony on society. The world in general, and Mexican society in particular, is composed of different kinds of people, and the relations between them have to be founded on respect and tolerance, things which appear in none of the discourses of the politico-military organizations of the sixties and seventies. (Marcos, "The Punch Card" 71)

So argues Subcomandante Marcos, in an interview with Gabriel García Márquez and Roberto Pombo. Marcos presents an alternative vision, founded on paradox, of the realities governing Mexico's impoverished Mayan communities in Chiapas: "Why a revolutionary army is not aiming to seize power, why an army doesn't fight, if that's its job. All the paradoxes we faced: the way we grew and became strong in a community so far removed from the established culture" ("The Punch Card" 71). The paradox (and challenge) of discarding the supposedly communal construct of nation for another form of communalism ("far removed from the established culture") is at the core of the critique of rights discourse we are advocating. How to truly think alternatives beyond the norms of the sociopolitical constructs firmly in place? And how to do so with a coherent critical consciousness informed by the deep historical and cultural contexts that have given shape to the present? Much of what follows in this book is an exploration of how Galeano's literary methods and ideas present a strikingly clear critique and practice of the kinds of critical consciousness necessary to producing such alternatives.

These methods and ideas are an expanded form of rights discourse within a profoundly literary aesthetic, at once independent of, yet simultaneously in deep conversation with, traditions of resistance and dissidence that for better or for worse have emerged out of the specific experience of the post-conquest Americas. Furthermore, we would advise readers ideologically disinclined from the views Galeano advances to resist jumping to reductive conclusions about the alternatives he proposes, especially in the critique of rights culture we are aligning with his project. Based on the passages just cited, for instance, a facile assumption might be that Galeano is offering outmoded and patriarchal notions of familial discourse as the alternative to state hierarchies. However, since he does not end his critique of oppression with the attack on the machinery of nation, such a hasty conclusion could not be further off the mark. A good instance of Galeano's strategy occurs in a passage entitled "Los Derechos Humanos" [Human Rights], which appears in both *Mujeres* and in *The Book of Embraces* under the heading "The Culture of Terror":

> Extortion,
> insults,
> threats,
> slapping,
> beating,
> thrashing,
> whipping,
> the dark room,
> the icy shower,
> enforced fasting,
> forced feeding,
> the ban on leaving the home,
> the ban on saying what you think,
> the ban on doing what you feel,

and public humiliation

are some of the methods of punishment and torture traditional to family life. To punish disobedience and discipline liberty, family tradition perpetuates a culture of terror that humiliates women, teaches children to lie and spreads the plague of fear.

"*Human rights should begin at home,*"Andrés Domínguez told me in Chile. (143)

An initial reading of this list suggests the violence done to a torture victim in a concentration camp or army barracks. Only at the end does the reader see the connection of that context with the home. Clearly, such a portrait of family domesticity is highly critical, condemning its structures as complicit with those of the nation-state, especially in relation to gendered structures of power that disadvantage women. The moral of the parable remains that human rights must begin at home, that is, such rights must gain expression as a function of the local rather than of the global. Building rights communities requires that the most local forms of community be responsive to, and exemplary of, issues of social justice, of which the treatment of women and children is one of many important markers. Patriarchal structures of prohibition, intolerance, and humiliation, wherever they are enacted (from the *campesino* to the *generalísimo*), must be overturned and supplanted by rights structures based on respect and freedom, not terror and prohibition.

Consistent with the critique we are suggesting of the nation-state as the norm, against which rights culture is to be measured, Galeano pushes for an alternative. But this alternative is not an easy one: the very structure of the anecdote, with its cascade of domestic offenses culminating in a highly condensed analysis, suggests an abiding pattern of terror and oppression that must be exposed ("the dark room") and overthrown. And coincident with such an alternative (that has yet to be fully enacted) is the need for both further analysis and action based on that initial analysis in order to produce a viable alternative structure of human rights governed by social justice. Moreover, the result (if not motivating feature) of such an analysis is a deep cynicism about how changeable such oppressive structures really are, let alone how viable they are as alternatives. Though Galeano does not say this himself, and may not even intend such an effect, the critical consciousness engendered by the vignette must necessarily question the very structure of the family itself as productive of the oppression associated with it.

Article 16 of the Universal Declaration declares that men and women "are entitled to equal rights as to marriage, during marriage and at its dissolution" and that the "family is the natural and fundamental group of society and is entitled to protection by society and the State" (Ishay 410). The reality, however, is very different. Such an entitlement remains entirely devoid of meaning in the contexts of the lived reality alluded to by Galeano, whose anecdote only hints at the many ways in which women are domesticated and abused —whether it be as a function of genital mutilation, the despicable practice of suttee, the unacknowledged economic benefits provided by women (as detailed in Marilyn Waring's *If*

Women Counted), the sexual exploitation of women in countless circumstances, and so forth. And, as Anne McClintock points out in her critique of the notion of postcoloniality, "Marital laws in particular have served to ensure that for women citizenship in the nation-state is mediated by the marriage relation, so that a woman's political relation to the nation is submerged in, and subordinated to, her social relation to a man through marriage. The global militarization of masculinity, and the feminization of poverty have thus ensured that women and men do not live 'post-coloniality' in the same way, or share the same singular 'post-colonial condition'" (92). McClintock further proposes that "In a world where women do 2/3 of the world's work, earn 10% of the world's income, and own less than 1% of the world's property, the promise of 'post-colonialism' has been a history of hopes postponed" (92).

The oppressive conditions that rights legislation has failed to resolve for a majority of women, even though women's groups are organizing globally in order to resist such conditions, are detailed by MacKinnon: "African women oppose genital mutilation. Philippine, Thai, Japanese, and Swedish women organize against the sex trade. Women in Papua New Guinea, the United States, and workers at the United Nations resist sexual harassment. Brazilian and Italian women protest domestic battery and 'honor' as a male excuse for killing them...Forced motherhood is opposed from Ireland to Germany to Bangladesh. Female infanticide and objectifying advertising are legislated against in India" (101-2). And in a critique of the gap between the Universal Declaration's language and actual practices, Susan Moller Okin confirms that "in many countries, violations of women's basic human rights are still commonplace" and that major rights instruments "such as the Universal Declaration of Women's Rights (1967) and the Convention on the Elimination of All Forms of Discrimination Against Women, or CEDAW (1979)—have been signed and even ratified by governments of countries whose laws or accepted practices are far from fulfilling the provisions of these conventions" (33).

Article 16 of the Universal Declaration, then, instates the notion of "equal rights" with little context and without the means to ensure the protection of the women it addresses, a deeply problematic structure that suffuses most human rights legal instruments. How would such a formulation operate in feminist discourse, for instance, where there exists a "rich concept of equality as lack of hierarchy, not sameness"? (MacKinnon 102). How is equality possible when one of the partners in the equation continues to enjoy long-held historical, economic, and political dominance that consistently mitigates against that equality? And why is equality all too often a trope for imitation and emulation, "a nonarbitrary recognition for meeting the dominant standard, integration over self-determination," as Mackinnon points out (104), when equality should ideally consist of precisely the freedom not to imitate or emulate male norms? In such circumstances, absolute equality, let alone relative equality, is decidedly an impossibility, an ethico-legal mirage. MacKinnon's sense of the differential in discourses of equality as a function of gender is noteworthy: "How equality is defined in the North American [feminist] movements, by contrast, is self-respecting but not isolationist, self-determinant but not segregationist, uncompromised but not absolutist, solid at the core but forgiving at the edges. Its equality is not absolute but relative to the best society has to offer, insisting on an expanded role for the subordinated in redefining standards from the point of view of those living under them" (106). The extent to which such a discourse is to be distinguished from non-North American feminist practice or from other ways of theorizing equality as a function of different cultural practices, modes of (dis)empowerment, historical circumstances, and so forth is a measure of the problem inherent in any overarching definition of what it means to be equal.

The vagueness, then, of the entitlements and protections offered by Article 16 works in inverse proportion to the actual entitlements and protections that accrue to families, howsoever defined. Similar pressure may be brought to bear on other Articles of the Universal Declaration. Article 4, for instance, states that "No one shall be held in slavery or servitude; slavery and the slave trade shall be prohibited in all their forms" (Ishay 408). How to reconcile such a far-reaching pronouncement with the following acerbic analysis made in Jim Goad's blistering attack on class relations in the U.S.?

> As much as we'd like to pretend that wage labor is somehow slavery's opposite, it is merely an ingenious mutation. Karl Marx, that pickle-faced commie bastard, didn't seem to think that wage labor represented much of an improvement over bound slavery. And Marx's ideological nemeses over at the Bank of England agreed that wage labor enriched the already wealthy. In an 1862 letter sent to his American investor chums, a Bank of England representative named Mr. Hazard hungrily rubbed his roach antennae at the prospect of an emancipated South:
>
>> Slavery is likely to be abolished by the war power, and chattel slavery abolished. This I and my European banker friends are in favor of, for slavery is but the owning of labor, and carries with it the care of the laborers, while the European plan, led by England, is that capital shall control labor by controlling wages. (106)

Goad is equally scathing with regard to Lincoln's motivations in ending slavery as a function of national self-interest rather than out of any ethical concerns about the disjunct status of blacks and whites: "[Lincoln] was also a white supremacist with no intention of ending slavery until 1863—two years into the Civil War—when he realized it would be a good way to shatter the South socially" (217). Goad cites the following excerpt from a letter Lincoln wrote to Horace Greeley as typical: "My paramount object in this struggle is to save the Union, and is not either to save or destroy slavery" (qtd. in Goad 218).

The rhetoric surrounding the abolition of slavery and servitude (furthered by the Universal Declaration's Article 4) is profoundly skewed by illusions of freedom that conceal severe restrictions. The problem with the Universal Declaration is precisely an interpretive (textual) one—"how" one defines slavery and servitude, as Goad's examples of Lincoln and Hazard show, profoundly effects how and what these terms mean. The Brazilian photographer Sebastião Salgado, who has made it his life's work to document migrancy, worker culture, the landless, and severely disadvantaged peoples, offers in a sequence of photographs included in *An Uncertain Grace* (which includes a short essay by Galeano in which he describes images that appear almost incomprehensible) extraordinary visual proof of the presence of slavery and servitude in the gold mine at Serra Pelado in northern Brazil: "bodies of clay. More than fifty thousand men...hunting for gold...they scale the mountain, slipping and sometimes falling, each fallen life no more important than a pebble that falls...Images of the pyramid builders in the days of the Pharaohs? An army of ants?" (*We Say No* 248-49). Brutal conditions that so disempower workers cannot be called anything less than an abuse of rights, a form of slavery and servitude to a system that undervalues their lives even as it overvalues the malleable element they extract from the clay. Again, this is the false image of the earth-born nobody, a historical deformation of the slave made over as a free worker seeking his or her fortune autonomously. The servitude that Galeano associates with life in the family is further troubled by such observations: the family becomes the extension, especially for women, of a form of servitude on which state culture is based, rather than a liberating principle of microcosmic social organization that establishes the most basic terms of human equality.

The struggle in liberal Western democracies to recognize alternative family structures (based on the sexual orientations of the parents, for instance) only hints at the degree to which family entitlement and protection in terms of equality are anything but guaranteed by so-called advanced cultures. How can such structures, governed by deep inequities, live up to their ideal when faced with the enormous pressures to sustain the inherent inequality in spite of universal declarations? Moreover, the discourse of family promoted by Article 16 suggests that it is actually a trope for an extension of the individual, an expanded individuality ("Men and women of full age...have the right to marry and found a family"), a concept that is highly questionable within the larger communitarian, liberal-democratic contexts in which a family may be said to operate. What if such a discourse promotes the monad (whether individual or family) decontextualized from, and at the expense of, the community that harbours the family?

It is no coincidence that the controversial Article 17 of the Universal Declaration, with its assertions that "everyone has the right to own property alone as well as in association with others" and that "No one shall be arbitrarily deprived of his property," occurs immediately following the Article on family, making a clear link between family and property in the logical order of the Universal Declaration's narrative of rights. This linkage is deeply questionable with regard to the gendered inequities that have so long defined family (for instance, women as chattel). But it is also a way of reinforcing the propertied monad at the expense of an expanded discourse that seeks to express communitarian rights principles based on solidarity. The propertied family, in other words, is deeply oppositional to community—a form of narrowing the circulation of communitarian energy that has consistently characterized the relationship between governmentality and domesticity (as an expression of deeply patriarchal and restrictive forms of exchange between genders, between the propertied and the unpropertied). What of alternative forms of kinship not based solely on property, or on limiting notions of what constitutes the "natural and fundamental group unit of society" (Universal Declaration, Article 16.3), not based on litigious structures of oppression, or on differential gendered power relations? Why are these alternatives—to which we will return in our last chapter —not figured in such a "universal" declaration? The question arises as much from Galeano's analysis as it does from thinking through alternative norms against which to devise alternative rights structures.

One of Galeano's key writing strategies is to restore to memory instances of resistance to colonial culture. For instance, in a brief passage from "The Revolution as Revelation," he notes that "Many Venezuelan children believe that Guaicaipuro, the hero of the native resistance against the Spanish conquest, is nothing but the name of an annual television award. The incident of Palmares, in which black slaves lived freely throughout the whole of the seventeenth century, defeating successive Portuguese and Dutch military expeditions, merits at best a couple of lines in the history books of Brazil" (15-16). To this may be added instances of alternative community-making by the displaced Cherokees in the nineteenth century, not to mention the formidable history of resistance associated with the Araucanians over several centuries, and the Haitian revolution led by Toussaint L'Ouverture in the last decade of the eighteenth century. Galeano's perspective is acute:

> *The history of America, the true, betrayed history of America, is a story of endless indignity.* On every single day some overlooked episode of resistance to power and wealth took place. But official history makes no mention of the uprisings of indigenous people or the rebellions of black slaves—or it mentions them in passing, when it mentions them at all, as episodes of misconduct. And it never mentions that some were led by women. (*We Say No* 215-16)

The question of deep context as a form of critical consciousness, then, needs to be permanently and rigorously embedded in all theorizing about human rights discourse. Further, such a deep context must be defined in the broadest of terms to include, among others, cultural, political, economic, gendered, ethnic, and historical narratives, all of which are nourished by multiple and complex streams of human experience and lived reality. Galeano's work, as one voice in the construction of such a deep context, is important insofar as it insists on alternatives to master narratives that refuse to address such deep contexts in the shaping of basic realities that determine how and why people live the lives they do, oppressed, disadvantaged, exploited, and bound by legal and economic norms not of their own making. What madness, for instance, produces the megalopolises of São Paulo and

Mexico City, whose urban growth is clearly unsustainable, not to mention profoundly destructive? As Galeano claims, "The inhabitants of Latin America's largest cities spend their days praying for rain to cleanse the air or wind to carry the poison elsewhere. Mexico City, the largest city in the world, lives in a state of perpetual environmental emergency" (*Upside Down* 237). The norms of squalor, pollution, unchecked development, and so forth can hardly be thought the true expression of how people choose to live and organize.

Dussel's comments on relative morality and absolute ethics are pertinent here: "What is good today can be evil tomorrow—not because the principle of good and evil is relative, but because circumstances can change. (And the first circumstance is the *cycle* of the prevailing system as an all-encircling totality)" (*Ethics and Community* 99). The system that is pervasive establishes contexts and norms as a function of the circumstances of the power it enacts. When these circumstances change, as they can through the forces of critique and resistance, the morally acceptable can be dramatically transformed into its other. Dussel, for instance, in a passage that resonates with many of the passages from Galeano that we have cited in this chapter, observes that

> The daily newspapers are filled with news of the actions and projects of persons, especially politicians, calculated to fall in perfectly with the intentions and principles of a particular social group. An example would be the United States' Strategic Defense Initiative [SDI], or "Star Wars." It is imperative that we learn to distinguish the absolute from the relative in all of these daily events. (*Ethics and Community* 99)

The supposed and spurious security produced by the SDI, as well as its association with a moral absolute, must be aggressively contextualized. One context that proffers itself is consistently articulated by Galeano and others horrified at the allocation of enormous economic resources and human energies to weapons technology when hunger and illiteracy are globally rampant. Drinan notes how the American Presidential Commission on World Hunger "comment[ed] that the vast sum spent by the United States and other nations on arms and armies (about $900 billion in 1986) made it almost impossible to feed the hungry around the world" (*Cry of the Oppressed* 184).

Galeano, too, connects the production of arms with the powers that control the United Nations, implicitly suggesting that the rights scenario produced out of such a context is duly compromised:

> Statistics compiled by the International Institute of Strategic Studies show the largest weapons dealers to be the United States, the United Kingdom, France, and Russia. China figures on the list as well, a few places back. And these five countries, by some odd coincidence, are the very ones that can exercise vetoes in the UN Security Council. The right to a veto really means the right to decide. The General Assembly of the highest international institution, in which all countries take part, makes recommendations, but it's the Security Council that makes decisions...In other words,

world peace lies in the hands of the five powers that profit most from the big business of war. (*Upside Down* 116)

Faced with such an appalling ethical inequity, only one of many others,[24] the allocation of priorities in wealthy nations that pride themselves on democratic principles can only be considered perverse and contrary to the most basic of human rights, the right to food. The facile association of democratic institutions and states with a form of moral absolutism dependent on the discourse of human rights, then, will remain crucially flawed so long as the underlying theories and terms that ground the association are uncritically accepted. Galeano provides a useful window on the necessity of this critique in offering the following historical synopsis of how context produces meaning:

> Until not so many years ago, historians of Athenian democracy never mentioned slaves or women, except in passing. Slaves were a majority of the Greek population and women half of it. What would Athenian democracy have looked like from their point of view?
>
> The U.S. Declaration of Independence declared in 1776 that "all men are created equal." What did that mean from the point of view of the half a million black slaves whose status remained unchanged after the declaration was made? And to women, who still had no rights? To whom were they created equal?
>
> From the point of view of the United States, engraving the names of citizens who died in the Vietnam War on an immense marble wall in Washington was a just act. From the point of view of the Vietnamese killed in the U.S. invasion, there are sixty walls missing. (*Upside Down* 115)

One standing wall for sixty non-existent walls. The aggressor memorialized as both victim and defender of freedom and democratic rights. The absence of solidarity between the victims on both sides of the war marked by the wall. Slaves' and women's servitude as the hidden structures on which democracy founds itself. And thus a concise history of inequality in the name of equality. Such iterations are barely the beginning of a vast context for producing meaningful structures of understanding that would preface change and that are a form of change themselves. To learn the questions that transform reality from an imposed cipher predicated on amnesia (that effaces detailed context) into a space where the rights and responsibilities coincident with such questionings are made manifest reality is the radical challenge posed by Galeano's writings.

The Unspeakable Legacy of Infinite Cruelty and Suffering: After Columbus, After Auschwitz, After...

With some notable exceptions, world order has been analyzed for centuries as if human suffering were irrelevant, and as if the only fate that mattered was either the destiny of a particular nation or the more general rise and fall of great powers. (Falk 173)

The conquest of the New World set off two vast demographic catastrophes, unparalleled in history: the virtual destruction of the indigenous population of the Western hemisphere, and the devastation of Africa as the slave trade rapidly expanded to serve the needs of the conquerors, and the continent itself was subjugated. Much of Asia too suffered "dreadful misfortunes." (Chomsky, *Year 501* 5)

Galeano's work makes striking affirmations about what it means to be human and to have rights, affirmations that replace the shameless instrumentality or benign neglect of legal and lexical definitions with an incisively different discourse. Galeano tells of alternative histories that put the question of rights and their actualization into a very different public context. This context is as much a function of aesthetic as of substantive choices made by a writer. In Galeano's case, it is instructive to examine how he addresses, for example, the year 1948, so crucial to seminal developments in the legal history of human rights because it was the year in which the Universal Declaration was ratified. 1948 is construed as the beginning of a new momentum in global sensitivity to human rights issues necessitated by the monstrous legacy of World War II (35 million dead), not to mention the unspeakable horrors of Auschwitz and all that for which it has become such a resonant symbol. These events are often cited as the crucial historical determinants in the creation of pan-global human rights instruments like the Universal Declaration: as MacKinnon remarks, "Horror at the Holocaust grounds modern morality" (99).

Further, Drinan observes that "In 1988, the [U.S.] State Department and the U.S. Holocaust Memorial Museum co-sponsored a conference in Washington attended by forty-four governments and thirteen nongovernmental organizations. The conference helped bring about the enactment of restitution laws in several European nations. *The Holocaust, the report notes, more than any other event brought about the human rights movement*; it is therefore necessary to move forward while the past is still a living memory" (*A Worldview of Human Rights* 92; our emphasis). The questions of how memory is neutralized or effaced, let alone how it is constituted and sustained, are critical to Galeano's work across a number of genres. For whom is memory alive? How is it sustained and narrated? What pressures exist to efface and reshape it to conform to particular ideological ends? The full ethical dimensions of a document like the Universal Declaration founded uniquely on "living memory" would, in such a context, be highly debatable, if only because it foundationally excludes the specificity of other memories and other agencies through which memory is expressed, human difference articulated. The otherness of the memories so excluded needs recuperation in order to extend the ethical dimensions of the Universal Declaration beyond its narrow Eurocentric focus, regardless of its supposed universality. As Galeano notes in a vignette entitled "Celebration of Contradictions/1," "Lively memory...is born every day, springing from the past and set against it. Of all the words in the German language *aufheben* was Hegel's favorite. *Aufheben* means both to preserve and to annul, and thus pays homage to human history, which is born as it dies and builds as it destroys" (*The Book of Embraces* 124).

But these comments suggest problems with historicizing rights primarily as a function of the events of World War II. One such problem is the way in which this form of historical logic implicitly erases other genocidal contexts in which the abuse of rights and human dignities has been extreme, foundational, and influential in the formation of Occidental moral, political, economic, and literary cultures. Take, for instance, the extraordinary events that unfolded in Cajamarca in 1532, where Pizarro, the conqueror of the Incas, led a massacre in the name of God that ultimately made him "the richest man in the world," bringing in "eighty-three kilos of solid gold" (Galeano, *Genesis* 89).[25] Eyewitness accounts of this "first encounter" by Francisco de Xerez and Cristóbal de Mena "estimated the Andean dead...[at] between 6,000 and 8,000" (Adorno, "Colonial Reform" 365). Galeano's telling of the story makes explicit the connections among religion, imperial culture, and the dream of infinite wealth, suggesting that the civil (rights) dimensions of encounter from the perspective of Spanish interests are utterly meaningless.

> The priest Vicente de Valverde emerges from the shadows and goes to meet Atahualpa [leader of the Incas]. He raises the Bible in one hand and a crucifix in the other, as if exorcising a storm on the high seas, and cries that here is God, the true one, and that all the rest is nonsense. The interpreter translates and Atahualpa, at the head of the throng, asks: "Who told you that?"
>
> "The Bible says it, the sacred book."
>
> "Give it here so it can tell me."
>
> A few paces away, Pizarro unsheathes his sword.
>
> Atahualpa looks at the Bible, turns it over in his hand, shakes it to make it talk, and presses it against his ear. "It says nothing. It's empty."
>
> And he drops it to the ground.
>
> Pizarro has been awaiting this moment ever since the day he knelt before Emperor Charles V, described the [Inca] empire as big as Europe that he had discovered and proposed to conquer, and promised him the most splendid treasure in human history...
>
> Pizarro yells and pounces. At the signal, the trap is sprung. From the ambush trumpets blare, arquebuses roar, and the cavalry charges the stunned and unarmed crowd. (*Genesis* 87-88)

The ensuing bloodbath establishes the terms of encounter as governed by the cynical extraction of wealth regardless of the cost in human lives. And it references a multitude of similar encounters that ground the foundation of the post-conquest Americas. While the dead letter of the Judeo-Christian bible does not speak to Atahualpa, Pizarro perversely dreams of conquering a territory as large as Europe, a curious, ironic anticipation of similar dreams that have led to the enormous suffering and cruelty in twentieth-century Europe. Thus, the title to this subsection places Galeano's various critiques—his critique of history from above, his economic and social critiques of the ways in which the Americas have developed, and his implicit critique of how literary culture has largely failed to address the enormous moral and ethical problems bequeathed by post-conquest America to the world—in relation to rights theories that largely evacuate the conquest from the historical contingencies to which they respond. Or, as Dussel frames it, after the conquest "The Indians had to recompose entirely their existence to endure the inhuman oppression that was their lot as the first victims of modernity, the first modern holocaust" (*The Invention of the Americas* 120).[26]

Dussel takes his use of "holocaust" from Russell Thornton's demographic study of aboriginal populations from 1492 to the twentieth century. Thornton argues that "In fact, the holocaust of the North American tribes was, in a way, even more destructive than that of the Jews, since many American Indian peoples became extinct" (xv-xvi). Thornton estimates "figures of 72+ million aboriginal American Indians in the Western Hemisphere and 7+ million north of the Rio Grande" as compared to a world population "circa 1500 [that] may have totaled around 500 million" (36). He goes on to suggest that "One of the more important demographic events in the history of the world may be Columbus's landing on Guanahani. Subsequently, as a direct result, the native peoples of the Western Hemisphere underwent centuries of demographic collapse and geographic concentration. Their total numbers were reduced to but a few million before a population recovery began" (42). Wright puts this slightly differently, stating that "Within decades of Columbus's landfall, most of these people [Native Americans] were dead and their world barbarously sacked by Europeans. The plunderers settled in America, and it was they, not the original people, who became known as Americans" (*Stolen Continents* 4). To limit the context of the cruelty and suffering to indigenous Americans, however, is insufficient: Falk notes that "[The] criminality of the West includes the genocidal ordeal of indigenous peoples who stood in the way of colonial conquerors; it extends to the horrifying reliance on slavery as the basis of economic development in the New World; and it relates to the deprivations and humiliations of the colonial era, to the continuing exploitation of the poor, and to the ecological plunder of the planet" (91). To this may be added the suffering experienced by the forced immigrants from Europe, who were sold into indentured servitude.

Dussel's likening of the conquest to a holocaust is deliberate and meant to address its status as an abstract referent for both the structures that enabled the conquest and the specific acts of cruelty associated with it that led to modernity. In this sense, he critiques any language system that confers upon the conquest an abstract, transcendental, and intangible quality. Theodor Adorno, writing after the holocaust of World War II, argued that "Thoughts intended to think the inexpressible by abandoning thought falsify the inexpressible. They make of it what the thinker would least like it to be: the monstrosity of a flatly abstract object" (110). This "monstrosity of a flatly abstract object" has multiple referents (suggested by the ellipses in the title of this section) that rights discourse must address as fully as possible in order to be in any way meaningful. When Adorno famously claimed that "After Auschwitz, our feelings resist any claim of the positivity of existence as sanctimonious, as wronging the victims" (361), an understanding of what this meant in relation to post-conquest modernity (insofar as the suffering of indigenous populations in the Americas is concerned) was almost entirely lacking from Occidental official discourse. Nonetheless, Adorno well understood that human suffering was not (could never be) contained by the trope of the holocaust, and that the right to express "perennial suffering" (362) was coincident with resistance to the indifference in which that suffering has habitually been framed. (Adorno's unfortunate phrase reads: "Perennial suffering has as much right to expression as a tortured man has to scream" [362].)

The unspeakable legacy of infinite cruelty and suffering to which "we" are heritors demands a response, not only to memorialize the breadth, range, and particularity of that cruelty and suffering (within the limits of the possible) but also to resist the perpetuation of the structures that continue to produce them. In no way do we mean to suggest that the post-Columbus genocide is an equivalent, lesser, or greater moral evil than is Auschwitz or any other catastrophic abuse of state power. The bases of such a comparison are (would be) odious and perverse if only for the way in which they eliminate the specificity of human agency in particular acts of egregious cruelty that are beyond reductive representation, beyond comparison.[27] Specific people with specific histories, genealogies, and cultural contexts make specific decisions that result in other people, also with specific histories, genealogies, and cultural contexts, suffering. Who are these people and what circumstances have produced such a perverse deformation of their humanity? The particularity of each such act, however irreducible and irrecoverable, and the choice to make another suffer are bound by the paradox that memorialization necessarily fails to be equivalent to the act itself, the particularity of the interaction between the tortured and the torturer.

The summary execution of indigenous populations in Guatemala in the early 1980s, the horrific genocide perpetrated in Rwanda in the following decade, and the Serbian torture of Muslim women in rape/death camps are instances that, in involving the partial witnessing of itemized acts of egregious cruelty done to specifically named people, can never approach the full scope of the barbarity of the acts in and of themselves, however specific the documentation.[28] The connection between such acts and the abstractions and transcendental principles of the Universal Declaration, not to mention other unenacted human rights instruments, is seemingly distant—that is, until one understands that rights instruments are all too often a function of discourses of state and national self-interest that have had insidious effects. Recall the words of Julio Simón (known as Julián the Turk in an especially sinister bit of racist nomination), a notoriously vicious Argentine thug responsible for extreme acts of cruelty for which he is unrepentant: "What I did I did for my Fatherland, my faith, and my religion. Of course, I would do it again" (qtd. in Feitlowitz 212). Recall, too, the words of Adolfo Francisco Scilingo, the man who publicly admitted to taking part in two death flights in Argentina in 1977, when 30 drugged, so-called subversives were thrown alive from navy airplanes into the Atlantic Ocean: "With regard to the subversives who had been condemned to death, Mendía [Vice Admiral Luis María Mendía, then Chief of Naval Operations] told us they 'would fly,' and that ecclesiastic authorities had assured him that this was a Christian, basically nonviolent form of death" (qtd. in Feitlowitz 195-96).

Both Simón and Scilingo make explicit the connection between national self-interest as expressed by state actions and egregious acts of cruelty. Both articulate the connection between institutional power and torture. To be clear, nation and religious authority combine to motivate and sanction extraordinary abuses in these men's testimonies. And such a structure, as we have already shown in some detail, has deep historical roots linked to the way in which post-Columbian acts of barbarity were carried out in the name of national self-interest. What to do when the understanding of such connections is itself barely present, acknowledged, or theorized in the construction of a response to cruelty evident in, for example, the burgeoning human rights discourse we have been describing throughout this chapter? What to do when the understanding that drives the response is only partial, repressed, or, for whatever reason, ideologically obscured or warped, dehistoricized, or historicized in only the most minimal and self-serving of ways?

In the case of Scilingo, Galeano tells the twisted story of how the Argentine state reacted after his confession:

> At the beginning of 1995, Captain Scilingo decided to make a public confession: he said he had thrown thirty people into the sea. Over the course of two years, he added, the Argentine Navy had thrown between fifteen hundred and two thousand political prisoners to the sharks.
>
> After his confession, Scilingo was imprisoned. Not for having murdered thirty people but for having passed a bad check. (*Upside Down* 194)

Impunity and indifference, the key evils Galeano implicitly identifies in this anecdote, mark the state's incapacity to address crimes against humanity, its moral and ethical cowardice, not to mention its profoundly skewed values clearly marked by the relative fate of Scilingo in relation to the political prisoners he murdered. Remember that to become a political prisoner under this régime was excessively easy. Mónica Brull, for instance, one of those "kidnapped, tortured, and subjected [by Julián the Turk] to mock executions," was part of a group that "had spearheaded legislation (unanimously passed by the [Argentine] Senate in 1975) to protect the handicapped from labor discrimination" (Feitlowitz 212). Subversion in this sense *is* the promotion of rights. Remember, too, that barely a year after Scilingo participated in "Christian" and "nonviolent forms of death" as sanctioned by ecclesiastical authorities, the then future U.S. president Ronald Reagan, in a syndicated column in the

Miami News (October 20, 1978), had this to say in support of the state-sponsored terror occurring in Argentina: "Jose A. Martínez de Hoz, [Argentine Minster of the Economy] said that Argentina had faced a well-equipped, disciplined force of 15,000 terrorists who were destroying the 'social fabric' of the country. 'What the government had to do was protect the human rights of 25 million people against a minority of people who had gone ideologically haywire,' he said" (qtd. in Drinan, *Cry of the Oppressed* 89). U.S. support for measures taken against so-called terrorists like Brull, who in another context would be hailed as effective human rights advocates, are well-known. As Galeano notes, the School of Americas (Fort Benning, Georgia) "had trained Latin American military officers in the arts of threat, torture, kidnapping, and murder" and that

> Their Latin American students numbered some sixty thousand…nearly all the officers responsible for the assassinations of the archbishop, Monsignor Oscar Arnulfo Romero, and four U.S. nuns were graduates of the School of Americas. So were those who carried out the murders of six Jesuit priests riddled with bullets in 1989…The greatest power in the world, the model, the democracy that inspires the most envy and imitation, acknowledged that its military nurseries had been growing specialists in the violation of human rights. (*Upside Down* 194-95)[29]

The rights implications of Galeano's vignette about Scilingo, let alone the connections between localized sovereign acts of cruelty supported in an international context by the "leader" in the advocacy of democratic rights, are profound. The matrix of stories we bring together here highlights the disregard of state structures (whether within a sovereign or an international context) for the kind of accountability implicit in the formation of universal rights instruments. If anything, then, the complicity of sovereign and international state structures with outrageous abuses of basic human rights after the passing of the Universal Declaration suggests that perhaps these are not the best forums in which to develop and enact meaningful rights instruments. Scilingo's case, like the sorry story of the judicial proceedings around the My Lai massacre (March 16, 1968) in which of the two officers charged with the murder of at least 128 Vietnamese civilians one was acquitted and the other had his sentence severely reduced (Lt. William Calley served three-and-a-half years), all this after a cover-up by the U.S. military, suggests the degree to which guarantees of state responsibility in the enactment of human rights justice are woefully inadequate. And this is especially so given U.S. self-promotion about being the foremost democracy in the world, the putative leader in advancing rights issues worldwide.

Moreover, in the broader historical context of modernity, state responsibility has taken on an unconscionably narrow meaning as a function of localized applications of the concept of liberty: as Dussel states, "Modernity has shown its double face even to this day by upholding liberty (the essential liberty of the person in Hobbes or Locke) *within* Western nations, while at the same time encouraging enslavement *outside them*" (*The Invention of the*

Americas 123). What to do when the meaning of rights (and by this "meaning" we understand that which is enacted, not merely understood in principle) is limited to the dominant countries that tolerate and even promote abuse beyond their borders? What to do when the same states that perpetrate egregious abuses of rights are the same states that devise the very instruments that nominally address those abuses? In this section, our intent is to examine how particular historical representations of the genesis of human rights discourse exclude an alternative genealogy, one that must be recuperated in good faith if the discourse of rights is to have any validity at all.

Again, Galeano's literary work cannot be underestimated, for it gathers the lost fragments of historical and literary narratives that reveal crucial aspects of indigenous and other marginalized cultures' post-conquest experiences. Those acts of memory insist on reinstating the fundamental knowledge of the enormity of the cruelty and suffering that have been the post-Columbian legacy to the world: "Since the colonial adventure of the Americas converted the Indians and the Blacks into slaves of European development, their cultures have survived the greatest process of annihilation in human history" (Galeano, "The Revolution as Revelation" 12). Or, more provocatively, consider Galeano's comments on the worldwide problem of hunger:

> Bodies out of camps. Auschwitzes of hunger. A system for purification of the species? Aimed at the "inferior races" (which reproduce like rabbits), starvation is used instead of gas chambers. And for the same price, a method of population control. The epoch of peace was ushered in with the atom bombs of Hiroshima and Nagasaki. For want of world wars, starvation checks population explosion…Sick with the plague of death, this world that eradicates the hungry instead of hunger produces food enough for all of humanity and more. (*We Say No* 251)[30]

Out of this insistence on the enormity of ongoing cruelty and suffering, which grounds Galeano's critique of how the Americas have been exploited, comes the possibility of imagining the space of the Americas anew. Ultimately, meaningful rights talk in regard to the Americas cannot occur until this legacy of cruelty and suffering is understood, however incompletely, then acted upon. To be clear, acting upon this legacy

Infinite Cruelty. From *The Book of Embraces*, 261, Eduardo Galeano.

requires attention to the infinitely small gestures of everyday life that ground community as an expression of reciprocal engagement with the other and to the grand historical gestures made by those charged with the responsibility of governance.

The genesis of a shared legal context for articulating human rights among a "community of nations" issues from a particular way of historicizing the world, which is also a particular way of producing narrative that has significant literary dimensions. In this case, the pre-Universal Declaration narrative effaces important historical referents related to the genocidal history from which the Americas emerged and that allowed the rapid transformation of Europe from a peripheral socioeconomic space into a central axis for the production and movement of world capital. The question Galeano implicitly asks is what legitimacy such a rights structure can have, especially in terms of ideals relating to fairness and universality, when it is so transparently a function of colonial American and Euro-centric narratives of what constitutes actionable horror and ethical provocation. This questionable legitimacy, no matter how laudable the language of the Universal Declaration, is especially troubled when apposed to a little-advertised fact. When the Universal Declaration was adopted as a resolution by the United Nations in 1948, "states that voted for its adoption did not bind themselves to adhere to its principles," though, as Drinan suggests, "it may be argued that it has become a part of the body of customary international law" (*Cry of the Oppressed* 32).

Nonetheless, the Universal Declaration purports to represent a "community of nations" even as it issues from a modernist European and American context in which community has meant the nation-state and in which the plurality of practices surrounding the production of community has been severely restricted in the name of national community. A good example of this occurs in the way in which monies are disbursed by the Pentagon for military uses, with little accountability to the plural practices of community in the U.S. that might be expected to have input into such disbursements: "The Pentagon assigns 80 per cent of its contracts directly to industrial corporations without public bidding. A good part of the citizen's budget, then, is spent on instruments of destruction without any competition...behind the public's back" (Dussel, *Ethics and Community* 165). This limiting of the community has had particular consequences for the marginalized, especially Amerindian and Black communities, who have seen persistent attacks on any form of alternative to community as defined by the legal and political orthodoxies associated with the modernist nation-state: "Nineteenth-century liberalism, however, struck a second fatal blow to the Indians by enshrining an abstract, bourgeois, individualist, civic life, instituting private property in the countryside, and suppressing communal modes of living" (Dussel, *The Invention of the Americas* 120).

Chomsky cites the example of the removal of the Cherokee from their lands "east of the Mississippi" to Oklahoma via the Trail of Tears in which "17,000 Cherokees were driven at bayonet point to Oklahoma by the U.S. Army" (*Year 501* 230) in 1838. By 1883, having survived complete displacement, the decimation caused by the forced removal and the Trail of Tears, as well as having built a community that was debt-free, had schools and hospitals, and had no homeless people (because of the principle of communal landholding), the Oklahoma Cherokee were subjected to legislation that attacked their right *not* to own property. Chomsky details how Senator Henry Dawes of Massachusetts argued that "Till this people will consent to give up their lands, and divide them among their citizens so that each can own the land he cultivates, they will not make much more progress" (qtd. in *Year 501* 232). The resultant legislation that prohibited communally-owned property and was introduced by Dawes led to dispossession, looting, and the "scatter[ing of the Cherokee] to remote urban areas where they suffered appalling poverty and destitution" (*Year 501* 232). Remember that this was for the crime of *not* owning property—an extraordinary abuse of rights and an attack on alternative notions of how communities sustain themselves. Seen in this light, Article 17, sections 1-2 of the Universal Declaration, which advocates the right to own property and not to be "arbitrarily deprived" of property, takes on sinister overtones: for the nineteenth-century Oklahoma Cherokee, this Article would have done nothing to protect their threatening notion of community, free as it was of the concept of individually-owned property.

Born of post-war ethical remorse that sponsored urgent debate about universal standards to prevent war and other affronts to human dignity and security (though cynics might argue that it was also born of a recognition that some serious PR was required to heal the wounds of the war) as well as out of a curious legal void in which its independent articles were non-enforceable, let alone non-binding, *to the states that voted for its adoption*, the 1948 Universal Declaration is indeed a curious and ambiguous document. The Universal Declaration and its correlated covenants, like the Convention on the Elimination of All Forms of Racial Discrimination (1969), the Convention on the Elimination of All Forms of Discrimination Against Women (CEDAW; 1979), the Declaration on the Right to Development (1986), and the Convention on the Rights of the Child (1989), have been particularly hindered in their instrumentality by the appalling record of the United States in the ratification of these documents. The self-righteousness and the moral hypocrisy of the United States in this regard have done great harm to the progress of the implementation of meaningful rights instruments worldwide. Many commentators have addressed this in considerable detail; suffice it to say that the United States has not ratified or supported the following, among others: the formation of the International Criminal Court (ICC) in June 1998 in Rome and "the U.N. covenants on economic rights, the rights of women, and the rights of the child" (Drinan, *A Worldview of Human Rights* 79). In the case of the Convention on the Rights of the Child, the "only other nation that [has] not ratified the treaty [is] Somalia" (*Human Rights Watch World Report 2000* 401) while the *Amnesty International Report 2000* states that "U.S. authorities continued to violate international standards protecting children" (252). Moreover, "[the United States] has not accepted the Inter-American Convention on

Human Rights (also known as the American Convention on Human Rights) or the Treaty on the Law of the Sea" (*Amnesty International 2000* 252). Additionally, the United States has "not returned to UNESCO, has declined to sign the world agreement on banning land mines [this despite it being the worst perpetrator of mining in the Western hemisphere around the American military base in Guantánamo, Cuba], and has not ratified the International Convention on the Elimination of All Forms of Racial Discrimination (even though 129 other nations have)" (Drinan, *A Worldview of Human Rights* 56).[31]

With regard to Guantánamo, it is important to know that "In 1903, the U.S. government used the Platt Amendment, imposed on Cuba as a condition of independence, to slice off 116 sq. km. of Cuban territory at the mouth of the Bahía de Guantánamo...The whole facility is surrounded by trenches, security fences, watch towers, and a 'no-man's-land,' where U.S. troops have laid 75,000 mines in 22 areas, the largest minefield in the Western Hemisphere" (Stanley 497). The hypocrisy of this situation in light of the U.S. paranoia around the ostensible threat posed by Cuba is staggering but predictable. In the case of the U.S. withdrawal from UNESCO, Galeano provides the following explanation:

> In the early eighties, UNESCO proposed an initiative based on the truth that news is not a simple commodity but a social right and that the communications media should bear the responsibilities commensurate with the educational purpose they serve. UNESCO set out to create an independent international news agency working from the countries that suffer the indifference of the factories of information and fear. Even though the proposal was framed in ambiguous and cautious terms, the U.S. government thundered furiously against such an attack on freedom of information. What business did UNESCO have sticking its nose into matters pertaining to the living forces of the market? (*Upside Down* 282)

The *Human Rights Watch World Report 2000* observes that as recently as 1999, "the U.S. continued to exempt itself from many of its international human rights obligations, particularly where international human rights law granted protections or redress not available under U.S. law. In ratifying international human rights treaties it typically carved away added protections for those in the U.S. by adding reservations, declarations and understandings. *Even years after ratifying key human rights treaties, the U.S. still failed to acknowledge international law as U.S. law*" (401; our emphasis).

The protectionism and isolationism behind these failures remains a huge hindrance to the instrumentality of human rights agreements, given the power and influence wielded by the American state. If a Pinochet or a Milosevic can be charged with crimes against humanity, the international community has the right to ask why a Kissinger will not be so charged (as Christopher Hitchens has forcefully argued), a person whose record in numerous instances, when judged in light of international human rights and international legal covenants, is more than worthy of interrogation. The same may be said for American president

Harry S. Truman's decision to bomb Hiroshima and Nagasaki using nuclear weapons, both cities civilian *not* military targets, and thus a staggering violation of international conventions governing the conduct of war. Chomsky categorically states that "Every [American president]...has been involved either directly or indirectly in atrocities and war crimes" (*Chronicles of Dissent* 264). The limitation of the concept of crimes against humanity to acts of war conducted by nation-states suggests a legal framework for the concept that is still inchoate and subject to further development in terms of theory and precedent. Why the concept would not extend to transnational corporations, for instance, is a good question worth further exploration, especially when such entities circumvent or degrade via various global trade agreements the legal, political, and economic structures that are definitive of national sovereignty.

The concept of crimes against humanity is especially relevant for corporate entities that commit egregious acts in violation of the environment, worker's rights, community health, and so forth. Important provisos must necessarily attach to such an expanded definition of crimes against humanity that builds on the operative conditions currently in place. For instance, the specific violation would have to have been conducted with the knowledge of specific agents within a corporate entity who either know or should have the responsibility of knowing about the harm that leads to grave personal injury for a large number of people. Thalidomide, Bhopal, and Love Canal are but a few examples of what might qualify for such a charge, as might be IBM's alleged complicity in facilitating the Final Solution (see Black). To this shortlist may be added McClintock's catalog of ecological disasters supported by the World Bank:

> ...the Indonesian Transmigrasi programme, the Amazonian Grande Carajas iron-ore and strip-mining project, and Tucurui Dam deforestation project, and so on. The Polonoreste scheme in Brazil carved a paved highway through Amazonia, luring timber, mining and cattle ranching interests into the region with such calamitous impact that in May 1987 even the President of the World Bank, Mr. Barber Conable, confessed he found the devastation sobering. (95)

Where conditions of reciprocal responsibility (thought in terms of broad outcomes related to health, security, freedom, to mention a few) between transnational corporations and international monetary organizations and the peoples with whom they conduct their business are disavowed in harmful ways, such an expanded legal concept of crimes against humanity may well provide an important transnational protection against such abuses. The necessary condition for civil conduct is reciprocal responsibility. Lack of such a standard connotes the absence of the civil as a meaningful condition of social organization. As the opening line to Aimé Césaire's *Discourse on Colonialism* suggests, "A civilization that proves incapable of solving the problems it creates is a decadent civilization" (9).

Part dream, part hope, part amnesia, part illusion, perhaps the most important effect of the Universal Declaration was to inaugurate the debate over how to theorize, historicize, and indeed narrativize the aspirations to build a consensus regarding meaningful human rights policies and instruments. Part of that debate has necessitated questioning, however painful and difficult, the underlying principles and *raisons d'être* of the Universal Declaration, something that Galeano has consistently (and implicitly) done in his published work for decades. In Galeano's historical conception, for instance, 1948 gets an entirely different focus than that of post-Auschwitz Europe. Galeano's alternative focus reminds readers about the difference between practice and ideal in the construction of rights theories and histories depending on context (in this case, Latin American as opposed to European). *Century of the Wind,* the third volume of the *Memory of Fire* trilogy, does not once mention the Universal Declaration in its 1948 segments, promoting instead an entirely different perspective. The first entry on 1948 focuses on the Ninth Pan-American Conference in Bogotá, Columbia. The meeting brought together Latin American foreign ministers desperate for development funds, General George Marshall—then American Secretary of State, originator of the Marshall Aid plan whose implementation was a crucial element in the reconstruction of post-war Europe, and soon-to-be winner of the Nobel Peace Prize (1953)—and John McCloy, head of the World Bank. Galeano scores the point that while Marshall "irrigates" Europe with cash, McCloy "warns: *'I'm sorry, gentlemen, but I didn't bring my checkbook in my suitcase'*" (131).

Galeano neatly encapsulates, in McCloy's own words, the hypocrisy about post-war economic disparities and allocation of resources that were to have a profound effect on the politics of rights, let alone the human development realities, in Latin America. The *Human Development Report 2000,* for instance, lists countries by a Human Development Index (HDI), which ranks countries by life expectancy at birth, adult literacy, and educational enrolment indicators. Even in a region as rich in resources, human and natural, the highest a Latin American country places out of 174 countries is 35th (Argentina), below such nations as Malta, Cyprus, Barbados, and the Bahamas.[32] Rawls makes an appalling argument using Argentina as an example of a resource-rich country that has "serious difficulties" by comparison with resource-poor Japan: "The crucial elements that make the difference are the political culture, the political virtues and society of the country, its members' probity and industriousness, their capacity for innovation, and much else" (108). The passage effectively slurs Argentina and its citizens while ignoring the external economic and historical factors that have produced its "serious difficulties," and unthinkingly propagates the stereotypes of the industrious Asians and the lazy Latins. The concepts of duty and responsibility are effectively evacuated from Rawls's formulation, predicated as it is on an isolationist ethic that compromises any "rights" discourse based on such premises.

Brazil, a target nation for American investment and growth, with enormous resources at its disposal, ranks a miserable 74th; Bolivia ranks 114th. Nancy Scheper-Hughes, the distinguished American anthropologist, notes that "Approximately one million children younger than five die each year in Brazil, or about forty children every hour. An estimated 25 percent of all infant deaths in Latin America occur in Brazil, and of these more than 50 percent take place in the Nordeste, which has an estimated infant mortality rate of 116/1,000 live births, one of the highest in the hemisphere and comparable to the poorest parts of Africa…And so despite the modernization of the Brazilian economy and its transformation into a world-class superpower, glossed in the 1970s as the Brazilian economic miracle…the rates of infant and child mortality did not show everywhere the expected decline" (279-80). What Scheper-Hughes calls the "modernization of child mortality" refers to the "containing of child death to one level of societyth—e very poorest, especially those millions of rural exiles now living in the teeming shantytowns and *mocambos*"—as well as to the fact that former causes of child death, primarily a function of infectious diseases, have been replaced by "infant malnutrition and diarrhea-caused dehydration, both related to bottle-feeding" (280). Further, as Galeano writes:

> Aid given by the North to the South is much less than the alms solemnly pledged before the United Nations, but it allows the North to dump its war junk, its surplus goods and development projects that underdevelop the South and spread the haemorrhage to cure the anaemia.
>
> Meanwhile over the last five years [1985-90], the South has donated to the North an infinitely larger sum, the equivalent of two Marshall Plans at constant prices, in the form of interest payments, profits, royalties and all kinds of colonial tribute. And meanwhile, the creditor banks for the North have gutted the debtor states of the South and ended up owning our public sector in exchange for nothing. ("The Other Wall" 8)

Galeano explicitly links the disparities he describes to being in the orbit of U.S. economic, political, and territorial interests in which reciprocal relations have *not* brought the promise but rather the lie of shared wealth. For Galeano, "Blinded by elitism, racism, sexism, and militarism, the Americas continue to ignore their own plenitude. And that's twice as true for the South: Latin America has the most fabulous human and vegetal diversity on the planet" (*Upside Down* 325).

Absence of self-recognition, especially as a function of cultural and biological diversity, the duplicitous discourses that deform human reality, the perpetuation of militaristic cultures, the economic exploitation in the name of development, all compromise the duty of (and right to) meaningful reciprocal relations and the just and equitable use of the plenitude of the Americas by its citizens. Here, Galeano advocates a shared responsibility to the diverse plenitude of the Americas. Implicit in his analysis is the importance of links between economic development and rights theories reluctant to address how historical inequalities and injustices are now so firmly entrenched as to make any meaningful rights discourse profoundly difficult to imagine, let alone enact.

But there are important qualifiers to be put in place with the language of development in relation to rights. For Galeano, development is far from the perverse economic model that depends on infinite expansion, growth, and progress as measured by purely economic indicators, as opposed to other standards that include widely disseminated literacy, quality of life as a function of the environment, infant mortality rates and health care generally, and a host of other factors that measure the "development" of quality of life. The co-extensive relationship between rights and development, seen in this latter light, is crucial to broadening human freedoms, dignity, and solidarity:

Human rights and human development are both about securing basic freedoms. Human rights express the bold idea that all people have claims to social arrangements that protect them from the worst abuses and deprivations—and that secure the freedom for a life of dignity.

Human development, in turn, is a process of enhancing human capabilities—to expand choices and opportunities so that each person can lead a life of respect and value. When human development and human rights advance together, they reinforce one another—expanding people's capabilities and protecting their rights and fundamental freedoms. (*Human Development Report 2000* 2)

This broadening of the contexts of rights, over and above the model based on state norms that we have been at pains to critique, is made explicit in Galeano's second 1948 episode in *Century of the Wind*, which in highly condensed form describes Jorge Eliécar Gaitán, leader of the Colombian Liberal Party, and provides a direct and intended contrast with the oligarchic state power represented by Marshall and McCloy.

The political country, says Jorge Eliécar Gaitán, *has nothing to do with the national country... What is the difference between liberal hunger and conservative hunger? Malaria is neither conservative nor liberal!*

This dignified leader, with the austere face of a statue, does not hesitate to denounce the oligarchy and the imperial ventriloquist on whose knee the oligarchs sit without life of their own or words of their own. He calls for agrarian reform and articulates other truths to put an end to the long lie. (132)

The scene set, Galeano's next vignette describes the *bogotazo*, a three-day street riot in Bogotá that follows upon the assassination of Gaitán on 9 April 1948. The catch to the story is that on that day "Gaitán has a date with one of the Latin American students who are gathered in Bogotá on the fringes of General Marshall's Pan-American ceremony." The meeting was set for 2:00 P.M.; "Gaitán's watch stopped at 1:05 P.M." (133). The student's name: Fidel Castro. With Marshall still in the city, all hell breaks loose and "After three days of vengeance and madness, a disarmed people returns to the old purgatory of work and woe. General Marshall has no doubts. The *bogotazo* was the work of Moscow. The government of Colombia breaks relations with the Soviet Union" (134-35). Subsequent vignettes devoted to 1948 point to further abuses of power in Latin America as a function of cold war antagonisms. Two detail the plight of the great Chilean poet Pablo Neruda, facing persecution in Chile, and travelling "from hideout to hideout" (136). In response, Pablo Picasso makes a speech "for the first and only time in his life" at a world congress of intellectuals for peace: "Picasso pays homage to *the greatest poet of the Spanish language and one of the greatest poets on earth, who has always taken the side of the unfortunate: Pablo Neruda, persecuted by the police in Chile, cornered like a dog*" (135-36).

As a coda to this sequence, Galeano shifts ground to Costa Rica and the six-week civil war there that culminates in José Figueres taking power. Figueres emblematizes the double standards with which Latin American governments are forced to live:

> [Figueres] outlaws the Communist Party and promises unconditional support to the struggle of the free world against Russian imperialism. But in an undertone he also promises to expand the social reforms the Communists have promoted in recent years...The anticommunist Figueres does not touch the lands of the United Fruit Company, that most powerful mistress, but nationalizes the banks and dissolves the army, so that money will not speculate, nor arms conspire. Costa Rica wants out of the ferocious turbulence of Central America. (136-37)

The choices made by Galeano in the sequencing of these vignettes are especially interesting in relation to the perspective that understands the Universal Declaration as one of the key events of 1948.[33]

Not only does Galeano move against a Eurocentric narrative of history, he also proleptically gestures toward the Cuban revolution as an extension of the resistant forces that temporarily emerge in reaction to Gaitán's assassination. Furthermore, the suspect coincidence of Marshall's presence in Bogotá with the assassination is implicit, as is the significance of the writer (Neruda) as an emblem of resistance to discourses of power, persecution, and injustice. And the Costa Rican civil war, with its highly ambiguous outcomes, hints at the Damocletian forces driving political decision-making in Latin America. Within the details of such a broad canvas, and set against a discourse of emergent rights, the sequence articulates a profound disconnection between the seeming forces of imperial benevolence and the actual conditions faced by Latin Americans resulting from their exploitation within a larger imperial context. As narrative sequence it is affective for the injustice it chronicles. But when juxtaposed with the Universal Declaration's appearance in the same year, it highlights not only the necessity of a meaningful discourse of rights but also the dangers in subscribing too quickly or uncritically to such a discourse, especially when it emerges from a context that disregards alternative (Latin American) realities.

Chomsky's analysis of U.S. policy in light of its human rights positioning, *The Umbrella of U.S. Power: The Universal Declaration of Human Rights and the Contradictions of U.S. Policy*, is instructive in its analysis of the Marshall Plan's "generosity and goodwill" (8):

For example, the fact that "as the Marshall Plan went into full gear the amount of American dollars being pumped into France and the Netherlands was approximately equaled by the funds being siphoned from their treasuries to finance their expeditionary forces in Southeast Asia," to carry out terrible crimes. And that under the U.S. influence Europe was reconstructed in a particular mode, not quite that sought by the anti-fascist resistance, though fascist and Nazi collaborators were generally satisfied.

Nor would it do to mention that the generosity was largely bestowed by American taxpayers upon the corporate sector, which was duly appreciative, recognizing years later that the Marshall Plan "set the stage for large amounts of private U.S. direct investment in Europe," establishing the basis for the modern Transnational Corporations, which "prospered and expanded on overseas orders...fueled initially by the dollars of the Marshall Plan" and protected from "negative developments" by "the umbrella of American power." (8-9)

Chomsky goes on to state that "Lars Schoultz, the leading academic specialist on human rights in Latin America, found that U.S. aid 'has tended to flow disproportionately to Latin American governments which torture their citizens...to the hemisphere's relatively egregious violators of fundamental human rights'...More wide-ranging studies by economist Edward Herman found a similar correlation world-wide, also suggesting a plausible reason: aid is correlated with improvement in the investment climate, often achieved by murdering priests and union leaders, massacring peasants trying to organize, blowing up the independent press, and so on" (10).

Chomsky's comments dramatically underscore the narrative choices made by Galeano in his resistant vignettes that recreate the year 1948: where the hypocrisy of Marshall in relation to Latin America is coincident with the murder of opposition politicians; where the influence of this hypocrisy on Castro in relation to the revolutionary roots of the Cuban revolution are ineluctably part of the skein of unfolding events; where the elaboration of universal rights is virtually meaningless in such a context, especially when those rights are an outcome of imperial states' self-interest; where the persecution of major literary voices of opposition is practiced in spite of powerful denunciations; and where the breadth of historical analysis is diminished by powerful master narratives that seek to control and eliminate alternatives like those proffered by Galeano. There are terrible ironies suggested by Galeano's narrative choices for 1948 that touch upon the incremental causes and effects that make history. The Colombian assassination obviously relates to Castro's revolutionary motivations, which is part of the context that leads to full-blown resistance to human rights abuses by the U.S.-sponsored Batista government in Cuba, which in turn spawns other forms of abuse in post-revolutionary Cuba as documented by Human Rights Watch. Despite its having been disallowed from visiting Cuba since 1995, Human Rights Watch chronicles a series of rights abuses that range from the death penalty to restrictions on labour rights to the surveillance of dissenters, the control of independent journalism, and the denial of "international human rights and humanitarian monitors access to the country" (*Human Rights Watch World Report 2000* 128). And these ironies, as both historical and literary effects, cannot be dissociated from those found in major human rights instruments that purportedly seek a form of universal justice. For these reasons, in the next section we will examine some of the stylistic features that characterize Galeano's writing practices, insofar as these relate to the intersection between emergent rights discourse and literary culture.

"We Say No": The Politics of Style

On 11 July 1988, two months prior to the plebiscite on General Pinochet's rule, Galeano delivered the opening speech to *Chile Crea* [Chile Creates], an international gathering of activists in support of democracy in Chile. The speech, made to a packed and emotional crowd under the watchful eye of the large military presence gathered outside the hall, outlines an oppositional politics that defines the central rights concerns of *We Say No*, Galeano's collection of essays, new journalistic pieces, speeches, interviews, letters, polemics, manifestoes, memories, and chronicles—the literary snapshots that have distinguished his approach to the forgotten and repressed histories of the Americas in tandem with his concern for issues that relate literary creation to human rights.

The question that consistently dominates Galeano's work in *We Say No* is how to articulate a politics of the word that averts and subverts its appropriation by those who seek to neutralize its latent powers. How to give voice to a politics that re-members and opposes the tortures, degradations, atrocities, and suffering that are a product of a politics that silences and elides its unspeakable nature? As Galeano proclaims, "We have a right to the echo, not to the voice, and those who rule praise our talent to repeat parrot fashion. We say no: we refuse to accept this mediocrity as our destiny…we say no to the neutrality of the human word" (243). The rights dimensions of this sort of discourse are far-reaching and need to be carefully examined if Galeano's multiple writing practices are to be understood more fully. In our reading, the politics of literary style as a practice of potential critique and resistance is fundamentally linked to the ways in which rights discourse imagines itself, gives itself textual presence.

The practice of negation and refusal implicit in the Galeano citation above operates in conjunction with the right to speak: that is, style shapes the enactment of the right to speech. When Jean-François Lyotard argues that "the capacity to speak to others is a human right, and perhaps the most fundamental human right" (140-41), he is careful to qualify this right in terms that distinguish between different kinds of interlocution:

…the interlocutory capacity changes into a right to speak only if the speech can say something other than the *déjà dit* (what has already been said). The right to speak implies a duty to announce. If our speech announces nothing, it is doomed to repetition and the conservation of existing meanings. The human community may spread, but it will remain the same, prostrated in the euphoria it feels at being on such very good terms with itself. It is the main function of the media today to reinforce the interlocutory consent of the community. They are boring to the extent that they teach us nothing. Interlocution is not an end in itself. It is legitimate only if, through others, the Other announces to me something which I hear but do not understand. (142-43)

Galeano's project is focused in the active phrase "we say no" since it not only engages in the act of interlocution but also "announces" its resistance to a community of deception marked by discursive homogeneity, what Lyotard might call communities of assent, what Rawls might call "relations of affinity" (112).

What good comes of an act of interlocution in which nothing is exchanged but an unthought, phatic, uncritical consensus that the world is as it should be? Such exchanges are as meaningful as white noise and silence emptied of interlocutory listening. Nothing passes from one to the other because the two are defined by their interchangeability, not by their capacity to show solidarity with the other's difference. Rather than passive exchange, then, which deadens and diminishes, active exchange implies learning to question and to wonder. Such a mode of speech (which also implies a mode of listening) has significant implications for rights discourse. Rights talk, whether legal or political, has largely been predicated on consensus with regard to overarching, universal principles like equality, inalienability, freedom, justice, and peace (as in the Preamble to the Universal Declaration). But what would emerge if such a discourse were supplanted by the productive dissonance of ongoing interrogation as a function of difference (whether in terms of gender, class, or historical context)? What if the universalism of such a hegemonic discourse of rights were to be foregone for the materiality of a non-essentialized process that produces and attends to difference as a function of reciprocal modes of listening and acting on that listening? In short, what if material outcomes as a function of ongoing critical evaluation of the sort offered by Galeano (and others) were privileged over unenforceable transcendental principles?[34]

Galeano's form of literary interlocution clearly follows the former model with its explicit gestures toward the materiality of language as an expression of the lived relations and experiences specific people produce as well as with his refusal to confine literary aesthetics to the generic and canonic orthodoxies that literature has traditionally offered. These pronouncements are designed to speak from the differential position of the South, the disadvantaged, the dispossessed, and so forth to the hegemonic centre that hears but does not understand (in Lyotardian terms)—yet. The redemption of the word's potencies in relation to colonial cultures that neutralize or marginalize the forms of textuality inimical to their survival, then, is central to Galeano's project and has bearing on how an alternative rights discourse might possibly be configured. The dream of "marvelous possessions" (as troped by Stephen Greenblatt, an American critic) has been supplanted by Galeano's realization that "We are no longer in the era of marvels when fact surpassed fable and imagination was shamed by the trophies of conquest" (*Open Veins* 11). The politics of quietism, silence, and imitative complicity have been displaced by the responsibilities of a speech that only provisionally narrates the certainties of its multiple misrepresentations.

Responsible speech recognizes its provisional nature, that it necessarily involves an interlocutor in a position of contingency and reciprocity: "Reciprocity respects not only the alterity of interlocution but the parity of the interlocutors. It thus guarantees their respective liberty and their equality before the word" (Lyotard 140). The word and one's relation to it are indicative of one's contingency, which, ethically acknowledged, enables the reciprocal conditions that lead to solidarity. Solidarity is an interlocutory form that recognizes the simultaneous right to reciprocal dissent, reciprocal consent. But—and this is an important proviso—it does so in the mode of an interlocution that attempts to speak *as if* from the position of the other, all the while recognizing the impossibility of so doing. The double gesture of *trying to* while recognizing the *impossibility of* is the beginning of solidary interlocution. It is not a speaking in the place of the other, but an attempt to engage with what it means to speak from the position of the other and thus an ethical recognition of the personhood of all the parties engaged in interlocution.

Linda Craft observes that testimonial discourse presumes a "collective subject in the so-called democratization of literature" and notes that Rigoberta Menchú "insists that she speaks as only one of many who have suffered oppression," appearing "to subordinate her own singularity to the identity of the community" (21). The opening lines to Menchú's *testimonio* state the problem explicitly:

> My name is Rigoberta Menchú. I am twenty-three years old. This is my testimony. I didn't learn it from a book and I didn't learn it alone. I'd like to stress that it's not only *my* life, it's also the testimony of my people...The important thing is that what has happened to me has happened to many other people too: My story is the story of all poor Guatemalans. My personal experience is the reality of a whole people. (1)

The point here is tricky: the speaker inevitably gets pegged as singular even as she insists on her solidary relation to the other; even as she states that it is *her* testimony she speaks in the name of community. Solidarity and community, in other words, are extraordinarily difficult acts to undertake with ethical regard for the integrity of the other and of one's own relationship to the other. Or, as Paulo Freire indicates, "Solidarity requires that one enter into the situation of those with whom one is solidary; it is a radical posture" (*Pedagogy of the Oppressed* 31). Furthermore, "the oppressor is solidary with the oppressed only when he stops regarding the oppressed as an abstract category and sees them as persons who have been unjustly dealt with, deprived of their voice, cheated in the sale of their labor—when he stops making pious, sentimental, and individualistic gestures and risks an act of love...To affirm that men and women are persons and as persons should be free, and yet to do nothing tangible to make this affirmation a reality, is a farce" (*Pedagogy of the Oppressed* 31-32). The latter statement is especially applicable to human rights instruments in which enactment (whether through legislative ratification or through interventions that guarantee the material reality of the right as principle) is so often detached from the abstraction that underpins the right. The recognition is a necessary condition for the historical revision required to produce a meaningful context for the understanding of human rights as a function of empowered, reciprocal speech. Galeano's texts demonstrate some of the possible forms taken by empowered speech that invite the collision of reciprocity and difference.

Pedagogy of the Oppressed. Photograph by Ricardo Azouri, from *We Say No* (front cover).

In the ideological space out of which Galeano writes, the anti-narratives of postcolonial theory and the historical revisions that arise out of that theory must address a culture beset by both the manipulations of the mass media, turning history into collective amnesia through the promise of an eternal electronic presence, and by a politics of (in)difference, neutralizing memory through the lure of the credit card and its promise of an open-ended future firmly cathected on consumerism. Galeano has distinguished himself in the construction of such an anti-narrative as much for his power to render "neutral" words potent as for his ability to transform vague echoes into vocal singularities, at once passionate and disruptive. For example, "We Say No," the critical speech delivered by Galeano at *Chile Crea*, articulates a politics of de-idealization dependent on the discovery of the foundational lies that have been perpetuated about the "Discovery" and its aftermath.

This culture of lies, which vulgarly speculates with human love in order to extract its appreciation, is in reality a culture of broken bonds: its gods are its winners, the successful masters of money and power, and its heroes are uniformed "Rambos" who use their influence while applying the Doctrine of National Security. By what it says and fails to say, the dominant culture lies when it claims that the poverty of the poor is not a result of the wealth of the wealthy, but rather the daughter of no one, originating in a goat's ear or in the will of God, who created the lazy poor and the donkey. In the same way, the humiliation of some men by others does not necessarily have to motivate shared indignation or scandal, because it belongs to the natural order of things: let us suppose that Latin American dictatorships form part of our exuberant nature and not of the imperialist system of power. (242)

At once cajoling, sarcastic, poetic, the passage typifies Galeano's project, which in conservative Hispanist circles has been ignored or dismissed for its Marxist pretensions as much as for its utopian deconstructions of a materialism devoid of humanity, and its radical critique of an America that has attempted unsuccessfully to obliterate the political traditions of communitarianism that antedate the conquest. The passage takes on meaning in relation to rights discourse because it interrogates the mythification of dominant structures' widely disseminated master narratives. Freire has remarked how people are made passive

...by the oppressors' depositing myths indispensable to the preservation of the status quo: for example, the myth that the oppressive order is a "free society"; the myth that all persons are free to work where they wish, that if they don't like their boss they can leave him and look for another job; the myth that this order respects human rights and is therefore worthy of esteem; the myth that anyone who is industrious can become an entrepreneur—worse yet, the myth that the street vendor is as much an entrepreneur as the owner of a large factory; the myth of the universal right of education, when of all the Brazilian children who enter primary schools only a tiny fraction ever reach university; the myth of the equality of all individuals, when the question: "do you know who you're talking to?" is still current among us; the myth of the heroism of the oppressor classes as defenders of "Western Christian civilization" against "materialist barbarism"; the myth of the charity and generosity of the élites, when what they really do as a class is to foster selective "good deeds"...the myth that the dominant élites, "recognizing their duties," promote the advancement of the people, so that the people, in a gesture of gratitude, should accept the words of the élites and be conformed to them; the myth that rebellion is a sin against God; the myth of private property as fundamental to personal human development (so long as oppressors are the only true human beings); the myth of the industriousness of the oppressors and the laziness and dishonesty of the oppressed, as well as the myth of the natural inferiority of the latter and the superiority of the former. (*Pedagogy of the Oppressed* 120-21)

Freire's analysis, in addition to being part of the larger intellectual context of which Galeano is a part, coincides with the pedagogical effect produced by the literary dimensions of the demythification that both Galeano and Freire propose. Meaningful rights structures can only exist where the illusion of well-ordered relations among humans is replaced by a critical discourse that acknowledges and accounts for the systemic lies and paradoxes that shape how people are in the world. Resistant critical stances are therefore a crucial element in defining rights discourse in a meaningful way.

Such resistant discourses are not necessarily an outcome of academic critical contexts. For instance, the American critic Stanley Fish advised an audience at UCLA in the October 1986 meeting of the Humanities Institute: "Act as you think you're supposed to act in the institution where you work!" (qtd. in Merod 242n21), a position that immediately eradicates dissent against the norm of institutional practices (themselves obviously aligned with state practices). What does such an instrumental and unethical position (which essentially permits the lie of bad faith) mean in a state like Chile?

> Since there was little official recognition of human rights abuses, it was possible for sheltered and incurious Chileans to remain ignorant of gruesome cases years after they had become household words in other social sectors and abroad...Some well-to-do citizens, initially horrified by reports of repression, were soon seduced by the comfort and order of authoritarianism. Across dinner tables and tennis courts, people agreed that Chile wasn't 'ready for democracy,' and few were willing to face the opprobrium of employers and peers just to salve a troubled conscience. One banker confided that for years he hid his concern for human rights in order to avoid jeopardizing his social and professional position. 'In meetings, I often said things I didn't believe, so as not to go against the tide,' he confessed. 'The truth is, we were all afraid.'" (Constable and Valenzuela 145)

Ignorance, the seductions of comfort, repressed consciences, and fear align rights inaction with institutional cultures of power that seek precisely that effect. The negation of these effects begins in the rhetorical moment in which "we say no" in solidarity with others who say the same, and establishes a community of resistance, a concept to which we will return in the last chapter of this book.

Galeano's positing of the resurrection of the pre-colonial in the postcolonial along with Freire's deconstruction of widely disseminated myths about structures of dominance are no doubt subject to possible attack for their putative naïveté, their dogmatism, and their refusal to recognize how the real of today has superimposed itself irrevocably on the imagined possibilities of the future. Diana Palaversich, for instance, classifies Galeano's writings as postmodern, a term she associates with a politically committed writing practice. Yet Palaversich subtly undermines that practice by labeling it as a form of Manichean (dualistic) analysis that is at once uniform but predicated on simplistic oppositions between good and evil, rich and poor, powerful and oppressed, and so forth. In short, Palaversich ends up reproducing in her analysis the very dualism of which she is so critical:

El rasgo narrativo más sobresaliente de la obra de este escritor que lo acerca a la estilística postmoderna es su predilección por la viñeta y el collage de fragmentos de la realidad latinoamericana. Si bien esta fragmentación significa una ruptura de la forma narrativa continua, no representa la destrucción de una imagen integrada y homogénea del mundo, lo que sí se implica en el uso postmoderno del mismo recurso. El universo literario de Galeano es seguro e uniforme, en cuanto sigue permanentemente polarizado entre los buenos y malos, explotadores y explotados, colonizadores y colonizados, ricos y pobres. (*Silencio* 246-47)

[The most salient narrative feature of this writer's work associated with the postmodern aesthetic is his predilection for vignettes and collages that incorporate fragments of Latin American reality. Although this fragmentation signals a break with continuous narrative form, it does not represent the destruction of an integral and homogeneous image of the world, which would be the implication when this same method is put to postmodern use. Galeano's literary universe is stable and uniform, in that it is forever polarized between good guys and bad guys, exploiters and exploited, colonizers and colonized, rich and poor.]

What sounds like an attack on Galeano's supposedly simplistic worldview is mitigated by being attributed to the societies in which postcolonial writers live. Why these societies should be radically different from First World societies is not examined, nor is the interdependence of all societies in a "global economy," even if one rejects the notion that economics explains everything. Palaversich's characterization of postcolonial society implies that postmodernism can only be practiced in affluent countries, the implicit assumption being that there is no polarization there:

La estructura maniquea de la narrativa de Galeano y otros escritores postcoloniales corresponde a la estructura maniquea de la sociedad en que viven...Rechazar la estructura binaria de la sociedad en que se vive significaría perder de vista las fuerzas políticas, sociales e ideológicas que rigen en el mundo y escamotear lo que Fanon en el contexto (post)colonial ha denominado como una lucha sanguinaria y decisiva entre dos protagonistas. (*Silencio* 250)

[The Manichean narrative structure of Galeano and other postcolonial writers corresponds to the Manichean structure of the society in which they live...To reject the binary structure of one's society would mean losing sight of the political, social, and ideological forces operative in the world and to shirk what in the (post)colonial context Fanon has called a bloody and decisive battle between two protagonists.]

In the next paragraph of her analysis, Palaversich reacts to Octavio Paz's apolitically universalist stance and contradicts herself again in attributing postmodernism to literary textuality and charging it with not having relevance in the extraliterary world, which is evermore polarized politically and where the old relations of power remain intact.

So where does this leave Galeano? In the final pages of her book, Palaversich deals cursorily with the *The Book of Embraces* and *Walking Words* in a way that gives the uneasy impression that she felt compelled to mention these books before she had a chance to absorb them fully:

El autor se aparta de la problemática socioeconómica; el tono de denuncia de la obra anterior se modifica o desaparece por completo y la escritura en general se vuelva lúdica, y aquí sí postmodernista, libre de las exigencias ideológicas. Estos textos buscan una unión más alegre con el lector, lo invitan a explorar las áreas misteriosas de la realidad más allá del sistema político. (*Silencio* 252)

[The author distances himself from socioeconomic issues; the tone of denunciation characterizing his previous work is modified or disappears completely and in general, his writing becomes more ludic, and now postmodern, free from ideological demands. These texts attempt a more happy union with the reader; they invite him or her to explore the mysterious regions of a reality beyond the political system.]

It becomes clear in reading such interpretations that dualism informs critical viewpoints to such an extent that the heterogeneity of Galeano's writing is denied because of its ethical commitment. Palaversich first describes Galeano's work as symptomatic of the embattled, Manichean society in which he lives, trapped in a worldview that can only grasp reality in reductive dualities in which the poor are opposed to the rich, the good against the evil, and so forth. Palaversich then goes on to describe his later work as devoid of any socioeconomic or political significance. She suggests that such significance is the opposite of mystery and a happy union with the reader, thereby implying that readers are unhappy when they are invited to explore socioeconomic issues. In our opinion, Galeano never stops exploring these issues, but he does so without separating them from the mysterious or wondrous dimensions of life, because this opposition is a meaningless abstraction.

But this kind of critical practice has been anticipated by Galeano, whose mastery of a prose style that accommodates, imitates, and plays to the enemy performs a radical deconstruction at the very heart of the ideology he is attacking. Evidence of this abounds. Consider, for example, the material production of Galeano's recent books and their introduction into the mainstream of American publishing by Norton, a publisher with vested interests in the production and dissemination of both the old and new literary canons. Consider also the stylistic inversions that typify Galeano's prose. Evident everywhere are the techniques of the television or radio sound bite, the abbreviated narrative masking its "true" dimensions in preparation for dissemination to a culture whose attention span has been conditioned by the sixty-second commercial: "The TV set is king. This familiar totem of our time immobilizes its devotees for more hours than any preacher and transmits ideology with an astounding power of diffusion and persuasion" (*We Say No* 154). In recognition of the communicative powers of this totem, Galeano has developed a precise literary style that rehistoricizes using the very tools of historical appropriation he is opposing. The prose is marked by its brevity, its journalistic "precision," its quotability, its polyvocality, and its use of an empirical method. But it is its canny eye for unforgettable tropes and ironic displacements, which verbalize the very doubleness of history as both the event mediated through different agencies and subjectivities *and* the event of the narrative displaced through the serial possibilities offered by language and textuality, that make Galeano's style more than a simple parody of the techniques of mass communication.

Furthermore, Galeano's style is composite. The pastiche and collage of the wildly dissimilar produce a fractured whole, a kind of literary scopophoria in face of the possibilities engendered when fragments of different narratives are brought together through the calculations of the author's vision. The figural cartographies that develop out of such mutative literary techniques are profoundly disturbing. They overlay the unclear palimpsest of history—if troping history as "palimpsest" is not itself a cultural overdetermination that reduces "history" to an empty category—with an agency that is single-minded in its will to efface blurry vision, single-minded in its accusatives, the demands it makes of both itself and the world in which it lives, yet evasively multiple in its presentation of the "other," the voices that lie at the periphery of access to dominating discourses.

Dussel's proposal to "overcome modernity through 'transmodernity,' a project of the future," responds to the limits of postmodernism's criticism of rationality and also offers a more appropriate framework for thinking through Galeano's project (*The Invention of the Americas* 12). The social commitment implied by Dussel's use of the term transmodernity is exemplified in the important shift from the myths of modernization that produced such tortured realities to a radical reconceptualization of liberation: "The act of liberation rationalizes modernity by transcending and deconstructing its irrational myth. As a practico-political program, liberation surpasses both capitalism and modernity in search of a new transmodernity characterized by ecological civilization, popular democracy, and economic justice" (*The Invention of the Americas* 117). This radical vision of a just future for all is only radical in relation to the pervasive injustice of the present. Galeano's commitment to a pedagogy that disseminates the wisdom required to think about justice in relation to the other cannot dispense with rational argumentation. To criticize his desire to discover (*des-cubrir*) what the system—mass media, politicians, corporations, academics—covers (*encubrir*) is not just naïve but dangerous. It is a common critical move to accuse thinkers (movers and shakers) like Galeano of naïveté because ironically, some postmodernist critics generalize their formalist-philosophical musings on the indeterminacy of language to account for all experience, thereby erasing the multiplicity of social realities in the name of difference. Dussel observes how "Even careful historians and philosophers"—and, we would add, literary theorists—"neglect the systematic linkages between postindustrial, service-oriented, financier, and transnational late capitalism and peripheral capitalism. Industrialized capitalism subsumes living labor by offering minimum subsistence salaries to competing marginalized ones who must sell themselves at subhuman prices, like the illegal *braceros* [migrant workers] in the United States" (*The Invention of the Americas* 131). How would the recognition of indeterminacy alter our reception of such an observation?

Is fetishizing the other not a form of reverse essentialism when we are speaking of suffering human others (the flesh named and revered by Dussel) and not the unconscious, indeterminate Other of psychoanalysis? Dussel, like Galeano, is clear on the need to comprehend the other's reason, not to appropriate but to allow that reason to speak of oppression and envision a way out: "Authentically liberating projects...require an amplified rationality which makes room for the reason of the Other within a community of communication among equal participants, as envisaged by Bartolomé de Las Casas in the 1550 Valladolid debate" (*The Invention of the Americas* 131). In a section from *We Say No* entitled "Othercide," Galeano—through strategies of irony and sarcasm and a subversive empirical method that produces historical revision—demonstrates the nature of colonial oppression by exposing its persistent creation of narratives that refuse to disrupt their own tendentious blindness. America after the "Discovery" is, after all, the America of disabled curiosity, the blind eye turning of a passive historicity, of forgotten chronicles of the community of "we" and of political resistance transliterated as "no," all of which constitute the absent presence instantiated in Galeano's discursive strategies. Two examples of the blindnesses constitutive of the contagion of absence that Galeano sees operative in conquest narratives are worth citing:

> On October 12, 1492, Christopher Columbus wrote in his diary that he wished to take a few Indians back to Spain *so they could learn to speak* (*"Que deprendan fablar"*). Five centuries later, on October 12, 1989, in a court of justice in the United States, a Mixtec Indian was considered "mentally retarded" because he did not speak proper Castilian. Ladislao Pastrana, a Mexican from Oaxaca, an undocumented *bracero* in the fields of California, was to be committed for life to a public asylum. Pastrana did not understand the Spanish interpreter, and the psychologist diagnosed "clear intellectual deficiency." Finally, anthropologists clarified the situation: Pastrana expressed himself perfectly well in his own language, Mixteco, spoken by the inheritors of a complex culture more than two thousand years old. (304)

From the point of view of the victors, which to date has been the only point of view, Indian customs have always confirmed their possession by demons or their biological inferiority. From the earliest days of colonial life:

> The Indians of the Caribbean commit suicide rather than work as slaves? Because they're lazy.

> They walk around naked, as if their entire bodies were faces? Because savages have no shame.

> They know nothing of the right of property, and share everything, and have no desire to accumulate wealth? Because they are closer to monkeys than to man.

They never hit their children and they let them run free? Because they are incapable of punishing or educating.

They believe in dreams and obey their voices? By influence of Satan or pure stupidity.

They make love when they wish? Because the demon induces them to repeat the original sin.

Homosexuality is allowed? Virginity has no importance at all? Because they live on the outskirts of hell. (310-11)

Othercide is an act of narrative conspiracy born out of a historically determined duplicity masking as history devoid of fiction. The other is deemed incapable, possessed by demons. Or, worse, the other is categorized as inferior and abject. All of these designations are arbitrary historical determinations made to service the ends of colonial ideology and its perverse narratives. Importantly, such arbitrary designations lead to material enslavement and sin against a fundamental law of the practice of rights as a speaking and listening to the other in the name of the reciprocal life of the community:

The law says: Thou shalt not kill. Which means: you shall not refuse to others the role of interlocutor. But the law that forbids the crime of abjection nonetheless evokes its abiding threat or temptation. Interlocution is authorized only by respect for the Other, in my words and in yours. (Lyotard 147)

This respect, however, does not impose an insurmountable distance between self and other, for when the concept of otherness is not essentialized either as demonic or fetishized alterity, it becomes the grounds for reciprocal interchange:

In transmodernity, the alterity, coessential to modernity, now receives recognition as an equal. Modernity will come into its fullness not by passing from its potency to its act, but by surpassing itself through a corealization with its once negated alterity and through a process of mutual, creative fecundation. The transmodern project achieves with modernity what it could not achieve by itself—a corealization of solidarity, which is analectic, analogic, syncretic, hybrid, and mestizo, and which bonds center to periphery, woman to man, race to race, ethnic group to ethnic group, class to class, humanity to earth, and occidental to Third World cultures. This bonding occurs not via negation, but via a subsumption from the viewpoint of alterity. (Dussel, *The Invention of the Americas* 138)

The terms used by Dussel to describe the co-realization of solidarity also apply to Galeano's "aesthetics," if by this we mean the material expression of a vision that is always multiple, dynamic, and provisional.

By opening the narrative space for the non-abjected other to speak and to be heard, Galeano restitutes the space of reciprocal interlocution as one of the steps requisite to the meaningful achievement of social justice and equitable rights. Galeano does so in resistance to the overwhelming shape given to modernity by the ideological underpinnings of the conquest, which framed the encounter with the other as the civilizing imposition of universal values:

> ...while the conquest depicted itself as upholding the universal rights of modernity against barbarism, the indigenous peoples suffered the denial of their rights, civilization, culture, and gods. In brief, the Indians were victimized in the name of an innocent victim and for the sake of universal rights. Modernity elaborated a myth of its own goodness, rationalized its violence as civilizing, and finally declared itself innocent of the assassination of the Other. (Dussel, *The Invention of the Americas* 50)

To be sure, the denial of rights (and the imposition of universal rights, arbitrarily designated as coincident with Eurocentric values) was enacted materially through specific acts of terror and brutality.

But the abuse of rights is also made possible by literary structures of narrative and ideology complicit in the demonization that produces banal untruths of the unthought stereotype invoked in the "barbarian other." Such a stereotype is a classic form of abjection that is a form of othercide, a silencing of the voice of the other that produces negative rights effects. Think of, to cite but one early modern example, Josuah Sylvester's translation of Guillaume de Saluste Sieur Du Bartas' *The Divine Weeks and Works* (1605), an hexaëmeral poem, and thus a poem with delusions of origin *and* a poem about the creation of myths central to the culture of appropriation and colonization. In a section entitled "The Colonies," Du Bartas/Sylvester elaborate on the commonly held myths associated with distinctions between Northern and Southern cultures. This is a *locus classicus*, if you will, of bigotry and racism told from the point of view of the victor and doubly reinforced by the highly charged contexts of the Judeo-Christian bible, more specifically, Genesis 1-2:

> The Northern-man is faire, the Southern foule;
> That's white, this black; that smiles, and this doth scoule:
> Th'one's blyth and frolike, th'other dull and froward;
> Th'one's full of courage, th'other fearefull coward:
> Th'one's plaine and honest, th'other all deceipt;
> Th'one's borne for Armes, the other Arts respecteth. (1. 458)

The classical binarisms associated with colonial subjugation and the myths necessary to perpetuate such a subjugation are played out here with disturbing ease. Northerners are fair, southerners foul. The northerner is courageous, the southerner a coward. The northerner is truthful, the southerner duplicitous. And finally, most damning of all, the northerner is born to arms, the southerner to arts. The latter stereotype is implicit in the extent to which those in the arts have been excluded from the policy-making dimensions of rights instruments.

Descriptions of absolute difference justify a reactionary ideology based on the demonization of such *false* differences. The colonial imperative depends on the articulation of alterities as fixed categories through the use of systemic misrepresentations in language. This latter recipe for the justification of the colonial imperative is as firmly in place here as it is in Las Casas's earlier *A Short Account of the Destruction of the Indies* (1552). In this text, Las Casas critically describes the European justifications for enslaving aboriginal youths, women and children after a successful battle: "The pretext under which the victims were parceled out in this way [enslaved] was that their new masters would then be in a position to teach them the truths of the Christian faith; and thus it came about that a host of cruel, grasping and wicked men, almost all of them pig-ignorant, were put in charge of these poor souls" (24).

The remedy Galeano proposes, if remedies are possible when the victors' narratives are so widely disseminated through media control of global culture, is a re-examination of the conditions that produce the colonial subject's gaze. Such a re-examination—also, necessarily, a self-examination—recognizes that the colonial imperative depends on the homogenization of the gaze as well as a monoculture that commodifies its own blinkered strategies of appropriation. If as Galeano ironically says "To civilize is *to correct*" (*We Say No* 315), then civilization is subject to a double-edged image of itself, for it both correctively distorts its vision of the world and allows for the corrective unmasking of that distortion. The question remains: which gesture has more transformational power and is more widely disseminated across the interstices of various cultural borders? The exposition of the doubleness of civilizing "correct[ions]" ultimately leaves Galeano's readership with a choice about the nature of its own vision of the civil state as given shape by Galeano's deconstruction of the colonial narrative. In the interstices between ignorance and recognition arises the possibility of the anti-narrative that voids the colonial master-narrative of its force. And without such an anti-narrative, the possibility of a truly informed, liberatory, and reciprocal rights discourse is moot.

The trope of "discovery," as it is used in North America both in reference to colonization and science, is particularly resonant in such a context. We now return to a seminal vignette, discussed early on in this chapter, about Father Ignacio Ellacuría, the Jesuit rector of University of Central America in El Salvador, who, to repeat and continue the story from where we left it off earlier,

...told me [Galeano] that to him the notion of the Discovery of America seemed absurd. The oppressor is incapable of discovery...

"It is the oppressed who discovers the oppressor."

He believed that the oppressor couldn't even discover himself. The true reality of the oppressor can only be seen from the point of view of the oppressed.

Ignacio Ellacuría was shot down for believing in that unpardonable capacity of revelation, and for taking the risks implied by his faith in the power of prophecy.

Did the Salvadoran military kill him? Or was it a system that cannot tolerate the gaze that gives it away? (*We Say No* 316)

The ironic discovery suspended in the passage is that the "Discovery of America" lies beyond the régime of colonial oppression: the discovery is always a function of the vision of the oppressed whose oppression grounds the ideological certainties—and thus, failures and blindnesses—of the oppressor. To oppress in this curious logic is to repress the unknowable elements that determine the agency of the oppressor, a fact Galeano ties directly to Ellacuría's brutal death (on 16 November 1989).[35] Failure to grasp the profound ethical import of this relation can only be undone by those who are subject to oppression, that is, subject to the discovery of the "true" nature of the oppressor.

The Ellacuría story, like the Pastrana incident cited earlier, chronicles the terrible human cost of oppression, the loss of specific agencies that bring relevant ethical knowledge to bear on rights issues. Beyond that, though, it also suggests a potential ground for the building of a rights discourse that recognizes differential power relations, not from the position of the powerful but from the position of those who least benefit from the exercise of power. What if the "us" determining rights structures was not the "us" of the American or European nationalist centre but the "us" of everything at its periphery? Imagine a rights discourse so grounded, based on the "gaze that gives [the system] away," based on the knowledge derived from the oppressed of the "other subjectivity" that is the "dominator, robber, torturer." In *Ethics and Community*, Dussel argues from the liberation theological perspective that "The 'flesh,' the 'flesh' of the other, his or her 'face'…is the only sacred thing in creation…Hence everything bound up in any way with 'flesh' (sexuality, sensibility, pleasure, and so on) is good, worthy, and positive, not to be rejected" (60). At the same time, then,

> If the "flesh" is something positive, something worthy and good, then hunger, thirst, homelessness, cold, and so on, will be evil. And their evil is not only physical, but ethical, political, communal, as well. These things are evil as the fruit of sin ["Sin is domination over the other" (61)], of injustice.
>
> The suffering of the starving or of the tortured…is experienced in the "skin," in the mucous lining of the stomach or in the muscles of one's members. The "flesh" cries out, suffers, undergoes pain. Thus "sensibility" serves notice, in the just who suffer oppression…of the reality of sin—the sin of the other subjectivity, the other pole of the relationship, as dominator, robber, torturer. (61-62)

Galeano's narrative choices reflect this Dusselian conception of the other, which challenges rights discourses incapable of imagining themselves in a relation to the other that is not grounded on domination or self-interest. The argument of French philosopher Emmanuel Levinas that the "human inversion of the in-itself and the for-itself (of 'every man for himself') into an ethical self…would take place in what I call an encounter with the face of the other" offers the flip side of the ethical position on rights proposed by Galeano and Dussel.

In Levinas's transcendental conception, which occurs in a context unrelated to extant relations of power (but which nonetheless implies them), the other "calls to me and orders me from the depths of his defenseless nakedness, his misery, his mortality. It is in the personal relationship, from me to the other, that the ethical 'event,' charity and mercy, generosity and obedience, lead beyond or rise above being" (202). The distinction between the two positions is important insofar as it bears on how different cultural contexts, determined by relations of power, figure the other in substantively different ways—one in the flesh, the other transcendental, one in a relation that begins with the self and moves to the other as opposed to the inverse. The two positions indicate how rights are conceived as a function of the most basic social unit involving two people in an interlocutory relation.

Imagine, then, as Dussel does, affirming "the reason of the Other as a step toward a transmodern *worldhood*" (*The Invention of the Americas* 26). Until such a denationalized positioning fully informs *all* discourses about rights, as Galeano implies in the Ellacuría vignette, the differential discourses of power will always be meaningfully blind to difference, incapable of entering into a truly interlocutory dialogue based on "ongoing dissensus," not consensus, what Murray Bookchin calls the "all-important process of continual dialogue, disagreement, challenge, and counter-challenge, without which social as well as individual creativity would be impossible" (17). Imagine a discourse based on a recursive, serial listening to the other with the ethical onus on *both* parties to carry forward such an interlocutory relationship, not necessarily based on a false or imposed consensus, but on an ongoing dialogue in which disagreement and the permutations of free expression it allows become the basis for enacting rights in relation to the other. We recognize, along with Edward Said, that "some dialectical oppositions are not reconcilable, not transcendable, not really capable of being folded into a higher, undoubtedly more noble, synthesis" ("The Public Role" 36). But we would add that such situations of apparent intransigence (exemplified in Said's argument by the struggle over Palestine) present the ethical horizon toward which recursive listening strategies beckon; they are the most extreme reality that such a strategy must address with a sustained patience tempered by the principles of discrepant engagement, reciprocity, and the understanding of differential and contingent relations of power. This position is especially important in situations characterized by persistent and extreme violence caused by historical circumstances that have complex origins, or in situations that threaten to inaugurate violent conflicts in which sustained interlocution based on recursive listening strategies is swept aside.

Default by any of the parties to the complex mediations called for by recursive listening increases the chance of a break (calamitous or not) from a position of reciprocal, egalitarian, and protracted interlocution that leads to material, meaningful change. That break can manifest itself as civil disobedience (in its myriad forms), increased state authoritarianism (as in the imposition of martial law and reduced civil liberties), localized insurgency, state-sanctioned war, full-blown revolution, and other expressions of extreme alienation.

The ethical challenge raised by such forms of dissent and discord lies in how to restore the conditions and contexts for recursive listening, even where, as Said suggests, if "synthesis" may be an impossibility, at least civil co-existence is not. Said's appeal to humanist intellectuals overlaps in many ways with Galeano's insofar as both see the work of "forestall[ing] the disappearance of the past" as crucial to producing a context that allows for the egalitarian reciprocity that grounds meaningful civil relations; both seek to "construct fields of coexistence rather than fields of battle as the outcome of intellectual labor"; and both advocate highly critical and reasonable "theoretical imperative[s] against the huge accumulations of power and capital that so distort human life" ("The Public Role" 34-35). Further, we would argue that both persist in questioning the power relations that lie behind apparent consensual discourse in the name of dissenting, critical, recursive listening.

A classic example of the arrogance of consensual discourse around rights occurs in Rawls's notion that "there is no society in the world—except for marginal cases—with resources so scarce that it could not, were it reasonably and rationally organized and governed, become well-ordered" (108). The marginal case he refers to is that of the so-called "Arctic Eskimos," whom he deems "rare enough, and need not affect our general approach. I assume their problems could be handled in an *ad hoc* way" (108). The precise point of the Ellacuría passage is that until so-called marginal cultures (say the Inuit or Inuvialuit) are no longer the *ad hoc* exception but are the basis for the norms governing an informed discourse of rights, hegemonic structures that fail to account adequately for human difference will persist. And rights as such will neither have broad application as an extension of notions of equality, let alone have meaning as a discourse that recognizes the plurality of human difference. Rawls's failure to even name Inuit culture properly, let alone his utter ignorance of the ways in which that culture is exemplary of a kind of sustainable long-term well-orderedness (in the face of extreme disadvantage), is typical of the supposed consensual policy-making voices that configure rights discourse in the name of hegemonic interests.

So long as such a structure (of analysis based on ignorance of difference) is in place, *all* rights discourse is severely compromised, mute in what it really has to say to difference. As Galeano suggests,

> In the dramatized versions of the Conquest of America still performed to this day by Indians of the Andes, the priests and conquistadors speak moving their lips but not uttering any sound. The conquerors speak, in indigenous theater, in a mute tongue. Today, the voices of the international system of power, broadcast by the dominant culture—what do they tell us?...The dominant culture expressed through the educational system and above all through the mass media does not reveal reality; it masks it. It doesn't help bring about change; it helps avoid change. It doesn't encourage democratic participation; it induces passivity, resignation and selfishness. It doesn't generate creativity; it creates consumers. (*We Say No* 211-12)

The theatrical gesture of silencing the priests and conquistadors is a powerful imaginative emblem of the kind of inversion to which Galeano's aesthetics are attuned. Implicit in the image is the world of power silenced so as to allow the other to speak and be heard, a radical gesture needed to initiate the interlocutory exchange in which difference is not addressed as a passive form of disempowerment. The reversal sets the necessary condition for any meaningful discourse of rights that is not just window dressing used to mask the realities governing how power achieves its ends. Whether it be through racist ignorance or through the failure of self-examination implicit in the pedagogical systems he critiques, Galeano, in numerous similar narratives of such failures, builds a startling portrait of the Americas crippled by the effects of the colonial imperative and thereby crippled in its power to enact rights and social justice on the same scale as the rights abjured, the injustices done.

But Galeano's portrayal of this state of relations is not one-sided. Throughout it is the power of speech that confirms the possibility of subverting such imperatives. Recognition is a crucial trope for Galeano, a metonym for the possibilities of multivalent human discourses, the cultures of resistance that resist structures of oppression. Conversely, the "lie" figures in Galeano's structural analyses of oppression as a metonym for the discourses of power:

> *The universal system of the lie practices amnesia.* The North behaves as if it had won the lottery. Its wealth, however, is not the result of good fortune, but of a long, very long historical process of usurpation, which goes back to colonial times and has been greatly intensified by today's modern and sophisticated techniques of pillage. The more resonant the speeches in international forums extolling justice and equality, the more prices of Southern products fall on the world market, and the higher the interest climbs on Northern money, which loans with one hand and steals with the other. (*We Say No* 211)

This "lie" founds the perpetuation of colonialist oppression by virtue of its rejection of any form of alternative history as much as by its rejection of differing imaginable futures. The writer exposes this fundamental condition of the colonial imperative by challenging the perpetuation of the lie, imagining different futures, and recuperating lost voices: "I am not a historian; I am a writer challenged by enigmas and lies, who would like the present to stop being a painful atonement for the past, who would like to imagine the future rather than accept it: a hunter of scattered voices, lost and true" (*We Say No* 256). Similarly, the exposition of "usurpation" is, in typically Galeanesque manner, a means of subverting systemic distortions in the representation of reality, a strategy that is consistently deployed throughout Galeano's oeuvre. This is why words and textualities are constantly invoked by Galeano for their potencies, their transformational energies, their crucial role in the reform of the North American colonial socius: "I think that a primordial function of Latin American literature today is the rescue of the word, frequently used and abused with impunity for the purpose of hampering and betraying communication...By writing it is possible to offer, in spite of persecution and censorship, the testimony of our time and people—for now and for later" (*We Say No* 142).

Galeano's writings contribute to the dissolution of the empowered fantasies and impotencies of the colonialist condition and especially its disregard for the failures buried in its own chronicles. What Galeano proposes is the vision of a world in which to speak is to remember the potencies that emerge from a vision of the dismembered "lie," which is to say, to write the potency of recognizing the misrepresentations by which "we" are defined and then to "say no" to such a vision. Ultimately, the theoretical implications of such a vision include a deep skepticism about the postcolonial, a word conspicuously absent from Galeano's creative lexicon. As McClintock caustically observes,

> "Post-colonial" Latin America has been invaded by the United States over a hundred times [in the twentieth century] alone. Each time, the US has acted to install a dictatorship, prop up a puppet regime, or wreck a democracy. In the 1940s, when the climate for gunboat diplomacy chilled, United States' relations with Latin America were warmed by an economic imperial policy euphemistically dubbed 'Good Neighborliness,' primarily designed to make Latin America a safer backyard for the US' virile agribusiness. (89)

From such a perspective, to put the "post" in "postcolonial" is to imply a historical fantasy, one in which Occidental culture both obscures and absolves itself from the various and ongoing modes of colonization and acculturation—economic, political, cultural, historical—by which it defines its relation to the other.[36] Galeano's response to this fantasy, then, is to chronicle the nested memories that the Americas in their national configurations repress in the persistent longing to sustain both the national subject and the nation *as* subject. Any rights discourse that resists such a longing—with its transcendental, delusive ethos of sovereign, national consensus based on self-interest as the normative basis for *thinking* rights, *being* human—must produce an alternative space in which the nation is no longer an illusory transcendental signifier for a unified ethical discourse.

Discrepant Engagements:
Solidarity, Critical Consciousness, and Reciprocity

To be Latin American and of my generation, those born between 1945 and 1955, the so-called generation of "disenchantment," implies being fully conscious of the dictatorships that invaded the southern Hemisphere in a systematic way for almost twenty years. The role of the writer, which is wholly integrated in the political tasks of these countries, is of extreme importance and complexity. What does a dictatorship signify and how does one document its traces? Up to what point is it feasible to make poetry about the tortured body? Who can say it is authentic for a writer to be responsible for the political violence of a country? (Agosin, "How to Speak with the Dead?" 214)

A passage from Galeano's *Upside Down* makes the following observation: "A McDonald's ad shows a boy eating a hamburger. 'I don't share,' he says. This dummy hasn't learned that now we're supposed to give away our leftovers instead of tossing them in the garbage. Solidarity is still considered a useless waste of energy and critical consciousness is but a passing phase of stupidity in human life" (310). The linkage Galeano makes here between solidarity and critical consciousness is crucial, the implication being that one cannot exist without the other. Solidarity is not an unthought way of being; critical consciousness is productive of something not unthought. Further on, in the same discussion, Galeano notes that

> When she died, Diana [Princess of Wales] was the head of eighty-one public charities. If she were still alive, she would make a great minister of the economy in any government in the South. After all, charity consoles but does not question. "When I give food to the poor, they call me a saint," said Brazilian bishop Helder Cámara. "And when I ask why they have no food, they call me a Communist." (*Upside Down* 311)

The capacity to question critically, so crucial an element in literary critical consciousness (and so often vitiated or betrayed by actual literary critical practices) is undeniably connected to the capacity to think in meaningful ways about human solidarity. The Princess Diana anecdote, with its formal compression, its interrogative narrative mode, its apothegmatic ethical conclusion that articulates the connection between structures of meaning and naming (charity that sanctions inequality as opposed to questioning the existence of inequality, the former worthy of canonization, the latter of demonization), highlights the crossover between literariness and mindfulness about rights that Galeano consistently addresses. This he does in a multiplicity of layered forms, some definitively literary texts, others hybridized narratives that question the very nature of literature. In this, the last section of this chapter, we undertake to examine what Galeano has to teach about thinking the relations between literary production and human rights initiatives.

Surprisingly little has been written in either the rights or literary domains about the ways in which the acute critical consciousness associated, perhaps, with a particular politicized reading of literature can be productively linked to the problems of human solidarity posed by the movement to think human rights into being. From our perspective, we see no distinction to be made between thought, implicit in critical consciousness, and action: thought is a form of action, action a form of thought.[37] The Chilean poet Marjorie Agosin, for example, in one of the rare essays that examines the crossover between rights theory and literature, cites Julio Cortázar's affirmation that "to write and to read is increasingly a possibility of acting extraliterarily, although most of our most significant books do not contain explicit messages nor do they seek ideological or political converts. To write and read is a form of action" (qtd. in "So We Will Not Forget" 177-78). Extraliterary solidarity and critical consciousness are reciprocal elements in literary and rights discourses that imagine the responsibility of being human in meaningful ways. We do not imply here a singular (simplistic), one-to-one correspondence between literature and rights that is necessarily explicit. Instead, we suggest that literature, in its most ethical and effective forms (which do not necessarily disclude highly aestheticized forms of writing), produces critical consciousness, a plural response to the contradictions of being and yet a form of solidarity at the same time. Rights discourse necessitates similar intellectual patternings: discursive interchange between sovereign states, the responsibility of entering into dialogue with the other (whether political, economic, or cultural), and a struggle to address contradictory human realities.

The most pertinent of literatures address these issues in the most varied of ways, just as the most crucial issues of rights discourse ask questions about our shared humanity, including the degree to which facets of humanity are truly shared from culture to culture, community to community. Again, at the risk of emphasizing the relevance of literature to rights discourse to the point of excess, we note the degree to which the critical literature in both disciplines is strangely short on meaningful commentary on their mutual relationship. Such a critical gap exists despite the burgeoning and loosely-knit groups of writers devoted to rights issues: PEN is but one example of such an formation, while organizations like Amnesty International employ writing in the project of advocating for justice in the treatment of political prisoners. This gap also exists despite the reliance of human rights advocacy groups, non-governmental agencies, and multi-national committees responsible for conceiving of and implementing human rights goals and policy on literary and philosophical points of reference as a means to animate and advocate policy. Some of the most relevant passages in Drinan's work on human rights issues, for example, depend on literary citation and narrative for their affect. A recent condemnation of the death penalty as a violation of human rights ends with a quote from Dostoyevsky's *The Idiot* ("To kill for murder is an immeasurably greater evil than the crime itself" [qtd. in Drinan, *A Worldview of Human Rights* 139]) while a distressing chapter on the right to food concludes with a testimonial letter from UNICEF: "No statistic can express what it's like to see even one child die [of hunger]...to see a mother sitting hour after hour, leaning her child's body against her own...to watch the small feeble head movements that expend all the energy a youngster has left...to see the panic in a dying tot's innocent eyes...and then to know in a moment that life is gone" (qtd. in Drinan, *Cry of the Oppressed* 186). The affect of passages such as these, as Galeano well recognizes, cannot be underestimated, for they challenge not only critical consciousness but also the capacity to imagine human solidarity in ways that interrogate one's (passive/active) relation to such narratives.

Galeano's place in this emerging intersection of disciplines is singular for many reasons: his challenge to literary genres is formidable in terms of how literature goes out into the world to create its effects. Moreover, Galeano blends the social scientific discourses that ground his cultural and political analyses with modes of narrative that are hugely indebted to the literary discourses of dissent and solidarity that have made Latin America so unique (whether in terms of Asturias, Cortázar, Conti, Benedetti, Neruda, García Márquez, Poniatowska, or Marcos, to mention only a few of the writers with whom Galeano might express some form of literary alliance). As a voice of moral outrage, highly critical of the conventions and forms of knowledge that circulate as unchallenged orthodoxies, and a teller of tales that deploy sophisticated literary tropes and structures, Galeano produces a distinctive discourse. His is one of a very few such voices with the combination of moral authority, critical consciousness, and discursive skill to gain widespread international attention. Moreover, his voice challenges the literary and the rights communities to think across entrenched boundaries that separate the two. Typically, the writer is prohibited from thinking as a maker of policy (traditionally a lawyer or a social scientist of some sort) and the lawyer is disenfranchised from the literariness of narratives that underscores and informs issues of social justice. Galeano's writing practices challenge this artificial divide in ways similar to what Nathaniel Mackey has termed discrepant engagement, which, "rather than suppressing resonance, dissonance, [and] noise, seeks to remain open to them. Its admission of resonances contends with resolution. It worries resolute identity and demarcation, resolute boundary lines, resolute definition...To see being as verb rather than noun is to be at odds with hypostasis, the reification of fixed identities that has been the bane of socially marginalized groups" (20). Mackey's phrase attacks impoverished epistemologies of social convention gathered in the term community, all too often used either as an index aligned with hegemonic interests or as a hopelessly utopian idealization of alternative social dispositions that can never be realized. Both senses of community place enormous pressure on the viability of the term as a meaningful signifier for alternative forms of engagement that produce human realities. And these pressures usually come from hegemonic, institutional culture itself, rather than from its so-called margins. In resistance to such reductive designations, Mackey's discrepant engagement precisely locates the differential (not always consonant) forces that trouble the sense of "community" as coincident with hegemonic power. Discrepant engagements point to the alignment of non-reductive alternatives that are always troubled and troubling, resistant and antithetical to the sort of top-down discourse that produces its own vitiated expression of human reality in both the discourse of rights and of literary analysis.

Mackey's "socially marginalized" (a term we use to include economic and class distinctions), it must not be forgotten, are globally in the majority. The resonance of their existence must be resolved in relation to the dissonance of the minority, those with power and wealth. This resonance is the defining problem of the human rights movement insofar as it seeks constructively to better the conditions of all peoples living as part of local, regional, and global communities: a problem of solidarity and critical consciousness, a problem of discrepant engagement that implies the necessity of thinking beyond traditional disciplinary modes. A good example of this need to "think beyond" occurs in Rawls's recent discussion about the control of nuclear and other weapons of mass destruction: "Yet so long as there are outlaw states—as we suppose—some nuclear weapons need to be retained to keep those states at bay and to make sure they do not obtain and use those weapons against liberal or decent peoples. *How best to do this belongs to expert knowledge, which philosophy doesn't possess*" (9; our emphasis). The affirmation affronts the very nexus between solidarity and critical consciousness we seek to establish via Galeano's writing practices. Critical consciousness in the face of such a statement might ask why nuclear weapons are necessarily needed to keep outlaw states at bay. And the logical flaw of associating weapons of mass destruction with the prevention of their dissemination and use surely requires comment. The summary exclusion of "philosophy"—which we would read as a synecdoche for the humanities generally—from "expert knowledge" is also striking for how it assumes reliance on an "expert knowledge" that can be excluded from the kind of critical consciousness a philosopher or writer might bring to bear on it. The very notion of disciplinary solidarity as a means to finding sophisticated solutions to complex problems is here abrogated, a profoundly skewed gesture in the face of the kind of alternatives proposed by Galeano. Moreover, the pressing moral problem of using evil means to suppress evil ends is not even addressed, the assumption being that reality demands such a disposition of forces to obstruct the spread of nuclear weaponry, genocide, and other forms of extreme challenge to human rights and social justice.

Jonathan Glover troubles the notion of an "unwavering...moral law" in the following way: "In a letter to a newspaper about the Gulf War, Father Denis Geraghty wrote, 'The use of weapons of mass destruction is a crime against God and man and remains a crime even if they are used in retaliation or for what is regarded as a morally justified end. It is forbidden to do evil that good may come of it.' Many other people, including some who are sympathetic to his opinions, will view Father Geraghty's tone with a mixture of envy and scepticism" (1). Amnesty International's policy regarding "adoption" of prisoners is based on a scrupulous opposition to the use of violence ("No person is adopted if he or she has used or advocated violence" [Drinan, *Cry of the Oppressed* 153]), a policy that led to the dropping of Nelson Mandela from its lists of adoptees. The examples highlight the problems engendered by moral certainties. Whatever the skepticism, let alone the theological origins of Geraghty's comment, the problem of the nature of the means to achieve specific ends so designated as "good" is extraordinarily relevant (whether in the contexts of weapons of mass destruction or in the contexts of discussions about the death penalty). To avoid it through the kinds of moves made by Rawls in this passage is antithetical to the kind of critical consciousness advocated by Galeano.

The crucial distinction that emerges from study of Galeano's thought is between moral absolutism (which in our reading Galeano does not advocate) and critical consciousness (which he does). For instance, take what Galeano has to say about the influence of European and North American cultures on the South: "It would be a delusion and an act of reactionary stupidity to propose the rejection of European and North American cultural contributions already incorporated into our heritage and into the universal heritage, arbitrarily reducing those vast and complex cultures to the machinery of imperialist alienation implicit in them. Anti-imperialism also is prey to infantile disorders" ("The Revolution as Revelation" 14). Galeano is equally categorical about the use of literature in a political context:

> I know I can be accused of sacrilege in writing about political economy in the style of a novel about love or pirates. But I confess I get a pain from reading valuable works by certain sociologists, political experts, economists, and historians who write in code. Hermetic language isn't the invariable and inevitable price of profundity. In some cases it can simply conceal incapacity for communication raised to the category of intellectual virtue. I suspect that boredom can thus often serve to sanctify the established order, confirming that knowledge is a privilege of the elite. (*Open Veins* 288)

In assessing television, Galeano is equally sanguine:

> Television per se should not be condemned, only television as a socially acceptable drug. Valium to deaden the mind. By the same token, neither should the messages be condemned simply because they come from the United States or other foreign countries. (*We Say No* 213)

This sort of critical (and reasonable) balance occurs throughout Galeano's oeuvre, though it is almost never commented on by the citics who have examined his work usually in support of the portrayal of him as a dogmatic ideologue.

How then to theorize, via the example of Galeano's writing practices, the relations between solidarity and critical consciousness, literature and human rights, criticism and community, and to do this in full recognition that each of these terms is problematic and meaningfully different to different constituencies? The sequence we propose to follow in subsequent chapters is thoroughly dependent on this question. From storytelling and *testimonio* (covered in the next chapter), both of which deploy narrative strategies that interrogate bourgeois literary modes of being (especially in relation to fact and fiction, chronicle and story, history from above and below), through to the following chapter on revisionary history as a means of thinking the literariness of historical narrative, through to our last chapter on alternative community making, the question of how solidarity and critical consciousness are at the core of an emergent discourse of which Galeano is representative will be addressed. In what follows, then, we examine how the kind of hybridized discourse of discrepant engagement that Galeano has painstakingly evolved over the last 45 years or so has relevance to rethinking the aims and relevance of literary culture. Moreover, we also address the use of that literary culture in relation to the similarly evolving human rights movement, which has emerged, perhaps not so coincidentally, in tandem with Galeano's own presence on the international scene.

Literary culture, for better or for worse, is a player in the scenario we describe. It is at once a crucial aspect of the instrumentality of the documents and actions by which human rights are effectuated: they are, after all, based in language and text and thus subject to the intertextual resonances and effects of discourse generally. Literary culture, moreover, is one of the ways in which human imagination constructs itself, thus making possible not only the imaginative detailing of the world as it is, but also of the world as it might be.[38] Galeano argues, for instance, that "To imagine the future instead of accepting it, I think it is necessary to be clear about the reigning power structure, which converts people and countries into commodities, condemns the majority of humankind to the hunger for bread, but which also condemns all of humanity, the many poor and the few rich as well, to the hunger of embraces" (Walljasper 35). The bridge between social analysis and affect is a notable aspect of how Galeano re-imagines such a reality, embodied in this example by the hunger for bread, the hunger for embraces. In this view, rationality is not promoted as an overweening value when placed in such an affective relationship; instead, critical consciousness and textual structures forge a unique alliance, part socio-economic analysis, part idealistic appeal to human affect: "In a world that reduces relations between individuals to relations between things, we all have a lot to learn from the vitality and the love of liberty of the African cultures, which do not divorce thought from emotion, and from the essential joy of religions that exalt the human body instead of censuring it" ("The Revolution as Revelation" 13).

The invitation to examine otherness as a force of contrarian example is consistently extended in Galeano's work, in resistance to racist and élitist structures of power: "As happens with *elitism*, the *racism* of the dominant cultures also saturates our societies in their entirety. How many times have we said, or heard someone say, *uncivilized* or *inferior* cultures in reference to indigenous and black cultures, and *dialects* in reference to their languages? How many times have we said, or heard someone say, *superstition* or *witchcraft* in reference to the native religions of America and Africa?" ("The Revolution as Revelation" 12). The critical consciousness necessary to produce such observations, let alone to act on them through the production of a full-scale literary discourse that resists élitist and racist structures deeply embedded in dominant culture, cannot be detached from its literariness, its textuality. Force of the imagination is what literary culture brings to discourses in which structures that unite affect and critique have been diminished, sublimated, or obliterated at the expense of a restrictive humanity in which reciprocity and solidarity are cant for abuse of power and economic and political debilitation.

Galeano's textual example with regard to the aesthetics of reciprocal responsibility, resistant representations, the mapping out of relations of dominance and oppression, and the reclamation of the imagination as a means of procuring human solidarity is distinctive if not interrogative of the way in which literary and rights discourses inform each other. That there is a specific politico-cultural context for this reciprocal engagement between the writer and the political realities of human rights activism has been noted by Agosin:

Throughout Latin America's literary history, since the nineteenth century, there has been a powerful alliance between the tasks of the writer and her political role...Both the political identity and the artistic identity were established as true occupations of politicians, thus converting the men and women of letters into public figures. Such were the cases of José Martí in Cuba, Che Guevara in Bolivia, Rómulo Gallegos, president of Venezuela, and Pablo Neruda, candidate to the presidency of Chile during the government of Salvador Allende. ("How to Speak with the Dead?" 214)

To this list could be added, among others, Vargas Llosa (despite his less than enlightened politics), Allende himself, and more recently Subcomandante Marcos, who has made a practice of combining the literary and the political as a means to effect dialogue and change.

Marcos's pronouncements on the affective power of the word and on the importance of silence in making the word meaningful are spoken from within the same general historico-literary frame as Galeano's. The following passage from Marcos's *Our Word Is Our Weapon* resonates with the kind of poetic logic evident in Galeano's *We Say No*:

Speaking and listening is how true men and women learn to walk. It is the word that gives form to that walk that goes on inside us. It is the word that is the bridge to cross to the other side. Silence is what Power offers our pain in order to make us small. When we are silenced, we remain very much alone. Speaking, we heal the pain. Speaking, we accompany one another. Power uses the word to impose his empire of silence. We use the word to renew ourselves. Power uses silence to hide his crimes. We use silence to listen to one another, to touch one another, to know one another.

This is the weapon, brothers and sisters. We say, the word remains. We raise the word and with it break the silence of our people. We kill the silence, by living the word. Let us leave Power alone in what the lie speaks and hushes. Let us join together in the word and the silence which liberate. (84)

From within such a textual context, meaningful interlocution takes on extraordinary political dimensions. It activates and enacts community, resists oppressive power, heals, renews, generates knowledge, and liberates. Marcos knows whereof he speaks, having been a key figure in the most successful direct actions to change the plight of the indigenous population in Mexico in the latter half of the twentieth century. Literature formed in this crucible is as thoroughly implicated in conceiving of human rights as any other discourse, more so because the new literary forms generated by revolutionary discourses are a crucial part of the way in which resistance is enacted. Further, literature is a crucial tool in what Drinan in *A Worldview of Human Rights*, borrowing on the work of Amnesty International, calls the "mobilization of shame," an affective technique that produces a politics responsive to shame, itself an outcome of a sense of moral responsibility born of reciprocity and solidarity. The latter two qualities are not features associated with the execution of power by hegemonic nations, one of the shocking derogations of duty to humanity that Galeano is intent to question. The correspondence between human suffering and profit, for example, may suit primitive cost-benefit analyses that give one nation relative economic advantage over another, but they simultaneously betray important principles of duty and reciprocity that underlie the human rights movement.

We wish to distinguish our argument here from Richard Rorty's position in a widely disseminated essay entitled "Human Rights, Rationality, and Sentimentality" that "most of the work of changing moral intuitions [necessary to achieving rights outcomes] is being done by manipulating our feelings rather than increasing our knowledge" (118). Rorty elaborates by stating that "the emergence of human rights culture seems to owe nothing to increased moral knowledge, and everything to hearing sad and sentimental stories" (119). Rorty's separation of moral knowledge from the act of hearing sentimental stories exhibits a total (if not typical) ignorance of the ways in which narrative (not necessarily sad or senti-mental) produces and transforms knowledge and then produces and transforms actions that result from that knowledge. The notion that a narrative must be sentimental in order to produce a meaningful affect is specious and vastly under-theorized, especially in the con-texts of emergent forms of writing like Galeano's, which work to overturn such ivory tower fantasies written in the paternalistic mode of transcendental truth-giving. Galeano's work is a sharp rejection of this mode, even as it makes use of techniques Rorty might categorize as sentimental.

We would argue for the use of the term affective, a term less loaded as a trope for effeminated discourse (that is, it is effeminate because it is sentimental, a subtle diminish-ment implicit in Rorty's formulations).[39] Moreover, the affective does not foreclose on forms of literary affect beyond the sentimental as nonetheless capable of having an instru-mental relation to human action and experience. Like many crucial words, "affect" has anti-thetical senses, and while it can also mean a false display of liking, the denotation that we are using here is "a feeling, emotion, or desire, especially as leading to action" (OED). Affect, in our sense, implies active critical empathy, as mediated by the force of critique, that enables action grounded simultaneously in thought and feeling. Rorty's universalization of the emotive capacity of literature under the rubric of the sentimental ignores the possibility that perhaps the most human form of knowing is a function of affect as a hybridized reflection of multiple ways of creating knowledge—whether through so-called rational modes, through emotive narrative modes, or through a blend of the two. The assumption that the rational and the sentimental are somehow alien to each other is a profound betrayal of lived reality. Rorty's pronouncement that "We are now in a good position to put aside the last vestiges of the ideas that human beings are distinguished by the capacity to know rather than by the ca-pacities for friendship and inter-marriage, distinguished by rigorous rationality rather than by flexible sentimentality" (132), derives from the discourse of mind/body split that is such a vitiated expression of human experience. The Cashinahua, for instance, to whom we have already referred in the previous chapter, associate "different kinds of knowledge" with "the hands, the ears, the genitals, and the skin, but the whole body knows and a 'wise person,' or *unaya*, has knowledge throughout his or her whole body" (Sault n.pag.).[40] And Galeano himself advocates a word coined by fishermen on the coast of Colombia, "*senti-pensante*" [from *sentir* meaning "to feel" and *pensar* meaning "to think"], a "thinking-feeling" language that "unites the head and heart. We are the victims of a fragmented culture which has taught us to separate thought from emotion, a culture that separates the soul from the body as if they were the beauty and the beast" (NACLA staff 19).[41] In such a view, which we share, critical consciousness (thinking) is not antithetical to affective depth (feeling) or to the corporeal experience of knowledge as a literal, affective embodiment (*senti-pensante*, thinking-feeling). And to suggest, as Rorty does, that thinking and feeling be made separate is to construct the sentimental subject as incapable of the critical consciousness that informs affect, a position that is powerfully aligned with disadvantaging the specific agency of the subject. Sentimentality in this reductive non-critical, non-rational mode all too easily justifies the most simplistic sorts of moral judgements used to justify heinous acts, whether in the name of nationalist or patriotic sentiment or in the name of individual self-interest.

In a rights context, such an idea is especially in need of debunking given the speed and range at which Rorty's ideas have been disseminated.[42] Note, for instance, the way in which an Indian NGO articulates the relations between affect and rational discourse as a function of a meaningful and effective rights strategy of interlocution:

> "We were not merely a struggle-oriented and slogan-shouting organization. We had the intellectual ability to put our case across solidly in the government's own terminology. The government had no alternative but to accept our conclusions since they were based on its own facts and figures." Such empowerment is invaluable—and is needed by all actors intent on promoting the realization of human rights. Holding actors to account for the human impacts of their policies and practices is central to the pursuit of justice—and using indicators is increasingly recognized as a tool central to that process. (*Human Development Report 2000* 107)

In such a context of informed and rational use of discourse, as one element in a plural mediation of rights, Rorty's claims ring especially hollow and superficial. As one more brick in the foundation of rights universalism that we have been at pains to criticize in this chapter via the example of Galeano, Rorty's depoliticized disavowal of the congruency between critical consciousness and affect is contrary to the notion of rights as a non-totalizing concept governed by the specificity of agency, whether historical, economic, or otherwise. Such a specificity (as opposed to the universalist discourse evident in rights sentimentality) is necessary in the construction of meaningful parameters for thinking and upholding rights as both discourse and as material practice. Emotions are a form of knowledge. And the actions they spawn can be highly rational, highly humanizing as they can be extraordinarily irrational and dehumanizing. Further, the battle to shape and control affect is a deadly endgame in which the loftiest human goals and the most despicable of outcomes are at stake. Compassion and abuse. Tolerance and intolerance. Love and hate. Joy and anger. Forgiveness and retribution. Such simplistic terms assume the essential purity of the content of our experience of emotions, which remain fundamentally irreducible, even as they suggest relative positions of power and disempowerment. But they also suggest that affect, in conjunction with the critical consciousness that is not necessarily dissociated from affect, determines specific choices that lead directly to actions that shape the legal and extra-legal rights lived on a daily basis by billions of people.

Rorty cites eighteenth-century Scottish philosopher and historian David Hume, who claims that "corrected (sometimes rule-corrected) sympathy, not law-discerning reason, is the fundamental moral capacity" (129), going on to advocate for what the philosopher Annette Baier deems a

> …'progress of sentiments.' This progress consists in an increasing ability to see the similarities between ourselves and people very unlike us as outweighing the differences. It is the result of what I have been calling 'sentimental education.' The relevant similarities are not a matter of sharing a deep true self which instantiates true humanity, but are such little, superficial, similarities as cherishing our parents and our children—similarities that do not interestingly distinguish us from many non-human animals. (129)

Rorty's displacement from one universal and essential structure to another ("true humanity" as opposed to "cherishing our parents and children") in the name of the sentimental is a vacuous theory of affect. It resolutely ignores the historicity of the specific domestic context that produces the affect. How would children who have been abused by a parent respond, let alone Argentine children of disappeared parents under the recent dictatorship who discover that their adoptive parents are actually complicit with the murder of their biological parent[s]? Furthermore, Rorty's analysis is predicated on presumptive social, cultural, and economic conditions that are far from shared universally. Here again is the totalizing language of the imagined family as arbiter of the normative, when in fact such a construct is deeply complicit, as we have already argued, with state values that require such homogeneous structures to insure a docile and coherent citizenry. The "revelation" that other people love their children as much as "we" do is surely predicated on suspecting other people (like communists?) of sending their children off to indoctrination camps to be brought up as "worker-bees" by specialists. But was separation not more representative of the British and other aristocratic Europeans who sent their children to faraway boarding schools for most of the year? And was not separating children from their parents one of the greatest weapons of destruction wielded by the colonizers who robbed Black slaves and indigenous peoples of the basic knowledge of parenting and communitarian ethics by destroying the family unit and its connection to community?

Parental and filial love is only a "revelation" in the aftermath of such paranoid and cynical events as "Operation Peter Pan," a "rescue mission" cooked up by the CIA, the U.S. State Department, American and Cuban religious institutions, and the Cold War propaganda machine. Forged copies of what was circulated as a new law announced a sinister plan to snatch children from their parents at the age of three to live in government-run homes or to be sent to Russia for indoctrination. In reality, the recently created "Oficina de Organización y Control de los Círculos Infantiles" [Office of the Organization and Management of Daycare Centres], an office of the Ministry of Labour, was conducting a survey to assess the needs of working mothers for a plan to build the first three hundred Daycare Centres in Cuba after the 1959 revolution (*Operación Peter Pan* 84-85). The U.S.-created *Radio Swan* broadcast this rather comic warning and novel image of Castro on 26 October 1960: "¡Madre cubana, no te dejes quitar a tu hijo! Es la nueva ley del gobierno quitártelo a los cinco años y devolvértelo a los 18 años y cuando te lo devuelvan serán unos monstruos del materialismo. Fidel se va a convertir en la madre suprema de Cuba" (90-91) [Cuban mothers, don't let them take your children from you! It is the new governmental law to take them from you when they are five years old and give them back to you when they are 18 and when they give them back to you they will be monsters of materialism. Fidel will become the supreme mother of Cuba]. As a result of the panic that ensued and the relentless harassment by U.S. based organizations, over 14,000 Cuban children and adolescents were flown from Cuba to Miami in the early 1960s.

Studies on Operation Peter Pan published by presses in the United States, where in recent years several people have come forward to give testimony about their transfer to the U.S., include those by Victor Andrés Triay and Yvonne Condé. Both admit that there is absolutely no evidence that the state had any intention or power to usurp "Patria Potestad" [paternal authority] in order to kidnap children from their families. Both base their justifications of U.S. intervention on the vague perceptions and false notions of upper-class parents, who felt that their rights were infringed upon by the abolition of private schools after the revolution, and the requirement that all children, regardless of social class, were to spend part of the year working on farms. The objective of producing more rounded individuals who would consequently be better able to identify with fellow citizens from different walks of life seems too incomprehensible for the authors to acknowledge. The scholarship in both publications is questionable and draws false parallels with other historical events, such as the Basque situation during the Spanish Civil War, transparently represented from a perspective whose only criteria is to propagate conspiracy theories of communist world domination. Condé appeals to the fact that "Lenin once stated, 'Revolution is impossible as long as the family exists,'" (25) translating this to mean literally that children would be taken from their families. She ignores the theoretical implications of Lenin's critique of the patriarchal and hierarchical structure that replicates the capitalist state's exploitation of an underclass that in domestic terms is occupied by women and children. More significantly, she ignores the pragmatic facts regarding the Cuban government's social policies and chooses to focus on paranoid fantasies without expressing the slightest suspicion about the role of U.S. propaganda in their perpetration. Condé sets the tone in her acknowledgments: "The Cuban Pedro Pans have their own Tinkerbell, Elly Vilano-Chovel, an officer in the Operation Pedro Pan Group, who sprinkles fairy dust everywhere she goes...Elly was invaluable in helping me locate many people, and with her fairy dust sprinkled my *animo* [spirit]" (viii).

Triay chooses a more apocalyptic tone, despite recognizing that the Cuban government was not responsible for the irrational behaviour that he puts into doubt at the same time that it implicitly informs his argument. He fails, however, to examine what forces triggered this doubtful action: "Although no evidence suggests that the regime was considering such a plan, it nevertheless produced a good amount of hysteria among some parents. Considering what they had witnessed [namely the abolition of élitist private schools and other class privileges], the stripping of *patria potestad* by the Cuban government seemed conceivable as a logical next step. A story of questionable validity coming out of Cuba in 1961 [published in *Time*] told of fifty mothers in the city of Bayamo who had signed a pact vowing to kill their children before handing them to Castro" (9).[43] The book closes with what Triay considers "the most interesting song" on an album whose proceeds go to Catholic Family Services' Refugee Resettlement Program:

We are Cubans—so listen to us well—
Who came in refuge and blame it on Fidel.
And to the Americans we want to tell,
That we are like brothers and get along well.
And to the Communists we want to say,
That from lovely little Cuba you must go away.
And to the Virgin of Charity we want to say,
That from lovely little Cuba you must take them away. (106)

The song is emblematic of the intellectual level and social vision of Condé's and Triay's books, which ultimately shed more light on Chomsky's thesis regarding the manufacturing of consent than on the conflict of state interests that resulted in Operation Peter Pan.

Ricardo Alarcón de Quesada cannot fail to note in his introduction to *Operación Pedro Pan* that "Se edita en medio de la batalla que libramos por la liberación de Elián González y por la eliminación de la Ley de Ajuste Cubano y las leyes Helms-Burton y Torricelli y toda la política anexionista que busca aniquilar al pueblo cubano y arrebatarle la patria" (xiii) [(This book) is being published in the midst of a battle that we are fighting for the liberation of Elián González and for the elimination of the Law of Cuban Adjustment and the Helms-Burton and Torricelli Laws and the entire politics of annexation whose objective is to annihilate the Cuban people and to seize their homeland]. Galeano's interpretation of "adjustment plans" provides a concise global context to the Law of Cuban

Adjustment, which ultimately aims at the restoration of U.S. economic interests in Cuba, a running subtext not only to Operation Peter Pan but also to the more recent Elián González case:

> When a criminal kills someone for an unpaid debt, the execution is called a "settling of accounts." When the international technocracy settles accounts with an indebted country, the execution is called an "adjustment plan." Financial capos kidnap countries and suck them dry even when they pay the ransom: in comparison, most thugs are about as dangerous as Dracula in broad daylight. The world economy is the most efficient expression of organized crime. (*Upside Down* 6)

Alarcón de Quesada identifies in no uncertain terms the connection between the propaganda campaign that dominated U.S. "news" with the battle over González and Operation Peter Pan, the strategy being to destabilize Cuban society through psychological warfare aimed at undermining support for the revolution. González (and his family) were so successfully exploited by the press precisely because the media representation of a poor child being seized from his American relatives by what appeared to be storm troopers *manipulated* emotions in accordance with Rorty's definition of sentimentality. This grossly exploited event shows how fraught the notion of family is in relation to rights, given that both the Miami relatives and the Cuban father and grandmothers made rights claims over González's fate.

Rorty's last major insight is that sentimentality is the only way to motivate the people in the hegemony who are empowered to activate change:

> The residual popularity of Kantian ideas of 'unconditional moral obligation'—obligation imposed by deep ahistorical forces—seems to me almost entirely due to our abhorrence for the idea that the people on top hold the future in their hands, that everything depends on them, that there is nothing more powerful to which we can appeal against them.
>
> Like everyone else, I too should prefer a bottom-up way of achieving utopia, a quick reversal of fortune which will make the first last. But I do not think this is how utopia will in fact come into being. (130)

In this view, the sentimental appeal to the "people on top" becomes the extent to which change can occur to push toward a utopian event-horizon; this change, astonishingly, would happen from within a democratic political context. In distinction from this deeply cynical, deeply naïve and patronizing position, the American critic Elaine Scarry affirms that "The work accomplished by a structure of laws cannot be accomplished by a structure of sentiment. Constitutions are needed to uphold transnational values" (302). Scarry's analysis of the effects that texts like Harriet Beecher Stowe's *Uncle Tom's Cabin* and E. M. Forster's *A Passage to India* had on their immediate historical contexts (the Reconstruction Amendments to the U.S. Constitution prohibiting "servitude," echoed in Article 4 of the

Universal Declaration, and the 1943 Independence Act of India) also suggests a fruitful area of relatively unexplored study in the relations between human rights theory and literary culture (290-91). Moreover, Scarry's examination of the conditions required to imagine otherness as a function of both literary imagination and constitutional (dis)empowerment articulates a productive line of inquiry linking human rights theory to literature.

Our caution would be that establishing constitutionality as the norm upon which rights need to be founded is highly problematic without the linked concept of critical consciousness and the ability to act upon that consciousness. As the *Human Development Report 2000* notes, "Every country needs to strengthen its social arrangements for securing human freedoms—with norms, institutions, legal frameworks and an enabling economic environment. Legislation alone is not enough. Laws alone cannot guarantee human rights" (7). There are multiple examples of (the potential for) constitutional failure and ample potential situations in which constitutionality is used to justify unethical actions. After all, the crucial aspect of a constitution is its textuality (which literally founds its implementability or not); hence, the interpretive capacity to act on its "meaning" is a social and cultural imperative that places literary and textual skills in a heightened relation to the legal structures that attempt to describe and circumscribe human rights.

In distinction from such constitutional legal empowerments, themselves suspect structures for providing adequate context for the enactment of rights, Rorty sees sentimentality as productive of rights enactments: the latter are based on Christian charity rather than empowered solidarity. Galeano's analysis of the relation between charity and solidarity, like Scarry's comments on the ineffectiveness of structures of sentiment by comparison with legal structures, presents an apposite counter to Rorty's argument: "Unlike solidarity, which is horizontal and takes place between equals, charity is top-down, humiliating those who receive it and never challenging the implicit power relations. In the best of cases, there will be justice, someday, high in heaven. Here on earth, charity doesn't worry injustice, it just tries to hide it" (*Upside Down* 312). Rorty's vision of top-down charity effectively discounts the plural social movements in which change has occurred via a combination of bottom-up, top-down, and horizontal, to borrow Galeano's trope, interlocutions (witness the ongoing history of the Zapatista insurgency). The disavowal of these latter forces is again a universalizing notion of how meaningful transformation actually occurs—not through monolithic, unilateral top-down actions but through highly mediated acts of specific human agency in dialogue with multiple factors of which the dominant hegemony is only one.

Contrary to such simplistic and deeply perverse structures of how sentiment produces trickle-down action, Galeano offers a much more nuanced alternative:

> The revolutionary value of a text can be measured by taking into account the things
> it triggers in the person reading it. The best books, the best essays and articles, the
> best novels, the most effective poems and songs, cannot be read with impunity. Lit-

erature that is directed toward consciousness acts upon it, and if accompanied by purpose, talent, and luck, it sparks the imagination and the will to change. In the social structure of the lie, to reveal reality is to denounce it. It implies its own denunciation. ("The Imagination and the Will to Change" 122-23)

Simple affect is not enough in such a perspective as the revelation of reality requires much more and can never be as unidimensional as Rorty imagines it to be. Galeano replaces the passive fantasy of sentimentality with a much more pragmatic notion of critique and resistance as a function of being acted upon (without impunity) by a literary text. Nor is this a sentimental self-aggrandizing writerly gesture. Galeano is careful to note that

It is said that one book does not change the world, and that is true. But what does change the world? A fast or slow process, depending on the situation, but always incessant, and with a thousand dimensions. The written word is one of them, and not merely an auxiliary wheel. To deny literature which is not part of an emergency is as serious a mistake as to despise the literary forms of expression which escape the boundaries of genre or which have no place on the altars of academic culture. ("The Imagination and the Will to Change" 123)

Thus, incremental, discrepantly engaged, multi-dimensional, non-orthodox, non-reductive, border-crossing forms of writing are a crucial aspect of how meaningful change is effected by textual means.

Critical Consciousness? José Francisco Borges, from *Walking Words* 29.

In short, then, the combination of affect with information is one of the ways in which textuality is empowering. Such empowerment becomes instrumental in how the world gets read, a reading that is overshadowed by the potential for engagement and reciprocity or disengagement and ignorance. A good instance of the latter case is provided by Chomsky, who notes John Taylor's work on how British arms sales to Indonesia increased "sharply under Thatcher as atrocities [in East Timor and Indonesia] continued" (*The Umbrella of U.S. Power* 59). Chomsky goes on to cite Alan Clark, defense procurement minister under Prime Minister Margaret Thatcher, whose less than enlightened position was that "My responsibility is to my own people. I don't really fill my mind much with what one set of foreigners is doing to another" (*The Umbrella of U.S. Power* 59). The ethical vacuity of such a position is defenseless; its pertinence to how human rights sensibilities need to be promulgated more effectively is manifest.

Reciprocity? José Francisco Borges, from *Walking Words* 310.

Galeano, like Chomsky, is blunt and effective in this shaming process that depends on narrative content and style. To tell the stories that inform critical consciousness is one aspect in the production of egalitarian reciprocity in the name of difference and engagement necessary to a meaningful rights discourse:

> Of every ten Guatemalans, for example, six are Indians, but in Guatemala the word "Indian" is used as an insult, and a man can be arrested for the simple crime of not speaking Spanish: to the public administration and the instruments of justice, autochthonous languages do not exist. While the tourist bureau issues invitations to visit the land of the Mayas, the grandchildren of the Mayas, principal victims of the "dirty war" of military dictatorship, are despoiled of their lands and assassinated and thrown into common graves under markers, which say "NN," for *Non Nato*, meaning "Unborn." (Galeano, "The Revolution as Revelation" 12)

Here, Guatemalan demographics, the deforming power of language, the refusal to recognize difference, the gap between the narrative told by tourist bureaus and lived reality, and the double death of those assassinated by the military all suggest the extent to which the alliance of critical consciousness and affect are given a unique register via the kind of literary discourse Galeano produces. In this last passage, literature is associated with the pedagogical practices necessary to produce an informed, ethical citizenry, one that opposes injustice as a function of the sophisticated critical consciousness its pedagogy produces.

By contrast, Peruvian author Mario Vargas Llosa, in an essay entitled "Social Commitment and the Latin American Writer," argues that

> Indigenist literature is very important from a historical and social point of view, but only in exceptional cases is it of literary importance. These novels or poems written, in general, very quickly, impelled by the present situation, with militant passion, obsessed with the idea of denouncing a social evil, of correcting a wrong, lack most of what is essential in a work of art: richness of expression, technical originality. Because of the didactic intentions they become simplistic and superficial; because of their political partisanship they are sometimes demagogic and melodramatic; and because of their nationalist or regionalist scope they can be very provincial and quaint. (131)

The dismissal of indigenous literature in this way, in an article on the social commitment of the writer no less, suggests that universalist, ahistorical, and Eurocentric standards of excellence distinguish the literarily important from that which is not. This extremely narrow view of literature as an aesthetic field with no relevance to anything but formal considerations is undermined by Galeano's writing practices, which place literary practices in relation to a range of historical, political, moral/ethical, aesthetic, and technical determinants. Literary "importance," itself a signifier for who decides on the shape of the canon (that is, who decides what gets read and taught and why) is never just a matter of richness of expression or technique. Both terms are extensions of a universalist discourse that disregards the contexts that produce such an evaluation. Moreover, by focusing on these as the exclusive guarantors of quality, other factors like the social commitment of the artist are diminished as measures for evaluating texts. Binding literary value to narrow understandings of literary disciplinarity (as exemplified in Vargas Llosa's ideas on indigenist literature) is no longer a viable option to achieve an informed understanding of how texts signify in a larger rights context.

Again we note—as does Galeano—literature's importance with no sense of privileging it as a discourse and with a keen sense of how literary writing, in both its creative and critical manifestations, has somehow been neglected from the larger perspective pertaining to the discussion of rights generally.[44] Galeano's example, then, is instructive and illuminating, part of a body of imaginative literary work that is emerging as an alternative response to state-defined rights. Neither wholly affective nor purely rational, Galeano's hybridized writings recognize what Freire means when he claims that "To deny the importance of subjectivity in the process of transforming the world is naïve and simplistic. It is to admit the impossible: a world without people. This objectivistic position is as ingenuous as that of subjectivism, which postulates people without a world" (*Pedagogy of the Oppressed* 32). State-defined rights, as we have seen in some detail, give the lie to unrealized notions of equality and other transcendental principles of governance, informed by a misdirected objectivism in the name of the universal, a world without people (as marked by their difference from the universal). Galeano challenges master narratives of rights that distract from the specificity of lived experience, the rich diversity of human difference, the interlocutory techniques of reciprocal yet discrepant engagements and critical consciousness, the relations between agency and (inter)subjectivity, and the alternative forms of memory and narrative that are as much a basis for communitarian ideals as any discourse produced by legal and political textualities that have proven themselves largely dead to the world.

Coda

As a final provocation, we invite readers to compare the following two statements, not only in relation to the discourses of enforcement and obedience that are so frequently aligned with rights discourse, but also in relation to discourses of freedom, imagination, and the recognition of complex, emergent, reciprocal realities, always contingent, always provisional. One is legal, the other literary. Which form of the gap between the two will inhabit and inform the rights policies of the future? Which poses the question of how narrative imaginings (whatever their genre) shape lived experience most pertinently?

> Governments therefore become just when they enforce the basic natural duties and protect the human rights flowing therefrom that constitute the social contract. And individuals become ethical when they freely acknowledge and affirm obedience to

these basic duties as a personal obligation and give their informed consent to respect and honor the human rights of all other human beings. (Grant 23)

On the woof and warp of reality, tangled though it be, new cloth is being woven from threads of many radically different colors. Alternative social movements don't just express themselves through parties and unions. They do that, but not only that. The process is anything but spectacular and it mostly happens at the local level, where across the world a thousand and one new forces are emerging. They emerge from the bottom up and the inside out. Without making a fuss, they shoulder the task of reconceiving democracy, nourishing it with popular participation and reviving the battered traditions of tolerance, mutual assistance, and communion with nature...These unarmed forces of civil society face frequent harassment from the powerful, at times with bullets. Some activists get shot dead. May the gods and the devils hold them in glory: only trees that bear fruit suffer stonings. (*Upside Down* 320-23)

NOTES

1. In general, we restrict our analysis of human rights and nation to the Americas, as constituted by North, South, and Central America, as well as the Caribbean basin. The basic form of this critique, as mediated by Galeano's writing practices, would be transferable—*mutatis mutandis*—to other contexts in which similar patterns of abuse and control are obvious, whether in China, Central Europe, Indonesia, or elsewhere.

2. The critique of universal rights principles precedes the Universal Declaration, with the American Anthropological Association's publication in 1947 of Melville Herskovits's "rejection of 'the applicability of any Declaration of Human Rights to mankind as a whole'" and his declaration that the "'rights of Man in the Twentieth Century cannot be circumscribed by the standards of any single culture, or dictated by the aspirations of any single people'" (qtd. in Preis 285-86). As Preis relates, Herskovits's "statement was submitted to one of the commissions of the United Nations, which...in 1947 carried out a theoretical inquiry into the foundations of an international declaration of human rights, drawing on a large number of individual philosophers, social scientists, jurists, and writers from UNESCO member states" (Preis 316n2).

3. Isabel Allende notes how Galeano has "opposed military dictatorships and all forms of brutality and exploitation, taking unthinkable risks in defense of human rights" (4).

4. James Cockcroft states that "Pinochet is on record as saying he does not recognize the existence of the concept 'human rights'" (Allende, *Salvador Allende Reader* 3). For the record, "when Chileans elected Allende to the presidency on September 4, 1970...Voter turnout was high—83 percent of the electorate. Allende garnered more than a million votes (36.3 percent), a plurality in a three-way race against the runners-up, the right-wing National Party's Jorge Alessandri (34.9 percent) and Tomic (27.8 percent) of the increasingly discredited PDC [Christian Democratic Party]" (11).

5. Article 1 of the Universal Declaration states: "All human beings are born free and equal in dignity and rights. They are endowed with reason and conscience and should act toward one another in a spirit of brotherhood" (Ishay 408). We note how universalist assumptions about "equality" and "brotherhood" are affirmed in a highly gendered language that undermines the very equality and brotherhood posited.

6. Preis, arguing from an anthropological context, states that "the notion of agency attributes to the individual actor the capacity to process social experience and to devise ways of coping with life, even under the most extreme forms of coercion. Within the limits of information, uncertainty, and other constraints (for example, physical, normative, or politicoeconomic), social actors are knowledgeable and capable" (312).

7. In fairness, Kropotkin's thesis in *Mutual Aid* presented a hard-won resistance to the Hobbesian and Kantian notions that war is either inevitable or makes a civilization better: "For individual progress...conquest over nature, mutual aid and close intercourse are, as they always have been, much more advantageous than mutual struggle" (306). Even in such a potentially admirable formulation, though, Kropotkin's discourse is dependent on the highly suspect language of progress, conquest, and the separation of humanity from nature.

8. See also Quijano and Wallerstein, qtd. in Mignolo, *Local Histories/Global Designs* 53.

9. Feminizing space does not always imply the will to exploit, for Galeano himself represents Latin America as a nurturing feminine space that has experienced both love and rape. In this case, the feminized territory evokes the "motherland" with the paradisaical connotations of being the spiritual and physical source of all being. The connotation responds to the will to reciprocate such generosity lovingly and not the will to exploit.

10. Mignolo, in the name of the struggle to recognize and reinstate radical heterogeneity on a planetary scale, offers a useful summary of the civilizing process:

If, as [Darcy] Ribeiro (1968) taught us, the last stage of the civilizing process (i.e., the early modern and early colonial periods) consisted in a massive "subalternization of cultures" that became—by the sheer effect of the discursive practices of modernity—the non-West, then "subaltern studies" may have as one of its horizons the rearticulation of the notion of civilizing processes, no longer conceived as subalternization of cultures but as plurilogic and pluritopic processes contributing to a planet in which similarities-in-difference could replace the idea of similarities-and-differences, manipulated by colonial and imperial discourses. While similarities-and-differences is the conceptual framework in which the very idea of Western civilization has been constructed (relegating the differences to the barbarian, the savages, the cannibals, the primitives, the underdeveloped, etc.), similarities-in-difference calls instead for a relocation of languages, peoples, and cultures where the differences are looked at, not just in one direction (the direction of the restricted notion of civilizing differences as the triumphal march of modernity), but in all possible directions and regional temporalities. *The* civilizing process is the triumphal march of the human species, of a variety of civilizing processes, and *not just* the global spread of European/Western civilizations under the banner of progress, civility, and development. (*Local Histories/Global Designs* 202)

The problem, as José David Saldívar puts it, is "How do we characterize non-Eurocentered transfrontier identifications? Is there any getting around a local/global opposition that, in James Clifford's formulation, 'either favors some version of globalism self-defined as progressive, modern, and historically dynamic *or* favors a localism rooted (not routed) in place, tradition, culture, or ethnicity conceived in an absolutist mode?'" (72).

11. Here Galeano is referring to a portion of the *Democrates secundus* by Sepúlveda in which these specific comparisons are made (see Pagden, *The Fall of Natural Man* 117).

12. Sepúlveda was a militarist who "saw virtue in military glory" and who had in 1529 exhorted Charles V "to mount another crusade against the Turk" (Pagden, *The Fall of Natural Man* 114).

13. To be clear, Indians for Sepúlveda are "'barbarous and inhuman peoples abhorring all civil life, customs and virtue'" (qtd. in Pagden, *The Fall of Natural Man* 116).

14. The Spanish *delirar* connotes madness, euphoria, delirium, and also visionary insight, meanings all but lost in the English verb "to rave."

15. This clichéd tag to presidential addresses, repeated unthinkingly, implicitly asks why a just god would only bless America (let alone why the leader of the so-called free world would only ask god to bless one and not *all* countries).

16. The title of Bell's doctoral dissertation, "Narratives of Treason: Postnational Historiographic Tactics and Late Twentieth-Century Fiction in the Americas," introduces her interpretive framework for Galeano's *Memory of Fire*, Margaret Atwood's *The Handmaid's Tale*, Carmen Boullosa's *Duerme*, and Leslie Marmon Silko's *Almanac of the Dead*.

17. Brunner is a Chilean academic who specializes in higher education reform; he has served as the secretary general to the Chilean president and cabinet.

18. Cockcroft observes how out of step U.S. policies were toward Chile in the international context. Because of American interests in U.S.-owned copper companies, the prospect of further developing U.S. business in Chile proved to be in direct conflict with respecting Chile's sovereignty, its democratically elected government, and even its peoples' basic human rights:

    While most of the world's governments refused to recognize the military dictatorship or broke off diplomatic relations in protest, the U.S. government immediately recognized General Pinochet as Chile's legitimate president and rushed in economic aid to his regime. Like the U.S. government, South America's dictatorships strongly backed the coup. At Santa Cruz, Bolivia, half a year earlier, Brazilian and Bolivian soldiers who had been trained at U.S. Army schools in the Panama Canal Zone instructed 250 Chileans in the techniques of terrorism. Recently released CIA and other U.S. government documents confirm extensive U.S. government foreknowledge of the military coup and its bloody aftermath. (Salvador Allende 19)

19. The Miskito, together with the Sumo and the Rama, are indigenous people inhabiting the Eastern Atlantic region of Central America, particularly Nicaragua and Honduras.

20. Fanon's critique of state interest in relation to rights is relevant here:

    ...the characteristic feature of certain political structures is that they proclaim abstract principles but refrain from issuing definite commands. The entire action of these nationalist political parties during the colonial period is action of the electoral type: a string of philosophico-political dissertations on the themes of the rights of peoples to self-determination, the rights of man to freedom from hunger and human dignity, and the unceasing affirmation of the principle: "One man, one vote"...Pacifists and legalists, they are in fact partisans of order, the new order—but to the colonialist bourgeoisie they put it bluntly enough the demand which to them is the main one: "Give us more power." (59)

21. Chomsky's comments echo what Hannah Arendt argues is "the most formidable form of...dominion: bureaucracy or the rule of an intricate system of bureaus in which no men, neither one nor the best, neither the few nor the many, can be held responsible, and which could properly be called rule by Nobody. (If, in accord with traditional political thought, we identify tyranny as government that is not held to give account of itself, rule by Nobody is clearly the most tyrannical of all, since there is no one left who could even be asked to answer for what is being done)" (*On Violence* 38-39). Galeano has a great deal to say about the "nobody," as we will examine later on in the book.

22. The speciousness of economic arguments on such issues is highlighted by a recent Philip Morris Co. economic analysis distributed in the Czech Republic, which suggests that the number of early mortalities caused by smoking actually "saved the Czech government between...$23.8 million to $30.1 million...on health care, pensions, and housing for the elderly in 1999" ("Silver Lining" 11). Though the company apologized for the study, it is clear that its manipulation of facts reveals as much about how it regards human suffering as it does about the outrageous distortion of economic data it uses to support its own interests. Chomsky takes this systemic distortion of fact a step further when he argues: "Facts that are inconvenient to the doctrinal system are summarily disregarded as if they do not exist. They are just suppressed" (*Chomsky on MisEducation* 19). Galeano's persistent attack on systemic structures elaborates in a similar key, showing how the disregard for inconvenient facts that is part of doctrinal pedagogies is connected to more widespread effects of the "System":

    Functionaries don't function
    Politicians speak but say nothing.
    Voters vote but don't elect.

The information media disinform.

Schools teach ignorance.

Judges punish the victims.

The military makes war against its compatriots.

The police don't fight crime because they are too busy committing it.

Bankruptcies are socialized while profits are privatized.

Money is freer than people are.

People are at the service of things. (*The Book of Embraces* 131)

23. The trope of "nature" in a rights context has a particular resonance related to Hobbes's seventeenth-century definition of the right of nature, which, as we have seen earlier, essentially means self-preservation at any cost.

24. Drinan, for instance, notes in 1987 that "Seventy percent of the world's people have only 10 percent of the world's resources available to them"; that "Fifty percent of the world's people lack clean drinking water"; and that "The developing nations now owe over $800 billion—two thirds of it to lending institutions in the United States" (*Cry of the Oppressed* 182).

25. Galeano points out that "Each soldier of the line gets more than Prince Philip makes in a year" (*Genesis* 89).

26. Elsewhere, in a discussion of the ethical problems posed by the Zapatista rebellion in Chiapas, Dussel argues that "Chiapas is a very serious ethical question, demanding an answer from the history of modernity. Latin America must answer; but Europe is also bound to respond, especially mindful of the genocide it carried out in the sixteenth century—the first Holocaust of modernity! Europe must recall the fifteen million dead Amerindians, and the fourteen million Africans sold into slavery. These are ethical situations that demand a solidarious co-responsibility with the oppressed, the poor, and the excluded" ("Ethical Sense" 56).

27. Jameson argues that "a politics of difference does not become possible until a considerable degree of social standardization comes into being, that is to say, until universal identity is largely secured. The genuine, radical difference that holds between Columbus and the peoples he encountered can never be articulated into a politics: at best an enslavement, at worst a genocide, and occasionally something like a compassionate attempt at an impossible tolerance (which is itself a form of patronizing condescension)" (*The Jameson Reader* 391). We would dispute these claims insofar as they rely on universalist notions that were always already in place, as we have shown, in early modern discourses of encounter, predicated as they were on assumptions about the demonstrable superiority of civil settler culture. Columbus and those who followed in his wake already had a politics of difference in place that permitted and fostered slavery, genocide, and intolerance. To equate a "politics of difference" with "universal identity" is to be complicit, however unwittingly, with the very structures that so vitiated early modern European encounters with indigenes (where the universality of the European worldview was assumed to be superior to the difference embodied in indigenous cultures).

28. See MacKinnon's essay (especially her footnote 5) in its entirety for some of the relevant details and sources of information in relation to the rape/death camps. The disjunction between the reports cited by MacKinnon and the Amnesty International Reports, which present conservative statistics on the abuse of women, is an issue related to witnessing and the validity given testimonial evidence. MacKinnon argues that it is "inexcusable that Amnesty International's October 1992 report on human rights violations in this war documents only three rapes, and these from an English newspaper rather than firsthand, as other atrocities are documented" (231). The more recent *Amnesty International Report 2000* suggests that there were "allegations of rape and sexual violence" but that "The need to protect victims and witnesses meant that the full extent of the abuses could not be determined" (265). Human Rights Watch's *World Report 2000* states that "Serbian police and paramilitaries, as well as Yugoslav soldiers, also committed rape against ethnic Albanian women. Despite the social taboos associated with rape, some women reported being dragged out of refugee columns and assaulted; in other cases women were separated from the village's men and held for as much as three days in private houses where they were sexually abused. The United States (U.S.) and British (U.K.) governments reported rape camps in Dakovica and Pec, but no hard evidence emerged to support those claims" (316).

29. Brian Loveman explains the cynical position of the Latin American military nationalists in relation to human rights advocacy, both as a critique of American economic imperialism and as an attack on sovereignty:

> Military nationalists saw U.S. support for human rights investigations, and even for introducing human rights courses in military curricula, as a deliberate effort to weaken or destroy the Latin American armed forces. Feigned concern for human rights by the world's strongest power barely masked its intention to subordinate Latin American *national* security and development to the United States' regional and international agenda…The armed forces' victory over subversion and the defense of the *patria* must not be undone by the creation of a new international order that destroys sovereignty. The armed forces…must defend themselves and their nations from the international human rights conspiracy whose victory would signify the demise of their nations. In the 1990s the armed forces sought to prevent the ploy of human rights and the return of 'politics' from destroying their institutions and their *patria*. (417-19)

30. The trope of the concentration camp is not used flippantly in the Latin American context, especially given the camps that existed in Chile and Argentina, for example, during the dictatorships that led to Galeano's exile. Cortázar uses the concentration camp in a discussion of the place of the intellectual in the public sphere as an image to describe Latin America generally. Behind the water fountains and light shows and World Cup soccer tournaments lie "ces énormes camps de concentration dissimulés" ("Réalité et littérature" 187) [these enormous hidden concentration camps]. Further, Cortázar argues that "Le pouvoir nous contrôle, que ce soit d'une manière sauvage ou conformément à des codes auxquels nous n'avons pris aucune part, nous freine, nous censure, et, ces dernières années, nous tue purement et simplement si notre voix dissone dans le choeur des conformismes ou des critiques prudentes" ("Réalité et littérature" 192-93) [Power controls us, whether brutally or in a way that conforms to laws that we had no part in making; it restricts, censures, or expels us, and, in recent years, kills us purely and simply if our voice sings out of harmony within the choir of conformity or of prudent critique].

31. To this list may be added further refusals to sign international agreements in the name of national self-interest and "the predatory nature of U.S. foreign policy" ("Lone Wolf Policy" 10): these would include the ABM treaty, the comprehensive test ban treaty, the biological weapons protocol, the small-arms convention (U.S. arms manufacturers account for over one-quarter of the world trade in small arms, or approximately 1.2 billion dollars), and the Kyoto accord on global warming (the U.S. is responsible for up to 25% of greenhouse gases produced worldwide), which the U.S. opposed in the face of 178 nations who supported the accord ("Lone Wolf Policy" 8-10).

32. Latin America, according to Drinan, "is one of the world's richest and most fertile regions. It has more arable land than any other continent. It has 16 percent of the world's cultivable land with only 6 percent of the world's population. But every fifth person in Latin America is a victim of severe malnutrition. One of the basic reasons is the need for land reform. In Latin America 7 percent of the people control 93.8 percent of the land. One-half of the land in Central America is used not to produce food for the 24 million people in the five nations of that region but to produce crops and cattle for export. Similarly Brazil, one of the world's largest exporters, has more acreage under cultivation than the United States, but more than 70 percent of the population suffers some degree of malnutrition" (*Cry of the Oppressed* 183).

33. 1948 marked not only the passing of apartheid legislation in South Africa but also marked, among other events, the year in which Gandhi was assassinated, the State of Israel came into being, the British welfare state was created, Indonesia gained its independence, the People's Republic of China was declared, and George Orwell's *1984* was published, with its ironic numerical inversion signaling a particular reading of the historical significance of 1948 vis-à-vis the future.

34. The Argentine jurist and philosopher Eduardo Rabossi takes the position that the "human rights phenomenon renders human rights foundationalism outmoded and irrelevant" (qtd. in Rorty 116).

35. Harlow notes how in 1969, 20 years before his death, Ellacuría "had argued that the 'third world is the prophetic denunciation of how badly arranged are the things of this world'"; she continues on to affirm that "Those political negotiations which Ellacuría endorsed and for which he struggled and died would

eventually lead three years later to the Peace Accords signed in Chapultepec, Mexico, on 16 January 1992" (*After Lives* 38). For a more complete study of Ellacuría's significance, see Whitfield.

36. For useful critiques of the term postcolonial as a less than effective term to describe the complex realities to which it potentially refers, see work by McClintock, Ella Shohat, Benita Parry, and the essays collected by Afzal-Khan in *The Pre-occupation of Postcolonial Studies*.

37. Paulo Freire argues the following: "Within the word we find two dimensions, reflection and action, in such radical interaction that if one is sacrificed—even in part—the other immediately suffers. There is no true word that is not at the same time a praxis. Thus, to speak a true word is to transform the world" (*Pedagogy of the Oppressed* 68).

38. A review of three Canadian writers' books (Michael Ondaatje, Catherine Bush, and Alan Cumyn) notes how their work "centre[s] on human rights issues" and the general assessment is that the novels "turn out to be more illuminating about *realpolitik* than a dozen foreign-policy documents or journalistic accounts" (Sandra Martin D10). Such an emergent genre of writing will necessitate new pedagogies and new intellectual formations to accommodate its critical relevance, perhaps in ways beyond the disciplinary imaginings of current traditional humanities and social scientific institutional configurations. And clearly, Galeano's work and the work of other writers in this emergent genre would necessarily offer unique pedagogical opportunities for rethinking the place of literature within a range of other institutional and pedagogical discourses.

39. Rorty appears ignorant of the degree to which the sentimental as a literary form does not connote a particularly effective genre, as exposed in the implicit and explicit critiques of the sentimental by people like Mary Wollstonecraft, Hannah More, Jane Austen, and so forth: "The word 'sentimental' came to mean 'false and self-indulgent feeling' after Schiller's division (1795) of poets into two classes, the 'naïve' and the 'sentimental': 'naïve writers are natural and instinctive; 'sentimental' ones are forced and artificial" (Ousby 845). Schiller's breakdown, in the context we have been arguing in relation to Galeano, is equally restrictive.

40. Kensinger, based on extensive fieldwork with the Cashinahua, states that "A wise person is not only one whose body knows based on past experience, but one whose knowledge continues to increase as knowledge is put into action. Knowledge is alive. It lives and grows in a body that acts, thinks, and feels" (246).

41. Galeano goes on to argue that "there must be a language capable of overcoming this false frontier, and of redeeming the essential unity of the human condition at a time when new generations are emerging into a supertechnological civilization which tends to tear the soul to pieces. So now more than ever, we need to put the pieces back together" (NACLA staff 19).

42. At last count, the essay that is the source of these ideas has been published in three major anthologies devoted to human rights issues, those by Hurley and Shute, by Ishay, and by the Belgrade Circle, all of which appear in our Works Consulted.

43. Similar sorts of exaggerations were used against Salvador Allende in Chile: "the rabid right-wing newspaper *Tribuna* filled its headlines with spurious tales of Allende's plans to burn nuns and assassinate priests...[and] *El Mercurio*, Chile's most influential paper, exaggerated the meat shortage with fictitious stories about the sale of sausages made of human flesh" (Rosenberg 343).

44. In researching this book we were consistently struck by the paucity of overt references in both literary critical discourses and in human rights writings to how literary and rights cultures inform each other. This gap exists despite elements of literary critical discourse that depend on thinking rights anew (for example, gay, lesbian, and queer criticism and other forms of criticism that focus on marginalized literary formations, whether a function of being indigenous, woman, decolonized, racially other, and so forth).

Chapter 3

Through the Looking Glass:
Story, Memory, and *Testimonio*

"The Light of Dead Stars Travels": The Writer as Storyteller

Telling stories—"*platicando*," a Mexican word for chatting that mysteriously connotes a particular experience of time (one cannot possibly "platicar" in a hurry to relay dry facts)—is the most fundamental of human activities, the basis of all art, communication, and community. There is no self without an other, no consciousness without dialogue. Storytelling intimates the magical source of identity. The word breathes life into human beings, who by telling each other stories create communities, histories, and the intricate bases of shared and disparate experiences. In the creation story "Language" (appearing in *Genesis*, the first volume in the *Memory of Fire* trilogy) Galeano speaks of how the First Father of the Guaraní created love and language, but there was no existence until the sacred hymn, marriage of music and words, gave life to women and to men. "So love became communion, language took on life, and the First Father redeemed his solitude. Now he accompanies men and women who sing as they go: *We're walking this earth / We're walking this shining earth*" (11). Bodies are animated by air that breathes life into them through words, poetry, incantation, song and stories, and the kinetic connection between earth and body symbolized for the Guaraní by the act of collective walking.

This animistic story generates both material and metaphorical reality, according to a vision that has not been sliced in two by the machete of Western reason. Trinh intuits the wisdom of the story, its originary wholeness/diversity prior to being violently split and hierarchized into two opposing objects, one inferior to the other that erects itself as judge, the institutionally controlled story that calls itself history.

The story depends upon every one of us to come into being. It needs us all, needs our remembering, understanding, and *creating what we have heard together to keep* *on coming into being...*They call it the tool of primitive man, the simplest vehicle of truth. When history separated itself from story, it started indulging in accumulation and facts. Or it thought it could. It thought it could build up to History because the Past, unrelated to the Present and the Future, is lying there in its entirety, waiting to be revealed and related. Story-writing becomes history-writing, and history quickly sets itself apart, consigning story to the realm of tale, legend, myth, fiction, litera-ture...fiction, not infrequently, means lies, and fact, truth. Did it really happen? Is it a true story? (Trinh 119-20; our emphasis)

This violent duality that reduces diversity to the number two (primitive other/superior me) whose legacy we are tracing through conquest, colonization, nationalism, capitalism, neo-colonialism, and neoliberalism is undone like an evil spell that finds its antidote in storytell-ing. Voices that suddenly explode and proliferate, uncontainable and contagious, break out of the nightmare of duality into the hopefulness of *soñar despierto* (wakeful dreaming), the endlessly inventive forms of storytelling that create and celebrate diversity, the source of life and human community.[1] Storytelling in this mode posits a form of community in which co-creation is contingent on the listening that enables creation as an expression of "hear[ing] together." The ceaseless enactment of this creative process ensures the possibility of "coming into being," a relentless ethical stance taken by the storyteller toward the world at large, in which "being" constantly calls upon its potential makers to be made through the mutual acts of listening and telling.

Like much of Galeano's writing, *Walking Words* transgresses generic boundaries in or-der to create a collective and shared history based on the oral traditions of storytelling. Yet *Walking Words* differs from his other work in that it appears to be more easily classifiable, the obvious story structure creating a first impression that the book belongs to the realm of "primitive" fiction whose relation to history is even less tenuous than that of contemporary narrative. According to Palaversich, "En *Las palabras andantes* desaparece todo interés en la situación política concreta en el continente. El "yo" del autor cede paso al narrador en tercera quien, acompañado por los grabados de José Borges, recrea los relatos de la tradición popular, y entre ellos los cuentos 'regalados' por sus amigos que simplemente celebran el misterio y maravilla de la vida humana" (*Silencio* 252) [In *Walking Words*, all interest in the concrete political situation of the continent disappears. The "I" of the author gives way to a third-person narrator who, accompanied by the woodcuts of José Borges, recreates tales be-longing to the popular tradition, and between them the stories 'given' by their friends all simply celebrate the mystery and marvels of human life]. Palaversich's interpretation draws from the clean division between history and story questioned by Trinh in the opening cita-tion. In light of these two quotations, we ask whether any popular tradition is ever com-pletely devoid of political interest, or whether it incorporates that interest in ways that free its significance from objectifying rhetoric.[2]

While many of the stories in *Walking Words* rely on fantastic elements characteristic of legends, they also have a political dimension in that they address poverty, the reality of being dispossessed of land and forced into urban exile, as well as homelessness and hunger: this hunger is not just for bread but for the mystery and marvels of life identified by Palaversich. Storytelling is holistic in that it does not dissect human experience, whether emotional, spiritual, or physical, into rationalized generic categories of inquiry. Perhaps it is for this reason that when faced with the rich concoctions speaking to all those dimensions, their political impact can be lost or lessened to different readers. Taken as a particular type of discourse, the purely political is incorporated (embodied) in the social by the storyteller who, instead of separating out the different threads of experience, weaves them together as they exist in the fabric of life. It cannot easily be denied that even the anonymous stories of those communities most tied to indigenous traditions speak not only about the mystery and marvels but also of the suffering and dignity motivating resistance and storytelling itself. If so, is it not paternalistic to assume that no desire for change and improvement exists in popular traditions? Such an assumption is based on a vision of the "primitive" as existing outside history, situated in an eternal (stagnant) mythic limbo where "primitives" happily celebrate the simple pleasures of life. The wisdom to be gleaned from storytelling is precisely that history and story cannot be separated, just as the desire for justice cannot be separated from the celebration of life. Candace Slater, U.S. academic and interpreter of Latin American culture, observes that

> ...if certain vertical alliances underlie many stories, the links between these and most people's experiences remain indirect. This is partly because, as Althusser suggests, the ideological manifestations evident in art forms are not merely the passive reflection of a particular political and economic reality. Rather, they are normally a far more complicated representation of largely imaginary relationships between men and the circumstances in which they find themselves. (211)

This appreciation of the complexity of the storyteller's vision of reality is recognized by Galeano and becomes a predominant factor in his approach to writing about Latin American reality, not just as the story of foreign exploitation but as a complicated fabric of literal and figural forces. These include memory, dream, prophecy, and myth—forces that allow him to reinvent a world appropriated by the conquerors' unidimensional history.

In *Walking Words*, Galeano looks to the Brazilian *cordel* tradition, a generic hybrid disseminated in written form and subsequently circulated among the illiterate by those who can read and recite the stories. The transmission of the stories relies on their musicality and poetic rhythm, further enhanced by the illustrations that accompany the verses. This form of storytelling crosses the generic boundaries characterizing most Western art through its performative, musical, visual, lyrical, and narrative components. This formal diversity is theorized by some to contain a relatively stable and hierarchical vision of the world, while other critics maintain that the *cordel* tradition continually transforms the stories to reflect changing attitudes and circumstances. The *cordel*'s hybrid character fuses literature with journalism and appeals to a public that is equally diverse, since it has something for everyone. As Marion Oettinger notes:

> In Brazil, where they continue to be used as major vehicles for Brazilian folkways, these pamphlets are sold by the thousands each week. There they are called *folhetos* or *literatura de cordel*, after the manner in which they are displayed by vendors—hanging over a string. Brazilian chap books deal with popular poetry, accounts of local catastrophes, popular legends, famous crimes, and infamous love affairs. *The Man Who Married a Donkey, The Son Who Murdered His Parents in Order to Get His Hands on Their Retirement Benefits, The Football Game from Hell*, and *The Overturned Bus Disaster* are examples of some of the alluring titles found in a typical marketplace. (82)

Galeano's incursion into this highly dynamic and versatile form of storytelling frees him to mesh history, gossip, myth, journalism, and "lying."[3] *Cordel* provides the perfect "set of guidelines," as Slater refers to its traditional formal aspect, to recuperate the holistic and democratic nature of storytelling. In Spanish, the word *historia* still retains the dual meaning of "history" and "story" that Galeano reunites in his writing. The result liberates the reader's interpretation from the conventional constraints of genre, consequently breaking down the categories that arbitrarily separate human experience and thought.

The open structure of *Walking Words*, evoked as process by the title even more obviously in the Spanish *Palabras andantes* (evocative of "wandering"), creates a free play of discourse and visual images that can be contemplated in any order. Reading is liberated from linearity even though some narrative threads are fragmentarily connected, as if they were different installments of the same story, ongoing with new titles. This kind of interruption of one story, that lapses for days and sometimes even months until being taken up again, is a feature of popular storytelling in Africa, and implies a very different reader reception from the compulsive "whodunit," "how does it end?" mode of reading. "Walking" becomes a metaphor for the material presence of the narrators who, like Borges, must physically displace themselves in order to disseminate their art. Words uttered enter into the condition of exile that is the storyteller's fate as he or she travels from place to place, story to story, audience to audience. Walking, too, is a metaphor for the exile's vision of human possibility, the resistance to any narrative that reduces or contains that possibility. In "Window on Utopia," Galeano cites the Argentine filmmaker Fernando Birri: "I walk ten steps and the horizon runs ten steps ahead. No matter how much I walk, I'll never reach her" (*Walking Words* 326). The nomadic walker attempts to reach a horizon that is infinitely regressive, yet the desiring movement towards it is empowering.

Walking Words oscillates between short, fragmentary stories, rendered as mythic encounters, and what Galeano has chosen to call "Windows," insights concentrated into a few poetic lines that frame an alternative non-narrative. Windows are used not only to break up the fragmentary sequence of mythic stories that form the bulk of the book but also to afford brief glimpses of reality transformed by the writer's craft. The structure, like that followed by the more testimonial and autobiographical *The Book of Embraces*, permits the clash of genres and produces the disorienting effects that result from such combinatory techniques. Thus, to enter the realm of myth, either as writer or as reader, requires dislocation from the norm of narrative sequence, which is at once a gesture towards the magic realism that expresses a wondrous relationship with the world and a transgression against the illusion of history as linear narrative. In Galeano's work, xenochrony (or "strange time") takes precedence over the bland linearity of narratives, whether fictional or historical, which ignore the presence of such strangeness in how people experience time. Galeano opposes the view that time is (and cannot be anything but) an ordered progression that reflects some rational norm, his work suggesting instead that the experience of historical or even literary time is always profoundly arbitrary, surpassingly contingent. For Galeano, history is a mirage, an event-horizon that dissolves into the discontinuities of the vision that produces the mirage. And *Walking Words* displays the ironic recognition of the writer as marker of that discontinuity: "For navigators who love the wind, memory is a port of departure" (113).

Readers of these mythic stories, fragmentary, lush with ambiguity, bizarrely detailed, will find that most of them have an in-built resistance to the simplicity with which they are told. In concert with the sparse eloquence of Borges's evocative woodcuts, Galeano has fashioned a dreambook that works on the level of psychic contagion. Like the writer refashioning the realm of myth, the reader cannot help but be refashioned by the transformative powers of language. Watch how prohibition becomes celebration in the following window:

On a wall in a Madrid eatery hangs a sign that says: *No Singing*.
On a wall in the airport of Rio de Janeiro hangs a sign that says: *No Playing with Luggage Carts*.
Ergo: There are still people who sing, there are still people who play. (94)

Writing is transformative but it is also memorial. Or better: writing transforms because it memorializes, shape-shifting moment into dream, reality into imagination. And vice-versa: the restaurateur's or the technocrat's dream of prohibition—no singing, no playing—becomes the imagination of those who transgress such inane prohibitions. The smug complacency of the sign betrays its own futility in the face of human resistance. Such insights typify Galeano's project as a writer who infuses the real with the lifeblood of imagination, combining words with the extra-verbal, the extra-literary, the unspoken shape of an inner voice that cannot be disclaimed or restricted. This freedom exposes the connections among actions, words, and thoughts that are usually veiled, alienating people from each other in order to create a docile citizenry resigned to solitude.

Galeano's readers find themselves in a participatory position, liberated from the narrative chronology that imposes a passive following of events unfolding seriatim in linear order. *Walking Words* resists being simply "consumed" as a cultural object because it invites the reader to make choices—however random, arbitrary, and subjective—to collaborate actively in making the text speak. Even contemplating the woodcut prints in relation to the written text implicates the reader in making connections, wondering about the origins and significance of visual elements, and allowing oneself to rest on the images or move along with the words. This play of image and word resists the universalizing structural analysis of folktales, a prevalent academic approach to deciphering "primitive" stories by reducing them to skeletal molds into which content is assumed to be poured and given shape in order to repeat the same message endlessly.

In her exploration of how such an approach misses the point of storytelling, Trinh exposes the simplistic mechanical structure, which is reflective not of the story but of the interpreter's obtuse perception:

> "A good story," another man of the West asserted, "must have a beginning that rouses interest, a succession of events that is orderly and complete, a climax that forms the story's point, and an end that leaves the mind at rest." No criteria other than those quoted here show a more thorough investment of the Western mind. *Get them*—children, story-believers—*at the start; make your point* by ordering events to a definite *climax*; then *round out to completion*; descend to a rapid close—not one, for example, that puzzles or keeps them puzzling over the story, but one that *leaves the mind at rest*. In other words, to be "good" a story must be built in conformity with the ready-made idea some people—Western adults—have of reality, that is to say, a set of prefabricated schemata (prefabricated by whom?) they value out of habit, conservatism, and ignorance (of other ways of telling and listening to stories). (142)

Contrary to this notion of the perfect recipe for cooking up an edifying falsehood, stories that have cultural significance are "true" in the sense that they speak of key events kept in memory through the telling, or they speak truths not limited to any specific time and place because they explore interactions that can occur in different contexts. Often, they do both. Stories in this mode are not meant to put children or insomniacs to sleep. Trinh's crucial differentiation between factual and truthful stories confounds the empirically narrow theories concerning truth claims in narrative. She shows how the Western tradition privileges factual over truthful representation in a reminder that

> ...literature and history once were/still are stories: this does not necessarily mean that the space they form is undifferentiated, but that this space can articulate on a different set of principles, one which may be said to stand outside the hierarchical realm of facts. On the one hand, each society has its own politics of truth; on the other hand, being truthful is being in the in-between of all régimes of truth. (121)

Galeano's writing occurs at the crossroads of these two conflicting paradigms: rather than fall under the reductive categories "truth" or "lie," his work is driven by the desire to articulate the experiences of people whose stories are only partially recognized as belonging to Latin American culture. This recognition often only happens when the state appropriates their stories and returns them to the people as mass culture to promote its own nationalistic agenda.

The fictive framework of *Walking Words* incorporates visual and literary elements of folk art to create truthful stories replete with creative energy. Galeano's continuous dialogue with Latin American popular culture lessens the monological solitude of writing, enabling him to envision storytelling as a collective project, a sharing of memory and creativity, and a form of resistance to the "universal culture" imposed by mass media on the Third World. Dussel uses the term "universal culture" to designate a phenomenon that is essentially a massive advertising campaign parading as culture: "Both the 'needs' and the means of their satisfaction are exported to the Third World, whose peoples, in all but total helplessness, contemplate not only the domination of their states, their armies, and their economies, but the destruction of their cultural objects, their customs, their symbols, the very meaning of their life" (*Ethics and Community* 201). The recuperation of these destroyed cultural objects is implicit in the engagement of *Walking Words* with Brazilian popular culture via the *cordel* tradition.

The first fragment of *Walking Words* tells of the genesis of Galeano's book and how it became a joint project with Borges. Galeano visits Borges's workshop in the town of Bezerros in the impoverished Sertão, the Northeastern hinterland of Brazil, a trip backwards in time or to a timeless space where *cordel* storytelling retains medieval troubadouresque elements and is also continually metamorphosing in tandem with the lived realities of many peoples. The description of Borges's workshop depicts a space outside modernity. The simplicity of the tools used by Borges establishes a clear distinction between mass and popular culture, terms often confused in so-called First World countries: "A makeshift table, some movable type made of lead or wood, a press that might have been Gutenberg's" (19). Galeano's choice to work with an artist who continues to illustrate his own stories with woodcuts is no simple foray into popular culture as if it were some homogeneous, static entity. In recent years, this type of illustration has fallen by the wayside, replaced by the glossy and soft-porn comic book images mass-produced by a publishing house in São Paulo (Rowe and Schelling 86-87). Popular artists like Borges struggle to keep their art alive even when they cannot realistically compete with the mass media "rip-offs" that the majority of the public actually prefers: "by contrast to the woodcuts, which reflect the poverty of the means of production, these technically sophisticated covers provide them [migrant rural workers] with a sense of participating in the fruits of modernity" (Rowe and Schelling 87).[4] The fact that individual artists continue to produce their own prints, even when this means sacrificing profits, attests to the active resistance of popular culture from being appropriated and emptied by "universal culture." *Walking Words* is a visual and literary hybrid because Borges and Galeano both cultivate traditional characters, motifs, and situations while also creating new ones. At first glance, Borges appears to be calling the shots by giving the book its basis in *cordel*, but it soon becomes apparent that while Galeano draws inspiration from traditional stories, he rejects their conservatism and elaborates their subversive, utopic potential.

The Storyteller. José Francisco Borges, from *Cordel* (1996): front cover.

Galeano records the slight awkwardness he experiences when first proposing this collaborative project to Borges: "his face like carved wood and he doesn't say a word...I venture my idea: his illustrations, his woodcuts, and my words. He is silent. I talk on, explaining. And he says nothing" (*Walking Words* 19). Galeano attributes Borges's silence to the fact that he is "explaining" instead of storytelling, and does not consider that perhaps Borges is silent because Galeano reserves the words for *his* part of the project. Given that Borges is not just a visual artist but a poet and storyteller himself, the reader is left wondering how this sudden division of labour makes him feel. This enigma aside, their collaboration results in a fertile embrace between popular rural artist and urban writer.

Borges's control of the various stages of production of the *cordel folhetos* is anachronistic in the modern age in which such control is usually usurped by institutional management in the service of ownership. But he and other artists practice their art alongside the partial technological appropriation of *cordel* literature that, in some positive instances, can also help these artists to disseminate their work. As Galeano explains, "In the TV era, Borges remains an artist of the old *cordel* tradition. In tiny booklets, he recounts events and legends: he writes the verses, carves the woodcuts, prints them, carries them from town to town on his back, and offers them for sale in marketplaces where he sings the feats of men and ghosts" (*Walking Words* 19). Galeano shares Borges's taste for manual production: Caleb Bach, calling Galeano "refreshingly old-fashioned when it comes to technique" (10), describes Galeano's rejection of computers in favour of writing by hand on scraps of paper before transferring them to final drafts on a manual typewriter. Galeano contrasts the physical-spiritual connection among handwriting, drawing, and collective storytelling with mass media, specifically television:

> The screen produces a ready-made reality. The viewer is passive. That's the problem of consumer culture: it consumes culture. Once the storyteller was universal to all people but gradually local cultures are being crushed by global culture imposed around the world. In the name of diversity, they are killing diversity. Control of the media is very undemocratic. (Bach 19)

A long poem explaining the roots, significance, and forms—both literary and performative—of the *cordel* laments the usurpation of traditional Brazilian culture by North American cultural models. The following excerpt from this poem, a kind of popular *Ars poética*, provides a more specifically nationalist interpretation of the clash between global and local referred to in Galeano's critique of media:

> *Era a música arrancada*
> *das raízes do Sertão*
> *quando o Brasil era puro*
> *sem ter muita inflação*
> *de caretas americanas*

que hoje endoidam a nação. (Cascon and Shadwick, *Cordel [Folheto]* n.pag.)

[*It was music drawn
from roots in the Sertão,
when Brazil was pure
without much inflation
no American manias
confusing the nation.*]

The producers of the booklet translate *caretas americanas*—literally "American masks"—to "American manias," but the more literal meaning evokes the issue of identity so prevalent in Galeano's work. As we have already seen, the second volume of *Memory of Fire* is subtitled *Faces and Masks,* while the cover of *Ser como ellos y otros artículos* [To Be Like Them and Other Essays], designed by Galeano, is a photograph of a puno mask from Perú representing the white colonizer. Galeano's diverse expressions of desires and worries shared by Latin Americans from different ethnic, social, and economic backgrounds emerges from his view that culture is communication between all sectors of society: "In order for it not to be mute, we thought, a new culture had to begin by not being deaf. We published texts about reality, but also, and above all, texts from reality. Words picked up in the street, in the countryside, in the caves, life histories, popular verses" (*Days and Nights* 147). This "mission statement," made in relation to editing the journal *Crisis,* is also relevant to Galeano's interest in popular storytelling. While in his various editorial positions he published others' stories, in *Walking Words* and *The Book of Embraces* he creates his own versions of tales that resonate with char-

Puno mask from Perú representing the white colonizer. From *Ser como ellos* (1997): cover design by Eduardo Galeano.

acters and happenings belonging to a collective repertoire to which they return by being read and retold. Slater's insights on the cordel can be transposed to examine Galeano's incursion into this form of storytelling, since they depict more accurately the narrative framework of Walking Words than the dualistic interpretation that differentiates between the "I"-centred discourse of "political" writing and the third-person narration characteristic of popular tradition. Slater explains that the structuralist approach to analyzing cordel literature recognizes the meshing of traditional form with the flexibility and individuality of specific authors: "cordel is not only a collection of stories but an underlying, quite particular vision of human life...there is within the tradition a basic structure capable of generating a wide variety of narratives. Less a preestablished mold than a set of guidelines demanding constant reelaboration, this sequence [the six-step sequence outlined by Slater] is something which each poet intuits, then manipulates at will" (58). Some of the salient features of cordel identified by Slater include "third-person narrative within first-person framework, individual authorship emphasized by devices such as final identifying acrostic; [and] reliance on 'eyewitness' or other corroborating source" (99).

This complex relationship between individual authorship and third-person narrative is incorporated into the "Story of the Female Avenger and the Archangel in the Palace of Sinners" in *Walking Words*, a metanarrative examining how the writer learns to become a storyteller meshed with the telling of the story. The story is attributed to an anonymous storyteller who mails it to the pathetic writer, together with bits of storytelling advice, and challenges him to configure the ingredients into a story deserving of the name. The story opens in the epistolary mode directed to "Dear Mr. Writer" and proceeds to insult, challenge, and instruct the writer in storytelling: "I am moved to write to you not out of admiration but out of pity for your minimal inspiration and limited imagination. In your prose, which is as proper as it is pedestrian, readers never find anything they haven't already read. This letter offers you the chance to reveal your normally hidden talent, that is, if you have some hidden somewhere" (29). Ironically, Galeano levels at himself as writer the criticism that he earned for his earliest works *Los días siguientes* (1965) and *Los fantasmas del día de león* (1967). These existential novels which left him feeling dissatisfied led to the writing of *Las venas abiertas de América latina* (1971) [*Open Veins of Latin America*], marking a radical change of perspective from individual angst to the economic analysis of imperialism and exploitation. But despite this book's radical challenge to the history of the conquerors and colonizers—Spanish, American, and multinational—and its enormous popularity among Latin American readers, in retrospect, Galeano "admits that *Venas* reduces history to a single economic dimension. These days he favors a description of history as life, something that 'sings with multiple voices'" (Bach 18). This dissatisfaction with European trends and genres gives Galeano the impetus to seek out new ways of seeing and telling. These grow from his own Latin Americanness even as they address his family's genealogy in Europe, thus accounting for his writing from a position as a cultural mestizo.

In the middle of the "Story of the Female Avenger and the Archangel in the Palace of Sinners," the letter-writer interrupts his narration to admonish the writer to move from sterile representation to the magical power that, when unleashed, gives the reader an authentic experience instead of a pale reflection:

> Please, I beg you, don't offend me by asking if this really happened. I'm offering it to you so you'll make it happen. I'm not asking you to describe the rain falling the night the archangel arrived: I'm demanding that you get me wet. Make up your mind, Mr. Writer, and for once in your life be the flower that smells rather than the chronicler of the aroma. There's not much pleasure in writing what you live. The challenge is to live what you write. And at your age it's time you learned. (35)

These ironic interruptions mesh reflections on storytelling with the actual story being told, illuminating the problems that face the artist who strives to reach his anonymous but discerning public. Since the *cordel* and other forms of popular storytelling have important dramatic elements involving performance and shared commentary, the effects of these elements are to be incorporated by the storyteller who wants to break out of the élite circle of bourgeois representation dominated by the writer's sensibilities and mediation. Authorship is not ownership in the collective context, and while individual storytellers are admired for their skill, the story is not received as a product of individual genius but as the expression of a shared repertoire of symbols and concerns.

The *cordel* tradition transcends the boundaries between popular and "high" culture by incorporating a wealth of biblical allusions, myths, legends, and historical references from around the world, as well as scrutinizing the most locally specific realities. Slater differentiates the *cordel*'s vast cultural repertoire from the mass media, despite the *cordel*'s appeal to members of all social classes:

> The *folheto*'s variety and often surprising freedom explains more than any other factor its continued survival in the midst of rapid change. Able to incorporate a two-thousand-year-old Buddhist parable, a local news event, or a recent best-selling novel with equal ease, the poet continues to write stories that mean something to the people who read them, that touch them in a way that other forms of entertainment do not. For all his interest in making a meager living, the *folheto* author does not toss them off in the same spirit as a writer of pulp novels. The reader does not throw away a *cordel* booklet he has finished reading like the Sunday supplement but hands it to a friend or slips it into a special drawer. The petty official flips through a stack of *cordel* stories with impatience, trying to pinpoint what annoys him in these "ingenuous" tales of saints and dragons. Were the *folheto* not full of disguised and yet transparent meanings, were it not imbued with what Miguel Arraes, former governor of Pernambuco, once called "the science of life's suffering," it would not have this power to console, inspire, and disturb. (226)

This power is coveted by internationally acclaimed authors who also see it as a source of inspiration to learn a form of expression that crosses class boundaries. The solitary writer looks to the *cordel* storyteller who, surrounded by his audience, gets immediate feedback and gratification. It is obvious why a writer like Galeano, who consciously writes "for the people whose luck or misfortune one identifies with—the hungry, the sleepless, the rebels, and the wretched of this earth," who writes against his own solitude "and against the solitude of others" (*We Say No* 130), would identify with a storyteller like "I am Joe No One." José Soares, who uses that descriptive stage name to identify with his traditionally popular and uneducated audience, explains how his stories differ from literature:

> And everyone likes me because I am just like them. There is no difference whatsoever between us, and still I can write *folhetos*. If I were a university graduate, if I had studied in some school, that would be something else. But I am no better than they are, and I still manage to write. Furthermore, they understand me. An educated person's writing is too fine, too pretty; it makes them feel silly and uncomfortable. (Slater 181)

The accessibility described here by Soares is not due to the "dumbing down" agenda of television and other forms of mass media but to a language that is clear and forceful despite its ambiguity, its allegorical and metaphorical intensity. Speaking to the Argentinian writer Héctor Tizón in an autobiographical moment, Galeano expresses a vision of writing and perception that accords well with what he later discovers in the *cordel* tradition:

> I tell Héctor I'm trying to write, to pin down, the little uncertainties that one continually conquers, before the whirlwind of doubt snatches them away—words that are like lion claws or tamarinds in the sand of swirling dunes. *Return to the joy of simple things*: the light of the candle, the glass of water, the bread I share. Humble dignity, clean world that is worthwhile. (*Days and Nights* 136; our emphasis)

Joy, dignity, and simplicity are the key components identified by Galeano as giving him pleasure and a sense of purpose. The gesture of sharing is central to his vision of writing against solitude and his commitment to gathering the voices of others to further enrich the collective sharing of stories. The link between Soares's popularity and Galeano's desire to "return to the joy of simple things" suggests that by becoming more like "I am Joe No One," "Mr. Writer" breaks out of solitude "to share that which gives happiness" (*We Say No* 130).

Trinh also identifies the principal motivation of storytelling as joy: "Let me tell you a story. For all I have is a story. Story passed on from generation to generation, named Joy. Told for the joy it gives the storyteller and the listener. Joy inherent in the process of storytelling. Whoever understands it also understands that a story, as distressing as it can be in its joy, never takes anything away from anybody" (119). Trinh associates storytelling with the figure of the Grandmother, the "keepers and transmitters": "Truth is when it is itself no longer. Diseuse, Thought-Woman, Spider-Woman, griotte, storytalker, fortune-teller, witch.

If you have the patience to listen, she will take delight in relating it to you. An entire history, an entire vision of the world, a lifetime story" (121). In *Walking Words*, the stories are attributed to a number of tellers who are also listeners: they collect the stories from the locals in order to disseminate them. Some of these, like the chronicler and the professor, may be ironic allusions to the educated writer who enters this realm as foreign investigator. Others, such as Sabino, the prophet poet in "Story of the Fatal Encounter between the Desert Bandit and the Repentant Poet," represent the historical and geographical roots of *cordel* storytelling. The stock character's identity is multiplied since he is associated with any "reciter of verses in marketplaces far from the coast" (55).

Central to *Walking Words* is the Grandmother who spins the thread without following the preordained patterns identified by structural analyses, sometimes relating stories that sound like native myths, and in other cases combining several different traits, as in the case of "Story of the Moon People": "I'm boring you. Grandma's always telling the same story. Come on, let's put the beans on to soak. You can't sleep? I never sleep. My whole life practicing and I still don't know how. Sit by me, the kitchen's the best place. Grandma knows. For a night without sleep, for a day without soul, it's the best. The stove never goes out. Never" (268). Like the stove, the story never goes out either. This story borrows from the *cordel* the many-layered context that defies being reduced to a structure that supposedly reveals a moral lesson with the didactic impetus of a punch line. While it recalls myths of origin in that the moon people seem to be the source and embodiment of music, the story overflows that formal framework. Grandmother tells about having to leave her region because of drought and how her people arrived in the city, represented through her eyes as alien yet recognizably allegorical for the reader: "People all bunched together, in a hurry. Automobiles in packs, howling like wild beasts. Machines chasing people, machines eating people. Everything forbidden. No corner to pee or sleep. Those who can read, read: 'Forbidden.' Those who can't, learn by blows, the poor man's school" (271).

There is much controversy among scholars of the *cordel* as to whether this genre reinforces or subverts the dominant ideology. Most well-wrought tales are too complex to express a rigid or unequivocal view, even when ending with an overt "moral." The most valued virtue in traditional stories is *firmeza* [steadfastness] contrasted with *falsidade* [deceit]: these moral traits can be embodied in characters regardless of their social class, thereby making it possible for a poor character to be morally superior to a wealthy authority figure.[5] Even in cases where the main narrative seems to represent justice within the limits of the status quo, details in the story can diverge from the story's overt intentionality to reveal dissatisfaction with and denunciation of the present state of affairs. While women characters often fall into the classical categories of the whore (embodiment of evil) or of the self-sacrificing virgin-mother, there is enormous variety in how these characters play themselves out. In most cases, even the woman who is to blame for her own downfall is given sympathetic treatment by the storyteller. Since the prostitute is a product of poverty, she is often represented as a victim with the storyteller's moral criticism tempered by compassion.

José Francisco Borges, "A Chegada da prostituta no céu"
[The Prostitute's Ascension], from *Cordel* (1996): 5.

Galeano makes use of stock characters such as the *cangaceiro* [bandit/desperado] and the prostitute in *Walking Words* in his appeal to the value of steadfastness, although its opposite—deceit—is almost completely absent or mitigated by social circumstances. Deceitful characters in *Walking Words* tend not to incarnate abstract evil or depravity, and those who oppress others are soon deflated, their power revealed to be illusory and transitory. The ideological thrust of the book, then, systematically disavows inequality and subordination. The representation of women is particularly interesting especially given the negative criticism that this aspect of Galeano's work has sometimes provoked. In Palaversich's interpretation of *Days and Nights of Love and War*, for instance, she remarks how Galeano's "confessional" references to women end up being counterproductive because they read like a list of sexual exploits. She also cites George Yúdice who, in an overview of Galeano's work, is especially critical of Galeano's "macho posturing" in representing himself as the hero who "enters" all kinds of women. While acknowledging Yúdice's observation, Palaversich gives Galeano the benefit of the doubt when these moments refer specifically to Galeano's relationship to Helena Villagra, opting for Cristina Peri Rossi's more generous and "innocent" reading of these episodes as moments representing the joy of survival and the surprising capacity to go on loving in the midst of war and terror (102-03).

There appears to be a real change of consciousness in the course of Galeano's work with respect to the representation of women, especially noteworthy in *Walking Words* (and in *Mujeres*). In his earlier writing, there is a tendency to represent women as passive objects of the author's own desire or at least to reduce their sphere of significance to sexual pleasure, however much Galeano privileges eroticism as an integral and highly valued aspect of human communion. In the later work, there is a widening of horizons, very much apparent in *Walking Words*, towards celebrating women in an all-encompassing vision of their independence, strength, creativity, and capacity for love.

Strong women protagonists populate the stories in *Walking Words*. Even when she is not the main character in the sphere of action, the woman provides the impetus for the male character to conquer all obstacles to fulfilling their love, however insurmountable and supernatural they may be. The "Story of the Seven Prodigies" exemplifies the typical folktale plot of challenges to be overcome by the male suitor who is initially rejected by the girl's father. In this case, the protagonist, who is dismissed by the father as being "nothing but skin and bones" (21), is also denounced by six other authority figures in a hilariously hyperbolic test of José's defiance of patriarchal rule. The richest landowner calls him a "penniless piece of shit," in response to which José miraculously gets his goat to shit mountains of gold. He then succeeds in defying María's boyfriend, her dead husband, the town priest, the policeman, and the judge.

The ending of this story subverts the usual restoration of patriarchal domination over the coveted woman by the successful suitor, a common structure that ensures the continued imbalance of gender power and the renewal of male power through the patriarch's submission to the young man. The girl for whom the great feats are performed is reduced to her exchange value in an exogamous economy in traditional tales. The "Story of the Seven Prodigies" ends with José's triumph and the requisite feast involving the community as collective witness and participant—confirmatory of the story's outcome. But Galeano subverts the outcome of the traditional European folktale or fairy tale by negating the law, both human and divine: "And everyone celebrated the humiliation of human law and the defeat of laws divine. María, still wet with tears, offered José a piece of cheese and a red rose. And José, naked champion, conquered conqueror, trembled at the knees" (25). This ending, punctuated by Borges's woodcut print of José and María face to face, both grasping the rose, with José on one knee, imbues both characters with fresh identities. María occupies a dominant position in moving from the traditional object of desire to conqueror, and José, dissociated from the patriarchal structure that he destroys through the seven prodigies, happily accepts his paradoxical identity of conquered conqueror. María's dominant position is not just a simple reversal of the submissive/dominant paradigm but signals a new dynamic altogether, given that she conquers not through force, violence, or manipulation but through inspiring love in the other. The couple's newly-found freedom is not limited to their identities as individuals, but rather it occurs in a social context liberated from laws. The result maintains the harmonious balance of individual and community common to traditional folktales while radically transforming the ideological valance of the story from the conventional restoration of order to liberation based on love.

The "Story of the Female Avenger and the Archangel in the Palace of Sinners" is another example of the complex interplay between popular storytelling and the subversion of traditional ideological paradigms. The protagonist, Calamity Jane, is a dynamic female character who not only discredits male figures, from the brothel owner to God, but also radically humanizes the terms of interaction in the process. While the division of town between church and brothel is a usual comic device in many cultures, in this story the latter is situated "high on a hill, in a white tower that reached the stars" (30), while the former is below. In Latin (Catholic) cultures, men often represent the brothel as a place of joyous celebration, as if the prostitutes and their clients participate equally in innocent erotic play. García Márquez and Federico Fellini, for example, often represent prostitutes as sensuous, maternal women who give themselves out of generosity and love of life, rather than as the result of poverty leading to sexual exploitation. At first, the narrator of "Story of the Female Avenger and the Archangel in the Palace of Sinners" seems ambivalent on this point and moves towards critiquing the situation. But then the anonymous storyteller intervenes: "I beg you not to spend too many words on this point, dear writer, given your notorious tendency to preach, and do allow Calamity Jane to come on stage right away" (30). There is wisdom in this advice. The author must renounce his tiresome authorship in order to create a complex feminine character who can assume control of the story and take it in surprising new directions. Calamity Jane empties the traditional dichotomy of virgin/whore by embodying both while redefining the attributes associated with each: "She crossed the mountains of three countries, guided by the reflections of her diamond ring on rocky canyon walls. Calamity brought along the ring, which disappeared the first night. And she also brought along her well-earned fame of having a mother's heart, a happy trigger finger, an infallible lasso, and marked cards" (31).

After challenging the brothel owner by shooting his hat off his head, Calamity Jane divests him of power and property by winning the brothel from him in a poker game and turning it into an oasis: "The brothel, which had been cold as a hospital and hard as a barracks, became filled up with birds and guitars, plants and colors" (32). The prostitutes now annex the church's role while also modifying the significance of confession to mean communion, thus uniting their erotic and spiritual activities: "They knew that behind every macho with balls hides a shipwrecked sailor begging for refuge...long lines of men waited their turn to pour out doubts and secrets and hidden fears, dreams and nightmares. The church couldn't compete. Priests, as you know, only hear the confession of sins, which is what people least need to confess" (32). Next, Calamity Jane bribes Mr. Government to decree the brothel a non-profit cooperative, a detail whose anecdotal objective is tax evasion, but can also be interpreted as another step in the feminization of business transactions and, in more general terms, of community practices.

True to the *cordel*'s layering of realistic and supernatural characters and events, the archangel appears as a headless horseman who turns out to be "an elderly dwarf with a red nose and the voice of a child, dressed by god to look like a headless devil and frighten licentious women" (35). The archangel soon switches alliance from God to the woman who listens to him and identifies with his complaints, once more subverting the conventional hierarchy of priest and sinner, transforming confession into a relationship of equality based on solidarity: "And, as everyone knows, archangels have souls; and a soul needs to confess, even if it doesn't sin. Calamity complained about the Wild West and the archangel complained about Heaven...And talking, they discovered they had spent their entire lives alone and hadn't realized it" (36). The hierarchies separating the oppressor from the oppressed, men from women, human from divine beings are all swept away, transforming society into community. In the open ending offered by the storyteller in the form of multiple options from which Mr. Writer can choose, the dichotomy between North and South is also eliminated, for while Calamity Jane enters the story from the North American West, "she doesn't go north, back to her origins. She continues the trip south toward her destiny" (37).

The subtle ideological subversions show the freedom of conventional *cordel* structure and the depth of characters who, despite exhibiting typical features, put them to new uses, thereby effecting fundamental paradigm shifts. Another example of this re-envisioning of story and world occurs in "Story of the Lizard Who Had the Habit of Dining on His Wives." The bizarre combination of human and animal characters engaged in fantastic relationships is typical of *cordel*. In this case, the mysterious woman who wears glasses and reads legends ends up devouring the lizard Dulcidio, who claimed to be "lord of that whole expanse of land and water and air, and also of the strip of sand on which she sits" (45). But even this ironic reversal of fortunes introduces a difference into the lizard's habit of destroying his victims. Before turning the tables on Dulcidio, the woman makes love to him in a way that inspires him to dream for the first time in his life. In eating him, the woman avenges the deaths of Dulcidio's many victims, but also liberates him from the "cruel destiny that wants to keep him a widower" (45). In a gentle feast performed as if it were a favour "she eats him as he sleeps. She swallows him bit by bit, from the tail to the head, making no noise and not chewing hard, careful not to wake him so that he won't have a bad impression" (48).

The intellectual woman, frequently disparaged in mainstream culture as asexual and boring, is visually identified by Borges with very prominent glasses on her nose, but there is nothing predictable about her in this story, where she goes from reading legends to being a legendary heroine. Her final performance is ambiguous. She destroys a destroyer of women whose name suggests that he kills sweet things ("*dulce*" means sweet and "*cidio*" is the suffix "cide," meaning "killer" in terms like "genocide"). But once again, instead of just inverting the submissive/dominant paradigm, her way of killing is gentle, even thoughtful. In a sense, she puts the monster out of his misery, gives him a vision of love, and saves herself and all his future victims. The deceptively simple story reveals the representation of a woman and a resolution that are both complex.

Other stories in *Walking Words* tell of impossible love between humans and natural elements, but instead of stressing hopelessness and resignation, they imitate traditional myths that tell how different natural phenomena came to be. The "Story of the Man Who in the High Heavens Loved a Star and Was Abandoned by Her" is a typically long title that describes the story and reveals the ending. This kind of "giveaway" title makes it clear that the significance of these stories is not contained in a surprise ending or in one that puts the mind to rest through happy resolutions. The impact of these stories does not depend on a climax, but on the surprising relationships that reveal the *firmeza*, or strength of character, that Galeano consistently associates with love: love of the other *and* of freedom. The radical ideology of encounter Galeano proposes in these stories is precisely that love of the other leads to freedom, a direct rebuttal of perverse encounter narratives based on subordination of the other in the name of one's own self-interest.

In the "Story of the Man Who in the High Heavens Loved a Star and Was Abandoned by Her," the division between heaven and earth is once more transgressed with stars coming nightly to rob a farmer of his best potatoes. Speaking for the silent protagonist, the narrator reconstructs the story of the man who died of sorrow after being separated from his celestial lover: "He was never able to tell the story. Not a word issued from his lips, which did not open even to eat. Perhaps because he had been starstruck, or perhaps because he knew that here on earth they would take his story to be an obvious lie or the hallucination of a poor mortal who thinks he's sitting on the throne of night's kingdom" (259). Ironically, the narrator appeals to the findings of scholars, starologists, and specialists who have all studied this particular case, citing one "who has spent his life photographing shooting stars" and who actually claims to have proof that all shooting stars are one and the same: "that one light, errant and wet, is the star that once knew the danger and joy of a human embrace" (260-61). The traditional structure of the creation myth woven through with humorously uncharacteristic scientific findings celebrates the interconnectedness of all being and the power of the dangerous embrace. The latter disrupts the hierarchy of order through the contagion of love. Instead of simply explaining the origins of natural phenomena, Galeano's myths represent origins as tales of cosmic empathy whose significance survives in the present as testimony to the potential of utopia.

The magic realism infusing these oneiric yet ideologically engaging stories undoes the narrative categories normally separating the *hic et nunc* of history from the universality of myth. Galeano combines the two visions of time—the specific moment in the past and atemporality—to cross-fertilize each other. On the one hand, mythologizing reveals the cosmic or global significance of events. Freed from their particular place and time they can illuminate other contexts through affinity. On the other hand, historical representation reveals the specificity of struggles and joys occurring in a particular community. The stylistic, kinetic energy of Galeano's prose, especially its rhythmic punch and lyric inflection, underlies his characteristically crafty play with the narrative perception that history and myth, history and story, illuminate each other. In "Story of the Time that Was," for instance, Galeano blends mythic nostalgia with a cunning historical reference in the manner of a modern-day Ovid telling of postmodern metamorphoses. The story begins: "Back in the time that's lost in time, the grandmother says, the deer was faster than the arrows that sought him" (111). By the fourth sentence, "the time of misfortune [has] arrived in Yucatán" (112)—a reference to the disappearance of the Mayan empire as well as a marker for the ongoing travails of indigenous Maya in the Yucatan—and the deer's eyes, "which provided the rest of the wounded with something to drink, were left moist and large forever" (112). By the eighth and last sentence of this concisely resonant story, one is left to ponder "this earth where the outcasts of heaven suffer in exile" (112). The mythographer always writes from a position of exile, but here it is an exile that finds community in a shared anomie, the inevitable suffering that makes of exile a familiar place, a touchstone for narrative otherness.

A similar meshing of myth and history occurs in Elena Poniatowska's representation of the disenfranchized Mexicans who are financially forced to abandon their rural homes to seek survival in Mexico City. She refers to them as *"Ángeles de la ciudad," "angelitos negros," "ángeles de la noche"* [Angels of the city, little black angles, angels of the night] in a book, evocatively entitled *Fuerte es el silencio* (1980) [Silence is Strong], that chronicles their trials and acts of resistance. The angel motif originates from a statue on Paseo de la Reforma that represents independence. But as Poniatowska points out, for a great many Mexicans this statue is interchangeable with their vision of the Guardian Angel. On 28 July 1957, an earth tremor sent the enormous angel crashing to the ground in pieces, destroying the landmark that, according to Poniatowska, was the first thing you saw (13). This mythic figure is replaced in the author's imagination by the little angels who are silenced and ignored by the affluent city dwellers:

> Sin embargo, desde 1957, los ángeles se han opacado en México. El esmog, siguiendo al pie de la letra los dictados de la canción, nos pinta angelitos negros. Allí los vemos alicaídos, tratando de pasar entre los coches, golpeándose en contra de las salpicaderas…Ya nada tienen que ver con aquellos ángeles de puro oro que se ríen en los altares barrocos de las iglesias del centro…Hoy por hoy los ángeles de la ciudad son todos aquellos que no saben que lo son. (14)

> [However, since 1957, the angels have become somewhat opaque in Mexico. The smog, loyally following the lyrics of the song, paints little black angels. There we see them with their drooping wings, trying to cross between the cars, hitting themselves against the fenders…They no longer bear any resemblance to the angels of pure gold laughing on the baroque altars of the downtown churches…These days the angels of the city are all those who do not know that they are.]

The mythic figure of the angel is made flesh and becomes the humblest and most desperate of city dwellers: the Indians who migrate seasonally to peddle their little heaps of seeds or to seek employment as maids and seamstresses often end up as street vendors of kleenex. Throughout the chronicle, Poniatowska's identification of the impoverished as angels evokes a kind of truthful insight about the divine nature of human beings who are phantasmal for being largely ignored but nevertheless divine in their earth-born anonymity. Galeano blends mythical and historical elements in similar representations that intuit the divine in the most desperate of society's outcasts.

The nightmarish existence of a street child, wrongly accused of committing a murder after he has robbed a corpse, is a reminder of the violent law of the jungle that dominates the lives of the millions of street children in Brazil alone. In "Story of the Hunter," El Gato [Cat], the protagonist, preys on absent-minded people. He is driven in his fight for survival by both his whining belly and Saint George, the warrior saint, who appears to him mounted on a Yamaha motorcycle in a glue-sniffing induced hallucination that is also a desperate fantasy of salvation. Even before coming upon the wealthy corpse, El Gato the hunter is also the hunted: "at dusk people in uniform corner him and almost catch him" (293). He no longer has a dog and wants nothing to do with strays, since a bullet meant for him once killed his dog instead. This little detail in El Gato's story echoes with the numerous murders of innocent street children by death squads, crimes that rarely make the headlines in Latin America or anywhere else. Real justice that would guarantee El Gato his basic human rights to shelter, food, and education is substituted for the grotesque charity of politicians who corrupt the Christian message that even Father Thomas Melville, once a Maryknoll priest in Guatemala, thinks is impracticable in the barbaric circumstances of misery. His testimony of the war against the poor in Guatemala closes Galeano's *Guatemala: Occupied Country*, but Melville's observations about the incompatibility of capitalism and Christianity are pertinent to any context that denies individuals their humanity:

> Today we hear community talked about on all sides: the Christian community. This is charity, love, translated into the local context. Some kind of real physical sharing, as well as the spiritual, has to be possible; some kind of a natural community has to exist, before Christianity can be planted. There is not much room in Latin America for the masses to practice this kind of sharing as things stand now, and the possibility becomes even more remote as the misery increases in proportion to the population growth, and the greater concentration of economic power in the hands of the minority. (150)

Galeano's meticulous documentation and political analysis of exploitation and violence in *Guatemala: Occupied Country* and *Open Veins of Latin America* results in an objectified historical perspective even when incorporating individual testimonies. The rhetoric of persuasion urging us to recognize the social, political, and economic causes of injustice turns to the seduction of the individual in *Walking Words*. The reader of "Story of the Hunter" is awakened to critical consciousness not through facts and disclosure but through insights into the consciousness and physical sensations of a particular child, El Gato, who in all sorts of ways is not easy to identity with; the otherness of a ragged, unkempt, stoned, potentially violent, desperate homeless person does not pose an easy invitation to exploring difference. El Gato's otherness represents an ethical challenge involving the recognition of our common humanity disguised and deformed by inhumane living conditions.

The corruption of the Christian notion of charity is carnivalized in the grotesque representation of appeasing the desperate that occurs throughout the world, First and Third. The drives calling for donations of food and toys during the Christmas season in North America are organized, orderly, hygienic, giving the impression of a smoothly running civic machine whose unsightly recipients are kept out of the picture. Better to focus on "our" own positive image of seasonal do-gooders than to ask how it is possible even in the most affluent societies for some parents not to have the means to feed and clothe their children, let alone succumb to Christmas consumerism. And let's not even worry about families of other faiths: are their children also eligible to experience the joy of Christmas? And if the real joy of Christmas is giving, then what joy is there for those who can only receive the anonymous donations? Father Thomas Melville feels defeated because "any capitalist system, whether it be 'laissez faire' or not, is based essentially on competition, rugged individualism, the profit motive, and it is difficult to see how such a system, though materially successful, can ever be supported by a Christian society that truly understands Christ's message of love" (Galeano, *Guatemala: Occupied Country* 153). Charity in such a perverse system is essentially no different from the frenzied scene evoked by Galeano in *Walking Words*, in which a politician usurps the part of Santa Claus:

> On the balcony, open to the sun, the mayor is sweating buckets. Down below in roaring commotion is a sea of children in rags, a foam of hands raised toward the sky: dressed up like Santa Claus, the mayor throws down toys from above. The toys rain down over the tumultuous crowd; poor children have a right to happiness too. These lucky kids dash and flail about, throwing punches and insults, stepping all over each other. A life-sized doll knocks over several; a space rocket strikes another right between the eyes; candies fall like rocks. (297)

This parable of despair cleverly converts the falling toys into dangerous projectiles, giving a humorous twist to the war on poverty in which charity feels like just another weapon in the arsenal against the poor. But despite being marginalized, El Gato identifies with the culture that denies him a human existence which demands not just the basics of survival but a popular culture in which creativity, identity, and solidarity flourish. Dussel observes, for instance, that dominant, élite, "universal culture" is in constant tension with popular culture:

The popular culture…basically structured around daily *work* (as "productive work" in the laboring and rural class; as "unproductive" work from the viewpoint of capital, in the ethnic groups, tribes, marginal groups, and other sectors that preserve their "outsideness"), is the nucleus of the people's practice of the centuries-old resistance to oppressors. With their songs, their dances, their living piety, their "underground economy" (their own consumption or production, invisible to the capitalist economy), their communal solidarity, their system of feeding themselves, and so on, they continue to do today what they have done for hundreds of years—bypass the oppressor's "universal culture." (*Ethics and Community* 202)

Galeano's story of El Gato does what El Gato himself cannot do, since his circumstances as abandoned street child only afford him the underground economy of the jungle where hunger and competition leave no room for communal solidarity. After stealing the rich corpse's wallet, El Gato seals his fate by buying "an immense color television, as big as the movies" (297), a suspicious action for a ragged street kid. While his extreme misery, attempts on his life, or the regular assassinations carried out by police and paramilitary groups to keep the streets "clean" of this type of non-consumer don't make the news, his capture for a crime he did not commit appears on the radios, the TV, the newspapers that proclaim the sensational investigation and a victory for the police: "With a number on his chest, El Gato confronts the black eye of the camera. The magnesium flash ignites, the shutter clicks" (299). El Gato, the hunter, becomes the trophy in a conspiracy among journalists, the organs of State terrorism, and an economic order that has no place for his kind.

"Story of the Hunter" is separated from "Story of the Second Visitation of Jesus" by a "Window on the City," which provides a glimpse of the system that turns people into circus freaks and charlatans begging for coins. Nevertheless, the latter maintain their hope of salvation, even when this is peddled by a prophet who sells the possibility of belonging to the chosen as a lottery ticket. The "Window" in this case bridges the story about hopeless poverty and crime and the story about the second coming of a Christ who looks as destitute as El Gato but offers a spiritual and practical way out of misery: "Look at heaven. Will it give you Paradise or will it give you a stiff neck? Where is the kingdom, if not in the exile that seeks it?" (304). While the two stories and the "Window" are discrete texts, they cross-relate to each other by providing different fragments that cumulatively form a vision of collective destiny. Galeano's storytelling is both an innovative vehicle for speaking about current social issues and a return to its traditional role of keeping memory alive. In a vignette from *The Book of Embraces*, the passion of speech assumes a mythico-magical dimension by which the storyteller "peoples" the world: "This man, or this woman, is pregnant with many people. People are coming out of his pores. With these clay figures, the Pueblo Indians of New Mexico depict the storyteller: the one who relates the collective memory, who fairly blossoms with little people" (20).[6]

The storyteller's identity is difficult to understand within the neoliberal framework governed by the paradigm of individualism that informs all human activities. When speaking of "literature" as understood in the European tradition, the focus tends to be on the author's individuality and the perception of art as property protected by copyright, a product sold for consumption like any other. This obsession with originality and intellectual property is alien to collective forms of storytelling that transmit pleasure and knowledge through repetition by multiple tellers, allowing the story to undergo modifications in its travels from mouths to ears. Because the storyteller is not a specialist or a professional who performs to a passive audience, storytelling is often a way of sharing impressions, a collective dialogue in which all participate as tellers and listeners: "The truth came out of the fire. On cold nights, men in ponchos curl up by the fire. In circles of maté and cane liquor, they smoke and tell lies that tell the truth. That's how they come in from the cold and from the foolishness of living, and that's how they spend the time that the day gathered for the night to fritter away" (*Walking Words* 323-24). The recent interest in storytelling even in (especially in) societies where stories tend to be read aloud only to children, and usually from written texts, expresses a longing to break out of the solitude of literature. The final window of *Walking Words* opens the book instead of closing it by suggesting that memory is a shared and vital experience. Independent of the individual performer, art extends far beyond the limitations of the mortal artist: "*The light of dead stars travels*, and by the flight of their splendor they look alive. The guitar, which does not forget its companion, makes music without any hand. *The voice travels on, leaving the mouth behind*" (328; our emphasis).

The Voice that Leaves the Mouth Behind:
Stories for the Young (and) Old

The stories that circulate freely and unpredictably instead of being reduced to thingness by being contained within the pages of a book tend to belong to popular culture (as we have argued earlier): "high" culture likes to categorize, canonize, and control the interpretation of texts to legitimize the élites who, in turn, legitimize the texts. Stories do sometimes break loose of libraries to join their cultural roots in popular culture where they are contaminated by indeterminacy to proliferate endless tellings (and singings). Those writings that recognize their sources often return to them, just as Galeano envisions receiving the voices and returning them to the collective after having intervened as writer to participate in his community. *The voice that leaves the mouth behind* expresses a different kind of freedom of expression: the empowered word overflowing individual utterance circulates to create memory and community. Can communities exist without shared stories telling about shared concerns? This question is crucial to countries where technology has all but appropriated the words to speak collectively, where concerns have been reduced to fantastic epics between good and evil battled by lonely superheroes. Cops and robbers on a universal scale provide the mass media with the almost exclusive paradigm for stories about conquering and defending property. Ethics and the hero's integrity function as window dressing to give the spectator's ego something personal with which to identify. This fantasy, however, offers no relief from solitude.

Why do we adults tell (read) children stories when they are so much better at storytelling than we? In Western societies, parents of all creeds and religions are frequently pressured to tell the dominant stories of European Christianity so that their children do not feel overlooked by the great gift-giver. But why do we tell children that Santa brings presents on Christmas Eve when we rarely indulge in making up imaginative stories any other time of the year (except, perhaps, Easter)? Most of the stories that we tell as truths have to do with giving, but this giving has become so materialistic that the original meaning is lost to a child whose pleasure is reduced to expecting presents from Santa, treats from the Easter bunny, money from the tooth fairy...The originary stories about giving and sharing are converted into promises of receiving. Instead of running wild, imagination is trained to imagine wealth. In this Western context, bible stories function as collective texts for some people but stories whose function is global proselytism are very different from local stories combining mythic and specific dimensions to keep memory alive. Some of the historical uses of the Judeo-Christian bible compromised the conditions of circulation and claim to universal truth of the stories it contains. This questionable status is represented in a humorous anecdote by Desmond Tutu, quoted by Galeano for being equally pertinent to America: "They came. They had the bible and we had the land. And they said: 'Close your eyes and pray.' And when we opened our eyes, they had the land and we had the bible" (*We Say No* 307). This colonialist heist recalls and contrasts with a simple truth that Trinh associates with story: that it "never takes anything away from anybody" (119). Storytelling springs from a local source of memory and significance. Popular stories are not imposed on one culture by another using either force or persuasion to change the listeners' worldview through asking them to renounce their traditional beliefs. The question arising in what Dussel calls "universal culture" is whether the Santa story holds some collective significance, or whether we tell it to conform to our neighbours' expectations and to avoid their wrath should our children reveal the lie to their children. The reversal of this pact involves not telling stories about love and sex so that our kids don't reveal the truth to theirs. Can these stories be told as truthful rather than factual in a society where truth is so confused with fact? No wonder, then, that children feel betrayed and bewildered when they learn that they have been lied to. The significance of giving is the truthful matrix of the story but once shopping malls become the dominant sites for acting upon the story, the story's truthfulness is overshadowed in the lie of frenzied consumption. The truthful aspect of the story concerning giving and love is undermined by the fact/lie dichotomy that dominates other representations in Western culture. Can we even think of stories that have collective significance that our neighbours might recognize? Those of us who were not bequeathed stories by our parents or even grandparents have no collective stories to pass on. Where do people turn to find stories that are complex enough to keep children and adults wondering, thinking, imagining on with the voice that leaves the mouth behind?

In the last years, the children's literature market has been swamped with folktales from all over the world. These, no doubt, communicate wisdom and wonder never found in the post-fairytale genre whose prime motive is to teach children virtues and good manners such as sharing, taking turns, and the use of words instead of fists. One of the more obvious differences between the folktale and, say, the Care Bears, is that the message in the folktale is harder to separate out from the other ingredients (and flow) of the story. While folktales also have a pedagogical dimension, this aspect cannot be translated to any simplistic pedagogy of good behaviour, since they often deal with attitudes that have many different manifestations, depending on context. The simple do's and don'ts of a lesson on proper conduct hardly inspire children to think beyond the most basic consequences of their actions. Trinh comments on how anthropologists miss the point, thinking that stories are just a substitute for knowledge among illiterate people:

> Primitive means elementary, therefore infantile. No wonder then that in the West storytelling is treasured above all for its educational force in the kindergarten and primary school. The mission of the storyteller, we thus hear, is to "teach children the tales their *fathers* knew," to mold ideals, and to "illuminate facts." For children to gain "right feelings" and to "think true," the story as a pedagogical tool must inform so as to keep their opinion "abreast of the scientific truth of the time, instead of dragging along in the superstitions of the past." But for the story to be well-told information, it must be related "in as fascinating a form as [in] the old myths and fables." (124)

In all fairness, Trinh's interpretation of Western didacticism is somewhat outdated, based here on Katherine Dunlap Cather's *Educating by Story-telling* (1926). Since Trinh's *Woman, Native, Other* examines the differences between Occidental and non-Occidental perceptions of otherness, she tends to contrast the worst examples of European rationalism with the storytelling traditions of Africa and Asia, and ends up underplaying the pedagogical dimension of the latter in order to strengthen the contrast. In *The Book of Embraces*, Galeano relates a funny anecdote about a father who tells a story to his stubborn daughter to get her to eat her soup. Instead of distracting her with an interesting story, he centres the story on the importance of nutrition and spins a babyish allegory in which a "birdy" represents his daughter: "There once was a birdy that didn't want to eat her dinny. The birdy had her beaky shut tight and her mommy said to her 'You're always going to be a tiny little birdy if you don't eat your din-din.' But the birdy didn't pay attention to her mommy and didn't open her becky..." (42). As if reading her father's frustration with her, and nonplussed by the thinly-veiled protagonist of the story, the little girl interrupts: "What a shitty little birdy" (42). The little girl humours her father by proving that she grasps his intention, but her *truthful* response also captures the father's hidden impatience toward her. Whether she actually ends up eating her soup is inconsequential: Galeano ends by giving the child the upper hand in the storytelling by having her reveal it as a sham to manipulate her behaviour instead of sparking her imagination. The anecdote, presented as a short vignette, encapsulates Trinh's critique of reducing storytelling to functionalism. Both Galeano and Trinh appreciate the truthfulness of the story over a didacticism that must get its point across instead of celebrating the complexities of relationships.

Walter Benjamin identifies the practical interests and concrete situatedness characterizing European folktales but puts a positive spin on what Trinh associates with narrow utilitarianism. In Benjamin's European context, the contrast is between the pragmatic, down-to-earth quality of the story and the abstract, universalizing tendency of literature. The story's capacity to give counsel is what attracts Benjamin's admiration. Benjamin's representation of the storyteller differs significantly from Galeano's image of the gauchos gathered around the fire to share their stories and, in many other instances, the grandmother who spins her yarns next to the stove. In Benjamin's context, the wisdom required for storytelling is attributed to a man, who counsels his readers: "But if today 'having counsel' is beginning to have an old-fashioned ring, this is because the communicability of experience is decreasing. In consequence we have no counsel either for ourselves or for others. After all, counsel is less an answer to a question than a proposal concerning the continuation of a story which is just unfolding" ("The Storyteller" 86). Here, Benjamin seems to coincide with Trinh's vision of storytelling as process, an unfolding that is more significant than the story's outcome: "The story is beautiful, because or therefore it unwinds like a long thread. A long thread, for there is no end in sight. Or the end she reaches leads actually to another end, another opening, another 'residual deposit of duration'" (Trinh 149). Trinh sees the "making material. [O]f composing on life" (129) as being effected by the magical and feminine power of speech. Beauty and wisdom are implicit in Trinh's vision of storytelling, and while Benjamin's counsel seems to share in those values, his concept of the story's earthiness diverges from Trinh's, towards functional interpretation.

Pedagogy, then, in the form of wisdom is the most essential aspect of the story according to Benjamin:

> Counsel woven into the fabric of real life is wisdom. The art of storytelling is reaching its end because the epic side of truth, wisdom, is dying out...It is...only a concomitant symptom of the secular productive forces of history, a concomitant that has quite gradually removed narrative from the realm of living speech and at the same time is making it possible to see a new beauty in what is vanishing. ("The Storyteller" 86-87)

The ethical challenges with which Galeano interpolates the reader suggest counsel in the more participatory mode of sharing wisdom instead of just passing it down. While the scope of the *Memory of Fire* trilogy can be loosely dubbed "epic," both Trinh and Galeano seem wary of the term given its historical function to idealize specific heroes associated with nationalist and colonialist agendas.

Storytelling is perhaps more resilient than Benjamin believed in a historical moment when all values and communitarian traditions seemed to have been annihilated by technology and fascism. And yet, it is in that very context that it begins to flourish again in Latin America where popular culture is still distinguishable from mass culture and where neoliberal neocolonialism is shown to be both highly technocratic and essentially totalitarian. Storytelling as a form of collective memory may have been lost to the descendants of Europeans, but the indigenous communities to which storytellers like Galeano and Marcos now turn for counsel safeguarded stories as part of their cultural legacy:

> Storytelling, the oldest form of building historical consciousness in community, constitutes a rich oral legacy, whose values have regained all importance recently, especially in the context of writings by women of color. She who works at un-learning the dominant language of "civilized" missionaries also has to learn how to un-write and write anew. And she often does so by re-establishing the contact with her foremothers, so that living tradition can never congeal into fixed forms, so that life keeps on nurturing life, so that what is understood as the Past continues to provide the link for the Present and the Future. (Trinh 148-49)

While Trinh speaks specifically about postcolonial women writers of colour, the need to return to a living tradition is relevant to a wider range of writers who, despite their differences, share this nonlinear view of time. Just as "Mr. Writer" strives to "un-learn the dominant language," Latin American writers (with a few notable exceptions like Vargas Llosa) are now turning to popular and indigenous culture in order to become participants in keeping memory alive and envisioning a collective future.[7] While not all these writers are people of colour or are mestizos whose ancestors belonged to both the colonizers and the colonized, memory in Latin America was silenced not only by colonization but more recently by fascist régimes backed by foreign intervention. Latin American writers from different ethnic backgrounds suffered persecution and witnessed the amnesia imposed through state terrorism. Galeano's description of the "system" in a vignette entitled "Divorces" extends the frame of reference from state terrorism to the alienated individualism of so-called democracies:

> Our system is one of detachment: to keep silenced people from asking questions, to keep the judged from judging, to keep solitary people from joining together, and the soul from putting together its pieces.
>
> The system divorces feeling from thought as it divorces sex from love, private life from public life, past from present. If the past has nothing to say to the present, history may go on sleeping undisturbed in the closet where the system keeps its disguises. (*The Book of Embraces* 123)

This terrible ending has its vital opposite in Trinh's vision of "life that keeps on nurturing life, so that what is understood as the Past continues to provide the link for the Present and the Future" (149), which is also Galeano's vision of memory as life force, cultural identity, prophecy. How to communicate that imposed solitude is evil because it cuts people off from each other and from the past, which is the source of life? Can such a warning be told to children in the form of a story, not a horror story but one that also celebrates identity? Could a child understand that identity is an accumulation of experiences (good and bad) and how this concept of identity differs from a mask that imposes a false identity?

While on first consideration these concepts may not seem age-appropriate for the young, mass media aimed at children do not make such distinctions. Instead, the mass media bombard children with sadistic and militaristic images of power and domination. These images are seen as acceptable so long as they follow the simple formula of good guys versus bad guys, us versus them, without getting too realistic, too specific about who "we" are and what makes "them" bad. The media relentlessly engineer objects of desire designed to mask children and to market them as rapacious little consumers. This same business also teaches contempt for anyone who does not fit the official image of youthful beauty together with an obsessive fear of maturation.

In the face of this massive alienation campaign, Galeano creates a children's story that rejects the fairytale ending in favour of reality and teaches us (children and adults) to honour our battle scars, to see through the inauthentic reflection of the looking glass. Written while Galeano lived in exile in Spain, *La piedra arde* [The Rock Burns], illustrated by Luis de Horna, is based on an idea attributed to Arkadi Gaidar, the early-twentieth-century Russian author of children's books and revolutionary hero.[8] The story centres on an exiled old man who befriends a not-so-nice little boy named Carasucia [Dirty Face]. Neither character is attractive at first sight. But the story leads us toward an understanding of why the old man chooses his own aged and scarred identity over the magical possibility of being transformed into a handsome young man. Dirty Face, who offers him this possibility in the form of a magic rock that he finds deep in the woods, learns along with the reader why the old man has no reason to go back in time. Upon discovering the magical rock, Dirty Face imagines how he will repay the old man for the kindness he has shown him instead of punishing him like others would have for stealing fruit from his garden. Dirty Face envisions how by smashing the rock, the old man will return to his youth: "¡El viejo bailará como un trompo y saltará como una pulga y volará como un pájaro! ¡No volverá a toser! ¡Tendrá las piernas sanas y una cara sin tajos y una boca con todos los dientes!" (n.pag.) [The old man will dance like a spinning top and he'll jump like a flea and fly like a bird! He won't cough anymore! His legs will be healthy and his face unscarred and his mouth full of teeth!]

The old man refuses to break the rock and to comfort the indignant boy he finally reveals the story of his life. It is the kind of story not usually told in children's books, despite the horrifying militaristic culture that is foisted upon children through television programs, movies, commercials, and toys that indoctrinate them in techno-militaristic culture:

> —Estos dientes no se cayeron solos. Me los arrancaron a golpes. Esta cicatriz que me corta la cara, no viene de accidente. Los pulmones…La pierna…Rompí esta pierna cuando me escapé de la cárcel, porque era muy alto el muro y había vidrios abajo. Hay otras marcas, también, que no puedes ver. Marcas que tengo en el cuerpo y no solamente en el cuerpo y que nadie puede ver…Si parto la piedra, estas marcas se borrarán. Pero estas marcas son mis documentos, ¿comprendes? Mis documentos de identidad. (n.pag.)

> [—These teeth didn't fall out by themselves. They were beaten out. This scar that crosses my face, isn't from any accident. My lungs…My leg…I broke this leg when I escaped from prison, because the wall was very high and had shards of glass on top. There are other marks that you can't see. Marks that I have on my body and not only on my body, ones no one can see…If I break the rock, these marks will disappear. But these marks are my documents, understand? My identification documents.]

The description of torture—partially graphic but mostly implied—is accompanied by a drawing of a prison that looks like a medieval castle with soldiers that look like the toy soldiers in the children's classic *The Nutcracker*. On the next page, the escaping prisoner dressed in the modern striped uniform is about to climb a barbed wire fence. Such images are familiar to children from other contexts (cartoons, comics, war movies) but here they leave the fictive adventure story genre to assume the weight of history. Images of prisoners are usually completely depoliticized in mass media, in that they tend to be criminals (and even those criminals who assassinate political leaders are not politically motivated but are simply insane). While the ideological struggle in this story is not explained in detail by the old man, aspects of his character from the first page onward reveal social values that relate indirectly to fighting for liberty. He weaves baskets and hemp slippers that he gives away to his neighbours and is offended if they try to pay him for these gifts because he supports himself by being the orchard watchman.

The message of cherishing one's identity instead of exchanging it for a more attractive image is applicable to both individuals and communities. The positive self-image is illustrated by the old man—hunchbacked, bald, balancing on his cane—smiling at himself in the mirror, speaking the words that link identity, liberty, and solidarity in simple yet complex enough terms to speak to a child's heart and mind:

> Me miro al espejo y digo: "Ese soy yo," y no siento lástima de mí. Yo luché mucho tiempo. La lucha por la libertad es una lucha de nunca acabar. Ahora hay otros que luchan, allá lejos, como yo he luchado. ¿Comprendes? Yo no quiero olvidar. No parto la piedra porque sería una traición. (n.pag.)

[I look at myself in the mirror and say, "That's me," and I don't feel sorry for myself. I fought for a long time. There is no end to the struggle for freedom. Now there are others who struggle, far away, just as I did. Understand? I don't want to forget. I can't split the rock because that would be a betrayal.]

Old Man and Mirror. Luis de Horna, from *La piedra arde* [The Rock Burns] (1980): n.pag.

Jacobo Timerman, a Jewish-Argentine writer who—in *Prisoner Without a Name, Cell Without a Number* (1981)—gives testimony about his imprisonment and torture for being a dissident and a Jew also speaks of these marks on the body that he associates with the gaze of fellow prisoners who mirror the torture victim's humanity back to him:

> Have you ever looked into the eyes of another person, on the floor of a cell, who knows that he's about to die though no one has told him so?...I have many such gazes imprinted upon me. Each time I write or utter words of hope, words of confidence in the definitive triumph of man, I'm fearful—fearful of losing sight of one of those gazes. At night I recount them, recall them, re-see them, cleanse them, illumine them. (164)

Like Timerman, the old man in *La piedra arde* incorporates in his own sense of identity the identity of others who have died, are exiled like him, or go on fighting. When he gazes at himself in the mirror, the image he sees does not circumscribe individual identity, for that singular image would express pure bravura at having escaped and survived—a mimicry of the typically Western lone hero. Instead, this image of self-contemplation is related to his past only because, like Galeano himself, he has become an exile. He is painfully aware that the past is still present for others and will be an inevitable future if memory is buried. Nowhere in the story is it necessary to explain that the old man is beautiful despite being old and ugly, because this is steadfastly revealed through his actions and words. To accept the new image offered by the proverbial fountain of youth would result in amnesia, alienation, and betrayal of self and others.

Galeano reveals through stories like *La piedra arde* how important it is for people not to forget. In other writings, he represents how the "system" lulls the affluent into satiated stupor, while the desperate whose senses are keen are kept in check through terror. Galeano uncovers the similarities between fascism and democracy as we know it. Chomsky focuses his attention on different forms of propaganda and censorship to show that so-called democracies engage in both through methods that are not as easily identifiable as totalitarian due to their transnational scope and the fact that political agendas are touted as pure economics. Galeano, too, draws the connections between amnesia and fear to show that fear is not limited to the victims of state terror but can be inculcated effectively through even less rational means:

Forgetting /1

Fear dries the mouth, moistens the hands and mutilates. Fear of knowing condemns us to ignorance, fear of doing reduces us to impotence. Military dictatorship, fear of listening, fear of speaking, made us deaf and dumb. Now democracy, with its fear of remembering, infects us with amnesia, but you don't have to be Sigmund Freud to know that no carpet can hide the garbage of memory. (*The Book of Embraces* 112)

In the Americas, infectious amnesia extends to the conquered indigenous cultures whose philosophy of life is forgotten, ignored, and actively persecuted. There comes the awareness, under dictatorship, that this genocide of memory has all happened before on a more massive scale. Galeano recalls how during a conversation between persecuted Chileans and indigenes the common denominator of oppression opens a new space for solidarity. During a trip through Chile, Galeano contemplates the Repocura Valley, a landscape that reminds him of a way of life that has been forcibly eradicated but continues to speak to the present:

> ...these lands no longer belong to everyone and to no one, as before. A decree of the Pinochet dictatorship has smashed the communities, forcing the Indians into isolation. They nevertheless insist on putting their poverties together and they still work together, are silent together, and speak together: "You people have had fifteen years of dictatorship," they explain to my Chilean friends. "We've had five centuries of it." (*The Book of Embraces* 133)

Oppression becomes a means of recognizing shared values that may be expressed in different languages, from different cultural perspectives. Both the Indians and the dissident Chileans who dreamed of a socialist future understand the common factors of each other's oppression. But the Indians' specific oppression reminds the leftists, whose struggle dominated the telling of history for decades, that the neocolonialism they fight—from the Indians' perspective—is an uninterrupted history of infamy since the conquest. The concise reminder of this difference implies that Galeano's Chilean friends had overlooked the Indians and did not connect their own struggle and aspirations to theirs. This lack of solidarity and communication among oppressed people has become an important focus in the actions and writings of Sandinistas and Zapatistas.[9]

In a communiqué, Subcomandante Insurgente Marcos summarizes the indigenous values that can serve as an admirable example of integrity to peoples of different cultural backgrounds. The commitment to these values (cynically appropriated by Western propaganda as paradigmatic of such countries as the U.S.) gives the Chiapanecans their spiritual orientation and inspiration to fight against annihilation and amnesia:

> Collective work, democratic thought, and majority rule are more than just a tradition among indigenous people; they have been the only way to survive, to resist, to be proud, and to rebel. These "bad ideas" (in the eyes of the big landowners and businessmen) go against the grain of the capitalist precept, "a lot in the hands of the few." It has been said, quite wrongly, that the rebellion of the people of Chiapas has its own tempo, which does not correspond to the rhythms of the nation. It is a lie...If the voices of those who write history are not accurate, it is because the voice of the oppressed does not speak...not yet. (*Shadows of Tender Fury* 46-47)

Here, indigenous resistance takes the form of recuperative story and restorative memory, a crucial model for understanding Galeano's writings, especially those he addresses to children, the heritors of memory and guarantors of future stories that will become memory.

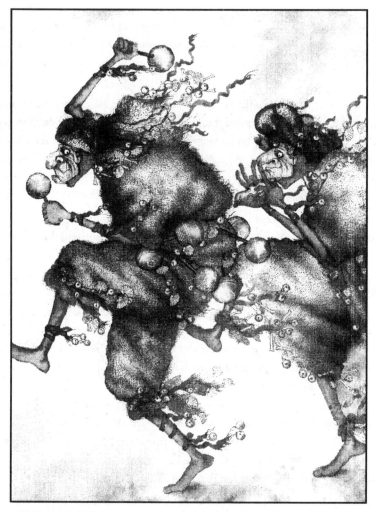

Trickster Gods. From *Las aventuras de los jóvenes dioses;* illustrated by Nivio López Vigil (1998).

Galeano returns to one of the many sources of indigenous philosophy and storytelling in his recreation for children of stories from the *Popol Vuh,* the sacred book of the Quiché Maya of Guatemala, entitled *Las aventuras de los jóvenes dioses* [Adventures of the Young Gods]. The book is illustrated by Nivio López Vigil, who has a special talent for expressing humour especially at the expense of the oppressors (who in this book are the lords of the Kingdom of Fear, recalling Galeano's many references to fear and forgetting). Like most adventure stories, this one involves several confrontations between good and bad characters. But the crucial aspect of the story is how it compels its readers to understand what differentiates the good from the bad. In many Western children's stories (including most Hollywood action films rated for adult viewing), the bad guys are bad simply by virtue of not belonging to "our" community, "our" country, "our" planet, "our" galaxy and, though only correlatively and very implicitly, they are bad because they do not share "our" values. Often, it is not at all clear what "our" values are and what "we" are fighting so heroically to defend, and so the distinction really comes down to expelling the invaders or conquering new territory. In *The Empire's Old Clothes*, Ariel Dorfman, exiled Chilean writer, cultural and literary critic, and Research Professor at Duke University, examines the evolution of the superhero and shows how what started out as an impulse that is "unquestionably rebellious and democratic" (106) gets progressively more vitiated:

> The superhero is fashioned in a manner that allows the common man to gain access to the workings of the State, exercising upon himself the internal military repression which quiets doubts, and all this without renouncing his resentment towards the public authorities. The protagonist's marginality expresses and concentrates a distance and distrust of the State while his superpowers and invincibility express and concentrate the awe and fear of state power used to carry out these tasks. No one is trying to destroy the State, just to do what it is supposed to do—only better, more efficiently, and first. (113)

In *Las aventuras de los jóvenes dioses*, Galeano creates a curiously new type of hero (given that these heroes come from an ancient book), but then he insists that "certain voices from the American past, long past, sound very futuristic" (*The Book of Embraces* 135). First, the singular hero is replaced by a pair of siblings, a boy and a girl named Hun Ahpú and Ix Balanqué.[10] These characters are taken from the *Popol Vuh*, the Mayan sacred book that tells of the creation of the world. In the original story about the dawn of life, however, they are twin brothers. Galeano borrows some of the characters, conflicts, and motifs from this dense and esoteric source to craft a story that has relevance to contemporary life and is comprehensible even for young readers. First, he adapts the principal characters to reflect gender balance, repeated in the representation of the most ancient of gods, the Old Man and the Old Woman, who created the heavens and earth. This originally hermaphroditic lord undergoes several transformations in its evolution to produce an ambiguous notion of gender. Both feminine and masculine identities are attributed to the gods as well as to "human males and the male heads of present-day patrilineages" by virtue of the name "mother-fathers," which is pronounced as a single word (Tedlock 349).[11]

In Galeano's story, the young pair of warriors live through a series of adventures in which they battle oppressive lords such as the *Soberbios*, a word that translates to "sovereign" and can be used figuratively to mean "magnificent" or "grand" but more relevantly denotes pride, haughtiness, and arrogance. In accordance with the structure of the *Popol Vuh*, "the first cycle deals entirely with adventures on the face of the earth" (Tedlock 34). The *Soberbios* offend the heavens and humiliate the earth. These characters recall Seven Macaw, who in the *Popol Vuh* rips off Hunahpu's arm (Tedlock 79), an episode recreated by Galeano, together with the replacing of Seven Macaw's teeth with corn (Tedlock 80). In Galeano's story, the first *Soberbio* oppresses nature by silencing rivers and birds so that the jingling of the golden bells adorning his bracelets and anklets can be heard by all. After injuring this *Soberbio* with his blowgun, Hun appeals for help to the two creators, who cure the *Soberbio* by extracting his eyes of silver and teeth of pearls and replacing them with grains of corn. Since in most indigenous creation myths humans are made of corn, this operation humanizes the haughty lord who proves his "conversion" by returning the arm he had earlier ripped from Hun's body.

The royalty in this story are consistently represented as being morally inferior to their victims. An ecological dimension to the story is also evident in the royalty's arrogant dominance of the world represented, in accordance with indigenous cosmogony, as an entity comprising both humanity and nature. While the first *Soberbio* suppressed rivers and birds, the second *Soberbio* is said to have killed four hundred children in a scheme of repression that weaves a web of solidarity between flora, fauna, humans, and gods. In the *Popol Vuh*, the killing of four hundred boys is carried out by Zipacna, the son of Seven Macaw: "And it used to be said that they entered a constellation, named Hundrath after them, though perhaps this is just a play on words" (Tedlock 84).

Pre-Columbian texts like the *Popol Vuh* are difficult to interpret: while they are replete with conflicts, intrigues, battles, and murders, the characters do not embody either good or evil. Even when the twins plot against Zipacna or Seven Macaw, they never represent their interest from an ethical perspective to justify attacking their enemy. The very concept of enemy is absent, thereby confounding interpretation based on ethical or ideological principles. The telling of the dawn of life is structured on opposites, but these are complementary in a harmonious scheme more similar to Eastern thought than the manicheism of Judeo-Christian traditions. It helps to remember that, despite their concrete references and fast-paced action, many of these stories are about time and astronomy:

> The continuing decipherment of Mayan hieroglyphic texts is another source of new light for the *Popol Vuh*, including the astronomical aspects of the story it tells. At times the astronomy is quite explicit, but the narrators often content themselves with allusions whose meaning is left to knowledgeable readers. Such is the case with their account of the cataclysm that ended the world preceding this one, where they mention that hearthstones came shooting out of a kitchen fireplace. Mayan fireplaces have three hearthstones arranged in a triangle, and we know that the contemporary Quiché have a hearthstone constellation consisting of a triangle of three stars in Orion. (Tedlock 16)

Galeano's recreation of the relationships among characters, recognizably borrowed from the *Popol Vuh*, infuses their mysterious actions and conflicts with an ethical and social significance that can be translated to a contemporary sphere of action. He nevertheless retains the magical aspects of the story, situating the socio-political conflict in a cosmic framework and ending in the recuperation of astronomical harmony.

The third *Soberbio* commits a sin against nature by killing for pleasure and not for food. After the heroic pair liberates the earth from these incarnations of greed, impunity, and arrogance, they receive an invitation to the Kingdom of Fear. In the *Popol Vuh*, this kingdom is represented as the underworld, "a region named Xibalba or 'Place of Fear'" (Tedlock 34), and situates the second cycle of the twins' adventures. The combination of the two cycles described by Tedlock is also applicable to the chronological order of events in *Las aventuras de los jóvenes dioses*:

> If the events of these two cycles were combined in a single chronological sequence, the aboveground episodes might alternate with those below, with the heroes descending into the underworld, emerging on the earth again, and so forth. These sowing and dawning movements of the heroes, along with those of their supporting cast, prefigure the present-day movements of the sun, moon, planets, and stars. (34)

While the twins are transformed at the end of Galeano's story into the sun and the moon, he spins an allegorical tale about the Kingdom of Fear, combining fantastic elements with features that characterize dictatorship and economic exploitation in contemporary terms:

> *Los señores del Reino del Miedo*
> *no producían maíz, ni chocolate, ni mantas.*
> *Ellos sólo producían miedo.*
> *Y con miedo pagaban a los hombres y a las mujeres*
> *que cultivaban la tierra*
> *y tejían el algodón.*
> *Quien protestaba, moría;*
> *Y también la duda estaba condenada. (Las aventuras de los jóvenes dioses* n.pag.)
> [*The lords of the Kingdom of Fear*
> *did not produce corn, nor chocolate, nor blankets.*
> *They only produced fear.*
> *And with fear they paid the men and women*
> *who cultivated the land*
> *and wove cotton.*
> *Whoever protested died,*
> *And even doubt was condemned.*]

The social factors characterizing this ominous place give it a tangible quality that opens the context to allow possible imaginative transpositions. Mythic elements that Galeano borrows from the *Popol Vuh* mesh with a historical reality that can be related to the situation in Chiapas and to any number of communities throughout Latin America and the world. Mythic language extends the boundaries of historical circumstances to create an allegory for economic exploitation and state terror, an allegory that nevertheless retains its concrete referents instead of becoming universally abstract and atemporal.

The sibling warriors then accept the invitation to the Kingdom of Fear and are condemned to a series of impossible challenges that they manage to overcome with the magical intervention of natural elements—that is, until the arbitrary lords decide simply to order them into a bonfire, to which Ix and Hun respond: "We know our destiny." The Lords of Xibalbá, painted on funerary vases of the Classic period, are described by Wright as arrogant and "rather louche…puffing on big cigars and surrounded by beautiful girls" (*Time Among the Maya* 188). In *Las aventuras de los jóvenes dioses*, López Vigil depicts them in a circle glaring menacingly at the reader (who visually occupies the twins' perspective). They are wrapped in black blankets and clutch what appear to be cow skulls. After their fiery death, at the hands of the Lords of Fear, the twins' bones are ground into fine dust and scattered at the bottom of a river. But, of course, the story doesn't end there.

Two raggedy old people arrive at the Kingdom of Fear to entertain the lords with exotic dances and magic. Their most popular act is the resurrection of the dead, which they demonstrate with a dog and with the bossiest of the bosses, after which all the lords want to be protagonists of this bizarre party and insist on also being dismembered. The trickster gods, who are really Hun and Ix in disguise, dismember the lords at the false fiesta, and never resuscitate them. Having fulfilled their mission on earth, Hun and Ix rise to heaven. "Y subieron al cielo, donde un falso sol estafaba a los días y una luna de mentira engañaba a las noches. Y desde entonces Hun Ahpú es el sol que anda nuestros pasos y su hermana Ix Balanqué es la luna que nos sueña los sueños" (n.pag.) [And they rose to the heavens, where a false sun used to defraud the day and a lying moon used to deceive the nights. And since then Hun Ahpú is the sun that walks our steps and his sister Ix Balanqué is the moon that dreams our dreams]. Heaven and earth are united; false gods, false lords, and false social systems are vanquished in an ending that is both mythical and political.

What counsel does Galeano's story offer children? It is impossible to interpret the fantastic actions of the two young warriors as exemplary in any simplistically mimetic sense. Nonetheless, their struggle against avarice, arrogance, and oppression implies that they struggle in order to defend the values of "collective work, democratic thought, and majority rule," earlier identified by Marcos as the basis of indigenous society (*Shadows of Tender Fury* 46). Marcos himself retells a Chiapanecan folktale suitable for young and old readers entitled *La historia de los colores* (*The Story of Colors*), in which the political dimension is much less obvious, since this is a creation myth about colour and human diversity. Ironically, this project was initially funded by the National Endowment for the Arts, but when it was discovered that the author was Marcos, the grant of $7,500 was quickly withdrawn.[12]

Reading the story against this action reveals the sad reality of a powerful government that refuses to recognize its part in causing the strife of indigenous Mexicans and also refuses to recognize the incontestably humane (and reasonable) appeal of both this book and the various communiqués issued by the Zapatistas. Consider, for instance, the following letter dated 13 January 1994, addressed to President Clinton, the North American Congress, and the people of the U.S.A.:

> We address you to inform you that the federal government of Mexico is using the economic and military aid that it receives from the people and government of the United States of North America to massacre the indigenous people of Chiapas...we have nothing to do with national or international drug trafficking or terrorism. We organized ourselves of our own volition, because of our enormous needs and problems. We are tired of so many years of deception and death. It is our right to fight for a dignified life...Our desire is the same as the rest of the world's peoples: true freedom and democracy. And for this passion we are willing to give our lives. Do not cover your hands with our blood by being accomplices of the Mexican government. (*Shadows of Tender Fury* 71-72)

While the most obvious reason for the American and Canadian governments to ignore the situation in Mexico is their prioritizing of the NAFTA (North American Free Trade Agreement) over any real consideration for human rights and environmental protection, Galeano's vignette entitled "Indians" identifies fear as a prime factor of racism against the indigenous population in the Americas.

Those who represent Native Americans as hopelessly degenerate, anachronistic phantoms who persist in holding on to a belief system that refuses to accept exploitation of land and people are primarily motivated by fear, the fear of the other holding up a mirror to reveal the degenerate mask of a "civilization" based on inequality. The oppressed other, the one in a position to know its oppressor, is also the one whose voice is prophetic and must be silenced at any cost:

Indians

> Language as betrayal: They shout *hangman* at them. In Ecuador, the hangmen call their victims hangmen: "*Indian hangman!*" they shout...Indians are stupid—vagrants, drunks. But the system that despises them despises what it does not know, because it doesn't know what it fears. Behind the mask of scorn is panic: Those ancient voices, stubbornly alive: What are they saying? What do they say when they speak? What do they say when they are silent? (*The Book of Embraces* 134)

The Zapatistas have broken this mysterious silence and speak lucidly about their needs and hopes. Not surprisingly, they still have a long way to go before they are reciprocated with the same kind of honesty and vision. In the meantime, the various forms of expression emanating from their culture provide windows to contemplate another way of seeing another possible world.

La historia de los colores was first sent from Marcos to the Mexican people in a communiqué dated 27 October 1994. It later became a bilingual book project that some critics classified as a children's book, although the categories appearing on the book jacket are "Latin American Literature/Folklore." *The Story of Colors* presents itself as a creation myth passed from Old Antonio's mouth to Marcos's ear, who in turn passes it on to whomever had the good fortune of finding a rare copy on the internet. Marcos is figured as first-person narrator and interpolator of Old Antonio, who is the actual narrator of the folktale about how colours came to be. Marcos represents himself as both belonging to the same community and as being slightly "out of step" with Old Antonio, who is in no hurry to escape the imminent rain Marcos sees in the gray mist when "Old Antonio points at a macaw crossing in the afternoon sky" (n.pag.). The difference between the two men is subtle: Marcos implies that Old Antonio's perception of beauty and desire to tell a story is a lesson in why *not* to be in a hurry: "While I'm lighting my pipe, I ask him, 'Do you think we'll get to the village before the rain starts?' Old Antonio doesn't seem to hear me. This time, it's a flock of toucans that's distracted him." Even before the title page, Marcos imagines the reader as listener in a chain of listeners and storytellers: "I light my pipe and, after three ceremonial puffs, I begin to tell you—just the way old Antonio used to tell it—." The sight of the macaw and the toucans triggers Old Antonio's memory of a mythic story about how the black and white world finally received the gift of colour.

Collaborative projects that bring together writers and visual artists (like the artistic linkage of Galeano and Borges in *Walking Words* that we discuss earlier in this chapter) open up the notion of authorship and result in hybrid works that cross generic and cultural boundaries usually separating artists from artisans, literature from storytelling, "civilization" from popular culture. Marcos collaborates on this book with Domitila Domínguez, a Mazatecan woman who, after spending years doing embroidery, suddenly felt the urge to paint a brown woman on the wall of her living room and couldn't stop herself from covering the room with figures. In *The Story of Colors*, Domínguez's striking images address visually the diversity and beauty of creation just as eloquently as the words of Marcos, Old Antonio, and the *pueblo*.

The gods in *The Story of Colors* have much in common with the gods in Galeano's *Las aventuras de los jóvenes dioses*: they are more human than those who first gave birth to the world. In this case, they are more quarrelsome, understandably since "the anger of the gods was a true anger because only the two colors took their turns with the world: the black which ruled the night and the white which strolled about during the day" (n.pag.). From the beginning of the story, the black and white world and, by extension, black and white perception is associated with strife while colours are linked with the beauty of difference.

The first colour, red, issues from a god's wound. While stumbling along pondering how to make the world more joyous for men and women, he trips over a rock and injures his head. The other colours have equally poignant origins that also resonate with vatic meanings for the future: green to paint the feeling of hope, brown from the heart of the earth, blue for the colour of the world that blinds another god when it gets stuck to his eyes, and yellow, a child's laugh snatched from him by a god who left him in tears ("That's why they say that children can be laughing one minute and all of a sudden they are crying" [n.pag.]).

The motif of making love appears several times in the story. Even when the world was still black and white, "the men and women were sleeping or they were making love, which is a nice way to become tired and then go to sleep"; this is also the way that the created colours engender an infinity of others. Left in a little box, not very tightly shut by the sleepy gods who had been indulging in some *pozol* (a maize drink), "the colors escaped and started to play happily and to make love to one another, and more and different colors were made, new ones." When the gods return, they assume that the ceiba tree, under which they had left the box, gave birth to the colours, and this is also how the ceiba becomes sacred: "You will take care of the world." The rambunctious gods climb the tree and start flinging the colours all over: "And it was a mess the way the gods threw the colors because they didn't care where the colors landed." It is hard to imagine a creation story that diverges more radically from the Genesis story of the Judeo-Christian bible, with its singular God who methodically creates one thing at a time in a temporally measured and spatially ordered universe.

The Chiapanecan folktale represents creation not as order, but as serendipitous chaos, a life-affirming playground where ludic gods frolic like spirited children and accidentally create beauty and difference. Chaos is also the very basis of community: "Some colors splattered on the men and women, and that is why there are people of different colors and different ways of thinking." In order to preserve this gift, the gods decide to pour all the colours on a macaw, "and so it goes strutting about just in case men and women forget how many colors there are and how many ways of thinking, and that the world will be happy if all the colors and ways of thinking have their place." The living bird is also a memorial, not to something dead and gone or to something abstract that can be preserved in scripture, but within nature, the divine source of knowledge for humans who, like the gods, are forgetful, irresponsible, and capricious, and who need the earth to give them roots.

Galeano's windows on theology in *The Book of Embraces* counterpoint the Mayan gods represented by Marcos in that the Christian god's solitude, perfection, and chastity inspire Galeano's pity. Throughout his work, he celebrates difference, joy, eroticism, and acceptance, the same themes that Marcos highlights in his story about the indigenous latter-day gods. Storytelling that imitates the oral tradition perhaps offers more than structures and techniques. The diversity of voices that this tradition incorporates by circulating freely, by being a shared means of expression, and a joyous way to while away the hours seems to accord with a worldview that is passed on along with the formal aspects. In returning to this tradition, writers do not simply borrow motifs, linguistic regionalisms, and stereotyped artifacts as they had in the past when trends such as *indigenismo* (Indianism) and *costumbrismo* (a genre that represented local customs and manners) skimmed the surface of culture by presenting it as a landscape to be admired or as a threatening otherness. How an author like Marcos functions within a culture that he joins by his own volition and how he transmits the many voices of the Zapatistas, whose messages he transcribes and disseminates, implies a hybrid kind of *testimonio* writing. His involvement in the community differs from the anthropological model of the interviewer who enters a community temporarily only to observe.

While Rosaura Sánchez speaks specifically of the narrowly defined genre of *testimonio*, her representation of how cultural artifacts circulate globally is applicable to the appearance of "Marcos's" collective story:

> In this age of information technology, with its attendant compression of time and space, rampant consumerism, and multinational/transnational capitalism, it is the cannibalization of a premodernist genre produced with late capitalist technology (tape recorders, camcorders, and so on) for commodification and sale on a world market by multinational publishers that best exemplifies the expansion of capital into even the most peripheral areas and signals most clearly the heterogeneous nature of cultural production in the Third World today. (7-8)

Thanks to the hype about the withdrawal of support from the National Endowment for the Arts, the initial price of $15.95 for a first edition of *The Story of Colors* quickly rose, reflecting the imbalance of demand and supply as well as the commodification identified by Sánchez. Similarly, by now almost all of the communiqués and open letters disseminated by Marcos and the Zapatistas have been collected and published in book form, translated into several languages, and consequently made available for institutionalization and canonization. The question remains, however, whether this process spells automatic appropriation and neutralization for all readers.

Ilan Stavans, novelist and critic, includes one of Marcos's letters in his anthology *The Oxford Book of Latin American Essays* published by Oxford University Press. While he expresses admiration for Marcos's "intellectually unsettling persona," he announces the demise of the Zapatista project, a gesture complicit with U.S. and Mexican national interests. His praise implies that we can now safely "shelve" Marcos's writings and not have to worry about any extra-literary consequences:

> While Subcomandante Marcos is obviously a *distinguished* member of the *tradition* of Latin American guerrilleros (Enriquillo, Ernesto "Ché" Guevara, Edén Pastora, and Abimael Guzmán are some others), he holds the unique position of *having used* the written word as his sharpest, most explosive weapon. The Mexican political establishment *was able to neutralize* the EZLN rebels, but it could not dismantle

Subcomandante Marcos's *intellectually* unsettling persona. He remains one of the most imaginative revolutionaries of this century and an *essayist* of the first order, and his writing exemplifies a true crossroads where Latin American politics and literature meet. (481; our emphasis)

Our Word is Our Weapon. From *Shadows of Tender Fury* (1995): 21.

Do politics and literature really meet when the politics are relegated to a past that has now been "neutralized" by the establishment? To what does this sanitized militaristic term refer? Have the Zapatistas been neutralized through the massacre of Mayas or through the negotiations that Marcos continues to invite? He does not, however, occupy the desperado's place in this invitation: "Let Fox designate a representative of his government with whom we can construct a dialogue. There's no hurry. A handshake with Vicente Fox is not among our wet dreams" ("The Punch Card and the Hour Glass" 74). Interestingly, this comment was made by Marcos in 2001, four years after the publication of Stavans's smug reference to the neutralization of the EZLN rebels, when according to Marcos the Zapatistas are in no hurry, let alone prepared, to acknowledge defeat. Is the "establishment" referred to by Stavans really only "political" in governmental terms, or is the anthologizing and institutionalizing of "essays" in this way also complicit with that "neutralization"? Is not "essay" a misnomer for a hybrid form of writing with quite different objectives than following a tradition or being worthy of publication by Oxford?[13]

Other academics in prominent Unitedstatian[14] universities go to great lengths to the-orize such problems, often adopting the defeatist/megalomaniacal attitude of neutralizing everything they touch. What these critics do not seem to realize is the insignificance of their self-inflicted censorship to anyone outside their magic circle. In his introduction to *The Real Thing: Testimonial Discourse and Latin America*, Georg Gugelberger recognizes that "when counterdiscourse is co-opted by mainstream discourse, new problems arise. These problems urgently require to be addressed" (12), but then he ends ambiguously, porten-tously declaring that

> ...every interpretation is a falsification, every truth an error. The subaltern may not write, but the subaltern undoubtedly will act. May we learn to observe more criti-cally even if the institutionalized bars behind which we work make the communica-tion very difficult, almost impossible. Pointing to this possibility of the impossible, realizing what we cannot do—namely, to identify with the subaltern in a gesture of solidarity—is a worthy experience of learning. (18)

While Gugelberger is clearly trying to be honest about the limitations of scholarly activities, his denial of identification "with the subaltern in a gesture of solidarity" paradoxically dis-misses Marcos's visionary appeal for solidarity, the precise objective of Marcos's writings even as he also takes material political action: those who identify with the Zapatistas' vision of a humane world are invited to join in stopping globalitarian colonization, regardless of the social position they occupy. Gugelberger's denial of solidarity and identification—let us say with the oppressed and not that highly abstract entity known among academics as the "subaltern"—also dismisses Freire's vision of *conscientização* [making conscious] and the pedagogy of the oppressed as well as Dussel's vision of solidarity as the basis for a communi-tarian ethics. This defeatist attitude, for all its intentions of scholarly integrity and clear-sightedness, also dismisses Galeano's call for the literal and figural embraces that can potentially transform a system based on detachment and alienation, whether intellectual, emotional, political, or historical.

The tenor of several of the essays on *testimonio* collected in *The Real Thing* privileges the academic legitimation of *testimonio* while sidestepping the issue of how *testimonio* is not intended exclusively or even primarily for academic "consumption"—and that it is perhaps the institution that seeks legitimation and not the texts that the institution supposedly le-gitimates. Elzbieta Sklodowska, for instance, remarks on "The fact that we, the interpretive community of academic critics, have agreed to 'recognize' *testimonio* and give it *institutional legitimation* is, arguably, one of the most important events of the past two decades in Span-ish American literary history" ("Spanish American Testimonial Novel" 84; our emphasis). The comment reveals both the flip side of defeatism and a skewed notion of community, as if academic legitimation, such as it is, somehow increases the value of the evidentiary texts (oral and written) that constitute *testimonio*. For all the hypersensitivity to the treacherousness of language, the academic rhetoric associated with this sort of analysis defaults into free-market lingo and represents the other as being motivated by the same self-serving and utilitarian objectives as any state propagandist. Referring to the Guatemalan Nobel prize recipient (1992) who made the plight of her Mayan community known through the seminal *testimonio* entitled *Me llamo Rigoberta Menchú y así me nació la conciencia* [*My Name is Rigoberta Menchú and Thus My Political Conscience Was Born*], John Beverley states that "someone like Rigoberta Menchú is also in a sense *exploiting her interlocutor* in order to have her story reach and influence an international audience, something that as an activist for her community she sees in quite utilitarian terms as a political task" ("The Margin at the Center" 33; our emphasis).

By contrast, other essays included in *The Real Thing* recognize the wider sphere of *testimonio*'s influence. Alberto Moreiras concedes that "testimonio provides its reader with the possibility of entering what we might call a subdued sublime: the twilight region where the literary breaks off into something else, which is not so much the real as it is its unguarded possibility. This unguarded possibility of the real, which is arguably the very core of the testimonial experience, is also its preeminent political claim" ("The Aura of Testimonio" 195). Moreiras's marking of his literary territory (beyond which lies a sublime, twilit region) might strike those who are not literary critics as a peculiar perspective, but his affirmation of the enunciative status of *testimonio* accords with our tracing of the connections between Galeano's interest in witnessing through *testimonio* and his envisioning an imperfect but possible utopian future. Moreiras also addresses the seemingly abject but self-interested academic discourse that gestures impotently beyond itself while subsuming every form of discourse as more fodder for theorizing, a critique that many of the essays in this same collection warrant:

> This essay on testimonio meta-critics only pretends to be a prolegomenon to that postliterary, or perhaps just postmodernist, disciplinary politics—and thus, in a way, a partial attempt to think through the implications of identity politics for those who, from a disciplinary perspective, have no relevant identity claim to make: those for whom an implication in disciplinary representational self-knowledge may have become, perhaps in spite of themselves, more powerful than any other form of belonging. (200)

Here, Moreiras suggests that academic trends like identity politics drive scholars to pursue forms of expression they are unable to identify with and must therefore theorize into abstractions that in the case of *testimonio* end up denying it any significance outside the academic sphere. Similarly, George Yúdice's "*Testimonio* and Postmodernism" is another essay in this collection that affirms *testimonio*'s significance beyond narrow academic parameters. Yúdice's reading of Menchú's testimony also contests the cynical neoliberal representation of Menchú peddling her story and manipulating readers in order to secure the political ends she seeks like any politician in a representational democracy. Contrasting the "hegemonic postmodern text in which the 'I' is expelled as vomit"—symbolic of the process of individuation that separates the child from its parents, and the body from nature—with Menchú's appeal to solidarity, Yúdice describes her text as "a testimonial of incorporation, embodiment" (56). This critic allows that solidarity is not necessarily an illusory and self-indulgent sentiment but a means of creating the conditions to listen to the other without fetishizing it as do "hegemonic postmodern text[s]" (57).

Abandoning the academic context altogether in order to examine the immediate pragmatic effects of *testimonio*, Lynn Stephen, in her afterword to María Teresa Tula's recounting of her formation as a Salvadoran activist, states that "La literatura testimonial es un género que permite a personas comunes hacer una lucha para el acceso a los medios de comunicación pública. Ellos desafían a los guardianes culturales ostendadores del poder y la producción cultural misma" (242) [Testimonial literature is a genre that permits common people to fight for access to the public media. They thus challenge cultural guardians who hold power and cultural production itself]. *Testimonio*, in this sense, resists the subalternization of people normally denied access to institutional means of communication. In no way can this gesture be equated with the kind of institutional legitimation imagined by Sklodowska or with the kind of analysis Beverley offers. Both refigure *testimonio* in terms of the centre recuperating the periphery; we would argue instead that *testimonio* demands that the ethical space of interlocution remain centred on the agency of the peripheral voice as a metonym for a wider community of shared experience. The periphery restores the ethical practice of reciprocal interlocution, from the position of the other to the centre.

The case of the Zapatistas, then, effectively puts into question some of these issues, especially the imposed problematic label "subaltern," given that they speak forcefully, effectively, and frequently. Are their accounts to be read as *testimonio* even if they are transmitted, sometimes translated, by Marcos? Does being categorized as a brilliant essayist mean that Marcos is really engaging in autobiography, even as he incessantly tells the story of the Chiapanecans? Ultimately, these questions highlight the limitations of literary taxonomies rather than shed light on what is meaningful about the Zapatistas' vision of community and communication.

Why would Marcos transmit this folktale, myth of creation, to the Mexican people? Clearly, the concept of living memory does not belong to a conventional history lesson or a multicultural vignette, and it is inseparable from the vision of a future that must rediscover its course. Galeano's testimonial approach to chronicling belongs to the same democratic vision shared by writers like Marcos and Poniatowska, whose stories combine personal artistic vision and multi-voiced participation in the act of storytelling. Like the first mythic grandfather of the Axé Indians in Paraguay who dug himself out of the earth with his nails, the indigenous people and all those who have been buried by the global *Soberbios* must dig themselves out of the cemetery of words.

"We Do Not Accept Humiliation":
Crisis, Democracy, and Freedom of the Press

It is not so much Galeano's style or format as his cast of characters that suggests an analogy with the testimonial genre. It is the marginal nature of Galeano's personae that gives his book its particular character, the voices that would not be heard beyond a small circle were there no interviewers or authors of "testimonies." (One is reminded of Neruda's Canto VII, "The Earth's Name Is Juan.") In this encyclopedic offering are included the kinds of individual voices that are sifted into categories by historical studies, voices that at last have found writers to transcribe them in their uniqueness and not for their mythical or emblematic qualities. (Kirkpatrick 171-72)

The full title of the journal in which Galeano collaborated as editor and occasional contributor from 1973 to 1976 is *Ideas, letras, artes en la crisis* [Ideas, Writing, Arts in Crisis], indicating an urgent situation requiring critical response. It is impossible to summarize the range of topics and approaches characterizing *Crisis*, especially in comparison to the narrow disciplinarity of most North American and transnational publications. Even those publications that have sections on the arts, film, interviews, and so forth, in addition to political and historical analyses, do not approximate how in *Crisis* such diverse topics are set into dialogical motion and not compartmentalized as discrete topics of interest. *Crisis*'s "mission statement" expresses a radically democratic vision of cultural communication: "We seek interlocutors, not admirers; we offer dialogue, not spectacle. Our writing is informed by a desire to make contact, so that readers may become involved with words that came to us from them, and that return to them as hope and prophecy" (*Days and Nights* 191). This journal on and from Latin American culture (in the widest sense of that term) had an extraordinary mandate related to memory and testimonial:

Culture didn't end, for us, with the production and consumption of books, paintings, symphonies, films, and plays. It didn't even begin there. We understood culture to be the creation of any meeting space among men, and culture, for us, included all the collective symbols of identity and memory: the testimonies of what we are, the prophesies of the imagination, the denunciations of what prevents us from being. For this reason *Crisis* published, among the poems and stories and drawings, reports on the deceptive teaching of history in the schools or on the wheelings and dealings of the large multinationals that sell automobiles as well as ideology. This is why the magazine denounced a value system that exalts things and scorns people, and the sinister game of competition and consumption that induces men to use and crush one another. For this reason we were concerned with everything: the sources of the landowners' political power, the oil cartel, the mass media. (*Days and Nights* 147)

Crisis 24 (1975): front cover.

primicia mundial: el informe de la
unesco sobre los medios de
comunicación en américa latina
los ciento veinte años de sigmund
freud "eché barraca y me equivoqué"
la muerte de martín güemes jabones
en polvo: los trapitos al sol hablan
los mapuches cuentistas y cuenteros
textos de tizón, zito lema, galeano,
girri, nepomuceno, kovadloff, rivera y
don verídico plástica: de la vega, deira,
del prete, paz, ruffinengo, sobisch,
tabaré y sábat

en este número:
índice de crisis

argentina $ 220,—   buenos aires, agosto 1976

40

Crisis 40 (1976): front cover.

In 1973, Uruguay suffered a military coup that created a dangerous environment for the publication of progressive ideas about freedom, justice, and equality. Galeano was imprisoned, after which he started his exile in Argentina, where the first issue of *Crisis* appeared in May of that same year. As far as state terror was concerned, Argentina was just one step behind Uruguay and after publishing monthly issues for four years, censorship became so repressive that the editorial board of *Crisis* decided that silence was preferable to being neutralized:

> The magazine is finished. In the morning I get everyone together to talk to them. I want to seem firm and talk hopefully, but sadness escapes through my pores. I explain that neither Fico nor Vicente nor I have made the decision; circumstances have decided. *We do not accept humiliation* as an epilogue to the beautiful adventure that has brought us together for more than three years. No one makes *Crisis* bow down: we will bury her erect, just as she lived. (*Days and Nights* 154; our emphasis)

Many of Galeano's collaborators, comrades, and closest friends were jailed, tortured, disappeared, or fled into exile. After a hiatus of ten years, in April of 1986, *Crisis* reappeared with a jubilant and visionary introduction by Galeano, who moved from a directorial to an advisory editorial position. In the introduction to the reborn *Crisis*, Galeano reflects on how the journal had always been cogent and coherent without the need to declare a specific agenda: "Ningún tema nos era ajeno, ningún pulso de vida, y en el vasto abanico de temas y personajes hubo siempre un lugar de privilegio para todo lo que ayudara a desenmascarar la realidad pasada y presente y todo lo que ayudara a descubrir la capacidad de maravilla de tierras y gentes despreciadas por la cultura oficial" (*Crisis* 41 [1986]: 3) [No topic was alien for us, no heartbeat, and in the vast panorama of topics and characters there was always a privileged spot for anything that would help to unmask reality, both past and present, and everything that would help to discover a capacity for the marvelous in lands and peoples disdained by official culture].

Leafing through issues of *Crisis*, one is immediately struck by the absence of hierarchical ordering that would privilege either high culture over popular culture or vice versa. World-famous authors like García Márquez appear frequently but on a completely equal footing with interviewees from marginalized sectors of society who give either anonymous testimonies or in-depth and detailed responses to complex situations. An example of the latter case is a long interview with native chief Saturnino Huilka, who speaks with great precision about the wisdom of his Inca ancestors Mamma Olla and Manco Capac. Huilka relates their insights to the present situation faced not just by his own people, but by all those who are oppressed (32 [1975]: 19-24). Often people are randomly interviewed about their reactions to an issue such as the politically motivated assassination in Argentina in 1974 of Father Carlos Mugica, a member of the *Movimiento de sacerdotes para el tercer mundo*. The interviews published in 1975 by *Crisis*, along with a *testimonio* by Father Mugica's colleague and friend Jorge Vernazza, were conducted in the slums where Mugica worked with the poor. A year after the event, the interview does not exploit the raw grief (or sensationalism and sentimentality) of immediate reportage. The responses are varied and even those interviewees who seem cynical reveal implicitly how the system has led them to perceive acts of kindness as asking for trouble. One interviewee declares that Mugica sought out his own death by worrying about other people's problems, by helping them, but insists that this means that Mugica "asked for it"—"*él se la buscó*" (26 [1975]: 18). Other interviewees attest to Mugica's selfless efforts on behalf of the poor while at the same time pointing to the slums where Mugica worked as being "el mundo al revés," a world upside-down—a trope Galeano has consistently used, as we have shown, throughout his work.

A regular feature of *Crisis* was interviews with children and marginalized people whose opinions on art are rarely considered in any context in North American journalism, except occasionally to ridicule art galleries for expenditures on paintings, whose value is not immediately apparent to the "common sense" wisdom of the guy-on-the-street. A 1975 issue of *Crisis* includes photos of mural paintings done by children in a harbour. Some of the young painters are interviewed as to where they got their inspiration, their motivation, and what kind of response they anticipate from the local fishermen. One child answers: "—Pintar en la pared ...? Me gusta...es como jugar a algo, pero no me importa si gano o si pierdo" [Painting on the wall? I like it...it's like playing something, but I don't care if I win or lose]. And as to whether the fishermen will also like the paintings: "—No sé, creo que no, son gente muy grande" [I don't know, I don't think so, they're big people]—an intuitive response further elaborated upon by one of the fishermen who clarifies that fishing is so intensive that he has eyes only for the sea: "Mire, si usted algún día se sube a las tres de la mañana en una de esas lanchas y se mete en el mar, y trabaja en el medio del mar, va a ver que luego para usted no hay otra cosa, todo cambia, y está en su casa y sólo piensa en volver al mar" (25 [1975]: 21) [Look, if one day you board one of these boats at three in the morning and go out to sea, and you work in the middle of the sea, you'll see that for you there will be nothing else, everything changes, and you're at home and only think of returning to the sea]. The questions are simple and direct, but formulated in a way to elicit more than the vacuously noncommittal "it's nice."

The responses reveal much about the nature of art, the cultural context in which it is discussed, and people's perceptions on important issues such as art's role in society and its effects on both individuals and communities. While the responses are not analyzed by the interviewer, they go beyond the individual's private reaction because many of the interviewees do grasp what is at stake. A kind of adult version of the mural painting follows. Large murals are executed on huge slabs of rock along a jetty in a desolate area where only working people go to the beach. Several of the people interviewed are not only heartened by the fact that talented artists bother offering their work in such a locale, but also by the fact that none of the murals is defaced or vandalized in any way; they interpret this as proof that art is for everyone and appreciated by the majority: "—Ojalá todos pintaran paredes y no cuadros. Esos cuadros que uno se entera por los diarios que valen millones y que ni siquiera podemos conocer de vista" (25 [1975]: 22) [If only everyone painted walls and not canvases. Those paintings that you find out about in the papers, that they are worth millions and we can't even see them first hand]. "—Yo de pintura no entiendo, pero le digo que ver esto me causa alegría" [I don't know anything about painting, but I can tell you that seeing this gives me joy]. The comments reveal an appreciation of beauty and the effort that went into painting the murals in such a difficult space. What is reflected upon frequently is how selfless is this will to give beauty anonymously to whoever happens to walk along the jetty.[15]

There is no effort on the part of the interviewer to combine negative and positive reactions according to the "pro/con" model of supposedly democratic opinion polls. The reactions are not pitted against each other with a view to catch the reader in a debate on what is right or wrong. And yet there is not necessarily a consensus, as opposed to an assortment of thoughtful reactions on which to reflect. Similarly, the journal frequently published photos of graffiti, which Galeano delights in gathering, and further disseminates in *The Book of Embraces* under the heading "The Walls Speak," as in, for instance:

> In Caracas, during a time of crisis, at the entrance to one of the poorest barrios:
> *Welcome, middle class.*
> In Bogotá, around the corner from the National University:
> *God lives.*
> And underneath, in a different hand:
> *By a sheer miracle.*
> And also in Bogotá:
> *Proletarians of all lands unite!*
> And underneath, in a different hand:
> *(Final notice.)* (101)

This gathering of voices, whose collective nature is further punctuated by the responses appearing beneath many of the original graffiti, functions as a synecdoche of Galeano's mission to chronicle Latin America through a myriad of sources from internationally-known public figures to the anonymous. The readers of this style of journalism do not entrust themselves to experts who play key roles in so-called investigative reporting that tends to turn a blind eye to historical causes and the powerful links connecting neocolonial countries with each other and their masters. According to Henry Kissinger, the "expert has his constituency—those who have a vested interest in commonly held opinions; elaborating and defining the consensus at a high level has, after all, made him an expert" (qtd. in Achbar 219). Chomsky agrees with this observation albeit ironically, especially the telling detail of the "vested interest," and de-neutralizes it in the reformulation: "An expert is someone who articulates the consensus of people with power" (qtd. in Achbar 219). *Crisis* is driven by this insight and provides a wide spectrum of views from people of diverse backgrounds. Their *testimonios*, personal accounts, oral or written, of lived experience, as well as poetry and stories, give *Crisis* a uniquely intense and fascinating diversity, especially when contrasted with the discourse of "specialists" and politicians dominating mainstream transnational journalism. Taken to its logical extreme, the fetishization of fact spells the end of democracy: "Shortly after the coup d'état, the military government dictated new regulations governing the mass media. According to the new censorship code, it was prohibited to publish street coverage and opinions on any subject given by non-specialists" (*Days and Nights* 148). *Crisis* was silenced as a result of this prohibition.

Both the exaltation of the expert and the rejection of expertise as source of information respond to pedagogical intentions. The expert specifies certain details, very often using a narrow focus, supposedly justified by the fact that the expert possesses extensive knowledge of a specific reality. Not all experts get equal say; some are even persecuted for disseminating their findings. The biotech industry, for instance, has become a hot topic because the consequences of its research affect all North American consumers, not just the faceless poor whose destiny never merits the same kind of media attention. Even those North Americans who naïvely claim to be apolitical or who conceive of politics in a narrowly nationalistic context sit up and pay attention when the government suddenly dismisses consumers' rights to know in favour of protecting biotech corporate interests. It has become evident even to the complacent consumer that experts who support the government's vested interests are widely disseminated to reassure the public, assumed by the same experts to be obtuse and superstitious, that genetically engineered food is safe. The inquisitive consumer almost has to be an expert in research methodologies to find dissenting scientific opinions, which mainstream newspapers either omit, ridicule, or neutralize by granting more space and the final word to the evidence proclaiming that "all is well and it's business as usual." The next step for people, who until now believed in the free press, is to realize that news that does not effect them directly is manipulated with an even higher degree of impunity.

Both Chomsky and Galeano have dedicated much of their work to exposing how mainstream mass media, the only source of so-called information for most people, is ideologically complicit with the "new" world order (which in fact is as old as the hills) and manipulates news coverage to confirm the global status quo:

> The Pope in Rome forcefully condemned the brief blockade, or threatened blockade, of Lithuania. But the Holy Father has never uttered a word against the blockade of Cuba, now in its thirtieth year, or of Nicaragua, which lasted a decade. That's normal. And it's normal, too, that since we Latin Americans are worth so little while still alive, then the value placed on our dead should be a hundred times less than on the victims of the now disintegrated Evil Empire. Noam Chomsky and Edward Herman have taken the trouble to measure the space we merit in the leading North American media. Jerzy Popieluszko, the priest murdered by state terror in Poland in 1984, took up more space than the sum total of 100 priests murdered by state terror in Latin America in recent years. ("The Other Wall" 9)

Crisis, like Galeano, rejects neutral words, openly questioning ideas, trends, and products from diverse critical viewpoints. These often *include* specialized evidence such as medical documentation, since the articles are well researched and offer in-depth analysis; however, these experts only furnish the requisite data to support commentaries whose primary focus is sociological and cultural. In a 1975 issue an article on feminine deodorants entitled "'su íntima seguridad' los desodorantes vaginales: un producto superfluo y peligroso" ['Your Intimate Security' Feminine Deodorants: A Dangerous and Superfluous Product] opens not with evidence of harm (which is well documented later on in the article), but with a sociological approach to gender and marketing issues. The laboratory is represented as a site of image-making and, in the case of women, the body is targeted to cause shame that leads to spending:

> En 1966, los gabinetes de investigación de la industria de la cosmética norteamericanos, hicieron un descrubrimiento que estuvo a punto de resquebrajar los fundamentos de la sociedad humana: la vagina olía; y para colmo de alarmas, olía mal. Los pacientes trabajos de los avezados científicos y técnicos yanquis habían desembocado en la misma conclusión a la que habían llegado, un siglo antes, la totalidad de los africanos que, sin ninguna formación científica, se acercaron al explorador inglés Stanley; el británico despedía un incómodo "olor a blanco." Lo cierto es que el cuerpo humano huele y olió siempre. (29 [1975]: 36)

> [In 1966, the research laboratories of the North American cosmetic industry made a discovery that nearly ripped apart the foundations of human society: the vagina smells; and to make matters worse, it smells bad. The patient labour of experienced Yankee scientists and technicians had led to the same conclusion reached a century earlier by all those Africans, who, without any scientific training, had been in close proximity to the English explorer Stanley; the Englishman gave off an unpleasant "smell of white man." The fact is that the human body smells and always has.]

The author of the article, Javier Font, then goes on to examine how this smell is not offensive in a healthy person, and how if an unusual smell indicates a disorder, there is even more reason to treat it instead of covering it up. The article openly identifies North America not only as the source of this kind of hazardous and useless product but as the centre of consumerism that it radiates to Latin America. Instead of being aimed specifically at women, the article is classified as relating to the theme of consumption (*consumo*), a category of reality that is represented as false or contrived. *Crisis* anticipates cultural studies because it deconstructs the ideological implications of things and activities that masquerade as necessity, without bracketing that focus off from historical, political, sociological, and artistic perspectives.

Dorfman explores how *Reader's Digest* is both a very special case of journalism and also paradigmatic of the American Way, representative of mass media generally in its banality and hidden agenda. Like the contributors to *Crisis*, Dorfman does not buy that democracy means freedom to consume:

> The inspiration behind the *Reader's Digest* is very clearly a political project, which—aside from the extreme conservatism of its public stance—can be noted in the type of communication that it suggests, in the type of relationship between reader and producer. It is democracy as it is practiced in industrial societies, but especially in the United States. To participate is, above all, to consume, to be a completely economic man. To participate in politics is to be a radio, television, or newspaper spectator; to participate is to deposit a vote every few years, certain that we are also voting when we dig into our pockets and wallets every day. (*The Empire's Old Clothes* 153)

Dorfman's main contention is that this kind of writing aimed at consumuption, rather than challenging the reader to think, speculate, and imagine, infantilizes the reader. Publications like *Reader's Digest* fragment the world and ration it out to the reader in bits and pieces of disconnected facts and anecdotes that never congeal into a knowledge that the reader could then apply to a different context in an accumulative process of learning and discovery. Dorfman contends that these disconnected anecdotes are offered as an evangelical message of salvation, based on the superiority of the rich and powerful in accordance with a Protestant ethic and the spirit of capitalism.

> Characters in the *Reader's Digest* are frequently besieged by hurricanes, packs of wild dogs, bears that have escaped from their cages, communist and Irish terrorists, collapsing buildings, Arctic and tropical climates, and they always succeed—thanks to their faith in God, thanks to their own integrity—in surviving…*Reader's Digest* is a tourist guidebook for the geography of ignorance…Every area is clearly delineated and set apart from the others, separated from any possible global cohesion. The apparent autonomy of the various chunks subterraneanly reinforces the image the reader has formed of his own cognitive potential in a world where everything changes at such a feverish rate, where specialization has grown to traumatic proportions, where nothing ever seems to reach a level of coherence or integration. (136-38)

But those like Galeano, Dorfman, and Chomsky, who perceive connections and can point them out and back up their findings convincingly to even non-experts, especially when it comes to connections between vested interests and exploitation, capitalism and poverty, U.S. dominance and political violence in Latin America, are quickly dismissed as simplistic. According to the *New York Times Book Review*:

> Chomsky is arguably the most important intellectual alive today. He is also a disturbingly divided intellectual. On the one hand there is a large body of revolutionary and highly technical linguistic scholarship, much of it too difficult for anyone but the professional linguist or philosopher; on the other, an equally substantial

body of political writings, accessible to any literate person but often maddeningly simple-minded. (qtd. in Achbar 19)

Is it "maddeningly simple-minded" or is it maddeningly revolutionary? Why is the linguistic scholarship deemed revolutionary (but too difficult to read) and the political writings not only simple-minded but completely unrelated to Chomsky's true genius? His politics are represented as an aberration of his intellect. The subtext clearly reads: "Chomsky should stick to the highly technical linguistic scholarship, much of it unreadable, because that is his specialization. He has no right to 'educate' anyone beyond the narrow confines of his discipline." But Chomsky refuses to be confined to his academic pigeonhole and has much to say about North American education, how highly selective it is about topics promoted as worth teaching, keeping them very close to home, reserving global interest strictly to business interests. In a dialogue with Donaldo Macedo, Chomsky asks:

How many American intellectuals have read anything written by the Central American intellectuals who were assassinated by U.S. proxy armies? Or would know of Dom Helder Camara—the Brazilian bishop who championed the cause of the poor in Brazil? That most would have difficulty even giving the names of dissidents in the brutal tyrannies in Latin America—and elsewhere—that we support and whose forces we train provides an interesting comment on our intellectual culture. (*Chomsky on MisEducation* 19)

Interestingly, a 1975 issue of *Crisis* features a long interview with Helder Camara and an extensive selection from other interviews and speeches made by the Brazilian bishop. The same issue includes two articles on the oil industry. The first exposes how a few weeks after the military coup, Minister of the Interior Eduardo Busso is seen giving an energetic handshake to Henry Holland of the U.S. State Department, ratifying a deal in which the cream of Argentina's oil reserves will be extracted by U.S. companies. The transaction is presented by mainstream media in Argentina as a necessary technical measure to extract the oil and by the Wall Street weekly *Business Week* as a business opportunity. But the *Crisis* article differs significantly from mainstream journalism in that it covers an extensive period, identifying and analyzing the milestone events along the way of foreign domination and exploitation. It turns out that the major American player, respected oil technician Walter J. Levy, can afford to give "free" advice to the Argentine government because he is on the CIA payroll. The article quotes official documents, newspapers both national and international, and specialized books like Julius Mader's *Who's Who in the CIA*, published in Berlin, reading the official truths published in the mainstream media of Argentina and the U.S. against each other. "Experts" are quoted, not to justify and explain events that defy common sense or ethical principles, but to expose their lies through their own discourse. Nevertheless, extensive specialized information on the oil industry is scrupulously documented. Experts certainly contribute the empirical evidence for the critical interpretation of a complex situation whose broadest implications are evaluated by a journalist who is not selling the reader a line. Instead of talking down to the reader by foreclosing on dialogue, which is the effect of the expert's paternalistic final word, these journalists and commentators openly state their suspicions, beliefs, and accusations. Their straightforward commitment to the topic provokes in the reader not the usual anesthetized acceptance but a range of responses from doubt and disbelief to outrage and a desire to know more.

This article on the petroleum industry also contains an insert entitled "Coincidental Deaths Do Not Exist," which examines in cultural and historical detail the various factions and relationships of power in the oil-rich Arab nations. The deaths of Feisal Ibn Aziz al Saud ("one of the pillars of North American influences in the region"), Adolfo Benito Cavalli (a retired Argentine, ex-member of *Sindicatos Unidos Petroleros del Estado* [National United Petroleum Unions]), and Tibor Berény (double-agent representing Shell while signing Argentine contracts with the U.S.) are represented in a global context instead of as singular and disconnected individuals. Contextualized in a global economic war, the story is not limited to exposing the sordid stories of shifty individuals, but reveals the real perpetrators to be monopolies that exercise global politics in which nations are puppet-territories to be exploited. Through detailing the national and personal histories of the three dead men, connections that would seem unthinkable in mainstream journalism emerge and hypotheses offered. There is no pretense of the kind of objectivity that refuses to consider the most obvious motivation of multinational corporations. The journalist, Carlos Villar Araujo, declares his belief openly and founds that belief not on any doctrine or supernatural revelation, but on hard, cold facts: "... creemos que la 'crisis del petróleo' es una gigantesca y audaz maniobra de los monopolios para hacer pagar a los propios pueblos de América del Norte y de Europa Occidental el costo de una profunda reconversión energética: desplazamiento de los yacimientos tradicionales hacia nuevas reservas ubicadas en los países centrales (Canadá, Alaska, Mar del Norte), desarrollo de fuentes alternativas de energía" (25 [1975]: 8) [We believe that the "oil crisis" is a gigantic and daring stratagem on the part of monopolies to make North Americans and Western Europeans pay the cost of a radical reconversion: displacement from traditional energy sources toward new reserves situated in the central countries (Canada, Alaska, North Sea), development of alternative sources of energy].

After offering a number of hypotheses on why Feisal was killed, Villar Araujo indulges in a little irony that addresses the journalistic practices of the not-so-free press and what happens to those who defy them:

O la última posibilidad de todas: que, en efecto, haya sido una muerte accidental, la obra de un insano solitario. Y bien, mientras no hayan pruebas abrumadoras, evidencias incontrastables, mientras quede el mínimo asomo de duda, siempre que haya petróleo de por medio *debe suponerse en prinicipio que las muertes accidentales no existen.* Es la ley del "determinismo petrolero". Si usted se entera que después de escribir estas notas al cruzar una calle me aplastó un colectivo, lector, piense mal y acierta. (25 [1975]: 8)

[Or the very last possibility: that it was in fact an accidental death, the act of a solitary madman. And so, until there is overwhelming proof, uncontestable evidence, while there remains the slightest hint of doubt, whenever oil is involved *one must start from the assumption that accidental deaths do not exist.* It's the law of "petroleum determinism." If you find out that after writing these notes I was hit by a bus crossing the street, reader, think the worst and guess right.]

This subjective tone would be scandalous in a mainstream journalist, let alone the suggestion that honest speculation based on the critical analysis of empirical evidence can cost a journalist his or her life. Galeano addresses the problem of objectivity when speaking about the extent of his personal involvement with the material while writing *Memory of Fire,* anticipating the criticism of those who believe that historiography is a purely objective task:

I mentioned this to José Coronel Urtecho: in this book I'm writing, however you look at it, backwards or forwards, in the light or against it, my loves and quarrels can be seen at a single glance. And on the banks of the San Juan River, the old poet told me that there is no fucking reason to pay attention to the fanatics of objectivity:

"*Don't worry,*" he said to me. "*That's how it should be. Those who make objectivity a religion are liars. They are scared of human pain. They don't want to be objective, it's a lie: they want to be objects, so as not to suffer.*" (*The Book of Embraces* 120)

Coronel Urtecho is generous in supposing that the fanatics of objectivity are trying to avoid their own pain. Even more to the point is Donaldo Macedo's observation that "Once intellectuals are adapted to the doctrinal system and rewarded by it, it becomes increasingly less difficult for them to live within a lie and ignore the true reality, even when faced with documented historical evidence" (*Chomsky on MisEducation* 174). Obviously, it is those who oppose the doctrinal system who suffer the consequences—and, in oppressed countries, journalists with integrity suffer persecution and are even assassinated, while in affluent liberal countries they are dismissed as inconsequential and simplistic and read by a minority who seek out "alternative" sources of information.

The next article in this 1975 issue of *Crisis* is on military spending by the world's "Super Powers," both state and private capitalists. A sidebar to this article reveals the spending on specified military equipment by companies that most North Americans in their innocence associate with cars and household appliances: Ford, Chrysler, General Electric, and American Motors right in there with missile and fighter jet producers like Hughes Aircraft and McDonnell Douglas. These investigative articles do not stop at reporting the facts, for facts are never simple unless one chooses not to follow the threads of the story to all the different places they lead. The writers speculate openly in a subjective tone that invites a similar response in the reader, instead of the idiotically passive acceptance of "official truths" paraded as incontestable data. After these three articles appears the section on graffiti and art entitled "Las naranjas son el alma" [Oranges are the soul] that we previously commented on, and the long interview with the Brazilian bishop.

At first glance, these texts may seem unrelated, fragments of reality as diverse and unconnected as those presented in *Reader's Digest*. But they all share in a desire to unmask reality of the pervasive lies concocted to protect multinational interests but to also unmask reality of the atrophied and tired gaze that *Crisis* aims to revitalize by featuring something as fresh and new as a child's painting of the sea or a mural painted for the sheer pleasure of expression. Despite the vast writing about exploitation and suffering, the dominant tone of *Crisis* is one of optimism and enthusiasm. This optimism, however, has nothing in common with the smug, pious optimism that Dorfman examines in *Reader's Digest*. *Crisis* does not propose simple solutions to the world's problems. The evidence it presents of corporate and state abuses is overwhelming. But the integrity of the contributors and the sanity of the numerous testimonies from the poor—usually silenced—majority prove that there are alternatives and that this kind of polyphonic inquiry and exploration of culture is an immensely valuable contribution to its revitalization. Instead of trying to be "up-beat" by featuring "feel-good" success stories or even human interest stories that celebrate the integrity, generosity, or bravery of a particular individual, the multiple voices in *Crisis* celebrate a multitude that expresses its values directly through testimony. The cumulative effect of these anonymous contributors ends up being much more inspiring in the long run than the occasional superhero.

As one last point of comparison, the high profile of indigenous culture in *Crisis* forms an integral part of envisioning a possible future through revisioning the cultural past that colonization attempts to annihilate.[16] Publications that disseminate the propaganda of "progress" represent non-European (especially tribal and communitarian) cultures as barbarian unless they assimilate to North American and European models of "civilization." In his reading of an article on "The Tabajara Indians: Musical Geniuses of the Jungle" in the April 1980 issue of *Reader's Digest*, Dorfman examines how this group of people receives paternalistic praise for their capacity to pass in an élitist bourgeois musical milieu. In a revealing statement innocently taken at face value by *Reader's Digest* as a primitive simile on the part of the Indians, the Tabajara explain that "we learned how to play classical music the same way parrots learn how to talk" (*The Empire's Old Clothes* 163). How they learned their traditional music is passed over in a brief parenthesis indicative of how insignificant this point is in the article on the Tabajaras' musical genius, itself a highly Eurocentric notion: "They still can't explain how they did it today" (*The Empire's Old Clothes* 163). Dorfman's point is that this attitude of cultural superiority recurs in every *Reader's Digest* article dealing with folk art or popular culture in the Third World:

Such a step from barbarism to Bach is symbolized in everything they do, including taking off their ponchos and feathers and putting on dinner jackets to play a toccata and fugue. This instantaneous transformation, taking place practically right in front of the television audience or those in the auditorium, is what the *Digest* offers, like Babar in a can, to its Third World readers. Fast food. Fast ideas. Fast development. They become "civilized," and as a reward they receive the applause (and recognition) of the public at the center of the world, and their immortality in *Reader's Digest*. (163-64)[17]

This immortality takes a radically different form in *Crisis*, where the extinction of specific peoples is examined in its historical and cultural contexts with a view to transform the mentality that permits and promotes genocide and cultural annihilation. The radical otherness of indigenous communities is not only respected but promoted as a necessary and desirable aspect of human diversity and rights. A moving example of this kind of heterodox journalism appears in a 1973 issue of *Crisis* entitled "*Las culturas condenadas*" [Condemned Cultures], a 31-page study of Paraguayan indigenous tribes combining their own testimonies, songs, and poems alongside the anthropological studies of international ethnographers who also give testimony to the persecution and slaughter of these peoples.

The first text about the Axé-Guayakí is written by Paraguayan Augusto Roa Bastos, one of the foremost writers of Latin American fiction, author of *Yo el supremo* (1974) (*I the Supreme*; trans. 1986).[18] Here again is a striking example of the cultural interconnectedness of literature, history, sociology, and politics characteristic of those Latin American writers who cannot turn their backs on history. Roa Bastos examines the many forms of exile experienced by these writers, including the violence of having to write in Spanish for those, like him, whose people speak an indigenous language (Guaraní is the second official language in Paraguay and is widely spoken by Paraguayans regardless of ethnic background). Roa Bastos defines the enormous project of writing in a literary void:

> ...[the writer] will always have something left that has not been expressed. This brings the Paraguayan writer face-to-face with the need to *make* a literature that as yet has no place in literature; to speak against the word, to write against writing, to invent stories that are the transgression of official history, to undermine, with subversive, demystifying writing, the language loaded with the ideology of domination. In this sense, the new generations of fiction writers and poets find themselves committed to the task of advancing this *literature without a past* that comes from a past without literature, of expressing it in their own language. (276)

While Galeano is not torn between languages, as an Uruguayan writer he belongs to the new generations that Roa Bastos addresses insofar as the history of Uruguay was shaped by colonization and again by a contemporary military dictatorship in conjunction with U.S. and multinational interests. In this sense, *Crisis* too faces "the task of advancing this literature without a past"; Roa Bastos's contribution, entitled "Un pueblo que canta su muerte"

["A People Who Sing Their Death"], introduces a complex drama that the editors piece together as a collage of testimonies in which the Axé songs and *testimonios* occupy centre stage. These oral lyrics are difficult to translate given that they speak of and from a cosmogony that is alien to Western modes of thought. Roa Bastos starts by explaining why he chooses to focus on the death song of the Axé and makes clear that the plight of this people is not isolated. He implies that what the reader is about to learn sheds light on global relations and the urgent necessity of setting a different course for history:

> El hecho de tomar la agonía de los Axé-Guayakí del Paraguay oriental como tema de esta selección de sus mitos y cantos, no significa parcializar en un solo pueblo indígena los padecimientos que, desde el comienzo mismo de la Colonia, han sufrido con mayor o menor virulencia las poblaciones vernáculas de nuestro Continente. Esta vieja tragedia de esclavitud, degradación y exterminio, que culmina en la actualidad con la inmolación de las tribus sobrevivientes, no puede ser comprendida en toda su significación sino en el marco global de nuestras sociedades basadas en el régimen de opresión y explotación de los estratos humanos que ellas consideran "inferiores" y los someten a una vida infrahumana; en el caso de los indígenas, a un rapidísimo proceso de aniquilamiento en masa mediante todos los recursos de su inhumano poder. De esta suerte, el etnocidio no es sino la fatal y fatídica resultante de esta ideología del privilegio y la superioridad racial—herencia del conquistador invasor—y sólo una de las formas del genocidio generalizado en la actualidad, no sólo en nuestro continente sino en varias partes del mundo, bajo el signo de la concepción nazi heredada y practicada por el imperialismo, en sus formas más crudas y degradantes, con la colaboración de las oligarquías locales. (*Crisis* 4 [1973]: 4)

> [By focusing on the agony of the Axé-Guayakí of Eastern Paraguay in this selection of their myths and songs we do not intend to isolate a single indigenous community in their suffering. Since the beginning of the Conquest, all the autochthonous communities of our Continent have suffered to a greater or lesser degree of virulence. This old tragedy of slavery, degradation, and extermination that currently culminates in the immolation of the surviving tribes cannot be fully understood except in a global framework. Our societies are based on a régime of oppression and exploitation of humans that are labeled "inferior" and subjected to subhuman existence. In the case of the Indians, they are subjected to a rapid process of mass extermination through every possible means of societies' inhuman power. Consequently, ethnocide is nothing but the fatal and ominous result of the ideology of privilege and racial superiority, inherited from the invading conquistadors. One of the many current forms of genocide, not only on our continent but in various parts of the world, it is carried out under the sign of Nazism, inherited and practised by imperialism in its cruelest and most degrading forms, with the collaboration of the local oligarchies.]

Typical of the global vision of *Crisis*, Roa Bastos offers an in-depth study of the Axé and of the reasons for their imminent disappearance in the local context. But he also identifies what he sees as the historical and ideological source of oppression and marginalization in the world, a problem that must be addressed by everyone everywhere. To represent the Axé as simply on the brink of extermination would not draw out the consequences of a terrible reality. By contextualizing their plight and recuperating their words, *Crisis* creates hope for changing the system that promotes modern-day slavery.

Roa Bastos explains the central place occupied by the word in the cosmogony of Guaraní Indians, which "conceived of human language as the foundation of the cosmos and the original nature of man. The nucleus of this myth of origin is the esoteric and untranslatable *ayvú rapytá* or *ñe'eng mbyte rã* as the very essence of *the soul-word*" (276-77; our emphasis).[19] The fusion of the divine, human, and natural realms in the Guaraní cosmogony creates communion where the Western *logos* identifies difference. Their primordial divinities "brought about the communion between knowing and doing, between unity and plurality, between life and death. Every man was God on the way to purification, and God—or the many gods of that theogony—was both the first man and the last. They did not impose exile, but the pilgrimage of the *multitude-person* to the *land-without-evil* that each one bore within and amid all" (277). We will return to these two key concepts—the "multitude-person," expressive of a communitarian vision of identity, and the "land-without-evil" as the ethical horizon of the future—in the last chapter. But for now, we point out that the terms are closely related to the vision that these contemporary writers are struggling to re-member and project as a viable, transformative future.

The ethnographer (León Cadogan), anthropologists and linguists (Bartolomé Meliá and Mark Münzel), Roa Bastos, and the Axé lyrics all converge in this fourth issue of *Crisis* on a vision that is difficult to comprehend from a Western perspective. Nevertheless, the combination of viewpoints that struggle to understand difference invites the reader to attempt the same, instead of simply accepting uncritically information doled out by "experts." Roa Bastos interprets one of the Axé's principal beliefs, showing how it informs their intellectual and spiritual wisdom and, ironically, becomes the basis of their extermination by white "civilizers":

El "civilizador" blanco, que utiliza a los Axé como perros de caza y señuelos para capturar a sus hermanos de raza probablemente no conoce el sentimiento mítico del Axé sobre *Jamó* (jaguar). Lo ignora o no le interesa saberlo, pero lo utiliza. Los Axé creen, según explica el mismo Münzel, que si son comidos por un jaguar mítico, se transforman a su vez en jaguares que deben seguir comiendo a sus hermanos. Por analogía piensan que al ser capturados se transforman en paraguayos, con la obligación de perseguir a los Axé. He aquí como hasta los mitos se "pasan al enemigo" de contrabando en el alma de los ratones silvestres convertidos en jaguares del blanco. (*Crisis* 4 [1973]: 9)

[The white "civilizer" who uses the Axé as hunting dogs and decoys to capture the brothers and sisters of their race are probably not familiar with the mythic feeling that the Axé have for *Jamó* (jaguar). He does not know anything about it and it does not interest him, yet he uses it. The Axé believe, as [Mark] Münzel explains, that if they are eaten by a mythic jaguar, they are transformed into jaguars that must go on eating their own brothers and sisters. By analogy, they think that when they are captured they are transformed into Paraguayans, with the obligation to persecute the Axé. This is how even the myths "go over to the enemy" as contraband in the souls of the wild rats of the jungle converted into the Whites' jaguars.]

Mark Münzel, German professor of ethnography at the University of Frankfurt, here mentioned by Roa Bastos, is the author of the article that follows, entitled "Tortuga persigue a tortuga" ["Turtle Persecutes Turtle"]. In it we find further evidence of how white Paraguayans exploit the Axé, whose pantheistic belief in reincarnation between humans and animals leads to a fatalistic acceptance of becoming non-human like their white hunters. Münzel's work examines the relationship between the "wild" Axé and the "tame" Axé. The latter assume what appears to be a mythico-magical non-identity, a kind of zombie-state in which they obey the white master and re-enact the myth of the jaguars who return to the tribe to hunt down the loved ones they miss. Münzel's ethnographic observations about the "tame" Axés' behaviour is all the more disturbing for its many metaphors of alienation:

Y como el Axé cautivo está decidido a transformarse en blanco, tiene que transformarse en cazador también. Para él, ignorante de nuestras costumbres y del sentido de nuestras acciones, transformarse en un blanco significa entrar en un mundo absurdo, grotesco, transformarse en animal. He observado, p. ej., cómo Axé "nuevos", recién llegados del monte, imitaron con exageración involuntaria y grotesca, las actitudes de los blancos, cambiando el modo de hablar axé, bajo y suave, por frases sin sentido, en voz alta; las reglas complicadas de la cortesía Axé por palmadas en el hombro y frases de saludo como "mbaé hora che?" (*Crisis* 4 [1973]: 10)

[And since the captured Axé is determined to be transformed into a white, he must also become a hunter. For the Axé, unfamiliar with our customs and the meaning of our actions, to be transformed into a white means to enter into an absurd and grotesque world, to be transformed into an animal. I have observed for example how the "new" Axé, recent arrivals from the mountains, imitated with unintentional exaggeration the gestures of the whites, changing the Axé way of speaking, low and soft, to meaningless phrases, uttered in loud voices; the complicated rules of Axé courtesy substituted by slaps on the back and greetings like "mbaé hora che?" (the Guaraní word meaning "what" combined with the deformed pronunciation of the word for "time" and the guaraní word for "mine" or "I" resulting in an incomprehensible question imitative of something like "what's up?").]

While Münzel's observations help to intuit the enormous conceptual leap made by the captured Axé into alienation, the reader is free to wonder why Münzel associates the absurd and grotesque world of the whites with the animal world. The Axés' poetry reveals their panmaterialist belief in metamorphoses between human and animal life, together with their veneration for certain animals like the Great White Anteater. These discrepancies make the Axé lyrics all the more compelling for the reader who is comparing the anthropologist's interpretation of observations with the words of the Axé themselves. A passive attitude is impossible to maintain in the face of such diverse and complex readings. The Axé lyrics challenge the reader to interpret their dense, metaphorical, and next to impenetrable meanings, since they speak with equal authority in this selection of articles as any of the "expert" commentaries. Despite their alien quality for most people who are entirely unaware of their cultural context, these lyrics are presented as speaking for themselves instead of being "demonstrations" to support the anthropologists' interpretations.

What allows the reader this degree of critical involvement is the consideration of the Axé's lyrics, which the *Crisis* editors intersperse alongside the essays by the anthropologists and linguists trying to fathom their reality and their vision. These songs are more challenging to interpret than any avant-garde or surrealist poetry or, for that matter, the scientific theses of experts. Few publications would expect their readers to engage with such material, but for *Crisis* it is a matter of principle to publish not just conventionally written discourse, but the discourses—however marginalized and alien—of those who have something to say or sing about their condition. The "Canción de airági," written by a "tamed" Axé, envisions a reunion with the author's people beyond death where the Axé will no longer be "domesticated" and enslaved. The identification between the Axé and the animals of the jungle is strong and the song tells of numerous metamorphoses:

Semejante a un Axé
el excelente pájaro cazador
se volvió un Axé.
El que perforó el labio,
el de la flecha con pluma de cañón blanco,
siempre acertaba;
nosotros lo hemos dejado atado por el monte,
entre los de antes, ahora nuestros enemigos. (*Crisis* 4 [1973]: 14)

[*Resembling an Axé*
the great bird of prey
turned into an Axé.
The one who perforated my lip,
the one with the white barreled feather,
always hit the mark;
we left him tied up on the mountain,
among the ones from before, who are now our enemies.]

This song speaks of the similarities between the Axé and animals like the *coatí* (a rain-forest mammal with elongated snout and long tail) and the tapir, revealing that Münzel's negative analogy of turning into an animal may be informed by the Western bias that the animal world is grotesque and absurd. The texts comprising this amazing and challenging presentation of tribes facing extinction are incredibly plurivocal, demanding the reader's participation and full engagement in ways that would be foreclosed by any single, reductive thesis.

While this particular series of texts on the "condemned" cultures of Paraguay deals with people who are near extinction or who have experienced a devastating assimilation that has erased almost all traces of their past, they are emphatically *not* the final word on indigenous culture in Latin America. The songs themselves tell a more hopeful story than the ethnographers' reports on the demise of the Axé. Despite the seemingly fatalistic prophecy that "el que está cautivo en las garras del jaguar, tiene que ser jaguar" (*Crisis* 4 [1973]: 11) [he who is captured by the jaguar's claws is to become a jaguar], other prophecies foretell a time beyond death where the Axé will be reunited and occupy their rightful place in the *land-without-evil*.

Since the articles and issues of *Crisis* are not presented as discrete entities having no relation to each other, the numerous other articles giving *testimonios* from different indigenous perspectives affirm a vibrant and prevailing presence, contrary to most journalistic representations of native peoples as anachronistic phantoms of an irretrievable past. The high profile given to issues of indigenous rights and culture in *Crisis* is especially significant given that the place of publication is Argentina, where the predominantly white population of Buenos Aires and other large urban centres tends to deny that indigenous people even exist in Argentina and in Uruguay. The interest in indigenous culture clearly expresses a Latin Americanist perspective encompassing countries where the large indigenous population has little access to or representation in the mass media.

Such feature articles as the interview with Chief Saturnino Huilke leave no doubt that indigenous peoples are not only surviving but are resisting those aspects of colonialist culture that clash with their communitarian ethics. True to its title, *Crisis* consistently published visionary material, new fiction, and poetry alongside socio-political analyses of every imaginable aspect of life in Latin America and beyond, seen from the perspective of the oppressed. The urgency and extreme need to respond to injustice implicated all those involved in the publication of the journal in a life-or-death situation that is hard to imagine in the context of mainstream journalism and mass media. Galeano remembers the consequences of this project, the brutal repression and the exhilaration of glimpsing what is truly possible:

> Fico Vogelius was the businessman who had financed the magazine *Crisis*, and he had put not only money but his soul and life into that venture and had given me the freedom to do whatever I wanted with the magazine. While it lasted—three years,

forty issues—*Crisis* managed to be a stubborn act of faith in the…word that is not, nor tries to be, neutral, the human voice that is not an echo or empty sound. For that crime, for the unforgivable crime of *Crisis*, the Argentine military dictatorship had kidnapped Fico, jailed him and tortured him. (*The Book of Embraces* 264-65)

Saturnino Huilka, from *Crisis* 32 (1975): 21.

The dedication shown by *Crisis* to disseminating a multiplicity of voices across Latin America—some well-known, others rarely heard—stems from the position, which we have discussed in previous chapters, that it is the oppressed who knows the oppressor and not vice versa. And it stems from the commitment to learn from the other who is vast and multiple, who remembers other ways of being and desires to share that memory.

Galeano represents this intuition of difference and what it has to offer as a desire for something lost and not yet discovered: "I'm nostalgic for a country which doesn't yet exist on a map" (*Days and Nights* 139). This is not an unreasonable realist's fantasy. Galeano's vision of writing as a creative recording of his own and others' testimonies contributes to breaking down walls that, like the ones surrounding the *ciudades perdidas* (the walled-in Mexican slums), attempt to disappear the oppressed without getting any blood on the oppressors' hands. *Testimonio* is often gut-wrenching as would be the evidence given by a witness before a jury deliberating over a heinous crime. But Galeano focuses on the spiritual strength that emanates from the voices of those who have suffered (unspeakably) but who have survived (impossibly):

> ...it helps me to remember what Chief Huillca said in Peru, speaking before the ruins. "They came here. They even smashed the rocks. They wanted to make us disappear. But they have not been able to, because we are alive, and that is the main thing." And I think that Huillca was right. To be alive: a small victory. To be alive, that is: to be capable of joy, despite the good-byes and the crimes, so that exile will be a testimony to another, possible country. (*Days and Nights* 175)

Similar to Roa Bastos's global accounting of genocide in his reading of the particular case of the Axé of Paraguay, Galeano reads Chief Huillca's insights as relevant to all those who share testimony and envision another possible country, the one that does not yet exist but is remembered nostalgically.[20] Read in relation to mounting repression and personal danger at the hands of death squads and police, Galeano's solidarity with Huillca becomes even more understandable. Returning to the dialogue between Galeano's Chilean friends and the Indians who remind them that they are just beginning to have a taste of oppression while the Indians have been under its rule for 500 years, here again, Chief Huillca and his people are given space to speak about what they have experienced first-hand and what all the victims of dictatorship are about to experience. Solidarity is both the recognition of a shared oppression and a shared destiny.

Given the limited number of *Crisis* issues as well as its extremely difficult publishing conditions, the diversity of voices is astounding. The *testimonios* of slum-dwellers, students, children, workers, mental patients, and countless others who participate in a true democracy inspire the hope that its editors set for themselves as their objective. It is telling that in countries where "freedom of speech" is taken for granted as the foundation of journalism, no publication anywhere even approximates the cultural scope and visionary democracy of a journal published on the brink of terror. Through the myth of freedom, North American journalism obliterates the voices of the marginalized and even of the majority, who are occasionally represented but rarely participate in telling their own stories when these contradict the official propaganda that everyone is free, happy, and prosperous. Understood in Galeano's broad cultural terms, *testimonio*—to give witness—is to participate in the formation of cultural identity, and in the writing of history as it happens to everyone, the only true expression of freedom and democracy. When practiced under a repressive régime, freedom and democracy have the value of prophecy, but on closer scrutiny of our own oppression, our "manufactured consent," our institutionalized miseducation, the prophecy speaks to all.

"The Future Has a Way of Coming from the Edges":
Revisioning the Past to Envision the Future

Testimonio has become a highly theorized genre in the North American academy, where new frontiers are constantly being sought, partly to escape the narrow élitist parameters of the literary canon, but ostensibly also to institutionalize, conquer, and consume forms of expression that nevertheless evade these discourses of power. While *testimonio* is read as a form of cultural resistance, it is rarely interpreted as heralding revolutionary change. *Testimonio*'s words are neutralized by the privileged class that denies its own power to envision the social change to which most *testimonio* appeals. By sharp contrast to the largely empty gestures of scholarly and predominantly theoretical (self-)interest, the circulation of *testimonio* in Latin America has the crucial function of reflecting images of shared identity to those who never see themselves in the mass media and those who see mirages of identity masked by repressive régimes.

Galeano goes so far as to proclaim that "I write for those who cannot read me: the downtrodden, the ones who have been waiting in line for centuries to get into history, who cannot read a book or afford to buy one" (*The Book of Embraces* 155). He goes on to explain why he bothers to write, by way of a personal experience. One night in Italy he attended a pantomime show with his partner Helena. They turned out to be the sole spectators, yet amazingly "the actors worked as hard as if they were basking in the glory of a full house on opening night. They put their hearts and souls into the performance and it was marvelous" (*The Book of Embraces* 155). This vignette is entitled "The Dignity of Art" and contrasts sharply with the business sense dominating mass media. The short piece ends by describing how the couple applauded until their hands were sore, an image of intimacy and shared pleasure between artist and active spectator. While such moments of face-to-face mutual appreciation are rare for writers, Galeano delights in repeating the story of a group of *Crisis* readers who once a month crossed the Río Uruguay to read the banned journal:

> There are about twenty of them. The group leader is a professor of about sixty who has spent a long time in prison. In the morning they leave Paysandú and cross over to Argentine soil. They all chip in and buy an issue of *Crisis* and then go to a café. One of them reads aloud, page by page. They all listen and discuss the material. The reading lasts all day. When it ends, they leave the magazine at the café as a present for the owner, and return to my country, where it is banned. "Even if it were just for this," I think, "it would be worthwhile." (*Days and Nights* 43)

In contrast to the highly detailed criteria by which academics define *testimonio*, Galeano is not interested in generic formulations, insisting that all authentic expression gives testimony: "no hay ninguna literatura que valga la pena que no dé testimonio de algo que merece ser contado. Como todo lo que proviene de la realidad, los sueños, los fantasmas, los misterios...Uno da testimonio siempre" (qtd. in Henriquez-Lagarde 97) [There is no literature that matters that does not give testimony of something that deserves to be told. Like everything that comes from reality, dreams, ghosts, mysteries...One is always giving testimony]. This flexibility and his refusal to even distinguish journalism from literature allow Galeano to gather the voices around and within him. This anti-structure is characteristic of *Days and Nights of Love and War*, in which the first-person autobiographical discourse engages in constant dialogue with others who are quoted as giving testimony. Hence, the usual differentiation between autobiography and testimony is also ignored, surpassed in a fluid interpolation of self and other. This approach to writing reminds Galeano of an old joke that he likes to tell in order to make a distinction he believes to be crucial: "masturbarse está bien, pero hacer el amor es mejor porque se conoce gente" (qtd. in Henriquez-Lagarde 101) [masturbating is okay, but making love is better because you get to know people].

Galeano started giving testimony in visual form as a political cartoonist and newspaper illustrator (in his early teens), thinking for awhile that drawing was his true vocation. He started to write regularly after suffering an emotional crisis that nearly led him to suicide but left him with his eyes cleared instead: "I saw the world for the first time and I wanted to devour it. Every day after that would be a gift. Now and then I forget, and I give this second life over to sadness. I let myself be expelled from Paradise, every now and again, by that punishing God who never finishes leaving you entirely" (*Days and Nights* 45). As a child, Galeano felt sorry for adults whose books of pure print looked unappealing, and he soon started to change that absence of sensorial pleasure by borrowing illustrations from popular artists and contributing his own skills as a graphic artist, a feature of his publications that continues to this day.

Galeano often shares the space on his pages with artists like José Guadalupe Posada (1852-1913), the engraver whose work is associated with the Mexican Revolution. Posada documented and commented on that period through the satirical use of a popular motif in Mexican culture dating back to pre-Columbian times: a grinning skeleton named *Calavera* engaged in myriad human activities. Octavio Paz describes Posada's subject matter as "the great theater of the world of man, at once drama and farce," pointing out that "Posada never took himself too seriously" while asserting that "he was a true moralist...an involuntary moralist; he shows without instructing" ("Will for Form" 32). Posada's engravings also provide the visual commentary in the English translation of the Zapatistas' communiqués entitled *Shadows of Tender Fury*, while serving as visual punctuation to (and comment on) Galeano's writings in his own rendition of Posadaesque *Calaveras* in *The Book of Embraces*. These images belong to popular culture and had their beginnings in nineteenth-century newspapers where they satirized politicians and bourgeois values as powerfully as the murals of Orozco. Posada, then, emblematizes the survival of popular art that speaks for those who were betrayed by the Revolution but who have not lost sight of its goals.

Galeano's own illustrations in *The Book of Embraces* are a tribute to Posada's vision and juxtapose the Mexican skeleton icon with details drawn from European-inspired classical art. In one instance, two cherubs carry an ornate mirror that reflects a singing skeleton strumming a guitar; in another, a couple of skeletons dressed in nineteenth-century finery are placed in a chalice. The latter motif also appears as ceramic sculpture in Mexican popular art, from miniature to two feet high figures representing ladies in bourgeois gowns and elaborate feathered hats beneath which grins the skull, combination of *memento mori* and social satire on the transitoriness of wealth and status. Inspired by the satirical power of this kind of visual art, Galeano juxtaposes images that take on new meanings, ideologically complex but as unambiguous in intention as his words. A text entitled "Advertisements" that combines ads from the classifieds of Uruguayan newspapers in 1840 (27 years after the abolition of slavery, as the parenthetical source clarifies), lists items for sale. Included are several human beings: "One halfbreed negress of the Cabinda race, for the sum of 430 pesos. Knows rudiments of sewing and ironing," "One nursing female. To be sold without offspring, has good and plentiful milk," indiscriminately listed with pieces of furniture, leeches, bottles of sarsaparilla, and "a lion, tame as a dog, will eat anything" (*The Book of Embraces* 79).

Skeletons. José Guadalupe Posada, from *Upside Down* 229.

In keeping with Galeano's concise archival historiography, this text needs no further comment—the horror of colonialism and slavery after its "official" abolishment is perhaps even intensified by the absence of commentary. The tone of normalcy in these advertisements reveals the degree of impunity and lack of humaneness in a society where the consumer class turns fellow human beings into products. On the opposite page (78), exploitation is given visual form and associates this perverse relationship of oppressor to dehumanized product with cannibalism. Galeano shows a balding and mustachioed man sitting at a dinner table set with bowls of food, condiments, and drink. The main dish appears to be a skinned human being, an image that seems to have been lifted from an anatomy textbook. He rises out of a dish from the waist up, face turned upwards, and arms extended in a dramatic pose. His exposed muscles are numbered. This same notion of the "charted" body recurs in another context, in the image of a cow, also standing on a plate, with cuts clearly delineated for butchering (117). The two images speak to each other and to the reader through an accumulative effect that widens the sphere of imaginative reference. Consumption of meat is transposed to the consumption of human beings through enslavement.

Gloria Anzaldúa describes how for the ancient Aztecs, the black and red ink with which they painted codices, for instance, was intimately connected to metaphor and symbol, since the colours themselves represented writing and wisdom ("Tlilli, Tlapalli" 33). The linking of image and word in an aesthetic that does not reduce image to mimetic representation is relevant to how Galeano's images, both literary and pictorial, encapsulate concepts and symbols and are comprehended immediately in metaphorical terms that amplify signification: "An image is a bridge between evoked emotion and conscious knowledge; words are the cables that hold up the bridge. Images are more direct, more immediate than words, and closer to the unconscious. Picture language precedes thinking in words; the metaphorical mind precedes analytical consciousness" ("Tlilli, Tlapalli" 34). The combination of image and word is thus an attempt to recapture the symbolic power of picture language and to bridge conceptual and emotional expression.

Galeano does not, however, represent this ability to bridge concepts and emotions as the result of artistic technique. He suggests that words and images find him to mysteriously join together of their own accord and create something that is beyond his own conceptualization or even authorial intention. While he sometimes calls himself a hunter of words, ultimately the words that he captures metamorphose into something else, to find their own shape and equilibrium. The wise storyteller knows and respects this fact. For this reason, Galeano prefers to be called a chronicler, despite his anti-historical sense of time: "I relate things that happen to me and to others: those things hound me until they find me; they decide what form they like best" (Yúdice, "Graffiti on a Bloody Wall" 48). Authorship, from this perspective, is as participatory as readership: "Reality speaks a language of symbols. Each part is a metaphor of the whole," says Galeano, contemplating the photographs of Sebastião Salgado (We Say No 249). There is no pretense of the author as God, inventing a reality free of the constraints of collective perception and experience. Galeano envisions the fusion of all creation in a mythical language that informs his sense of purpose and destiny as a writer, never letting his passion for communication to be neutralized by the system that seeks to separate and alienate beings, to make them more compliant and resigned to their present fate as producers and products.

The Devourer Devoured

The squid has the eyes of the fisherman who hooks him. The man who will be swallowed by the earth that feeds him is himself made of earth. The child eats its mother and earth eats sky every time it sucks rain from its breasts. The gluttonous flower closes over the beak of the bird, hungry for its honey. The awaited is also awaiting and the lover is both mouth and mouthful, devourer and devoured: lovers eat each other whole, from head to toe, every last bit, all-powerful, all-possessed, without leaving even the tip of an ear or the smallest toe. (*The Book of Embraces* 99)

Clearly there is no one-way gaze for Galeano, no complete conquest of the other. All experience and communication are reciprocal. Followed through to all its social consequences, this vision of interdependence—not just as necessity but rather as the very essence of being—prophesies the end of exploitation, the necessary end of a global system in which "a few countries squander resources that belong to everyone," in which "the richest 6 percent of humanity devours a third of all the energy and a third of all the natural resources consumed in the world" (Bowden 121-22).

In *The Book of Embraces*, the visual representation of humans, animals, and inanimate objects displaced from their usual contexts and juxtaposed into new relationships serves to express both evil and the hope of overcoming its reign. A particularly evocative image depicts the gradual growth of a cornstalk from a few leaves to several leaves until, on the last page in the series, the tip of the plant flowers into a human eye. The story Galeano recuperates simultaneously evokes indigenous creation myths that tell how human beings were made of maize (223-29). Galeano also tries his hand at images that evoke Borges's woodcuts, juxtaposing in one densely intertextual instance three little demons holding sticks or knives on one page (127), with Superman on the opposite page (126). The (U.S.) Superman becomes a negative image in its juxtaposition with the popular Mexican hero, *Superbarrio*, highlighted in the text "Chronicle of the City of Mexico" to reveal the vacuous fantasy of power characteristic of mass media. *Superbarrio* is unknown to most North Americans since he battles crimes on the streets of Mexico and is such a clear parody of fantasies of empowerment represented by Superman:

Superbarrio has a pot belly and bow legs. He wears a red mask and a yellow cape. He does not do battle against mummies, ghosts or vampires. At one end of the city, he confronts the police and saves some starving people from eviction while at the other end, at the same time, he leads a demonstration for women's rights or against the poisoning of the air. (126)

The page, illustrated by the three woodcut demons and appropriately titled "The Clash of Symbols," refers specifically to the anecdote on that page: a pair of bronze shoes atop an enormous pedestal in Havana, a strange but expressive monument to the people who toppled the rest of the statue of Estrada Palma, president under the colonial occupation of the U.S. (127). But the title's significance extends to the two juxtaposed images as well: the American superhero, mass media image of power and escapist fantasy, and the three little demons wielding primitive weapons, evocative of Borges's artisanship.

Journalism again meets image in the work of the internationally known Brazilian photographer Sebastião Salgado, whose *An Uncertain Grace* includes a preface by Galeano. Salgado's photographs are overwhelming in their depiction of the extreme inhuman conditions that people (migrants, landless, homeless, dispossessed children, Third World workers) endure. They are also extraordinary in their haunting beauty. Galeano helps the viewer meet the powerful gaze of Salgado's subjects in a way that recalls one of his own vignettes. "The Function of Art" tells the story of a young boy whose father takes him to see the ocean for the first time: "When the child and his father finally reached the dunes after much walking, the ocean exploded before their eyes. And so immense was the sea and its sparkle that the child was struck dumb by the beauty of it. And when he finally managed to speak, trembling, stuttering, he asked his father: '*Help me to see!*' (*The Book of Embraces* 17). Something oddly similar happens in the way that Galeano helps us see Salgado's art. While many of the photographs depict people who are suffering extreme poverty, are dying or are already dead, the poetic power of Galeano's commentary speaks to both the horror and the beauty:

> Salgado's photographs, a multiple portrait of human pain, at the same time invite us to celebrate the dignity of humankind. Brutally frank, these images of hunger and suffering are yet respectful and seemly. Having no relation to the tourism of poverty, they do not violate but penetrate the human spirit in order to reveal it. Salgado sometimes shows skeletons, almost corpses, with dignity—all that is left to them. They have been stripped of everything but they have dignity. That is the source of their ineffable beauty. This is not a macabre, obscene exhibition of poverty. It is a poetry of horror because there is a sense of honor. ("Salgado, 17 Times" 8)

Galeano dedicates this preface to his partner Helena Villagra, "who saw with me" (15). Seeing is infused with shared meaning and contrasts sharply with the usual passivity that this verb implies in consumer culture, where sight is overwhelmed by advertising and the senseless, disconnected propaganda of alienation, "the great communications media that uncommunicate humanity" (14). Like Salgado, Galeano gives testimony so that his readers can also see with him all that is carefully omitted from the screens and billboards cluttering up the view. He collects and disseminates words that hardly ever reach us because they do not serve the interests of transnational media. For instance: "An African economist, Davison Budhoo, resigned from the International Monetary Fund. In his farewell letter he wrote: 'There has been too much blood, as you know. It runs in rivers. It has befouled me completely. I sometimes feel that there isn't soap enough in the world to wash away what I have done in your name'" (14).

Conscience speaks once eyes see beyond the lies. Many such eyes are being extinguished unnecessarily, unpardonably every minute. Salgado's empathic and reciprocal gaze, together with Galeano's words, implies that we must try to see through those dying eyes as well: "Eyes of a child looking on death, not wanting to see it, unable to look away. Eyes riveted on death, snared by death—death that has come to take those eyes and that child." Those eyes interpolate the other's gaze, giving testimony on behalf of a multitude whose global story is a "chronicle of a crime" (12). Galeano helps us to understand that those eyes are not begging for charity, for a drop of relief in a bottomless bucket of need. Like the African economist who suddenly sees that he has been working for the enemy, Salgado also moves from the willful blindness of the "expert," the economist who manufactures statistics to cover up how economic growth benefits a tiny minority while it spreads poverty, violence, and death throughout the globe:

Salgado was an economist before he found out he was a photographer. He first came to the Sahel [a region of North Africa] as an economist. There, for the first time, he tried to use the camera's eye to penetrate the skins reality uses to hide itself. The science of economics had already taught him a great deal about the subject of masks. In economics, what appears to be, never is. Good fortune through numbers has little or nothing to do with the greater good. Let us postulate a country with two inhabitants. That country's per capita income, let us suppose, is $4,000. At first glance, that country would seem to be doing not at all badly. Actually, however, it turns out that one of the inhabitants gets $8,000 and the other zero. Well might the other ask those adept in the occult science of economics: "Where do I collect my per capita income? At which window do they pay?" (15)

"Simplistic!" scream the experts, not just the economists (who probably don't read Galeano or contemplate Salgado's images) but also the historians, the literary critics, and all those whose sight is overwhelmed by the fragmented, disconnected reality transmitted by the media. The propaganda machine does not even have to conspire; there is no global conspiracy because that would require cooperation and coherence to produce a unified image. Disjunction can proliferate on its own, without direction, and as long as the media exclude those who perceive connections that experts cannot, the world order is almost effortlessly maintained. Unable to see any pattern, for instance the connection between military spending and children dying of hunger (isn't it due to drought?), the passive observer is convinced that reality is too complex to comprehend in socially ethical terms. The structure of the fragment also informs humanity, reduced to isolated individuals who cannot grasp each other's reality and are therefore limited to the abstract ethics of neoliberal individualism.

Galeano also contributes an afterword to a very different work of photojournalism, prophetically entitled *Juárez: The Laboratory of Our Future* by American writer and cultural critic Charles Bowden. The book documents the immediate effects of NAFTA on Juárez, twin city to El Paso and a major site of maquiladora production, in images and critical commentary that contradict all the good news promoted by politicians and mainstream media. The book, prefaced by Chomsky with commentary throughout from Mexican critics and writers like Carlos Monsiváis and Elena Poniatowska, is a collective project with numerous photographers, all of whom intervene to give "testament to the bleak underside of industrial development, where alleged progress seems to have gone cancerous" (back cover). These eyes and voices are not afraid to make connections and to identify the most powerful perpetrators of crimes against "all the children, teenagers, women, and men who have been victims of the violence and poverty in Ciudad Juárez" (n.pag.).

Detail from "The Little Revenge from the Periphery," by José Bedia; from Ivo Mesquita, *Cartographies* (1993): 88.

Ciudad Juárez is a huge industrial complex situated in a polluted wasteland where the workers from the maquiladoras and their families live in shacks constructed of cardboard and other materials salvaged from the garbage dump. The few schools are "housed" in similar makeshift constructions. The images portray a modern version of a mythic hell. Here, images do reveal decomposing corpses robbed of all dignity, photographers are photographed taking shots of recently slaughtered victims or bodies found bloated in the Río Grande, half mummified in desert graves or lying spread-eagled in the middle of a busy street. But the text ensures that the images cannot be exploited by the tourism of poverty. Horrifying as they are, they embody both resistance and the prophetic vision of what neoliberal capitalism will bring to the poor countries that it claims to develop. This Mexico is the very opposite of the *turista*'s Mexico, as Bowden observes: "We do not wish to look at Juárez, we do not vacation there, we do not speak of the place. When it briefly comes to our attention, we dismiss it as a grotesque exception to what matters, what is, and what will be. We believe or profess to believe that the present and the future are more palpable in cyberspace than on the ground by the river that divides the United States from México" (48).

But Bowden, like Galeano, begs to differ from this "we's" dismissal of Juárez and foresees the city's prophetic significance from the perspective of its victims and not those who profess that "free" trade frees workers and helps "developing" nations on the road to global prosperity. Bowden sees this borderland as "a huge ecotone [borderland between two biological zones] of flesh and capital and guns...rubbing up against itself as two cultures and two economies and two languages meet and mingle and erupt into something we cannot yet name" (48-49). While the place defies definition, Bowden is convinced of its global significance and its prophetic message: "I have a hunch about Juárez, and my hunch is that this ignored place offers the real 'Windows' on the coming times. *The future has a way of coming from the edges, of being created not in the central plaza but on the blurry fringes of our peripheral vision*" (49; our emphasis). The edges, the marginalized spaces, are barely perceived because the "small screen" of mass media shrinks our vision as it pretends to bring the world into our living rooms. Bowden suggests that Juárez, space of chaos, is created by the economic centres of world order, and that the order of the centre depends on the chaos of the periphery. This laboratory of *our* future is a monstrous experiment in high-tech slavery that the current economic system intends to impose throughout the world but always in remote places that to North American and European eyes are peripheral, barely there. Bowden's windows relate precisely to how Galeano uses that term to signify apertures, insights, brief but illuminating. Galeano's structural use of windows contrasts radically with the disconnected fragments, shards of debris scattered helter-skelter by mass media. Despite their fragmentary concision, windows are penetrating snapshots and sudden visions perceived in times of crisis, ones that Walter Benjamin refers to as "the genuine historical image as it flares up briefly" ("Theses" 256). We will return to Galeano's archival and testimonial chronicling in relation to this conception of prophetic and empathic historiography in the next chapter.

Galeano's vignettes, windows, snippets of conversations, and *testimonios* implicate readers in a participatory mode of reading that depends on making associations and engaging in a collective project to reassess the past and envision the future. It is not a matter of assembling the pieces of a puzzle into a single coherent image, because the many voices chronicled by Galeano intervene in what Yúdice calls a "polylogue," the very language of multiplicity, but a multiplicity in search of communication ("Graffiti on a Bloody Wall" 32). This structure is given organic, human form in the metaphor of the book as house, asylum, and sanctuary accessible through windows that look out over multiple realities, windows necessarily framed by perspective, context, the situatedness of the observer and the observed. Galeano's description of the structure of *Memory of Fire* applies to the chronicling method characteristic of all his work. He explains that the brief chapters "are the windows of a house; there are as many possible houses as there are readers ... 'The branch has its faithful birds,' wrote the poet Salinas, 'because it does not bind, it offers.' The reader comes and goes at will in this house of words" (*We Say No* 257). A historiography of windows, which open onto the past, partially and fleetingly glimpsed as memories, stories, *testimonios*, reveals the fissures in the walls built by hegemonic discourse, be it historical, commercial, political, or literary. Galeano's house of windows rejects the concept of hegemony altogether in favour of seeing together what the system tries to hide from sight, seeing through the looking glass of a distorted reality that diminishes our shared humanity. Before being shared, the past must be recuperated from the keepers of official histories, witnessed together through all the stories that circulate in fragments, half-forgotten, forbidden, but alive. Rooted in storytelling, Galeano's historiography gathers the many peripheral voices of the Americas that speak from the past to the future.

NOTES

1. Sherene Razack offers a useful reading of aspects of Trinh's work on storytelling that break down simplistic dichotomies between mind and body, reason and emotion. According to Razack, Trinh offers a "third category, 'instinctual immediacy' ... instinct does not stand opposed to reason; it requires us to relate to the world with immediacy, to allow 'each part of the body to become infused with consciousness.' Instinct requires us to reactivate the 'radical calling into question in every undertaking, of everything that one takes for granted'" (53). We would associate "instinctual immediacy" with the appeal made to *soñar despierto* (wakeful dreaming) in Galeano's work.

2. We would argue that *Memory of Fire* effects a more obvious discursive break with the historiographic approach of *Open Veins of Latin America*. While Palaversich's observation of a discursive change in Galeano's historiography is recognized by Galeano himself as a move away from focusing too exclusively on economic interpretations to a more comprehensive vision of social forces, her bracketing of the political as contrary to storytelling confuses these issues. In this instance, her critical methodology depoliticizes popular forms of narrative and relegates the political to the realm of empty rhetoric, instead of recognizing that all human expression necessarily includes political issues even when they are not explicitly identified as such. Third-person narrative issuing from a collectivized source is just as implicated in political relations as a first-person narrative; the difference is not limited to form, but manifests itself in the breadth of focus. We will examine Galeano's historiographic strategies in detail in the next chapter.

3. Within a Western context, fiction is usually trivialized and denied validity in relation to fact and history. Moreover, as Trinh argues, "Men appropriate women's power of 'making material' to themselves and, not infrequently, corrupt it out of ignorance. The story becomes *just* a story. It becomes a good or bad lie" (129). This bias is reflected in the *cordel* tradition as well, and the *folheteiro*, storyteller or seller of the little pamphlet stories called *folhetos,* is also referred to as "*contador de mentiras*" [teller of lies], as depicted in an eponymous woodcut print by Borges.

4. Rowe and Schelling attempt to problematize the concept of "popular" by rejecting what they refer to as "essentialist" in favour of positing it as "denoting the relations of cultural power between dominant and subordinate groups" (87). What is insufficiently examined in the discussion, however, is the question of foreign domination and systematic destruction of local tradition for economic gain. Their pragmatic interpretation of culture buys into the hierarchical grouping of dominant versus subordinate, begging the question of how the dominant is enforced by "universal culture" in order to create a subordinate group.

5. Slater states that *firmeza* "may be loosely translated as 'character.' *Falsidade*, its opposite, suggests hypocrisy, deceit, slander, and double-dealing. A person who embodies *firmeza* will be solid and centered; one characterized by *falsidade* will be hollow, light, unbalanced, and subject to change" (71).

6. The first edition of *The Book of Embraces* (1992) in English relates this vignette to the "Hopi," changed to "Pueblo Indians" in subsequent editions.

7. Doris Meyer's anthology *Lives on the Line: The Testimony of Contemporary Latin American Authors* is an excellent source for viewpoints on the significance of writing and the writer's relationship to community. We note that Vargas Llosa exploits Argueda's suicide to promote his own aversion to indigenous culture and the concept that literature is rooted in popular culture. See Vargas Llosa's essay "Social Commitment and the Latin American Writer" (128-36) in which he proposes that Arguedas was driven to suicide by the Latin American cultural imperative to write socially committed literature, and not by the clash of cultures that, according to Isaac Goldemberg and others, is felt in the heart of every Peruvian (Meyer 303).

8. "Timur and his Team" ("Comrades," "Gang," or "Squad," depending on the various translated editions in which the story appears) is one of Gaidar's best-known stories and may have been the primary influence on Galeano for this book. While there are no similarities at the anecdotal level, the spirit of Gaidar's work is solidary, exemplified in this story of a gang of do-gooders who perform radical and spontaneous acts of kindness under the cover of anonymity. The old man in Galeano's work shares in this communitarian ethos by supplying the neighbourhood with baskets and *alpargatas* [slippers].

9. The Sandinistas toppled the Somoza dynasty and took power in Nicaragua as a result of a popular insurrection in 1979. The revolutionary process they launched amidst constant U.S. intervention lasted ten years until the Sandinistas were defeated in 1990. They continue to be the most powerful political force in Nicaragua by working with the coalition headed by Violetta de Chamorro. Galeano openly expresses his support for the Sandinista revolution in "In Defense of Nicaragua" (*We Say No* 200-04) and has written several essays on witnessing the fruits and frustrations of the revolution, some of which are collected in *El descubrimiento de América que todavía no fue y nuevos ensayos* [The Discovery of America Yet to Come and New Essays; (1991)]. The Zapatista National Liberation Army (EZLN; Ejército Zapatista de Liberación Nacional) initiated a rebellion in the state of Chiapas, Mexico that began on 1 January 1994, the same day that the NAFTA went into effect, which outlaws indigenous systems of collective land ownership. The predominantly Mayan population rose up in arms against the white ranchers and displaced farmers streaming to this region from other areas of Mexico because of the government's inability to address issues of land reform. The EZLN's lack of interest to gain state power contrasts markedly with other insurrection movements. The Zapatistas are distinguished by how they reach out to sympathizers around the world calling for a global movement of "Humanity Against Neo-liberalism." Galeano (together with other well-known writers) was contacted by lead Zapatista spokesperson Subcomandante Insurgente Marcos and has been monitoring the progress of their cause and actively speaking out on their behalf. For Galeano, the Zapatista movement blends issues of social justice, indigenous rights, the unmasking of realities that have long oppressed indigenes, and broader questions of human transnational solidarity: "En la patria de la solidaridad, no hay extranjeros" (Galeano, "Una marcha universal" n.pag.) [In the homeland of solidarity there are no foreigners]. Galeano's analysis of the situation in Chiapas takes into account the literary abilities of Marcos in relation to the political and economic exploitation the Zapatistas seek to overturn:

> Mexico is not a democracy because the Mexican economy is not democratic; that is clear. But, politically, Mexico has made major advances in the direction of democracy. To a considerable extent, those advances are the result of pressure from the Zapatistas. They have harnessed and directed the energies of civil society. And they have had a tremendous impact internationally—thanks, in large part, to the *language* of Marcos. In my view, it's a splendid language, a language that contains indignation, poetry, and, above all, a sense of humor. We need humor as much as we need food or water. That's his greatest merit as a writer. (Sherman 7)

10. The definitive edition of the *Popol Vuh* in English is translated and commented on by Dennis Tedlock. The Glossary to this edition gives the following definitions for the two protagonists:

> HUNAHPU *Junajpu*, sometimes *xjunajpu* or "little Hunahpu," a hunter and ballplayer, the elder twin brother of Xbalanque. Their mother is Blood Moon and their fathers, who jointly conceived them, are One and Seven Hunahpu. The astronomical roles of Hunahpu include that of the planet Venus, which still bears his name when it appears as the morning star, and that of the sun that appeared on the first day of the present age...XBALANQUE *Xb'alanq'e*, a hunter and ballplayer, the younger twin brother of Hunahpu...The astronomical roles of Xbalanque include that of the night or underworld sun and that of the full moon that rose when the sun set on the first day of the present era. His name means "sun's hidden aspect" in Kekchí (a Quichean language). (344, 361)

Galeano simplifies this astronomy by ending the story with Hun Ahpú occupying the role of sun, and the feminized Ix Balanqué that of moon.

11. The balance between feminine and masculine elements is present in the *Popol Vuh* in the concept of "Masters of Ceremonies," one lord bearing this title in each of the three leading lineages who are referred to as "Mothers of the Word" and "Fathers of the Word." As Tedlock notes, "the combination of 'Mother' and 'Father' suggests the contemporary daykeepers called mother-fathers, who serve as the ritual heads of patrilineages" (57).

12. After the chairman of the National Endowment for the Arts canceled the grant to publish *The Story of Colors*, the Lannan Foundation stepped in to support the project. This is the same organization that awarded Galeano the first Lannan prize for Cultural Freedom in 1999.

13. In a more recent essay entitled "Unmasking Marcos," Stavans reiterates his views on the defeat of the Zapatistas in a triumphant tone (from the dominant point of view), despite his expressed admiration for Marcos. In contrast to Marcos's focus on the dignity of the Chiapanecans, Stavans dismisses both

Marcos and the Maya in one sweeping statement of impotence: "His [Marcos's] real task, the best he can do, is to call attention to the misery of miserable men and women" (*The Essential Ilan Stavans* 182). By the end of the essay, Stavans dismisses all political action for change, stating that Marcos would do best by becoming a novelist since "after all, Latin America is depressing in its politics, but vivid in its imaginings" (191). As in the Oxford collection, Stavans suggests that literature wins the day, and that the plight of starving and persecuted peasants should be relegated to the pages of an imaginative novel. Of equal concern is the extent to which Stavans so naïvely separates writing and imagining from political action.

14. We have not introduced this term before because its use is still very limited, but we use it now because it appears in *The Real Thing: Testimonial Discourse and Latin America,* to which we now turn. This new denomination for the citizens of the U.S. is an effort to relinquish the name that the U.S. appropriated from all the other inhabitants of the Americas. As Gugelberger points out, "it obviously is drawn from the Spanish *estadounidense"* and is developed by Michael Kearney in "Borders and Boundaries of State and Self at the End of Empire" (19).

15. As an extension of this democratization of the access to art, one of the innovative features of *Crisis* involved the inclusion of removable inserts of reproductions of art by well-known Latin American visual artists. *Crisis* also typically included historical documents that were not easily accessible, as did its related journal *Cuadernos de Crisis,* the latter usually devoted to single issue coverage of people, artistic genres, or historical and political analyses (*Cuadernos* included issues on Che, on the tango, and on the U.S. Marines, for example).

16. The sheer richness and diversity of materials in *Crisis* merits a full-length book treatment in relation to issues of freedom of the press both in democratic and non-democratic contexts, the nature of truly independent investigative reporting, and the practical methodologies of reportage that depends on heterogeneity rather than homogeneity.

17. The reference to Babar relates to another essay in *The Empire's Old Clothes* entitled "Of Elephants and Ducks," in which Dorfman argues that underdevelopment is treated like childhood from the European perspective of progress, and that the series of stories about Babar the Elephant by Belgian writer Laurent de Brunhoff endlessly reiterates the message that Babar (the African barbarian) must assimilate to European life.

18. Information on two Paraguayan groups, the Mbyá-guaraní and the Axé-guayaquí, is attributed to the ethnographer León Cadogan in the editorial note to *Crisis* 4 (1973) (Cadogan had died just before the publication of this issue of *Crisis*). Cadogan recuperated the stories, both mythical and historical, and revealed the extermination of these peoples after having spent 20 years learning from (not about) the Guaraní. The information on Cadogan's work in Paraguay, provided in an obituary alongside one of his writings, reveals that he had much in common with the protagonist of Jorge Luis Borges's short story "El etnógrafo" ["The Ethnographer"]. An expert by virtue of his academic training, Cadogan however preferred to be "el discípulo y oyente de quienes en el Paraguay tienen todavía una palabra original y creativa, repetidamente inspirada: los indios guaraníes" (*Crisis* 4 [1973]: 18) [a disciple and listener of those in Paraguay who still have an original and creative word, repeatedly inspired: the Guaraní Indians].

19. The Guaraní (ethnographically divided into three groups, Kaiová, Xiripá, and Mbyá) live in the eastern lowland area of South America (including Paraguay, Argentina, Brazil, and Bolivia); there are approximately four million people who speak the Guaraní language. Semi-nomadic, they are also communal farmers and people of the forest, their word for "paradise" being *yvága* ("place of abundant fruit trees"). Tupang, Tupâ, Tupavé, or Tenondete is their principal god, who is incapable of doing evil and who protects the natural world. Their belief system also suggests that life on earth is not final. Chiefs reside patrilocally but other men live in their wives' houses and perform bride-service. Their language is distinctive for its onomatopoetic reproduction of forest sounds and for its minimalism.

20. Spelling of indigenous names like Huillca/Huilke/Huilka varies considerably in Spanish given that they are phonetic approximations of words whose cultural transmission is not based on an alphabetic system.

Chapter 4

Dissonant Histories, Literature, and the Reinvention of the Americas

Neither criminality nor repression can hold back history. (Salvador Allende 240)

Inequality before the law lies at the root of real history, but official history is written by oblivion, not memory. We know all about this in Latin America, where exterminators of Indians and traffickers in slaves have their statues in city plazas, while streets and avenues tend to bear the names of those who stole the land and looted the public purse. (Galeano, *Upside Down* 201)

What do historians *fabricate* when they become writers? Their very discourse ought to betray what they are doing. (de Certeau 88)

History as Resistant Critique

 Imagine a history that elided or betrayed the infinite richness and detail of your life—of *any* life. Imagine almost any history that refuses to address this elision or betrayal. Obituary history: family and institutional genealogy, documented public accomplishment, cause of death. A generic snapshot trapped by the linear conventions of its own discourse. Now imagine a form of dissonance to this sort of history making. Another story: lost conversations, small acts of compassion and humanity, silences, dreams, forbidden thoughts, undocumented desires. An irretrievable jumble of synchrony and diachrony. An impossible taxonomy of sentiment, action, inaction, and an irreducible skein of shifting, contingent inter-relations. Now imagine those who have the wealth, power, and self-interest to leave the narrative trace of an obituary and those who do not—those without obituaries or tombstones, phantom presences haunting memory and story. Which history is truer to the form a life takes? Which history more in need of recuperation and writing? Which form more complacent regarding the story it tells? The assumptions about the forms of its telling? Which story more dangerous and potentially dissonant? Which story more suspicious of its narrative assumptions?

The tension between obituary, "official" history and all that lies beyond its particular event-horizon—the impossible, irreducible, polyphonic, and interrelated complexity of *all* forms of historical agency (recognized and unrecognized, fictive story and documentable memory)—distinguishes Galeano's dissonant alternatives to official, obituary history. Official history designates history from above, the kind of monolithic and widely disseminated history that refuses to examine the sources of its own judgements about naturalized power relations of advantage and disadvantage. Official history, in Galeano's terms, is coincident with the amnesia that forgets the conditions that produce inequality and injustice, as he argues in the second epigraph to this chapter. Elsewhere, Galeano describes official history as the "key link in the chain of dominant culture" and as an "instrument of separation. We are taught histories that are divorced from one another. The history of each part of Latin America has little or nothing to do with that of the other parts: these handfuls of the same earth only meet in battle" (*We Say No* 217). Galeano's interrogation of official history occurs through the use of non-linear synchronic (syncretic) narratives that exemplify unexpected

conjunctions, alternative archives, found materials, highly allegorized and condensed retellings of familiar events, indigenous myths, and a host of other strategies and techniques, many clearly a function of literary discourse. Moreover, his critique of official history advocates the ethical responsibility inherent in the historical present as a necessary predicate to the conditional, potentially transformable future that remains to be made.

South African writer Bloke Modisane tells the story of being taught as a young black student that his ancestral Zulu heroes were bloodthirsty, savage psychopaths:

> A group of us confronted our teacher.
> 'My lessons come from the history books,' he said. 'This is only a historical phase, the situation may be reversed tomorrow and the history may have to be rewritten.'

Official History. From *Crisis* 55 (1987): 13.

'How did it happen?' I said. 'Why?'

'Your history lessons may answer that.'

The question has not been fully answered, but the history revealed that truth may have a double morality standard; the white man petitioned history to argue his cause and state his case, to represent the truth as he saw it; he invoked the aid and the blessing of God in subjugating the black man and dispossessing him of the land. It was impossible to understand history, it showed a truth I could not accept, so I learned my history of South Africa like a parrot. (41)

Mimicry here is the expression of being masked, of involuntarily assuming the false identity of a stranger to whom one is forced to assimilate in order to avoid being slaughtered. The result? Not being able to say "I am." Modisane's parroting of an incomprehensible text is a recurrent metaphor throughout the colonized world. It recalls Münzel's observations, discussed in the previous chapter, about the grotesque mimicking of white people's gestures and speech by captured Axé, who on a mythic level believe that they are metamorphosed into their captors, condemned to repeat their crimes. But we have seen that the songs of the Axé are more complex than the single-mindedly coherent interpretations of even the most empathetic ethnographers. Parroting also functions as camouflage, as hidden resistance: it humours the oppressors' belief that the history lesson has been learned just as it was taught. And because the powerful take their power for granted, the resulting illusions of grandeur and superiority have a large component of naïveté. But while the subjugated are dutifully parroting the subjugator, their memories may be silently active. Parroting can also have a subversive function: when it is consciously intentional, it parodies its object without necessarily even modifying its discourse, which is unintentionally a self-parody generated by the illusion of power. The colonized all over the world frequently don masks and costumes to parody whites, whether as ethnographers or conquistadors, a carnivalesque gesture whose significance has nothing to do with imitation or assimilation. Often these events are "theatrical productions" associated more with shamanistic power than the Western concept of representation; they revise official history by telling the story as it was meant to be told by its participants.

Galeano's dissonance from official history begins with the assumption that in the case of the Americas, virtually all "official" history is in need of reinvention. The three epigraphs to this chapter signal issues we will address via Galeano's resistant writing practices in relation to official history. No matter what constraints are placed on history—in its actual making and in the act of narrating that making—dissonant history shows that "official history" is a dominant genre that has small concern for memory, rooted as it is in violent, apocalyptic modes that betray memory. Galeano's writing also affirms that the making of history—as a discourse that is also a fabrication—must reflect on the identity of the historian/writer. These ideas presume a fundamental shift away from what official history deems appropriate for study (grand narratives, important personages, highly canonical texts) to an expanded notion of history as a text that includes radically diverse signifying forms and expressive practices. Where Dominick LaCapra argues that "Rarely do historians see significant texts as important events in their own right that pose complex problems in interpretation and have intricate relations to other events" (38), we would add that even more rarely do historians understand so-called non-significant texts as worthy of the same scrutiny. The underlying value judgements that produce the categorical distinction between significant and non-significant are addressed by the dissonant historian: the basis of these distinctions itself forms a narrative (of history, of writing, of the writing of history) worthy of investigation.

Taken together, then, these ideas form the basis for a dissonant practice of the writing—and thus the (re)making—of history that is especially evident in Galeano's work. Galeano is distinctive insofar as he locates himself in a discourse of resistance produced out of the post-conquest Americas, a specific historical vision that is at once an astringent anti-narrative and an encompassing theoretical critique of the way in which history is (un)made and remembered. In this regard, Galeano's historical project takes its place in the creation of what Jacques Rancière calls heretical history and what we would call dissonant or dissident history. For Rancière, "There is history—an experience and matter of history—because there is speech in excess, words that cut into life, wars of writing. And there is a historical science because there is something written that quells these wars and scars these wounds by coming back onto the traces of what was already written. There is a history of mentalities because there is heresy and its sanction" (88). Galeano's historical writings conform to Rancière's association between excessive speech (the writing wars in which the shape of the narrative battleground is at stake) and the recursive return to the traces implicit in what has already been written. These latter spaces of heresy and resistance are opened by the dissident historian in the name of forgotten experiences, histories of mentalities and affect, and material histories of corporeal experience. In what follows, we examine Galeano's revisionary history of the Americas, *Memory of Fire*, by way of the much earlier work, *Open Veins of Latin America*, as well as the more recent *Upside Down*, all of which study the pervasive effects of colonization on the Americas.

Galeano's historical method is intimately aligned with two streams of thought: Benjaminian historiography and its offshoots and Dusselian historiography as influenced by liberation theology. Both Benjamin's and Dussel's historiographic methods are marked by two predominant motifs: the first is the recognition of the literariness of historical narrative, which throws into question its truth content. The second is the acknowledgement of the ethical imperatives governing the choices made in shaping historical narratives, especially as a function of the recognition of the relations of dominance (the covert ideologies that sanction) implicit in such narratives. Galeano's historiography presents an extraordinary synthesis of "words that cut into life" via a hybridized literary and historical discourse *and* an attack on sanctions governing traditional historiographic theory. In this light,

Galeano's historiography *is* a form of radical theory (a narrative in its own right) that commingles literary and historiographic dimensions. The overlap between the two constitutes a field in which the truth-value of fictional or historical narratives is radically interrogated. Before examining examples of how these motifs operate in Galeano's specific writing practices, a brief summary of some crucial theories relating to our reading of Galeano in historical terms is needed.

Theory, in its derivation from the Greek noun *theōria*, means a looking, a seeing, an observing or a contemplation, hence a speculation. There are histories to those specular acts that constitute theory, just as there are histories to the histories themselves, what may be called narratives about narratives (or metanarratives). If history (in its derivation from *historia*) is a "finding out" and historiography is a narrative of that "finding," then the intersection of theory as a speculative seeing and of history as a narrative of finding has a great deal to tell us about how we see what we see and how we find what we find. Whether narrative is a function of speculation, the constructedness of a seeing (that seeks to efface how it comes to that seeing), or a way of perpetuating various forms of cultural amnesia, or even a gesture toward the (im)possibility of a social practice that seeks to inscribe memory, theories of history and histories of theory posit a heterology. Rancière calls heterology "a logic of the other, a position between words and things" (98), which is to say an epistemology that destabilizes the certainty of narratives, whether historical or theoretical, and a poetics of knowledge that puts to the question representation itself. If history is, as Rancière claims, "an unmentionable *mimēsis*," a fraudulent representation of "what it is not admissible to represent" (54), then history marks the failure of representation. But is that failure always necessarily a *failure*?

Galeano's work posits a radical answer to this question. For Galeano, within the recognition of the limits of historical writing practices so theorized, the possibility of unmasking the fraud in the name of an ethical recuperation of what is unmentionable *is* possible. That possibility is always informed by ethical and narrative limits, which must be foregrounded by the dissonant historian as an example of an ethical writing practice that is adequately informed by its theoretical relation to material reality. Theory and history, then, are discourses whose primary narratives signal toward (even as they seek to occlude) the metanarratives that underlie their form and function. And the history of history-making is a narrative of a rhetorical paralepsis (that is, a disregard or omission), an unspeakable theoretical *mimēsis* that refuses representation even as it compulsively reiterates that refusal (whether as a foundation of a putative narrative meaning or as a symptom of the uncertainty produced by all meaning effects). History is always profoundly heterological, founded on the logic of an otherness that cannot be compelled into representation. Radical historians like Galeano seek to reinstate and restitute that otherness, all the while recognizing that the specificity of agency associated with that otherness can never fully be recuperated.

History in this radical sense, then, is deeply related to the material structures of story, the materiality of the storyteller as a presence, the materiality of the actions invoked by the storyteller. The radical historian allows materials to erupt in narrative without necessarily laying claim to them, thus using a methodology that is necessarily polyphonic. This methodology is not institutional so much as it is a way of life, a way of using "words that cut into life":

> If structure, as…[Roland Barthes] pertinently defines it, is 'the residual deposit of duration,' then again, rare are those who can handle it by letting it come, instead of hunting for it or hunting it down, filling it with their own marks and markings so as to consign it to the meaningful and lay claim to it. '*They see no life / When they look / they see only objects.*' The ready-made idea they have of reality prevents their perceiving the story as a living thing, an organic process, a way of life. (Trinh 143)

Seeing no life in the act of seeing (making theory), the historian destroys the very object of historical scrutiny. A radical historiography (writing on/study of the writing of history; meta-history, the history of history making) recognizes the life of the object as it is trapped in the prison house of language and seeks to liberate it through the eruptive story, the story that makes war on the sanctions governing the lifeless object of "official history." The residual deposit of duration—structure—which assumes a materiality (a "deposit") can either be seen as a speculation contingent upon the disappearance of the witness or as the evanescent, discluded material of historical life that the radical historian seeks to address and restore (within the limits of the possible).

We recognize that the use of history as a "master" signifier must address how such a trope evacuates the particularities of story, thus perpetuating an illusion of discursive mastery where no such mastery is possible. Galeano's resistance to any linkage of his work with any specific genre coincides with this recognition. Trinh argues that "Truth does not make sense; it exceeds meaning and exceeds measure. It exceeds all regimes of truth" (123), further noting that the "truthfulness of the story…does not limit itself to the realm of facts" (144). The truth, like history, is always within parentheses, always contingent on an unseen or unspoken supplement. Institutional seeing, the making of theories of seeing and knowing that is historiography, evacuates the parentheses, giving "truth" an illusory narrative stability that serves institutional epistemologies. Master signifiers presume a régime of truth, one in which no supplement is possible to the master discourse. This becomes one of the dangers in producing an institutional notion of historicization in which the supplement that lies beyond the institution is thought to have been "mastered." Trinh argues, heretically and in line with the kind of historical telling practiced by Galeano, that "Storytelling as literature (narrative poetry) must…be truer than history. If we rely on history to tell us what happened at a specific time and place, we can rely on the story to tell us not only what might have happened at a specific time and place, but also what is happening at an unspecified time and place" (120).

Galeano's work, then, generally operates in the interstices between the historical and the fictive storytelling practices we discussed in the preceding chapter. Galeano retropes writing as history and history as writing, recognizing all the while that such a revisionary act has historical, literary, and, ultimately, political and ethical consequences. Further, Galeano's work unsettles received ideas about what a historian is, who is authorized to write history, and what histories are important. This unsettling recognizes the lived context that the historical writer introjects into another time and disseminates to a readership with its own historical agendas, ennuis, and blindnesses. For Galeano, the possibility of making history, either in the proactive sense of historical action or in the sense of commenting on history through writing, is always present. The two notions of history are interdependent and co-productive, potent in the possibility of their effects. Eugene Rosenstock-Huessy's notion that "The historian certainly is not the onlooker of an event but the last man whom the event produces" (58) would impose for Galeano an unthinkable form of closure on the possibility of historical action. There is (currently) no "last man" or woman; to say so would be to reduce the historical to the realm of a literary mode, the apocalyptic, with its notion of linear progression to an (the) end. To propose a limit on what is historically imaginable is contrary to the arbitrariness of human freedoms and the intersection of those freedoms (restricted or not) with specific but not necessarily knowable historical contingencies. Though not necessarily knowable as fact (itself determined by subjectivities, biases, and contexts that need acknowledgement) historical contingencies are potentially knowable as fiction (story), or as a hybrid expression of fact that informs fiction. Galeano's historiographic method thinks beyond the reductive limits imposed by such terms as fact and fiction, all the while recognizing that powerful historical master narratives are at work to justify (however illusorily) human suffering even as they produce the delusion of diachronic linearity in the face of the multiply fragmented existences on which history is predicated. The historian can either be the passive onlooker or the active participant—in short, the person who acts in accord or disaccord with the recognition of the problem of narrating historical contingency.

In our chapter on the relations between literary and rights discourses, we noted in Galeano's work the remarkable absence of master tropes that have gained theoretical currency in the West, perhaps the most notable absence, given Galeano's own context, being that of the terms "postcolonial" and "postcolonialism." The rush to proliferate various critical "posts"—postmodernism, postcolonialism, posthumanism, postfeminism, post-theory, *posthistoire*—signals a theoretical panic that is perhaps a futile response to the overpowering sense of historical belatedness, or to the overpowering arrogance of modernity that sees a cynical novelty in commodifying nostalgia. Moreover, this form of historical belatedness revels in (depends on) the repeatability of its master narratives, suggesting therefore that real difference (or change) from these narratives is impossible. This denial of the possibility of change is evident in the unimaginative affirmation that there are only two options open to the writer: to fetishize the master narrative or to long nostalgically for ideologies that this type of reactionary criticism pronounces dead, apparent in Gladys Rivera-Ocasio's dismissal: "La 'armadura' del texto de Galeano responde al deseo de fetichizar, no ya las grandes ideas o relatos, sino las partículas, al imperativo ecológico de que todos los residuos deben ser reciclados: los mil sesenta y tres retazos, piezas, de *Memoria del fuego* surgen de los escombros de las ideologías y utopías difuntas, conceptos, ideas trasnochadas" (197) [The 'framework' of Galeano's text responds to the desire to fetishize not the grand ideas or stories but the particular ones in accordance with the ecological imperative that all garbage must be recycled: the one thousand sixty-three remnants, pieces, of *Memory of Fire* rise from the debris of dead ideologies and utopias, stale concepts and ideas]. Such a method, then, would reduce the potency of historical absences (forgettings, phantom memories, oral echoes of events, and so forth) to the shelf-life of a sound bite, or to a product whose obsolescence is its very attraction (because it is "garbage"). The more cleverly one engineers historical obsolescence, the more quickly one reduces memory to a by-product of a momentary recognition that is always commodifiable, a reliable resource always present, always being renewed. Galeano's counter-historiography is significant precisely for how it resists these sorts of pressures.

In the case of what has been called *posthistoire* (posthistory), Lutz Niethammer suggests that

> Two aspects distinguish the posthistorical cluster of arguments from writings which may, in some respects, be quite similar: first, their reference back to, and self-location within, a tradition of the production of meaning for which they no longer see any social future; and, second, their avoidance of thinking about death, especially about the danger that modern civilization will annihilate itself and the world, which is the central preoccupation of other writers. Instead, the picture that looms for theorists of posthistory is of a mortal life lived without any seriousness or struggle, in the regulated boredom of a perpetual reproduction of modernity on a world scale. The problematic of posthistory is not the end of the world but the end of meaning. (3)

Niethammer suggests that posthistory is concerned with "the negative utopia of a life continuing without meaning" (4). Moreover, he argues for the very literariness of the form, suggesting that "In the metaphors of the interpretative conjuncture...we must discover the content of that unutterable life-historical sensibility [the posthistorical] which, like a catalyser, takes otherwise disparate elements from the spiritual household of the age and combines them in a transcending global interpretation" (4). We would caution that this form of post-historiography is in line with Galeano's only insofar as both take into account the threat of historical master narratives as a form of "global interpretation" and the literariness associated with configuring such a threat. The threat lies precisely in how such master narratives are complicit with an analysis that vacates struggle and resistance in the name of an illusory global homogeneity, thus removing "meaning" from the actual process of event, reductively understood in relation to the world-scale dissemination of modernity. Galeano rhetorically recasts this form of abject, postmodern historiography in the name of resistance: he does so using multiple narratives and writing strategies that undermine any totalizing view of historical process complicit with modernity, which arises as a function of colonial relations of encounter.

Walter Mignolo's use of the term "colonial relations" is explained by Gustavo Verdesio as "the situation in which an ethnic minority, technologically advanced and practicing Christian religion, imposed itself on an ethnic majority, technologically less advanced and practicing non-Christian religions. Colonial situations are shaped by a process of transformation in which members of both the colonized and the colonizing cultures enter into a particular kind of human interaction, colonial semiosis, which, in turn, contributes to the conformation of the colonial situation" (108). We would argue with the value-laden notion of technological advancement, which almost always refers indirectly to military technologies or technologies that enable militarism, as opposed to other forms of *tekhnē* (the Greek root of technology, meaning an art or craft) in which colonized cultures may be seen as equally accomplished. The difference between pre-conquest Tenochtitlan and virtually any early modern city in Europe amply supports this point. The sense of amazement conveyed by Bernal Díaz's account of the Cortés expedition into Tenochtitlan underlines the *tekhnē* evident in what the conquistadors saw: "And when we saw all those cities and villages built in the water, and other great towns on dry land, and that straight and level causeway leading to Mexico, we were astounded...It was all so wonderful that I do not know how to describe this first glimpse of things never heard of, seen or dreamed of before" (214). The description that follows is distinguished by words like "splendour," "marvellous," "diversity," "remarkable," and so forth, followed by the perfunctory comment: "But today all that I then saw is overthrown and destroyed; nothing is left standing" (215).

A similar discourse of wonder at the Araucanians' military *tekhnē* occurs in Alonso de Ercilla's sixteenth-century epic poem *Araucana* (*The Historie of Aravcana*; 1569-1590), which tells the story of the Spanish conquest of the Araucanians, a resistant and highly organized indigenous group that dominated the Southern and central parts of what is now known as Chile:[1] warriors were "furnished ether wth Bowes and arrowes, Pikes and Halberds, clubs, Maces, barred wth Iron, Axes, swords, dartes, slings, and suche like: vppon there boddies for defence they Carrye Corseletts, Compleate made of Lether wth Cuysses [thigh pieces], Greves, poldrons [shoulder plates], vambraces [forearm armour], gantelets, gorgetts and Morions, so hardened by art, as they are sword and pike free" (2). Importantly, the recognition of military technology is one of the first detailed descriptions in the *Araucana* (Canto 1.2), suggesting an anxiety about the reality of Spanish military superiority.[2] Wonder at the urban marvels of Tenochtitlan and acknowledgment of anxiety-producing military technologies were not the only forms of recognition by the conquistadors that indigenous culture had the capacity to make. The discussion by Garcilaso de la Vega of the sophisticated record-keeping and accounting of the Inca known as *quipu*, based on knotted textiles, as well as the oral record-keeping done by *quipucamayus* (those "who had charge of the accounts" [331; see 329-33 for a more complete description]) suggests another form of accomplishment largely unrecognized by European culture, and still largely misunderstood and unacknowledged within that context.

A culture that uses textiles and formalized methods of allegorical, oral storytelling as a community-based form of record-keeping (that includes historical data) has a great deal to teach a culture that relies (almost) uniquely on numeric and alphabetic systems to track the records it deems important. Examples such as these are easily proliferated (Mayan astronomers' discovery of zero, for instance) in spite of the destruction wrought on indigenous archives by the conquistadors, let alone the ethnographic biases present in the transmission of indigenous cultural knowledge and achievement. As Mignolo points out in a chapter entitled "Record Keeping Without Letters," with few exceptions Castilian and European historians "[held] that there is a natural and substantial complicity between history and alphabetic writing, and that record keeping *without* letters does not have the same authority as record keeping *with* letters" (*The Darker Side* 162-63). Mignolo's discussion of Bernardo Boturini Benaducci, "an Italian knight…who arrived in Mexico during the first half of the eighteenth century and authored *Idea de una nueva historia general de la América Septentrional* (1746)" (*The Darker Side* 3), is particularly insightful. Boturini Benaducci produced the subversive insight that "every human community had its own manner of recording the past and that the connivance between alphabetic writing and history was a regional invention of the West" (*The Darker Side* 147).

Rather than reading their own ignorance when faced with alternative modes of memory, post-conquest European culture generally read ignorance into the other, a doubly false gesture that undermined the ethics of encounter. This interpretive gesture—in which knowledge of the other is produced as "your" own in distinction from "their" ignorance—cannot be underestimated as a deep colonial structure that has compromised thinking encounter in any other way but as imperial conquest. Las Casas is one of the few to escape this rhetoric, however incompletely and however problematically, in such observations as the following: "[Indians] are so skilled in every mechanical art that with every right they should be set ahead of all the nations of the known world on this score, so very beautiful in their skill and artistry are the things this people produces in the grace of its architecture, its painting, and its needlework" (*In Defense of the Indians* 44). The complicity of so-called sophisticated technologies with the colonial enterprise is not to be underestimated, whether in terms of military technologies, record keeping technologies, or "related forms of scientific and technological knowledge": "The modern techniques of land surveying were invented by the English in India in order to tax on the basis of land ownership...Similarly, the Portuguese created the mathematics and technology of high-seas navigation in order to reach the sources of trade goods" and "Spaniards created demographic lists of indigenous people in order to tax on an individual basis (tribute)" (Seed 188-89). In all these instances, the notion of technological advancement is highly compromised, usually understood in terms that privilege the dominant culture, however incorrect such an evaluation of dominant culture's superiority may be.

Mignolo argues for the use of colonial semiosis as opposed to colonial discourse to map the range of signifying practices deployed in a colonial situation. Verdesio defines colonial semiosis as the "totality of symbolic messages and exchanges in colonial situations" whereas colonial discourse resonates as "an expression that limits the corpus to verbal messages, whether oral or written" (85). Again, we would argue that, whatever the theoretical semantics, one should not exclude any form of signifying from such a study. Semiosis is equally reliant on textual signification as is discourse, with discourse also being used open-endedly to refer to a broad range of verbal and non-verbal significations (as in visual discourse, musical discourse, gestural discourse, and so forth). The bottom line is understanding the range of signifying practices (whether verbal or not) produced by a particular encounter situation. Galeano's historiographic project, with its reliance on fictive and imaginary recreations of events and their affect, constantly points to the limits of language and of all semiotic practices, while nonetheless enacting a form of discourse/semiosis. The point is that such limits must be referred to if one is to even approach being historically accurate, since it would be inaccurate to represent historical narratives as a linear totality without multiple non-diachronic supplements. At the same time, the imaginary that produces historical narratives within this frame must be open to the broad range of signifying practices that produce historical information. Galeano's historiographic method fulfills both terms of these formulations in relation to the "colonial situation."

The colonial situations governing the inception of modernity in the Americas enacted a staggering concentration of wealth that permitted what Dussel identifies as the "first stage of modernity: world mercantilism" ("Europe, Modernity, and Eurocentrism" 470) associated with a specific nation-state: as Dussel argues, "Spain, as the first 'modern' nation, had the following attributes: a state that unified the peninsula, a top-down national consensus created by the Inquisition, a national military power (since the conquest of Granada), one of the first grammars of a vernacular language (Antonio de Nebrija's Castilian *Gramática* in 1492),[3] and the subordination of the church to the state, thanks to Cardinal Francisco Jiménez de Cisneros" (470). As practiced by Spain, world mercantilism permitted the development of new technologies, new modes of production, and military consolidation of European power in which, for example, the "silver mines of Potosí and Zacatecas (discovered in 1545-46) allowed the Spaniards to accumulate sufficient monetary wealth to defeat the Turks at Lepanto in 1571" (470). Moreover, for Dussel, "Europe's superiority [is] the offspring of its accumulation of riches, experience, and knowledge derived from the conquest of the Latin American continent" (471). Though we would modify this position slightly to include all of the Americas as the source for modern Europe's move from the periphery to the centre of world-systems, the staging of this move clearly prepared the ground for "modern European ethnocentrism…pretend[ing] to claim universality for itself" (471).

Necessarily, such an ethnocentric pretense and claim require a historiographic model to support and enable them, one predicated on the forgetting, distortion, or absolution of the conquest and its effects, especially in relation to the concentration of capital that has permitted the current world-system to develop as it has.[4] Dussel notes that

> Five hundred years after the beginning of modern Europe, the *Human Development Report 1992*…issued by the United Nations reveals that the wealthiest 20 percent of humanity (principally Western Europe, the United States, and Japan) consume 82 percent of the world's resources. Meanwhile the poorest 60 percent (the historical periphery of the world-system) consume only 5.8 percent of these resources. This amounts to an accumulation never before seen in the history of humanity, a structural injustice never imagined on a world scale. Is this not the offspring of modernity, of the world-system started by Western Europe? ("Europe, Modernity, and Eurocentrism" 475)

To this bleak picture may be added the consequences of such devastating inequality, one such being that the "deaths of more than 30,000 children every day from mainly preventable causes goes unnoticed. Why? Because these children are invisible in poverty" (*Human Development Report 2000* 8). Behind such an assertion are specific faces and lived experiences: there *are* specific corporeal incarnations to this unimaginable suffering. Further, that suffering is located in particular groups: "Indigenous peoples are still the most deprived in economic, social and cultural rights—in both developing countries such as India and industrialized countries such as Australia, Canada, and the United States" (*Human Development Report 2000* 33).

Imagine the colonial no longer as a function of nation per se so much as a function of the concentration of capital no longer necessarily tied to specific national sites—transnational capital, as it were. In such a context, then, to speak of the "postcolonial" is a significant deformation of reality such as it is. Rather, we would suggest the transnational hypercolonial as a more appropriate term, one that might fit Galeano's historical understanding (in sync with Dussel's) of emergent and extremely concentrated forms of the colonial imperative articulated transnationally. Galeano, citing Ignacio Ramonet (editor of *Le monde diplomatique*), calls this "globalitarian power" in which the "logic of the market imposes totalitarian dogmas on a national scale" (*Upside Down* 153). Moreover, Galeano notes how this formation, born of the history of the conquest of the Americas, operates with impunity, despite unimaginable crimes: "No judge can send a global system to jail for killing by hunger, but a crime is a crime even when it's carried out as the most normal thing in the world" (*Upside Down* 154). Galeano establishes a clear historical analysis of this system of impunity as itself the key aspect of power. And he does so using the words of the system itself, thus making his analysis doubly forceful: "What is power? An Argentine business-man, Alfredo Yabrán, defined it unmistakably: 'Power is impunity'" (*Upside Down* 206). But in Galeano's historiography, impunity as a sign of power is also the "child of bad mem-ory" (*Upside Down* 211), that is, a function of the regulation of historical narratives that suit the powerful. Galeano enumerates how "bad memory" comes to be using the trope "history of burnings," which references how indigenous knowledges were systematically eradicated and how compromising information related to the historical (bad) conduct of nations has been suppressed:

> ...the history of burnings is a long one, dating from 1562 in Maní de Yucatán when Father Diego de Landa threw Mayan books into the flames, hoping to reduce indig-enous memory to ashes. To mention only a few bonfires: in 1870, when the armies of Argentina, Brazil, and Uruguay razed Paraguay, the historical archives of the van-quished were torched; twenty years later, the government of Brazil burned all the papers that testified to three and a half centuries of black slavery; in 1983, the Argen-tine brass set fire to all the records of their dirty war against their countrymen; and in 1995, the Guatemalan military did the same. (*Upside Down* 211)

The eradication of memory has from the start been a key feature of the colonial situation, one that is coincident with the cultural inferiority ascribed to indigenous cultures. Louis de Vorsey argues, for instance, that

> ...there were sophisticated methods of record keeping operating within most native societies. These oral systems (often incorporating such mnemonic devices as wam-pum belts, notched sticks, and scribed bark or shell) relied upon human memory to transfer knowledge from one generation to the next, with designated elders serving as the primary repositories of tribal lore. Unfortunately, when many of those elders died in the wave of epidemics that followed the arrival of the Europeans, the cultural loss suffered by the natives was tantamount to the wholesale burning of libraries. (709)

Further, the very structure that enacts power, defined as the capacity to restrict or efface his-tory with impunity, ensures its self-perpetuation through economic structures based on ex-ploitation and disadvantage:

> The globalitarian order steals with its trade hand what it lends with its finance hand. Tell me how much you sell and I'll tell you what you're worth. Latin America's ex-ports aren't even 5 percent of the world's total, and Africa's add up to 2 percent; what the South buys costs more and more, and what it sells is worth less and less. To buy, governments go further and further into debt, and to comply with the usury on the loans, they sell grandma's jewelry and then grandma herself. (*Upside Down* 154)

The rights dimensions of such a historical distortion are striking. The *Human Development Report 2000* states, for instance, that,

> …little in the current global order binds states and global actors to promote human rights globally. Many least developed countries are being marginalized from the expanding opportunities of globalization. As world exports more than doubled, the share of least developed countries declined from 0.6% in 1980 to 0.5% in 1990 to 0.4% in 1997. And these countries attracted less than $3 billion in foreign direct investments in 1998. The global online community is growing exponentially —reaching 26% of all people in the United States but fewer than 1% in all developing regions. (9)

The end of history in such an economic context is submission; no history is possible or relevant in the accumulative logic of transnational capital. Meanwhile, the end of the writing of traditional history has been to ignore (with few exceptions) and justify inequality and injustice on this massive scale. History in this mode reinforces the impunity of the system, an unjust structure that Galeano is at pains to attack for the way in which it perverts rights discourse. Further, the history of effective resistance to the impunity of the system is effaced from history told as the story of its own end.

The widely unreported water uprising in Cochabamba, Bolivia is a striking example of this resistance, which is important in relation to both how history is made and how the making of history has significant rights dimensions. "In 1998," as Maude Barlow tells it, "the World Bank refused to guarantee a $25 million loan to re-finance water services in Cochabamba unless the government sold the public water system to the private sector and passed the costs on to consumers. Only one bid was considered" (6). A company called Aguas del Tunari, a subsidiary of a Bechtel conglomerate (a major U.S. engineering firm) took over and in December 1999 doubled water prices. The privatization resulted in water costing more than food (in one of the poorest countries in Latin America) and the scandalous fact that "Peasants and small farmers even had to buy permits to gather rainwater on their property" (6). Even the gods, who thought they had seen everything, laughed. But the measures taken by Aguas del Tunari prompted such outrage that tens of thousands of Bolivians marched to Cochabamba in a showdown that culminated in the directors of Aguas del Tunari and Bechtel abandoning the country and company, after which Bechtel launched a $40 million suit against Bolivia at the World Bank's International Court for the Settlement of Investment Disputes (6-7).[5] In the meantime, the citizens' group that had opposed the privatization (*La coordinadora de defensa del agua y de la vida* [The Coordinating Committee for the Defense of Water and Life], led by Oscar Olivera) took over control of the local water service, its first act being to open a "huge water tank in the poorest southern neighborhoods" (6) of the city. The story was virtually ignored in the mainstream North American media, even though (or perhaps because) it represented a significant victory for communitarian principles based on basic human rights (the free access to potable water) over transnational corporate privateers' capacity to operate with impunity.[6] Cochabamba, if anything, showed that history had far from reached its end.

Meaningful rights instruments (and the implementation of those instruments) cannot exist without the coincident structures of historical analysis that articulate systemic hypocrisy and abuses, especially when the system that creates the legal contexts for implementing rights is also the system that abuses them:

> In Uruguay, the Statute of Limitations for Punitive Claims, enacted at the end of 1986, declares that the tortures, kidnappings, rapes, and murders committed by the recent military dictatorship are to be forgotten, *as if* these terrorist acts perpetrated by the state had never taken place. The people of Uruguay preferred to call it the Law of Impunity and intervened with a petition of protest containing more than 600,000 signatures. Shortly before this law absolving the torturers was passed, the government of Uruguay signed and ratified the International Convention Against Torture, which obliges it to punish them. This also happened in Argentina. The convention explicitly denies the right to claim to have been following orders. The Argentine government signed and ratified it and went right on to whitewash the tortures carried out at the direction of the high command. In our countries, international conventions carry the same legal weight as national laws. *But the fact is that some laws call for human rights to be respected while others authorize their violation: some pretend to exist, others exist in fact.* (*We Say No* 207)

Seeing through the looking glass of official history entails critical structures that recognize the disparity between respect and violation, pretense and fact. Without such a critical faculty rights discourse masks the way in which it protects those who abuse with impunity, while giving the illusion that some form of justice has been achieved. The end of revisionary history in the dissonant mode proposed by Galeano is to address and expose orthodoxies about "historical reality" as duplicitous and complicit with the power that is impunity.

Revisionary histories of the sort created by Galeano, then, have direct bearing on rights discourses generally, which, as we have shown earlier, have been reluctant to address and include history as a means of contextualizing rights. To be clear, though, Galeano's historical method is not the only one, as Galeano himself implicitly recognizes. For instance, the 1999 report of the Guatemalan Truth Commission (*Comisión para el esclarecemiento histórico* [CEH]) investigated thirty years of political repression and laid the blame for "more than two hundred thousand political murders" (Grandin 391) and for the genocide that had occurred squarely on the Guatemalan state. The Commission thus established an important precedent for the use of "dissonant" history in a rights context:

> The report's use of history is a breakthrough in human rights documentation. The delight with which it was received by human rights groups in Guatemala, despite

their previous fears, calls to mind one of Walter Benjamin's historical theses: "To articulate the past historically…means to seize hold of a memory as it flashes up at a moment of danger"…If any country lives in a perpetual moment of danger, it is Guatemala, as demonstrated by the killing of Bishop Juan Gerardi in April of 1998. Gerardi was the head of the Catholic Church's historical memory project, a three-year investigation of human rights violations committed during the war. Two days after the project released its report, *Guatemala: Nunca más*, Gerardi was bludgeoned to death. (Grandin 400)

Gerardi's history does not end with his death. Bishop Mario Rios Montt—brother of General Efrain Rios Montt who presided over the very genocide documented in the report of the *Comisión para el esclarecemiento histórico* and whose so-called democratic régime was supported by the U.S. under President Reagant—ook over the same office once held by Gerardi as head of the Catholic Church's human rights office in Guatemala (May 1998), whose task it is to investigate the genocide. Alternative histories with powerful rights motivations are dangerous because they threaten impunity with disclosure and unsettle official memory with counter-narratives based on documentary evidence and other forms of narrative.[7] They convert the indifference of the executioner and the facelessness of the victim into the recognition of a historical moment in which human agency is enacted in grievous and heinous ways.[8]

Alternative histories, then, are not easily dismissed. Official history with its easy assumption of the comprehensive linearity of narrative (as in, for example, "it is legal therefore it is just"), not to mention its facile confidence in the veracity of the narrator (and the deep reluctance to question the contexts that produce that veracity as a discursive effect rather than a "truth"), is more often than not dissimulative. Any rights discourse predicated on historical discourse that is so deformed would itself be highly compromised—hence, the importance of the historical revisionism practiced by Galeano as a form of solidarity with other alternative writing practices necessary to create the deep context for meaningful, truly democratic and enabling rights discourse.

"History Is an Incessant Metaphor": The End of the End of History

Francis Fukuyama's 1992 *New York Times* bestseller proclaimed *The End of History and the Last Man* as its title, with history understood as "a single, coherent, evolutionary process" (xii). Moreover, Fukuyama argued "that a remarkable consensus concerning the legitimacy of liberal democracy as a system of government had emerged throughout the world over the past few years, as it conquered rival ideologies like hereditary monarchy, fascism, and most recently communism" (xi). The extension of this argument is that "liberal democracy may constitute the 'end point of mankind's ideological evolution' and the 'final form of human government,' and as such constituted the 'end of history'" (xi). But who gave that story its beginning and what propels it to its end, its naïve reliance on the universality of a structure oscillating between beginning and end? Whose voices form the consensus to which Fukuyama refers? And if the rival ideologies had in effect been conquered (a signifier we read as especially imperial given Fukuyama's U.S.-centric views), why was the world less than a better place?

Galeano's response to Fukuyama's ideas, contained in a short piece published in *New Internationalist,* is worth examining in some detail. Its polemical tone (itself a form of historical intervention) combines with a methodic exposition of the master narratives that "lie" behind the notion of the end of history using concise historico-literary tours de force to deflate Fukuyama's triumphalist rhetoric.[9] In this sense, Galeano clearly understands the "critical moment" in Benjaminian terms as one in which the "status quo threatens to be preserved" (Benjamin, *The Arcades Project* 474), a moment that therefore calls for the disruption of the fantasy of historical stasis proposed by Fukuyama's thesis:

The End of History. José Guadalupe Posada, from *Upside Down* 161.

The end of history. Time has been pensioned off, the world has stopped turning. Tomorrow is another name for today. The places at the table are set, and Western civilization denies no-one the right to beg for crumbs.

Ronald Reagan wakes up one day and says: "The Cold War is over. We've won." Francis Fukuyama, a functionary in the US State Department, achieves sudden fame and success by discovering that the end of the Cold War is also the end of history. In the name of liberal democracy, capitalism becomes the last port of call for all journeys, "the final form of human government."

Hours of glory. The class struggle no longer exists, and to the East there are no longer enemies but allies. The free market and the consumer society have won universal consensus, no more than delayed by the historical diversion of the communist mirage. Just as the French Revolution wanted it we are now free, equal and fraternal. And property owners too. Kingdom of greed, paradise on Earth.

Like God, capitalism has the highest opinion of itself and has no doubts about its own immortality. ("The Other Wall" 7)

To this scenario, motivated by the triumphalism evinced in the West after the fall of the Berlin Wall in 1989, Galeano responds with the image of the "other wall." History on this resistant plane is made with inverted tropes that transform one form of narrative into another. The other wall "separates the poor world from the opulent world" and is "higher than ever":

The Berlin Wall has died a timely death. But it lived no more than 30 years. The other wall will soon be celebrating its fifth centenary. Unequal exchange, financial extortion, capital bleeding away, monopoly over technology and information, cultural alienation—these are the bricks that build up day by day, as wealth and sovereignty drain ever faster from the South to the North of the world...

Economic neo-liberalism, imposed by the North on the South as "the end of history," as the only and ultimate system, consecrates oppression under the banner of freedom. In the free market the victory of the strong is natural and the annihilation of the weak is legitimate. Racism rises to the status of economic doctrine. The North confirms divine justice: God rewards the chosen people and castigates the inferior races, condemned by their biological make-up to violence and inefficiency. In a single day a worker from the North earns more than a worker from the South can in half a month. ("The Other Wall" 8)

The linkages between implicit racism and economic doctrines that favour the dominant North are but one form of hypocrisy needing exposure, if only because the condition of being disadvantaged economically is not a biological given so much as a historical condition produced out of a specific sequence of events.

As we have seen, narratives of indolence and weakness are expedient in covering over the historical contexts that continue to produce disadvantage. Similarly, the staggering resources devoted to military expenditure are produced out of an equally perverse structural deformation of narrative history:

> If the Iron Curtain has melted away and the bad guys of yesterday are the good guys of today, why do the powerful continue to manufacture and sell weapons and fear?
>
> The budget of the US Air Force exceeds the total of the budgets for the education of all children in the so called Third World. A waste of resources? Or resources to defend waste? Could the unequal organization of the world, which pretends to be eternal, be sustained a single day longer if the countries and the social classes that have bought up the world disarmed?
>
> This system, sick with consumerism and arrogance, which launched so voraciously into the destruction of land, sea, air and sky, now mounts guard at the foot of the high wall of power. It sleeps with one eye open and with good reason.
>
> The end of history is its message of death. The system that sanctifies a cannibalistic international order tells us: "I am everything. After me, nothingness." ("The Other Wall" 8-9)

The hypocrisy evident in so-called epochal historical moments (like the fall of the Berlin Wall) that do *not* produce change in the deep structures associated with militarism, the shocking disproportion between military expenditure and education, the attack on nihilist consumerism, and the self-absorbed production of an apocalyptic master narrative ("the end of history") that disallows alternatives—all suggest to Galeano that the trope of the "wall" is very much *in* place, more than ever a narrative mask that distorts the lived relations of people in terms of advantage and disadvantage. The sequence of ideas Galeano maps out in his short essay is fully in line with the historiographic method we have linked with him. There, the space of the inverted trope, the alternative narrative, the polemical intervention become the means by which dissonance and revision take root in the name of resistance to historical lies told as truths.

The exile of the lie from the truth and of the truth from the lie produces a mode of forgetting that empties the infinitely complex energies of interaction and reaction that make giving voice to human activity such a troubled project. This is not to suggest that forms of historical truth do not exist, but rather that transcendentalized notions of essentialist, timeless historical truths are spurious or in desperate need of critical interrogation. As Benjamin puts it:

> Resolute refusal of the concept of "timeless truth" is in order: Nevertheless, truth is not…a merely contingent function of knowing, but is bound to a nucleus of time lying hidden within the knower and the known alike. This is so true that the eternal, in any case, is more the ruffle on a dress than some idea. (*The Arcades Project* 463)

Galeano has been critiqued for producing "a more allusive, fragmented, Benjaminesque—or should we call it postmodern?—mosaic...[that] may be less a philosophical-aesthetic adjustment than a more old-fashioned inability to call things by their name" (Martin, "Hope Springs Eternal" 157). Martin here refers to Galeano's apparent lack of acknowledgement of the "massive, historic defeat for the Latin American Left," which, according to Martin, Galeano registers but does not analyze, producing instead an "elegiac incantation in unison. But Latin America is not and never has been united, at least not in any simple way. Unity is a desirable objective, and long-awaited; but there is little virtue in pretending that in some ghostly way it already exists" (156-57). We disagree with this understanding of Galeano's historical method. It assumes a unitary response where there is none (we have cited ample evidence throughout this book of Galeano's contradictory practices, including his own recognition of these practices), and it attaches virtually empty political signifiers (like the Left) to a wide array of ideological practices in which no essentialist core exists. Moreover, we would posit that it is not so much unity in some "alternative nostalgic-utopian world" that Galeano seeks to achieve so much as the recognition of historical difference as the fundamental precondition for a solidarity that allows dissensus, dissonance, and discrepant but reciprocal engagement.

Thus, to produce the reductive master narrative of a coherent defeat of the "Latin American Left," as Martin wishes Galeano to do, is to foreclose on emergent processes (the Cochabamba resistance, the Zapatistas, the ongoing survival of Cuba in spite of heightened political and economic pressures, the making of alternative histories based on *testimonio*, and so forth) that make such a singular vision premature. Martin further accuses Galeano of "giving us a montage of brief historical snippets because he cannot for the moment bring himself to give us the whole picture" ("Hope Springs Eternal" 157). As we have seen, though, Martin has missed the point in his reductive conclusion: the precise point of Galeano's historical method is to alert the readers to the fact that the "whole picture" is a deceptive trope used by powerful master narratives that need undoing. Thus, one of the functions of the multiple perspectives, voices, and narratives is to suggest a fragmented whole, an archive of disarray out of which contradictory topoi can be discerned. The key point to be made here, which Martin misses, is that Galeano's historical method is intensely literary, thus open to ambiguity, allusion, indirection, affect, narrative fact *and/as* fiction, narrative fiction *and/as* fact.

Galeano argues that the "brief moments of history" articulate myriad experiences in which "each situation symbolizes many others, grand events are revealed through small ones, and the universe is viewed through a keyhole. Reality the unsurpassable poet, speaks in a language of symbols...*history is an incessant metaphor*" (*We Say No* 258; our emphasis). In such a scheme, style and substance align to resist any single narrative, any reductive collocation of historical fact. In his suspicion of "fact" Galeano displays the kind of historical virtue described by Friedrich Nietzsche in "On the Utility and Liability of History for Life."

There, the human being (described in androcentric terms) "rebels against that blind power of facts, against the tyranny of the real, and he subjects himself to laws that are not the laws of those historical fluctuations. He always swims against the historical tide, either because he struggles against his passions as those stupid facts closest to his existence, or because he commits himself to honesty while the glittering nets of lies are being spun all around him" (145). For Nietzsche, "true historical natures" are "those who were little troubled by the 'That's how it is,' but instead pridefully followed a 'This is how it should be'" (146). We reiterate our argument that Galeano's historiography represents an extraordinary confluence of ideas in which no one idea predominates, especially as a function of the historical and geographical space in which he writes in the Americas.

When reality speaks in the language of metaphor and symbol, though, is the historian ready to listen? From Galeano's perspective, it is not enough to see non-symbolic event as the stuff of history. Rather, history must be read (and produced) symbolically, which necessarily entails literary structures of meaning and interpretation. Galeano's historical method thus responds to E. P. Thompson's affirmation, in his essay "Agenda for Radical History," that historians have "had an insufficient vocabulary for examining the structure of power relations through symbolism, from the awe of empire or monarchy to the awe today of nuclear weapons" (362). No surprise then that the key trope through which Galeano articulates his historical method is that of "incessant metaphor," the relentless referentiality of one thing to another—and another and another: "Reality speaks a language of symbols. Each part is a metaphor of the whole" (*We Say No* 249). Seeing through the keyhole (an image like that of the perforated mirror that we have associated with the wisdom of the *tlamatinime*) allows the symbolic spectacle of an inverted world. In the upside-down world, the dominant narratives are supplanted by so-called "small" events as part of a historical understanding that is neither static nor reductive, the very master narrative that Martin wants Galeano to produce in the mode of a defeatist rhetoric.

Martin argues that Galeano "simultaneously asserts that there can be no objective knowledge while also implying that he knows the truth" and that he is after a "coherent utopian narrative" ("Hope Springs Eternal" 153). Again, we would disagree. Galeano recognizes "knowledge" but always mediated by context, that is, by the "incessant metaphors" that transform one thing into another. The only truth in such a context is unstable, highly contingent, and reflective of the fragmentary, contradictory reality Galeano brings to life. Coherence in such a context reduces historical narrative to a dead, duplicitous letter. Conversely, in her reading of *Memory of Fire*, Tomassini observes that Galeano's "making present" of historical moments privileges space over time. The resulting impression of synchronicity sidesteps the historian's claim to an omniscient gaze that sweeps through time, taking account of events chronologically and comprehensively while implicitly imposing cause and effect links motivated by unacknowledged ideological readings. The aim of Galeano's synchronic and spatial representation is to capture (as in a snapshot, an image that tells a thousand words) the living, breathing presence of historical vision:

> *Memoria*...no manifiesta ni implica propósito explicativo, sino la modesta intención autorial de "hacer que la historia viva y respire"...En general, la obra convierte temporalidad (condición de la historicidad) en espacialidad, limitando la narración a los microcontextos...pero estos microcontextos no están conectados a la manera de la novela histórica, o de la épica; en cambio, guardan entre sí relaciones paradigmáticas de homología o de heterología, a manera de los contrarios o los repertorios. (Tomassini 114)

> [*Memory*...does not reveal or imply any objective to explain, but rather the modest authorial intention of "making history live and breathe"...In general, the work converts temporality (the condition of historicity) into space, limiting the narration to micro-contexts...but these are not connected as they are in the historical novel or the epic; on the contrary, they are linked by paradigmatic relationships of homology or heterology, as in the case of opposites or repertoires.]

Though there is a recognition of the passing of diachronic time (as in, for example, the rough chronological ordering evident in *Memory of Fire*), Galeano consistently resists the coherence implicit in diachronic accounts of historical sequence. This stance is perfectly consistent with Galeano's critique of the illusion of historical "progress" as a sort of post-Darwinian tale of evolutionary betterment in which the survival of the fittest justifies present cruelties and injustices. Martin's vision of Galeano spinning a "coherent utopian narrative" is particularly misguided. If anything, Galeano resists utopianism (in the sense of describing the "no place" or the "good place") in the name of the here and now, which is a complicated synthesis of different constituencies struggling for different visions of the world, some admittedly utopian, some radically dystopian.

Though we return to this idea at some length in our last chapter, we would situate Galeano's historico-literary method in relation to Carlos Fuentes's comments on García Márquez's *One Hundred Years of Solitude*. Fuentes resists facile generalizations about value-laden and over-determined concepts like utopia in favour of a specific relationship to history put in simple and direct terms—"this *is* happening, this *could* happen":

> The true re-vision of epic and utopia is the literature and art of our time: the demonized power of the dead time of historiography to enter, without undesirable burdens, into the total time of the present. Borges and Paz, Carpentier and Cortázar, Cuevas and Botero, Lam and Gironella, Matta and Rojo confront the positivist time of the epic past...and the nostalgic times of utopia...with the absolute present time of myth: this is happening, this could happen. (qtd. by Kirkpatrick 167)

In this perspective, both epic and utopia stand in need of revision via artistic means. Historiographic time, the mortuary time of master narratives bound to epic and utopian genres (both severely compromised by their relations to European conquest and imperial culture) must be refashioned in the "total time of the present." Positivism and nostalgia must be displaced by myth in the name of the "absolute present time." Michel de Certeau, the French cultural theorist and historian, argues that "Historians metamorphose the environment through a series of transformations which change the boundaries and internal topography of culture...[and that] an increasing mass of historical books are becoming novelistic or mythic. Such books no longer produce these transformations in the fields of culture, while in contrast 'literature' intends to work upon language and make a 'text' stage what Raymond Roussel describes as a '*movement of reorganization,* a mortuary circulation which engenders as it destroys'" (72). The internal topography of a culture is chronicled, in part, by the production of those mythic texts and textualities, which form a metanarrative that counterpoints the multiple ideological positions possible in any given culture. Literature figures significantly in such chronicling because it registers the imaginary in a manner with which no form of traditional historiography can compete. The freedom of this imaginary is at stake in Galeano's historical writings, which reproduce de Certeau's notion of how literary language works upon the historical to "stage" a transformative reorganization that "engenders as it destroys."

Where Martin argues that "memory must be complete, and accurate, not mythological" ("Hope Springs Eternal" 156), Fuentes leans more toward the necessity of being-in-the-present that myth necessitates if only because it requires an active relationship between story and participant in the moment. Complete and accurate memory is an impossibility, a construction governed by overdetermined master narratives, whereas the pejorative sense of the "mythological" deployed by Martin misunderstands how the very literariness of myth presumes an interpretive politics *in* the historical moment. Again, "this *is* happening, this *could* happen." Myth understood in this way locates the "nowness" of the present, the historical possibility inherent in that present, as a conditional "could." Martin observes elsewhere that Galeano's vision "is much closer to literature than to history, and closer to myth than to either" ("Preaching to the Converted" 183), with no sense of how one of the main goals of Galeano's historiographic method is to disrupt the imagined disciplinary boundaries supposedly separating history from literature from myth, shattering the specific master narratives that deform or obliterate deep cultural memory in their own amnesia. Amnesia, for Galeano, "is not the sad privilege of poor nations alone. Wealthy nations also teach oblivion. Official history does not mention—among many other things—the source of their wealth. No wealth is innocent of another's poverty" (*We Say No* 262). In the same light, Dussel argues that "Marx's stock is particularly low since he explains how the misery of the people (indigenous peoples, Africans, mestizos, peasants, laborers) of peripheral nations is proportional to the wealth of the rich within both peripheral and central capital. The myth of modernity ignores all this" (*The Invention of the Americas* 130). Here, the overlap between Galeano's historical analysis and Dussel's is explicit. Understood in this light, then, Galeano operates somewhere between the two extremes presented by Martin and Fuentes, recognizing that the multiple-voiced present is imbricated in the past, but at the same time mindful that the present conditions the potential future: "*Memory of Fire* would like to multiply the voices that fly at us from the past but sound like the present, and speak to the future" (*We Say No* 263).

History's "Refuse": Benjamin, Galeano, and the "Power to Create"

Alvaro Barros-Lémez reads the concept of the historical narrator in Galeano's work from an indigenous point of view that escapes Western historiography. The speaker is a collective entity akin to the Guaraní notion/word "multitude-person," and the authority of that person lies only in the communitarian realm.[10] While Barros-Lémez refers specifically to *Days and Nights of Love and War*, his opposition to such misreadings as Martin's is equally pertinent, in our opinion, in reference to *Memory of Fire*:

> Una visión superficial podría señalar lo obvio: la argamasa que une esta diversidad de temas, personajes, lugares, situaciones y sensaciones, es el propio Galeano-narrador, como testigo privilegiado, testimoniador a través de sí mismo de una historia que es social. No compartimos esa visión. A nuestro entender, lo que busca Galeano es validar, darle certificación a hechos ocurridos en la vida del personaje central de esta historia: los pueblos de la América Latina. El eje en la búsqueda de la forma en que se manifiesta lo protagónico en este texto, debe trasladarse del Galeano-narrador a "lo que es narrado." Eso que se narra crea un protagonista que es social, que es múltiple tanto en fisonomía como en nacionalidad, sexo y edad, que—además—percibe la realidad circundante de diferentes formas. Será esa calidad "social," esa fisonomía múltiple y esa percepción diversa, la que contribuirá a crear un texto que, más allá de tener un aparente narrador individual, en verdad tendrá un narrador plural que se manifestará—como en las antiguas culturas indígenas de nuestro continente—a través de un "shamán," de un "amauta", que hará las veces de bocina resonadora de esas voces múltiples, que será su vocero y a la vez su memoria. (45)

[A superficial vision might indicate the obvious: the mortar holding together all these diverse subjects, characters, places, situations, and sensations is the Galeano-narrator himself, as privileged witness, dispenser of testimony through himself of a history/story that is social. We do not share that vision. To our understanding, what Galeano seeks to validate, to attest to, are the events that occurred in the life of the main character of this history/story: the peoples of Latin America. The axis of the search for the form in which the protagonist reveals itself must shift from the Galeano-narrator to "that which is narrated." This is what creates a protagonist that is social, multiple in terms of features, nationality, gender, and age, that—in addition to these distinctions—perceives the reality around it in different ways. This "social" quality, multiple physiognomy, and diverse perception contribute to creating a text that despite having an apparently individual narrator, has plural narrators who manifest themselves—as in the ancient indigenous cultures of our continent—through a "shaman," an Inca elder, who is at times a resounding mouthpiece of those multiple voices, at other times their spokesperson and their memory.]

We would insist, though, that the imprecision and non-reductiveness of this polyvocal historical method is precisely its virtue since it destabilizes traditional, "official" narratives of the past. Moreover, this method posits a historical narrator that refuses any reductive subject-position, either as someone who speaks only for him- or herself or as someone who always speaks for everyone. The tense relation between these two extremes is played out in Galeano's writings, which posit the problem of how to speak for oneself, how to speak for another in ways that do justice to the interlocutory relations that exist between the individual and the community of which he or she is a part. Galeano's vision of the writer's ethical responsibility to history may be apposed to comments made by Julio Cortázar in a letter to Roberto Fernández Retamar, the editor of the Cuban literary journal *Casa de las Américas*:

> If once upon a time, a man could be a great writer without feeling like a participant in the immediate history of mankind, this is no longer true. No one can write today without this participation: it is a responsibility and an obligation. Works that assume this obligation, even though they are imaginative works displaying the entire gamut of games writers can invent, are the only ones that can approach greatness. Even though they never allude directly to that participation, in some ineffable way they will contain that tremor, that presence, that atmosphere that makes them recognizable and awakens in the reader a sense of contact and closeness. ("Letter to Roberto Fernández Retamar" 81)

As we have already seen, participatory history from Galeano's perspective avoids the trap of any single master narrative, whether defeatist (all is lost) or triumphalist (history has ended). Instead, he multiplies the possibility of story and interpretation as a form of action that makes history an active, material process, resistant to reductive historiographic methods that foreclose on anything but spectatorship and distance from the making of history. As in Cortázar's evocation of that which produces in the "reader a sense of contact and closeness," Galeano insists upon the reader's responsibility as historical actant: history is not to be passively received as coherent "truth" but to be made by the interpreter in material relation to the alternative historical method exemplified by Galeano's approach.

In this last regard, then, Galeano's method is closely aligned with Benjamin's notion of historical materialism. Benjamin himself claims, in his great unfinished work of historiography *The Arcades Project*, that he "aspires to neither a homogeneous nor a continuous exposition of history…since the different epochs of the past are not all touched in the same degree by the present day of the historian (and often the recent past is not touched at all; the present fails to 'do it justice'), continuity in the presentation of history is unattainable" (470). Further, "Historical materialism must renounce the epic element in history. It blasts the epoch out of the reified 'continuity of history.' But it also explodes the homogeneity of epoch, interspersing it with ruins—that is, with the present" (474). In such an understanding, then, "Progress has its seat not in the continuity of elapsing time but in its interferences—where the truly new makes itself felt for the first time, with the sobriety of dawn" (474). These ideas, framed in the fragmentary form that characterizes *The Arcades Project*, anticipate the shape Galeano gives to his own historical method.

Benjamin clearly understood the historical force of literary texts, describing his own historiographic method as "literary montage" (460) in which "I needn't *say* anything. Merely show. I shall purloin no valuables, appropriate no ingenious formulations. But the rags, the refuse—these I will not inventory but allow, in the only way possible, to come into their own: by making use of them" (460). Further evidence of the literary dimensions of his historiography occurs in Benjamin's citation of a passage from André Monglond's *Le préromantisme français* (1930): "The past has left images of itself in literary texts, images comparable to those which are imprinted by light on a photosensitive plate. The future alone possesses developers active enough to scan such surfaces perfectly" (482). Galeano, knowingly or not, has clearly taken on Benjaminian literary montage as a form, a way of "making use" of the materials history presents to him. But he does not privilege literary textuality over other forms of textuality, his approach being attuned to a wide range of texts and documentation, much in the same way that Benjamin's trope of "the rags, the refuse" signals an alternative form of historical archive in need of actualization, a crucial Benjaminian term. Historical creation makes use of refuse, the literal and figural "stuff" official history disallows. That said, Galeano deploys literary structures and sensibilities consistently as part of his historiography, very much in line with Monglond's metaphor of the "developer" scanning literary texts for historical images.

Furthermore, Galeano's historical writing is clearly in line with Benjamin's argument that the "materialist presentation of history carries along with it an immanent critique of the concept of progress" (476), that "as soon as [progress] becomes the signature of historical process *as a whole*, [it] bespeaks an uncritical hypostatization rather than a critical interrogation" (478). Benjamin overturns the sense in which "basic historical concepts" are understood, a strategy coincident with Galeano's method: "Catastrophe—to have missed the opportunity. Critical moment—the *status quo* threatens to be preserved. Progress—the first revolutionary measure taken" (474). Historical master narratives are linked by Benjamin with their inversions—both suspect inventions requiring critique: "Overcoming the concept of 'progress' and overcoming the concept of 'period of decline' are two sides of one and the same thing" (460). Benjamin further argues that "historical materialism has every reason to distinguish itself sharply from bourgeois habits of thought. Its founding concept is not progress but actualization" (460). These ideas attack historical passivity and link "progress" with "revolutionary measure[s]" enabled by resistance to both passivity and the status quo. Progress as master trope for a "historical process" that is manufactured by official history is supplanted by progress as an interrogative interruption of this ideological relay.

Galeano consistently deploys this sort of interrogative interruption. Consider, for instance, his association of progress with an economic language that evacuates the suffering and disadvantage of the "poor masses" in the name of social "costs," a dehumanizing language that effectively commodifies suffering: "the singular debasement of things through their signification...corresponds to the singular debasement of things through their price as commodities" (Benjamin, *The Arcades Project* 22). The logic of a system that thinks in such terms—making progress an overweening master narrative while at the same time debasing human suffering through its commodification—requires interrogation via the kind of skeptical historical method exemplified in the following passage:

> After all, human dignity depends on the weighing of costs and benefits, and sacrificing the poor masses is nothing more than the *social cost* of Progress.
>
> What might be the value of that *social cost*, if it could be measured? At the end of 1990, *Stern* magazine made a careful assessment of the damage caused by development in Germany today. The magazine estimated, in economic terms, the human and material cost of automobile accidents, traffic jams, air and water pollution, food contamination, the deterioration of green areas, and other factors, and concluded that the value of these damages was equivalent to a quarter of the entire gross national product. The spread of misery obviously was not included among the damages, because for the past several centuries Europe has fed its wealth on foreign poverty, but it would be interesting to know how far such an assessment would go if it were applied to the catastrophes of modernization in Latin America. (*We Say No* 296-97)

Progress here is shown to be illusory by Galeano's critical interrogation of economic measures that are inadequate to the task of addressing human suffering. History made from such a master narrative, tied to its illusory vision of infinite progress and development, does not even begin to address the deceptions it practices.

Benjamin's historiography accounts for such deceptions in the following way:

> To historians who wish to relive an era, [French historian] Fustel de Coulanges recommends that they blot out everything they know about the later course of history. There is no better way of characterizing the method with which historical materialism has broken. It is a process of empathy whose origin is the indolence of the heart,

acedia [laziness, torpor, apathy], which despairs of grasping and holding the genuine historical image as it flares up briefly…The nature of this sadness stands out more clearly if one asks with whom the adherents of historicism actually empathize. The answer is inevitable: with the victor…There is no document of civilization which is not at the same time a document of barbarism. And just as such a document is not free of barbarism, barbarism also taints the manner in which it was transmitted from one owner to another. A historical materialist therefore dissociates himself from it as far as possible. He regards it as his task to brush history against the grain. ("Theses" 256-57)

Benjamin's insight, via de Coulanges, has especial meaning in the Americas, whose conquest gave birth to the notion of infinite progress as a function of the enormous, seemingly unlimited wealth it contained. The "progress" master narrative that dominates historical methodologies recapitulates the era of seemingly unlimited wealth, in spite of the realities imposed by knowledge of later history (namely that the world has finite resources, that sane development is not about infinite growth so much as about sustainability). Benjamin's much quoted idea that any document produced by civilization is also a document that is tainted unremittingly by the barbarism it signifies as it is passed from "one owner to another" is entirely relevant to Galeano's historical method, which he aligns with an African proverb: "Until lions have their own historians, histories of the hunt will glorify the hunter" (Bach 19). Galeano consistently brushes against the grain of received historical wisdom via the kinds of archival choices he makes and the narrative forms he deploys. Palaversich has noted how the vignette, the narrative form that dominates throughout the *Memory of Fire* trilogy,

…being one of the smallest self-contained narrative forms, is an ideal vehicle for the capturing of [the] fragmented and multilayered history of the continent. The vignette enables the writer to perform spatial and temporal shifts and changes of focus without having to provide narrative links between scenes. It also permits a non-linear, random reading, given that each narrative unit is a self-sufficient story perfectly understandable when read independently of the others. ("Eduardo Galeano's *Memoria del fuego*" 137)

As well, Galeano uses the vignette to show how the incremental weight of evidence taken over an enormous range of time and narrative (appropriately condensed via the vignette form) tells a story contradictory to traditional master narratives about the Americas. The polyphonic form destroys monologic narratives in favour not of the self-sufficient narrative unit so much as of the specificity and "democratization" (Palaversich, "Eduardo Galeano's *Memoria del fuego*" 139) of historical agency. For Galeano, historical agency is implicated in an extraordinary skein of intertextual meaning and action only fragmentarily represented by the author. The incremental density of the historical fragments used by Galeano is no replacement for the historical agents he describes, the larger resistant narratives he tells.

Truthful History. Carlos Alberto Estévez Carasa, "El juego preferido de Dios" and "La verdadera historia universal" (1995). *1er Salon de Arte Cubano Contemporaneo* 53.

Fueled by an approximative historical method, though, Galeano's narratives consistently address their own incomplete status even as they insist on this incompleteness as a referent for the lost histories that they seek to redress. Again, the literary trope of "incessant metaphors" governs this historiographic project more than does any aesthetic of self-sufficiency. All story is intertwined: "The consciousness of shared roots, the knowledge of a historical process intimately intertwined, should open new doors leading out of reciprocal incommunication—or at least help to do so" (*We Say No* 218). Galeano's sense of the intimate intertwinings of historical process is congruent with Eric Hobsbawm's notion that "all human collectivities necessarily are and have been part of a larger and more complex world." This idea forms part of a larger critique Hobsbawm makes of historians who succumb to the "temptation to isolate the history of one part of humanity—the historian's own, by birth or choice—from its wider context" (365).

Where Hobsbawm argues from this point of view toward universalism ("Historians, however microcosmic, must be for universalism" [365]), Galeano, as we have seen, resists universalist history in the name of anti-narratives that show how such universalism is made on the backs of forgotten (and profoundly interconnected) historical agents, oppressed and marginalized collectivities. We fully understand that such anti-narratives can be read as universalist in their own right, a universalism that is undercut by the fact that it opposes any form of historical reduction that distracts from the struggle for justice and equity. In this sense, Galeano's historical writings are congruent with Edward Said's notion of universality as "taking a risk to go beyond the easy certainties provided us by our backgrounds, language, nationality, which so often shield us from the reality of others" (*Representations of the Intellectual* xiv). Galeano's perspective is informed by José Martí's notions, expressed in his essay "The Truth About the United States," which opens with a critique of essentialist discourse while also proposing its own form of essentialism based on the "permanent duel between constructive unselfishness and iniquitous hate":

> In our America it is vital to know the truth about the United States. We should not exaggerate its faults purposely, out of a desire to deny it all virtue, nor should these faults be concealed or proclaimed as virtues. There are no races; there are only the various modifications of man in details of climate and history in which he lives, which do not alter the identical and the essential...how all nations are boiling in the same stew pot, and how one finds in the structure and fabric of them all the same permanent duel between constructive unselfishness and iniquitous hate. (*José Martí Reader* 172)

The sheer lack of widely disseminated historical alternatives to histories of the Americas, until very recently, mitigates against this sort of theoretical argument that an anti-narrative of the sort produced by Galeano is equally a master narrative and therefore equally redundant and reductive.

These observations, then, in tandem with the kinds of critical interrogations to which Galeano subjects his distinctive archive, disintegrate the boundaries separating history from literature, the factual from the fictive. The disruptive powers of literary creation, particularly in the revision of histories and historiographies in which Benjamin's notion of "empathy" with the victor is the norm, bring the critic face to face with the possibilities, limits, responsibilities, and failures of history as an enacted relation to the world. Galeano's historical texts explicitly theorize those possibilities, limits, responsibilities, and failures via a form of dissonant history based on the identification of historical counter-narratives. The key premise underlying this method is the Benjaminian notion that the subject-position of the teller of the story determines the way in which the story is made. Perhaps this is an obvious truth, but it is also one largely ignored through the persistent misrecognition of historical writing as objective and factual as opposed to literary, fictive, or counterfactual. Palaversich refines this point in arguing that

...if the true referent of history is yet another text there is no reason why works of fiction could not enjoy the same legitimacy as, say, archival documents. However, such an approach is inadequate because Galeano's highly eclectic documentation undermines the traditional notion of the historically relevant document and is a product of the ideological demand for a particular body of texts, an *archive*, in the Foucauldian sense of the term, for those groups who do not possess their own histories. ("Eduardo Galeano's *Memoria del fuego*" 143)

The naming of this misrecognition of the histories of the Americas is a pre-eminent aspect of Galeano's writing: indigenous experience is the crucial missing dimension that needs to be restored to historical consciousness in the Americas:

Civilization? History changes according to the voice that sings it. In America, in Europe, or in any other place. What for the Romans *was the invasion of the barbarians*, for the Germans was *the migration south*.

It's not the voice of the Indians that has told, thus far, the history of America. Just before the Spanish conquest, a Mayan prophet, mouth of the gods, announced: *When greed is done away with, the face will be untied, the hand will be untied, the feet of the world will be untied*. And when the mouth is untied, what will it say? What will the *other* voice say, the one never heard?

From the point of view of the victors, which to date has been the only point of view, Indian customs have always confirmed their possession by demons or their biological inferiority. (*We Say No* 310)

Even those groups said to "possess their own histories" do not necessarily possess much more than a deceptive and incomplete version of an already told tale. Thus, the construction of an alternative archival model is of crucial importance for how received wisdom about widely disseminated cultural narratives ("land of the free, home of the brave," "land of opportunity," "liberty and equality") is to be shaken loose from a non-critical relationship to its own secure sense of historical emplacement.

As we have just seen, in putting critical pressure on how all historical narratives are potentially "incessant metaphors" for the inter-relatedness of other narratives (forgotten, untold, deliberately obscured, neglected), Galeano's historiography argues toward a radical deconstruction of all histories. This latter move occurs in the name of a basic critique of the premises, underlying stories, and unthought assumptions that ground different expressions of culture as a function of historical narrative. It is no coincidence, then, that the inaugural gestures of *Memory of Fire*'s first volume place the reader in the domain of indigenous myth and story (64 pre-conquest vignettes), sourcing the history of the Americas in the allusive literariness of the largely unknown referents of those myths and stories. The point Galeano makes in this unconventional gesture is that history is grounded (such as it is) in mythic time and in the literariness of the stories that remain to be recuperated from that time. History is not based on narrative homogeneity but on difference, the acknowledgement of difference as it erupts into the mythic story that becomes history: that is, the story of making story *is* history. LaCapra observes that "The multiple roles of tropes, irony, parody, and other 'rhetorical' devices of composition and arrangement generate resistances to the construal of texts in terms of their 'representational' or narrowly documentary functions, and they disclose how texts may have critical or even potentially transformative relations to phenomena 'represented' in them" (38). Literature, as such, cannot be separated from history any more than can myth from literature.

Dissonant history acknowledges myth as one element in history's multi-literary dimensions, a recognition that history is interpretive insofar as it is composed of the tropes and rhetorical strategies that potentially transform the passive spectacle of history into an act of collective making (via reader and writer). Where the "official" historian "writes for an audience that already accepts his basic values and assumptions" (Gossman 39), the dissonant historian writes to challenge the assumptions of that anticipated audience. Lionel Gossman argues that "Although at times historical narrative and fictional narrative may seem to have been straining in opposite directions, they have both traditionally accepted the essential conditions of classical narrative and have operated within the framework these provide" (21). The radical historian not only undoes the conventions of classical historical narrative but also undoes the conventions associated with fictional, literary narratives.

Literariness in the conveyance of narrative is no guarantor of dissonance, especially if it is coincident with classical historical narrative modes. And even if it dissents from those modes, as in the case of French nineteenth-century historian Jules Michelet, literariness is no guarantee that historical writing will necessarily change or come to a realization of the importance of its own literariness as a way of transmitting knowledge. Gossman states that

> Of the historical writings I know, the one that comes closest to breaking the historical code is perhaps Michelet's *La Sorcière*, which appeared over one hundred years ago. Yet the historians who have recuperated Michelet from the domain of literature, to which he had been banished by their Positivist predecessors, have been attentive above all to the range of questions he asked of the past, to his acute sense of the richness of historical phenomena. They have hardly commented on all the peculiar features of a text of unusual density and complexity, in which the account of events is so shot through with lyrical and confessional writing, and fiction is so intimately interwoven with traditional historical narrative, that the reader is disoriented and made uncertain as to what is dream or poetic effusion, what is a narrative of past events (*histoire*) and what belongs to the situation at the time of writing or enunciating and to the subject of the enunciation (*discours*). (37)

The recognition that multiple perspectives are conflated, knowingly or not, in historical writing practices is a key aspect of the dissonant historical discourse produced by Galeano.

History, in such a context, is an allegory of memory, a story told about the making(s) of memory. Because of this, no purely historical discourse is possible, though strongly tendentious writing tries to elide this fact (often successfully as a function of how readers read uncritically).

All discourse, historical and literary, is referential in unexpected ways beyond the full control of the person creating the discourse. A classic example of this occurs in Ercilla's previously mentioned *Araucana*. Even though the ideological intent of the poem is fairly clear as a narrative of Spanish imperial culture, fissures can be observed, some no doubt introduced by the fact that George Carew's translation heightens the critique of the Spanish conquistadors as a function of his own English nationalism. Note, for instance, the critique of Spanish greed, their "Imoderatt desire of Rule in so muche as 1000 Leagues of Land was nott able to satisfie the greedie appetites of ten persons" (4), in which Pedro de Valdivia (the Spanish conquistador authorized by Pizarro to conquer Chile and the "founder" of Santiago)

> ...was so subiected to avarice as his Judgement was in a manner Lost, and forgettinge the meane quallitie he was in, thought himsellfe poore, when he had 50000 slaves workinge in his mynes, whose Labours was daylie worthe vnto him sellfe *12:markes* [12:markes is 3:pound weight] of golld, and not contented wth his fortune to satisfie hius vnlimitted Covetousnesse, he layed suche grievous taxes vppon the miserable Indians, as they growinge into despayre of Ease, hardened there harts, wch begatt the rebellion. (9-10)[11]

Though a literary epic written by (and for) the conquerors, the historical information to be gained from such a passage is not negligible. The passage mounts an explicit critique of the conduct of the Spanish and explicates, perhaps unwittingly, the justifiable indigenous rebellion detailed through the rest of the poem: 50,000 slaves working in mines; three pounds of gold issuing daily from the mines; excessive taxes; surpassing greed for land; immoderate desire to rule—the passage documents a range of facts and analyses that justify the Araucanian rebellion even as these same details condemn the Spaniards, which is *not* the overt ideological intent of the epic taken as a whole. Same book, in other words, but different stories. To diminish the historical content of the passage we have cited in the name of its literariness would be to deform the multiple forms of information it conveys. Further, the designation "literary," as we have remarked in the previous chapter, can be used to neutralize writers whose words erupt from spaces of difference, writers whose relation to the public sphere is *not* merely writerly (as in the case of people like Galeano, Neruda, Poniatowska, and Marcos). Disruption of form (and therefore of content) in both historical and literary modes is a crucial tactic deployed by dissonant writers who refigure the very ways in which stories deemed historical are told. Both literary and historical convention are interrogated by those writers who, like Galeano, argue toward a resistant critique of any settled form, especially those fixed by narrow academic and disciplinary boundaries that evacuate the full signifying richness texts like Ercilla's incarnate.

The defamiliarization that occurs at the beginning of *Memory of Fire* through the use of indigenous myths and story is one example from a range of tactics deployed by Galeano, for whom temporal shifts, tone, indirection, sarcasm, authorial distance, the revelatory documentation that arises from the archival choices he makes, and so forth all figure. Galeano is explicit about the importance of myth in his historical method:

> Myths, collective metaphors, collective acts of creation, offer answers to the challenges of nature and the mysteries of human experience. Through myths, memory lives on, recognizes itself, and acts.
>
> Throughout the pages of the trilogy, historic experience is interwoven with myth, as it is in life. The first part of *Memory of Fire*, however, is based exclusively on indigenous myths transmitted from parents to children by oral tradition. I found no better way to approach the America that existed prior to Columbus's arrival. In any event, practically all the documentation of this period ended up in the bonfires of the conquistadors.
>
> These indigenous myths, keys to the most ancient memories of America, perpetuate the dreams of the conquered—lost dreams, scorned dreams—and return them to a history that is alive: they come from history, and to history they return.
>
> In 1572, when the Spaniards cut off the head of Túpac Amaru, the last king of the Inca dynasty, a myth was born among the Indians of Peru. This myth proclaimed that the severed head would one day be rejoined to the body. Two centuries later, the myth returned to the reality from which it came, and prophecy became history: José Gabriel Condorcanqui took the name Túpac Amaru and led the largest indigenous revolt of all time. The severed head found its body. (*We Say No* 258-59)

The story of Túpac Amaru's resurrection in Condorcanqui is typical of the historical strategy Galeano deploys so effectively. A myth, born of a specific event (Túpac Amaru's execution), takes on its own prophetic reality with material consequences to the struggle to make history.

But myth can also lead to a recursive relation to the past in which, for example, the unanswerable question of human origins yields a way of understanding mortal reality. The first myth told in *Genesis*, "The Creation," frames history and humanity's relations to it through allegory:

> The woman and the man dreamed that God was dreaming about them.
>
> God was singing and clacking his maracas as he dreamed his dream in a cloud of tobacco smoke, feeling happy but shaken by doubt and mystery.
>
> The Makiritare Indians know that if God dreams about eating, he gives fertility and food. If God dreams about life, he is born and gives birth.

In their dream about God's dream, the woman and the man were inside a great shining egg, singing and dancing and kicking up a fuss because they were crazy to be born. In God's dream happiness was stronger than doubt and mystery. So dreaming, God created them with a song.

"I break this egg and the woman is born and the man is born. And together they will live and die. But they will be born again. They will be born and die again and be born again. They will never stop being born, because death is a lie." (*Genesis* 3)

Dreamtime is historical time insofar as it is a referent for an imagined relation between the secular and the divine coincident with a particular culture, in this case the Ye'kuana or Makiritare Indians.[12] Galeano's recreation of the myth uses literary echoes, especially the tropes of happiness, mystery, and doubt, to underline the affirmative potential of being born anew. Here, resistance to the fixity of "death" is a referent for the making of history itself. The myth that inaugurates *Memory of Fire*, in other words, prophesies reinvention and resistance, locating them not only in dreamtime but also in an indigenous god's wish for renewal as a key component of an originary story. The prophecy maps itself not only onto historical time writ large but also onto the discursive reinvention that will proceed from this inaugural moment. The myth as prophecy becomes the "incessant metaphor" of history, the constant possibility of the resurrection of memory in both dream narrative and material action. Material action is always implicit in this mythic mode of historical narrative and method and can yield unexpected and dissonant consequences, like the material, imaginative challenge *Memory of Fire* cumulatively represents to the ossified narratives of official history.

Mythic story connotes the dream of unstoppable renewal, in spite of the certainty of death. When God declaims that "death is a lie," however extravagant such a claim seems, the allegory affirms the collective (over individual) experience of renewal that history in this mode enables. The affirmation effectively announces an allegory of the historical method Galeano will pursue and sustain throughout the allegorical and polyphonic narratives of the trilogy. Gerald Martin suggests that

In Latin America…the 1920s demonstrated that any artist attempting to represent the region's realities under the sign of the future was now obliged to engage with this perspective of rebellion and redefinition, if he or she was to resolve within a textual structure the acutely contradictory, heterogeneous or plural elements and discourses generated within uneven development. The most thoroughgoing attempts to do this were Asturias's *Men of Maize* (1949) and Neruda's *General Song* (1950). Later versions, such as Fernández Retamar's *Caliban* (1971) or Galeano's *Open Veins of Latin America* (1971) and *Memory of Fire* (1982-86), though undoubted classics, were beginning to sail against the contrary winds of history, and the ideological timbers were beginning to creak. These works were simple negations, mere inversions of an ideology, whereas the 'Ulyssean' masterworks of the era, from *One Hundred Years of Solitude* [García Márquez] to *I the Supreme* [Roa Bastos], tended to be more dialectical, to see synthesis as a question of raising rather than reducing. (*Journeys Through the Labyrinth* 361)

We would argue that Galeano's historical work is neither the mere inversion of an ideology nor a matter of reduction, precisely because (as we have argued throughout this chapter) it is so polyphonic, syncretistic, and allegorical—impossible to summarize as a total object of critical scrutiny and profoundly suspicious of all forms of literary or historical master-narratives. As such, it represents a (rare) hybridized response to the post-Conquest encounters that have shaped the Americas. Dussel explains that "If the *meeting* (*encuentro*) of two worlds were to signify the new hybrid, syncretistic culture that the mestizo race is articulating, its content would be acceptable. Popular culture in its own creative consciousness would then be producing this meeting, and not the brutal event of conquest" (*The Invention of the Americas* 57). The anti-narrative of the myth we reproduce here from Galeano's *Genesis* restructures the shape of the encounter in an allegory that puts the very premises governing the representation of the encounter to the question.

Galeano observes that the final volume of *Memory of Fire* was "built around the figure of Salvadoran revolutionary Miguel Mármol, his eleven deaths and eleven resurrections. Miguelito, so many times killed and reborn, is the most telling metaphor of Latin America. Our collective memory remains stubbornly alive: a thousand times slain, a thousand times reborn in the hiding places where she licks her wounds" (*We Say No* 264-65).[13] Resurrection and insurrection. Prophecy and (re)vision. These form the matrix of unexpected synergies and transformative energies that history in Galeano's perspective attempts to locate. This practice registers the alterity that the imaginary engenders at the same time as it destroys the orthodoxies of the familiar. Stories that invert and trouble reality through myth are one source of such transformative energies, as are stories that dig in behind the façade of received wisdom, which more often than not translates into a form of cultural amnesia. Cultural amnesia takes different historical forms, one of which is captured in José Antonio Burciaga's strikingly concise (hi)story of the Christmas flower known as the Poinsettia in English but as *la cuetlaxochitl* in Nahuatl. As Burciaga shows, the blood-red colour was associated by the Aztecs with sacrificial blood, an association it would unwittingly take on when the *cuetlaxochitl* was appropriated by North American culture (from the Mexica) as a sign of Christmas. The plant was brought to the North by Joel Poinsett, the American ambassador to Mexico, who had been Secretary of War prior to his ambassadorship: "He increased the size of the army by a third, and many of his soldiers helped transport Indians westward. During Poinsett's term as secretary of war, more Indians were displaced than at any other time" (43). The irony of the flower symbolizing both pagan and Christian sacrificial blood is made doubly so as a function of having been appropriated to the North by the "blood sacrifices of a U.S. Secretary of War" (44). Burciaga concludes his highly condensed, ironic attack on cultural amnesia by suggesting that "Five hundred years after the encounter between Europe and this continent, we should attempt to recapture the history and contributions of the indigenous peoples. It would be a noble act to give the flower its original name, *cuetlaxochitl*—'Flower that withers, flower that perishes like all that is pure'—as a reminder of wounded Mother Earth" (44).

For Galeano, this sort of historical imagination "opens new doors to the understanding of reality and foresees its transformation; it anticipates, through dream, the world to be conquered, at the same time that it challenges the immobility of the bourgeois order. In the system of silence and fear, *the power to create and invent strikes at the routines of obedience*" (*We Say No* 171; our emphasis). Disobedient, dissonant history then becomes the means to mobilizing alternatives to the "routines of obedience" that govern the "system of silence and fear." History as practiced by Galeano resists this deeply structural fear in the name of witnessing those who have been disappeared from history, making the power to create, the power to transform history's refuse, into the rejection of abjected memory and historical amnesia. It is to the matter of those disappearances that we now turn.

"Deaths Without Relays":
Stories about Memory and Disappearance

Galeano's experience of disappearance and fear are not incidental to his resistant historical method. In 1973, Galeano went into exile in Argentina (after the June 27 military coup in Uruguay) where he edited the celebrated radical journal *Crisis*, one that blended, as we have already seen, wildly different modes of writing, subject matter, and types of writers and artists before its offices were closed and its staff was threatened with disappearance. Haroldo Conti, one of the editors of *Crisis* and one of Argentina's most prominent writers, was disappeared (in April 1976) after publication of an open letter in *Crisis* to the Argentine dictatorship. Galeano states that not one line was printed in the Argentine newspapers about Conti after he was disappeared, despite his prominence: "As was the case with many thousands of Argentinians, Chileans, Guatemalans, and Uruguayans, the earth swallowed him up" (*We Say No* 172). The targeted disappearance of prominent critics of dictatorships is not limited to "Third World" spaces, the assassination by car bomb of Orlando Letelier and his aide, Ronni Moffitt, in Washington, D.C. (1976) being a particularly egregious example of the lengths taken to silence critics. Letelier was the exiled Chilean opposition leader who had mounted an effective campaign against Pinochet's dictatorship from the U.S. As Christopher Hitchens reports: "The man responsible for arranging the crime, the Chilean secret policeman General Manuel Contreras, has since stated in an affidavit that he took no action without specific and personal orders from Pinochet" ("The Case Against Henry Kissinger, Part Two" 51). Hitchens also notes how the promise of surveillance of Latin American dissidents in the United States was offered by American intelligence to Operation

"Condor," an organization of "cross-border assassination, abduction, torture, and intimidation coordinated among the secret police forces of Pinochet's Chile, Alfredo Stroessner's Paraguay, Jorge Rafael Vidala's Argentina, and other regional caudillos" (50).[14] Galeano's work on *Crisis* took place in this oppressive context and no doubt influenced subsequent writing projects substantially.

Ricardo Burton, "El país del Minotauro", 1984, Villa Devoto

Deaths Without Relays. Ricardo Burton, "El país del Minotauro" [The Minotaur's Country] (1984), from *Crisis* 43 (1986): 29.

Shortly after Conti's disappearance, Galeano fled Argentina to Catalonia before returning to Uruguay in 1985.

Buenos Aires, November 1975:
I Like to Feel Free and Stay Here if I Want

The telephone rings and I jump. I look at my watch. Nine-thirty in the evening. Should I answer or not? I answer. It's the José Rucci Commandos from the Argentine Anticommunist Alliance.

"We're going to kill you, you bastards."

"The schedule for calling in threats, sir, is from six to eight," I answer.

I hang up and congratulate myself. I'm proud of myself. But I want to stand up and I can't: my legs are limp rags. (*Days and Nights* 78)

How many historians write out of such circumstances? How many histories are written from a perspective where the material experience of fear is embedded in the very structures of thought and feeling that make this sort of history? How many historians would recognize the "incessant metaphors" present in the preceding narrative, however truncated or fragmentary? And yet the absence of such disappearances, paradoxically, is the very stuff of traditional history as told by those who have the power to do the disappearing with impunity, or as told by those who do not even recognize such disappearances as relevant.

The disappearance of indigenous languages (and all the coincident human knowledge associated with those languages), barely on the horizon as an issue worthy of academic or political attention, is but one example of this sort of traditional history-making that excludes the matter of disappearance from its purview. Daniel Nettle and Suzanne Romaine detail how, for example, "*The Ethnologue* counts 27 Quechuan languages in Peru…while the Peruvian government accords only six of these the status of language. The government's decision is political rather than linguistic" (30). Nettle and Romaine state that "linguists estimate the number of languages in the world to be between 5,000 and 6,700" (27) and that "fewer than 4 percent of languages have any kind of official status in the countries where they are spoken" (39). The disappearance of these presences from historical accounting—let alone official status—is an enormous threat to human biolinguistic and historical diversity even as it announces a form of linguistic imperialism at the service of globalitarian transnational culture, itself largely a product of colonizing cultures. An early colonial example of this imperial logic is to be found in Antonio de Nebrija's comments on why he wrote his Castilian grammar. In the prologue to the grammar, when the Castilian monarch asks Nebrija to outline the potential benefits of his work, Bishop de Avila jumps in and asserts the imperial and colonialist motives before Nebrija can respond:

…el mui reverendo Obispo de Ávila me arrebató la respuesta; y, respondiendo por mí, dixo que después que vuestra Alteza metiesse…debaxo de su iugo muchos pueblos bárbaros y naciones de peregrinas lenguas, y con el vencimiento aquellos ternían necessidad de recebir las leies quel vencedor pone al vencido, y con ellas nuestra lengua, entonces, por esta mi Arte, podrían venir en el conocimiento della, como agora nos otros deprendemos el arte de la gramática latina para deprender el latín. (101-02)

[...the most honourable Bishop of Ávila seized the response; and, answering for me, said that after your Highness has placed...beneath his yoke many barbarian peoples and nations with nomadic languages, and with the victory they would have to receive the laws that the victor imposes on the vanquished, and with them our language, for this purpose my Art would serve them just as we presently learn Latin from the art of Latin grammar.]

The conquest of "barbarian peoples" here is clearly associated, at a crucial historical juncture, with the imposition of the colonists' language, which implies the space of colonial homogeneity predicated on the disappearance of difference ("nomadic languages"). Irving Leonard argues, in a similar mode, that

...throughout the length and breadth of the continents [of the Americas] the ways of thinking, feeling, and of imagining have an identical source, a common storehouse of legends, myths, themes, and ideas which were drawn upon in the invention of local stories, ballads, and diversions. This collective fund was the medieval and renaissance lore of Catholic Europe, brought from the earliest times by the printed page as well as by oral means and passed from mouth to mouth among the unlettered. (328)

In this reading, the source of regional Spanish-American culture is imagined to be European universal culture. Moreover, the "unobstructed circulation of practically all books, save those of Protestant heresy, of course, was an effective aid in implanting the language of Castile as the universal idiom of Spanish America" (328). Though hybrid cultures no doubt formed as a result of encounter, to state things as Leonard does is to miss out on the enormous repository of indigenous cultural materials already in place *prior* to encounter.

Trinh provides a discerning synopsis of the logic of historical disappearance from the perspective of the prisoner: "Always recurring in the prisoner's mind is the fear of a time when the witnesses themselves die without witnesses, when History consists of tiny explosions of life, and of *deaths without relays*" (67; our emphasis). Traditional history does not witness the dispossession of the prisoner, a dispossession guaranteed by history that then becomes a form of death without relay. Trinh's prisoner whose death goes unnoticed in a series of similarly unmarked deaths is particularly resonant in the specific historical context from which Galeano's historiography has emerged. The Argentine disappearances to which we have already referred, in which political prisoners were sedated and thrown from planes into the sea (while the Argentine government denied such actions taken in its name), stands as a horrific reminder of the fate of the prisoner in relation to historical memory.

To "deaths without relays" Galeano poses unstoppable memories given over as story: "Neither criminality nor repression can hold back history" (Salvador Allende 240). A poignant passage from *The Book of Embraces*, in which Galeano describes how Uruguayan political prisoners communicated despite severe restrictions, encapsulates the power of story to interrupt oblivion:

> Their hands were tied or handcuffed, yet their fingers danced, flew, drew words. The prisoners were hooded, but leaning back, they could see a bit, just a bit, down below. Although it was forbidden to speak, they spoke with their hands. Pinio Ungerfeld taught me the finger alphabet, which he had learned in prison without a teacher:
>
>   *"Some of us had bad handwriting,"* he told me. *"Others were masters of calligraphy."*
>
> The Uruguayan dictatorship wanted everyone to stand alone, everyone to be no one: in prisons and barracks, and throughout the country, communication was a crime.
>
> Some prisoners spent more than ten years buried in solitary cells the size of coffins, hearing nothing but clanging bars or footsteps in the corridors. Fernández Huidobro and Mauricio Rosencof, thus condemned, survived because they could talk to each other by tapping on the wall. In that way they told of dreams and memories, fallings in and out of love; they discussed, embraced, fought; they shared beliefs and beauties, doubts and guilts, and those questions that have no answer.
>
> When it is genuine, when it is born of the need to speak, no one can stop the human voice. When denied a mouth, it speaks with the hands or the eyes, or the pores, or anything at all. Because every single one of us has something to say to the others, something that deserves to be celebrated or forgiven by others. (25)

Ungerfeld, Huidobro, Rosencof. And many others who remain unnamed. Echoes of other disappearances. The names of these prisoners animate the story of speech in the space of the prison, where the dream of speech made impossible reigns. Galeano's historical method *names* names, a recuperation that historicizes the official relays in which such facts are negated. But more than that, Galeano recuperates the irrecuperable experience of being a political prisoner in a system that seeks to brutalize by restricting communication, once again interpolating story into fact. Galeano's version of history inverts the oblivion of the prisoner in the name of voices that will not be denied. Resistance, celebration, forgiveness, and hope gather in the *story* that is this *history*, all tropes that interrupt the unrelayed deaths marking official history's version of the past.

Official history has deep structures of oblivion at its core, eradicating events, peoples, and active tropes of resistance in the name of a master narrative that naturalizes oblivion.[15] Galeano notes, for instance, how "Indigenous rebellions, which did not let up from 1493 on, receive little or no mention in the texts that teach America's past. Equally ignored are the continuous black slave revolts, which began from the moment Europe gloriously founded hereditary slavery in America" (*We Say No* 259). Acts of surpassing state cruelty shown for what they are, or of rebellion in the just cause for freedom from servitude, or the (un)making of histories from which such acts are expunged are all clearly associated by Galeano with radical acts of memory. Radical memory reinstates the narrative relays necessary to memorialize the prisoner, here an "incessant metaphor" for the very condition of being "in" traditional history as a phantom presence held incommunicado. Galeano's historiography has noteworthy overlaps with Benjamin's notion that "To articulate the past historically does not mean to recognize it 'the way it really was' ([Leopold von] Ranke). It means to seize hold of a memory as it flashes up at a moment of danger. Historical materialism wishes to retain that image of the past which unexpectedly appears to man singled out by history at a moment of danger. The danger affects both the content of the tradition and its receivers" ("Theses" 255). The instantaneity of memory precipitated by the moment of danger makes history as a function of how the dangerous now is implicated in the memorial past it generates. History in this sense is not and can never be "the way it really was," which implies a static past that has no bearing on the present. Instead, history is what emerges from the collision of the present moment of danger and the memory that erupts from that moment.

History, then, as crisis: in the moment, of the forgotten moment, of the relation between "the content of the tradition and its receivers." "Crisis," the root word for critic and criticism, is the Latin translation of the Greek word *krisis*, meaning a sifting, an ability to discern, a critical relationship to the act of seeing. Seeing, theory, history: acts of narrative crisis in the face of the danger of forgetting, all the while recognizing that the counter-narrative produced by this crisis will not reinstate "the way it really was." As we have argued in the chapter on human rights and literature, no act of representation, historical or otherwise, can reinstate the specificity of agency occuring in the "now" of the past. The representation of agency is critical to the making of meaningful narratives that put pressure on the "now" of the present. Where Benjamin argues that things are debased through their signification, Galeano recognizes that historical signification is a thing-in-itself. The dissonant historian resists this debasement (of memory, of historical agency) by interrupting the persistence with which particular master narratives gain credence in the market of historical ideas, restituting memory in place of degraded and repetitive narratives whose commodification as cultural capital goes largely unquestioned. The production of effective counter-narratives that interrupt Trinh's unwitnessed "deaths without relay," for instance, satisfies one of the conditions for the sort of radical historiography articulated by Galeano. Witness the following vignette from Galeano's largely autobiographical *Days and Nights of Love and War*, detailing his experiences with tyranny and dictatorship:

The System

Extermination plan: destroy the grass, pull up every last little living thing by the roots, sprinkle the earth with salt. Afterward, kill all memory of the grass. To colonize consciences, suppress them; to suppress them, empty them of the past. Wipe out all testimony to the fact that in this land there ever existed anything other than silence, jails, and tombs.

It is forbidden to remember.

Prisoners are organized into work gangs. At night they are forced to whitewash the phrases of protest that in other times covered the walls of the city.

The steady pelting of the rain on the walls begins to dissolve the white paint. And little by little the stubborn words reappear. (178)

Official history flirts with archival fantasies of a total narrative of temporal ordering where the interpretants of normative archival and temporal structures produce master narratives whose interests align with that of the state. History in this mode simultaneously holds to myths of continuity in the very fragments that make its dislocations apparent when subjected to Galeano's historiographic method. Though it is "forbidden to remember," the "stubborn words reappear." The official historian, like Fukuyama, dissimulatively retropes the disunity of the past as the historian's present mastery of fact and figure. Which is not to say that it is impossible to speak of time, place, event, and human activity in a meaningful way. Literature has always recognized this. Homeric narrative, for instance, articulates a narrative of conquest (and therefore of dispute and battle) or of foundation (of the nation or imperial state, again a function of militarized discourse) through "discovery" (as in the *Iliad*). And similar arguments could be advanced in relation to the Judeo-Christian bible and other foundational texts associated with early Occidental historiography.

These literary topoi—conquest, imperial foundation, discovery—dominate foundational texts in historiography. Herodotus, for instance, begins the first book of *The Histories* by stating his purpose in recording "what were their [the Greeks and the Barbarians] grounds of feud"; he follows this with the assertion that "According to the Persians best informed in history, the Phoenicians began the quarrel" (5).[16] Book one of Thucydides' history *The Peloponnesian War* also locates its narrative as a function of war. Thucydides states that he "prepared a written account of the war that was fought between the Peloponnesians and the Athenians," suggesting this "was the greatest ferment ever to sweep the Greeks and many of the barbarians—in other words, the majority of the human race" (4). Astonishingly, Thucydides goes on to claim: "I have been unable to obtain accurate information about the period that preceded the war or about epochs in the still more distant past; but on the basis of the most reliable evidence I could find after the most painstaking examination, I do not consider those times to have been very important as far as either war or anything else is concerned" (4). Without any accurate information, Thucydides is still able to dismiss the past as unimportant, a kind of cart-before-the-horse logic that effectively disappears the past. The strategy will come to typify official history's constriction of narrative to only that which pertains to its normative values as a function of state self-interest. The unapologetic Hellenocentrism—not to mention the sheer (anti-historical) refusal to confront the past as having any relevance to the present—sets the stage for Occidental historiography, which will rely on national identifications (Eurocentrism) and the forgetting or eradication of the other from what it deems relevant. Here is the arrogance of a language system, a purported science of fact and figure, relayed by a reliable narrator whose veracity is unquestioned. This arrogance abrogates to itself the quantitative dimension of human experience, even when that experience surpasses and destroys the possibility of reductive narratives, a fact suggested by the incomplete phrase that "ends" Thucydides's master narrative ("He [Tissaphernes] first went to Ephesus and sacrificed to Artemis..." [350]).

Galeano's anti-historiography affirms that the essence of the past, that which makes it what it is, cannot be supplanted by any objective measure of the diffuseness of human energies at specific synchronic historical junctures. This is why the literariness of Galeano's historical method is so important—"history is an incessant metaphor." Moreover, synchrony is itself never simply a self-contained narrative in a linear diachronic chain. Multiple synchronic moments swell time with meaning at the same time as they point to the limitations of narrative methods that are not faithful to the density of synchronic time, its jumble of event and meaning. Further, no synchronic juncture has priority over any other in its potential to reveal, among others, horror, accomplishment, mystery, or inertia. History in such a context is mirage, an event-horizon that dissolves into the discontinuities of the vision by which that mirage is produced. History. Blindness. Disappearance. The blindness of historical discourse to everything that circumvents its audacious claim to everything. The blindness of discourse to everything that envelops it in a barely penetrable cocoon of unspoken event, forgotten gesture, furtive imagination of possibility.

The crisis of history for Galeano, then, is the crisis of grand metanarratives supplanting the local stories and anonymous interventions that are refused historicization through master narratives. Much like Mignolo's critique of Eurocentric critiques of Eurocentrism (*Local Histories/Global Designs* 37), the problem with defining alternative histories lies in historiographic models that recapitulate their own structures in the name of productive analysis. That those structures are profoundly tied to repeated structures of colonialism, imperialism, expansionism, and so forth has been largely overlooked by practitioners of traditional historiography, including some of the most sophisticated proponents with the keenest of theoretical tools at hand. There is little surprise in this observation to anyone who has examined the opening pages of foundational historiographic documents (in Occidental discourse) like Herodotus's *Histories* and Thucydides's *The Peloponnesian Wars*. As we have just shown, both these texts locate their originary moments in profoundly colonial and militaristic models of historiography, structures that will be repeated in later histories and historiographies in which the same topoi are explored.

Galeano's history-making presents a radical break with the tradition we have briefly sketched. This radical break is exemplified in Galeano's skepticism over "the frontiers that, according to literature's customs officers, separate the forms" (*Genesis* xv). As a function of the hybridity and the formal border crossing he intends, Galeano then suggests that "There is nothing neutral about this historical narration [in *Memory of Fire*]" (xv), nonetheless affirming that "each fragment of this huge mosaic is based on a solid documentary foundation. What is told here has happened, although I tell it in my style and manner" (xv). By the last book of the trilogy, Galeano's prefatory comments affirm that "The author relates what has happened, the history of America, and above all, the history of Latin America; and he has sought to do it in such a way that the reader should feel that what has happened happens again when the author tells it" (*Century of the Wind* xvii).

These prefatory comments articulate a spare historical method that is radical in a number of ways. First, it shifts the ground of history to writing generally, suggesting a writing practice open to the possibilities that extend beyond any one genre or discipline. Second, it abjures neutrality yet advocates a meticulous documentary foundation based on multiple sources.[17] Contrary to the accusations made of historical naïveté, Galeano acknowledges writing that translates history as having a non-neutral facticity—events happen but they are shaped by the observer's perspective as much as they are shaped by the observer's "style and manner." Thus, a willful recognition of the materiality of events is juxtaposed with the circumstances that shape the response implicit in the events' narration. Third, Galeano iterates his desired relation to the reader, an acknowledgement of the place of the reader's response traditionally missing from historiographic methods where objectivity reigns at the expense of figuring the act of remembering implicit in the act of reading history. Obviously, such a remembering is not necessarily so for the reader whose knowledge of particular circumstances is not extant. So here, by arguing for a narrative method that makes the reader feel as if "what has happened happens again," Galeano is clearly pointing to another cornerstone in his anti-historiography, one that suggests a form of affective pedagogy. Furthermore, the kind of Thucydidean turning away from the past because it has no bearing on the present is decisively revoked by Galeano. Instead, the necessity of interpretation and critical understanding is invoked in the name of possible transformations that arise from such a critical consciousness:

> *Open Veins* seeks to portray the past as something always convoked by the present, a live memory of our own day. A search for keys in past history to help explain our time—a time that also makes history—on the basis that the first condition for changing reality is to understand it. This is no catalog of heroes, dressed as if for a masked ball, who die in battle making solemn pronouncements; rather it probes for the sound and footprints of the multitudes who traced the paths we walk today. (*Open Veins* 288-89)

The epigraph to the third volume of *Memory of Fire*, *Century of the Wind*, cites Juan Rulfo's line "and clawing ourselves out of the wind with our fingernails," which suggests the extent to which the battle to find place in history is a struggle of epic proportions. The vortex of events flows on relentlessly. The historian in this mode claws forth the actors and events that have traditionally been subsumed in the vortex as an act "convoked by the present," as a necessary precursor to being in the present meaningfully. Galeano repeatedly resorts to literary tropes to figure this relation of absence to presence, of making the absent palpable in the present. Moreover, Galeano further radicalizes this anti-historiography by arguing for "shared identity" and "collective memory" that ground identity, collective and individual. Identity and collectivity have rightly been critiqued by literary theorists for their easy assumptions of a reductive, essentialist state, not to mention the political uses (usually authoritarian) to which such terms conform. Galeano well understands this critique, offering in its stead resistance to the logical extension of the critique, which suggests (equally reductively) that identity and collectivity are terms entirely empty of value or meaning. Implicit in the affirmation of shared, collective identity is the notion that what is lost to history as a function of the distortions caused by dominant culture is always recuperable if one is capable of "clawing" oneself out of the wind, reading the "thousand signs," remembering one's place in the construction of historical space and time:

> A thousand signs, a thousand reasons and arcana tell me that I am a small drop in a certain sea, a fistful of a certain soil, a brick of a certain house to be built: *the national culture, shared identity, collective memory, comes from history and returns to history unceasingly*, transfigured by the challenges and requirements of reality. Our identity lies in history, not in biology, and it is made by cultures, not by races; but it lies in *live* history. The present does not repeat the past; it contains it. But from what footsteps do we draw our direction? The dominant cultures distort history and lock it up in museums; our dominant classes, threatened, want an immutable world. (Galeano, "The Revolution as Revelation" 15)

Immutability, like apocalyptic, reduces the historical actant to a passive spectatorship, bound by the certainty that all action is futile because nothing changes, or by the certainty that if things change they do so at the risk of apocalyptic annihilation. Galeano utterly rejects both master narratives firmly embedded in traditional historiography and argues instead for the radical dissonance that recognizes how all people(s) can (do) potentially share in the construction of history, not as spectacle but as a lived process of transformation. For Galeano, the relations between history and repetition need thinking, not only for how historiography is itself predicated on a repeatable methodology that reinforces the narrative's claims to veracity, but also for how the repetition of historical narratives oppresses the capacity to think beyond what those narratives say: "repetition can easily be taken for fate" (Grandin 401).

> Does history repeat itself? Or are its repetitions only penance for those who are incapable of listening to it? No history is mute. No matter how much they burn it, break it, and lie about it, human history refuses to shut its mouth. Despite deafness and ig-

norance, the time that was continues to tick inside the time that is. *The right to re-member does not figure among the human rights consecrated by the United Nations, but now more than ever we must insist on it and act on it. Not to repeat the past but to keep it from being repeated.* Not to make us ventriloquists for the dead but to allow us to speak with voices that are not condemned to echo perpetually with stupidity and misfortune. When it's truly alive, memory doesn't contemplate history, it invites us to make it…A memory that's awake is contradictory, like us. It's never still, and it changes along with us. It was born to be not an anchor but a catapult. A port of de-parture, not of arrival. It doesn't turn away from nostalgia, but it prefers the dangers of hope. (*Upside Down* 210-11; our emphasis)

The (unrecognized) right to remember is also the right to be an active maker of history. Re-membrance facilitates hope, enacts contradiction. Memory is both then and now, nostalgia for the past and the present "danger" of a future to be made. Memory and the stories we tell about memory preserve the "time that was" in the "time that is," implicating both story-teller and audience in the collective vision co-created by acts of speaking and acts of listen-ing. The storyteller telling the story of memory here and now always embodies the potential to refigure official history through an act of making that is not ventriloquism or repetition when produced in the dissonant mode proposed by Galeano. Thus, history, such as it is, recognizes that presencing is always, paradoxically, a referent for disappearance, a metaphor for a supplement that demands the historian's ethical attention: "North American blacks, the most oppressed of peoples, created jazz, the freest of all musics. Don Quixote, the most errant of knights, was conceived in the confines of a prison…'*The military respects the consti-tution,*' says the Minister of Defense on the eve of the coup d'état" (*The Book of Embraces* 129).

Galeano proliferates examples of how official history's presences always point to rele-vant disappearances, arguing, in a familiar turn of speech, that "Past history is topsy-turvy because present history is upside down" (*We Say No* 261). A particularly telling comparison between historical presence and absence is made in Galeano's short anecdote about Teddy Roosevelt, the American president and national hero who argued that "War purifies the soul…and betters the human race. And for this, he was awarded the Nobel Peace Prize" (*We Say No* 261). Galeano compares Roosevelt's historical recognition with that received by Charles Drew, a "scientist whose research on the storage and transfusion of blood saved mil-lions of lives" and who served as the director of the American Red Cross. In 1942, this orga-nization "refused to use blood from African-American donors for transfusions. Drew, who was black, resigned." Galeano pertinently asks: "But who in the United States has heard of Charles Drew?" (*We Say No* 261). The recuperation (however partial) of that which has been disappeared enacts the dissonance that refashions ossified histories, betrayals that do little justice to the ineluctable richness of human experience. In the next section, we examine how specifically literary modes of analysis coincide with the creation of the dissonant histories that ultimately lead to the alternative possibilities upon whose threshold Galeano places his readership.

Dissonant History:
The Carnival of Desire and Loss

Is it possible to conceive a writing of carnival that addresses the celebratory potential of human community, a writing that *is* carnivalesque? How can the spectacle of the page articulate the spectacle of community releasing its collective experiences of desire, loss, joy, rebirth? Questions such as these haunt Galeano, whose texts address the historical vision of Latin American culture struggling with the spectres of desire and loss that define its collective narratives. Galeano writes toward carnival through chronicles of desire and loss. In so doing he offers, as we have already seen at some length, alternative histories, alternative representations, to the histories of stereotype and convention that have traditionally qualified the experience of the Americas. Carnival has been refashioned as an American popular cultural (and now academic) cliché. It defines the irrepressible, "primitive" spirit of Latin American culture, the unabashed eroticism, the celebration of body and movement in rhythmic dance music, the "quaintly" creative folklorism, the tribalism and cultism, the masks and floats, the disruption of the illusory order of society, the spiritual vitality that North America longs to possess in order to assimilate, refashion, and commodify. But it is the production and the widespread dissemination of such stereotypes that mark the processes of assimilation and destruction as already begun.

As a writer of dissonant histories, Galeano's perspective offers unique insights into the nature of the carnivalesque. In his terms carnival is *not* an expression of a collective forgetting in a brief-lived moment of misrule. Nor is it a passionate embrace with the nihilistic joy that emerges from such a forgetting. Instead, carnival—or, more precisely, carnivalesque writing—is an encounter with the phantasms of the disappeared (*los desaparecidos*)—it is restorative writing that celebrates the recuperative power of memory. Recording the desire and loss that constitute the hitherto unwritten historical narrative of the Americas, carnivalesque writing produces discordant, nonconformist alternatives to official narratives. It subverts oppression through the potent acts of naming and remembering that fracture the complicit silences of "official" history. Carnival, then: the writing of the spectacle of disappearance through the memorial acts by which those who have disappeared reappear, dancing in the very texts that defy and transfigure loss.

But carnival, too, as a vivid symbol of the way things could be as opposed to how they actually are:

> Dark skins, white wigs, crowns of lights, cloaks of silk and jewels: at the Rio de Janeiro carnival the starving dream together and for a while are Kings and Queens. For four days the most musical people in the world live out their collective delirium.

And on Ash Wednesday, at midday, the party is over. The police arrest anyone who stays in disguise. The poor take off their feathers and paint, rip off the visible masks, the masks that unmask, the masks of fleeting freedom, and put on different, invisible masks, negating the human face: the masks of routine, obedience and misery. Until the next carnival, the Queens go back to washing dishes and the Princes to sweeping the streets. (Galeano, "The Other Wall" 7)

Tactical Frivolity. José Guadalupe Posada, "A la cuerda los que quieran echar una maroma para caer parados (detalle)" ["Hop up to the tightrope whoever wants to perform a pirouette and land on their feet"—meaning "to climb on the bandwagon and perform a political balancing act (detail)"].

Registering the disappearances of history, how the "human face" is negated in the aftermath of carnival, is in Galeano's terms a key end of resistant histories.[18] How and why that disappearance has all but been evacuated from traditional history are the implicit questions Galeano asks of traditional historiographic methods. The ethical drive of such a passage not only resists dominant modes of shaping memory but also exposes a deep structure of hypocrisy and disadvantage. Carnivalesque writing attacks such structures through the voice of the *tlamatini*, the one who gives face to the faceless. Galeano does not name names in this passage, nor does he give specific narrative details. Instead, the structure of disappearance as founded on disadvantage ("routine, obedience, and misery") is foregrounded, as are the different ways in which masks (visible and invisible) operate in relation to carnival and the real.

But Galeano does violate the law of silence that governs the structure of disappearance. Carnivalesque play is always circumscribed by restrictions, not the least of which is the silence that is complicit with its containment. Hence, "collective delirium" and "disguise" are limited by police surveillance. The collective that registers alternative identities is returned to decentred fragments that ensure anonymity and disempowerment. But there are names to those who vanish into facelessness, and names to those who condemn them to this disappearance. The "incessant metaphors" of history *do* have material referents, the larger structures of disappearance and control referencing the specific circumstances and agencies of people caught in those structures. This is the lesson that carnival teaches, the incessant metaphor it enables.

The city that gives its name to carnival, Rio de Janeiro, is also the city of death, prostitution, and brutality for street children.[19] The phantom apparitions of the anonymous, masked carnival goers (condemned to return to their facelessness) reference the bodies and names of children disappeared in the carnival of death produced by an upside-down world. Here, murdered children become the incessant metaphor of history in which one form of facelessness references another.

Michel de Souza (06.01.87; 6 years old).

Marco Antonio C. de Farias (15.01.87; 15 years old).

Renata G. Mello (28.01.87; 2 years old).

Again, names forgotten by official history. A wall in Rio de Janeiro is covered in names such as these, the names of street children assassinated between January 1987 and September 1988 (Dimenstein 18): "In Rio de Janeiro alone, from January to July 1989, 184 children and adolescents were murdered" by death squads known without irony as *justiceiros* (the Portuguese adjective *justiceiro* suggests the somewhat contradictory qualities of being just, impartial, inflexible and severe; the Portuguese verb *justiçar* means "to execute"), often with the reason that their deaths are warranted because they have no future, often because being a *justiceiro* is financially rewarding since the killers are paid by businesses and others looking to "cleanse" the streets (20). In Rio de Janeiro, children abandoned in life are adopted by parents in death, who allow for an anonymous child's corpse to be buried *with* a name, *their* name: "'It is a sad irony, a macabre game. A boy who spent his life on his own gets a father only after he's dead,' comments Maria Tereza Moura, ex-coordinator of Rio de Janeiro's Street Children movement" (25).

Are the names of Michel, Marco, and Renata the masks for yet another form of faceless complicity with this carnival of death? The preposterous inversion is real: to be legally buried the system must recognize the faceless dead even if such a recognition is itself a profound masking of the real. A wall in Recife implores and asks: "Don't kill my kids. Who is to blame?" (Dimenstein 72). Again, the incessant metaphor of history. There is a history of responsibility for these horrors, a history of implication and complicity in the creation of a system that sanctions such cruelty. Names are to be named. Faces to be identified. Unwritten conversations to be imagined and recorded. As Mikhail Bakhtin, one of the key scholarly figures in the twentieth-century recuperation of carnival as a crucial metaphor of human reality, argues, "All peoples still have enormous spheres of unpublicized speech, nonexistent from the point of view of literary written language" (421). The absence of that unpublicized speech is not only literary but historical. Only a hybrid language that is neither one nor the other (literary or historical) can approximate the sound of that speech, a key theoretical underpinning to Galeano's writing strategies. Histories of choices made require explication, are deserving of memory. Bakhtin further suggests that "That which stands behind negation is by no means nothingness but the 'other side' of that which is denied, the carnivalesque upside down...the nonbeing of an object is its 'other face,' its inside out" (410). The other side, inside out, upside-down of facelessness, in other words, *has* a face—the other of the other.

But if the incessant metaphor of anonymity references structures that produce that anonymity, then the upside-down of carnival also references the potential for restitution of identity when that identity is recuperated in the collective possibility that carnivalesque delirium releases: as Bakhtin affirms, "Carnival celebrates the destruction of the old and the birth of the new world—the new year, the new spring, the new kingdom" (410). Bakhtin's words unwittingly reference the old world in the new, the carnival dimensions of post-conquest making that was born of destruction. Carnival, however, is not statically complicit with that structure since it suggests the endless possibility of overturning, of confronting that which is denied with its other face, a structure that Galeano consistently deploys in his dissonant history making. Carnival, in this latter sense, reveals the "opposition to the official world and all its prohibitions and limitations," a "game of negation" that "may also serve utopian tendencies" (Bakhtin 412). Bakhtin suggests a tense, libratory relation between the official and the unofficial, between the new world that is anti-carnivalesque and the yet-to-be-born world that celebrates the collective energies of negation and resistance. The point to inversion as a tool for framing historical circumstance in relation to how the "nonbeing of an object is its 'other face,' its inside out"—to how that facelessness remains to be recuperated within the limits of the writer's possible.

Similar analyses are to be found throughout Galeano's work, which takes note of how anonymity, nobodying, and othercide are systemic disappearances that destructure and vitiate the materials of history. The master narrative of the "someone" is preferred to that of the "nobody," with little or no consideration of the contextual structures that turn one person into a "someone," the other into a "nobody." The absence of regard for the ways in which these evaluations of identity presence are made suggests an arbitrary privileging of one master narrative over another as a function of power relations, not as a matter of the potential value of (and respect for) all memory. But Galeano, typically, takes this logic one step further by suggesting that even those who think of themselves as "someone" are profoundly deluded by structures that empty that identity of systemic meaning too. Where the collective integration that carnival enables is displaced by the fragmentary disconnectedness of the structures of everyday life, identity is impossible, except as an empty and delusional trope.

Consider the following two passages, the first of which describes the "nobody," the second of which describes "someone." Both operate out of an ironic literary mode that visualizes the "nobody" or the "someone" as abstract categories that essentially describe the same condition of historical anonymity. Both depict these figures in relation to a history from which they have been erased, an ironic mobilization of memory that effaces even as it exposes:

> The nobodies: nobody's children, owners of nothing. The nobodies: the no ones,
> the nobodied, running like rabbits, dying through life, screwed every which way.
> Who are not, but could be.
> Who don't speak languages, but dialects.
> Who don't have religions, but superstitions.
> Who don't create art, but handicrafts.
> Who don't have culture, but folklore.
> Who are not human beings, but human resources.
> Who do not have faces, but arms.
> Who do not have names, but numbers.
> Who do not appear in the history of the world, but in the police blotter of the local
> paper.
> The nobodies, who are not worth the bullet that kills them. (*The Book of Embraces*
> 73)

1969: Any City
Someone

On a corner, by a red light, someone swallows fire, someone washes windshields, someone sells Kleenex, chewing gum, little flags, and dolls that make pee-pee. Someone listens to the horoscope on the radio, pleased that the stars are concerned about him. Walking between the tall buildings, someone would like to buy silence or air, but doesn't have the cash. In a filthy barrio, amid swarms of flies above and armies of rats below, someone hires a woman for three minutes. In a whorehouse cell the raped becomes the rapist, better than making it with a donkey in the river. Someone talks to no one on the phone, after hanging up the receiver. Someone talks to no one in front of the TV set. Someone talks to no one in front of a one-armed bandit. Someone waters a pot of plastic flowers. Someone climbs on an empty bus, at dawn, and the bus stays empty. (*Century of the Wind* 204)

In each vignette, both "nobody" and "someone" are faceless and anonymous, yet they embody the multitude's experience of exclusion and alienation. Both texts play on the complicit irony between chronicler and reader, since we know that the emptying out of identity parodies the oppressors' blindness. The "nobody" and the "someone" are allegories of systemic obliterations of historical agency, parodic stereotypes that expose the lie of debased personhood while reclaiming the very agency that has supposedly been lost. Graffiti on a wall in Guelph, Ontario (written anonymously) produces this very effect of critique and reclamation of agency through the invocation of the "Nobody."

Vote for Nobody.
Nobody will keep election promises.
Nobody will listen to your concerns.
Nobody will help the poor & unemployed.
Nobody...cares!
If Nobody is elected, things will be better for everyone.
Nobody Tells the Truth.

Galeano's practice of naming people whose testimony he retrieves breaks with this ironic anonymity, and puts a face, as such, on experiences that official history excludes.

One possible source of the word "carnival" lies in the Medieval Latin *carnelevamen*, which signifies, quite literally, a taking away of flesh, disappearance incarnate, being nobodied. Another source lies in the Italian *carne*, thus the festival of flesh, the celebration that precedes the purgative fasting of Lent to mark the Christian biblical story of Christ's fast in the wilderness prior to his death and resurrection at Easter. Evidently, carnival marks potent intersections among death, the celebration of flesh, the movement toward spiritual resurrection, and absence. All of these figure in Galeano's writings as expressions of the experience of the Americas, an experience traditionally confined either to the sardine can of official history as told by the conquerors, or of history as an otherwise unwritten text, a tradition of silent forgetting and orgiastic disavowal.

In place of these narratives, Galeano, for whom "all memory is subversive" (*Open Veins* 308), proposes a carnival of memory. In such a carnival, the fragmentary dialogues of the dispossessed, the dead, the disappeared, the forgotten, and the living come together in celebration of the fact that "every act of destruction meets its response, sooner or later, in an act of creation" (*Open Veins* 308). Writing is thus a dialogic and creative act of carnival that memorializes the silent history of the Americas: "One writes in order to deflect death and strangle the specters that haunt us; but what one writes can be historically useful only when in some way it coincides with the need of the collectivity to achieve its identity" (*Days and Nights* 185).

Writing that has historical purpose, then, is polyphonic writing that enters into a dialogue (or heterologue) with collective identity and need. Such writing vents the communitarian spirit that infuses carnival with its collective vitality, its incarnation of a humanity always threatened or defined by loss, and the desire to void such a loss. Carnival coalesces the individual with the collective in a manner that sustains the identity of each. As such, it represents an idealized, perhaps utopic, version of human community that subverts—ideologically, politically, culturally—what Galeano calls the "system," that is, the state machine that wants no such coalescence because it threatens the reigning and pervasive structures of political, economic, and military oligarchy. Carnival, whether as a street or as a textual performance of social inversion, is always inherently political, an expression of competing views of the *polis* (the state) and the *politēs* (the citizen).

Hence, carnival, death, and desire are inseparable in Galeano's writing. He imagines his own death, for example, as communion with those who will collectively "tread" upon his tomb. The image is not morbid but carnivalesque since it expresses the continuity between life and death, community and the individual. And this, in the fragmentary narrative that Galeano writes, gives way to a memory of desire, the "first little kisses":

> Under which streets would I like to lie when I'm sent to die? Underneath whose treading? Whose footsteps would I like to hear forever?
>
> We waited for the summer, and in the summer party time, carnival.
>
> The eucalyptuses blossomed, Mars shone red in the sky, and the hot earth was warm with little toads.
>
> We roamed the quarries in search of good clay for mask making. We would knead the molds—pointed noses, bulging eyes—and dip them in plaster. We would shape the masks with wet newspaper and then Aunt Emma would help us paint them. We would hang an old pot around our necks and the masked orchestra would set out to wander around the carnival parade.
>
> Every neighborhood had a stage, sometimes two. Among the gigantic colored dolls the carnival groups sang at night.
>
> In the shadows under the stage, with the commotion above, the first little kisses happened. (*Days and Nights* 125-26)

The passage moves from death to desire, both occurring beneath the street or stage in which the "commotion" of carnival is enacted. Much of Galeano's writing emerges from moments of carnival contact. The result subverts traditional writing aesthetics that exclude the testimony of marginal voices. Galeano consistently expresses the desire to "return the word" to those who have been silenced or excluded, thus validating the power of writing to shape community, ethos, history, and identity.

The carnivalesque circulation of social energies is exemplified in dialogue. Words emerge from communitarian experience into the writer's vision, then return to the community transformed into hope and prophecy. Interlocution, as we have seen in our chapter on rights, is actively sought, discrepant engagements articulated. In *Days and Nights of Love and War*, street war (symbol of collective expression and oppression) is pitted against soul war (symbol of individual expression and oppression). Again, there is continuity between the collective and the individual that emerges from carnivalesque writing. Carnival is the meeting place of the individual with the collective, puts into action joy, the celebration of aliveness. And, necessarily, carnival inverts. Carnival is thus a "tactic and strategy of resistance" at the same time as it "is unyielding in its demand for participation" and in its explicit abolition or inversion of hierarchy (Jordan and Whitney 24-25). Galeano rejects melancholic self-involvement, the smothering passivity of grief, for the carnivalesque "courage" of joy, the potential that joy brings as an active and subversive force, a denial of nihilism. This is not to trivialize or diminish the suffering that Galeano chronicles, often in painful detail. Writing inevitably expresses loss and desire, but joy too, the celebratory sharing of belief in what it means to be human. This anti-apocalyptic, anti-nihilistic, anti-abject recuperation of the enacted force of resistant writing typifies Galeano as a carnivalesque writer. The pain of desire and loss can be memorialized in the multiple voices that celebrate the durability of human experience in the face of such pain. It is in this sense that the resistance embodied in expressions of carnival is also, as John Jordan and Jennifer Whitney argue, the "secret of joy" (24-25).

It is not surprising, then, that Galeano frequently resorts to images of collective memory, of embrace, of conflict, to validate such a positioning, especially in the myriad voices and telling anecdotes that he chronicles. For example, in *The Book of Embraces*, a brief segment on José Luis Castro, a local carpenter, and his father who has died and whose death is being celebrated at a wake, ends with an admonition: "'*The important thing is to laugh,*' the old man taught him, '*and to laugh together*'" (217). Death and loss provide an opportunity for communal remembrance and celebration. For Galeano, then, the continuity of decay and rebirth is most vividly embodied in such moments, moments that recall Marx's dictum that "In history, as in nature, decay is the laboratory of human life." Here, Galeano is very much in accord with Bakhtin, who suggests "Laughter and the material bodily element...as a degrading and regenerating principle" (79). Out of death a community of memory is born, a memory that invokes the power of laughter, the power of communitarian expression that restores and gives meaning to individual identity.

In a passage describing a trip to the market, again a symbol of communitarian exchange, Galeano writes:

The spices in the market are a world apart. They are minuscule and powerful. Meats unfailingly get excited and give off juices when penetrated by spices. We are always aware that if it had not been for spices we would not have been born in America and magic would have been lacking at our tables and in our dreams. After all, it was they who spurred on Christopher Columbus and Sinbad the Sailor. (*Days and Nights* 176)

The market locates sensuality, historical convergence, magic, dream, birth. All unite in Galeano's creative vision, which superimposes the diverse materials of experience in the carnival disorder and energy of the marketplace. Such a writing is recuperative, ever mindful of how identity can be breached and reconstituted by the sensual experience of disorder. The aggregate effect of a writing that persists in uncovering moments of loss and desire, of magic and dream, of birth and renewal, is to restore a version of history that is marked by the subjective identity of its maker. Instead of the Borgesian nightmare vision—"Now, the teaching of…harmonious history, full of stirring episodes, has obliterated the history which dominated my childhood. Now, in all memories, a fictitious past occupies the place of any other" (Borges 21)—Galeano proposes a chronicle of significances that are perpetually on the threshold of disappearance.

In the second of Franz Kafka's eight Blue Octavo Notebooks, Kafka suggests that "The history of the world, as it is written and handed down by word of mouth, often fails us completely; but man's intuitive capacity, though it often misleads, does lead, does not ever abandon one" (9). Galeano's work testifies both to the failures of history and to the dissonant insights the writer can restore to such failed histories. Writing celebrates the carnivalesque play of desire and loss, the redemptive acts of memory and imagination that restore the possibility of a dissonant history, unmade of false harmonies and fictitious memories promoted in official history's self-interest. Dissonant history always remains to be remade by the life forces and redemptive ethics to which carnival and carnivalesque writing attest.

Coda

We end with the African proverb brought to the Americas by slaves, which Galeano uses as the epigraph to the first volume of *Memory of Fire*: "The dry grass will set fire to the damp grass" (*Genesis* n.pag.). Returning to this epigraph later in his career, Galeano comments that it expresses an "ancient truth that we all have two memories. Individual memory is vulnerable to time and passion and, like us, condemned to die. Collective memory, like us, is destined to survive" (*We Say No* 262). The sense of an immanent collectivity that underpins Galeano's historical discourse is a radical challenge to narratives that imagine the individual as central to history or to theories that think of the subject "as originator" instead of "analyzing the subject as a variable and complex function of discourse" (Foucault, "What Is An Author" 118). Radical history restores the collective memory by divesting itself (within the limits of the possible) of principles of exclusion sanctioned by official history in the name of the individual who speaks for the "official." Hegel remarks in his *Philosophy of History* that "the state is the universal spiritual life, to which individuals by birth sustain a relation of confidence and habit, and in which they have their existence and reality" (104). The dissident historian condemns the discourse that underlies this affirmation with its totalitarian regard for the state as the "universal spiritual life," its regard for the individual as subsumed in this state-defined universality. The dissonant historian recognizes that such narratives are complicit with state interests that are not necessarily those of the community, a crucial distinction Galeano persistently affirms, and one we have elaborated upon earlier as part of our critique of rights discourse generally.

Radical history sets fire to stories that potentially restore community in the name of an ethics of solidarity that is also an ethics of remembering. Such an ethics exceeds (and critiques) the supposed autonomy of the state as universal (self-interested) arbiter of the individual's relations to others. The reinvention of the Americas, crucial as it is to Galeano's project as a writer, will involve the transmission of memories that restitute principles of community alien to the official histories that speak in the name of sovereign self-interest. History, in Raymond Williams's sense, "*teaches* or *shows* us most kinds of knowable past and almost every kind of imaginable future" (148). The lack of an imaginable future justifies the killing of street children in Brazil just as it justifies the master narrative of the triumphant end of history that condemns us to the world as it *is*, as it (in dominant fantasies) always *will*

be. But the death of the future is premature and a lie produced by discourses that seek to conform memory and story to that lie. We now turn to aspects of Galeano's work that invoke notions of alternative community, the world as it *could* be. These alternatives suggest an "imaginable future" that is a radical break with the "end" of history as a trope for the impossibility of change.

NOTES

1. The Araucanians, who include three distinct subgroups—the Huilliche, the Picunche, and the Mapuche—currently number over 300,000 people who live primarily in Chile and in Argentina. They have an extensive history of resistance to the conquest and by 1598 had eradicated most Spanish settlements south of the Bío-Bío River. Major rebellions against settler culture occurred in the eighteenth century and a war against white settlers in 1880-81 ended with the Araucanians' defeat. Galeano details some of the history of these resistances in *Genesis*; see especially 119-20, 127, and 128. We use the condensed and incomplete prose translation of Ercilla's *Araucana* by the Elizabethan statesman George Carew, which was probably done in the "late sixteenth or the early seventeenth century" (vii).

2. Galeano marks the dissemination of this wonder throughout Europe in a short vignette about Albrecht Dürer, the great German painter (1471-1528). Dürer, in Brussels in 1520, had a chance to examine the remnants of Cortés's booty (that had not been melted into gold ingots) from the conquest of Tenochtitlan. Galeano describes his reaction as follows: "These things must be emanations from the sun, like the men and women who made them in the remote land they inhabit: helmets and girdles, feathers, fans, dresses, cloaks, hunting gear, a gold sun and a silver moon, a blowgun, and other weapons of such beauty that they seem to have been made to revive their victims. The greatest draftsman of all the ages does not tire of staring at them" (*Genesis* 70).

3. While couched in terms of facilitating trade relations, Nebrija's insistence on the study of Castilian by neighbouring peoples as a diplomatic necessity is aligned with the overtly imperial imperative of subjugating the enemies of the faith: "I cierto assí es que no sola mente los enemigos de nuestra fe, que tienen ia necessidad de saber el lenguaje castellano, mas los vizcainos, navarros, franceses, italianos, y todos los otros que tienen algún trato y conversación en España y necessidad de nuestra lengua, si no vienen desde niños a la deprender por uso, podrán la más aina saber por esta mi obra" (102) [And it is certain that not only the enemies of our faith have the necessity of knowing our Castilian language, but also the Biscayans, Navarrese, French, Italians, and all others who have dealings and conversation with Spain need our language, should learn it in childhood, and can avail themselves of my work].

4. McClintock summarizes how
   The international monetary system set up at the Bretton Woods conference in 1944 excluded Africa (still colonized) and most of what is now called the Third World, and was designed to achieve two explicit objectives: the reconstruction of Europe after World War II, and the expansion and maintenance (especially after decolonization) of international trade in the interests of the colonial powers and America. The President of the World Bank and the deputy managing director are always American, while by tradition the managing director is European. (98)

5. The showdown included an extreme response from the Bolivian military: when martial law was declared on 8 April 1999, President Banzer imposed a state of siege involving "crack military units," army officers in civilian clothes firing pointblank into the crowds (Jorge Crespo, a 17-year-old, was killed and many others wounded), and the 80,000-strong protesters were labeled as drug traffickers (López Levy 17).

6. The degree to which the media exclude discussion of alternative social movements is discussed by Galeano in his interview with David Barsamian. Galeano briefly addresses the "popular movement in Mexico called El Barzón," largely unknown outside Mexico, which has grown into a movement of "more than one million persons" resisting "the pressures of Mexican banks" (9). Galeano sarcastically states that "when a delegation of El Barzón went to Washington, it was received by the vice president of the International Monetary Fund. I suppose this is such an important man he doesn't even speak to his wife, but he received El Barzón" (9).

7. Harlow's discussion of truth commissions argues that "A recording of facts and events, of abuses of individual lives and national histories, as well as an effort to correct an 'official record' that has systematically obscured those abuses, the writing of human rights draws by necessity on conventions of narrative, autobiography, and biography, of dramatic representation, and of discursive practices" ("Sappers in the Stacks" 182).

8. Here, we are referencing Theodor Adorno's comment that
   What the sadists in the camps foretold their victims, "Tomorrow you'll be wiggling skyward as smoke from this chimney," bespeaks *the indifference of each individual life that is the direction of history.* Even in

his formal freedom, the individual is as fungible and replaceable as he will be under the liquidators' boots. (362; our emphasis)

9. See also Galeano's extended analysis of the military coup in Brazil, which deposed Jango Goulart at the end of March 1964 ("Brazil: the Defeat and After" [1964]). Galeano concludes, long before Fukuyama's book was published, that "One cycle has been completed, possibly; the methods and the men will change. But the night of March 31st did not end history" (76).

10. For more on the "multitude-person," see Roa Bastos, especially 276-77. By contrast, the Mexican author Homero Aridjis writes about indigenes as alone in the midst of multitudes, a reference to historical conditions that alienate and isolate indigenous realities from official history. In a poem entitled "Imágenes Indias" [Indian Images], Aridjis states: the Indian "Nace solo, / come solo, / fornica solo, / defeca solo, / duerme solo, / envejece solo, / muere solo, / en medio de la multitud" (117) [is born alone, / eats alone, / fornicates alone, / defecates alone, / sleeps alone, / ages alone, / dies alone, / in the midst of multitudes].

11. The relevant passages from the Spanish version read as follows:
    El felice suceso, la vitoria,
    la fama y posesiones que adquirían
    los trujo a tal soberbia y vanagloria,
    que en mil leguas diez hombres no cabían,
    sin pasarles jamás por la memoria
    que en siete pies de tierra al fin habían
    de venir a caber sus hinchazones,
    su gloria vana y vanas pretensiones. (*La Araucana* 26)
    And:
    A Valdivia mirad, de pobre infante
    Si era poco el estado que tenía,
    Cincuenta mil vasallos que delante
    Le ofrecen doce marcos de oro al día:
    Esto y aun mucho más no era bastante,
    Y así la hambre allí lo detenía:
    Codicia fue ocasión de tanta guerra
    Y perdición total de aquesta tierra. (*La Araucana* 45)

12. The Ye'kuana are a river people whose territory covers approximately 30,000 square kilometres in the Venezuelan states of Amazonas and Bolívar (which include the Orinoco river). Their name means "people of the *curiara*," the canoe made from a hollowed-out tree trunk used to navigate the river systems along which they live: "ye" for wood, "ku" for water, and "ana" for people.

13. Mármol's story, told in a *testimonio* by Roque Dalton, the Salvadoran poet and revolutionary (who was assassinated in 1975 for his alleged collaboration with the CIA), centres on the *matanza* or massacre he witnessed in January 1932 in El Salvador, which involved a peasant uprising that was brutally suppressed by General Maximiliano Hernández Martínez (30,000 civilians were killed). Miraculously, Mármol, aged twenty-six, survived his own execution in 1932 by Martínez's firing squad, an incident recounted in gruesome detail in *Century of the Wind* (92).

14. According to Keith Slack, "these repressive regimes exchanged information on 'subversive' groups or individuals operating within their countries; and ultimately coordinated the detention, deportation, torture, and killing of political prisoners. In addition to this exchange of information and prisoners, Operation Condor also served as a source of international hit squads (such as the one that killed Letelier) that struck at enemies of the participating regimes—Argentina, Chile, Bolivia, Uruguay, Brazil, and Paraguay" (492). Slack's article examines the "Archive of Terror" discovered in 1992 by a "group of Paraguayan jurists, led by Judges José Augustín Fernández and Luis María Benítez Riera" (493).

15. Barbara Harlow, in *Resistance Literature*, details how the "demand on the part of critics and readers, against historical necessity, and through an appeal to universality, posterity and the human condition, is among those 'strategies of containment' that [Fredric] Jameson examined in his work *The Political Unconscious*" (17). Insofar as literary culture removes itself from the historical conditions that produce it (in

the name of universal truths about the human condition), it is complicit with the form of official history that is so tied to the kind of oblivion Galeano critiques.

16. Herodotus's response to cultural difference—"[which] expressed wonder at the strangeness of 'their' ways, [but] never denied their right to act and believe as they wished" (Pagden, *European Encounters* 183)—may be opposed to Aristotle's view that "the optimum condition for all mankind was some kind of mean of which European culture was the obvious instantiation" (183). But a historiography that grounds its master narrative in imperial conquest and war mitigates any such seemingly progressive position, because the right to act and believe as you wish is always potentially at the mercy of imperial force.

17. Palaversich elaborates that

> *Memoria del fuego* displays an impressive bibliography of approximately 1200 consulted sources, but when examined more carefully, it becomes evident that this "base documental rigurosa" [rigourous documentary base] consists of very heterogeneous sources. Besides the conventional historiographical documents such as chronicles and histories, the bibliography also includes nineteenth and twentieth century novels, various collections of poems and songs, ancient myths and legends as well as personal diaries and oral testimonies, all of which in their turn become bona fide documents given equal importance and legitimacy. ("Eduardo Galeano's *Memoria del fuego*" 142)

18. Carnival and resistance are closely intertwined, as Teresa Gisbert shows in her discussion of the *Tragedia del fin de Atahuallpa* [The Tragedy of the End of Atahualpa], the Inca leader executed by Pizarro in 1533: "The permanence of Amerindian culture can be seen in various artistic constructions that over the centuries have defied obliteration and loss of memory. Much has been written about the *Tragedia del fin de Atahuallpa*, which was edited by Jesús Lara and which is performed in Oruro [Bolivia] on Sunday morning during Carnival time" (661). The persistence of such memories in different forms, and their association with "Carnival time," may also be identified with writing practices that make use of carnival as a metaphor of resistance and of an inverted world. Such strategies are not limited to writing practices as the "Carnival Against Capital" direct actions have shown in recent demonstrations against globalization: absurdist actions like the launching of teddy bears from medieval catapults at the Americas Summit in 2001 in Québec City or the throwing of pies, cross-dressing, and other manifestations of "tactical frivolity" articulate forms of carnivalesque critique. When 50,000 Indian farmers staged a demonstration that involved a day of laughing outside the State Government offices in the southern state of Karnataka the government collapsed within the week (see Jordan and Whitney 25).

19. Galeano does not limit the narratives concerning the neglect of children to Rio de Janeiro; see *Upside Down* 235 for an evocative "window" on street children in Córdoba, Argentina. Also, in "To Be Like Them," an afterword to the devastating pictorial chronicle of maquiladora culture by Charles Bowden, Galeano states that "Street children practice private enterprise through crime, the only field open to them. Their only human rights are the right to rob and the right to die" (126). In the same essay Galeano notes how "between January and October 1990, the police murdered more than forty children in the streets of Guatemala City. The bodies of these children, beggar children, robber children, garbage-picking children, turned up without tongues, eyes, or ears, tossed in the dump" (128). For Galeano, state culture is responsible for such heinous crimes and, moreover, incites them: "In the 1986 Brazilian elections, Afanásio Jazadji won a seat in the state congress of São Paulo in one of the greatest landslides in Brazil's history. Jazadji earned his immense popularity on the radio. His program loudly defended the death squads and preached in favor of torture and the extermination of delinquents" (128). How so-called democratic, civil culture can produce ethical delinquency of such a magnitude is one of the significant historical dilemmas to which Galeano persistently directs his readers' attention.

Chapter 5

Imagining Elsewhere as Here:
Utopian Ideals, Communities of Resistance, and a
Time Beyond Infamy?

After all, community, the community-based mode of production and life, stubbornly heralds another possible America. This prophetic voice speaks from the most ancient of times, and still resounds despite five centuries of attempts to impose an obligatory silence. Community is the oldest and the most obstinate of all American traditions. As much as it pains those who decry socialism as a foreign notion, our deepest roots are in community: communal property, communal labor, shared lives, lives based on solidarity. Private property, on the other hand, a way of life and work based on greed and selfishness, is indeed an import, brought by the conquistadors since 1492. (Galeano, *We Say No* 263)

Writing That Conquers:
"New" Worlds, "Ideal" Commonwealths, and Other Colonial Fictions

 In this last chapter we will argue toward two convergent points that emerge from Galeano's writing of story and memory as they relate to the Americas. The first is that utopian constructs issuing from the European tradition, historical and literary, are deeply complicit with structures of conquest—what we call, echoing French historian Michel de Certeau, writing that conquers. Galeano does not necessarily recognize this, a symptom of the extent to which the utopianism associated with Sir Thomas More's famous fiction is pervasive as a trope for alternativism. Nonetheless, utopian thought recasts itself in the contemporary Latin American context, taking its inspiration from communitarian ethics instead of from idealized colonial practices of assimilative encounter. Second, and largely based on the kind of stories and memories invoked by Galeano, we argue that the post-conquest Americas have effectively become a space in which alternative communities have been limited and neutralized in the name of discovery and the "new world," now mutated into the "new world order." Galeano brings forth extensive and devastating evidence to this effect as the grounds for the necessity of reinventing the Americas via acts of memory and story that recuperate these neutralized resistances in the name of re-igniting memory as a trope for possibility and meaningful change. Both structures have foreclosed on the possibility of imagining a true elsewhere as here; as such, our argument deliberately shifts the grounds of thinking the no-place or good place of European utopia (*eutopia*) into a thinking of the elsewhere that is always potentially here.

Where we argue that Galeano's historical method of inscribing memory and telling stories in dissonant ways results in a potential reinvention of the Americas, obviously such a reinvention is far from a reality, much less thinkable as a homogeneous concept or even a political agenda shared by a majority of people. Galeano's writings, then, posit the question of what it means to produce an alternative history/story, writing practice/politics as an act of the imagination. And, as we argued at the end of our previous chapter, this act of the imagination, historical or otherwise, places the reader on a threshold that begs interrogation: Where am I now? Where is this elsewhere that could be here? What are its distinctive features? Where are others in relation to me? Where are others in relation to this elsewhere that I imagine? What must I do to move the imaginary of elsewhere into closer proximity to others and me? And: What conditions of reciprocal relations in a community of interest must be agreed upon in order to achieve meaningful change in the face of the historical injustices recounted by Galeano, in order to undo the deep structures of institutional and cultural learning that work against the possibility of imagining anything else but the given of the moment in which I (we) live? Like history, utopia is an allegory of crisis and power, a response to predecessor texts, and an interpretive writing praxis.

There is a significant (and largely unstudied) overlap between the ways in which utopic and colonial encounter narratives—what we designate as the key predecessor texts to utopian fictions—respond to otherness. The utopian response to encounter has had far-reaching consequences for how the Occident has addressed alterity and difference. The "no-place" of the "new" world depicted in early modern encounter literature both parallels and inverts the "no-place" of the "ideal" commonwealth outlined in utopian texts. The fiction of the "new" is overwritten and mirrored in the trope of the "ideal," thus enacting de Certeau's "*writing that conquers*...[in which the] New World [is used] as if it were a blank, 'savage' page on which Western desire will be written" (xxv). Simply put, utopia functions as an associative term for the "ideal," but that "ideal" is based upon (and emerges from) structures of empowerment first deployed in the formation of modernity through colonial conquest. Utopia recapitulates encounter. But it does so in terms that preclude encounter's otherness: that is, utopia produces a story of an otherness that is seemingly different but is in fact made over in the name of the self-same. Utopian fiction presents an alternative that is no alternative because it has been formed in the crucible of colonial imperatives that had given shape to early modern Europe's wealth and power—Europe's move, in Dusselian terms, from the periphery to the centre.

Utopian elsewhereness, in other words, is really "here and now." Under the pretense of being the nowhere that is a good place, European utopian fiction masks an agenda that promotes colonial imperatives related to reinforcing the power relations that allow for dominance and subordination. Utopianism, then, is a deceptive fictive structure complicit with foreclosing on the possibility of the centre thinking beyond itself through to its alterity. It is most emphatically *not* positioned as a discourse that thinks from the position of the other and therefore is highly troubled as a meaningful signifier for alternative thinking—the thinking of the elsewhereness of the other, the thinking of the other's potential for shaping alternatives to the present reality. Which is not to say that utopian narratives operate exclusively in this manner, nor that they cannot possibly contain a critique of their alignment either with dominant culture or hegemony. In this section we address early modern rationalist utopianism and will turn in the latter part of this chapter to (re)visionary utopianism in the contemporary context where alternative communities are not predicated on extant power structures. Instead, alternative communities oppose such structures by rediscovering what the conquest left undiscovered or covered over.

Colonialist utopianism naturalizes its own dystopianism, making palatable the facts of conquest and colonialism via a literary structure that suggests there is (almost) no alternative. Its invocation as a trope for change, then, is highly compromised and aligned with stasis (the Benjaminian position of the victor) in telling the story of encounter with difference. In what follows, we examine a range of encounter ("new" world) texts in relation to key early modern imaginings of an "ideal" commonwealth as an expression of utopianism. Galeano's take on Sir Thomas More's *Utopia* (1515/16), itself based on Amerigo Vespucci's (1451-1512) account of his "discovery" of "America" (or rather Vespucci's non-discovery of the self-same in a space of difference),[1] is a useful place to begin, if only for how it is symptomatic of a reading that early modern utopian fiction invites.

1515: Antwerp
Utopia

The New World adventures bring the taverns of this Flemish port to the boil. One summer night, on the waterfront, Thomas More meets or invents Rafael Hithloday, a sailor from Amerigo Vespucci's fleet, who says he has discovered the isle of Utopia off some coast of America.

The sailor relates that in Utopia neither money nor private property exists. There, scorn for gold and for superfluous consumption is encouraged, and no one dresses ostentatiously. Everybody gives the fruits of his work to the public stores and freely collects what he needs. The economy is planned. There is no hoarding, which is the son of fear, nor is hunger known. The people choose their prince and the people can depose him; they also elect the priests. The inhabitants of Utopia loathe war and its honors, although they fiercely defend their frontiers. They have a religion that does not offend reason and rejects useless mortifications and forcible conversions. The laws permit divorce but severely punish conjugal betrayals and oblige everyone to work six hours a day. Work and rest are shared; the table is shared. The community takes charge of children while their parents are busy. Sick people get privileged treatment; euthanasia avoids long, painful agonies. Gardens and orchards occupy most of the space, and music is heard wherever one goes. (*Genesis* 61)

The only source Galeano cites for this passage is a bilingual edition of *Utopia,* suggesting that the vignette is in fact a reading (an interpretation) by Galeano of More's text. It is unclear whether Galeano's reading accepts the positive description of Utopia at face value, or whether he chooses to ignore the parodic, cynical thrust of the text in order to highlight his own democratic practices and ideals. Crucial information is missing from the vignette that throws the reliability of the narrator, in whom Galeano seems to have placed his trust, into doubt. Raphael Hythloday, the sailor/narrator on whom More's fictional character in the story depends for the production of his own narrative (at second hand), uses a Greek pun in the construction of his surname, which means "skilled purveyor of nonsense." The in-joke—apparent only to the educated early modern humanists More is implicitly addressing (in Latin)—is that the narrator's tales are hardly to be trusted and that the society he describes, with all its echoes of encounter with indigenous America, is a fancy, a nonsensical impossibility. More structures the narrative at several removes from his own voice to mount a critique of monarchic practices in early modern Europe, even as the structure he uses for the critique is spoken largely in the voice of a "skilled purveyor of nonsense." Utopia is thus a self-limiting critique, based on a self-canceling structure. The attack on arrogant kingship is couched in nonsensical terms, a parody of the possible that ultimately results in *Utopia*'s tense balancing of the possible against the impossible, the hegemonic makers of sense against the non-hegemonic purveyors of nonsense.

Though it is beyond the scope of this present discussion to go into a detailed reading of *Utopia,* a few key moments are worth examination in order to outline the colonialist origins of a term whose significance is indeterminate enough to later free it from this context and to be recuperated to name an ethical horizon for imagining forms of communitarian existence (beyond infamy). First, More explicitly opens *Utopia* in relation to his own monarch "Henry VIII, the unconquered king of England" (the first words a reader encounters in the translation [3]). He then suggests to Raphael that he should show concern for "public affairs" by counseling "some great prince...for the springs of good and evil flow from the prince, over a whole nation, as from a lasting fountain" (8). Utopian discourse, in its inaugural moment, is always already political discourse disguised as fiction, even though, as Jameson argues, "the Utopian text is mostly nonnarrative and...somehow without a subject-position" (*The Jameson Reader* 384).[2] *Utopia* installs the fantasy of the absolute monarch as the source for nationhood in the powerful trope of the "lasting fountain." In other words, the structure in which utopian discourse operates is, from its inaugural appearance, aligned with structures of power, even if it represents itself as a critique or even a parody of a critique (which More could well have argued had he been charged with seditious writing) of those same structures. Deeply ambiguated by this form, which is also an ingenious rhetorical strategy for subverting any absolute reading position, More presents Hythloday with the opportunity to be useful in public affairs. But Hythloday responds to this admonition by suggesting that

> I have not that capacity that you fancy I have, so, if I had it, the public would not be one jot the better, when I had sacrificed my quiet to it. For most princes apply themselves more to affairs of war than to the useful arts of peace; and in these I neither have any knowledge, nor do I much desire it: they are generally more set on acquiring new kingdoms, right or wrong, than on governing well those they possess. (8)

Hythloday concludes his long reflection on the uselessness of attempting to change power structures by arguing, specifically in relation to England, that "though they willingly let go all the good things that were among those of former ages, yet if better things are proposed they cover themselves obstinately with this excuse of reverence to past times" (9). Thus, the preamble to *Utopia* is framed so as to reinforce the top-down relations of hegemon to subordinate (in the name of nation and the commonwealth) while at the same time suggesting that critique is pointless—a position that many so-called "realists" might take today.

In this sense, then, *Utopia* enshrines political stasis as recognition of *realpolitik*: this is the way it is and change is impossible. Though critique can be offered, it will not be heeded or it will be subject to severe restrictions. David Weil Baker, for example, states that "despite their practice of religious toleration, the Utopians are unwilling to allow the dissemination of any religious idea. The diversity of Utopian religious beliefs cannot all be expressed publicly. Thus, for instance, Utopians who do not believe in the afterlife cannot articulate those opinions...Rather, such opinions must be confined to an audience composed primarily of an elected and lettered sacerdocy" (74). The argument from past precedent will be used selectively to reinforce hegemonic practices in Utopians' own interests (even as those practices ignore or transform "good things" from the past). The reading problem *Utopia* presents at this juncture, and one no doubt that Galeano faced when addressing this text in *Memory of Fire*, is whether Hythloday is in fact purveying nonsense or whether his nonsense is reasonable. The former seems to be the case when Hythloday recounts his adventures *in* Utopia but not when he argues with More *about* civic duty. If this reading is correct (and it may well not be given the highly ambiguous structure More deploys), then *Utopia* becomes a self-canceling structure of critique. One critiques but it goes nowhere; one critiques obliquely (through parody or through convoluted narrative structures or through both) with little hope of real transformation to the "ideals" (such as they are) expressed in the text. *Utopia* can be read as a limited affirmation of the reality of the status quo, even as it presents a genealogy of the disappearance (or virtuality) of the critic's ability to present meaningful alternatives to the status quo. The latter are clearly impossibilities, with much in the actual description of Utopian customs to suggest an alliance between the structures being critiqued in early modern absolutism and the way in which Utopia is itself governed.

Though Utopians "detest war" (Baker 75) and seem to be religious libertarians, passages at the conclusion of the fiction throw both these aspects of enlightened politics into some doubt. Again, the politics of ambiguity are at stake in a narrative that addresses notions of encounter through its idealizations. The questions, though, are to what extent these ideals are genuinely brought forth as an act of political difference (by the skilled purveyor of nonsense) and to what extent these ideals are masks for a more insidious programme related to conforming difference to a state norm. Again, we are concerned here to show how apparent structures of political difference, alternative community making, work to support colonial logic based on homogeneity and self-sameness.[3] A crucial passage at the end of the narrative addresses how Utopians offer up solemn prayers to,

> ...God in a set form of words; and these are so composed, that whatsoever is pronounced by the whole assembly may be likewise applied by every man in particular to his own condition; in these they acknowledge God to be the author and governor of the world, and the fountain of all the good they receive, and therefore offer up to Him their thanksgiving; and in particular bless Him for His goodness in ordering it so, that they are born under the happiest government in the world, and are of a religion which they hope is the truest of all others...*But if their government is the best, and their religion the truest, then they pray that He may fortify them in it, and bring all the world both to the same rules of life, and to the same opinions concerning Himself.* (95; our emphasis)

The passage reiterates that this view of Utopian government as the "best" is only so if God ordains it to be so, and that Utopians would be amenable to a better form of religion or government if God were to direct them to either. What is curious is how this represents a sort of escape clause against any charge of totalitarian thinking on the part of the Utopians—if there's a better way and God ordains it, so be it. But what appears to be an escape clause is in fact a reinforcement of the principle of a metaphysical being imposing a rule of order on humanity in the name of "His" superior form of knowing. This is precisely the principle on which early modern absolutism was founded. The king as medium between the commonwealth and the divine was empowered to speak in the name of God in order to achieve political ends. Moreover, the passage clearly creates a form of thinking governmentality that suggests a hierarchy, from best to worst, without thinking the possibility of alternatives to this hierarchy. Effectively, difference is eradicated in the name of the "happiest government in the world." And the justification for colonial power is clearly invoked in the last phrase quoted above.

The colonial logic of such a passage is clear. If we are of the opinion that our form of government is superior, and moreover authorized by the Christian God—that most elusive transcendental signifier—then we are fully authorized to "bring all the world to the same rules of life" and "to the same opinions concerning Himself." This formulation recapitulates the logic behind the *Requerimiento*, the odious document read by conquistadors in the name of God, the Catholic Church, and the Castilian crown. And it recapitulates the missionary logic behind Christianizing indigenous populations and imposing the so-called rule of law upon them in the post-conquest period. A telling passage from Bernal Díaz's *The Conquest of New Spain* lets slip that "Whilst we [the conquistadors] were fighting the Indians, the priest González took possession of the chests, the idols, and the gold, and carried them to the ship. In the skirmish we captured two Indians, who when they were afterwards baptized received the names of Julian and Melchior. Both were cross-eyed" (19-20). Theft in the name of God, kidnapping, and a jibe at physical imperfection: Díaz's conquistadors are empowered to do so in the name of God, in the name of possession to which they are entitled by virtue of their religious and military superiority. Little wonder that after the prayerful solemnities described in the passage from *Utopia* cited above, the Utopians go off to "spend the rest of the day in diversion or military exercises" (95), in direct contradiction of their apparent aversion to war. Also, little noted in this last passage is the fact that "diversion" requires leisure, and that leisure is itself a product of the accumulation of capital that was enabled by colonization. Galeano's distance from such a positioning in his take on *Utopia* is symptomatic of the extent to which this makeover structure—in which difference eventually leads to the self-same—has been ignored in utopian fiction as a response to (and justification of) encounter narratives of colonial power.

Another passage in *Utopia* makes clear the Utopians' take on colonial relations and encounter. When over-population threatens, the Utopians draw

> ...a number of their citizens out of the several towns, and send them over to the neighboring continent; where, if they find that the inhabitants have more soil than they can well cultivate, they fix a colony, taking the inhabitants into their society, if they are willing to live with them...But if the natives refuse to conform themselves to their [the Utopians'] laws, they drive them out of those bounds which they mark out for themselves, and use force if they resist. (45)

Conscription to colonize followed by the fixing of a colony in a neighbouring continent, and the "taking in" (assimilation) of its inhabitants. Here, refusal to conform produces expulsion of the native inhabitants followed by the use of force if resistance is met. Nothing could more clearly summarize the colonial logic used by Europeans in their encounter with the Americas. "Alter the native" rather than "alternative" was the primary mode of colonial encounter then, an aspect of encounter that Galeano persistently exposes and critiques: "At first, pillage and 'othercide' were carried out in the name of God in heaven. Now [they are] done in the name of the god of Progress" (*We Say No* 303). The colonial makeover depends on assimilative policies in which force is justifiable, as is expulsion, a logic that anticipates the indigenous removals in the United States in the nineteenth century, not to mention the ongoing justification of settler colonies' displacement of indigenous populations from the inception of the history of post-conquest America. As if this were not enough, utopian imperialism is predicated on an evaluation "that the inhabitants have more soil than they can well cultivate" rather than on an evaluation of whether or not the inhabitants of the neighbouring continent desire the presence of the Utopians. Read in light of the Utopians' use of slavery and mercenaries (67, 79) and of their being a creditor nation ("For besides the wealth that they have among them at home, they have a vast treasure abroad, many nations round them being deep in their debt" [78]), the fantasy of utopian difference from colonial power structures is a textual sleight of hand that More fabricates. A key passage on slavery in *Utopia* is one of the few places in the text where More overtly slips up and exposes a cynical agenda with less than ethical behaviour by the Utopians:

> The slaves among them are only such as are condemned to that state of life for the commission of some crime, *or, which is more common, such as their merchants find condemned to die in those parts to which they trade, whom they sometimes redeem at low rates; and in other places have them for nothing.* They are kept at perpetual labor, and are always chained, but with this difference, that their own natives are treated much worse than others. (67; our emphasis)

Slavery *is* practiced in Utopia. Further, slaves are procured from criminals (which assumes a "just" and equitable legal system) or, more importantly, from traders who buy death-row prisoners "at low rates" or who, better yet, "have them for nothing." The full passage articulates an ethical positioning that appears to be enlightened ("They do not make slaves of prisoners of war, except those that are taken in battle; nor of the sons of their slaves, nor of those of other nations" [67]) but is most emphatically *not*. The death penalty becomes an excuse to acquire free and "perpetual labor," while distinctions of treatment are used to demean. So the apparent restrictions on slavery merely disguise a structure that permits slavery (there is no larger attack on the actual institution of slavery in *Utopia*) that is perfectly coincident with the kinds of arguments we have already discussed in relation to the School of Salamanca. In short, in *Utopia* the other is a commodity to be treated in conformity with one's own norms and standards—and there is no space for difference from this process of colonial assimilation. Mimicking this logic is Utopia's spatial location in proximity to the American continent, "but separated from it by a man-made channel built on the instructions of Utopus, the conqueror of the territory" (Goodwin and Taylor 142). In other words, Utopia's spatial difference comes of its own experience of conquest, which produces the channel, at the same time as its proximity signals its potential non-difference. The symbolic cut of the channel allows Utopians to think themselves differentiated, which in turn authorizes the establishment of their own cultural norms as those to be imposed on all other groups, a radical fantasy of total empowerment over the encounter with difference that is a familiar allegory of colonization. For instance, a document from the *General Archives of the Indies* entitled "Against Those Who Deprecate or Contradict the Bull and Decree of Pope Alexander VI," which authorized the subjugation of the Indies, clearly articulates that the encounter with difference is to be made only on the colonists' terms: "And if they say that, although the conquest is just, it should be abandoned because of all the evil and the injuries done because of it to the barbarians, to this it is already responded and proved that the benefit from this conquest, spiritual as well as temporal, is far greater than the damage done to them" (Jara and Spadaccini, *1492-1992* 420). This sort of cost-benefit analysis is typical for how it relies on measures defined by the invader culture with little or no recognition of the evaluative measures that indigenous cultures might apply to the same analysis.

The penultimate passage in *Utopia* reinforces the logic of making all over into the same, a fantasy of absolute empowerment that echoes the notion of the end of history we have already explored in the previous chapter. In that view, the new world order of globalitarianism supplants any alternatives to (differences from) it with its own implacable logic. All seek to imitate it in the name of a commotionless world given over to consumption and amnesia:

> And therefore I am glad that the Utopians have fallen upon this form of government, in which I wish that all the world could be so wise as to imitate them; for they have indeed laid down such a scheme and foundation of policy, that as men live happily under it, so it is like to be of great continuance; for they having rooted out of the minds of their peoples all the seeds both of ambition and faction, there is no danger of any commotion at home; which alone has been the ruin of many States that seemed otherwise to be well secured. (98)

Again, a scheme and foundation of policy in which a docile citizenry happily goes on its way masks the fear of disorder and ruin of the state. The fact that the Utopians find it necessary to root "out of the minds of their peoples all the seeds both of ambition and faction" suggests little acceptance for difference, little ability to think of alternatives to the current state of affairs. In this view, stasis guarantees state harmony even as it eradicates difference.

Utopia ends with More dismissing the absurdity of how the Utopians make war, their notions of religion, and their conception of communal life without money:

> When Raphael had thus made an end of speaking, though many things occurred to me, both concerning the manners and laws of that people, that seemed very absurd,

as well in their way of making war, as in their notions of religion and divine matters; together with several other particulars, but chiefly what seemed the foundation of all the rest, their living in common, without the use of money, by which all nobility, magnificence, splendor, and majesty, which, according to the common opinion, are the true ornaments of a nation, would be quite taken away. (98-99)

This closural disagreement (between More and Hythloday in which More gets the last word) is not to be set aside as an empty rhetorical move, but rather one that reinforces that what is "good" about the Utopians is not worth attending to ("seemed very absurd"), while what is "bad" (as in the reading we have just given in which homogeneity and proselytization are virtues to be sought and imposed "on all the world") remains uncritiqued—a crafty spider in the convoluted web of this text. The fact that *Utopia* was written shortly after the "discovery" and that it obviously makes use of discovery narrative structures and details, linking it in particular with Vespucci (who gave his name to the Americas), is no coincidence. The sin against nobility of "living in common, without the use of money" is the perceived sin of the Americas, one that the conquistadors sought to eradicate expeditiously.

An enormous historical irony addressed by Galeano is that More's utopian society actually *did* form the basis of an attempt at alternative community directed by Vasco de Quiroga, an Audiencia judge who later became the bishop of Michoacán, Mexico. Quiroga "had arrived in Mexico [in] 1530 and quickly developed collective work farms, hospitals and asylums, public granaries and warehouses, work schedules, and small home crafts" (Baptiste 10).[4] Galeano describes the attempt at utopian community in the following way:

> Primitive Christianity, primitive communism: the bishop of Michoacán draws up ordinances for his evangelical communities. He was inspired in founding them by the *Utopia* of Thomas More, by the biblical prophets, and by the ancient traditions of America's Indians.
>
> The communities created by Vasco de Quiroga, where no one is master of anyone or anything and neither hunger nor money is known, will not multiply throughout Mexico as he wished. The Council of the Indies will never take the foolish bishop's projects seriously nor even glance at the books that he obstinately recommends. But here utopia has returned to America, where it originated. Thomas More's chimera has been incarnated in the small communal world of Michoacán; and in times to come the Indians here will remember Vasco de Quiroga as their own—*the dreamer who riveted his eyes on a hallucination to see beyond the time of infamy.* (*Genesis* 132; our emphasis)

Here, Galeano persists in his reading of More's utopian society as an ideal world, though already it has been turned into a hybrid creature, a mestizo form of social organization that ironically incarnates the sources of More's fiction in encounter narratives. The point, moreover, is that even European culture is incapable of instituting its own view of utopia in any meaningful way. And the indigenous population, not in need of such an imposition, is still capable of understanding Quiroga's vision of a time beyond infamy, thus suggesting their capacity to enter into meaningful dialogue about the desired (ideal) forms given to human community.

Further examples of the relationship between utopian fiction and encounter narratives are to be found spread through any number of early modern utopian fictions, texts that certainly deserve a full study in their own right. For our purposes here, however, we wish to examine briefly one later version of utopian fiction that enumerates similar patterns, if only to show that instead of transforming itself, the genre of utopian writing consolidated its position as an alternative space of (generally) unrecognized self-sameness. Margaret Cavendish's *The Description of a New World, called The Blazing World* (1666) explicitly makes the connection between "discovery" and the utopia she describes, the newness of America being transposed onto Cavendish's "New Blazing World" (121). The prefatory poem to the fiction, written by Cavendish's husband, William Cavendish, Marquis and later Duke of Newcastle, compares Columbus's having "Found a new World (America 'tis named: / Now this new World was found, it was not made" [121]) with Cavendish's own power of fabrication: "But your creating fancy, thought it fit / To make your world of Nothing, but pure Wit" (121). From the start, America's "discovery" is the source of the ability to be creative (to "make"), in William Cavendish's highly Eurocentric terms, a diminishment of how America itself was constructed as an imaginary space of finding, one not already made by others. America allegorizes being found (and therefore acted upon), whereas Margaret Cavendish, as an exemplar of civil European culture, exemplifies the capacity to make a "World of Nothing," the capacity to act upon nothing with something. How this structure reinforces colonial relations of relative power and disempowerment is obvious; this structure persists throughout Cavendish's utopian fiction.

Though the details of Cavendish's utopia differ from those in More's, similarities abound in relation to fantasies of colonial empowerment. One aspect of this fantasy entails the notion of a homogeneous culture with a familiar disposition: "the Duchess answered…[that] she would advise her Majesty [of the Blazing World] to introduce the same form of government again, which had been before; that is, to have but one sovereign, one religion, one law, and one language, so that all the world might be but one united family, without divisions; nay, like God, and his blessed saints and angels" (201). Like More, fantasies of state and sovereign power are intertwined with divine authorization, here not so subtly achieved through simile. Encounter narratives are full of this sort of gesture, in which divine authority is used to envision a unified world where difference has been obliterated. A particularly sobering example occurs in Fray Diego Durán's account of the last days of Tenochtitlan after Hernan Cortés had definitively defeated Moctezuma. The chapter heading, with no irony, "treats of how Don Hernán Cortés, Marqués del Valle, after having con-

quered Mexico-Tenochtitlan left that city in good order" (558), the actual chapter going on
to describe how "after the city had been leveled" Cortés "saw to it that the natives were in-
structed in the things of the faith. He indicated sites where churches were to be built, where
crosses and images were to be set up, and he ordered that the Indians be taught the doctrines
of our Holy Catholic faith" (559).[5] This occurs after the preceding chapter closes with the
image of "over forty thousand men and women" dead who, "rather than fall into the hands
of the Spaniards, knowing of the cruel death they could meet at the hands of those men and
their Indian allies, threw themselves and their children into the canals. The stench of the
corpses was so great that, even though bodies were continually disposed of outside the city,
many were left and the evil smell continued for a long time" (557).

   Despite the stench of the dead and its having been razed, the city is deemed in good
order because of the institution of religious symbols and teachings that will make over difference into the self-same. The explicit authority for this carnage comes in the following
passage, which describes how Cortés's actions are endorsed by the Virgin Mary, as well as by
no less than the patron saint of Spain, Santiago,[6] both of whom appear on the scene of the
crime:

> Valiant Don Hernán Cortés conquered Mexico-Tenochtitlan on the feast of Saint
> Hippolytus, three days before the Assumption of the Most Blessed Virgin, Our
> Lady. It is said that She appeared during the conquest in order to aid the Spaniards.
> It is also said that the glorious patron of Spain, Santiago [or Saint James], appeared
> also, just the same as his image is now seen in the church of Tlatelolco. (558)[7]

Colonial encounter narratives frequently modulate into narratives of destruction and assimilation in the name of a divinely sanctioned order. This pattern is replicated in Cavendish's
utopian fiction (and hinted at in More's *Utopia*), which imagines heavenly order (itself an
illusion, a rhetorical sleight of hand) to be the appropriate basis for earthly order.

   Where Cavendish deviates significantly from More is in the explicit transformation of
the Blazing World into a military and imperial force driven by the intent "to make you the
most powerful nation of this world" and to "destroy all your enemies" (210).[8] The promised
land is to be achieved by force. The language in the passage where this intent is expressed reiterates the fantasies of imperial paranoia, destruction, and domination with the narrator
stating that the Empress will not "return into the Blazing World, until she had forced all the
rest of that world to submit to that same nation" (211). Submission to the space of utopia
signals submission to an absolute monarchic government made over as the homogeneous,
divinely authorized space of the Blazing World's utopia, again seeming difference masking
the self-same. Literally and figuratively, this form of utopian narrative is writing that conquers. As such, it tells the story of conquest as an allegory linking the utopianism of the
Blazing World with the ideal commonwealth (England), which turns out to be nothing
more than a system of power relations that is a replica of what is *always already* in place.

Cavendish's Blazing World achieves its victory using submarine-like vessels ("ships that could swim under water" [205]) and "fire-stones" that ignite in water (211). The means of victory clearly vindicates the alliance between scientific and military technology that was not only characteristic of encounter narratives but of succeeding structures of capital and policy that used the wealth of the "new" world to produce the egregiously militaristic nation-states of modernity.

And so, with Cavendish as with More, utopia reinstates powerful narratives of control and subordination even as these narratives give the appearance of providing an alternative ideological space. Our point in relation to Galeano is that he largely eschews utopianism of this sort (this in spite of his reading of *Utopia* that we discuss above) for the very alternative forms of storytelling and documentation that restitute lost memories. Galeano's project is not to think of "no-place" as a "good place"; rather, he asserts that elsewhere is here, that the possibility of thinking alternatives does not need to be located in a fictive utopian otherworld that is nowhere or elsewhere. In fact, material alternatives (political, historical, cultural) are already deeply embedded in the history of the Americas, needing restitution and recuperation from the historical amnesia that has displaced them, processes that radically change the use of the term "utopia" in the contemporary Latin American context. When translated through a communitarian ethics arising from the particular space and experience of colonized Latin America, utopianism comes to mean a thinking through the materials of lost or disavowed histories in the name of story and memory, reinvention and critique, resistance and transformation.

"Burn Even the Memory of It":
From *Utopia* to Communities of Resistance

Colonialist utopianism relies on fantasies of otherness that replicate the disposition of power relations born of colonial encounter narratives in which the other is "converted" into the image of the colonizer. Conversion is a crucial colonial trope (as it is in utopian fiction), in which seemingly empty gestures of assimilation produce the illusion of a cultural makeover.[9] Rather than pursue this route as a viable way of thinking about alternatives, Galeano's writing practices recuperate historical materials that show that alternatives have existed and continue to exist in spite of enormous state pressures to eradicate or limit them. Instead of static utopias comfortably aligned with state interests, then, Galeano chronicles active communities of resistance, suggesting that their extraordinarily marginal place in official history is inversely proportional to the potential for transformation they embody. The notion of community, to which we now turn, is specifically linked by Galeano to an official culture that criminalizes alternative forms of human interaction that resist state practices or bypass them altogether. A long history of this struggle is enacted in the Americas, which in Galeano's conception effectively become the battleground over how to define community in opposition to the nation-state and the forms of governmentality that such a notion of community produces. It is important to distinguish Galeano's views from the misnomer of community as a signifier for power relations structured in the name of exploitative self-interest. Such a debased notion of community can be found at either the national or the local level, as June Nash has shown in her anthropological fieldwork in Chiapas. There she found that "The ideology of corporate community founded in the rituals carried out by brotherhoods responsible for each of the saints recognized in the community continues to motivate behavior, but now in a system of class stratification in which the exploiters exist among the indigenous populations [of Chiapas]" (16). Local community is vitiated by cor-porate structures in which *caciques* [traditional leaders] manipulate *ejidos* [small plots of land allotted to families as a function of land reform] in the name of self-interest (and often at the expense of indigenous populations who are forced to move [Nash 16]). Galeano ar-gues for an altogether different notion of community, one that is processual, based on non-exploitative principles that look beyond narrow perspectives of self-interest, that recu-perates indigenous and other alternative visions of community (many of which have been obliterated from official history), and that seeks to establish the well-being of all its mem-bers in a just, equitable, and ethical way.

When the Digger colony was founded on 1 April 1649 and attempted to establish a commune on Saint George's Hill, Surrey (England) based on the collective cultivation of the common land, it was brutally repressed by the very forces that had launched an attack on the English monarchy that would culminate in the beheading of Charles I. In his *Selected Writings*, Gerrard Winstanley imagines a world in which "the earth should be restored and become a common Treasurie for all mankind" (53) and articulates a vision of "True Reli-gion" whose aim is "To make restitution of the Earth, which hath been taken and held from the Common people, by the power of Conquests formerly, and so *set the oppressed free*" (81).[10] For expressing such radical ideas (in the midst of a revolution), the Diggers were sub-jected to multiple abuses, including repeated imprisonment, houses pulled down, farming implements destroyed, animals kidnapped or hurt, beatings (including a memorable inci-dent in which they were beaten by "*men in women's apparel*"), and fields of corn destroyed (96-97)—all this for the crime of community and its explicit critique of property. Galeano describes an extraordinarily violent response (as facilitated by military technologies) to an-other community based on similar principles, this time in Brazil in 1937:

1937: Cariri Valley
The Crime of Community

From planes they bomb and machinegun them. On the ground, they cut their throats, burn them alive, crucify them. Forty years after it wiped out the community of Canudos, the Brazilian army does the same to Caldeirão, verdant island in the northeast, and for the same crime—denying the principle of private property.

In Caldeirão nothing belonged to anyone: neither textile looms, nor brick ovens, nor the sea of cornfields around the village, nor the snowy immensity of cotton fields beyond. The owners were everyone and no one, and there were no naked or hungry. The needy had formed this community at the call of the Holy Cross of the Desert, which saintly José Lourenço, desert pilgrim, had carried there on his shoulder. The Virgin Mary had chosen both the spot for the cross and the holy man to bring it. Where he stuck in the cross, water flowed continuously.

According to the newspapers of distant cities, this squalid holy man is the prosperous sultan of a harem of eleven thousand virgins; and if that were not enough, also an agent of Moscow with a concealed arsenal in his granaries.

Of the community of Caldeirão nothing and no one is left. The colt Trancelim, which only the holy man mounted, flees into the stony mountains. In vain it seeks some shrub offering shade under this infernal sun. (*Century of the Wind* 108-09)

Not only does Caldeirão represent an attack on private property, it also usurps that symbol of conquest, the Virgin Mary, who as we have seen earlier sanctions the destruction and brutalization of the Mexica in Tenochtitlan but who now also becomes the source from which this community's origins (and water) flow. The destruction of Caldeirão is justified by a trumped-up charge of being an "agent of Moscow" and the implausible notion that the dispossessed stockpile arms (in addition to growing corn and cotton). And despite the destruction, the example proves that recent history has produced material examples of people who gather into communities based on real alternatives to the nation-state.

Communities such as these only threaten insofar as they pose the potential to supercede the nation-state with another form of communal organization, one that does away with the underlying premises of the nation-state in the name of different forms of human solidarity. The passage conveys both the risk of imminent destruction that the people who form these communities undertake, but also and perhaps most importantly the fact that people do undertake to explore alternatives in real and substantial ways. Like the situation we discussed earlier in this book involving the Oklahoma Cherokee who in the nineteenth century founded, despite extreme privation, a successful alternative community based on egalitarian principles of non-ownership, Caldeirão restitutes the memory of the potential to transform—even as it also signals the incapacity of the nation-state's violent self-interest to allow for such transformations.[11] Galeano's rhetorical strategy here is especially effective: "Look at how these communities actually existed. Look at how they were brutally destroyed for the crime of expressing themselves differently. What meaning can democracy have in the face of such examples?" The latter question is especially pertinent in Galeano's case because the multiple examples of alternative community-making that he recounts are almost always counterposed as seeming threats to democracy, though the message is clearly that democracy threatens itself in how it deals with alternative forms of community-making:

Democracy is not what it is but what it appears to be. Ours is a culture of packaging. The packaging culture holds the contents in contempt...Slavery has supposedly been outlawed for a century, but a third of Brazil's workers earn little more than a dollar a day and the social pyramid is white at the peak and black at the base: the richest are the whitest, and the poorest the blackest...

For something to not exist, one merely has to decree that it does not exist...the Guatemalan dictator Manuel Estrada Cabrera decreed in 1902 that all of the volcanoes were dormant, while violent eruptions from the Santa María volcano were burying more than a hundred villages in the vicinity of Quetzaltenango under avalanches of lava and mud. The Congress of Columbia enacted a law in 1905 determining that no Indians lived in San Andrés de Sotavento and other districts where oil gushers had suddenly sprouted; the Indians living there were thus made illegal, and the oil companies could kill them with impunity and seize their lands. (*We Say No* 206)

Even communities that exist within the confines of the nation-state are not immune from extinction should they be deemed expendable or non-existent.[12] And government decrees that pervert reality are a sad legacy of the sovereign state, which fantasizes about pure utopian spaces in which sovereignty goes unchallenged.

Examples such as Caldeirão are proliferated throughout Galeano's work, showing the range and persistence with which such communities have sought to find expression.[13] Their marginalization from official history as a "crime" underlines alternative communities' symbolic potency and their eradication signals their profound difference from the kinds of utopian fiction we discussed earlier. Utopias always survive—a fantasy of their own making. In the case of the alternative communities portrayed by Galeano, they always disappear under brutal circumstances, their disappearance paradoxically signaling the extent to which they persist in the material world. Alternative communities of resistance are real because they are destroyed. Fictional utopian communities are unreal because they fantasize about an illusory survival in a perfect state that is completely unreal. Contrarily, the source of real alternatives to human community does not emerge from philosopher kings speaking the language of civilization but from the disenfranchised, oppressed, and marginalized. In the case of women, for instance, Galeano notes how "No mention is made—even in passing—of certain black and Indian captains, women who gave a tremendous beating to the colonial troops long before the wars of independence. There is one honorable exception to this law of silence: recently Jamaica recognized Nanny as a national heroine. Two and a half centuries ago, Nanny—a fierce slave, half woman, half goddess—led the Windward maroons to freedom, leaving the British army defeated and humiliated" (*We Say No* 260).[14]

Galeano also tells the story of Palmares, a community of villages founded in Brazil by escaped black slaves that flourished in the seventeenth century:

On some nights when there is lightning, the incandescent crest of this mountain range can be seen from the Alagoas coast. In its foothills the Portuguese have exterminated the Caeté Indians, whom the pope had excommunicated in perpetuity for eating the first Brazilian bishop; and this is where fugitive black slaves have found refuge, for the last many years, in the hidden villages of Palmares.

Each community is a fortress. Beyond the high wooden palisades and the pointed-stake traps lie vast planted fields...The blacks of Palmares eat much more and better than the people of the coast, where all-devouring sugar-cane, produced for Europe, usurps all of everyone's time and space.

As in Angola, the palm is king in these black communities: with its fiber they weave clothing, baskets, and fans; the fronds serve as roof and bed; from the fruit, the flesh is eaten, wine is made, and oil for lighting is extracted; from the husk, cooking fat and smoking pipes are made. As in Angola, the chiefs perform the noble office of blacksmith, and the forge occupies the place of honor in the plaza where the people have their assemblies.

But Angola is multiple; still more Africa as a whole. The Palmarians come from a thousand regions and a thousand languages. Their only common tongue is the one heard from the mouths of the masters, accompanying lash-delivered orders on slave ships and in canefields...

Since the Dutch were expelled from Pernambuco, the Portuguese have launched more than twenty military expeditions against this land of the free. An informant writes from Brazil to Lisbon: *Our army, which could tame the pride of Holland, has produced no result against those barbarians on its many and frequent incursions into Palmares...*

The Dutch had no better luck. Its expeditions, too, were without glory. Both Dutch and Portuguese have burned down empty villages and gotten lost in the thickets, turning this way and that like madmen in the violent rains. Both have made war against a shadow, a shadow that bites and runs; and each time they have claimed victory. Neither has succeeded in crushing Palmares nor in stopping the flight of slaves who leave King Sugar and his court without labor, although the Dutch crucified rebellious blacks and the Portuguese flog and mutilate to instill fear and set an example. (*Genesis* 241-42)

Astonishingly, the first military expedition of more than 40 against the Palmarians occurs in 1602. Galeano tells the story of how "the commander of the expedition, Bartolomeu Bezerra, announces in Recife: *The core of the rebellion has been destroyed.* And they believe him" (*Genesis* 175). Almost a century later, it will take a mercenary born of an Indian mother, Domingos Jorge Velho, to utterly destroy Palmares in 1694 using "the biggest army yet mobilized in Brazil" (*Genesis* 274) and cannon power:

Flames devour the capital of Palmares...the huge bonfire can be seen burning throughout the night. *Burn even the memory of it.* Hunting horns unceasingly proclaim the victory.

Chief Zumbí, wounded, has managed to escape. From the lofty peaks he reaches the jungle. He wanders through green tunnels, seeking his people in the thickets. (*Genesis* 274)

As told by Galeano, Palmares exemplifies the sustainability of alternative communities—in this case one that survived for a century and thrived on the different cultures that came together in its space. Palmares also exemplifies the persistence with which such communities have come under attack in the name of civilization, and its destruction constitutes an accusation against a civilization that compulsively disallows any form of alternative, any perceived threat to its sovereign self-interest.[15] More than that, though, Palmares, with the constant propaganda that was issued announcing its defeat, emblematizes survival—hence, the edict to "*burn even the memory of it*," destroy it so totally that its restitution in story and memory will be impossible.

Even after it has been so utterly destroyed, the narrative that Galeano tells is one in which the potential for resurrection remains wandering "through green tunnels" seeking out the community of people. The literary allegory is resonant here, but it must not be forgotten that this story, the memory of Palmares, is also rooted in material circumstances of specific historical agents who created Palmares in response to oppression and slavery. The core of the rebellion, in other words, will never be destroyed. Complete and utter destruction (like endless survival) are fantasies that only a fictive utopia can contain.[16] But Palmares is not the colonialist Utopia of More's imaginings and instead contributes to the historical roots of a utopian vocation that resurfaces in Caldeirão. Fredric Jameson alludes to this continuous enactment of the memory that fuels the utopian need to activate possible alternatives through concrete examples of resistance:

> ...what is often imperfectly called a group or collective "identity" in a specific tradition of oppression and in a (necessarily constructed) historical past...is an identity that must be based fully as much on solidarity as on alienation or oppression, and it necessarily feeds on those images of primitive or tribal cohesion which were however always the spiritual property of the Utopian tradition proper: what was once called "primitive communism," what is refracted out culturally in pictures of the horde or the clan, the *gens*, the village, even the monorial family—whatever collective structures seem to resist the anomie of the modern industrial state and to offer some negative and critical power over [and] against the larger and more diffuse demographies in which the group's current oppression is practiced. (*The Jameson Reader* 391-92)

Though Jameson's rhetoric is riddled with negative diction (suggestive of the extent to which the vocabulary to express oppositional alternatives effectively is lacking) and avoids reference to indigenous examples, the point he makes is clear enough: utopian solidarity depends on both a sense of alienation and the possibilities proffered by concrete examples of alternative community-making. Hence, in spite of the destruction wrought on Palmares, Zumbí's community of resistance carries forward as a marker of the historical power of his example. Galeano makes this point in his description of what happens to Zumbí (as an embodiment of community identity) after he has been assassinated by a traitor and had his head implanted on a stake to rot in the plaza at Recife:

> The vanquished dream about Zumbí; and the dream knows that while one man may remain owner of another man in these lands, his ghost will walk. He will walk with a limp. Because Zumbí had been lamed by a bullet, he will walk up and down time and, limping, will fight in these jungles of palms and in all the lands of Brazil. The chiefs of all the unceasing black rebellions will be called Zumbí. (*Genesis* 275)

Zumbí's spectral dream presence confirms the persistent threat to freedom and the existence of evil in the world in the twin infamies of slavery and repressive colonization. His limp signals his vulnerability, his sacrifice on behalf of the oppressed and vanquished. And he gives his name to a genealogy of rebellion that enables the persistence of communities of resistance.

Names travel through story and memory and in their travelling confirm that the struggle to achieve basic rights produces community. This is the open secret that utopian conquest narratives cannot obliterate, that drives their anxious and paranoid imaginings of the perfectibility of the sovereign state through the eradication of difference. Galeano suggests that it is "high time America discovered herself" and that this

> ...necessary discovery, revelation of the face hidden behind the masks, rests on the redemption of some of our most ancient traditions. It's out of hope, not nostalgia that we must recover a community-based mode of production and way of life, founded not on greed, but on solidarity, age-old freedoms and identity between human beings and nature. I believe there is no better way to honor the Indians, the first Americans, who from the Arctic to Tierra del Fuego have kept their identity and message alive through successive campaigns of extermination. Today they still hold out vital keys to memory and prophecy for all of America, not just our Latin America: Simultaneously, they bear witness to the past and cast the light of fresh fires on the path ahead. If the values they embody were of only archaeological interest, the Indians would no longer be objects of bloody repression, nor would the powerful be so anxious to separate them from the class struggle and from the people's liberation movements. (*We Say No* 227-28)

It is to this vision of hope, memory, prophecy, and solidarity brought forth on behalf of communities of resistance forcefully reiterated in Galeano's writings that we now turn.

From Solitude to Solidarity:
Love in the Time of Globalization

Once the notion of utopia has left its point of origin in colonialist fantasy to embrace a communitarian democracy that emerges from the hybrid colonial space, it fuels activities as seemingly different as the writing of literature and armed insurrection. The title of this section draws from the work of García Márquez—his novel *One Hundred Years of Solitude*, his acceptance speech for the Nobel Prize, and his more recent novel *Love in the Time of Cholera*—and suggests with a fair bit of irony that, at least from the perspective of the colonized, globalization is about as desirable as cholera. The love expressed by Galeano's "dangerous and fertile embraces" characterizes his writing generally in that it reaches out to the other (both testimonial sources and readers) while respecting the other's difference. Dussel associates this kind of love with the Greek term *agape*: "It is a very special love; it is love for the other *as other*, for the sake of that other and not for my own sake, with a respectful attitude toward the person of the other as something sacred and holy" (*Ethics and Community* 10).

Such a notion of love necessarily overflows the dualism of self and other in Dussel's and Galeano's communitarian ethics, since persons are persons by virtue of their interrelationships. *Agape*, and not concensus, is the foundation of community that embraces diversity and opposes any kind of self-interested rule, including majority and representational government. In Dussel's vision of community, individual rights are not pitted against collective interests because the individual as person is a community member, just as human beings are inseparable from the materiality of the earth that produces them. Simplistic binaries are rejected: duality is placed in a relationship of reciprocity and complementarity that only seems paradoxical from the Western rationalist perspective. A *logos* that compulsively situates dual terms in a hierarchical disposition invariably conceives of one term dominating (by being better, morally superior) or denying the other. In Dussel's vision of community "all individuals are persons *for* one another. Their relationships are 'practical,' and this praxis is that of the love that is charity: each serves the other for that other, in the friendship of all persons in all things...community in which individuality is expressed in full and uncoerced communication. *The community is the real, concrete agent and mover of history*" (*Ethics and Community* 11; our emphasis). Dussel's discourse of resistance links the political and spiritual dimensions of an anti-apocalyptic prophecy. He accuses the present world order of being sinful and encourages those seeking liberation to envision and strive towards a place of possibility that recalls the Guaraní's *land-without-evil*:

> In the times in which we live, the prophets, the martyrs, and the heroes must be able to recognize the difference between the prevailing moral legality of the dominator, and the communal ethical legality or the legality of liberation. They must be able to endure the social illegality conferred upon them by a system of sin, and proclaim before the principalities and powers of "this world" the madness of the communal le-

gality of the reign of God, the land of promise, the "new land where justice shall dwell" (2 Pet. 3:13). (*Ethics and Community* 75)

Clearly, Dussel recognizes a higher order of ethics than the judicial systems that are only as democratic as the governments they serve. Like Galeano, he appeals to conscience as "mad" visionary insight that must see beyond the sordid lies imposed by the system. This vision (inextricably linked with a Christian liberation theological perspective) glimpses the possible utopia based on the solidarity of liberated individuals living communally without the divisions caused by private ownership and inequality.

Debating the causes of solitude together with the possibility of solidarity is a collective project engaging many Latin American writers and activists. We will address this vast area of cultural activity by focusing on four visionaries (García Márquez, Nahuel Maciel, Galeano, and Marcos) who agree that the one characteristic shared by Latin Americans is hope, the

capacity for wakeful dreaming (*soñar despierto*). For Galeano, the previously mentioned Spanish expression *abrigar esperanzas* is crucial to his argument that "Hope needs to be *abrigada*, protected" (Barsamian, "Eduardo Galeano" 9). Again, no simplistic view of reality comes of this seemingly simple directive:

> [Hope is] fragile, and a little delicate, but she's alive. I have friends who say, "I'm entirely hopeless. I don't believe in anything." But you go on living. How is it? I hope I never lose hope, but if that day comes and I'm sure that I have nothing to expect, nothing to believe in, and that the human condition is doomed to stupidity and crime, then I hope I will be honest enough to kill myself. Of course, I know that the human condition is something at once horrible and marvelous. *Estamos muy mal hechos, pero no estamos terminados.* We are very badly made, but we are not finished. (Barsamian, "Eduardo Galeano" 9-10)

Soñar despierto. From *Crisis* 41 (1986): 68.

In the name of the "*mal hechos*," which we would translate as the "shoddily made," Galeano offers up memory, prophecy, and the embrace of community, all tempered by the kind of resistant, secular, and self-critical qualifications that we have identified throughout this book as a consistent feature of Galeano's work. In the following section, we intervene in the ongoing dialogue about memory and prophecy by considering a long interview with García Márquez entitled *Elogio de la utopía* [In Praise of Utopia] and an open letter sent to Galeano by Subcomandante Insurgente Marcos in response to *Walking Words*.

In his book on ecology (*Úselo y tírelo,* 1994), Galeano speaks about 500 years of solitude to summarize a millennial retrospective on Latin America:

> Fin del siglo, fin del milenio, fiesta de cumpleaños. El mundo de nuestro tiempo—mundo convertido en mercado, tiempo del hombre reducido a mercancía—ha celebrado los quinientos años de su edad. El 12 de octubre de 1492 había nacido esta realidad que hoy vivimos a escala universal: un orden natural enemigo de la naturaleza y una sociedad humana que llama "humanidad" a la quinta parte de la humanidad. (22)

> [End of the century, end of the millennium, birthday party. The world in our time—world converted into a market, human time reduced to product—celebrated turning 500 years old. The 12th of October 1492 saw the birth of the reality that today has become universal: a natural order antagonistic to nature and a human society that reserves the name of humanity for one fifth of the earth's population.]

Clearly, this is not an optimistic picture of history or the present state of affairs, a cynicism echoed in García Márquez's fatalistic joke that "The day shit has any value, the poor will be born without bums." And yet both Galeano and García Márquez are adamantly anti-apocalyptic and opposed to the notion that we have reached the end of history.

García Márquez, Galeano, and Marcos share a vision of the role of the writer, not as an individual expressing personal genius but as a creative medium who channels the fears and hopes, memories and aspirations of the community. In Galeano's case, this sense of purpose is most clearly expressed in the essay "In Defense of the Word," where he affirms that "One writes out of a need to communicate and to commune with others, to denounce that which gives pain and to share that which gives happiness. *One writes against one's solitude and against the solitude of others*" (*We Say No* 130; our emphasis). But, as we have seen, Galeano puts into question the term "others," for when it refers to readers, it excludes those who are illiterate. Galeano avoids the pitfalls of abstract lamentations about the uselessness of literature by clearly establishing the social context that suppresses communication, yet simultaneously ignites the desire to break out of the silence of solitude. For the North American or European urban dweller, the term "solitude" may conjure up the image of a peaceful retreat, a place of healing and relaxation, while its meaning in the Latin American lexicon connotes loneliness and lack of community. Solitude and silence are politically loaded terms related to oppression, to societies where solitude springs from alienation, silence from repression.

Pondering some of the unhappy consequences of development in colonized territories, Galeano observes that "Latin American scientists emigrate, laboratories and universities have no funds, industrial 'know-how' is always foreign and exorbitantly expensive," and then asks the ironically macabre question: "why not recognize a certain creativity in the development of a technology of terror? Latin America is making inspired universal contributions to the development of methods of torture, techniques for assassinating people and ideas, for the cultivation of silence, the extension of impotence, and the sowing of fear" (*We Say No* 131-32), an idea he echoes in a found graffiti from the Uruguayan city Melo, which proclaims "*Assist the police: torture yourself*" (*The Book of Embraces* 209). It is in this particular context, what he calls "our republics of silence" ironically troped as the site of technical progress and foreign intervention, that Galeano defines the significance of literature as the voice of denunciation and hope (*The Book of Embraces* 137). In his vision, "writing springs from the wounded consciousness of the writer and is projected onto the world; the act of creation is an act of solidarity...Our writing is informed by a desire *to make contact*, so that readers may become involved with words that came to us from them, and that return to them as hope and prophecy" (*We Say No* 139-40; our emphasis). Bobbye S. Ortiz lukewarmly translates the Spanish verb *comulgar*, used in this passage, as "to make contact." But there are other Spanish words meaning to share, to sympathize, and to agree with. Galeano uses the word *comulgar* with its extensive Christian connotations of giving and taking communion, transposed into a communitarian context where the divine source of the word is not the Christian god but humanity.

One of the windows of *Walking Words* takes us back to the subject of utopia, not as a static, rational space of perfection, but as a processual metaphor associated with hope and the desire to advance toward the goal of liberation. The horizon that is continually displaced is an ethical limit that ensures the good faith of the process of those attempting to achieve utopian ideals. The horizon of perfection is unreachable in human terms yet functions, in a metaphor we have seen earlier in the book, as a metonym for human desire: "She's on the horizon, says Fernando Birri. I go two steps closer, she moves two steps away...What good is utopia? That's what: it's good for walking" (*Walking Words* 326). The Americas offer particularly fertile ground for envisioning and implementing utopian projects, as García Márquez argues in a dialogue on utopia with Nahuel Maciel:

> Ninguna otra región del globo, al ser descubierta, encontrada o *develada* ha sido bautizada Nuevo Mundo, privilegio de comienzo y de génesis de un tiempo y un espacio del que es dueña, no sin cierta ambigüedad, América. Por esta razón, su territorio ha propiciado a la objetivación de la Utopía y buena parte de las esperanzas frustradas en Europa se han concentrado en el Nuevo Mundo, donde la tábula rasa de una historia abierta al futuro ha potenciado planes y proyectos de toda índole.
> (*Elogio de la utopía* 38)

[No other region in the world, upon being discovered, found, or *unveiled,* was baptized the "New World," a privilege of beginnings, genesis of time and space attributed to America, not without a certain degree of ambiguity. For this reason, its territory has given rise to the objectification of Utopia, and many of the hopes frustrated in Europe have been concentrated in the New World, where the *tabula rasa* of a history open to the future has favoured all kinds of plans and projects.]

History, for the pioneer and colonizer, is to be made anew. But what of the history of those who were already here? Ancient cultures, despite undergoing continuous change, maintain their roots in a past in which history and myth are intertwined in ways that are difficult to comprehend from a European perspective. The European vision of utopia may crystallize into an oppressively static space in reaction to the fragmentation and speed of modernity whose myriad "posts"—postmodernism, post-colonialism—signal that the present is always so far ahead that the names lag behind identifying what is thought to have been surpassed.

As we have seen, the "New World" was built over top of a world that did not voluntarily relinquish its past. Sacred places had to be desecrated and burned, cathedrals erected over the rubble. And the majority of Europeans who envisioned these continents as new were also incapable of relinquishing their pasts, institutions, religious and political beliefs, and racism. In the nineteenth century, and repeatedly whenever history is pregnant with utopian tension, "America" seems to be what Hegel identified as "the country of the future" (Maciel, *Elogio de la utopía* 171). Thus, there is an evident correlation between envisioning this space as propitiously utopian and negating its historical character, forgetting its past.

For Galeano, in a position we have examined in some detail in our earlier chapter on history, the past is the seed contained within the present and the future, one vital for interpreting the experiences and desires of the individuals and communities of the Americas. The visionary revisionist does not flee from the past (like the persecuted Europeans) but instead searches it for traces that can reconstitute an identity that has been distorted by lies, past and present, and amnesia: "We say no to the lie. The dominant culture, which the mass media irradiates on a universal scale, invites us to confuse the world with a supermarket or a racetrack, where one's fellow man can be merchandise or competition, but never a brother" (*We Say No* 242). Galeano's description of Latin Americans infuses the stereotypes with new and unexpected meanings: "Dicen que hemos faltado a nuestra cita con la Historia, y hay que reconocer que nosotros llegamos tarde a todas las citas" (*Úselo y tírelo* 118) [They say that we missed our appointment with History, and admittedly, we do arrive late to all appointments]. Galeano ironically echoes those who conceive of history as capital development and dismiss traditional communitarian social structure as backward and anachronistic. He cites Mario Vargas Llosa as a prime example of this double-faced complex: superiority in relation to the indigenous population, inferiority in relation to the American and European model of metastatic, cancerous economic growth: "Kill the Indian and save man, advised the pious U.S. colonel Henry Pratt. And many years later, Peruvian novelist Mario Vargas Llosa explained that there is no other way to 'save' the Indians from hunger and misery than to modernize them, even if their cultures must be sacrificed" (*We Say No* 305-06). Vargas Llosa implies, taking it completely for granted, that misery and hunger are products of indigenous culture and not the result of systemic persecution, exploitation, and genocide.

Ronald Wright seconds this interpretation of Vargas Llosa's commitment to white supremacy: "The smooth and intellectual Vargas had immense appeal for foreign dilettantes who did not know, or chose to ignore, his long antagonism to Andean Peru. ('I've never liked the Incas,' Vargas once admitted in the *New York Times*.) Peruvian voters, many of them illiterate Indians who would have been denied the vote if Vargas's political friends had had their way, were not so easily fooled" (*Stolen Continents* 291). Nor is García Márquez entirely free of the kind of racism that presents facile stereotypes of indigenes. In *One Hundred Years of Solitude* and in interviews about Columbia, he repeatedly sets the African influenced culture of the coast, which he privileges as life-affirming, against the Indian highland culture that he represents as sombre, cruel, unpredictable, and complicit with the military. While it is true that the armies in many Latin American countries are predominantly made up of Indians and mestizos, such a militaristic choice is made for reasons of political, economic, and psychological oppression. Galeano examines this apparent paradox and in the case of Guatemala concludes that the army first turns the Indian recruits into cockroaches by brutalizing them and stripping them of their cultural identity and human dignity, after which they are turned into birds of prey and unleashed on their own Mayan communities (*We Say No* 234).

To continue with Galeano's characterization of the Latin American stereotype: "Los latinoamericanos tenemos una jodida fama de charlatanes, vagabundos, buscabroncas, calentones y fiesteros, que por algo será. Nos han enseñado que, por ley del mercado, lo que no tiene precio no tiene valor, y sabemos que nuestra cotización no es muy alta" (*Úselo y tírelo* 119) [We have the shitty reputation of being charlatans, vagabonds, troublemakers, randy party animals, and there must be some reason for this. The law of the market has taught us that things without a price have no value, and we know that the quote on our price is not very high]. Self-image and the image of the other are thrown by a distorting mirror in the form of billboards and TV screens promoting consumerism as the only lifestyle, even to those spectators who are utterly destitute or, like the majority of Latin Americans, those who survive at a subsistence level with no "disposable" income. "Lifestyle" as it is currently used in advertising and the media in general reduces the application of this word to affluent or "wannabe" ways of living; only those who can choose their style have lifestyles. The poor don't have lifestyles, just life for what it's worth—and Galeano fervently claims that it is worth more than the lifestyles of those who have renounced "being" in favour of "having."

He searches for the roots of the alienation suffered by Latin Americans, both rich and poor, and finds it partially in the media images that promote the American Way of Life to those who are excluded from being "Americans" even by the U.S.-centric usage of the term reduced from its pan-American meaning to an exclusively nationalistic one.

Hope breathes life into the Latin American stereotype. Passion can turn from violent self-destruction to solidarity through an imaginative re-evaluation of the past and the uncovering of value that has no relation to the market: "Llevamos quinientos años aprendiendo a odiarnos entre nosotros y a trabajar con alma y vida por nuestra propia perdición, y en eso estamos; pero todavía no hemos podido corregir nuestra porfiada costumbre de abrazos, nuestra manía de andar soñando despiertos y chocándonos con todo y cierta tendencia a la resurrección inexplicable" (*Úselo y tírelo* 119) [We've been learning to hate each other and to dedicate body and soul to our own perdition for five hundred years now, and that's where we're at; but we still haven't been able to correct the obstinate habit of embracing each other, our passion for dreaming while we're awake and banging into everything, and a certain tendency towards inexplicable resurrection].

It is worth recalling here that utopia for Galeano is a horizon that beckons and incites to walk relentlessly. But this journey is not just a linear movement toward the future. The myth of progress, as we have seen in the previous chapter, is one of the lies that Galeano debunks most vigorously because it erases Latin America's history and blames Latin Americans for their poverty, financial debts, and so-called "underdevelopment." This future-oriented lie dangles the carrot of prosperity before the noses of "Third World" countries, beckoning them to join the so-called First World. It is now considered politically incorrect to refer to Latin America as "underdeveloped," but acceptable to call it "developing"—in Spanish "*en vías de desarrollo*," in the "process of developing"—or to refer to it as an "emerging economy." As Galeano points out, this linear (but never causal) image represents Latin America and all impoverished countries as occupying the infant stage of human development. Infants mature by imitating adults, and here all utopian aspirations of renewal are subsumed under a reactionary prerogative to obey the law of the jungle imposed by multinational corporations and foreign interests on Latin America, the law of global hegemonic exploitation. Galeano's writing mirrors different identities for Latin Americans and throws open windows on realities usually hidden from sight.

Walking Words moves the imagination of Subcomandante Insurgente Marcos, who sends Galeano an open letter telling him that the part of the book entitled "Window on the Word" is still dancing in his head. First, Marcos describes in detail the circumstances in which he contemplates these dancing words: he lies smoking with a rifle for a pillow, his boots on, his pistol by his side, the rain pouring torrentially outside his makeshift tent, reducing the crickets to silence. And in this perpetual state of alert, Marcos muses on the incessant question: "Do words know to fall silent when they can't find the time or place for which they're called? And the mouth, does it know how to die?" (qtd. in *Our Word Is Our*

Weapon 254). What Marcos reveals about his sleeping habits gives urgent poignancy to his doubts and his desire for justice, at the same time drawing a symbolic distinction between sleeping deeply and dreaming while awake or vigilant. He explains that he has constructed himself a cot made of branches and forked props, fastened with liana, and that he cannot get too comfy in a hammock since deep sleep would be a luxury that could cost him dearly. His cot of sticks is sufficiently uncomfortable to ensure that he barely catches a wink (*Our Word Is Our Weapon* 254). In this half-waking state, he has passed several nights mulling over the question of whether the moment to fall silent has arrived, whether the moment has passed and it is no longer the place, whether it is time for the mouth to die. But immediately following these troubling questions left elliptically open-ended, he writes a long description of how they celebrate the Day of the Child in Mexico and, more precisely, in the mountains of Chiapas to which the children of the Zapatistas have been displaced by thousands of soldiers who have occupied Mayan territory in order to defend national sovereignty.

Significantly, Marcos includes himself among the children: "We Mexican children celebrate the day, more often than not, despite the adults" (255). By this token, childhood would seem to be not an inferior stage of underdevelopment but a privileged state of mind. The conquest continues, writes Galeano, and the contempt too: "the mass media teach self-hate to the vanquished. In the age of television, Indian children play cowboys and Indians, and it's hard to find anyone who wants to play the Indian" (*We Say No* 263). In Marcos's testimony, the Mayan children do not suffer this form of alienation, for while they suffer great deprivation and danger, they are as a consequence aware of their historical circumstances. The cliché of little boys playing war is invested with new energy, signaling not aggression but a sense of justice. Their games, like all children's games, reflect their reality but also their desires:

> The children of the masters of the government spend the day at parties surrounded by gifts. Zapatista children, masters of nothing if not their dignity, spend the day at play; they play at war, they play at being soldiers who take back the land the government has stolen from them, of being farmers who sow their corn-fields and gather wood, of being the sick whom no one cures, of being the hungry who must fill their mouths with song instead of food. (*Our Word Is Our Weapon* 255-56)

Marcos's description slips from realistic testimony to charged metaphor and back again to a favourite song about walking towards the horizon: "Now we can see the horizon, / Zapatista combatant, / the path will be marked / for those who come behind" (256).

His tone in this letter is at once intimate, playful, and talkative, surprising attributes given the electronic medium he uses and the adverse circumstances in which he writes. His words give him a physical presence that ground his message in a specific reality while also bridging the gulf dividing the clandestine writer of communiqués and his readers, whoever they may be. There is no abstract discourse here, no philosophy or political science or economics. Every word congeals into a tangible image, an immediate reality traversed by past and future. After a long and lovingly detailed description of the local children, whose play typically reflects both conflict and solidarity, Marcos makes a characteristic comment on how that was not what he had really wanted to tell Galeano. His discourse is consciously serpentine and anti-linear, taking detours to gather anecdotes that situate his thoughts in relation to the people to whom he has decided to dedicate himself. The style ensures that his ideas about justice never ring abstract. What he really wanted to tell Galeano was a story he heard from an old man, the proverbial Old Antonio, the storyteller we have already encountered in *The Story of Colors*. Marcos in turn asks Galeano to retell the story to others as part of the chain of story that forms community. Again, memory is central to the story, as is the request to repeat an oral story in written form. Marcos looks to Galeano as both a repository and a voice that will help circulate the old man's words and the historical insights that are represented as a valuable lesson:

> Old Don Antonio taught me that you are as big as the enemies you choose to fight, and as small as the fear is big. "Choose a big enemy and it will make you grow so you can confront him. Lessen your fear because if it grows, it will make you small," Old Don Antonio told me one rainy May afternoon, in the hour when tobacco and words reign. The government fears the Mexican people; that's why it needs so many soldiers and police. Its fear is very big. Consequently, it is very small. We're afraid of oblivion, which we have made smaller with our pain and blood. Consequently, we are big. (*Our Word Is Our Weapon* 257)

Galeano discloses that the Guatemalan army hunts down children and old people with the objective of leaving the Maya "without seeds," as explained by Colonel Horacio Maldonado Shadd. The fact that Marcos learns histories from Old Antonio is significant: "in every old person there lurks a transmitter for the unpardonable community tradition and the no less unpardonable tradition of identifying with nature" (*We Say No* 234). In his letter to Galeano, Marcos encourages him to retell this story in writing and offers to share Old Antonio with him in a way that goes beyond the mere borrowing of a tale: "Say that Old Don Antonio told you all this. We've all had an Old Don Antonio at some point. But if you never had one, you may borrow mine this time. Tell them how the indigenous of the Mexican Southeast lessen their fear to make themselves big, and choose colossal enemies to make themselves grow and get stronger" (*Our Word Is Our Weapon* 257).

The horizon that incites to walking (not running, driving, speeding down the information highway, or flying business class) must have a different orientation. Galeano sees urban life as an ecological and social hell, not understanding how "First World" sites can be perceived as desirable, normative, or prescriptive: "When a Latin American president in his speech says, 'We are becoming part of the First World,' in the first place he's lying. Second, this is practically impossible. And in the third place, he should be in jail because this is an incitement to crime. If you say, 'I want Montevideo to become Los Angeles,' you are inviting the destruction of Montevideo" (Barsamian, "Eduardo Galeano" 3). To become like the U.S. is seen, by Galeano, as unethical and ultimately nihilistic: "We cannot become them. If the entire world has the same quantity of cars as the U.S. with its one-person, one-car [lifestyle], then the planet will explode. We have poisoned the air, poisoned the earth, poisoned the water, poisoned human souls. Everything is poisoned" (Barsamian, "Eduardo Galeano" 3). In short, the "First World" is apocalyptically close to being the last, and to emulate it would spell the end of history with no horizon. So in what direction does that utopian horizon beckon us to walk?

Prefaced by Galeano, *Elogio de la utopía* is a dialogue between García Márquez and Nahuel Maciel, an Argentine journalist whose vision of journalistic writing is informed by the indigenous Mapuche culture of the province of Neuquén. The "self-portrait" he offers of himself on the book's back cover surpasses the genre of the "blurb" in its rich conception of purpose, history, and reception:

> *Kerruf* significa *paisaje que anda*, es decir, viento. Cuando una persona logra comunicarse con otra más allá de las palabras, cuando se logra conversar con las manos y escuchar con los ojos, se dice *Huerque*, es decir *mensaje*...Cuando aprendí estas palabras, supe que quería ser un huerque y que quería ser un paisaje que anda, es decir, un hombre con un mensaje propio acuñado en los diversos paisajes que lo contenían...Pero lo que nosotros sentimos, no es el lenguaje del viento: es la respuesta de nuestro paisaje al viento. Diría que cada cosa reza, en sus palabras, lo que el viento libera en ella al empujarla. Engrasen el eje del molino y habrá una plegaria menos en las noches tibias. Asesinen a un árbol y habrá una palabra ausente al paso del viento. Quizá por esto yo sea, hoy, periodista, es decir: un hombre en busca de un paisaje para mi huerque. (Maciel and García Márquez n.pag.)

> [*Kerruf* means *walking landscape*, in other words, wind. When a person succeeds in communicating with another beyond words, when they manage to converse with their hands and listen with their eyes, we call this *Huerque*, meaning *message*...When I learned these words, I realized that I wanted to be a *huerque* and a walking landscape, in other words, a man with his own message created in the diverse landscapes that contained him...But what we feel is not the wind's language but our landscape's response to the wind. I would say that each thing prays, in its own words, what the wind's pushing against it liberates. When they grease a windmill's axle, there is one less prayer on warm nights. When they assassinate a tree, a word is absent as the wind blows by. Perhaps this is why today I am a journalist: a man in search of a landscape for his message.]

Maciel's vision of journalism sets the tone for an "interview" that strives to liberate this intuitive "message" about Latin America's destiny. Maciel and García Márquez challenge the reader to "find an incentive, some model for theoretical reflection on utopian intentionality, the latent *Novum* underlying history, veritable expedition *in terram utopicam*…in order to extend the limits of historiography, beyond the causality of economics and sociology to which it is condemned by a reductive and exclusively actual analysis" (51-52). Utopia is not a Promised Land one can flee toward, leaving persecution, injustice, and misery behind. On the contrary, utopia as an ethical horizon incites confrontation with injustice in the hope of effecting radical change in the name of community and egalitarianism. Galeano defines himself as a utopianist, as someone who indulges in wakeful dreams ("*soñar despierto*"). This capacity to dream is the utopianist's source of inspiration, a mode of being contrary to accepting the present as defined by García Márquez: "In short, the characteristic common to all utopias is the author's rejection of the contemporary system and society. The capacity to say *no* to *his/her* reality is inherent to *homo utopicus*" (104).

Galeano's 1988 speech "We Say No," which we have already discussed at some length, bears revisitation in relation to the kinds of utopian thinking we locate in Galeano's work, especially in terms of the materiality with which the word is used to forge an alternative vision of reality. The resounding "no" hurled repeatedly against "the praise of money and of death," against a "system that assigns prices to people and things," and against fear and "the neutrality of the human word" expresses a community's opposition to organized political crime on a global scale. The speech does not stop at denouncing or simply negating "the suicidal egotism of the powerful" (*We Say No* 241-44). The word "no" contains and is propelled by its opposite, the "yes" springing from hope and the utopianism that perceives the horizon well beyond the chimera of democracy held up by the "First World" as an example and an ideal:

> By saying no to dictatorships, and no to dictatorships disguised as democracies we are saying yes to the struggle for true democracy, one that will deny no one bread or the power of speech, and one that will be as beautiful and dangerous as a poem by [Pablo] Neruda or a song by Violeta [Parra]. By saying no to the devastating empire of greed, whose center lies in North America, we are saying yes to another possible America, which will be born of the most ancient of American traditions, the communitarian tradition that the Chilean Indians have defended, desperately, defeat after defeat, during the last five centuries. (*We Say No* 243-44)

The oxymoron of wakeful dreaming situates hope in the present, but the memory of the communitarian tradition underlies the hope for solidarity in the future.[17] García Márquez sees utopias as premature truths, a future whose point of departure is the rich potential of humanity (*Elogio de la utopía* 116). Implicit in his vision is the "no" to how things are in the present and the need to work on how things should be. And he insists on the need for permanent heresy, another expression of dissidence that envisions ways of being in peace which, according to Galeano, do not necessarily have to be invented from scratch. This form of utopianism clearly contradicts the colonialist dream, discussed earlier in this chapter, of a rigidly ordered community where all citizens are subjugated to sameness and complete consensus.

Biblical heaven is represented by Galeano as another example of this oppressive view of a static utopia that, in this case, entraps even God. Utopia as visionary and dynamic growth is then humorously developed as God's dream, another much needed corrective to Judeo-Christian scripture. Returning to a series of vignettes titled "Theology" (that we discussed earlier in relation to God's loneliness and how he is misunderstood by his human creatures), Galeano plays with the idea of tempting God to partake of the carnivalesque reality that is banned from the static utopia of heaven. First, God ponders his own shortcomings and is impressed by human love, freedom, and independence: "*Later, I admit, I felt envy. Just as no one can give me orders, I know nothing of the dignity of disobedience. Nor can I know the boldness of love, which requires two*" (*The Book of Embraces* 90). Alienated from his creations, God only experiences the greatest of human attributes while dreaming, when he acquires the characteristics of the plural imperfect gods of religions that Judeo-Christian traditions refer to as pagan: "And I like sleeping, I really do, because when I sleep, I dream. Then I become a lover, I burn myself in the brief flame of fleeting love, I am a strolling player, a deep-sea fisherman, or a Gypsy fortune teller; I devour even the leaves of the forbidden tree and drink and dance until I'm rolling on the ground" (91). Clearly, for Galeano, order, perfection, and authority are not ideals to impose on human society or for human society to emulate. They are instead the symptoms of failure characterizing a lonely god who passes his biases and blindness on to his children. Consequently, utopia in its fresh recuperated sense is not guided by these principles.

But this god is not a hopeless case, for "he" perceives himself, his inverted image, in the mirror of his creation. His solitude echoes the narcissistic and incestuous solitude of the Buendía oligarchy in *One Hundred Years of Solitude*, condemned to die out apocalyptically because they exist only as the élitist power recorded in the biblically structured parchments of Melquíades and not in the collective memory that circulates endlessly. The Old Testament god mourns himself: "When I wake up, I am alone. I have no one to play with because the angels take me so seriously, nor have I anyone to desire. I am condemned to desire myself. I wander from star to star, growing bored in the empty universe. I feel very tired, I feel very alone. I am alone—alone for all eternity" (*The Book of Embraces* 91). Galeano suggests that the mythic and the historical unconsciously intermingle in the Western tradition as well, where the intransigent God that he recalls from his childhood as his "superfather castigator" is linked to a social system governed by punishment and intimidation, the "chief of police of the universe" (89). This authoritarian master is transposed from the divine to the political realm and is incarnated in the chief of police of the state. And if we push the analogy further in relation to modes of obligatory transnational totalitarianism, dissimulatively renamed "globalization," then we are back to the chief of police of the universe, God converted into an idol. Galeano speaks openly in the autobiographical mode of losing his Catholic faith early on in life. But he is specific about that faith having been in the Christian god, for whom he feels sorry and whose melancholy confidences he still hears: "He is perhaps the only god that has never made love out of all the gods of all the religions in the history of the world" (89). Making love, which celebrates the unity of body and earth, is linked to solidarity and communitarian ethics, the "dangerous and fertile embraces" incomprehensible to this lonely monotheistic God and his equally lonely people.

Despite this apparently anti-Christian stance, Galeano makes a clear distinction between the official church representing the oligarchy and liberation theology. The latter is committed to removing the imperial mask from God's face and to returning him to the people who live in accordance with the vision of early communitarian Christianity. In his testimonial history of the war against the Maya in *Guatemala: Occupied Country*, Galeano includes the testimonies of guerrilla leaders, soldiers, and the liberation theologians of the Maryknoll order. He quotes Ernesto Cardenal, the Nicaraguan poet, utopianist (who founded a commune on the island of Solantiname based on early Christian ideals), Marxist liberation theologian: "The liar commits a sin…because he robs words of their truth" (*The Book of Embraces* 229). But instead of speaking of the Christian basis of community, Galeano prefers to go further back in the American tradition to recuperate the indigenous vision that he projects into the future as utopian destiny: "Back around 1524, Fray Bobadilla made a great bonfire in the village of Managua and threw the Indians' books on the flames. The books were made of deerskin with images painted in two colors: red and black. Nicaragua had been lied to for centuries when General Sandino chose those colors, unaware that they were the colors of the ashes of the national memory" (*The Book of Embraces* 229). This vignette belongs to a series entitled "Resurrections" and is illustrated with a corn stalk flowering into a human eye, which suggests that the past be intuited even in instances when memory fails or has been eradicated.

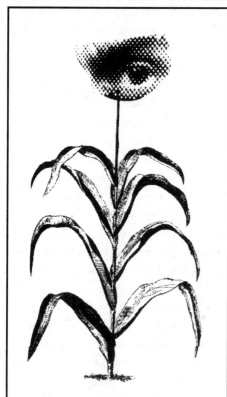

Resurrections. Eduardo Galeano, from *The Book of Embraces* 229.

We will now turn to Central America and the Caribbean as utopian sites of imminent resurrection despite the fact that very recently the revolutionary projects in El Salvador (1979-1982/83) and Nicaragua (1979-1990) have been crushed, just as they were in Chile, by U.S. intervention in aid of the parasitical oligarchy that sells the people and resources of its own nation in exchange for military protection and personal wealth. Galeano writes prolifically of the possibilities, the achievements, and the enemies of these *pueblos* and of Cuba, privileged site of hope, despite being under perpetual threat of invasion, demonized and punished by the God of capital who cannot fathom such disobedience to the imperial directives governing world order.

"Our Pyramids Are Words":
Insurrections, Resurrections, and Magical Marxism

Despite his understanding that writing is political ("Just give me the name of any writer in history who was not political" [Barsamian, "Eduardo Galeano" 6]), Galeano has repeatedly rejected being referred to as a political writer. The rejection of such a convoluted term is understandable since "political" is used in the same reductive terms as "history" to refer exclusively to a handful of players who have the power to manipulate and control the vast majority whose memory, reality, and hopes are ignored, appropriated, or annihilated. The term "political" is also too reductive to describe Galeano's writing style since the latter manifests a profoundly democratic diversity that cannot be contained in any doctrine or genre. Moreover, the "political" does not adequately name the intersection of humane letters with dissenting reflection on rights, story, and history that typifies Galeano's work.

In a vignette entitled "Celebration of Continuous Birth," Galeano converses with Salvadoran revolutionary Miguel Mármol. Mármol, discussed in the previous chapter, is an important symbolic figure for Galeano. Like the mythical Inkarí, he is a fusion and reincarnation of earlier mythical heroes like Atawallpa, Manku, and Tupac Amaru—"the truest metaphor for Latin America. Like him, Latin America has died and been born many times. Like him, it goes on being born" (*The Book of Embraces* 223). In another historical example pregnant with mythic significance, Galeano celebrates the resurrection of Augusto César Sandino: "había sido asesinado por el viejo Somoza, el primero de la dinastía, cuarenta y cinco años antes. La dictadura prohibió su nombre y su imagen. El que fue héroe de la resistencia nacional y voz de los pobres, se escapó del cementerio" (*El descubrimiento de América* 77) [he had been assassinated by the old Somoza, the first one of the dynasty, forty-five years before. The dictatorship prohibited his name and his image. The one who was the hero of national resistance and the voice of the poor escaped from the cemetery]. How to interpret such resurrections? Mármol says it is pointless to talk about it: "*Catholics tell me it has all been pure Providence. And the communists, my comrades, tell me it's been pure coincidence,*" to which Galeano responds with his characteristic heterodoxy: "I propose that we jointly found Magical Marxism: one half reason, one half passion, and a third half mystery" (*The Book of Embraces* 223). The playful alogical mathematics and recuperation (defamiliarization) of a literary term (Magical Realism) associated with Latin American fiction provides much food for thought: while to the best of our knowledge this is the only reference Galeano ever makes to Magical Marxism, it strikes a richly evocative balance among wonder, anti-positivism, and the historical materialism characteristic of Galeano's own writings.

The literary term magic realism is often misconstrued as referring to rhetorical or aesthetic techniques characterizing fiction in which supernatural events are presented in the same tone as documented historical or mimetically plausible ones. García Márquez, perhaps the author most associated with this term, refers to this tone as a straight-faced (*cara de palo*) recounting of things of wonder. The term, coined by the Cuban writer Alejo Carpentier in his preface to *Kingdom of This World*, refers not to a way of storytelling but to the very reality that is narrated. Thus, according to Carpentier, García Márquez, and, we suspect, Galeano, Latin American reality exceeds the boundaries of predominantly rationalist European discourse and representation. García Márquez explains that Latin American reality cannot be conceived of as objective reality because Latin Americans include spiritual beliefs, superstitions, dreams, visions, and all kinds of other "paranormal" phenomena in their accounts of reality. Their expression of such a richly diverse reality—subjective, objective, collective— can only be expressed by combining the magical, or inexplicable, with realism, the literary commitment to represent the (shared) world that exceeds any purely objectivist description.

Magical Marxism borrows from this literary context, the fundamental notion that Marxism in Latin America must be rooted in a multifarious reality that exceeds the European imagination and European models. Galeano chronicles numerous indigenous ways of life to show that communism (in its de-Europeanized sense) is the most ancient of American traditions. The argument has its place too in the liberation theology movement, which argues that Christian communitarianism (in its scriptural sense) is a form of social organization that overlaps with indigenous American traditions of shared and reciprocal community. Ironically, such a view might come as a shock to those Americans whose vision of American tradition is representational democracy and individual freedom. Miseducation and ignorance reinforce the belief that communitarianism is equivalent to the threatening ideological configuration known as communism, anathema to the so-called American Way of Life. The Cold War mentality is precious to the U.S. precisely *because* it promotes the lie that all communitarian models are Soviet (communist/Stalinist) transplants that have no real cultural basis in the Americas. This lie is also dear to many national governments in Latin America for the same reasons. Socialist revolutionaries, even when they are indigenous leaders of agrarian reform or ecological movements, are systematically dismissed as foreign agents or as the misled puppets of such agents. A prime example is the representation of the Nicaraguan revolution in the press—not just in the U.S., as Galeano observes, but in Europe as well. Spanish newspapers, for instance, quote "well-informed sources" that are never named to accuse Tomás Borge and the Sandinistas of being directly involved in Basque terrorism (*We Say No* 181-82).

The international denial, then, of the possibility of social change in Latin America and other impoverished areas is based on the most simplistic of analyses. The first involves the defeatist illusion that the world has been divided in two and is therefore ruled by two masters, and the second involves the more recent notion that one of the masters has fallen and, as a result, socialism has been eradicated:

> Everything that is happening in Nicaragua has been reduced to the geopolitics of blocs, a game of East versus West: the game belongs to Moscow, which is sticking its nose in where it doesn't belong, and, in that way, is changing the delicate balance of power that guarantees world peace. The *contras* are not, therefore, mere paid mercenaries working for the restoration of the colonialist past and a dethroned dynasty; they aren't Business Fighters, but Freedom Fighters, heroes of a threatened civilization, Western civilization, which, on the eve of the Apocalypse, turns to God and to the Rambos it can pay. (*We Say No* 203)

The most obvious piece of evidence, and one that is rarely addressed by the Western press, is the fact that in such cases as Cuba (during both the Revolution and the Bay of Pigs invasion) and Nicaragua the people were armed and defended the revolution instead of turning their weapons against their revolutionary leaders. The mass media, in their complicity with U.S. state interests, represent the demise of revolutionary governments in Chile, Guatemala, Nicaragua, and El Salvador (in other words, anywhere in the U.S.'s immense sphere of egregious influence) as a result of their own failure. In fact, these democratically supported revolutionary governments were under perpetual threat from the U.S. and had to dedicate debilitating sums of money to defend themselves from invasion: "Actually, the revolution that overthrew the Somoza family dictatorship did not have a moment's respite over ten long years. Every day Nicaragua was invaded by a foreign power and its hired criminals. It faced the unrelenting siege from the bankers and the commercial masters of the world" (*We Say No* 274-75).

It is all too easy for the mass media to represent U.S. intervention as a heroic struggle for democracy. This is especially so given the general ignorance of North American people concerning other countries, combined with a totalitarian patriotism that is inculcated not through the easily recognizable channels of state propaganda but through what the naïve perceive as simply entertainment or "infotainment."

> El dictador era loco por los baños y los espejos. Dieciséis baños tenía la casa que ocupaba antes de refugiarse en el bunker [...] el más perfecto símbolo del sistema. En el bunker vivió Somoza sus últimos tiempos en Nicaragua. El garaje está al lado del dormitorio y los baños tienen teléfono. Entre plantas de plástico y muchos espejos, el dictador leía *El misterio de la bondad*, por Elena G. de White, los últimos

best-sellers norteamericanos y el *Management Information Systems Hand-book.* Afuera ardía el mundo, pero el bunker era una estructura de acero a prueba de sonidos, un gran ataúd forrado de terciopelo donde no se escuchaba la lluvia, ni los gritos, ni los tiros. "Hay que estimular el turismo," ordenaba el dictador en plena guerra. (*El descubrimiento de América* 76)

[The dictator was nuts about bathrooms and mirrors. The house he owned before barricading himself in the bunker had sixteen bathrooms. The bunker is the most perfect symbol of the system. There, Somoza spent the end of his stay in Nicaragua. The garage is beside the bedroom and the bathrooms have phones. Among plastic plants and many mirrors, the dictator read *The Mystery of Kindness* by Elena G. de White, the latest North American bestsellers, and *Management Information Systems Handbook.* Outside the world was burning, but the bunker was made of soundproof steel, a great coffin lined in velvet where the rain could not be heard, nor the shouts and bullets. "Tourism must be stimulated," ordered the dictator in the middle of the war.]

This description belongs to magic realism and could easily form part of García Márquez's novel *The Autumn of the Patriarch.* Somoza's virtual alienation from reality echoes the alienation of those who do not see and cannot understand what is going on beyond the mirrors that reflect their own blank gazes, their bathrooms that could house entire families, their artificial (and, no doubt, imported) plants in the middle of a tropical paradise. Nor would the dictator's reading materials inform him of what was going on right under his nose. Those who disssociate themselves from the starving majority of illiterate people without access to even basic education tend to turn up in Miami with Cubans who share similar ideological tendencies: "el chillón paraíso de los millonarios latinoamericanos y de la clase media que quiere y no puede pero hace como que puede. Este es el santuario de los dictadores y sus matones, incesante festival del consumismo…Vea a los hombres que son o han sido amos de otros hombres, arrodillándose ante las cosas" (*El descubrimiento de América* 73) [the tacky paradise of Latin American millionaires and the middle class that wants to be but cannot, but makes like it can. This is the sanctuary of dictators and their thugs, incessant festival of consumerism…See the men who are or have been the masters of others, kneeling down before things].

What position does Cuba occupy in Galeano's revisions and prophecies? What position does it occupy in the Latin American imagination? This country is mythologized by both its enemies and its idolatrous admirers (who, as Galeano points out, wax ecstatic when it comes to talk but rarely lift a finger to actually offer aid). Galeano has written numerous essays on Cuba, including his own testimonies of traveling to the island, in one instance, by the most convoluted route imaginable (resulting from the embargo that dictated no air access from anywhere in the Americas). He chronicles the testimonies of Cubans from all walks of life as well as Fidel Castro's 1970 speech on the challenges, mistakes, and hopes for the future delivered during one of the most difficult periods of the revolution following the failure of a 10-million-ton sugar-cane harvest. Galeano tries to capture both Castro's dilemma and the understandable tension of the Cubans, whose long-term deprivations begin to erode their hope for survival and the building of a socialist country condemned to meagre subsistence:

> "The enemy says that in Cuba we have difficulties," said Fidel. The faces and fists of the crowd, which listened in silence, tightened. "The enemy is right about that. The enemy says that in Cuba there is discontent," he added. "And the enemy is also right about that. But there is one thing that the enemy is mistaken about!" And then he stated that the past would not return; in a thunderous voice he stated that Cuba would never return to the hell of the colonial plantation and the whorehouse for foreigners, and the multitude responded with an earthshaking roar…I had the luck to have been there and I do not forget it. (*Days and Nights* 162)

The past puts the present into perspective, but Galeano's dynamic re-evaluation never lets that past crystallize into an alibi for abuse or impotence. His writing returns to Cuba time after time to reconsider whether justice, freedom, and equality are being advanced, in the hope of discovering the same participatory democracy that he would like to see globally. In more recent re-evaluations, Galeano expresses disappointment with Castro's bureaucratic government and calls it a "sistema de ecos de los monólogos del poder" (*Apuntes para el fin del siglo* 54) [system of echoes of the monologues of power], but he does not reject the dream that Cubans envision together with all those Latin Americans who believe in equality. His careful consideration of internal and external factors, comparative analysis of benefits and drawbacks, and contextualizing of Cuba within the Americas despite U.S. measures to isolate Cuba from the world lead Galeano to conclusions that are both realistic and hopeful. He appeals to Castro's repeated expressions of self-criticism and openness to evaluating mistakes committed along the way, applying the best of Castro to critique his increasing alienation from the people.

In the case of Cuba, Galeano demythologizes in order to approach a reality that deserves honest evaluation because of its constantly changing responses to new challenges: "Nunca he confundido a Cuba con el paraíso. ¿Por qué voy a confundirla, ahora, con el infierno? Yo soy uno más entre los que creemos que se puede

The Embattled Caribbean. Eduardo Galeano, from *The Book of Embraces* 109.

quererla sin mentir ni callar" (*Apuntes para el fin del siglo* 54) [I have never confused Cuba with paradise. Why should I now confuse her with hell? I am one among many who believes that we can love her without lying or falling silent]. Galeano understands the authoritarianism and bureaucratic stagnancy as a function of what he calls Cuba's tragic solitude, the unjust external factors that inevitably lead to internal consequences:

> Cuba did not import a prefabricated model of vertical power from Moscow, but was obliged to transform itself into a fortress to keep from ending up on the dinner plate of its all-powerful enemy…Now is a time of tragic solitude for Cuba. A time of danger. The invasion of Panama and the disintegration of the so-called socialist camp are, I am afraid, influencing its domestic politics in the worst way, abetting bureaucratic obduracy, ideological rigidity, and the militarization of society. (*We Say No* 276)

But this evaluation was written in 1990 and is tellingly republished and uncensored in a collection of essays under the prophetic title *El tigre azul* [The Blue Tiger] in 1996 by the Social Sciences Press of Havana. Much has changed in Cuba since the 1980s, and it seems that despite its tragic solitude, its windows are open to the resistant currents blowing from El Salvador, Nicaragua, Chiapas, and other places where people envision solidarity and participatory democracy as the basis for a just world. While the very existence of Cuba is an inspiration to Latin American revolutionaries who struggle to achieve sovereign governments and social systems, they in turn inspire Cuba to continue "the project of the Sierra Maestra" (cradle of the Cuban revolution), despite the forty-year embargo that attempts to annihilate it (*Apuntes para el fin del siglo* 54). In a chronicle of the Sandinistas' achievements and challenges evocatively entitled "Siendo" ["Being" in the progressive tense indicating a process of becoming], Galeano makes the point that solidarity is more contagious than the plague "cuando se libera la energía colectiva" (*El descubrimiento de América* 87) [when collective energy is liberated]. Through solidarity's gaze, the world is an integrated ecosystem involving not only biological and environmental issues but political and social ones as well:

> El planeta es uno, de todos, y a largo plazo nos costará a todos por igual—cada árbol del Amazonas crucificado es un centímetro cúbico menos de oxígeno, también, para el banquero neoyorkino—. Aunque ahorita, en lo inmediato, los costos sociales—miseria, desnutrición—tengan actores de ojos saltones (vientres hinchados, piel y hueso) y otros de ojos vidriosos (panzas desbordantes, cuerpos sin forma) por el despilfarro—. La solidaridad, de polo a polo, de mar a mar de Corinto hasta Corinto, dando vuelta entera alrededor del globo—no es más que una forma de la conciencia crítica de la humanidad. Un enorme fenómeno virtuoso que encontró en Nicaragua un rinconcito para germinar y denunciar la existencia de 7 mil millones de ojos saltones y secos de tanto llorar. Solidaridad…forma madura de hacerse responsable por el planeta de todos. (Ferrari 112)

[We have one planet that belongs to all, and in the long run we will all suffer or en-joy the same consequences—each crucified tree of the Amazon means one cubic centimeter less oxygen, even for the New York banker—. Although right now, the social costs—misery, undernourishment—are roles filled by actors with bulging eyes (distended bellies, skin, and bone) and others with glassy eyes (obese stomachs, shapeless bodies) due to extravagant waste—. Solidarity, from pole to pole, from sea to sea from Corinth to Corinth, circling the entire globe—is nothing but a form of humanity's critical conscience. An enormous virtuous phenomenon that found in Nicaragua a little corner in which to germinate and denounce the existence of seven thousand million people with bulging eyes, dry from so much weeping. Solidar-ity…the mature form of being responsible for the planet that belongs to all of us.]

This global vision of solidarity expressed by Sergio Ferrari, the progressive Argentinian his-torian who compiled dialogues and testimonies from Nicaragua, El Salvador, and Haiti (*Sembrando utopía* [Sowing Utopia], 1992), is an attempt to envision a radically humane future. Similarly, Galeano's historiography pulls down the covert ideological barriers that compartmentalize people and historical events in order to erase continuity, macroscopic cause and effect, and, ultimately, solidarity. A previously discussed essay from *We Say No*, poetically titled "Othercide: For Five Centuries the Rainbow Has Been Banned from America's Sky," contains Galeano's summary of how racism and capitalism go hand in hand to ensure the hegemony of a voracious minority. The essay is written in a style that can well be described as Magical Marxism: it is simultaneously a critique of exploitation and a visionary recuperation of the values that survive, however marginally, whispering prophe-cies of a future that remains to be invented through communitarian solidarity. Galeano's humorously caustic summary of history reveals how disoriented the Europeans were from the start. Navigational errors are metaphorically transposed to the Europeans' lack of ethical bearings: "Columbus thought Haiti was Japan and Cuba was China. And he believed that the inhabitants of China and Japan were Indians from India" (*We Say No* 303).

This ignorance of the other is strikingly similar to general North American ignorance of anything beyond the U.S. borders—as Gates notes, "Twenty-five percent of a sample of high school seniors in Dallas did not know that Mexico was the country bordering the United States to the south"; "One in seven American adults cannot locate the United States on a world map" (112). Galeano's essay moves from disclosing ignorance to the inverted gaze that we keep returning to as the vision of true knowledge and communication: Ignacio Ellacuría's notion that the oppressed discovers the oppressor (*We Say No* 316) and that the "third world is the prophetic denunciation of how badly arranged are the things of this world. A society that makes possible the third world is an unjust society, an inhuman soci-ety, a society appallingly badly arranged" (qtd. in Whitfield 41). In between, Galeano un-folds a concise history of the oppression of earth and non-European others, Christian colonizers shown to develop "naturally" into capitalist neocolonizers:

After five centuries of business from all of Christianity, one-third of the American forest has been annihilated, a lot of once-fertile land is sterile, and over half of the population eats infrequently. The Indians, victims of the greatest thievery in world history, still suffer the usurpation of their remaining bits of land, and are still condemned to the negation of their *distinct* identity. They are still prohibited from living the traditional way; their right to be themselves is still denied. At first pillage and "othercide" were carried out in the name of God in heaven. Now it is done in the name of the god of Progress. (*We Say No* 303)

Furthermore, by insisting that communism is an imposition of Russian imperialism, anti-communitarian governments draw an imaginary divide between Amerindian cultures and the rest of the oppressed majority. To proclaim, as Galeano does, that socialism (communism or communitarianism) belongs to the First Nations and that it is systematically attacked by imperial culture seems heretical because it reduces the U.S. to a colonial extension of European bourgeois culture even as it assumes world hegemony. Together with the Cold War mentality (kept alive through the relentless harassment of Cuba), the representation of the Amerindians as a folkloric souvenir of frontier times is essential to obfuscating the mutual communitarian interests of the vast and diverse peoples exploited by imperial economic interests.

Like the Brazilian photographer Sebastião Salgado, Galeano captures the particular image whose expressive power exceeds the particular and appeals to humanitarian ethics in a global context. While he does analyze and accuse the oligarchic power of globalitarianism, more often he focuses on the disenfranchised in terms of their dignity, determination, and democratic instincts. In a window entitled "The Landless," we glimpse cultural solidarity with the poor, their desperation and courage, and the forces of the world order that attempt to defeat them:

Sebastião Salgado photographed them, Chico Buarque sang to them, José Saramago wrote about them: five million families of landless peasants wander the deserted vastness of Brazil "between dreams and desperation."

Many of them have joined the Movement of the Landless. From encampments improvised by the sides of roads, rivers of people flow through the night in silence into the immense, empty farms. They break the padlocks, open the gates, enter. Sometimes they're greeted by bullets from hired guns or soldiers, the only ones working on those unworked lands.

The Movement of the Landless is guilty. Not only does it show no respect for the property rights of sponging landlords; even worse, it fails to fulfill its duty to the nation. The landless grow food on the lands they occupy when the World Bank commands the countries of the South not to grow their own food but rather to be submissive beggars on the world market. (*Upside Down* 322)

Squatters's settlements are hardly utopic alternative communities, and yet the act of occupying and laying claim to land on the basis of cultivating it, reminiscent of the earlier cited Diggers' Movement in early modern England, expresses not just desperate need but a vision of basic human rights over property rights. More and more testimonial and journalistic stories that emerge seem to belong to futuristic dystopian narratives. From the streets of Toronto, where in 2000 the homeless occupied a contaminated plot of industrial land belonging ironically to Home Depot, to the sewers of Mongolia, where entire communities live underground (including children that were born in the hot, steamy, mosquito and rat infested labyrinths), squatters are a global human phenomenon. In Spanish, they are called "*colonos*" and more humorously "*paracaidistas*" [parachutists]. The communities they build are "*colonias*" [colonies], an ironic twist on "colonization," returned to the most innocently communitarian use of the term. The process of occupying and colonizing land that owners allow to remain fallow in countries where the majority goes hungry is a form of agrarian reform that does not wait for governmental legislation, or even revolution, and in this sense squatting expresses a vision of justice and perhaps the most grassroots form of alternative community.

We now turn to another gatherer of the silenced voices that have been written out of history, Mexican writer Elena Poniatowska. While her texts differ from Galeano's vignettes in length and novelistically developed detail, her voice chronicles Mexico as Galeano's chronicles Uruguay and Argentina. Both writers share many affinities and their texts converse within a growing literary community based on common concerns. While Poniatowska is most often studied in literature departments as a writer of short stories and novels, much of her work belongs to the hybrid genre of *testimonio*, as Galeano practices it, that is, obviously filtered through the author's own gaze and voice that travels leaving the mouth behind. Hers is a writing practice that has no pretense to be journalistic nor to agonize about whose discourse it may be appropriating. Speaking about her testimonial novel *Hasta no verte, Jesús mío* (1969) [Here's Looking at You, Jesus], Poniatowska explains that though she conducted an extensive series of interviews with the woman who becomes the protagonist of the novel, her approach and intentions were primarily literary rather than anthropological or sociological:

> I made use of the anecdotes, the ideas, and many of Jesusa Palancares's expressions, but I would never be able to assert that the narrative is a direct transcription of her life because she herself would reject that. I killed off the characters who got in my way, I eliminated as many spiritualist sessions as I could, I elaborated wherever it seemed necessary to me, I cut, I stitched together, I patched, I invented…I limited myself to *divining* Jesusa. ("And Here's to You, Jesusa" 151)

Instead of attempting an illusory objective recording of events, Poniatowska makes her authorial presence felt as participation, sometimes solidary, at other times critical, often ambiguous. One of the most moving chronicles of a squatters' settlement is her account of "La colonia Rubén Jaramillo" [The Rubén Jaramillo Colony] in the state of Morelos, Mexico (in *Fuerte es el silencio* [Silence Is Strong]). The text includes photographs of agrarian reform leaders starting with Emiliano Zapata, as well as documentation on the construction of homes, school, the sewage system, the inhabitants, the army invasion that put an end to the dream in September 1973, and the final image of armed peasants deciding to take refuge in the mountains until the government addresses their needs. (They are still waiting.)

Poniatowska's narrative techniques have nothing in common with the self-effacing anthropological model of interviewing natives. Instead, she exploits a full arsenal of fictive narrative structures, from a seemingly omniscient narrator (her possible presence is only intimated at the end of the text) to fast-paced dialogue, drama, and suspense. A charismatic hero ambiguates people's motives for embracing ideas and suggests that affect (as we examined in our first chapter) is intrinsic to understanding. This is concretely expressed in the women *colonos'* own *testimonios* that reveal infatuations with El Güero Medrano that are both ideological and erotic. Conflict between different factions that lead the reader into theoretical questions are played out by the characters instead of being developed through analytic discourse. Finally, all these elements, together with Poniatowska's own sly involvement as one of the characters who at the same time is an outsider (unless she is gossiping with the women about the charismatic hero), contribute to "La colonia Rubén Jaramillo," being a gripping narrative that defies generic classification.

The first paragraph opens with a seeming statement of fact but immediately turns to the discrepancy between writing and reality and to the presence of the protagonist, Maoist revolutionary, anti-intellectual peasant leader, passionate and imperfect El Güero Medrano:[18]

> La invasión se hizo a las siete de la noche. Para la madrugada del 31 de marzo de 1973, habían tomado la tierra. En la libreta del Güero Medrano aparecían setecientas familias—él mismo las apuntó—, pero a la hora de la cita sólo se presentaron seis mudanzas. A las nueve, dos horas más tarde, llegaron algunas gentes con sus triques a cuestas. El Güero Medrano gritó irritado:
> —¿Qué pasó con los demás?
> Aquileo Mederos Vásquez alias el Full, su segundo, aventuró:
> —Parece que les dio miedo. ¡Tanta patrulla que anda por aquí!
> —Pero si habían quedado.
> —Pues sí, pero luego la gente es rete rejona—filosofó el Sin Fronteras.
> Al darse cuenta que los hombres no le respondían como lo pensaba, el Güero Medrano tomó una motocicleta y esa misma noche se dio a la tarea de recorrer todos los tugurios de la ciudad de Cuernavaca. En cada cuarto de vecindad pegaba el grito: "¡Recuerden el compromiso que tienen conmigo, ahora vamos a cumplir!" (*Fuerte es el silencio* 181)

[The invasion took place at seven in the evening. By daybreak on 31 March 1973, they had occupied the land. According to El Güero Medrano's booklet, there were seven hundred families—he had jotted them down himself—but at the moment of truth, only six presented themselves ready to move. At nine, two hours later, people arrived with their gear on their backs. El Güero Medrano, irritated, bellowed:

—What happened to the others?

Aquileo Mederos Vásquez, alias the Full, his second in command, ventured:

—It seems that they got scared. So many patrols around here!

—But they committed to it.

—Well, yeah, but people are such chickenshits—philosophized Borderless.

Realizing that the men were not responding as he had expected, El Güero Medrano grabbed a motorcycle and that same night set himself to combing all the slums in the city of Cuernavaca. In each neighbourhood he hollered: "Remember what you promised me. Now we're going to do it!"]

No heroics or rhetoric. The leader—far from being a noble revolutionary—seems more like a bully in relation to his half-hearted followers. And in the course of the story, he wins the reader's admiration but also reveals how easily power corrupts: El Güero's mood swings cover the full range from authoritarian megalomania to insightful solidarity. The land destined to be another of many resorts for the rich named "Villa de las Flores" [Villa of Flowers] is slowly occupied with people eventually having to squeeze themselves into ever-smaller lots to make room for more arrivals. This reality gives occasion to reflect on how difficult it is to set aside personal aspirations to show solidarity toward fellow *colonos*. While the community is run as a participatory democracy with regular assemblies where people can voice their concerns directly, El Güero reigns. Though he is criticized by some for his lack of theoretical coherence, he is knowledgeable about history and political science and has even taken a trip to China (through party affiliation and financial support from the Chinese government) to examine the organization of farms first-hand. In short, El Güero sets himself the task of teaching the illiterate peasants about the ideological implications of their struggle.

Choosing a meaningful name for the community recalls similar entries in Galeano's *Century of the Wind*. An entry for 1984 records the stolen name of a community that had originally been named after the popular Chilean singer of protest and love songs Violeta Parra: "The dictatorship of General Pinochet changes the names of twenty bone-poor communities, tin and cardboard houses, on the outskirts of Santiago de Chile. In the rebaptism, the Violeta Parra community gets the name of some military hero. But its inhabitants refuse to bear this unchosen name. They are Violeta Parra or nothing" (277). And in the next vignette, entitled "The Found Name," a Huichol Indian named Carlos González, from a community with no name in the mountains of Nayarit in Mexico, accidently finds a book in a garbage dump. Flipping through it he sees that it tells a recent story about "a man who had kept his word." Upon returning to his community he reads the book aloud, which takes him almost a week, after which the hundred and fifty families vote in favour of adopting that man's name as their own: "This community bears the name of a worthy man who did not doubt at the moment of choice between treachery and death. '*I'm going to Salvador Allende*,' the wayfarers say now" (277-78).

The *colonia* chronicled by Poniatowska finds itself in a similar situation. After "invading" the land and establishing a new community, the squatters must change the typically idyllic resort name of "Villa of Flowers" to a meaningful name that will also give them a sense of rootedness and historical continuity. El Güero proposes that they change the name to "Colonia Proletaria Rubén Jaramillo," to which the *colonos* respond with silence. He then launches into a history lesson and explains that the term "proletariat" identifies them as a colony of poor or dispossessed people, and that Rubén Jaramillo was a peasant like them and an agrarian leader who was assassinated by order of Adolfo López Mateos in 1962. When he mentions that Jaramillo was a captain of the Zapatistas, the listeners immediately grasp his significance. Poniatowska infers that memory is more meaningful to this group of people than political reasoning:

> (...entonces sí hubo entre los rostros cansados y las miradas torpes un relámpago de interés, algunos alzaron la vista que habían tenido baja, otros canjearon su expresión ausente por una mirada más alerta, porque en los mítines los campesinos siempre tienen cara de estar eschuchando algún rumor lejano, como que ladean la cabeza, cuando no de plano cierran los ojos, atentos sólo a un viento interno, a algo que no tiene que ver con los presentes). (*Fuerte es el silencio* 191)

> [(...then all of a sudden something like a lightning bolt of interest passed over the tired faces and stunned expressions. Some looked up instead of contemplating the ground, others focused their eyes and looked alert, because in meetings, peasants always look like they are listening to some distant murmur, tilting their heads to one side or even completely closing their eyes, receptive only to an internal wind, to something that has nothing to do with those around them).]

The anecdote frames the tension between peasants who want to farm the land and live in accordance with a distant, almost mythical memory of community before they were dispossessed and betrayed by their national leaders, and those who see a need to forge a new consciousness. But ultimately, the vision of peace comes from both the past and the prophesied future and expresses the flip sides of being conscious. The peasants hear the "internal wind" blowing from memory, while the revolutionary students and political leaders feel it blowing from the future.

The new consciousness that El Güero and his circle of community leaders discuss in these assemblies is called in socio-political terms "*concientización*" [making conscious]. This "making conscious" of the political dimension of community is seen as a necessary aspect of the defense of rights when traditional community structures have been eroded or repressed by the dominant culture. Within such a paradigm, the peasants are fully aware of their repression, but since the dominant culture is alien to them, they lack a coherent perspective of the enemy's identity and are able only to give testimony of specific abuses. In response to a squabble that breaks out among the assembled *colonos*, El Güero reminds them (at the top of his lungs) that while they are arguing, the dangerous enemy is stalking them. Their response illustrates the difference between El Güero's ideological conception of the enemy and the peasants' atomized view of the same: "Ahora sí todos se miraban desconcertados. —¿Quién es el enemigo, Güero, pa'que sepamos de quién vamos a defendernos, contra quién vamos a pelear? ¿Qué trazas tiene pa'reconocerlo? (*Fuerte es el silencio* 192) [Now everyone really looked confused. Who is the enemy, Güero, so we know who we are defending ourselves from, who we are fighting against? What are the signs to recognize him by?]. When an elderly woman ventures a memory of once being chased off the land by firefighters wielding high pressure hoses, El Güero explains to them that whoever eventually appears to persecute them will have been sent by the landower. The *colonos* respond incredulously: they assume that they have somehow, miraculously, acquired the right to remain because they have committed themselves to the land (193).

In accordance with Galeano's belief that history can reveal itself, Poniatowska allows the *colonos* and different factions within the community to express their views and their contradictions without interfering through direct interpretation. One of the few instances in which the omniscient narrator intrudes reveals what the ostentatious governor Felipe Rivera Crespo thinks of the *colonos* and their mangy dogs: "'Cómo puede ponérsele Golondrina a una perra negra y escurrida? Así, se ven a sí mismos como lo que no son.' Estos hombres eructaban acedo y se empanzonaban y se les aflojaban los músculos de aquí y de allá, los del vientre primero, y se les abultaba el cuello, se les encorvaban los hombros, porque la vida les pesaba muy pronto, sin embargo les ponían a sus perros pelones y feos: 'Golondrina'" (*Fuerte es el silencio* 213) ["'How can they name a bony black dog "Swallow"? That's how they see themselves; as something they're not.' These people belch and they grow fat bellies and their muscles turn to flab all over, first on their gut, their necks are swollen and their shoulders curved, because life starts weighing on them early on, nevertheless they call their ugly bald dogs 'Swallow'"]. Since officials like the governor are not worthy of giving testimony, Poniatowska takes liberties to intuit and interpret the contempt they feel for "este mar de carne morena, ajada y sucia" (213) [this sea of dark flesh, withered and dirty]. The "fictionalizing" of the governor's thoughts suggests that he is not a legitimate protagonist in history in the same way that the *colonos* are, since they are allowed to reveal themselves through their own discourse, one imitative of *testimonio*.

By presenting the story of Jaramillo as a drama that unfolds in the present of our reading, Poniatowska manages to turn a collective experience silenced by government and history into a riveting drama, one whose representation is dominated by its actual protagonists despite Poniatowska's authorial presence. The narrative framework is ambiguous, making it unclear how the text came to be. The character Elena shares the author's first name, seems to share in the writing of the chronicle, and is El Güero's biographer—activities that overlap ambivalently with Poniatowska's role as author-chronicler:

> Una noche el Güero la siguió, sacó la hoja de la maquina de escribir:
> —Eres espía.
> —No. Estoy escribiendo tu vida.
> —¿Mi vida? ¿Por qué?
> —Porque te quiero. (243)

> [One night El Güero followed her, pulled the sheet of paper out of her typewriter:
> —You're a spy.
> —No. I'm writing the story of your life.
> —My life? Why?
> —Because I love you.]

This Elena leaves her notebook (presumably containing the story of the *colonia* and its leader) in Jaramillo the day it is invaded by 3,000 soldiers, 500 police, and 300 judiciary agents. Newspapers announce the death of El Güero shortly after, and while we are given a testimony of the details, these are said to be rumours due to the lack of actual eyewitnesses. There is no one left to give witness, since the *colonos* have either been arrested or have fled into the mountains. The anonymous accounts, however, carry the weight of collective memory in which desire, myth, prophecy, and fact intermingle, giving full expression to a sense of identity that is under constant persecution but foretold to resurface at the next opportunity to assert freedom.

By the final section of the chronicle, El Güero has been converted into a legendary hero (like the Palmarian hero Zumbí discussed earlier), celebrated by a carnivalesque procession led by a magnificent queen dressed in ermine and red velvet and a retinue of children in white who sing: "Y aquí en Morelos, / Florencio Medrano / intrépito vencerá" (*Fuerte es el silencio* 278) [And here in Morelos, / Florencio Medrano / intrepid will overcome]. The song is overheard by a first-person narrator who comes in search of stories about El Güero and the founding of the Colonia Jaramillo, and while the locals are elusive and reserved in their interactions with strangers, there are always those who will divulge the memory of their ephemeral but dignified past:

> De lejos, sobre su loma, la Jaramillo parece una costra como bien lo dijo el cantinero Urbano. Bajo las costras, hay una herida, una enfermedad que a la larga cicatriza o revienta. Todos guardan silencio cuando alguien de afuera pregunta por el Güero o por Lucio Cabañas. Se ponen a rascar el suelo con una varita de huizache, haciéndose los desentendidos. Sin embargo, cuando termina la junta de colonos y se

van a su casa no falta una mujer que diga: "¿Usted es la que anda preguntando por el Güero? Véngase conmigo, yo lo conocí y si quiere, le cuento." (278)

[From afar, on the hillock, Jaramillo looks like a scab, as the bartender Urbano had aptly described it. Beneath the scabs, there's a wound, a disease that in the long run will either heal or explode. Everybody remains silent when an outsider asks about El Güero or Lucio Cabañas. They feign ignorance, distractedly scratching the ground with a stick of *huizache* [a native plant]. However, once the meeting of *colonos* is over and they all head home, there is always bound to be a woman who asks: "Are you the one who was asking around about El Güero? Come with me: I knew him, and if you like, I'll tell you about him."]

Poniatowska has chronicled major historical events in this tireless process of "asking around" and gathering the voices of countless witnesses and participants who ordinary newspaper reporters usually pass over in silence (since they prefer to quote so-called "experts"). The complex results of conflicting accounts and perspectives on such events as the 1985 earthquake in Mexico City, the massacre and detention of students, workers, political leaders, and sympathizers of all ages in Tlatelolco (1968), hunger strikes and other forms of protest by women, all democratize historiography and journalism. By re-envisioning the role of chronicler as gatherer and disseminator of multitudinous voices that are allowed to contradict each other, Poniatowska has preserved the stories of the Mexican people denied them by censorship and official history.

Both Galeano and Poniatowska believe in the power of the oral tradition, which is a kind of historical accumulation of memorable conversation. In a dialogue with her, Galeano reminisces about an evening spent with three great Mexican writers who were also great conversationalists: "eran muy buenos conversadores, que es un modo de narrar, ¿no? La narración oral es tan importante en la vida y en la historia americana, porque buena parte de nuestras mejores energías de vida han sido transmitidas por tradición oral. *Hay una expresión muy linda de los indios mapuches de Chile que dice: 'Pirámides aquí? Ninguna. Nuestras pirámides son las palabras'* (Poniatowska, "Preparo libros" 25) [they were very good conversationalists, which is a form of narrating, isn't it? Oral narration is so important in the life and history of the Americas because a good part of our best life energies have been transmitted through the oral tradition. *The Mapuche Indians of Chile have a lovely saying that goes: 'Pyramids here? Not one. Our pyramids are words'*].

Galeano's vision of *testimonios* as the pyramid-like building blocks for reconstructing the past and shaping the future is not unique and therefore not solitary but solidary. The hope for democratization depends on the encounter and cross-fertilization of voices that multiply and proliferate in order to recuperate the vast territories of knowledge and experience that media and capital try to monopolize and silence (just as the bio-prospectors and water traffickers try to gain total property rights to the planet and even, as we have seen in one particular case, the rain clouds overhead). Form and content, medium and message mesh, while the individualistic doctrine of globalitarianism that fights for complete control against communities is countered by collective discourse that reveals it to be an odious deformation of human interests and communication.

In accordance with indigenous visions of the human individual integrated into community, which in turn is integrated into nature, Galeano's historical vision does not separate ecological, sociological, and political concerns. The result is an indictment of capitalism that surpasses the narrow leftist agenda of representing the "proletariat" (a hopelessly reductive term that evacuates the very specificity of human agency that Galeano seeks to recuperate) as the new hegemony to which the indigenous population would still have to assimilate. Galeano privileges native culture as a source of American communitarianism, suggesting implicitly (by never using the term himself) that the "proletariat" should not be reduced to this industrial term, too closely associated with what he represents as the "system" (whether referring to state or private capitalism) that reduces human beings to their function as factory workers.

In response to the predictable criticism that we cannot go backwards, based on the assumption that indigenous people belong to the past and that technology must continue developing in order to exploit the globe and ensure permanent economic growth, Galeano turns to the ecological proof that current concepts of development (infinite quantifiable progress as determined by macro-economic and techno-militaristic indicators) are suicidal and indefensible:

> "Archaic techniques" in the hands of communities had made the deserts of the Andes fertile. "Modern technologies" in the hands of private export plantations have turned the fertile lands of the Andes and everywhere into deserts. It would be absurd to go five centuries back in technology; but it is no less absurd to ignore the catastrophes caused by a system that wrings people dry and demolishes the forest and rapes the earth and poisons the rivers, all in order to make the highest profit in the shortest time. (*We Say No* 312)

In "Funeral for the Wrong Corpse," Galeano strikes back at the simplistic and complacent notion that socialism is buried globally because Eastern Europe turns from state totalitarianism to the global totalitarianism of the so-called "Free Market." Just as the colonized image in the mirror is a mask that must be removed in order to reveal the true face of Latin America, Galeano denies that Stalinism was the only alternative to capitalism: "Our face was never in that mirror" (*We Say No* 274). While it is undeniable that Eastern Europe was not only sympathetic to socialist revolutions but also provided advisors, arms, technicians, and humanitarian aid to establish socialism in Cuba, Caribbean revolutions have a strong autochthonous character and cannot be written off as the results solely of foreign intervention or dogmatic, Eurocentric socialist theory.

The Caribbean revolutionaries from Tomás Borge (Commander of the Nicaraguan revolution) to Jean Bertrand Aristide (President of Haiti's fleeting democratic republic) make an important distinction between "Real Socialism" and the "Democratic Socialism" that most Latin American revolutions strive to achieve. Borge insists on not throwing the baby out with the bathwater, thinking it as ludicrous to disavow Marx's prophecies and egalitarian vision as it is to disavow the significance of Christ. Borge, who held the most honorific post in Sandinismo, would have been a priest had it not been for his recognition that he could not honestly take the vow of chastity. Together with Aristide and poet-priest-revolutionary Ernesto Cardenal, Borge asserts that all true Christians are revolutionaries and that those who go to church to show off their new clothes and throw coins into the alms box are not Christians but Pharisees (Ferrari 79). According to the same logic, real socialism is a lie because although (in Eastern Europe) it addressed some basic problems—health, education, unemployment—(problems that were never resolved and are on the rise in so-called First World countries), "el hombre no vive sólo de bienestar material. Requiere de libertad, y esa libertad les fue negada" (78) [man does not live by material well-being alone. He needs freedom, and that freedom was denied]. Galeano, too, accuses Eastern Europe of the same hypocrisy that characterizes U.S. propaganda:

> With respect to Panama, Nicaragua, or Cuba, the U.S. government invokes democracy as the Eastern governments invoked socialism—as an alibi. Latin America has been invaded by the United States more than a hundred times in this century. Always in the name of democracy and always to impose military dictatorships or puppet governments to rescue money in danger. The imperial system does not want democracies. It wants vassals. (*We Say No* 276)

Galeano's vision is that democracy, like America, has yet to be discovered. In so-called First World countries, the poor, like the slaves in Ancient Greece, do not enter the equation because, according to U.S. mythology, everyone gets an equal chance and therefore those who do not succeed have only themselves to blame. What each competitor begins with—money, education, ethnicity, class connections, level of greed or ambition—is, of course, of no consequence, since materialist interpretation is only for Marxists. Why does the term "democracy" not fall out of style when it is so emptied of meaning by the undeniable evidence of inequality and poverty associated with it? Galeano maintains that the terms "socialism" and "imperialism" name pertinent realities and cannot be dismissed as anachronistic. His analyses reveal the motives behind terms that camouflage the powerful, replaced by the neutralized lexicon that attempts to forge images of a happy global family where everyone is free to trade: "The term 'socialism' is applied in the West as makeup for injustice; in the East it evokes purgatory or maybe hell. The word 'imperialism' is out of fashion and is no longer to be found in the lexicon of mainstream politicians, even though imperialism does exist and pillage and kill" (*We Say No* 279).

Galeano observes that at summit meetings the presidents of the Americas invoke the anthem to free trade as a term synonymous with democracy. But the conditions limiting freedom are only expressed in armed retaliation against those who practice free trade with the wrong partners, those whose business does not benefit First World countries or transnationals. Two prime examples are Guatemala and Cuba, punished through U.S. military invasion for buying Soviet oil, or as Galeano puts it, for forgetting "que su libertad de comercio consistía en aceptar los precios que los Estados Unidos le imponían" (*Apuntes para el fin de siglo* 52) [that their freedom to trade meant accepting the prices imposed by the U.S.]. Galeano's careful chronicling of such contradictions reveals the sheer improbability of the alibis presented in transnational media to explain these acts of aggression against Latin American sovereignty, the "War on Drugs" being an especial favourite (although it does not work in the case of Cuba). Both the Zapatistas (initially represented as targets of military aggression justified by the false charge that they were drug trafficking) and the fact that drug lords throughout Latin America are prospering more than ever since free trade have revealed the hopeless contradictions in which mainstream politicians and media ensnare themselves in their dishonest intermingling of drug trafficking, political insurrection, and free trade. Galeano's fragmentary chronicling imitates the concise brevity of journalistic articles only in structure. But even the briefest vignettes throw open windows on vast expanses of reality liberated from the myopically incomplete stories told by official culture at the expense of those whose political interests are not served by the media.

To speak of the free market is abhorrent to anyone like Galeano, who sees that its freedom is reserved for a handful at the expense of multitudes. Besides, the term appropriates a cultural practice belonging to the local level of economy and applies it to methods of exchange that contradict what is popularly known as the marketplace. Galeano does not split hairs on this count: "For us capitalism is not a dream to be pursued, but a nightmare come true. Our challenge lies not in privatizing the state but in deprivatizing it. Our states have been bought up at bargain prices by the owners of the land, the banks, and everything else. And for us, the market is nothing more that a pirate ship—the greater its freedom, the worse its behavior" (*We Say No* 278).

Why not despair of a scenario that seems to get progressively worse? How to go on writing when language is being appropriated by a new form of Orwellian "newspeak," the word "freedom" appropriated to authorize extortion and pillage? As Galeano states emphatically, "Sometimes I feel as though they have stolen even our words" (*We Say No* 278). How can people like the Sandinistas, defeated after a ten-year struggle to progress toward their vision of a social utopia in the midst of military and economic intervention, assert that it is capitalism that has failed? All those who, like Galeano, say no to the lie refuse to accept the hegemony of the few over the vast majority that has no real say, except for the virtually meaningless ballot-in-a-box, play-acting at democracy that is increasingly the norm. They say no to "representative" democracy and read history, culture, and the media politically to deconstruct the undemocratic manufactured consent identified by critics like Chomsky and Galeano:

> We are all neighbors in this world of multinational programs and simulcasts via satellite, but as Orwell would say, some are more neighbors than others. Communications are centralized. Everything that happens on the planet gets translated in the centers of power, translated into the language of the Universal System of the Lie, and then returned to the world converted into sounds and images for mass consumption. Objectivity? *We distrust an objectivity that reduces us to objects.* (*We Say No* 210-11)

The other face of this reading against the grain is to re-evaluate the potential of canonical texts that have been "kidnapped" to represent the interests of institutional élites, whether the politburo or the Christian church. Borge has reached the conclusion that both the Judeo-Christian bible and Marx's *Capital* have to be read with free will, not schematically, a point that stresses the importance of critical reading practices as metonyms for social practices (whether freedom or oppression). Even after losing the elections to U.S.-backed Violetta de Chamorro, the Sandinistas are optimistic that the loss was a temporary setback and that the meek (poor) shall inherit the earth, not in the afterlife but after the collapse of capitalism. Is this also an outmoded term in the era of transnational corporations and capital? Far from being insular or parochial, the Sandinistas debated and continue to debate the failure of capitalism in Latin America, North America, and Europe, together with their own failures to radically democratize society.

This debate occurs in the face of a globalitarian triumphalism that overlooks the millions of impoverished victims in a "new world order" and dismisses the majority of the population as collateral damage. Success is gauged only from the perspective of corporations and highly partial statistics that monitor industrial growth. And those who have compelling evidence that the free market is a failure not only in the Third World but in North America and Europe as well are dismissed despite such evidence of the homeless, the unemployed, and the unemployable whose numbers are growing parallel with the "growth" of each country's economy. According to Cardenal, the mainstream media that hail the end of socialism should also announce the failure of capitalism: "Es el falso socialismo el que ha fracasado—no el cumplimiento auténtico del socialismo—. En cambio, el capitalismo que ha fracasado es el auténtico capitalismo" (Ferrari 138) [It was the false socialism that failed—not the carrying out of authentic socialism—. On the other hand, the capitalism that failed was authentic capitalism]. Among the many examples that Cardenal cites in his critique are the numerous homeless people sleeping in Lafayette Park in front of the White House in Washington, D.C.

Comandante Víctor Tirado López of the Sandinistas subverts the paternalistic paradigm of the North's preaching democracy to its indebted vassals and expresses the optimistic vision that democracy, conceived of as a process of conscience formation, will inevitably spread to the U.S. and throughout the world:

En la nueva situación, Estados Unidos también tendrá que democratizarse. En ese país el multipartidismo es casi una ficción...Las minorías sociales, étnicas, políticas no tienen voz directa en el Gobierno y en el Parlamento...Estados Unidos también debe democratizar sus relaciones con el mundo y especialmente con América Latina. En las nuevas condiciones, la política de Estados Unidos basada en la fuerza, la agresión, la amenaza, las represiones, el chantaje, los bloqueos financieros y comerciales no tienen futuro. Es un anacronismo, una política que no acepta el mundo y la mayor parte de los gobiernos latinoamericanos. (Ferrari 55)

[In the new situation, the United States will also have to become democratic. In that country the multiple party system is practically a fiction...The social, ethnic, and political minorities have no direct voice in the Government and the Parliament...the United States should also democratize its international relations, especially with Latin America. Under the new conditions, U.S. politics, based on force, aggression, threats, repression, blackmail, financial and commercial blockades, has no future. Anachronistic, this politics is unacceptable to the rest of the world and to the majority of Latin American governments.]

These views are not restricted to the "victims" of U.S. and transnational policies, since, as Holly Sklar argues in *Chaos or Community*, the citizens of the U.S. are in some cases more victimized by "free" market economics than the countries usually designated Third World that at least secure work contracts even if the working conditions and wages are extremely exploitative. Sklar opens her first chapter "Wealth and Poverty" (a cause and effect paradigm similar to Galeano's assertion that there are poor countries *because* there are rich countries) with the following statement:

One out of four children is born into poverty in the United States—according to the official measure. The United States is the world's wealthiest nation, but much of that wealth is concentrated at the top. The combined wealth of the top 1 percent of American families is nearly the same as that of the entire bottom 95 percent...Such obscene inequality befits an oligarchy, not a democracy. The income gap in Manhattan, New York is worse than Guatemala's. (5)

Sklar, too, appeals to the notion of local and global solidarity as the only hope for a future in which the vast majority is not enslaved and children are not exterminated as the enemy condemned to poverty under the present economic régime. She asserts that people *are* working together to oppose the dehumanizing trends of exploitation and to promote just alternatives. Sklar also names a heartening number of examples in which people are trying to take control of their collective destinies—from community-based organizations to cross-border coalitions to international non-governmental organization forums. In accordance with the

Latin American views on the interdependence of nations that must now think of defending their sovereignty from the purely nihilistic effects of corporations whose only interest is their own profits, Sklar envisions the exploited of the world recognizing their mutual interests and the need to view each other not as competing enemies but rather as allies for survival. Her reasoning debunks the claims of free trade agreements that give corporations license to exploit resources and people with limited legal restrictions:

> We have to understand the growing linkage between working conditions and wages in the United States and those abroad. Wages and costs in many Third World countries are kept low by denying workers the right to organize unions, or recognizing only subservient unions. Health and safety regulations are minimal or nonexistent. Repression is widespread. But there is also widespread activism. American workers have a direct stake in supporting better wages and working conditions for Third World workers; otherwise corporations will continue freely trading on cheap labor to transfer jobs and diminish wages and working conditions in the United States. (169)

One of the most important keys to the future identified by Sklar is environmentally sustainable development in relation to which she calls for the democratization or abolition of such organizations as the International Monetary Fund, World Bank, and World Trade Organization, an end to "structural adjustment" and reduction of Third World debt since, as she states, "it is time to recognize that the 'debt' has been more than repaid through colonialism, neocolonialism and usurious interest" (173). This kind of global thinking is a forceful antidote to the other globalization envisioned by those whose only concern is to line their own pockets. The work of "intellectuals" such as Galeano (who, as we have seen previously, eschews any form of reductive categorization as a writer), Sklar, and a myriad of others who are not even published in English and do not conceive of themselves as intellectuals but as peasants and workers who happen to understand their own plight gives a much more accurate and optimistic picture of the scope of dissident and visionary, utopian historiography.

   While a linear view of history whose outcome is globalitarianism would appear to be inevitably eschatological, thus making any form of dissension, activism, or revolution seem destined to failure, Galeano's reading of history taps potential sources of inspiration and hope in the process of meaningful democratization:

> After all we've seen, we know for sure that history makes mistakes: she gets distracted, she falls asleep, she gets lost. We make her and she looks like us. But she's also, like us, unpredictable. Human history is like soccer: her finest trait is her capacity for surprise. Against all predictions, against all evidence, the little guys can sometimes knock the invincible giants for a loop…across the world a thousand and one new forces are emerging. They emerge from the bottom up and the inside out. (*Upside Down* 320-21)

This dynamic and, some would say, utopian vision of how the course of history may suddenly change to favour those whom official history systematically writes out of reality "deobjectifies" and humanizes events by infusing them with prophetic hope. And yet Galeano insists on a form of objective empiricism that rejects the historian's quasi-objectivity, his or her erasure of self as narrator, interpreter, and manipulator of reality: "It occurred to me that history could talk about itself," he says, reflecting on the "window" structure of the *Memory of Fire* trilogy (Bach 17). The privileging of marginalized voices and silenced events manifests Galeano's will to revision and retell stories that represent the conscience and determination of the oppressed, whether they are oppressed on the basis of gender, ethnicity, class, or sexual orientation.

To consider the indigenous traditions of democracy necessarily involves an altered form of vision that does not separate what Western culture categorizes as history and myth. Popular media images of indigenous people tend to dwell on the effects of decadence, alcoholism, incest, and all the other social ills that are not often historicized to explain how specific groups of people were forcibly stripped of their identity and their cultural bearings by the consequences of conquest and colonization. Galeano recuperates the sources of identity and vision to show that they are not just distant memories but rather that they continue to manifest in lived experience. Instead of relegating indigenous peoples to the sphere of myth (making implicit that they do not belong to the present, to history, or to the future), Galeano's revision searches out the strongest roots of communitarian democracy and appeals to the prophecies that inform current acts of resistance and revolution: "In 1523, Chief Nicaragua asked the conquistadores: '*And your king, who elected him?*' The chief had been elected by the elders of the communities…Pre-Columbian America was vast and diverse, and it had forms of democracy that Europe was unable to see and of which the world remains ignorant" (*We Say No* 311).

Is It Tomorrow?:
The Dream of the Blue Tiger

The Guaraní have a myth of destruction that is also, in Galeano's reading, a "promise" of a better America. Not so much a narrative of apocalypse but a story of renewal and rebirth, the myth of the blue tiger that destroys the world asks the question "Is it tomorrow?" Has the current state of affairs reached the point where the destructive forces that allow for creation and rebirth can be unleashed? Is the future here? The ethics of such a question address the most fundamental questions of being-in-the-world, how one *is* in relation to one's surroundings: Whether one recognizes the pain and suffering in the infamy of the now. Whether one embraces the work that always remains to be done in the present as an ethical response to the past and as a vindication of the potential of the future. Whether one dreams of utter apocalyptic destruction or of rebirth in the potential of tomorrow that is today. Whether one is willing to surrender a transcendental, apocalyptic vision of eschatological salvation for the materiality of an elsewhere that is here and now. While we recognize that Galeano's critical positions can seem (to some) bleak and disturbing, such a response is produced through no fault of his own. The documentation from story, memory, *testimonio*, and archive assembled by Galeano is too diversely sourced and polyphonic to be dismissed as untrue (within the limitations of what any single authorial vision can produce).

The Blue Tiger: Is It Tomorrow? From *Crisis* 58 (1988): 59.

But this is not to say that Galeano's vision of the future (Is it tomorrow?) is not strongly opposed to the forces that have conspired to make the world such as he describes it. And, in this respect, Galeano's writing practices advocate an anti-apocalyptic, life-affirming theory of the possibility of community and human solidarity that is deeply contextualized in the indigenous cultures of the Americas, but not to the exclusion of other influences.[19] Consider the following excerpt from the vignette that opens the second volume of *Memory of Fire, Faces and Masks*:

The blue tiger will smash the world.

Another land, without evil, without death, will be born from the destruction of this one. This land wants it. It asks to die, asks to be born, this old and offended land. It is weary and blind from so much weeping behind closed eyelids. On the point of death it strides the days, garbage heap of time, and at night it inspires pity from the stars. Soon the First Father will hear the world's supplications, land wanting to be another, and then the blue tiger who sleeps beneath his hammock will jump. (3)

Galeano describes the Guaraní's nomadic way of life in mythic terms as a search for paradise, that is, as a model for imagining another world. That search produces the following vision:

> They have skirted jungles and mountains and rivers in pursuit of the new land, the one that will be founded without old age or sickness or anything to interrupt the endless fiesta of living. The chants announce that corn will grow on its own and arrows shoot into the thickets all by themselves; and neither punishment nor pardon will be necessary, because there won't be prohibition or blame. (3)[20]

The ethical function of this vision is direct in its challenge to readers. How far are you prepared to go in acknowledging an indigenous world of difference that makes such claims? How to read this allegory of enacted difference in relation to other visions of the "promised land"? How does such a far-fetched story address the potential of thinking otherness in ways that produce meaningful transformation, the incarnate energy that difference releases?

In sharp contrast to the Western-Christian concept of apocalypse, *pachakuti* belongs to a vision of radical change that both accounts for the conquest of the indigenous people by Europeans and foresees an end to their hegemony. This concept maintains the apocalyptic distinction between those who will be annihilated and those who will be liberated. At the same time, *pachakuti* addresses historical and political contingency in a way that perhaps the myth of Revelation in the Christian bible did at the time of the Christians' persecution by the Romans but which has now been lost to metaphysics in the Western tradition. The myth of eternal return takes on entirely new meaning when instead of referring to the natural life cycle, it is associated with human affairs, political domination, and submission:

> The Incas believed that history was a succession of ages divided one from another by a cataclysmic epoch—a *pachakuti*—an "overturning of the world"...Just as the Maya used prophecy to contain and subvert the invasion, the Incas employed their scheme of revolving ages to imply that the new order—unnatural and destructive from the Andean point of view—could not be accepted and would one day be reversed. For the past order is not irrevocable; it remains latent in the underworld, awaiting a return: one *pachakuti* demands another. This is the meaning of the words in the elegy for Atawallpa: "The elders and the people buried themselves alive." Nearly five centuries later, Andeans still expect the righting of their world. (Wright, *Stolen Continents* 181)

If the new "World Order" is also deemed unnatural and destructive from the silent majority's point of view and for this reason cannot be accepted, will it one day be reversed? When the mass media and other mouthpieces for globalitarianism suggest there is no other reality possible, can the oppressed resist abjection by remembering that the past order is not irrevocable? The nostalgic vision of a past in which people were tougher and more honest when they had to work hard is only ostensibly a meaningful memory for those who are being worked to death and still cannot support their children. And so we turn to the other America that according to Galeano has yet to be discovered.

Wright explains a cosmogonic vision that is both prophetic and historical. The vision gives way to a Mayan discourse that combines pre-Columbian and post-Columbian history in a hybrid form Wright calls "prophecy-history," a term that we would apply to Galeano's own vision of a history that cannot be put behind us, a history that is pregnant with prophecy in a more significant way than what is usually meant by simply not repeating the mistakes of the past. This vision of a history that speaks to the future served two purposes for the Maya and conceivably can do the same now: "it is a powerful indictment of the European invasion, and its very seamlessness is a proclamation of resistance, an assurance that the Maya world continues" (165). Prophetic denunciation of the conditions that have produced what Ellacuría calls "a region maltreated since the armed Conquest made by Spanish Christendom, a region that, without losing its heart, has a face that is disfigured and hardly recognizable as human" (qtd. in Whitfield 224) bears thinking in relation to the lived realities utopian thought addresses. Teresa Whitfield, in her book on Ellacuría, argues that "What is denounced by the prophecy is precisely that which makes necessary the utopia. Prophecy impels the force of history that the utopia attracts and ensures that the utopia does not become an evasion of reality" (224).

Something very similar emerges from the writings of contemporary Latin Americans who turn to *testimonio* for personal accounts of collective experience, inspired by the belief that the *pueblo* is a lived, inescapable reality and, despite being largely written out of history, that it is the true repository of memory as a form of urgent prophecy that links the materials of history with utopian vision. This is no passive role for the *pueblo*: living people are not mere archives and memory implicitly engenders a desire for collective "self"-affirmation, denunciation, resistance, and even revolution in the name of a possible, imagined future. This vision of "prophecy-history" is linked to radical change for the indigenous population that awaits the turning of the tables in the march toward a utopian horizon. And since the "proletariat" poor have no democratic past to project into the future, it is clearly of collective interest for them to look to what Galeano calls "traditions of the future."

The term "utopia," then, undergoes a significant conceptual-spiritual metamorphosis when it passes from European usage to the Latin American context, where it becomes permeated with the indigenous connotations of *pachakuti*. As such, its very hybridity signals the mestizo reality that emerges from bringing together the different streams of democratic thought and practice that suffuse European and indigenous visions of an ideal world. This is not the fanciful, arrogant invention of a reality that never was and is therefore nowhere. And this may also be the reason why Galeano acknowledges the good in the utopic visions of More and Las Casas despite the blind spots that mark their texts. It is perhaps a sign of solidarity to grant the Europeans their insights into justice and to accept their vision as (necessarily) marred by the ideological baggage that makes it difficult to comprehend the other's point of view, culturally impossible to ask with humility like the *tlamatinime* do in a passage we have already cited: "we ignorant people contemplate you...And now what are we to say? What should we cause your ears to hear?" (León-Portilla, *Aztec Thought and Culture* 63).

From a purely social perspective, the *pachakuti* might resemble the concept of hegemony; Inca hegemony prophesied as replacing Spanish hegemony, a pan-American "sácate tú para ponerme yo," loosely translatable as "get lost it's my turn," a cynical political allusion referring to politicians taking their turns at the trough. But the native representation of their sovereignty diverges in significant ways from Western philosophies of power, in that they recognize that "white" domination exploits not just the vanquished people but the earth itself, the source of all life. All indigenous cultures, by contrast, once had worldviews that integrated their humanity with nature; thus, they suffer doubly from seeing themselves and the world humiliated:

> *On that day, dust possesses the earth,*
> *On that day, a blight is on the face of the earth,*
> *On that day, a cloud rises,*
> *On that day, a mountain rises,*
> *On that day, a strong man seizes the land,*
> *On that day, things fall to ruin,*
> *On that day, the tender leaf is destroyed,*
> *On that day, the dying eyes are closed.* (Wright, *Stolen Continents* 164)

Wright cites these verses to show how ambiguous these references are from a purely historical perspective: "A European mind asks, What day is this? Does it lie in the past or future? Is it the day the Toltecs invaded Yucatán? Is it the day the Spaniards arrived? Is it the Day of Judgement? Is it the war of the end of the world? To a Maya mind it is all of those" (*Stolen Continents* 164). The prophecy of overcoming this blight is also envisioned in mythic terms, releasing the symbolic potential of reality and language in a way that frees the indigenous images from a narrow sphere of interest to foresee the future of the world. Remember lines from Galeano that we have already quoted: "When the greed is done away with, the face will be untied, the hand will be untied, the feet of the world will be untied," to which Galeano adds a question in the spirit of the *tlamatinime*, the spirit of listening to the other: "And when the mouth is untied, what will it say? What will the other voice say, the one never heard?" (*We Say No* 310).

Augusto Roa Bastos expresses a similar attitude in turning to the Guaraní to recuperate a snychronic conception of time and space in which utopia is both a memory and a horizon that unites each individual with him/herself, the community, and the divine:

> Their primordial divinities did not fulminate punitive laws against one who aspired
> to wisdom. They brought about the communion between knowing and doing, be-
> tween unity and plurality, between life and death. Every man was God on the way to

purification, and God—or the many gods of that theogony—was both the first man and the last. They did not impose exile, but the pilgrimage of the *multitude-person* to the *land-without-evil* that each one bore within and amid all. (277)

The vision of cosmic harmony is threatened when the languages capable of expressing opposites held in balance (*multitude-person*) are forcibly replaced by the European languages that can only express these concepts in the awkward approximations of hyphenated pairs. As an exiled writer, Roa Bastos finds the key to reconstructing collective identity and a literature of human solidarity in the indigenous insights that were passed on from mouth to mouth. Perhaps without even realizing it, what he says about exile is applicable to all those who have lost their sense of community, their connection to a fertile and promising past, even if they have never suffered war or physical displacement: "For those writers subjected to internal exile, as for those forced to scatter in the diaspora, the work of literature once again means the imperative need to embody a destiny, to find their place once more in the vital reality of a collectivity, their own, in order to nourish themselves in its profoundest essences and aspirations, and from there go on to embrace the universality of humankind" (277).

In his massive chronicling of the last five hundred years of "agravios, revueltas y profecías" [injustices, revolts and prophecies] in Chiapas, Antonio García de León ends *Resistencia y utopía* [Resistance and Utopia] with a prophetic retelling of the eruption of the volcano Chichonal in 1982. After a detailed history woven together from archival material, periodicals, oral stories, and "marvelous" events (in the Latin American sense of rationally inexplicable events that are nevertheless believed) and ending with what García de León identifies as a general war waged by imperialist governments against all of Central America, the final narrative is told in the voice of gossip, storytelling, rumour, and oral history: "*Cuentan que* cuando sobrevino el estallido, todo quedó a oscuras y como suspendido en el

Lying in Wait. Crisis 42 (1986): 41.

mismo éter de los días de la creación: los pájaros callaron por primera vez en siglos, las reses flotaban semicalcinadas en las aguas turbias de ríos que cambiaron de cauce" (438; our emphasis) [*They say* that when the eruption occurred, everything was plunged into darkness, as if suspended in the ether of the first days of creation: the birds fell silent for the first time in centuries, cattle floated half-burned in the turbid waters of rivers that changed their courses]. While a traditional apocalyptic vision of a luminous city descending from heaven is heralded from house to house by an old woman ("*madre de los dioses*" [mother of the gods]), a parallel reality of rebirth here on earth suggests that both natural phenomena and history invite allegorical and prophetic readings: "Pero el día siguiente, los insectos fueron los primeros en abandonar sus refugios y empezaron de nuevo el ritual cotidiano y tenaz para reorganizar los ciclos rotos del universo mundo" (438) [But the next day, the insects were the first to abandon their refuges and once again initiated the tenacious daily rituals to reorganize the broken cycles of the universe world]. What does this insect world have to do with the account of genocide in Central America, which García de León obliquely links to this story with ellipses?

It is left to the reader to move from political history to biology, to glimpse the communion between knowing and doing, unity and plurality, life and death, in a prophetic reading of the erupting volcano (one of the favourite metaphors of Central American poets):

> Su nacimiento fue de nuevo precedido de visiones proféticas y vino a unirse como un anuncio más a las piezas de este inmenso rompecabezas, al mapa de esta pausada guerra de movimientos, a esta secuencia en apariencia inmóvil que sólo es posible medirla con la vara de los siglos. Su estremecimiento colosal (su bostezo de "relámpagos, truenos ensordecedores, terremotos y fuertes granizadas"), que quedará como mojonera en la memoria de las generaciones futuras, anunciaba solamente la impaciencia de las fuerzas minerales y telúricas que empujaban por salir de nuevo a la superficie. (García de León 439)

> [Its birth was once more preceded by prophetic visions and it came to join, like one more sign, the pieces of this immense puzzle, the map of this slow and deliberate war of movements, this apparently immobile sequence measurable only with the yardstick of centuries. Its colossal tremor (its yawn, "flashes of lightning, deafening thunder bolts, earthquakes, and heavy hailstorms"), which would stick like a landmark in the memory of future generations, only announced the impatience of mineral and telluric forces that were pushing to break through to the surface once again.]

The innocent eruption that releases pent-up forces seeking to resurface vaguely recalls the *pachakuti* and is more obviously a metaphor for human desire breaking out of oppression. But by "metaphor" we do not wish to suggest that this passage should be reduced to the purely symbolic language of allegory. Rather, it holds the human and the telluric in balance, suggesting that they consequently share similar traits. The telluric does not stand in for the human but provides the cosmic context for telling the story of radical change.

Where is this situated in time? As a story of geological movements, its historical dimension would really only be constructed by the human perspective on those who were displaced and harmed by the eruption (in this case the Zoque communities). Otherwise, it is atemporal in its eternal cycles, hence the biblical language that relates it to the Judeo-Christian story of Genesis. But García de León's meticulous chronicling of human tensions is represented in a language that, like Galeano's, rejects neutrality and unabashedly judges, accuses, envisions, and expresses the urgency of the insight that "we have reached tomorrow." This revelation can be apocalyptic or utopian depending on whether we choose the law of the urban jungle that condemns us to solitude or choose to open our ears to the voices that remember community and speak about/in solidarity.

Martin Luther King told the same prophecy—that "tomorrow is today"—before he was silenced, but as we have shown through the numerous stories examined in this book, individuals who are solidary are not so easily eliminated because they express the aspirations of a multitude that never forgets and only seems to resign itself while it gathers strength: "We are now faced with the fact that tomorrow is today…We still have a choice today: nonviolent coexistence or violent coannihilation. This may well be mankind's last chance to choose between chaos and community" (qtd. in Sklar 2). Mythical and prophetic thinking infuse historical process with hope. Revolutionary martyrs don't die; they germinate and are reborn, like the legendary and historical figures of Zumbí or Tupac Amaru.

Inca emperor Tupac Amaru I banned Christianity and as a result was beheaded in 1572. Wright describes how Francisco de Toledo, the Spanish viceroy who was determined to destroy the Inca free state, "had Tupa Amaru's head stuck on a pike, whereupon thousands gathered each night to venerate it…Europeans usually left their trophy heads to rot; in Tupa Amaru's case they took it down and buried it. But as we shall see, the Inca's head still lives" (*Stolen Continents* 186-87). Content that they had buried the memory of Tupac Amaru, whose son died shortly after, the Spanish did not understand that the head and the memory would germinate to resurface 200 years later in the great-great-great-grandson José Gabriel Kunturkanki [Condorcanqui] Tupac Amaru. The name and the memory had been kept alive by Diego Felipe Kunturkanki, who had assumed it as his own when he married the first Tupac Amaru's daughter, Juana. After failing to better the lot of his people through legal channels, José Gabriel proclaimed himself Tupac Amaru II, hanged the corregidor of Tinta in 1780, and led the greatest Andean revolt of the century with the promise: *Manañam kunanmanta wakchakayniykiwan wiraquocha mikhunqañachu!* "From this day forth, no longer shall the Spaniard feast on your poverty!" (Wright, *Stolen Continents* 195). Galeano's entry in *Faces and Masks* for 1780 represents this hero from the point of view of the liberated man who further immortalizes Tupac Amaru in a painting that commemorates solidarity:

Antonio Oblitas, slave of the magistrate Arriaga, hoisted a strong rope, hangman's rope, mule's rope, in the plaza of this town of Tungasuca, and for a whole week the wind rocked the body of Arriaga, boss of Indians, owner of blacks, owner of Antonio. This hand that paints is the hand that hanged. Antonio Oblitas is painting the portrait of the man who ordered the freedom of all the slaves in Peru...creating color over the rough wood, come and go the brushes of Antonio, hangman of his master, nevermore a slave. Túpac Amaru poses on a horse, out in the open...The painting is born between two battles, during the armed truce...The painter immerses himself in this long moment of truce. Thus the artist and his model escape from time; stave off, while the work lasts, defeat and death. (52)

The legend of Inkarí (fusion of Atawallpa [Atahualpa], Manku, and Tupac Amaru), whose head is slowly growing a new body that upon completion will initiate a new *pachakuti*, gives symbolic significance to historical acts conceived of as a continuum in the Andean people's quest for justice. The most recent incident involved the massacre of some of the Peruvian rebels who have, once again, taken the name of Tupac Amaru. In response to the smug news reports of the mass media, Subcomandante Marcos writes on 25 April 1997:

Some days ago we heard on the radio news of the military assault on the Japanese embassy in Peru. The great international Power decided upon a new crime in Latin American lands and ordered the assassination of the rebels of Tupac Amaru (who, let us not forget, were negotiating a solution to the crisis with the government of Fujimori)..."A clean operation," said the news programs, and described Fujimori as smiling and happy. And, way above him, the supranational powers, which had given the order for annihilation, also smiled...that is how they are, Power and its neoliberal governments; they pretend to dialogue and negotiate, when in reality they only seek the opportunity to exert their violence...But a lot of history still remains to be written. (*Our Word Is Our Weapon* 184)

Ending on a note that throws open a window on the history that remains to be written and made, Marcos denies defeat. This denial involves the recognition that the seemingly natural order of things is an aberration that must be reversed through myriad activities to promote the true interests of humanity. The First Intercontinental *Encuentro* held by the Zapatistas in July and August 1996 (in the Chiapanecan town of La Realidad) was attended by delegations from approximately forty-three countries in five continents.[21] How many people saw this event covered in any detail on television, heard the talks on radio, or read transcripts or reports in the mainstream media? Such events, especially when they are conducted peaceably, typically do not make "news." The mainstream media are largely silent about stories that articulate alternative analyses of events that critique hegemonic interests. Adrienne Rich, poet and feminist theorist, in the short prologue she writes to *First World, Ha Ha Ha!: The Zapatista Challenge,* addresses this very issue:

When we do and think and feel certain things privately and in secret, even when thousands of people are doing, thinking, whispering these things privately and in secret, there is still no general, collective understanding from which to move...But these thoughts and feelings, suppressed and stored-up and whispered, have an incendiary component. You cannot tell where or how they will connect, spreading underground from rootlet to rootlet till every grass blade is afire from every other. This is that "spontaneity" that party "leaders," secret governments, and closed systems dread. (n.pag.)

The union of feeling and thinking—*senti-pensante*—that unexpectedly creates incendiary networks of solidarity also describes a vision in which mythic imagination is aligned with solidary social aspirations that seek to change the world as it has become. This phenomenon is especially prevalent in Latin America, informed by the attributes of magic realism, which admits different forms of consciousness instead of suppressing them through rationalization. The cultural heritage of the indigenous peoples has endured despite the extreme solitude to which the European colonialists and present-day neocolonialists have condemned them. The regenerative power of their memory, kept alive by word of mouth, independent of the writings and images destroyed in numerous bonfires over the centuries, speaks in Galeano's vision for humanity (with the exception of those who evaluate people and resources in terms of market value, and even in this case, if the memory does not speak *for* them it can still speak *to* them).

Can we answer the most fundamental of questions when we are interpolated by a memory that "has always, always been" and could not have been forgotten?:

¿Que tiene dueño la tierra? ¿Cómo así? ¿Cómo se ha de vender? ¿Cómo se ha de comprar? Si ella no nos pertenece, pues. Nosotros somos de ella. Sus hijos somos. *Así siempre, siempre.* Tierra viva. Como cría a los gusanos, así nos cría. Tiene huesos y sangre. Leche tiene, y nos da de mamar. Pelo tiene, pasto, paja, árboles. Ella sabe parir papas. Hace nacer casas. Gente hace nacer. Ella nos cuida y nosotros la cuidamos. Ella bebe chicha, acepta nuestro convite. Hijos suyos somos. ¿Cómo se ha de vender? ¿Cómo se ha de comprar? (Galeano, *Úselo y tírelo* 38; our emphasis)

[Does the earth have an owner? How so? How can she be sold? How can she be bought? She does not belong to us but we to her. We are her children. *This is how it has always, always been.* Live earth. The way she raises worms is the same way she raises us. She has bones and blood. Milk, too, and she nurses us. She has hair, grass, hay, trees. She knows how to bring forth potatoes. She creates homes. She creates people. She takes care of us and we take care of her. She drinks *chicha,* accepting our offer. We are her children. How can she be sold? How can she be bought?][22]

We have seen that this vision of the "earth-born" as a constitutive basis for understanding humanity remains unacknowledged by the legal and institutional contexts of the nation-state. This vision has meant ongoing persecution and suffering for indigenes because it exposes structures of self-interest that are sacrilegious, a form of collective suicide that disavows our earth-born contingency. To hear such an assertion is not to sentimentally discover personal enlightenment and fulfillment, but rather it is to be situated in a moment of historical crisis, an urgent wake-up call coming from the past, prophesying the future.

As we have seen throughout this book, prophecy requires fortitude and memory, represented by Galeano in an animistic image that recalls the promise of the blue tiger: "Our collective memory remains stubbornly alive: a thousand times slain, a thousand times reborn in the hiding places where she licks her wounds" (*We Say No* 265). Echoing the blue tiger lying beneath the first father's hammock, this image of temporary retreat is a propitious sign of the divine power embodied in humanity to transform the world. The Guaraní belief that the *multitude-person* is a god walking towards the *land-without-evil* reveals that utopian change is both divine and human, one that involves a collective effort to reach an ethical event-horizon. Which is to say that utopia invokes that most obstinate of American traditions—community. Western fantasies about salvation starring the individual superhero (whether epic historical figure or Hollywood icon) implicitly deny the power of collective will and vision. The disempowered are wholly dependent on the messianic figure who battles evil single-handedly. And though we know that this story belongs to escapist fiction, our own (manufactured) cultures do little to imagine a more realistic and realizable scenario in which an ineluctable destiny is shown to be a mirage.

In a vignette entitled "Traditions of the Future," Galeano weaves together the many narrative threads that we have followed through his writings to come full circle to a critical moment of truth:

There is just one place where yesterday and today meet, recognize each other, and embrace, and that place is tomorrow.

Certain voices from the American past, long past, sound very futuristic. For example, the ancient voice that still tells us we are children of the earth and that our mother is not for sale or for hire. While dead birds rain on Mexico City and rivers are turned into sewers, oceans into dumps and forests into deserts, this voice, stubbornly refusing to die, heralds another world different from this one that poisons the water, soil, air and soul.

The ancient voice that speaks to us of community heralds another world as well. Community—the communal mode of production and life—is the oldest of American traditions, the most American of all. It belongs to the earliest days and the first people, but it also belongs to the times ahead and anticipates a New World. For there is nothing less alien to these lands of ours than socialism. Capitalism, on the other hand, is foreign: like smallpox, like the flu, it came from abroad. (*The Book of Embraces* 135)

Returning to the issues that we addressed earlier in our chapter on rights and literature, Galeano suggests that the lists of human rights proclaimed by the United Nations are woefully disconnected from reality and, judging by the alternative list he offers his readers, they are also ineffectual, pedestrian, and unimaginatively modest: "Suppose we start exercising the never-proclaimed right to dream? Suppose we rave a bit?" (*Upside Down* 334).

We end with Galeano's invitation to "set our sights beyond the abominations of today to divine another possible world." This gesture of solidarity, so characteristic of his work, is followed by a list of visions—at once magical, playful, and intuitively familiar:

...the air shall be cleansed of all poisons except those born of human fears and human passions;

in the streets, cars shall be run over by dogs;

economists shall not measure living standards by consumption levels or the quality of life by the quantity of things;

politicians shall not believe that the poor love to eat promises;

food shall not be a commodity nor shall communications be a business, because food and communication are human rights;

no one shall die of hunger, because no one shall die of overeating;

we shall be compatriots and contemporaries of all who have a yearning for justice and beauty, no matter where they were born or when they lived, because the borders of geography and time shall cease to exist. (*Upside Down* 334-36)

Galeano's prophesies invoke the seeds of the past to be sown in the future, which is *always already* upon us. They encapsulate his faith in and hope for the restitutions enabled by both memory and imagination, the two poles of energy fused in his work as critique and visionary voice. Works that result from critical integrity, aesthetic sensibility, historical crisis, and a solidary sense of justice revolutionize art by freeing it from the canons and genres that have traditionally claimed it for an élite, to return it to the people to whom Galeano listens and for whom he writes. The spirit of his work sends his interlocutors gathering other voices, other circles of incendiary story and memory that spread like wildfire. Galeano's defence of the word imagines a collective transformation of the solitude that the system attempts to impose by deforming words, silencing memories, and turning away from the formidable potential of wakeful dream and imagination.

The chronicler and storyteller—*multitude-person, tlamatini*—obstinately writes to recuperate words, memories, and whispered dreams, returning them to their collective source as a gift of hope, a discrepant engagement, a marriage of heaven and earth. When Pachacamac, the son of the sun, murders his newborn baby brother, then fearing the anger of his father chops the baby into pieces and scatters these about the world, a strange thing occurs: "From the teeth of the dead baby, corn grew; from the ribs and bones, cassava. The blood made the land fertile, and fruit trees and shade trees rose from the sown flesh. Thus the women and men born on these shores, where it never rains, find food" (*Genesis* 28). Out of an evil, cowardly act are hope and life ineluctably born? Or is this the creation of both the earth-born nobody and *Pachamama*, the feminized union of heaven and earth without which those who think themselves divinely created dominate and spoil the earth in their all-conquering blindness? Until the divine is united with the earth-born through the death that allows for rebirth, creation is imperfect and static. The union of dis-membered flesh and vegetal life (corn and cassava) nourishes and animates human society. The Inca allegory could not be clearer: the evidence of murderous destruction scattered over the world does (can) *not* prevent dynamic hope from being restored to human community as the legacy of loss and evil.

Through re-membered stories such as these, Galeano shatters the looking glass that reflects an upside-down world created by the masters of the mirage, and offers in its stead other windows and mirrors through which to contemplate ourselves as other than we are made out to be. His vision takes in terrifying realities but also announces humanity's collective potential in the disorder of everyday life: "Reality is not destiny, it's a challenge" (Sherman 6). Utopianism is no longer an illusory dream of perfection but rather a recognition of the urgency of being in *this* moment, in *this* world—collectively, imperfectly, discrepantly, critically: "Perfection shall remain the boring privilege of the gods, while in our bungling, messy world every night shall be lived as if it were the last and every day as if it were the first" (*Upside Down* 336). The dream of a time beyond infamy—*land-without-evil*, imperfect and possible utopia—references an imaginable future ethically lived fully in the here and now. Message of hope and responsibility, vision and critique, its voice carries on a speaking wind birthed in flames, laughter, and a blue tiger's roar.

Is it tomorrow?

NOTES

1. In 1499, Vespucci, who was neither pilot nor navigator, launched an expedition to the "new" world, exploring the coast of Venezuela. Vespucci did not lend his name directly to the Americas but rather had the Latinized rendition of his first name (Americus) given to the American continents by a German cartographer, Martin Waldseemüller. Interestingly, Waldseemüller knew of Vespucci through a distorted interpretation of Vespucci's travels that had used forged versions of his letters. The European appropriation of the "new" world (in name and in cartographic reality) was in its origins based on forgery and distortion. Such an ironic detail is worth remembering in relation to Galeano's project of restitution and reinvention, as well as in relation to the issue of fiction masquerading as historical truth.

2. Jameson further argues that in utopian discourse, "one of the constraints of the form would seem to be the incompatibility within it between action or events and that timeless map-like extension of the non-place itself: in other words, if things can really happen in Utopia, if real disorder, change, transgression, novelty, in brief if history is possible at all, then we begin to doubt whether it can really be a Utopia after all, and its institutions—from a promise of the fulfillment of collective living—slowly [begin] to turn around into their opposite, a more properly dystopian repression of the unique existential experience of individual lives" ("Of Islands and Trenches" 16-17).

3. Wallerstein notes that one of the elements one should not miss in utopia is "its homogeneity" (*Unthinking Social Science* 171) and cites the opening lines that describe Utopia's fifty-four cities all built to the same plan, with identical language, customs, institutions, and law. Wallerstein's take on utopia is useful in relation to Galeano's insofar as he advocates a notion of utopias as "always ideological" (*Unthinking Social Science* 183). In acknowledging the possibility of justice and social dynamism, Wallerstein argues that

   > Here Engels (and Marx) was right, provided one remembers that they were wrong in the implicit utopia involved in believing that there could ever be an end to history, a world in which ideologies no longer existed. If we are to make progress, it seems to me we have not only to accept contradiction as the key to explain social reality, but also to accept its enduring inescapability. Our utopia has to be sought not in eliminating all contradiction but in eradicating the vulgar, brutal, unnecessary consequences of material inequality. This latter seems to me intrinsically a quite achievable objective.

   > It is in this sense that utopia is a process, always defining the better in a way that is critical of existing reality. (*Unthinking Social Science* 183-84)

4. Quiroga's utopian organization (as described by Baptiste) seems to anticipate a curious kind of paternalistic infantilization of indigenes that has had significant negative effects, whatever Quiroga's intentions may have been. Galeano discusses an example of the small home crafts that the women in the Mexican village of Ocumicho make. The extraordinary clay sculptures, which the women sometimes stamp with a name not their own or choose not to sign at all, can be seen as an extension of Quiroga's utopian vision in which crafts reflect an imagined limit on indigenous cultural achievement (folklorism), or they can be seen as an inspired expression of community and ongoing rebellion (through the ability to create in spite of extreme hardship) in the face of different forms of repression.

   > In dark, windowless houses the Ocumicho potters model these luminous figures. Women tied to an endless chain of children, prisoners of drunken husbands who beat them, practice a new free-style art. Condemned to submission, destined for sadness, they create each day a new rebellion…

   > They don't understand this business of solitary glory. In their Tarascan Indian community, all are one when it comes to this sort of thing. *Outside the community, like the tooth that falls from a mouth, one is nobody.* (*Century of the Wind* 227; our emphasis)

   Ocumicho's community of makers is important because resistance (in the form of creative expression) is possible but not because it has done away with structures of exploitation and oppression. That is, it represents an art-based form of community production that survives in spite of tremendous internal and external pressures.

5. This account differs significantly from that found in Fray Bernardino de Sahagún's *Conquest of New Spain* (the 1585 revision), which states that Cortés's first orders of business included "finding the gold the Spaniards lost when they retreated from Tenochtitlan," the appointment of a ruling body, and the "collection of tribute" (140). The gold seems to have been a major issue and Sahagún reports that "a dili-

gent inquiry was made" and that the "gold that had been gathered in the conquest of Mexico was recovered, but not the treasure that [the Indians] robbed when the Spaniards fled from Mexico" (141). The interesting turnabout here that makes the native population thieves of their own possessions is worth noting, yet another demonstration of how rhetoric was deployed to produce ideological effects that reinforced the conquest. The difference between Durán's and Sahagún's accounts suggests the way in which official history has left plenty of contradictory fissures in its supposedly monolithic structure.

6. Cortés's letters make frequent references to divine providence interceding on his behalf during his military campaign against Tenochtitlan: "But each day Our Lord God gave us victory, and they always suffered the worst of it" (254). The logical emptiness of this sort of repeated declamation has little to do with its rhetorical power to reinforce the sense of authorized state action on behalf of a greater power that was clearly at issue for the conquistadors. Similar formulations are to be found in phrases like "God Bless America" or "In God We Trust."

7. Santiago's image in Tlatelolco is particularly ironic given that Tlatelolco became the site of a bloody massacre on 2 October 1968, when the Mexican government fired on its own people as a function of student and popular pressure to democratize. Though exact numbers of people killed and injured are a matter of debate, and Mexican newspapers reduced the number of dead to between 20 and 28, *The Guardian*, after a thorough investigation, estimated the number of dead to be approxiamately 325. An even larger number of people were wounded, and approximately 2,000 people were jailed (Poniatowska, *Massacre in Mexico* 207): "the blood of hundreds of students, of men, women, children, soldiers, and oldsters tracked all over Tlatelolco has dried now. It has sunk once again into the quiet earth. Later, flowers will bloom among the ruins and the tombs" (208). Poniatowska's chronicle of these events bears thinking in relation to Galeano's historical method. Octavio Paz argues that this form of chronicling "far surpasses a theory or hypothesis" and that Poniatowska's "'collage' of 'voices bearing historical witness'…shows us history before it has congealed and before the spoken word has become a written text" (Introduction vii). The link between alternative forms of chronicle like Poniatowska's and Galeano's and thinking through meaningful forms of alternative social dispositions cannot be emphasized enough.

8. Marina Leslie suggests that "Each utopian fiction enacts a deliberate revision and reworking of its predecessors to establish a new model commonwealth in a new site" (3), a position with which we would agree, though we would add that the underlying structure of utopian fiction as a response to colonial encounter narratives follows a precise logic in which the imperial eradication of difference guarantees the security of the self-same state. Leslie cites a passage from Robert Burton's early modern epic *The Anatomy of Melancholy* in which self-interest is the literal source for Burton's utopian vision: "I will yet, to satisfy and please myself, make an Utopia of mine own, a New Atlantis, a poetical commonwealth of mine own, *in which I will freely domineer, build cities, make laws, statutes, as I list myself*. And why may I not?" (qtd. in Leslie 3; our emphasis). In stating things so baldly, Burton was exposing a structure of power relations that underlie the utopian genre.

9. The mass baptisms in early post-conquest Mexico are a good example of this drive to convert, one example being Francisco de Las Navas's venture into the Popoloca region east of Puebla where "he baptized 12,000 in two months" (Baudot 450). How meaningful such baptisms were to those people who underwent the experience is moot, since the real point of such a spiritually vacant undertaking was to produce an illusion of assimilation, closely linked with fantasies of homogeneity to be found in utopian texts (as echoes of colonial encounter narratives).

10. Though Winstanley is often cited as a lone example of this sort of thinking, he was not. The anonymous author of a treatise entitled *Tyranipocrit Discovered* (Rotterdam, 1649) argued for, among other things, the fair distribution of wealth:

A reformation that will establish tyranny and slavery, and make the rich richer and the poore poorer, that is the reformation that the devil would have, but a reformation *sine* partiallity [without partiality], that would give unto every man alike meanes to live on, and that would cause all able persons to labour according to Gods commandement, and agreeable to reason, and that would maintaine and cherrish all old, weake, and impotent persons, so well the poore as the rich, &c. (17)

Further:

...if all men had alike meanes, then every man might have alike education, and then one man could not by arts or languages so easily deceive his artlesse neighbours, as now they do, then warres would cease concerning goods and lands: for if any person that either by fraud or force, had augmented his estate, that at the yeers end, or in a shorter time, all his new addition of goods should be taken from him, and shared amongst his poorer neighbours. (49)

11. Galeano gives other examples of the kind of repression faced by the Cherokee in an essay entitled "The Blue Tiger and the Promised Land":

To justify usurping the lands of the Sioux Indians at the end of the [nineteenth] century, the United States Congress declared that "community property is dangerous to the development of the free enterprise system." And in March 1979, a law was promulgated in Chile requiring the Mapuche Indians [the Araucanians] to divide up their lands and turn themselves into small landowners with no links among them; the dictator Pinochet explained that the communities were incompatible with the nation's economic progress. The U.S. Congress was right. So was General Pinochet. From capitalism's point of view, communal cultures that do not separate human beings from one another or from nature are enemy cultures. But the capitalist point of view is not the only one. (*We Say No* 229)

12. An often overlooked aspect of the Zapatista insurrection in Chiapas is that it is taking place in a province that "produces more than half of Mexico's hydroelectric power, an increasing portion of which flows north to the maquiladora zone on the Mexico-US border. Yet, even including its major cities of Tuxtla Gutiérrez and San Cristóbal de las Casas, only half of Chiapanecan households have electricity or running water" (Sanders 18). Furthermore, the Selva Lacandona, the Chiapanecan rainforest, "where real indigenous autonomy has been in place ever since the 1994 Zapatista uprising," is also the site of Montes Azules Biosphere Reserve, the Selva's last virgin forest. The site is the target of bio-prospecting (bio-piracy) by "transnational biotech corporations that hope to profit from the region's genetic wealth" (Weinberg 23). The extraordinary military presence in Chiapas cannot be separated from these facts. The militarization of these spaces is inseparable from the extent to which the use-value of native communities benefits the North, which increasingly depends on exploitative manufacturing zones like the maquiladoras or on the extraction of biogenetic information from areas inhabited by indigenous populations at minimal cost to achieve immense profits. Similarly, the long and brutal civil war in Guatemala cannot be dissociated from its containing the "largest oil deposit in Central America," thus leading to the Guatemalan army's vicious campaign "bombing villages and evicting communities so that Texaco, Hispanoil, Getty Oil and other companies can survey and exploit the oilfields" (*We Say No* 233).

13. For instance, Galeano cites the Guaraní, to whom we return later in this chapter, where "chiefs were chosen in assemblies of men and women—and assemblies deposed them if they failed to carry out the collective mandate" (*We Say No* 311). Similarly, in "Iroquois tradition, men and women governed on an equal footing. The chiefs were men, but it was the women who elected and deposed and the council of women held decision-making power over many fundamental aspects of the entire confederation. Around 1600, when the Iroquois men went to war on their own, the women went on a love strike. And before long the men, obliged to sleep alone, submitted to shared government" (*We Say No* 311-12).

14. Galeano includes a vignette about Nanny in *Faces and Masks*, where he describes her mythic persona as a "woman of fiery clay, mistress of the gods, [who] wears nothing but a necklace of English soldiers' teeth...She squats with her back to the enemy, and her magnificent ass catches the bullets. Sometimes she sends them back with interest and sometimes she turns them into balls of cotton" (23).

15. Dussel discusses the persistence of resistance to slavery as well as the "systematic brutality" of colonial interests: "The slaves...resisted continually, and many finally attained liberty. The thousands of Afro-Brazilians populating the *quilombos* (hiding places of runaway slaves; the word's meanings, both conventional and colloquial, include brothel, "a fuck-up" [*follón*], and disorder) and defying colonial armies and the many Jamaican slaves who took refuge along the Pacific coasts of Central America provide evidence of the resistance" (*The Invention of the Americas* 123).

16. E. M. Cioran figures utopia as a "monstrous fantasy" because of its abstract "need to associate happiness...with becoming, and to coerce an optimistic, aerial vision" (31), whereas its monstrosity lies more precisely in its dream of a homogeneous, material stasis, an endless purity and survival that justify re-

morseless tactics of assimilation and destruction. Cioran's cynical take on utopia sees it as linked with notions of social organization:

A great step forward was made the day men understood that, in order to torment one another more effectively, they would have to gather together, to organize themselves into a society. If we are to believe the utopias, they succeeded in doing so only by halves; the utopias therefore offer to help them, to furnish them a context appropriate to the exercise of a complete happiness, while requiring, in return, that men abdicate their freedom or, if they retain it, that they use it solely to proclaim their joy amid the sufferings they inflict upon each other. Such seems the meaning of the infernal solicitude the utopias show toward men. Under these conditions, how can we fail to envisage a reverse utopia, a liquidation of the infinitesimal good and the enormous evil attached to the existence of any social order whatever? (92)

Cioran's frustrated anarchism turned misanthropic cynicism silently reads the social in relation to Eurocentric notions of state governance, whereas Galeano argues toward a version of the social based on communities of resistance derived primarily from marginalized and oppressed social formations. Perfection is never at issue in these alternative communities as it is so obviously a form of totalitarianism that reduces human difference and dissidence. But this is not to say that such communities disperse the "enormous evil" Cioran associates with "any social order whatever." Nor is it to say that though better, such formations are not capable of evil or injustice. The failure to distinguish between different ways of being social, which is to say the failure to theorize communitarianism adequately, is implicit in Dussel's comments about the difference between capitalism and socialism, both of which he critiques: "The sin of capitalism is to have taken work—which is an actual, living human being—and turned it into merchandise. The sin of socialism is that the human being is transformed into an 'instrument of production' of the *social*—but not the *communal*—whole" (*Ethics and Community* 185).

17. Dussel articulates this same idea in a reading of Marx: "For Marx human societies exemplified communitarian relationship[s] prior to modern, capitalist individuality. Marx extrapolated beyond such relationships to the utopian communitarianism of the full individual in the full community" (*The Invention of the Americas* 182).

18. "Güero" is a non-pejorative nickname given in some Latin American countries to people who are fairer in complexion than the *mestizo* or indigenous majority.

19. Galeano, addressing the Columbian quincentenary celebrations, argues that "we shall have to celebrate the vanquished, not the victors. The vanquished and those who identified with them, like Bernardino de Sahagún, and those who lived for them, like Bartolomé de Las Casas, Vasco de Quiroga and Antonio Vieira, and those who died for them, like Gonzalo Guerrero, the first conquered conqueror, who ended his days fighting at the side of the Indians, his chosen brothers, in Yucatán" (*We Say No* 234-35).

20. Galeano repeats this story of the rebirth of difference in the "festival of life" at the end of "The Blue Tiger and the Promised Land" (*We Say No* 227-35).

21. The Second *Encuentro* for Humanity and Against Neoliberalism was held in Spain in 1997, again initiated by the Zapatista leadership seeking to build global networks of resistance, communication, and enacted solidarity.

22. *Chicha* is a traditional alcoholic drink of the Andes, made of fermented corn.

Works Consulted

I. By Eduardo Galeano

Books

Galeano, Eduardo. *Apuntes para el fin de siglo*. Santiago: LOM Ediciones, 1997.

—. *Las aventuras de los jóvenes dioses*. Illus. Nivio López Vigil. Mexico: Siglo Veintiuno Editores, 1998.

—. *The Book of Embraces*. Trans. Cedric Belfrage with Mark Schafer. New York: Norton, 1991.

—. *La canción de nosotros*. Mexico: Editorial Hermes, 1975.

—. *La chanson que nous chantons*. Trans. Régine Mellac and Annie Morvan. Paris: Albin Michel, 1977.

—. *China 1964: Crónica de un desafío*. Buenos Aires: Jorge Alvárez, 1964.

—. *100 relatos breves*. 2nd ed. San José, Costa Rica: Educa, 1998.

—. *Contraseña*. Buenos Aires: Ediciones Del Sol, 1986.

—. *Conversaciones con Raimón*. Barcelona: Granica, 1977.

—. *Crónicas latinoamericanas*. Montevideo: Editorial Girón, 1972.

—. *Days and Nights of Love and War*. Trans. Judith Brister. New York: Monthly Review, 1983.

—. *El descubrimiento de América que todavía no fue y nuevos ensayos*. Caracas, Venezuela: Alfadil Ediciones, 1991.

—. *Los días siguientes*. Montevideo: Editorial Arca, 1965.

—. *Días y noches de amor y de guerra*. Montevideo: Arca, 1986.

—. *Entrevistas y artículos (1962/1987)*. Montevideo: Ediciones del Chanchito, 1988.

—. *Los fantasmas del día del león: y otros relatos*. Montevideo: Editorial Arca, 1967.

—. *Guatemala, clave de Latinoamérica*. Montevideo: Banda Oriental, 1967.

—. *Guatemala: Occupied Country*. Trans. Cedric Belfrage. New York: Monthly Review, 1969.

—. *Memoria del fuego I. Los nacimientos*. 1982. 10th ed. Mexico: Siglo Veintiuno Editores, 2000.

—. *Memoria del fuego II. Las caras y las máscaras*. 1984. 8th ed. Mexico: Siglo Veintiuno Editores, 2000.

—. *Memoria del fuego III. El siglo del viento.* 1986. 5th ed. Mexico: Siglo Veintiuno Editores, 1987.

—. *Memory of Fire: I. Genesis.* Trans. Cedric Belfrage. New York: Pantheon, 1985.

—. *Memory of Fire: II. Faces and Masks.* Trans. Cedric Belfrage. New York: Pantheon, 1987.

—. *Memory of Fire: III. Century of the Wind.* Trans. Cedric Belfrage. New York: Pantheon, 1988.

—. *Mujeres.* Madrid: Alianza Editorial, 1995.

—. *Open Veins of Latin America: Five Centuries of the Pillage of a Continent.* Trans. Cedric Belfrage. New York: Monthly Review, 1973.

—. *Patas arriba: La escuela del mundo al revés.* Mexico: Siglo XXI Editores, 1998.

—. *La piedra arde.* Salamanca, Spain: Lóguez, 1980.

—. *Ser como ellos y otros artículos.* Mexico: Siglo Veintinuno Editores, 1997.

—. *Soccer in Sun and Shadow.* Trans. Mark Fried. New York: Verso, 1998.

—. *El tigre azul y otros artículos.* La Habana: Ediciones Políticas; Editorial de Ciencias Sociales, 1996.

—. *Upside Down: A Primer for the Looking-Glass World.* Trans. Mark Fried. New York: Metropolitan, 2000.

—. *Úselo y tírelo: El mundo del fin del milenio visto desde una ecología latinoamericana.* Buenos Aires: Biblioteca de Ecología, 1994.

—. *Vagamundo.* Buenos Aires: Ediciones de Crisis, 1973.

—. *Vagamundo y otros relatos.* Montevideo: Ediciones del Chanchito, 1987.

—. *Ventana sobre Sandino.* N.p.: Ediciones Raiti, 1985.

—. *Violencia y enajenación.* Mexico: Nuestro Tiempo, 1971.

—. *Voces de nuestro tiempo.* San José, Costa Rica: Educa, 1983.

—. *Walking Words.* Trans. Mark Fried. New York: Norton, 1995.

—. *We Say No: Chronicles 1963-1991.* Trans. Mark Fried, et al. New York: Norton, 1992.

Book Chapters, Forewords, and Afterwords

Galeano, Eduardo. "All the World's a Ball 8/10-17/98." *The Best of The Nation: Selections from the Independent Magazine of Politics and Culture.* Ed. Victor Navasky and Katrina vanden Heuvel. New York: Thunder's Mouth/Nation, 2000. 550-53.

—. "For Haroldo Conti." Trans. Mariana Valverde, Audrey Campbell, and Patricia Veras. *The Writer and Human Rights* 13-17.

—. Foreword. Gelman xi-xii.

—. "The Imagination and the Will to Change." Trans. Mariana Valverde. *The Writer and Human Rights* 121-23.

—. "In Defense of the Word: Leaving Buenos Aires, June 1976." Trans. Bobbye S. Ortiz. Simonson and Walker 113-25.

—. Preface. Menchú, *Rigoberta: La nieta de los mayas* 7.

—. "Salgado, 17 Times." Trans. Asa Zatz. Salgado, *An Uncertain Grace* 7-15.

—. "To Be Like Them." Afterword. Bowden 121-29.

Journals

Crisis. Vols. 1-45, 54-55, 58. Buenos Aires: 1973-1976; 1986-1988.

Cuadernos de Crisis. Vols. 1-15. Buenos Aires: 1973-1975.

Journal Articles

Galeano, Eduardo. "Abrazos." Trans. Cedric Belfrage. *Grand Street* 10.1 (1991): 11-22.

—. "All the World's a Ball." *The Nation* 10-17 Aug. 1998: 41-42.

—. "The Blue Tiger and the Promised Land." *NACLA Report on the Americas* 24.5 (1991): n.pag.

—. "Brazil: The Defeat and After." *Studies on the Left* 4.4 (1964): 55-76.

—. "Capitalist Realism." *The Nation* 11 Oct. 2000: 61.

—. "Crash Course on Incommunications." *MediaChannelOrg.* 27 Nov. 2000 <http://www.mediachannel.org/views/oped/galeanonew.shtml>.

—. "Las dagas bajo la capa del imperio." *Temas de izquierda* 1 (1967): 3-106.

—. "Economics for Children." *The Nation* 1 Jan. 2001: 34.

—. "Être comme eux." *Le monde diplomatique* Oct. 1991: 16-17.

—. "The Impunity of the Sacred Car." *Conjunctions* 33 (1999): 55-65.

—. "An Invitation to Flight." *Bomb* Fall 1999: 109-10.

—. "The Living Thought of Military Dictatorships." *The Nation* 8-15 Jan. 2001: 42.

—. "Marvel in Daily Life." Trans. Tracey Hill. *Artforum International* 27 (1989): 122-23.

—. "El mensaje de los jóvenes." *Enciclopedia uruguaya* 57 (1969): 122-26.

—. "My Life and the Beautiful Game." *Harper's Magazine* June 1998: 36-38.

—. "The Other Wall." *New Internationalist* Nov. 1990: 7-9.

—. "The Revolution as Revelation." Trans. Walter I. Bradbury. *Socialist Review* 65 (1982): 7-16.

—. "The Story of the Lizard Who Made a Habit of Having His Wives for Dinner." Trans. Alastair Reid. *Grand Street* 11.2 (1992): 183-88.

—. "A Tale of Ambiguities." *Index on Censorship* 24.3 (1995): 33-36.

—. "El teatro del bien y el mal." *Patria Grande.* 1 Oct. 2001 <http://www.patriagrande.net/uruguay/eduardo.galeano/escritos/el.teatro.del.bien.y.el.mal.htm>.

—. "Una marcha universal." *Patria grande.* 1 Oct. 2001 <http://www.patriagrande.net/uruguay/eduardo/galeano/escritos/una.marcha.universal.htm>.

—. "Upside Down: The End of the Millennium as Promise and Betrayal." Trans. Mark Fried. *El Andar* 63 (2000): 66-70.

—. "Vers une société de l'incommunication?" *Le monde diplomatique* Jan. 1996: 16.

—. "Windows." Trans. Mark Fried. *Grand Street* 16 (1997): 39-41.

—. "Windows 1: Words." *New Internationalist* 323 (2000): 5.

—. "Windows 2: Images." *New Internationalist* 326 (2000): 5.

—. "Windows 3: Voices." *New Internationalist* 329 (2000): 5.

—. "A World Gone Mad." *Progressive* Dec. 2000: 30-32.

—. "Yuletide All the Time." *The Nation* 22 Jan. 2001: 32.

II. Sources About Eduardo Galeano

Allende, Isabel. "Breath of Hope: On the Writings of Eduardo Galeano." *Monthly Review* 48.11 (1997): 1-6.

Alston, Philip, and Henry J. Steiner, eds. *International Human Rights in Context: Law, Politics, Morals.* 2nd ed. Oxford: Oxford UP, 2000.

Armijo, Jorge. Rev. of *Les veines ouvertes de l'Amérique latine: Une contre-histoire*, by Eduardo Galeano. *Études internationales* 12.1 (1982): 201.

Bach, Caleb. "Eduardo Galeano: In Celebration of Contradiction." *Americas* 44.5 (1992): 16-21.

Barros-Lémez, Alvaro. "Cantares que de gente en Gente Quedan: La América Latina: lucha, exilio y narrativa en la obra de Eduardo Galeano." *Escritura* 12.23-24 (1987): 167-90. Rpt. *Casa de las Américas* 166 (1988): 35-46.

Barsamian, David. "Eduardo Galeano." *Progressive* July 1999: 35-38.

Bell, Douglas. "Inside Planet Football." *Globe and Mail* 13 June 1998: D18.

Bell, Virginia Ellen. "Narratives of Treason: Postnational Historiographic Tactics and Late Twentieth-Century Fiction in the Americas." Diss. U of Maryland, College Park, 1997.

Berrett, Jesse. Rev. of *Upside Down: A Primer for the Looking-Glass World*, by Eduardo Galeano. *Mother Jones* Sept.-Oct. 2000: 86.

Borge, Tomás, Gabriel García Márquez, et al. "Para, de, con Julio Cortázar." *Casa de las Américas* 25 (1984): 145-46.

Bowden, Charles. *Juárez: The Laboratory of Our Future.* New York: Aperture, 1998.

Burns, Jimmy. "When beauty turns to duty." Rev. of *Football in Sun and Shadow*, by Eduardo Galeano. *Financial Times* 21 Feb. 1998.

Cabrera, Vicente. "La intertextualidad subversiva en *La mujer habitada* de Gioconda Belli." *Monographic Review / Revista monográfica* 8 (1992): 243-51.

Campanella, Hortensia. "La memoria insustituible." Rev. of *Días y noches de amor y de guerra*, by Eduardo Galeano. *Cuadernos hispanoamericanos* 346 (1979): 236-40.

Cason, Jim, and David Brooks. "Se debe describir la parte del hoy que omitirá la historia: Saramago." *Jornada de Enmedio* 26 Oct. 2000: 2a.

Castillo, Alvaro. "Cinco narradores rioplatenses." *Cuadernos hispanoamericanos* 299 (1975): 479-83.

Childress, Boyd. Rev. of *Upside Down: A Primer for the Looking-Glass World*, by Eduardo Galeano. *Library Journal* 1 Sept. 2000: 236.

Crespi, Roberto. "State Terror, the Radical Nationalist Intellectual, and the Class Question." Rev. of *Days and Nights of Love and War*, by Eduardo Galeano. *Latin American Perspectives* 13.4 (1986): 86-99.

Davies, Pete. Rev. of *Football in Sunshine and Shadow*, by Eduardo Galeano. *Eye of Monday* 15 Dec. 1997.

Davis, Thulani. "Eduardo Galeano's History con Sabor." Rev. of *Memory of Fire: Century of the Wind*, by Eduardo Galeano. *Voice Literary Supplement* May 1988: 24-25.

De Gaudemar, Antoine. "Le foot, c'est le pied." *Libération* 12 Feb. 1998.

"Einzigartiges Lese—und Sehbuch: Ein Fest der Phantasie." Rev. of *Wandelnde Worte*, by Eduardo Galeano. *Stadt Anzeiger* 18 Dec. 1997.

Faudree, Paja. Rev. of *Soccer in Sun and Shadow*, by Eduardo Galeano. *Voice Literary Supplement* June 1998: 74.

Figurelli, Roberto. "Eduardo Galeano e a revista *Crisis*." *Cadernos Hispano América (Curitiba)* 2 (1987): 71-82.

Fischlin, Daniel. "Dissonant History: Eduardo Galeano and the Carnival of Desire and Loss." *Border Crossings* Fall 1994: 49-51.

—. "Eduardo Galeano and the Politics of Style." *Ariel* 24.4 (1993): 89-99.

—. "History's 'Refuse': Benjamin, Galeano, and the 'Power to Create.'" *Revista canadiense de estudios hispánicos* 26.1-2 (2001).

—. "Psychic Contagion." Rev. of *Walking Words*, by Eduardo Galeano. *Border Crossings* Fall 1995: 82-84.

Fonseca, Isabel. "A Land in Exile From Itself." Rev. of *Upside Down: A Primer for the Looking-Glass World*, by Eduardo Galeano. *New York Times Book Review* 12 Nov. 2000: 32.

Franco, Jean. "The Raw and the Cooked." *The Nation* 14 Feb. 1987: 183-84.

Gamboa, Humberto. "América Latina al fin del milenio." *¡Exito!* 20 May 1999: 20-21.

—. "Galeano: Premio a la libertad intelectual." *¡Exito!* 22 Apr. 1999: 15.

Gonzalez, Barbara Renaud. "The truth be told." *San Antonio Express News* 18 Apr. 1999: 1H+.

Gutschke, Von Irmtraud. "Musik der Mondmenschen." *Neues Deutschland* 25 Apr. 1997.

Hackl, Erich. "Geschichte erzahlen?: Anmerkungen zur Arbeit des Chronisten." *Literatur und Kritik* 291-292 (1995): 25-43.

Henríquez-Lagarde, Manuel. "Las huellas de la pelea." *Casa de las Américas* 30.174 (1989): 90-101.

Holley, Eugene, Jr. Rev. of *Soccer in Sun and Shadow*, by Eduardo Galeano. *Hispanic* May 1999: 66+.

Jímenez, Arturo. "La vena literaria de Galeano." *Jornada semanal.* 2 Apr. 2000. 1 Oct. 2001 <http://www.jornada.unam.mx/2000/abr00/000402/sem_galeano.html>.

Kirchhoff, H. J. Rev. of *Soccer in Sun and Shadow*, by Eduardo Galeano. *Globe and Mail* 17 July 1999: D16.

—. Rev. of *Walking Words*, by Eduardo Galeano. *Globe and Mail* 29 Mar. 1997: D15.

Kirkpatrick, Gwen. "Scholarship and Passion: Myth and Historiography in the New World." *Common Knowledge* 1.3 (1992): 165-72.

Rev. of *Upside Down: A Primer for the Looking-Glass World*, by Eduardo Galeano. *Kirkus Reviews* 15 July 2000: 1009.

Rev. of *We Say No: Chronicles 1963-1991*, by Eduardo Galeano. *Kirkus Reviews* 1 May 1992: 585.

Lagos-Pope, María-Inés. "Testimonies from Exile: Works by Hernán Valdés, Eduardo Galeano, and David Viñas." *Exile in Literature.* Ed. María-Inés Lagos-Pope. Lewisburg, PN: Bucknell UP, 1988. 121-37.

Lewis, Joel. "Don't understand soccer? He'll give you a hand." Rev. of *Soccer in Sun and Shadow*, by Eduardo Galeano. *Newark Star-Ledger* 19 July 1998.

López, Ruth. "Triumph over oppression." *Pasatiempo* 16-22 Apr. 1999: 58+.

—. "Uruguayan writer to get cultural freedom prize." *Santa Fe New Mexican* 21 Apr. 1999: B1+.

Lopez-Baralt, Mercedes. "Eduardo Galeano: Diálogo sobre *Memoria del fuego*." *Revista de estudios hispánicos* 9 (1992): 449-74.

Lovell, W. George. "Re-membering America: The Historical Vision of Eduardo Galeano." Rev. of *Memory of Fire* (3 volumes), by Eduardo Galeano. *Queen's Quarterly* 99.3 (1992): 609-17.

Manrique, Jaime. "Eduardo Galeano." Trans. Eva Golinger. *Bomb* 75 (2001): 54-59.

Martin, Gerald. "Hope Springs Eternal: Eduardo Galeano and the History of Latin America." *History Workshop Journal* 34 (1992): 148-58.

—. *Journeys Through the Labyrinth: Latin American Fiction in the Twentieth Century.* New York: Verso, 1989.

—. "Preaching to the Converted." Rev. of *Memory of Fire: Century of the Wind*, by Eduardo Galeano. *Third World Quarterly* 11.1 (1989): 182-84.

Martínez, Pedro Ángel. "Eduardo Galeano: habló de un mundo incomprensible en la Feria." *Ultima hora* 4 May 1997: 31.

Rev. of *Football in Sun and Shadow*, by Eduardo Galeano. *Maxim* 1 Nov. 1997: 209.

More, Michael. "Salgado/Galeano." *Pasatiempo* 3-9 Nov. 2000: 16+.

NACLA staff. "Eduardo Galeano." *NACLA: Report on the Americas* 20.5-6 (1986): 14-19.

Nargin, Natasha. "Galeano Believes Smaller Is Better." *Journal North* 3 Nov. 2000: 1+.

Nepumuceno, Eric. "Nao, o Brasil Nao Conhece Eduardo Galeano, o Escritor." *Minas Gerais, Suplemento Literario* 26 Apr. 1975: 3.

Nikiforuk, Andrew. "Globalism: the new Great Satan." Rev. of *Upside Down: A Primer for the Looking Glass World,* by Eduardo Galeano. *Globe and Mail* 27 Jan. 2001: D5.

O'Doherty, Ian. "Football tales off-side." Rev. of *Football in Sun and Shadow,* by Eduardo Galeano. *Irish Independent* 29 Nov. 1997: 7.

"Open Veins of Latin America." Rev. of *Open Veins of Latin America,* by Eduardo Galeano. *Monthly Review Press.* 11 Sept. 2000 <http://www.igc.apc.org/MonthlyReview/-opveins.htm>.

"Our 25 Favorite Books of 2000." *Voice Literary Supplement* Dec. 2000: 7.

"La página de Eduardo Galeano." *Patria grande.* 1 Oct. 2001 <http://www.patriagrande.net/uruguay/eduardo.galeano/index.html>.

"Palabras pronunciadas por Eduardo Galeano ante la reunión anual de los libreros de los Estados Unidos, American Booksellers Association. Publicado en el papel literario de EL NACIONAL." 29 Aug. 2001 <http://www.multimedia.com/palabras.htm>.

Palaversich, Diana. "Eduardo Galeano: entre el postmodernismo y el postcolonialismo." *Indiana Journal of Hispanic Literatures* 1.2 (1993): 11-24.

—. "Eduardo Galeano's *Memoria del fuego* as Alternative History." *Antipodas* 3 (1991): 135-50.

—. "Postmodernismo, postcolonialismo y la recuperación de la historia subalterna." *Chasqui* 24.1 (1995): 3-15.

—. *Silencio, voz y escritura en Eduardo Galeano.* Montevideo: Luis A. Retta Libros, 1995.

Pavón, Alfredo. "La lucha contra el poder: 'La canción de nosotros.'" *La palabra y el hombre* 18 (1976): 93-95.

Paz, Francisco Moraes. "História e literatura em *Memórias do fogo.*" *Cadernos hispano América (Curitiba)* 2 (1987): 47-54.

Pelaez, Vicky. "Ese hombre llamado Eduardo Galeano." *La Prensa* 6 Nov. 2000: 32.

Pendleton, Richard. Rev. of *Football in Sun and Shadow,* by Eduardo Galeano. *Four Four Two* 1 May 1998: 148.

Pérez Montaner, Jamie. Rev. of *La canción de nosotros,* by Eduardo Galeano. *Chasqui* 6.2 (1977): 90-94.

Pogolotti, Graziella. "La ciudad subterránea." *Casa de las Américas* 16.92 (1975): 91-93.

Poniatowska, Elena. "El periodismo no es el suburbio de la literatura, dice Galeano." *La jornada* 6 Mar. 2000: 33.

—. "Preparo libros abiertos para que el lector se sienta libre: Galeano." *La jornada* 5 Mar. 2000: 25-26.

Prida, Dolores. Rev. of *Upside Down: A Primer for the Looking-Glass World,* by Eduardo Galeano. *Latina* Oct. 2000: 38.

Rev. of *Football in Sun and Shadow,* by Eduardo Galeano. *Publishers Weekly* 23 Mar. 1998.

Rev. of *Upside Down: A Primer for the Looking-Glass World,* by Eduardo Galeano. *Publishers Weekly* 18 Sept. 2000.

Rama, Angel. "Galeano en busca del hombre nuevo." *Camp de l'arpa* 27 (1975): 23-25.

Ramsay, John G. "Galeano 101." *Ruminator Review* Fall 2000: 24+.

Richler, Daniel. "In the Studio: Eduardo Galeano, April 22, 1991." *One on One: The Imprint Interviews.* Ed. Leanna Crouch. Toronto: Somerville, 1994. 27-35.

Riva, Hugo. *Memoria viviente de América latina: La obra de Eduardo Galeano.* Buenos Aires: Editorial Lumen, 1996.

Rivera-Ocasio, Gladys. "La novela histórica hispanoamericana actual: Carpentier, Fuentes y Galeano." Diss. Yale U, 1998.

Roman, Peter. Rev. of *Open Veins of Latin America*, by Eduardo Galeano. *Science & Society* 39.4 (1975-1976): 497-500.

Rossi, Christina Peri. "El amor y la guerra." *Triunfo* 23 Dec. 1978: 12.

Ruiz, Ramón Eduardo. Rev. of *Open Veins of Latin America*, by Eduardo Galeano. *Pacific Historical Review* 44 (1975): 581-82.

Saad, Gabriel. "Eduardo Galeano: La literatura como una pasión latinoamericana." *Cuadernos hispanoamericanos* 324 (1977): 454-69.

Saz, Sara M. "Breath, Liberty, and the Word: Eduardo Galeano's Interpretation of History." *Secolas Annals* 21 (1990): 59-70.

Schoefer, Christine. Rev. of *Soccer in Sun and Shadow*, by Eduardo Galeano. *Express Books* Aug. 1998: 10.

Rev. of *Football in Sun and Shadow*, by Eduardo Galeano. *Scotsman* 29 Nov. 1997: 16.

Sharpe, Tom. "Cultural, ecological problems are focus of seminars." *Santa Fe New Mexican* 11 May 2000: B1+.

Sherman, Scott. "'Words That Must Be Said.'" Trans. Sherman Prince and Amy Prince. *The Atlantic Online.* 1 Oct. 2001 <http://www.theatlantic.com/unbound/interviews/ba2000-11-30.htm>.

Smith, Dinitia. "In Its Debut, A Big Prize For Freedom Helps Writer." *New York Times* 21 Apr. 1999: B1.

"Subcomandante Marcos—Carta a Eduardo Galeano, 2 de mayo de 1995." 29 Aug. 2001 <http://spin.com.mx/~hvelarde/Mexico/Marcos/galeano-19950502.htm>.

Taylor, Robert. "Game's mythology goal of soccer book." *Californian* 21 June 1998.

Todaro, Lenora. "Conscientious Objector." *Village Voice* 5 Dec. 2000: 78.

Tomassini, Graciela. "Historia y ficción en *Memoria del fuego* de Eduardo Galeano." *Texto crítico* 3.4-5 (1997): 111-23.

Torres-Fierro, Danubio. "Los mercaderes de la virtud." *Vuelta* 16.190 (1992): 57-59.

Valdés, Marcela. "A Life Spent Turning Lead into Air." *Library Journal* 1 Sept. 2000: 235.

Verani, Hugo J. "Los restos del naufragio: *La canción de nosotros* de Eduardo Galeano." *Revista de crítica literaria latinoamericana* 7.13 (1981): 61-70.

Villaplana, Alvaro Carvajal. "Sobre ética y derechos humanos." *Revista de filosofía de la Universidad de Costa Rica* 34.83-84 (1996): 395-400.

Villepique, Greg. Rev. of *Upside Down: A Primer for the Looking Glass World*, by Eduardo Galeano. 23 Nov. 2000 <http://www.salonmag.com/books/review/2000/10/12/galeano/>.

Walljasper, Jay. "Rethinking the Left." *Social Policy* Spring 1996: 20-35.

Weinhardt, Marilene. "A canção de nossa gente: Um romance latino-americano." *Cadernos Hispano América (Curitiba)* 2 (1987): 55-70.

West, Paul. Rev. of *Memory of Fire: Century of the Wind*, by Eduardo Galeano. *Latin American Literature and Arts Review* 39 (1988): 61-63.

Williams, Richard. "The beautiful game dissected." *Guardian* 30 May 1998: 9.

Wilson, S. R. "Eduardo Galeano: Exile and a Silenced Montevideo." *Chasqui* 9.2-3 (1980): 30-38.

—. Rev. of *Días y noches de amor y de guerra*, by Eduardo Galeano. *Journal of Spanish Studies Twentieth Century* 8.1-2 (1980): 192-94.

—. Rev. of *Memoria del fuego I: Los nacimientos*, by Eduardo Galeano. *Latin American Literary Review* 11.22 (1983): 105-08.

—. Rev. of *Memoria del fuego II: Las caras y las máscaras*, by Eduardo Galeano. *Chasqui* 14.2-3 (1985): 76-77.

Wolff, Maria Tai. Rev. of *Memory of Fire: Genesis*, by Eduardo Galeano. *Center for Inter-American Relations Review* 36 (1986): 64-65.

Wright, Ronald. "Discovery is theft." Rev. of *Memory of Fire* (3 volumes), by Eduardo Galeano. *New York Times Literary Supplement* 20-26 Oct. 1989: 1165.

Yeomans, Matthew. "Goooooooooooal!" Rev. of *Soccer in Sun and Shadow*, by Eduardo Galeano. *New York Newsday* 5 July 1998: B12+.

Yúdice, George. "Graffiti on a Bloody Wall." Rev. of *Days and Nights of Love and War*, by Eduardo Galeano. *Latin American Literature and Arts Review* 32 (1984): 48-50.

Zeitz, Eileen. "Eduardo Galeano: el oficio de la revelación desafiante." *Chasqui* 9.1 (1979): 88-91.

III. General Sources

Achbar, Mark, ed. *Manufacturing Consent: Noam Chomsky and the Media*. Montréal: Black Rose, 1994.

Achebe, Chinua. *Morning Yet on Creation Day: Essays*. London: Heinemann, 1975.

Achugar, Hugo. "El exilio uruguayo y la producción de conocimientos sobre el fenómeno literario." *Ideologies and Literature* 4.16 (1983): 224-41.

Adorno, Rolena. "Arms, Letters and the Native Historian in Early Colonial Mexico." Jara and Spadaccini, *1492-1992* 201-24.

—. "Colonial Reform or Utopia: Guaman Poma's Empire of the Four Parts of the World." Jara and Spadaccini, *Amerindian Images* 346-74.

Adorno, Theodor W. *Negative Dialectics*. Trans. E. B. Ashton. New York: Continuum, 1990.

Afzal-Khan, Fawzia, ed. *The Pre-Occupation of Postcolonial Studies*. Durham: Duke UP, 2000.

Agosin, Marjorie. "How to Speak with the Dead?: A Poet's Notebook." *Human Rights Quarterly* 16 (1994): 214-23.

—. "So We Will Not Forget: Literature and Human Rights in Latin America." Trans. Janice Molloy. *Human Rights Quarterly* 10 (1988): 177-92.

Allende, Salvador. *Salvador Allende Reader: Chile's Voice of Democracy*. Ed. James D. Cockcroft. Trans. Moisés Espinoza and Nancy Nuñez. Melbourne, NY: Ocean, 2000.

Amnesty International Report 2000. London: Amnesty International, 2000.

Anderson, Benedict. *Imagined Communities: Reflections on the Origin and Spread of Nationalism*. Rev. ed. London: Verso, 1991.

Andrea, Bernadette. "Columbus in Istanbul: Ottoman Mappings of the 'New World.'" *Genre* 30 (1997): 135-65.

The Annals of the Cakchiquels/Title of the Lords of Totonicapán. Trans. Adrián Recinos, Delia Goetz, and Dionisio José Chonay. Norman: U of Oklahoma P, 1953.

Anzaldúa, Gloria. *Borderlands / La Frontera: The New Mestiza*. San Francisco: Aunt Lute, 1987.

—. "Tlilli, Tlapalli: The Path of the Red and Black Ink." Simonson and Walker 29-40.

Arendt, Hannah. *On Violence*. San Diego: Harvest, 1970.

—, ed. *Illuminations: Essays and Reflections*. Trans. Harry Zohn. New York: Schocken, 1969.

"Argentina struggles to reverse decay." *Globe and Mail* 18 Oct. 1994: A11.

Aridjis, Homero. *Imágenes para el fin del milenio & Nueva expulsión del paraíso*. Mexico: Joaquín Mortiz, 1990.

Armstrong, Nancy, and Leonard Tennenhouse, eds. *The Violence of Representation: Literature and the History of Violence*. London: Routledge, 1989.

Axtell, James. *After Columbus: Essays in the Ethnohistory of Colonial North America*. New York: Oxford UP, 1988.

Baker, David Weil. *Divulging Utopia: Radical Humanism in Sixteenth-Century England*. Amherst: U of Massachusetts P, 1999.

Bakhtin, Mikhail. *Rabelais and His World*. Trans. Helene Iswolsky. Bloomington: Indiana UP, 1984.

Baptiste, Victor N. *Bartolomé de Las Casas and Thomas More's Utopia: Connections and Similarities: A Translation and Study*. Culver City, CA: Labyrinthos, 1990.

Barlow, Maude. "Water War!" *Briarpatch* Apr. 2001: 5-7.

Barnet, Michel. *Canción de Rachel*. Buenos Aires: Galerna, 1969.

Barsamian, David. *Noam Chomsky: Chronicles of Dissent*. Vancouver: New Star, 1992.

Bass, Thomas A. "The lives and times of the selfish gene." *Globe and Mail* 18 Oct. 1994: A27.

Baudot, Georges. *Utopia and History in Mexico: The First Chronicles of Mexican Civilization, 1520-1569*. Trans. Bernard R. Ortiz de Montellano and Thelma Ortiz de Montellano. Niwot: UP of Colorado, 1995.

Beer, Gabriella de, and Raquel Chang-Rodríguez, eds. *La historia en la literatura iberoamericana: Memorias del XXVI Congreso del Instituto Internacional de Literatura Iberoamericana*. Hanover, NH: Ediciones del Norte, 1989.

Belnap, Jeffrey, and Raúl Fernández, eds. *José Martí's "Our America": From National to Hemispheric Cultural Studies*. Durham: Duke UP, 1998.

Benhabib, Seyla. *Situating the Self: Gender, Community and Postmodernism in Contemporary Ethics*. New York: Routledge, 1992.

Benjamin, Walter. *The Arcades Project*. Trans. Howard Eiland and Kevin McLaughlin. Cambridge: Belknap P of Harvard UP, 1999.

—. "The Storyteller: Reflections on the Work of Nikolai Leskov." Arendt, *Illuminations* 83-109.

—. "Theses on the Philosophy of History." Arendt, *Illuminations* 253-64.

Beverley, John. "The Margin at the Center: On *Testimonio* (Testimonial Narrative)." *De/Colonizing the Subject: The Politics of Gender in Women's Autobiography*. Ed. Sidonie Smith and Julia Watson. Minneapolis: U of Minnesota P, 1992. 91-114.

—. "Postmodernism in Latin America." *Siglo XX / 20th Century (Critique and Cultural Discourse)* 9.1-2 (1991-1992): 9-29.

—. "'Through All Things Modern': Second Thoughts on *Testimonio*." *boundary 2* 18.2 (1991): 1-21.

Black, Edwin. *IBM and the Holocaust: The Strategic Alliance Between Nazi Germany and America's Most Powerful Corporation*. New York: Crown, 2001.

Bobbio, Norberto. *The Age of Rights*. London: Blackwell, 1995.

Bodmer, Beatriz Pastor. *The Armature of Conquest: Spanish Accounts of the Discovery of America, 1492-1589*. Trans. Lydia Longstreth Hunt. Stanford: Stanford UP, 1992.

Bollinger, William, and Georg M. Gugelberger. "Interview with Miguel Mármol, Los Angeles, May 23, 1988." *Latin American Perspectives* 18.4 (1991): 79-88.

Bookchin, Murray. *Social Anarchism or Lifestyle Anarchism: An Unbridgeable Chasm*. Edinburgh: AK, 1995.

Borges, Jorge Luis. "Tlön, Uqbar, Orbis Tertius." Trans. Alastair Reid. *Ficciones*. New York: Knopf, 1993. 5-21.

Brotton, Jerry. *Trading Territories: Mapping the Early Modern World*. Ithaca: Cornell UP, 1998.

Burciaga, José Antonio. *Drink Cultura: Chicanismo*. Santa Barbara: Joshua Odell, 1993.

Caceres, Leonardo. "Memoria del fuego americano." *Araucaria* 27 (1984): 193-98.

Campa, Román de la. *Latin Americanism*. Minneapolis: U of Minnesota P, 1999.

Canary, Robert H., and Henry Kozicki. Introduction. Canary and Kozicki ix-xv.

—, eds. *The Writing of History: Literary Form and Historical Understanding*. Madison: U of Wisconsin P, 1978.

Canclini, Néstor García. "Cultural Reconversion." Trans. Holly Staver. Yúdice, Franco, and Flores 29-43.

Carey, Alex. *Taking the Risk Out of Democracy: Corporate Propaganda versus Freedom and Liberty*. Ed. Andrew Lohrey. Urbana: U of Chicago P, 1997.

Caruth, Cathy. *Unclaimed Experience: Trauma, Narrative, and History*. Baltimore: Johns Hopkins UP, 1996.

Cascón, Ana, and W. F. Shadwick. *Cordel [Folheto]*. With prints by J. Borges. Bezerros, Brazil: Borges, 1996.

Castañeda, Jorge G. *La utopía desarmada: Intrigas, dilemas y promesas de la izquierda en América Latina*. 2nd ed. Mexico: Joaquín Mortiz, 1995.

Castillo, Debra A. *Talking Back: Toward a Latin American Feminist Literary Criticism*. Ithaca: Cornell UP, 1992.

Cather, Katherine Dunlap. *Educating by Story-telling*. New York: World Book, 1926.

Cavendish, Margaret. *The Blazing World and Other Writings*. Ed. Kate Lilley. London: Penguin, 1994.

de Certeau, Michel. *The Writing of History*. Trans. Tom Conley. New York: Columbia UP, 1988.

Césaire, Aimé. *Discourse on Colonialism*. Trans. Joan Pinkham. New York: Monthly Review, 1972.

Chapman, John W., and J. Roland Pennock, eds. *Human Rights*. New York: New York UP, 1981.

Chevigny, Bell Gale. "Twice-Told Tales and the Meaning of History: Testimonial Novels by Miguel Barnet and Norman Mailer." *Centennial Review* 30.2 (1986): 181-95.

Chomsky, Noam. *Chomsky on MisEducation*. Ed. Donaldo Macedo. Lanham, ML: Rowman & Littlefield, 2000.

—. *Perspectives on Power: Reflections on Human Nature and the Social Order*. Montréal: Black Rose, 1997.

—. *Rogue States: The Rule of Force in World Affairs*. Cambridge, MA: South End, 2000.

—. *The Umbrella of U.S. Power: The Universal Declaration of Human Rights and the Contradictions of U.S. Policy*. New York: Seven Stories, 1999.

—. *Year 501: The Conquest Continues*. Montréal: Black Rose, 1993.

Cioran, E. M. *History and Utopia*. Trans. Richard Howard. Chicago: U of Chicago P, 1998.

Cohen, Ralph. "Genre History, Literary History, and Historical Change." Perkins 85-113.

Collier, George A., with Elizabeth Lowery Quaratiello. *Basta!: Land & the Zapatista Rebellion in Chiapas*. Rev. ed. Oakland, CA: Food First, 1999.

Collins, Jane Lou. *Unseasonal Migrations: The Effects of Rural Labor Scarcity in Peru*. Princeton: Princeton UP, 1998.

Columbus, Christopher. *The Four Voyages*. Ed. and trans. J. M. Cohen. London: Penguin, 1969.

—. *Journal of the First Voyage*. Ed. and trans. B. W. Ife. Warminster, Eng.: Aris & Phillips, 1990.

Condé, Yvonne M. *Operation Pedro Pan: The Untold Exodus of 14,048 Cuban Children*. New York: Routledge, 2000.

Constable, Pamela, and Arturo Valenzuela. *A Nation of Enemies: Chile Under Pinochet*. New York: Norton, 1991.

Cooper, Marc. "Chile and the End of Pinochet." *The Nation* 26 Feb. 2001: 11+.

Cortázar, Julio. "Letter to Roberto Fernández Retamar." Trans. Jo Anne Englebert. Meyer 74-83.

—. *Nicaraguan Sketches*. Trans. Kathleen Weaver. New York: Norton, 1989.

—. "Réalité et littérature." *Temps modernes* July-Aug. 1981: 183-94.

Cortés, Hernán. *Letters from Mexico*. Trans. and ed. Anthony Pagden. Rev. ed. New Haven: Yale UP, 1986.

Craft, Linda J. *Novels of Testimony and Resistance from Central America*. Gainesville: UP of Florida, 1997.

Crespo, Ramón Torreira, and José Buajasán Marrawi. *Operación Peter Pan: Un caso de guerra psicológica contra Cuba*. Havana, Cuba: Editor Política, 2000.

Dalton, Roque. *Miguel Mármol*. Trans. Kathleen Ross and Richard Schaaf. Willimantic, CT: Curbstone, 1987.

Dash, Robert C. "Testimony of Gloria Daysi Alonson Jaimes: Resistance and Struggle." Trans. Robert C. Dash and Irma Fernández Dash. *Latin American Perspectives* 18.4 (1991): 89-95.

Deleuze, Gilles, and Félix Guattari. *Anti-Oedipus: Capitalism and Schizophrenia*. Trans. Robert Hurley, Mark Seem, and Helen R. Lane. Minneapolis: U of Minnesota P, 1983.

Derrida, Jacques. *Specters of Marx: The State of the Debt, the Work of Mourning, and the New International*. Trans. Peggy Kamuf. New York: Routledge, 1994.

Díaz, Bernal. *The Conquest of New Spain*. Trans. J. M. Cohen. London: Penguin, 1963.

Díaz, Gisele, and Alan Rodgers. *The Codex Borgia: A Full-Color Restoration of the Ancient Mexican Manuscript*. New York: Dover, 1993.

Dieterich, Heinz. *Noam Chomsky habla de América Latina: con documentos inéditos de los National Archives*. Habana, Cuba: Casa Editora Abril, 2000.

Dimenstein, Gilberto. *Brazil: War On Children*. London: Latin American Bureau, 1991.

Dorfman, Ariel. "Código político y código literario: el género testimonio en Chile Hoy." Jara and Vidal 170-234.

—. *The Empire's Old Clothes: What the Lone Ranger, Babar, and Other Innocent Heroes Do To Our Minds*. New York: Penguin, 1983.

dos Santos, Carlos Roberto A. "*As veias abertas da América Latina*: análise historiográphica." *Cadernos Hispano América (Curitiba)* 2 (1987): 37-46.

Drinan, Robert F. *Cry of the Oppressed: The History and Hope of the Human Rights Revolution*. San Francisco: Harper & Row, 1987.

—. *A Worldview of Human Rights: The Mobilization of Shame.* New Haven: Yale UP, 2001.

Du Bartas, Guillaume de Saluste Sieur. *The Divine Weeks and Works.* 2 vols. Trans. Josuah Sylvester. Ed. Susan Snyder. Oxford: Oxford UP, 1979.

Dupriez, Bernard. *A Dictionary of Literary Devices.* Trans. Albert W. Halsall. Toronto: U of Toronto P, 1991.

Durán, Fray Diego. *The History of the Indies of New Spain.* Trans. Doris Heyden. Norman: U of Oklahoma P, 1964.

Dussel, Enrique. "Beyond Eurocentrism: The World-System and the Limits of Modernity." *The Cultures of Globalization.* Ed. Fredric Jameson and Masao Miyoshi. Durham: Duke UP, 1998. 3-31.

—. "Ethical Sense of the 1994 Maya Rebellion in Chiapas." *Journal of Hispanic Latino Theology* 2.3 (1995): 41-56.

—. *Ethics and Community.* Trans. Robert R. Barr. Maryknoll, NY: Orbis, 1988.

—. "Ethics Is the Original Philosophy; or, The Barbarian Words Coming from the Third World: An Interview with Enrique Dussel." Interview with Fernando Gómez. *boundary 2* 28.1 (2001): 19-73.

—. "Europe, Modernity, and Eurocentrism." *Nepantla: Views from the South* 1.3 (2000): 465-78.

—. *The Invention of the Americas: Eclipse of "the Other" and the Myth of Modernity.* Trans. Michael D. Barber. New York: Continuum, 1995.

Early, Edwin, et al. *The History Atlas of South America: From the Inca Empire to Today's Rich Diversity.* New York: Macmillan, 1998.

Ercilla, Alonso de. *La Araucana.* Mexico: Editorial Porrúa S.A., 1972.

—. *The Historie of Aravcana.* Ed. Frank Pierce. Manchester: Manchester UP, 1964.

Ewell, Judith. "Venezuela's Cappucino Socialists: The History of the MAS." *Latin American Perspectives* 18.4 (1991): 113-17.

EZLN: Documentos y comunicados 3: 2 de octubre de 1995/24 de enero de 1997. Mexico: Ediciones Era, 1997.

Falk, Richard A. *Human Rights Horizons: The Pursuit of Justice in a Globalizing World.* New York: Routledge, 2000.

Fanon, Frantz. *The Wretched of the Earth.* Trans. Constance Farrington. New York: Grove, 1963.

Feitlowitz, Marguerite. *A Lexicon of Terror: Argentina and the Legacies of Torture.* Oxford: Oxford UP, 1998.

Ferrari, Sergio. *Sembrando utopía: Reportajes y conversaciones.* Managua, Nicaragua: Ediciones Nicarao, 1992.

Fiss, Owen. "Human Rights as Social Ideals." Hesse and Post 263-76.

Flanagan, Tom. *First Nations? Second Thoughts.* Montréal: McGill-Queen's UP, 2000.

Foucault, Michel. "Governmentality." Trans. Pasquale Pasquino. *The Foucault Effect: Studies in Governmentality.* Ed. Graham Burchell, Colin Gordon, and Peter Miller. Evanston: U of Chicago P, 1991. 87-104.

—. "Of Other Spaces." Trans. Jay Miskowiev. *Diacritics* 16.1 (1986): 22-27.

—. "What Is An Author." *Foucault Reader.* Ed. Paul Rabinow. New York: Pantheon, 1984. 101-20.

Franco, Jean. *Critical Passions: Selected Essays.* Ed. Mary Louise Pratt and Kathleen Newman. Durham: Duke UP, 1999.

—. "Going Public: Reinhabiting the Private." Yúdice, Franco, and Flores 65-83.

—. "¿La de quién?: La piratería postmoderna." *Revista de crítica literaria latinoamericana* 17.33 (1991): 11-20.

Freire, Paulo. *Pedagogy of the Oppressed.* Trans. Myra Bergman Ramos. New York: Continuum, 1995.

Freire, Paulo, with Antonio Faundez. *Learning to Question: A Pedagogy of Liberation.* Trans. Tony Coates. New York: Continuum, 1989.

Fuentes, Carlos. *The Buried Mirror: Reflections on Spain and the New World.* Boston: Houghton Mifflin, 1992.

—. *El espejo enterrado.* Mexico: Fondo de Cultura Económica, 1992.

—. *Gabriel García Márquez and the Invention of America.* Liverpool: Liverpool UP, 1987.

Fukuyama, Francis. *The End of History and the Last Man.* New York: Avon, 1992.

García de León, Antonio. *Resistencia y utopía: Memorial de agravios y crónica de revueltas y profecías acaecidas en la provincia de Chiapas durante los últimos quinientos años de su historia.* 2nd ed. Mexico: Ediciones Era, 1997.

García Márquez, Gabriel. *El asalto: El operativo con que el FSLN se lanzó al mundo: Un relato cinematográfico.* Managua, Nicaragua: Nueva Nicaragua, 1983.

—. *Clandestine in Chile: The Adventures of Miguel Littín.* Trans. Asa Zatz. Cambridge: Granta, 1990.

García Márquez, Gabriel, and Nahuel Maciel. *Elogio de la utopía.* Honduras, Argentina: El Cronista Ediciones, 1992.

Gates, Henry Louis, Jr. *Loose Canons: Notes on the Culture Wars.* New York: Oxford UP, 1992.

Gelman, Juan. *Unthinkable Tenderness: Selected Poems.* Ed. and trans. Joan Lindgren. Berkeley: U of California P, 1997.

Gewirth, Alan. "The Basis and Content of Human Rights." Chapman and Pennock 119-47.

Gill, Lesley. *Teetering on the Rim: Global Restructuring, Daily Life, and the Armed Retreat of the Bolivian State.* New York: Columbia UP, 2000.

Giordano, Al. "Zapatistas on the March." *The Nation* 9 Apr. 2001: 6+.

Gisbert, Teresa. "Art and Resistance in the Andean World." Jara and Spadaccini, *Amerindian Images* 629-77.

Glover, Jonathan. *Humanity: A Moral History of the Twentieth Century.* London: Pimlico, 2001.

Goad, Jim. *The Redneck Manifesto: How Hillbillies, Hicks and White Trash Became America's Scapegoats*. New York: Touchstone, 1998.

Goldman, Emma. *Anarchism and Other Essays*. New York: Dover, 1969.

Goodwin, Barbara. *The Philosophy of Utopia*. London: Frank Cass, 2001.

Goodwin, Barbara, and Keith Taylor. *The Politics of Utopia: A Study in Theory and Practice*. New York: St. Martin's, 1982.

Gossman, Lionel. "History and Literature: Reproduction or Signification." Canary and Kozicki 3-39.

Gramsci, Antonio. *The Modern Prince and Other Writings*. New York: International, 1957.

Grandin, Greg. "Chronicles of a Guatemalan Genocide Foretold: Violence, Trauma, and the Limits of Historical Inquiry." *Nepantla: Views from the South* 1.2 (2000): 391-412.

Grant, Robert. "The Social Contract and Human Rights." *Humanist* 60.1 (2000): 18-23.

Greenblatt, Stephen. *Marvelous Possessions: The Wonder of the New World*. Chicago: U of Chicago P, 1991.

Gruzinski, Serge. *Painting the Conquest: The Mexican Indians and the European Renaissance*. Trans. Deke Dusinberre. Paris: Flammarion, 1992.

Gugelberger, Georg M., ed. *The Real Thing: Testimonial Discourse and Latin America*. Durham: Duke UP, 1996.

Gugelberger, Georg, and Michael Kearney. "Voices for the Voiceless: Testimonial Literature in Latin America." *Latin American Perspectives* 18.3 (1991): 3-14.

Gusfield, Joseph R. *Utopian Myths and Movements in Modern Societies*. Morristown, NJ: General Learning, 1973.

Harbury, Jennifer. *Bridge of Courage: Life Stories of the Guatemalan Compañeros and Compañeras*. Montréal: Véhicule, 1994.

Harlow, Barbara. *After Lives: Legacies of Revolutionary Writing*. London: Verso, 1996.

—. *Resistance Literature*. New York: Methuen, 1987.

—. "Sappers in the Stacks: Colonial Archives, Land Mines, and Truth Commissions." *Edward Said and the Work of the Critic: Speaking Truth to Power*. Ed. Paul A. Bové. Durham: Duke UP, 2000.

Hegel, Georg Wilhelm Friedrich. *The Philosophy of History*. Trans. J. Sibree. New York: Dover, 1956.

Herodotus. *The Histories*. Trans. George Rawlinson. New York: Knopf, 1997.

Herrera, Hayden. *Frida Kahlo: The Paintings*. New York: HarperPerennial, 1993.

Hertzler, Joyce Oramel. *The History of Utopian Thought*. New York: Cooper Square, 1965.

Hesse, Carla, and Robert Post, eds. *Human Rights in Political Transitions: Gettysburg to Bosnia*. New York: Zone, 1999.

Hitchens, Christopher. "The Case Against Henry Kissinger, Part One: The Making of a War Criminal." *Harper's Magazine* Feb. 2001: 33-58.

—. "The Case Against Henry Kissinger, Part Two: Crimes against Humanity." *Harper's Magazine* Mar. 2001: 49-74.

—."Covenant with Death." *The Nation* 14 May 2001: 9.

Hobbes, Thomas. *Leviathan*. Ed. Michael Oakeshott. Oxford: Basil Blackwell, 1955.

Hobsbawm, Eric. *On History*. London: Abacus, 1998.

Hoffman, Stanley. "Human Rights as a Foreign Policy Goal." *Human Rights. Daedalus* 19-50.

Holiday, David. "Guatemala's Precarious Peace." *Current History* Feb. 2000: 78-84.

Hulme, Peter. *Colonial Encounters: Europe and the Native Caribbean 1492-1797*. New ed. London: Routledge, 1992.

Human Development Report 2000: Human Rights and Human Development. New York: Oxford UP, 2000.

Human Development Report 2001: Making New Technologies Work For Human Development. New York: Oxford UP, 2001.

Human Rights. Daedalus: Journal of the American Academy of Arts and Sciences. Fall 1983. Issued as Vol. 112, Number 4 of the Proceedings of the American Academy of Arts and Sciences.

Human Rights Watch World Report 2000: Events of 1999 (November 1998-October 1999). New York: Human Rights Watch, 1999.

Hurley, Susan, and Stephen Shute, eds. *On Human Rights: The Oxford Amnesty Lectures 1993*. New York: Basic, 1993.

Ignatieff, Michael. "Human Rights." Hesse and Post 313-24.

—. *The Rights Revolution*. Toronto: Anansi, 2000.

Ishay, Micheline R., ed. *The Human Rights Reader: Major Political Essays, Speeches, and Documents From the Bible to the Present*. New York: Routledge, 1997.

Jameson, Fredric. *The Jameson Reader*. Ed. Michael Hardt and Kathi Weeks. Oxford: Blackwell, 2000.

—. "Of Islands and Trenches: Neutralization and the Production of Utopian Discourse." *Diacritics* Summer 1977: 2-21.

Jara, René, and Nicholas Spadaccini, eds. *Amerindian Images and the Legacy of Columbus*. Minneapolis: U of Minnesota P, 1992.

—. *1492-1992: Re/Discovering Colonial Writing*. Minneapolis: U of Minnesota P, 1989.

Jara, René, and Hernán Vidal, eds. *Testimonio y literatura*. Edina, MN: Society for the Study of Contemporary Hispanic and Lusophone Revolutionary Literatures, 1986.

Jordan, John, and Jennifer Whitney. "Resistance is the Secret of Joy." *New Internationalist* 338 (2001): 24-25.

Kafka, Franz. *The Blue Octavo Notebooks*. Ed. Max Brod. Trans. Ernst Kaiser and Eithne Wilkins. Cambridge: Exact Change, 1991.

Kant, Immanuel. *On History*. Ed. Lewis White Beck. Trans. Lewis White Beck, Robert E. Anchor, and Emil L. Fackenheim. New York: Macmillan, 1963.

Kappler, Brian. "Donner tome sheds light on reserves." *Montreal Gazette* 26 May 2001: A18.

Katzenberger, Elaine, ed. *First World, Ha Ha Ha!: The Zapatista Challenge*. San Francisco: City Lights, 1995.

Keane, John. "Who's In Charge Here? The Need For Rule of Law to Regulate the Emerging Global Civil Society." *Times Literary Supplement* 18 May 2001: 13-15.

Kearney, Michael. "Borders and Boundaries of State and Self at the End of Empire." *Journal of the Historical Society* 4.1 (1991): 52-74.

Kensinger, Kenneth M. *How Real People Ought to Live: The Cashinahua of Eastern Peru*. Prospect Heights, IL: Waveland, 1995.

Kissinger, Henry A. "The Pitfalls of Universal Jurisdiction." *Foreign Affairs* 80.4 (2001): 86-96.

Klein, Ernest. *A Comprehensive Etymological Dictionary of the English Language*. Amsterdam: Elsevier, 1971.

Kropotkin, Peter. *Kropotkin's Revolutionary Pamphlets: A Collection of Writings*. Ed. Roger N. Baldwin. New York: Dover, 1970.

Kruger, Barbara, and Phil Mariani. *Remaking History*. Seattle: Bay, 1989.

Kumar, Krishan. *Utopianism*. Buckingham, Eng.: Open UP, 1991.

Kumar, Krishan, and Stephen Bann, eds. *Utopias and the Millennium*. London: Reaktion, 1993.

LaCapra, Dominick. *History & Criticism*. Ithaca: Cornell UP, 1985.

Landesman, Charles. "The Problem of Universals." Introduction. *The Problem of Universals*. Ed. Charles Landesman. New York: Basic, 1971. 3-17.

Las Casas, Bartolomé de. *In Defense of the Indians: The Defense of the Most Reverend Lord, Don Fray Bartolomé de Las Casas, of the Order of Preachers, Late Bishop of Chiapa, Against the Persecutors and Slanderers of the Peoples of the New World Discovered Across the Seas*. Ed. and trans. Stafford Poole. DeKalb: Northern Illinois UP, 1992.

—. *A Short Account of the Destruction of the Indies*. Ed. and trans. Nigel Griffin. London: Penguin, 1992.

Lasky, Melvin J. *Utopia and Revolution: On the Origins of a Metaphor, or Some Illustrations of the Problem of Political Temperament and Intellectual Climate and How Ideas, Ideals, and Ideologies Have Been Historically Related*. Chicago: U of Chicago P, 1976.

Lauren, Paul Gordon. *The Evolution of International Human Rights: Visions Seen*. Philadelphia: U of Pennsylvania P, 1998.

Le Goff, Jacques. *History and Memory*. Trans. Steven Rendall and Elizabeth Claman. New York: Columbia UP, 1992.

Leonard, Irving. *Books of the Brave: Being and Account of Books and of Men in the Spanish Conquest and Settlement of the Sixteenth-Century World*. Berkeley: U of California P, 1992.

León-Portilla, Miguel. *Aztec Thought and Culture: A Study of the Ancient Nahuatl Mind*. Trans. Jack Emory Davis. Norman: U of Oklahoma P, 1963.

—. "Word and Mirror: Presages of the Encounter." Jara and Spadaccini, *Amerindian Images* 96-102.

Leslie, Marina. *Renaissance Utopias and the Problem of History.* Ithaca: Cornell UP, 1998.

Levinas, Emmanuel. *Entre Nous: Thinking-of-the-Other.* Trans. Michael B. Smith and Barbara Harshav. New York: Columbia UP, 1998.

"Lone Wolf Policy." *The Progressive* Sept. 2001: 8-10.

López Levy, Marcela. "The Damn Water is Ours!" *New Internationalist* 338 (2001): 16-17.

Loveman, Brian. "Human Rights, Antipolitics, and Protecting the *Patria*: An (Almost) Military Perspective." Loveman and Davies 398-423.

Loveman, Brian, and Thomas M. Davies, Jr., eds. *The Politics of Antipolitics: The Military in Latin America.* Rev. ed. Wilmington, DE: Scholarly Resources, 1997.

Lyotard, Jean-François. "The Other's Rights." Hurley and Shute 135-47.

Maciel, Nahuel, and Gabriel García Márquez. *Elogio de la utopía.* Honduras, Argentina: El Cronista Ediciones, 1992.

Mackey, Nathaniel. *Discrepant Engagement: Dissonance, Cross-Culturality, and Experimental Writing.* Tuscaloosa: U of Alabama P, 2000.

MacKinnon, Catharine A. "Crimes of War, Crimes of Peace." Hurley and Shute 83-109.

Mann, Mary. Preface. Sarmiento 7-20.

Mannheim, Karl. *Ideology & Utopia: An Introduction to the Sociology of Knowledge.* Trans. Louis Wirth and Edward Shils. San Diego: Harvest, 1985.

Manuel, Frank E., ed. *Utopias and Utopian Thought.* Boston: Houghton Mifflin; Cambridge: Riverside, 1966.

Marcos, Subcomandante Insurgente. *Our Word Is Our Weapon: Selected Writings.* Ed. Juana Ponce de León. New York: Seven Stories, 2001.

—. "The Punch Card and the Hour Glass." Interview with Gabriel García Márquez and Roberto Pombo. *New Left Review* 9 (2001): 69-79.

—. *Shadows of Tender Fury: The Letters and Communiqués of Subcomandante Marcos and the Zapatista Army of National Liberation.* New York: Monthly Review, 1995.

—. *The Story of Colors / La historia de los colores: A Folktale from the Jungles of Chiapas.* Illus. Domitila Domínguez. Trans. Anne Bar Din. El Paso, TX: Cinco Puntos, 1999.

Marín, Lynda. "Speaking Out Together: Testimonials of Latin American Women." *Latin American Perspectives* 18.3 (1991): 51-68.

Marshall, Peter. *Demanding the Impossible: A History of Anarchism.* Hammersmith, Eng.: Fontana, 1993.

Martí, José. *José Martí Reader: Writings on the Americas.* Ed. Deborah Shnookal and Mirta Muñiz. Melbourne, NY: Ocean, 1999.

Martin, Gerald. *Journeys Through the Labyrinth: Latin American Fiction in the Twentieth Century.* London: Verso, 1989.

Martin, Randy. "Theater after the Revolution: Refiguring the Political in Cuba and Nicaragua." Yúdice, Franco, and Flores 115-40.

Martin, Sandra. "No refuge between book covers." *Globe and Mail* 10 June 2000: D10.

McClintock, Anne. "The Angel of Progress: Pitfalls of the Term 'Post-Colonialism.'" *Social Text* 31-32 (1992): 84-98.

Menchú, Rigoberta. *I, Rigoberta Menchú: An Indian Woman in Guatemala*. Ed. Elisabeth Burgos-Debray. Trans. Ann Wright. London: Verso, 1998.

—. *Rigoberta: La nieta de los mayas*. Madrid: El País S.A.—Santillana S.A., 1998.

Merod, Jim. *The Political Responsibility of the Critic*. Ithaca: Cornell UP, 1987.

Mesquita, Ivo. *Cartographies*. Winnipeg: Winnipeg Art Gallery, 1993.

Meyer, Doris, ed. *Lives on the Line: The Testimony of Contemporary Latin American Authors*. Berkeley: U of California P, 1988.

Mignolo, Walter D. *The Darker Side of the Renaissance: Literacy, Territoriality, and Colonization*. Ann Arbor: U of Michigan P, 1995.

—. *Local Histories/Global Designs: Coloniality, Subaltern Knowledges, and Border Thinking*. Princeton: Princeton UP, 2000.

Millett, Kate. *The Politics of Cruelty: An Essay on the Literature of Political Imprisonment*. New York: Norton, 1994.

Mills, Kenneth, and William B. Taylor, eds. *Colonial Spanish America: A Documentary History*. Wilmington, DE: SR, 1998.

Modisane, Bloke. *Blame Me On History*. London: Thames and Hudson, 1963.

Mohanty, Satya P. "Colonial Legacies, Multicultural Futures: Relativism, Objectivity, and the Challenge of Otherness." *PMLA* 110.1 (1995): 108-18.

—. *Literary Theory and the Claims of History: Postmodernism, Objectivity, Multicultural Politics*. Ithaca: Cornell UP, 1997.

Monsiváis, Carlos. *Amor perdido*. Mexico: Biblioteca Era, 1977.

—. *Mexican Postcards*. Ed. and trans. John Kraniauskas. London: Verso, 1997.

Montaigne, Michel de. *The Essayes of Montaigne*. Trans. John Florio. New York: Modern Library, n.d.

More, Thomas. "*Utopia*." *Ideal Commonwealths*. New York: Colonial, 1901. 1-99.

Moreiras, Alberto. "The Aura of Testimonio." Gugelberger 192-224.

Morsink, Johannes. *The Universal Declaration of Human Rights: Origins, Drafting and Intent*. Philadelphia: U of Pennsylvania P, 1999.

Mukherjee, Arun Prabha. *Oppositional Aesthetics: Readings from a Hyphenated Space*. Toronto: TSAR, 1994.

Narayan, Uma. "The Project of Feminist Epistemology: Perspectives from a Nonwestern Feminist." *Gender/Body/Knowledge*. Ed. Alison M. Jaggar and Susan R. Bordo. New Brunswick, NJ: Rutgers UP, 1989. 256-69.

Nash, June. "Global Integration and Subsistence Insecurity." *American Anthropologist* 96.1 (1994): 7-30.

Nebrija, Antonio de. *Gramática de la lengua castellana*. Ed. Antonio Quilis. Madrid: Editorial Nacional, 1984.

Neruda, Pablo. *Canto General*. Trans. Jack Schmitt. Berkeley: U of California P, 2000.

Nettle, Daniel, and Suzanne Romaine. *Vanishing Voices: The Extinction of the World's Languages*. Oxford: Oxford UP, 2000.

Niethammer, Lutz. *Posthistoire: Has History Come to An End?* Trans. Patrick Camiller. London: Verso, 1994.

Nietzsche, Friedrich. "On the Utility and Liability of History for Life." *Unfashionable Observations*. Trans. Richard T. Gray. *The Complete Works of Friedrich Nietzsche, Volume 2*. Ed. Ernst Behler. Stanford: Stanford UP, 1995. 83-167.

Oberhelman, Harley D. *García Márquez and Cuba: A Study of Its Presence in His Fiction, Journalism, and Cinema*. Fredericton: York, 1995.

Oettinger, Marion, Jr. *The Folk Art of Latin America: Visiones del Pueblo*. New York: Dutton Studio, 1992.

Okin, Susan Moller. "Feminism, Women's Human Rights, and Cultural Differences." *Hypatia* 13.2 (1998): 32-52.

Ortega y Gasset, José. *Man and People*. Trans. Willard R. Trask. New York: Norton, 1957.

Ousby, Ian, ed. *The Cambridge Guide to Literature in English*. Cambridge: Cambridge UP, 1993.

Pagden, Anthony. *European Encounters with the New World: From Renaissance to Romanticism*. New Haven: Yale UP, 1993.

—. *The Fall of Natural Man: The American Indian and the Origins of Comparative Mythology*. Cambridge: Cambridge UP, 1982.

Parry, Benita. "Problems in Current Theories of Colonial Discourse." *Oxford Literary Review* 9.1-2 (1987): 27-58.

Partridge, Eric. *Origins: A Short Etymological Dictionary of Modern English*. New York: Greenwich, 1983.

Payne, Douglas W. "Mexico and Its Discontents." *Harper's Magazine* Apr. 1995: 68+.

Paz, Octavio. Introduction. Poniatowska, *Massacre in Mexico* vii-xvii.

—. "The Telltale Mirror." Meyer 164-78.

—. "Will for Form." Introduction. *Mexico: Splendors of Thirty Centuries*. Boston: Bulfinch; New York: Metropolitan Museum of Art, 1990. 3-38.

Pelupessy, Wim. "Economic Adjustment Policies in El Salvador During the 1980s." Trans. John F. Uggen. *Latin American Perspectives* 18.4 (1991): 48-78.

Perkins, David, ed. *Theoretical Issues in Literary History*. Cambridge: Harvard UP, 1991.

Perry, Michael J. *The Idea of Human Rights: Four Inquiries*. New York: Oxford UP, 1998.

Peters, Jeffrey N. "The Cartographic Eye/I: Champlain and the Uses of Early Modern Geographic Discourse." *Genre* 30 (1997): 79-104.

Peterson, Jeanette Favrot. *The Paradise Garden Murals of Malinalco: Utopias and Empire in Sixteenth-Century Mexico*. Austin: U of Texas P, 1993.

Poniatowska, Elena. "And Here's to You, Jesusa." Meyer 137-55.

—. *Fuerte es el silencio*. Mexico: Ediciones Era, 1980.

—. *Luz y luna, lunitas*. Mexico: Ediciones Era, 1994.

—. *Massacre in Mexico*. Trans. Helen R. Lane. New York: Viking, 1975.

—. *La noche de Tlatelolco: Testimonios de historia oral*. Mexico: Ediciones Era, 1971.

Powell, Philip Wayne. *Tree of Hate: Propaganda and Prejudices Affecting United States Relations with the Hispanic World*. Vallecito, CA: Ross, 1985.

Preis, Ann-Belinda S. "Human Rights as Cultural Practice: An Anthropological Critique." *Human Rights Quarterly* 18.2 (1996): 286-315.

1er Salón de Arte Cubano Contemporáneo. La Habana, Cuba: Centro de Desarrollo de las Artes Visuales, 1995.

Rabasa, José. *Inventing America: Spanish Historiography and the Formation of Eurocentrism*. Norman: U of Oklahoma P, 1993.

Rabossi, Eduardo. "Hobbes: derechos naturales, sociedad y derechos humanos." *Cuadernos de filosofía* 20 (1989): 37-46.

Rama, Carlos M. "De la fragilidad de la democracia latinoamericana: El caso uruguayo." *Cuadernos americanos* 234.1 (1981): 19-30.

Rancière, Jacques. *On the Shores of Politics*. Trans. Liz Heron. London: Verso, 1995.

Randall, Margaret. "Reclaiming Voices: Notes on a New Female Practice in Journalism." *Latin American Perspectives* 18.3 (1991): 103-13.

Rawls, John. *The Law of Peoples with "The Idea of Public Reason Revisited."* Cambridge: Harvard UP, 1999.

Razack, Sherene H. *Looking White People in the Eye: Gender, Race, and Culture in the Classrooms*. Toronto: U of Toronto P, 1998.

Reed, Jon. "'The Dictatorship Has Taught Me the Road': Interview with Nineth de García, Leader of GAM." *Latin American Perspectives* 18.4 (1991): 96-103.

"Report on the Nicaraguan Indian Peace Initiative: A Search for Indian Rights Within the Arias Peace Plan." *Fourth World Documentation Project*. 7 Sept. 2001 <http://www.halcyon.com/pub/FWDP/Americas/ariaspax.txt>.

Rivero, Eliana S. "Testimonial Literature and Conversations as Literary Discourse." Trans. C. Alita Kelley with Alec Kelley. *Latin American Perspectives* 18.3 (1991): 69-79.

Roa Bastos, Augusto. "Metaphor for Exile." Meyer 274-78.

Robinson, Darryl. "Defining 'Crimes Against Humanity' at the Rome Conference." *American Journal of International Law* 93.1 (1999): 43-57.

Rorty, Richard. "Human Rights, Rationality, and Sentimentality." Hurley and Shute 111-34.

Rosales, F. Arturo. *Testimonio: A Documentary History of the Mexican American Struggle for Civil Rights*. Houston: Arte Público, 2000.

Rosenberg, Tina. *Children of Cain: Violence and the Violent in Latin America*. New York: Penguin, 1992.

Rosenstock-Huessy, Eugene. *I Am an Impure Thinker*. Norwich, VT: Argo, 1970.

Rowe, William. "Liberalism and Authority: The Case of Mario Vargas Llosa." Yúdice, Franco, and Flores 45-64.

Rowe, William, and Vivian Schelling. *Memory and Modernity: Popular Culture in Latin America.* London: Verso, 1991.

Rushdie, Salman. *The Jaguar Smile: A Nicaraguan Journey.* London: Pan, 1987.

Sahagún, Bernardino de. *Conquest of New Spain: 1585 Revision.* Trans. Howard F. Cline. Ed. S. L. Cline. Salt Lake City: U of Utah P, 1989.

Said, Edward W. "Nationalism, Human Rights, and Interpretation." *Freedom and Interpretation: The Oxford Amnesty Lectures, 1992.* Ed. Barbara Johnson. New York: Basic, 1993. 175-205.

—. "The Public Role of Writers and Intellectuals." *The Nation* 17-24 Sept. 2001: 27-36.

—. *Representations of the Intellectual.* New York: Vintage, 1996.

Saldívar, José David. *Border Matters: Remapping American Cultural Studies.* Berkeley: U of California P, 1997.

Salgado, Sebastião. *The Children: Refugees and Migrants.* New York: Aperture, 2000.

—. *Migrations: Humanity in Transition.* New York: Aperture, 2000.

—. *Terra: Struggle of the Landless.* Poetry by Chico Buarque. London: Phaidon, 1997.

—. *An Uncertain Grace.* Essays by Eduardo Galeano and Fred Ritchin. New York: Aperture, 1990.

—. *Workers: An Archaeology of the Industrial Age.* New York: Aperture, 1993.

Sánchez, Rosaura. *Telling Identities: The California testimonios.* Minneapolis: U of Minnesota P, 1995.

Sanders, Jerry W. "Two Mexicos and Fox's Quandary." *The Nation* 26 Feb. 2001: 18+.

Sargisson, Lucy. *Utopian Bodies and the Politics of Transgression.* London: Routledge, 2000.

Sarmiento, Domingo F. *Life in the Argentine Republic in the Days of the Tyrants or, Civilization and Barbarism.* New York: Collier, 1961.

Sault, Nicole. "Many Mirrors: Contrasting Models for Illness and Healing." 29 Aug. 2001 <http://www.raiz.org/mirrors/contrast.html>.

Savic, Obrad, ed. *The Politics of Human Rights.* London: Verso, 1999.

Scarry, Elaine. "The Difficulty of Imagining Other Persons." Hesse and Post 277-309.

Scheper-Hughes, Nancy. *Death Without Weeping: The Violence of Everyday Life in Brazil.* Berkeley: U of California P, 1993.

Seed, Patricia. *Ceremonies of Possession in Europe's Conquest of the New World, 1492-1640.* Cambridge: Cambridge UP, 1995.

Sen, Amartya. *Development as Freedom.* New York: Anchor, 2000.

Sevilla-Casa, Elias. "Notes on Las Casas' Ideological and Political Practice." *Western Expansion and Indigenous Peoples: The Heritage of Las Casas.* Ed. Elias Sevilla-Casas. The Hague: Mouton, 1977. 17-29.

Shohat, Ella. "Notes on the 'Post-Colonial.'" *Social Text* 31-32 (1992): 99-113.

Sibley, David. *Geographies of Exclusion: Society and Difference in the West.* London: Routledge, 1995.

"Silver Lining." *The Progressive* Sept. 2001: 11.

Simonson, Rick, and Scott Walker, eds. *The Graywolf Annual Five: Multicultural Literacy.* St. Paul: Graywolf, 1988.

Singer, Daniel. *Whose Millennium?: Theirs or Ours?* New York: Monthly Review, 1999.

Sklar, Holly. *Chaos or Community?: Seeking Solutions, Not Scapegoats For Bad Economics.* Boston: South End, 1995.

Sklodowska, Elzbieta. "Spanish American Testimonial Novel: Some Afterthoughts." Gugelberger 84-100.

Slack, Keith M. "Operation Condor and Human Rights: A Report from Paraguay's Archive of Terror." *Human Rights Quarterly* 18.2 (1996): 492-506.

Slater, Candace. *Stories on a String: The Brazilian* Literature de Cordel. Berkeley: U of California P, 1989.

Sommer, Doris. "Rigoberta's Secrets." *Latin American Perspectives* 18.3 (1991): 32-50.

Spivak, Gayatri Chakravorty. "Can the Subaltern Speak?" *Marxism and the Interpretation of Culture.* Ed. Cary Nelson and Lawrence Grossberg. Urbana: U of Illinois P, 1988. 271-313.

Stanley, David. *Cuba.* Melbourne, Eng.: Lonely Planet, 2000.

Stavans, Ilan. *The Essential Ilan Stavans.* New York: Routledge, 2000.

—, ed. *The Oxford Book of Latin American Essays.* New York: Oxford UP, 1997.

Sternbach, Nancy Saporta. "Re-membering the Dead: Latin American Women's 'Testmonial' Discourse." *Latin American Perspectives* 18.3 (1991): 91-102.

Stille, Alexander. "Slow Food: An Italian Answer to Globalization." *The Nation* 20-27 Aug. 2001: 11-16.

Stobbart, Lorainne. *Utopia Fact or Fiction?: The Evidence from the Americas.* Phoenix Mill, Eng.: Alan Sutton, 1992.

Tedlock, Dennis, trans. *Popol Vuh: The Definitive Edition of the Mayan Book of the Dawn of Life and the Glories of Gods and Kings.* Rev. ed. New York: Touchstone, 1996.

Teitel, Ruti. "Millennial Visions: Human Rights at Century's End." Hesse and Post 339-42.

Teixeira, Cecilia. "Para uma gramatica do terror: Dois momentos da facção platina." *Letras (Curitiba)* 25 (1976): 65-75.

"This is Your War on Drugs." *Harper's Magazine* Oct. 2000: 17-21.

Thompson, E. P. *Making History: Writings on History and Culture.* New York: New, 1994.

Thornton, Russell. *American Indian Holocaust and Survival: A Population History Since 1492.* Norman: U of Oklahoma P, 1987.

Thucydides. *The Peloponnesian War: A New Translation, Backgrounds and Contexts, Interpretations.* Trans. Walter Blanco. Ed. Walter Blanco and Jennifer Tolbert Roberts. New York: Norton, 1988.

Timerman, Jacobo. *Prisoner Without a Name, Cell Without a Number.* Trans. Toby Talbot. New York: Vintage, 1988.

Tocqueville, Alexis de. *Democracy in America.* New York: Knopf, 1994.

Todorov, Tzvetan. *The Conquest of America: The Question of the Other.* Trans. Richard Howard. Norman: U of Oklahoma P, 1999.

Triay, Victor Andres. *Fleeing Castro: Operation Peter Pan and the Cuban Children's Program.* Gainesville: UP of Florida, 1999.

Trinh, T. Minh-ha. *Woman Native Other: Writing Postcoloniality and Feminism.* Bloomington: Indiana UP, 1989.

Tula, María Teresa. *Este es mi testimonio.* With Lyn Stephen. Boston: South End, 1994.

Tyranipocrit Discovered. Ed. Andrew Hopton. London: Aporia, 1990.

Valdés, Gina. *Puentes y fronteras.* Trans. Katherine King and Gina Valdés. Tempe, AZ: Bilingual Review, 1997.

Valle-Castillo, Julio. "La transcripción del fuego." *Nicaráuac* 14 (1987): 145-51.

Vargas Llosa, Mario. "Social Commitment and the Latin American Writer." Meyer 128-36.

Vega, Garcilaso de la. *Royal Commentaries of the Incas and General History of Peru.* 2 vols. Trans. and introd. Harold V. Livermore. Austin: U of Texas P, 1966.

Verdesio, Gustavo. "Forgotten Territorialities: The Materiality of Indigenous Pasts." *Nepantla: Views from the South* 2.1 (2001): 85-114.

Vidal, Gore. *The Decline and Fall of the American Empire.* Berkeley: Odonian, 1992.

Vidal, Hernán. *Crítica literaria como defensa de los derechos humanos: Cuestión teórica.* Newark, DL: Juan de la Cuesta—Hispanic Monographs, 1994.

—. *Cultura nacional chilena, crítica literaria y derechos humanos.* Minneapolis: Institute for the Study of Ideologies and Literature, 1989.

Vorsey, Louis de, Jr. "Silent Witnesses: Native American Maps." *Georgia Review* 46 (1992): 709-26.

Walker, John. *A Critical Pronouncing Dictionary and Expositor of the English Language.* London: Thomas Tegg & Son, 1836.

Wallerstein, Immanuel. *The Modern World—System I: Capitalist Agriculture and the Origins of the European World-Economy in the Sixteenth Century.* San Diego: Academic, 1974.

—. *Unthinking Social Science: The Limits of 19th Century Paradigms.* Cambridge: Polity, 1991.

—. *Utopistics: Or, Historical Choices of the Twenty-first Century.* New York: New, 1998.

Waring, Marilyn. *If Women Counted.* New York: HarperCollins, 1990.

Weinberg, Bill. "Bio-Piracy in Chiapas." *The Nation* 20-27 Aug. 2001: 23.

White, Hayden. *Metahistory: The Historical Imagination in Nineteenth-Century Europe.* Baltimore: Johns Hopkins UP, 1973.

Whitfield, Teresa. *Paying the Price: Ignacio Ellacuría and the Murdered Jesuits of El Salvador.* Philadelphia: Temple UP, 1995.

Wilkinson, James. "A Choice of Fictions: Historians, Memory, and Evidence." *PMLA* 111.1 (1996): 80-92.

Williams, Raymond. *Keywords: A Vocabulary of Culture and Society*. London: Fontana, 1989.

Wilson, S. R. "*El Cono Sur*: The Tradition of Exile, The Language of Poetry." *Revista canadiense de estudios hispánicos* 8.2 (1984): 247-62.

—. "Nicaragua: The Struggle for History." *Chasqui* 9.2-3 (1982): 23-27.

Winstanley, Gerrard. *Selected Writings*. Ed. Andrew Hopton. London: Aporia, 1989.

Womack, John, Jr. *Rebellion in Chiapas: An Historical Reader*. New York: New, 1999.

Wood, Denis. *The Power of Maps*. New York: Guilford, 1992.

Wright, Ronald. *Stolen Continents: The "New World" Through Indian Eyes*. Toronto: Penguin, 1993.

—. *Time Among the Maya*. New York: Grove, 2000.

The Writer and Human Rights. Ed. Toronto Arts Group for Human Rights. Toronto: Lester & Orpen Dennys, 1983.

Yúdice, George. "Postmodernity and Transnational Capitalism in Latin America." Yúdice, Franco, and Flores 1-28.

—. "*Testimonio* and Postmodernism." Gugelberger 42-57.

Yúdice, George, Jean Franco, and Juan Flores. Introduction. Yúdice, Franco, and Flores vii-xiv.

Yúdice, George, Jean Franco, and Juan Flores, eds. *On Edge: The Crisis of Contemporary Latin American Culture*. Minneapolis: U of Minnesota P, 1992.

The Zapatistas. *Zapatista Encuentro: Documents from the 1996 Encounter for Humanity and Against Neoliberalism*. New York: Seven Stories, 1998.

Zimmerman, Marc. "*Testimonio* in Guatemala: Payeras, Rigoberta, and Beyond." *Latin American Perspectives* 18.4 (1991): 22-47.

IV. Filmography

Chile crea: Una semana en julio. Dir. Frank Diamond. Stichting Derde Cinema, 1988.

Eduardo Galeano: Mi palabra hoy. Producción general: Tauro Video. Producción y edición: HDTV Video Productora. N.D.

Entre Líneas. With Vicente Parra. Prod. José M. Cueto. Dir. Vicente Parra. TV E.S.A., 1989.

Galeano, Eduardo. Video interview. With Malcolm Guy. Productions Multi-Monde, 30 Aug. 1995.

Index

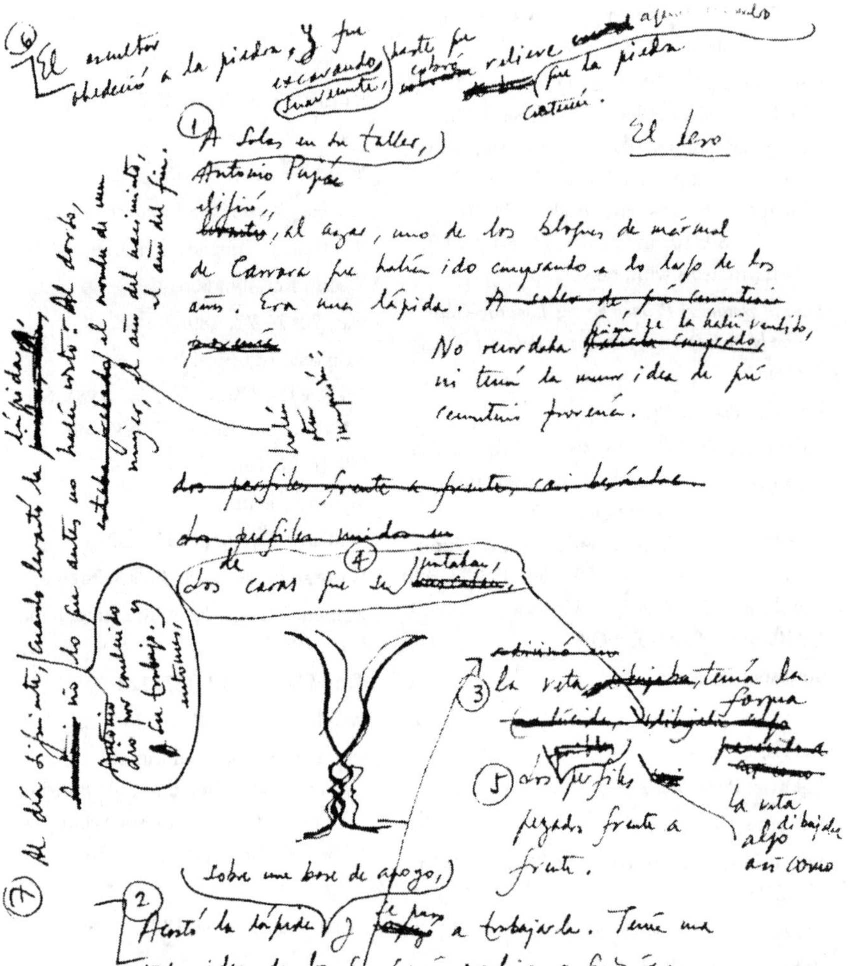

⑥ El escultor obedeció a la piedra, y fue escavando suavemente, hasta que cobró relieve lo que la piedra contenía.

El beso

① A solas en su taller, Antonio Pujía eligió, al azar, uno de los bloques de mármol de Carrara que había ido comprando a lo largo de los años. Era una lápida. No recordaba [illegible] ni tenía la menor idea de qué cementerio provenía.

④ dos caras que se juntaban,

③ la vista [illegible] tenía la forma

⑤ dos perfiles pegados frente a frente.

sobre una base de apoyo,

② Acostó la lápida y se puso a trabajarla. Tenía una vaga idea de lo que quería esculpir, o quizás no tenía ninguna. Empezó por borrar el nombre de un hombre, el año del nacimiento, el año del fin. Después, el cincel penetró el mármol, y Antonio encontró una sorpresa, que lo estaba esperando piedra adentro:

⑦ Al día siguiente, cuando levantó la lápida, vio lo que antes no había visto: al dorso, estaba grabado el nombre de una mujer, el año del nacimiento, el año del fin.

Holograph of a Galeano manuscript in progress.

BOOKS of RELATED INTEREST from

BLACK ROSE BOOKS

Beyond O.J., *by Earl Ofari Hutchinson*
Certainties and Doubts, *by Anatol Rapoport*
Cure of the Mind, *by Theodore Sampson*
Culture and Social Change, *Colin Leys, Marguerite Mendell, editors*
Decentralizing Power: On Paul Goodman, *Taylor Stoehr, editor*
Defending the Earth, *by Murray Bookchin*
Designing Utopia, *by Michael Lang*
Dissidence: Essays Against the Mainstream, *by Dimitrios Roussopoulos*
Images and Words, *by Ioannis Stavrianos*
Islamic Peril, *by Karim H. Karim*
Legacy of the New Left, *by Dimitrios Roussopoulos*
Nationalism and Culture, *by Rudolf Rocker*
Perspectives on Power, *by Noam Chomsky*
Public Place, *by Dimitrios Roussopoulos*
Rethinking Camelot, *by Noam Chomsky*
Year 501, *by Noam Chomsky*

send for a free catalogue of all our titles
BLACK ROSE BOOKS
C.P. 1258, Succ. Place du Parc
Montréal, Québec
H3W 2R3 Canada
or visit our web site at: http://www.web.net/blackrosebooks

To order books:
In Canada: (tel) 1-800-565-9523 (fax)1-800-221-9985
email: utpbooks@utpress.utoronto.ca
In United States: (tel) 1-800-283-3572 (fax)1-651-917-6406
In UK & Europe: (tel) London 44(0)20 8986-4854 (fax)44 (0)20 8533-5821
email: order@centralbooks.com

Printed by the workers of
MARC VEILLEUX IMPRIMEUR INC.
Boucherville, Québec
for Black Rose Books Ltd.